ONCE SHE HAD LOVED ZAVEL, THE MAN CALLED 'WOLF' . . . NOW, SHE FEARED WHAT HE COULD DO TO HER . . .

Wolf took hold of her arm. "Marya, I can grab enough opportunities for the two of us." His grip tightened.

She refused to look at him. "Let go, Zavel. You're hurting me . . ."

He spun her around to face him. "I'd like to know what's behind this fierce push of yours? What happened to you in Russia before I met you? I'd give a lot of money, Marya, to know what has made you so cold and resistant. One day I'll know."

Her eyes snapped with resentment. "How many times must I tell you? Nothing happened. Nothing at all. I was just left on my own. . . ."

"But you're not on your own anymore. You're my wife. Why can't you be satisfied with being a wife and mother . . . like your friend Leah?"

Marya thought of Leah who lived next door and wanted to laugh in Wolf's face. She and Leah had come from such different backgrounds. Yes, they were both Jews. But Leah had been born here. Leah was the kind of woman who was content to speak Yiddish to her children and to satisfy herself with running their lives. That was all fine for Leah, Marya thought, but not for her. Life was too full of chance . . . everything changed. A child disappeared; another child died; a husband was killed; parents were killed; you came to a new country; a new husband came along; a new husband no longer loved you. At any time it could all be gone. . . .

She had to accomplish as much as possible . . . while she could . . .

SHARON STEEBER

Published by
Banbury Books, Inc.
37 West Avenue
Wayne, Pennsylvania 19087

Dell ® TM 681510, Dell Publishing Co., Inc.

ISBN: 0-440-04248-8

Printed in the United States of America

First printing—September 1982

To the *mishpocheh*
Alice, Don, John, Donna

PART I

"... I sought him whom my soul loveth;"
from "The Song of Songs"

1883-1893

Prologue

Marya sat on the bench, waiting. In front of her the winter sun, half-hidden by the clouds, shone on the East River, turning it milk white. Exhausted by the realization of what she had just done, she closed her eyes and started to sink inside herself. The others would come looking for her soon, probably Michael or Sadie. They would be worried and wouldn't know how to tell her what she already knew.

She wished she could stop the trembling of her hands. Was it because she was old now—sixty-seven years was old? Or because of what had just happened that her hands trembled? She wondered how the sun could be shining so brightly one moment, then completely disappear behind the clouds the next. But there was nothing unusual in that, she supposed. It was part of nature. Was what she had just done part of nature too? She shut her eyes more tightly.

The air had a chill to it, and she pulled her jacket close around her. Somewhere in the distance behind her, the bells of a church started to strike. One, two, three, tolled the bells. Marya could feel the bells in time with her heartbeat.

The bells struck five, then six. She felt the rhythmic sounds taking her away, lulling her deeper into drowsiness. Seven. Eight. The ringing filled her head. It was getting louder and louder. Suddenly her heartbeat started to quicken. Her head and ears were throbbing with the sound. The bells . . . the bells . . . they were pulling her far away again, taking her back.

Chapter 1

Once again she was sixteen years old. She was running as fast as she could. Her heart was hammering in her chest as she ran over the stones and ruts in the dusty road, oblivious to the sharp edges and roughness. The czar's soldiers were coming! The Gentiles were ringing the bells again to warn them. Hide! Hide! But where? The bells kept ringing. . . .

Dragging, pulling, she yanked David along behind her. His small legs stumbled along the ground, and he was screaming in terror. What was wrong with his mother? Why was she crying and yelling at him at the same time? Never before had she been so rough with him or acted so angry. What had he done wrong?

Marya heard cries and shouts to her right and left as she ran through the twisting streets of Petrovichi. A woman darted right in front of her and grabbed a young girl by the braids, pulling her across the street into an open doorway. Two old men who had been praying jerked their eyes open at all the commotion and tried to run, their limbs stiff with age. An old woman, her arms full of cabbages and potatoes, was trying to crawl under a horse cart along the side of the road.

Over the din of the bells and shouts, Marya could hear another sound, the neighing of the Cossacks' horses and the pounding of their hooves on the packed dirt. Louder and louder it grew until she was certain they were right behind her.

David screamed, and his legs went out from under him. As Marya turned to scoop him up, she saw a Cossack on a tall grey horse racing around the corner.

The soldier was quick to spot the pretty young girl with one thick auburn braid already hanging loose from her *kokochniki*. He was aware of her slim but rounded body as she struggled with the wailing child. What a prize she'd be! He rode his horse straight at the two of them, all the time holding her terrified gaze.

Marya stood as if paralyzed. She could not take her eyes from his menacing stare. She could see clearly all the jagged lines and creases of his big square face with its loose skin and drooping mustache.

As the pounding horse came nearer, David wailed and twisted his small body until his hand slipped from hers.

"Go! Run!" screamed an old woman behind her. The woman reached out long, bony arms and scooped David up in a single motion.

Marya tried to turn in the old woman's direction. She could feel on her shoulder the hot breath of the horse as the Cossack rode between her and the boy.

He must have her! He leaned over in his saddle and strained toward her, ready to grab her hair, her arm, her dress, whatever he could.

Marya saw the cracked black leather of his gloves as they came closer and closer. She could smell the mingled sweat of man and beast. She screamed, turned and tried to run behind him.

But he was too fast for her. In a moment he had shot his arm out and swept her up. Holding her in one arm, he kept her pinned against the side of the horse while her feet dragged in the dust.

Marya could feel the muscles moving in the

horse's powerful flanks as it charged up the street. Suddenly she was filled with an animal fury of her own. She would not let this happen! She would not be hauled away like a piece of furniture or other booty to be . . . her mind exploded in a flash of white anger.

Elated with his conquest, the Cossack threw back his head and whooped. His whoop changed to a yell as Marya sunk her teeth into his arm. She twisted and turned in his grasp and tore at his hand with her fingernails until the blood ran. He felt her slipping from him. He tried to tighten his grip but found it useless as Marya writhed and squirmed in a passion of hate and resentment. He swore as she fell to the ground.

His eyes glinting, his face washed in sweat, he reared his horse and looked back over his shoulder at the girl lying in the dust. The horse, caught by the sudden stop, pawed the air with its hooves.

Marya looked back down the street for some sign of David and the old woman. All around her was a tumult. She saw fathers dragging their wives and children, men in flight, their long beards flying, women crying. To one side a band of young men had started to hurl rocks at the tide of soldiers.

Marya jumped to her feet and spun to dodge a rock meant for a Cossack. She saw the soldier riding toward her again, his face contorted in anger. She gathered her long skirts up in her hands and ran toward a narrow opening between two buildings, hoping this was where David and the old woman had disappeared.

"My son, my son," she sobbed aloud, running desperately as the Cossack swerved at her again. She felt his glove graze the side of her face and jerked herself backward. She had to find David. Where was the old woman? She edged her way into the passageway as fast as she could.

It led to another street, this one strangely quiet. She looked up and down—no David. She knew she had to do two things: hide and find her child. But she couldn't do both at the same time. She ran to the end of the road and cut through to Vitebsk Street again, back into the midst of the soldiers. Angling her way through the turmoil, she twisted her head from side to side as she searched everywhere for some sign of the boy. One of her braids had come loose and half her hair was strewn down her back in tangles. Her face was streaked with dust and tears, and her dress was soiled with dirt and blood from where she had fallen. She had to find her son.

"Maidele." Someone touched her sleeve.

Marya screamed and spun around. It was only an old man, withered with age. He gently took her by the hand and without a word led her down one street and another until they came to the building that Marya recognized as the synagogue.

"No, we can't." She pulled back. "That would be the worst place to hide."

"That's why it is the best," he said. He climbed the steps and turned to look at her. She paused. But what else could she do? It wasn't likely David was still out in the streets anyway. Surely the old woman had hidden him away. And it was too dangerous for her to return home yet.

The inside of the synagogue was cool and quiet. Marya huddled in the dark, not daring to move. The room was crowded and she could hear the frightened breathing of the others who had come there to hide. Nobody lit a lamp or made a sound. Outside they could still hear screams and the splintering of wood as the soldiers rode their horses into the houses and smashed the furniture and dishes.

Hidden by the dark of the synagogue, Marya put her head in her hands and tried to make sense of what was happening to her. It had all come too fast. Last year the Cossacks had charged into the Jewish sector of Mogilyov, the town where she and David were then living with her mother and father. It had been whispered in the streets for some time that Alexander II had been assassinated and the Jews were to blame. The soldiers wanted vengeance in blood. When they'd broken into her parents' house, she and David had hidden in the closet. She had stuffed rags into David's mouth to keep him from crying out. Had he made a sound, they would have been slaughtered on the spot.

But maybe that would have been for the better, she now thought bitterly. From her hiding place she had been forced to watch as three burly soldiers grabbed her mother and started to rip her blouse. Like a crazed animal, her father had bellowed and charged at them with a meat cleaver in his hand.

They had killed him with a single blow on the head. From where she hid she could see his legs grow rubbery and all the fury drain out of his face as he fell to the dirt floor. Then the soldiers threw themselves like beasts on her mother, and Marya had closed her eyes tightly. But she couldn't close her ears to stop the sounds that invaded them. Over and over came waves of mingled screams and grunts. It was as if an evil and ugly demon were unleashed from the men, and she knew that when she thought of men and women together, she would not be able to erase the memory of it from her mind. She had to bite the insides of her mouth until the blood came to keep herself from crying out. When they left the house, her mother was dead, and the bloody taste in Marya's mouth wouldn't go away.

She couldn't get out of her mind the faces of her father and mother. She saw her mother's face in the marketplace when she went to shop, in the streets, and in every room and object of their small house. She saw her father as he had looked when he had taken her at dawn into the autumn forests of birch and fir to look for wild mushrooms. Wrapped in his thick cloak, rucksack in hand, and shaking with excitement, he had pulled her from clump to clump of damp leaves where they might find the buttery brown growths. She could see his face as she had begged him for three straight years to teach her to read and write as the boys who went to the yeshiva, the school, could, and how his face slowly had softened over those years at the frivolous notion and he had given in.

Finally, the memories of her parents were so thick that she could no longer stand to be in Mogilyov. She had written to her husband, Gershon, that there she had nobody except kindly neighbors, and the memory of her parents was everywhere. She told him she was going to get what money she could for her parents' ramshackle house and journey to Petrovichi to be with his parents, and where maybe she could help out in their small embroidery business.

Her in-laws had welcomed her and their only grandchild, and she had thrown herself into the work in the shop as a way to forget. One day a young man had burst in full of excitement and waving a small paper booklet. It was a brochure put out in Yiddish by the Morris & Co. Steamship Line. It proclaimed the joys of living in America and the type of life newcomers could find there. America, it said, was a land rich with milk and honey where all, Jew and Gentile, were treated with respect and dignity. In this vast, enlightened country a man could live wherever he wanted, do whatever work he liked, send his children to the university, and make more money than he could ever dream.

Marya slowly read the brochure and permitted herself the first glimmer of hope since the murder of her parents. That night she had written again to Gershon. She knew it was risky to say such things, but they must go to America. There was no future for him in the czar's army. He would have to spend the next twenty-five years there, and like the other Jews, he wouldn't be allowed to rise above the rank of private.

His letter to her was like all his others. He told her a little of his daily routine and asked about David.

Then he told her how much he missed them both. There was no mention of America.

It was at that time she began to have disquieting dreams. One night she woke up in a sweat and couldn't stop trembling. In her dream she had seen a hunter, dressed as a member of the aristocracy, shoot at a flock of geese in the winter sky. One bird was hit, and as it plunged downward, it was transformed into a young man and hit the ground with a sickening thud. She hadn't been able to recognize the man's face, but she had awakened with a burning pain in her stomach.

Two days later, Marya wrote Gershon again, and her words were filled with urgency. When was his next leave? She must see him, they must talk, they must plan.

A short time later she had received an official letter on heavy yellow parchment. In large black letters it informed her that Gershon Bonarsky, aged 21, from the town of Petrovichi, had regrettably been killed on the Russian-Afghan border in the service of the czar, fighting against the Turkish Emirate. She had held the letter in her hand and stared at it until the black letters started to squirm like snakes. Never again would she see this blond, burly man her parents had chosen for her. She ached to think that no more would she feel his warm body next to hers, or see him striding toward her, his face in a huge grin, or sit along the river bank on *Shabbas*, the Sabbath, and watch him toss David into the air and catch him.

So she was sixteen and a widow. She was no longer a wife, but she was a mother. David had become her whole reason for living. The thought that now something might have happened to him turned her world dark and barren.

Finally, hours later and into the night, there came silence from outside the synagogue where Marya was still hiding. The next morning when she and the others dared to step from their hiding place, they found the streets were sparkling white, like snow. But the white was feathers from the beds the soldiers had sliced apart as they rifled through the houses looking for money. Amid the feathers were littered pieces of broken pottery, bits of furniture and here and there a dead dog or cat. She hurried through the streets to the house of her husband's parents, the house that had become her home, too. They would help her search for David.

"Isaac! Rose!" she called as she ran into the wooden house set off by itself on the edge of town. There was no answer. She stopped and knew at a glance the soldiers had been there. But nobody was there now. She felt as if she were reliving a nightmare.

Quickly she ran back into the center of town where the embroidery shop stood. Boxes full of spools, red, yellow, blue, green, were still lined up on the floor. In the middle of the room was a table where a design lay ready on a piece of mesh, waiting to be traced. To the left was the big embroidery machine. All the shelves were in order. Thank God nothing had been destroyed! But at the same time the quiet in the shop was so eerie it made her shudder.

She raced out into the street and looked for a familiar face but saw none in the people milling about. Everyone seemed to be searching for someone. She told herself probably Isaac and Rose were also out hunting frantically for her and David.

Marya spent the next two days alone, searching for David, the old woman, Isaac, Rose. She tried to ask questions: Had anyone seen an old woman and a two-year-old boy with hair about the color of hers? But Petrovichi was full of old women and full of young boys—red hair, brown hair, black. Everyone had seen them and no one had seen them.

She talked with the other merchants in the town. Had they seen Isaac or Rose? For two days she hadn't spoken to them or had word. But people were too busy looking after their own to be of any help to her.

The third day Marya went to the glass shop behind Isaac's store. Judah, the glass blower, stood up and came to her at once. "*Oy*, Marya. It hurts my heart to have to tell you this." He placed his arm around her shoulder.

Marya stopped breathing. "What is it? What do you have to tell me? Say it quickly before I fall dead to the floor."

"They have found them." He squeezed his eyes shut in an expression of silent grief.

"Them? Who?" Marya heard herself screaming. "David?"

"No, the *zeyde* and *bubbe*, Isaac and Rose," Judah said, referring to the boy's grandfather and grandmother.

"And David?" she cried. "Has anyone seen my son?"

Judah meant to be kind. "His body will turn up in time, child, like the others."

Marya waited two more months, staying alone in Isaac and Rose's house. She felt she might be going crazy. Every day she haunted the streets, staring at faces, looking for a thatch of dark red hair or for an old woman with long, bony arms—but what kind of clue was that? Now all the neighbors began to say he must be dead. But she would have more children, they assured her. She was young. Such a beauty any man would want. Life was long, and there would be many other babies. The death of a child was not such an unusual event. Always more babies died than lived. If it hadn't been the soldiers, it might have been the fever. She should marry again as soon as possible and have another child. It would be the best thing to soothe her pain.

On the eighty-seventh day the body of a boy was brought to her. "It's not David," she said dully.

"*Nu*, well? She cannot accept it," said those around her.

At the end of one hundred days Marya was

possessed by a desire to feel clean, to be released from
the obsession of what had happened to her. Bitterness
ate at her and took over her mind until she could not
call it her own. First she sold the embroidery shop to a
young man from a neighboring village who had just
married a girl from Petrovichi. She collected the
money, then walked to Isaac and Rose's house. She
gathered together their clothing, took it to their nearest
neighbor, some distance away, and gave everything
away. Then she returned to the small house and began
to tear at her clothing. With her sharp nails she pulled
at her blouse until it began to rip. Then she tore at her
skirt and the tuniclike sarafan, and finally her chemise,
until all her garments were hanging in pieces about her.
Having followed the old custom of rending her garments to express mourning, she was now ready to put
all that, all the old ways, behind her.

She struck a match and threw it onto the floor of
the bedroom. She watched the small flames start to lick
around the edges of the coverlet on the bed. They grew
slowly at first and then crawled up and caught the
mattress. As if hypnotized, she could not take her eyes
from the flames as they now leapt about the bed. She
took off her rent garments and piled together all her
clothes, saving out only one overskirt, a chemise, and a
heavy cape. All else—shawls, felt boots, skirts, sarafan,
babushkas, blouses—were sacrificed to the flames.
Next she threw all of David's clothes onto the bed. As
the flames grew taller, she watched all her past life disappear before her. Finally she removed from her head
the *kokochniki*, the elaborate headdress that hid the
hair of a married woman to make her less appealing,
and threw it onto the fire. Married life and motherhood, that was all behind her now. Quickly the fire
caught the headdress and devoured all its cloth in a
single swoosh.

Next the table by the bed caught and then a chair.
Marya refused to save even the Sabbath candlesticks
with which she'd faithfully marked the beginning of the

Sabbath every Friday evening, as her mother and mother's mother had done before her. Now completely naked, she stared into the orange and yellow center of the fire and felt a strange purging. There must be a better way. She was going to find it. But she knew it wasn't here in Russia. The czar? Who was the czar to her? Nothing but a mad butcher.

She grabbed from the wall the embroidered picture of Alexander III that Rose had hung, as did most of the Jewish families, just as a precaution against the interrogations of the Cossacks. She flung it into the burning pile and stood under a spell as the brilliant colors melted together and then vanished. In the white heat of the fire flamed up an image, a glimpse, of how her life could be, of a place where she might walk the streets without fear and do whatever her wits and determination would allow her to do. Never, she vowed, would she think of Russia again. She would put behind her both her religion and her country; neither had given her anything but bitterness and grief. Never would she talk again of this country that had taken from her everyone she loved.

She quickly dressed, slammed the door of the smoldering house, then began to walk in the direction of Smolensk, some fifty miles to the north, where there was a train that could take her to the city of Vilna, near the border.

Chapter 2

Out of the corner of his eye Wolf watched the young woman poking through her small bundle.

The room was crowded. Tension hung in the air like cobwebs. In the corner three or four people sprawled on the floor murmuring in hushed tones. Others sat on the plain wooden chairs or stood against the wall.

He saw her pull out a small wooden comb and start to unwind her long braids. Slowly she untwisted the strands of hair and started to draw the comb through them. She worked in a rhythm, and the deep red of her hair glinted in the half-light of the room. He watched the rise and fall of her breasts each time she lifted her arm, and could not help but notice how slim but roundly formed she was. There was something about her that made him want to touch her.

She knew she should have her head covered and not be revealing her hair like this. But that was part of the old customs, she told herself, and if her behavior was improper, then so be it. She was turning her back on the old ways—what had they brought her but misery and disillusion?—and she was going to a new country, the *goldeneh medina*, the golden land, where she'd learn new customs, better ways. She took her time combing out the long strands, and only when her hair was completely combed to her satisfaction did she put her head covering back on.

A man, the agent, came in, slamming the door behind him. His face was florid, and he pulled his fleshy body about like a great weight. Instantly the room became silent. "We leave tonight at eleven." His voice droned. He had said this many times before to other groups gathered here. "The smallest sound from just one of you could mean death for everyone." He pointed to a large woman with a big sack on the floor next to her. "You! Empty out that bag."

She did as she was told. Out tumbled an array of old clothing, down pillows, copper pots, candlesticks for *Shabbas* and a samovar.

"Those metal things, wrap them in clothing or get rid of them. They'll rattle and give us away." He turned to a family with a boy about three and a girl eight. "Can they keep their mouths shut?" he barked at the startled father. Both the father and mother nodded their heads vigorously. The man circled about the room, glaring at each person in turn while he asked questions and issued warnings.

He stopped in front of the young woman who had been combing out her braids, and Wolf could see him size her up appreciatively. "Traveling alone?" he asked.

She nodded curtly and said nothing, returning his stare. She recognized the look in his eyes. She had seen it too many times recently on the faces of men, times she didn't want to think about anymore. But she refused to move her eyes away first.

As she held his stare, the man apparently could think of nothing more to ask her and moved on.

Angling toward the group again, he slid his tongue over his large lips, and said, "Once we start, no one's to ask questions. No one's to complain. No one's to doubt me. So if you've got questions, ask them now." He waited.

Someone wanted to know how long the crossing would take. Another said he couldn't swim, he hoped there'd be no swimming required. Another asked if they'd have to walk the whole way or would a cart carry them. There had been a cart when his brother-in-law went across last year.

The man answered the questions in a monotone and without elaboration. Five hours, no swimming, no cart. This would be a "legal" crossing. He had passports for all of them. They would notice that the ages and sexes didn't match theirs, but it didn't matter; the guards knew what to do.

"Now let's go," he said.

The room came alive with the sound of shuffling as they gathered up their packs and boxes tied in string. Just before he went out the door, the man turned to face the group again. "Remember, if the German soldiers hear a comment or a question, they have to shoot, whether they want to or not, even though we've paid them. They'll do it to save their own necks."

Wolf also knew that the guards, even having been bribed, sometimes changed their minds and shot just for the sport of it. Or that the agents like this one could take their money and betray them anyway. Stories abounded of thwarted attempts to jump the borders. Mother Russia had made their leaving hard enough by prohibiting emigration. Human nature's greed and caprice made it even harder. Wolf knew the success of what they were about to do was completely subject to human whim.

The band of a little less than twenty made its way through a field of high grass. As they walked, the countryside began to look more and more familiar to Wolf. When he was a boy, he had often come with his father and uncles to hunt in nearby forests outside the town of Tovrick. Wolf looked up and saw that the moon was hidden by clouds. He was thankful it wasn't full. That would have made their undertaking so much more difficult. It was good that it was a warm autumn night, the kind the Russians called *babiye leto*, old woman's summer.

Slightly ahead of him walked the young woman with the deep red braids. Her *povoiniki*, the headdress that revealed her uncovered hair, told him she wasn't married, and the colors and pattern of the *poneva* she wore over her chemise came from the region where the republics of White Russia and Great Russia met. Although he could tell from her clothing that she was from the Pale of Settlement, that vast western area where the majority of Jews were forced to live, she did not carry herself like the typical woman from a small town or village. Instead she seemed unusually self-possessed and even aristocratic as she walked with her back straight, her head high. He wondered why she was traveling alone.

They came to a barn and the agent went in first to make sure no one else was there. Then he motioned the others to come in. When all were inside, he shut the barn door and lit a torch. The barn was sweet with the smell of hay. They dropped their bundles on the dirt floor and flopped down into the hay.

"Try to get an hour of sleep," the agent said. "You'll need it." He settled down in the hay not too far from the young woman who was traveling alone.

The woman was immediately aware the agent had dropped down next to her and that his choice of spot wasn't accidental. Before the agent put out the torch, she turned and realized another man was coolly watching her and the agent. The last thing she wanted was a man next to her, or even one looking at her. She knew her feelings were showing on her face, and she was glad. She pointedly arranged her bundle between her and the agent, then closed her eyes to try to rest.

Suddenly her eyes jerked open. She must have fallen into a deep sleep. Something was different. Then she heard the breathing of someone—it must be the agent—right next to her. He had rolled toward her in his sleep. She lay with her eyes wide open and stared up toward the rafters in the dark. His labored breathing seemed to be coming closer as she tried to decide what to do. It was too dark in the barn to see a thing. She turned and reached for her bundle to draw it closer to her. Then she felt his hand on her, grasping her tightly by the wrist. She tried to pull her arm away. He clamped down all the harder and now it started to hurt.

"Stay close to me tonight," he wheezed, "and you won't get hurt."

His fierce hold on her and the tension she sensed in his body brought back a sharp image of the Cossack who had held her pinned against his horse. With all her strength she pulled her hand from his and was instantly on her feet. She snatched up her bundle and stumbled across the other bodies strewn about the barn until she found an area where no one else seemed to be.

Wolf, unable to see in the dark barn, had heard the rustling and was aware that someone, a woman?—the tread was light—was moving about. Then he heard a man get up and follow her. Wolf carefully got to his feet and made his way over to where the stirring had come from. At the sound of approaching footsteps, the agent pulled back from the girl. Wolf set his bag down between them. "Get your hands off her," he said. His voice was low and controlled. "That's my wife."

All three knew it for a lie. All the agent could make out in the dark was the outline of muscular shoulders and a powerful frame, but he knew which one of his travelers it was. The agent lumbered to his feet, ignoring them both, and immediately resumed his role of leader. He snapped his fingers. "It's time," he said. "Let's go."

At once the travelers awoke, shook themselves and began to collect their things.

Wolf turned to the girl to ask her name. "Why don't you leave me alone?" she said through clenched teeth. She distrusted this man and his motives. She distrusted the masculinity he exuded and that he was tall, strong and rugged. Here was another vulture, she thought bitterly, chasing off one scavenger so that he might have the prey for himself.

Wolf had started to extend his hand to help her up but drew it back at her sharp retort. Ignoring him, she busied herself with gathering up her belongings, then followed the others out into the night.

They tramped through the fields for what seemed like hours. It would not do for them to be seen or heard by the Russian patrols that roved the borders. They looked exactly like what they were, people fleeing the country, and if they were spotted, they'd all be rounded up and then who knew the worst that might happen? Once or twice in the beginning someone had said a few words, only to be angrily silenced by the agent. No one spoke now.

The fields gave way to a forest, and when they came to a small clearing, the agent signaled them to stop. A man came toward them, and the agent went forward to meet him. Wolf moved to the edge of the group where he could hear the two men talking low in German. They were far enough away that he could catch only fragments of what they were saying, but it was enough to make him suspicious. The agent turned and motioned to the group to stay there until he returned with the passports they would need to show the border guards so that they could enter into Germany's Polish corridor, the narrow strip of land that ran across the north of Poland from Germany eastward to the Russian border, and that Germany had claimed as its own.

The minutes passed slowly as the members of the group shifted restlessly and tried to keep from talking. Minutes turned into half an hour, then an hour. By now the silence had been broken. People talked among themselves, wondering what was taking the agent so long, estimating how far they must be from the border, complaining that they'd be crossing at dawn, at the rate they were advancing.

When one of their group, a tall, imposing young man, stepped forward and began to speak to them in a hushed but firm voice, they didn't know what to think. He wasn't dressed like one of them, they could see. His shirt was of silk rather than homespun, and wasn't embroidered with bright flowers or animals. His hat and jacket were of finer fabric than they could buy. Obviously he was from the city, not to be trusted. And they remembered how he had held himself apart from them, talking to no one when they sat waiting for the agent in the small house in Tovrick. Nor had he spoken on the train from Vilna to Shavl, nor on the horse and wagon ride from Shavl to Tovrick. Now what was this he was saying, standing up in front of them as if he were the agent or their leader?

Wolf spoke to them in Yiddish. He cautioned them to remain quiet even if they didn't agree with what he was about to say. "We are in greater danger than we realize, and to make a commotion will intensify our predicament."

At first they only gaped at him, open mouthed. A woman somewhere in the group started to whimper softly, but Wolf put up his hand for silence. It was clear, he saw, that they were on their own. The agent wasn't coming back. "Now here are our choices. We can turn back and risk being arrested. And that means you can count on getting nothing for the fifty rubles you each paid the agent to get you across the border."

There was a stirring and mumbling among them. He held up his hand again. "Or, we can continue on our own. We are not more than an hour from the crossing point."

"Or we can stay right here and wait for the agent," belligerently put in the man who had been afraid of swimming. "He said he'd be back."

"To stay here means to be arrested by the Russian patrols," said Wolf. "We've been swindled, can't you see? If he were going to lead us across, we'd be on our way by now. He'd take no chances of our not clearing the German border guards and entering the Polish corridor well before dawn and before there's a lot of other people about to notice us."

"To go on means to be shot by the Germans," countered the same man. "We'll never get through without the passports. And we'll never get the passports without the agent."

"What makes you think we can make it?" asked the young woman with the red hair. Her face was insolent, her manner defiant. But she was recalling the agent's words to her when he grabbed her, words that at the time were cryptic but now, with what this man standing in front of them was saying, were starting to make some sense.

So, Wolf thought, she was deigning to talk to him now. Still, she was the first to show any real interest in his proposal. Something in her voice suggested that she would go along with his plan if he could satisfy her question. He met her stare full face. "I know these woods. When I was a boy, I came here from St. Petersburg to hunt with my father. We can make it through the forests and fields and avoid the checkpoint all together. We'll be able to make do without the passports."

"And how long ago was that?" sneered a man in the back. "What does a child remember?"

Wolf looked at him steadily. "Woods don't change. I still know where the border is and about how long it'll take us to get there. I know how we can avoid the armed patrols. Now the most important thing is time. We have to leave immediately." Always, thought Wolf, the most important thing in his life, in any endeavor, seemed to be time. It was imperative he impress upon them the necessity of starting at once.

"What are you trying to do, get us killed?" rebuked someone.

"Crazy man, *meshuggener*," muttered another.

Wolf was not daunted. "I could hear bits of what the agent was saying in German. That and the fact that he hasn't come back are enough to tell me he won't, or at least not without bringing trouble," he continued.

Ah, the young man knows German, they said to themselves. So he was educated. So maybe he wasn't a *meshuggener* after all. He must be a scholar, a wise young man from the city. He might know more of things outside the *shtetl*, the pale, than they. Perhaps he could be trusted a little.

"Those who want to come with me, stand over here," Wolf said, motioning to a large tree on his right. He watched as the group divided and redivided.

The young woman traveling alone swung her belongings without hesitation across her back and came to stand next to him. She had not come this far to take any chances of turning back. Behind her was nothing. She would rather die than not go ahead. If this man knew what he was talking about and could just lead them across the border, she knew she could take it from there.

The family with the two children came to stand by the tree, as did the large woman with the big, ungainly bundle. Three young men joined them. Another couple, the woman holding in her arms an infant swaddled in what must have been every piece of clothing it owned, came too.

Some seven people hadn't moved and were still standing in the same place. Wolf addressed them. "Those of you who aren't coming, I recommend you turn back this minute. If the agent comes back at all, he'll return with soldiers. You'll be lucky to be arrested. Most likely you'll be shot on the spot instead."

Those remaining immediately began to confer among themselves. As Wolf was about to lead his band away, the man who had argued most belligerently detached himself from the other group and ran to join them.

As Wolf led them into the forest, he tried to

assess each person to foresee possible difficulties. The young men would be no problem, and they'd be able to help with the others. The fat woman would be the one who'd need their help the most, but she appeared to have the right attitude and shouldn't be any trouble if she could just manage to hang on to that oversized bundle of hers. The family with the two children looked healthy and strong enough, and he could sense that the father and mother were determined to do whatever was necessary to pass out of Russia. One problem might be the other couple's baby. They'd have to find a way to keep it from crying out. And, of course, there was the pretty young woman who was on her own. He figured that after the sharp way she had spoken to him, she must be sufficiently spirited to handle whatever came along, and for an undertaking like this one, that was good. Of them all, she seemed the most driven, the most determined, and he couldn't help wondering what made her that way.

They walked another half hour into the woods, then angled sharply to the left and into a meadow. After a while they began to hear the sound of running water.

The man who had joined them at the last hurried alongside of Wolf, clearly upset. "I already said I can't swim. Now I hear a river. How am I to get across?" He turned to the nearest person, who happened to be the fat woman. "Can you swim?" Without waiting for an answer, he kept talking. "I knew it. I should have stayed to wait for the agent. Now I won't be able to cross the river, and I'll have to wait around on this side and try to get back somehow, and I'll probably get arrested anyway."

Suddenly he felt Wolf's hand tighten on his arm.

His voice was low and controlled. "Do exactly as I say, step by step, and no harm will come to you," he said and tightened his grip on the man's arm even more. "Do you have that?"

"Yes," said the man, "but . . ."

"Good. Then the first thing we'll start with is silence. Got that?"

The man nodded. Wolf turned to the woman who held the infant and asked if he could hold it. Uncertain, the woman slowly held it out to him. From his bag he took a bottle of schnapps and started to feed it to the infant. Panic flashed on the mother's face as she instinctively grabbed at Wolf's arm to stop him.

"This will keep the baby quiet," he said. "We can take no chances of his crying out now."

The mother nodded reluctantly and stepped back. As Wolf handed the infant back to the mother, he caught a glimpse of the red-haired girl watching him as if in a trance. Had he been able to read her mind, he would have been as surprised as she was when unbidden there came to her a sudden memory of her lost son.

A volley of shots, some distance away, suddenly rang out, then another. Their eyes flickered across each other's faces in a reflex of fear, followed by an instant realization of what had happened. Nobody said anything, nobody stopped walking.

A short time later Wolf suddenly turned and made a sign for everyone to stop. He listened to the quiet, waiting to hear what he thought he had heard just a few moments before and what he had been expecting. They were being followed, but he knew he couldn't tell the others or someone might panic. He didn't hear what he was listening for, but he couldn't take any chances. Motioning for everyone to wait there for him, he went to investigate the depth of the river on his own. The night was still too dark for him to make out exactly where the shore was, and he had to use the sound of the water to guide him.

He waded into the cold rushing water and found to his relief that it was more of a stream than a river, and the water came no higher than his armpits. He hurried back to the group, which had taken advantage of his absence to sprawl out on the ground, and signaled for them to follow him quickly.

At the water's edge he again heard the sounds he had heard earlier. Someone was coming along behind them. As fast as he could, he began to organize the crossing. Holding their belongings high above their heads, one by one they waded into the river. The current was stronger than he had realized, and each person had to be escorted across by another whose sole responsibility it was to help that other person keep upright in the rushing waters. He watched as the redhaired girl stepped into the stream. Her foot slipped, and Wolf grabbed hold of her arm to support her.

She could feel herself tighten at this man's touch. She tried to tell herself that he was helping her, that was all. He meant her no harm. He wasn't like the others. But she still couldn't stop the instinctive recoiling to protect herself.

Seeing that she wasn't tall enough to have any strength in the river at all, Wolf suddenly stepped out into the water and scooped her up. He could feel her body tense in his arms, and she stared away from him into the dark. Where the current was strongest in the middle, he had to toss her over his shoulder to better balance himself as the water tugged at him. The suddenness of his move surprised her and she made a slight sound and seemed to relax for a second or two before stiffening her body again. She felt so light in his arms, almost like a child, it was hard for him to keep in mind she was such a sharp-tongued bundle of anger. By the time he set her down on the opposite bank, he wondered if he only imagined that she seemed somehow less resisting, less angry. He returned to the other side and continued helping the others over to the opposite bank.

The girl positioned herself on a rock along the side and watched as Wolf hoisted the three-year-old boy on his shoulders. That image of him, with the boy straddled over his broad shoulders as he carefully made his way through the water, burned itself into her memory and later would come back to her, even though she did not want it to. Then, in spite of herself, she would think of things she didn't want to think about ever again.

As Wolf began to cross the river for the last time, he heard the sound of horses coming nearer. He waded through quickly and motioned his band to position themselves behind nearby trees and remain perfectly still. There they remained until Wolf was totally certain that whoever had been following them had lost their trail and continued along the other side of the stream.

It would be dawn in another hour or so, and the air had grown colder, chilling to the bone their bodies that were already wet from fording the stream. Wolf hurried them along now, partly to keep them warm, partly to get them to the border before daylight.

As the forests opened out into fields of high grass, he signaled to them to get down on their hands and knees and start to crawl. The going was slow and was made slower because they had to drag their packs along with them. They were nearing exhaustion, but Wolf would not let them stop. "Only another twenty minutes," he whispered to the person behind him, and the word was passed.

When they came to the barbed wire, their hearts began to beat faster. This must be it! The group moved as a single body now, its movement made fluid by concentration and anticipation. How far they were from the German border guards, they didn't know, but they weren't taking any chances. They moved silently and quickly.

Wolf held up the barbed wire for Marya to crawl under, and she in turn held it for the fat woman who held it for the belligerent man who held it for the next person until everyone of them had slipped through. On the other side they tried to stop so they could hug and congratulate each other, but Wolf pulled them ahead. He no longer knew where he was, but he was looking for some sign of refuge. He knew it wouldn't do for them to look suspicious, for none of them had passports and could easily be escorted back to the Russian border. He led them to the edge of the road and motioned them to stay out of sight. They waited. Eventually a farmer came by in a large wagon piled high with hay, and Wolf stepped out into the road and hailed him.

From where she hid in the bushes, Marya could see Wolf hand the man something. Then he turned and motioned for them to come out and get into the wagon. As they crowded into the hay, exhaustion dropped over them, and they fell asleep. Every bone in Marya's body ached now, and she was too tired to mind that she was falling asleep next to Wolf.

Wolf slept only lightly. In fluent Polish he had told the farmer he was taking his workers back to Friedland from the border town of Tilsit, where he had lent them out to another farmer, and that one of the peasants, a complete idiot, hadn't tethered the team tightly enough when they stopped to rest for the night. The horses had got loose, and now his workers had no way westward to his farm outside of Friedland. He didn't know whether the farmer believed his story, but the gold pieces appeared to dismiss any doubts he may have had and to encourage him to help a countryman in need.

Marya stirred in her sleep and opened her eyes to see Wolf looking down at her. "Oh," she said, startled.

He held out his hand. "Shall we try again?"

She remembered how she had responded to him after he had helped her get rid of the agent in the barn, and she felt embarrassed.

"My name's Zavel," he was saying. "That means wolf in Hebrew. So everybody calls me Wolf. Wolf Luminov."

She raised herself up onto one arm and slowly extended her hand. "Marya," she said. "That's all. Marya." She quickly withdrew her hand as soon as they had shaken. Even though she knew she was being abrupt to this man who had done nothing but help her, she couldn't stop herself.

He noticed that she did not give her full name, or say where she was from, and that again she drew back from his touch. He was surprised, then, when she kept looking into his eyes.

She saw that his eyes were black and intense and were watching her closely, just as they had during the night in the barn. Yes, she was thinking, his name suited him well. There was a wildness about him. His face was broad, with high, prominent cheekbones and a straight, strong nose, and his black hair was thick and untamed. He had something of an animal's energy and instincts, coupled with a strong intelligence, and she found that combination unsettling. At the same time it drew her, against her will, and she found herself still talking to him.

"Where are we going?" she asked. Now that they had crossed into German territory, she was anxious to get on the right road that would eventually take her to Hamburg, where she could make arrangements for her steamship passage. She did not know the exact way but had heard enough tales in Petrovichi to know what towns to use as her guideposts.

He sensed her impatience and wondered what was pushing her. But then what was pushing any of them? Everyone on this wagon had a story to tell, a reason that compelled each one of them to wrench up everything and risk beginning anew. He suspected most were, like him, headed for Austria, where the current reign was said to be more enlightened toward Jews.

"Where do you want to go? To Vienna? That's where I'm going. If you'd like, maybe I could help you get there." As soon as the words were out of his mouth, he wondered why he had bothered to offer; anyone as reluctant to be near him as she had appeared to be would most certainly not want to travel with him any more than she had to. Still, he could not pull his eyes from her and was aware of the curve of her hip, the softness of her shoulder as she lay on her side next to him.

"I'm going to America."

"To America?" He was surprised by how far she was journeying. He had heard about the opportunities in America, and he knew that more and more people were leaving Russia to go there, but he somehow had not thought that she, traveling alone, would be going someplace so distant. "Then you have family there?" he said, and could picture a bearded father with dark, watchful eyes and a short, fat mother with a sharp tongue, even sharper than hers.

"No."

He was surprised. "Friends?"

She shifted and rearranged herself in the hay, giving the impression she didn't want to continue the conversation. "No," she said.

For the next few minutes they both were silent, and the only sound they heard was the clacking of the wagon wheels on the dirt.

As the road disappeared in a blur beneath them, Marya looked out on the Polish countryside which she could just begin to see in the early light. Never had she been so far from home before, and she was curious to see this country she had only heard vague reports about. Already they had passed numerous lakes and in the distance she could see dense forests. She watched the soft hills and open fields go by. At the same time she couldn't get from her mind the awareness of Wolf's long legs not too far from hers, and the span of his shoulders as he lay propped on his elbow above her. Unbidden, the image came to her again of how he had been with the children as they forded the stream.

Then she heard herself say, "That was a good idea to give the baby schnapps," and wondered why she was even bothering to have a conversation with someone who made her feel slightly uneasy and whom she would probably never see again as soon as they got to the first town.

"You mean you're going by yourself to America, and you don't know anyone there?" he asked.

Marya ignored his question. "The mother wasn't too happy at first, but then she seemed to see the sense of it," she continued. Then she actually found herself starting to laugh. "You should have toasted *L'chayim*, though."

"Then you must have a job waiting for you there," Wolf persisted.

Marya smiled and shook her head. "No, I don't have a job yet, but I know I'll get one, and you certainly stick to one topic of discussion. I want to talk about what we just went through, and you want to talk about America."

"Not about America, I don't know much about America. I want to know about you in America." He looked at her sharply. "And I think you're deliberately teasing me. That baby and the schnapps, you're not really interested in going on about that, are you?"

"No, but I don't have much to say about what I'm going to do in America either."

"You don't have anything to say about where you're from, and you don't have anything to say about where you're going. That doesn't leave us much to talk about, it appears."

Marya laughed again. She was even enjoying talking to this man. True, she still didn't trust him; he was too cunning, too much of a physical presence for her taste. But it was a soothing surprise to find herself talking to a man and not feel it a frightening ordeal.

"Why are you going to Vienna?" she asked him.

"I'm going ahead of my family to get a job. Then once I'm established, I'll send for them to come." It was his turn to shift in the hay and look away.

"Now I'll ask you the same questions. Do you know anyone in Vienna?" She saw a closed look drop over his features.

"What does it matter? Russia is no home for a Jew, or for anyone who is so presumptuous as to imagine that he has something to offer his country and would like to serve on the town council, or become mayor. There will never be anything here for us under the rule of the czars." His voice had become bitter and stern.

The gentleness she had begun to see when he had first asked her about herself was gone. Now he was the fierce wolf again.

"Yes," she said, and looked down, trying to keep her own memory of the past year's events away. She looked up at him again, but from the dark look on his face he still appeared to be lost in his thoughts. She felt a sudden urge to reach out and touch him, to see if she could get back the other side of him she had had such a brief glimpse of, so different from the cool command he had shown as they crossed the border. Her urge was almost strong enough to push away the uneasiness she had felt in his presence, but still something held her back.

He looked at her and saw that she was watching him. For the first time he could see her eyes clearly in the morning light and was startled at the color, a light, luminous green that stood out against the fairness of her skin and the deep red of her hair. She held his gaze and slowly smiled. He felt his breath catch as he returned her look and she didn't turn away.

Then they both felt the wagon begin to slow down, and immediately Wolf was back in charge.

Marya watched as he jumped from the wagon and strode forward to talk to the driver. She caught the word "Pastek" and knew they were coming into that town. From there she would get to Berlin, and from Berlin by train to Hamburg. Everything became a blur of motion as people began to climb out of the wagon, dragging their packs, bundles and boxes with them. They shook hands and exchanged names, then broke into smaller groups according to where they were going. While Wolf was occupied with translating and dispersing directions, she gathered her belongings and looked about the small town, trying to decide where she might go to hire a cart to take her to the nearest place where she might catch the train to Berlin.

As she began to walk down the street, Wolf was suddenly at her side. "Marya, good luck in America." He held out his hand.

She took it, and as she felt the warmth of his touch a strong presentiment came to her. "Wolf . . . Zavel," she said, and her words seemed to tumble over one another as she felt a flush come over her face. "I feel we'll see each other again. Sometimes I get a picture in my mind, just a fragment or glimpse of what will be." She laughed a little, almost self-consciously. "I guess I get it from my grandmother, may she rest in peace. But I know we'll meet again somewhere before we die." She saw that his expression didn't change, and it was almost as if he hadn't heard her. She felt a little foolish and began anew, more formally this time. "Thank you for bringing us out of Russia. We'll . . . I'll never forget that. And I hope you get your family to Vienna right away." She added the familiar expression of luck, "*Gey mit die riechter fuss!* (May you step out with the right foot!)" Then she turned and continued down the street alone.

The next morning, as Wolf sat on the train, he made a sudden decision. He wasn't alarmed, for all his best decisions were made quickly, even impulsively. He got off the train at the next stop and caught one in the opposite direction for Hamburg, even though it seriously depleted his money.

He couldn't get the girl with the long red hair out of his mind. He laughed a little to himself, as he thought about the young women he had known in St. Petersburg. They were beautiful and polished and poised, yet they were like elegant portraits, prettily painted but without substance and life, to be admired perhaps, as one admires a beautiful work of art, but not to be mistaken as real.

He was going after Marya. He was going to America.

Chapter 3

Wolf entered New York City with three dreams: one was to make of himself a man his father would be proud of, a man of position and achievement. Another was to send for his parents and brothers and sisters as soon as possible; once he was established here and they knew they had someone they could depend on, they'd surely come.

The third dream was to find the girl with the green eyes and red hair who saw "pictures."

As he stood under the trees on the edge of Battery Park, it excited him to think Marya was here somewhere in this city that rose up before him. Maybe she was just a few miles away, maybe less than that. He might turn a corner and there she'd be, dropping apples into her shopping bag or seated in a glass-plated shop window and sipping tea through a sugar cube in the Russian style. He could look up in a few minutes and she'd be standing right in front of him, all smiles. This very moment she might even be thinking of him and feeling sad that she would never see him again, believing he was somewhere in Vienna.

Behind him were the canal boats that bobbed their way across the Hudson River. He had just crossed the Jordan, he said to himself, to the Promised Land. Yesterday, as the ship had pulled into the harbor, the setting sun had cast a burnished haze over the ragged skyline of the city. Now, in the early morning light, the city was harder edged, clearer. How he wished his father could be here with him to see this city as it stirred to life.

As he began to walk up South Street, he recalled his last conversation with his father in St. Petersburg.

Amid the gleaming crystal and polished mahogany of the family dining room he had told his story of how that morning he had seen a group of Russian boys in Shavli Street shove two old men to the ground and shave off their long beards. The two men and the crowd that watched uneasily were all Jewish, and not one person had dared to stop the young men for fear of reprisals. Wolf had charged at the bullies, who were about his age, but they had already finished their handiwork and now turned their attention to him. Three of them had stood together and laughed as the fourth grabbed at his jacket and tried to spin him to the ground. But Wolf was too big, too strong, to be flung down like an old man. He felt a blow on the side of his face and then became like a madman. He yelled out and pushed his attacker to the ground while one of the others, almost as tall as he, shoved at him from behind. He spun and caught the ruffian square in the jaw with his fist. Now they all came at him at once. They beat and kicked at him until his legs went out from under him, and he staggered to the ground. Then they picked up their wounded and hurried away, swearing loudly among themselves.

After he told his tale, Wolf waited for his father to speak. He realized that here in the refined elegance of his family home, such an account sounded out of place, made up, even coarse and inappropriate, like the bruise on his face and the cuts on his hands. The soft chiming of the massive grandfather clock in the hallway filled the silence. To Wolf each chime, each tick said, "Time, time, time is running out."

Wolf remembered that his father had picked up the small silver bell on the table and rung it lightly. At once a servant appeared to remove the first course of the meal.

Trying to hide the urgency in his voice, Wolf renewed the discussion he had had with his father many times before. But he could see his own face in the ornate mirror along one wall of the room and knew his eyes were narrowed, barely concealing his anger. "Father, it is time we left Russia. Every day there are more taunts from the pogromchiks, those czarist-inspired hordes. There are more outbreaks of violence, more killings."

Dov Luminov sighed deeply and patiently. "Yes, Zavel, there have always been such problems. But the Jews will endure. This is nothing new, especially in Russia." His father was a big man, almost as large as his son, with a severe countenance and piercing eyes. He had raised Zavel to challenge and question things he didn't understand or that didn't seem right, all in the long tradition of the Jewish scholar. Now Dov Luminov was feeling what it was like to have that rapier he had forged held against him.

Wolf recalled how he had shifted in his chair and put his bruised fist on the table. "The situation is worse now. At every minute there are people being killed, businesses being destroyed."

His younger sister, Tamara, could not resist joining in. She shook her dark curls and, unlike the others, felt no fear of her glowering older brother whom she adored. "What would you have us do, Zavel? Fight back with sticks and clubs? That would mean certain death and—"

Wolf had pounded on the table. "We could move to Vienna like hundreds of other families are doing. We could start a new life. We don't have to leave forever, just until these pogroms stop, until things become better. And, who knows, we may not want to come back. We may find a better life. . . ."

His father had put up his hand for silence. "Better life? What better life could we possibly have? Our family is not like those others. We are well known and respected by everyone. Luminov Pharmaceuticals is solid and successful. Such a family, be it Gentile or Jewish, does not just pick up and leave. Our life—your life—is here. Our livelihood is here. For farmers and peasants such a change matters less. They have little to lose. We have a place in this city, Zavel. We have many friends, highly placed friends. I have done much for them. They would do much for us, too, if it came to that, you can be sure."

Wolf had struggled to keep his voice from rising. "It is only because our family is useful to the government that we have those friends. We pay more than one thousand rubles in taxes each year, more than we should. That is why our windows haven't been broken. That is why our clothes haven't been strewn in the street like those of the poor families. That is why our company has not been 'sold' to a Gentile family." His heart was pounding, and his face felt flush from his need to make his father see. He tried to control himself. Above all, he did not want to insult his father or show disrespect in his home.

"The hard times come and go," his father said patiently. "Just now the government is stirred up because of the assassination of the czar. So life for some Jews is a little harder now. You're impulsive, Zavel, so you got involved this morning and got hurt. But better times will come, you'll see."

Wolf had gone for a walk after dinner, he remembered. He couldn't get over what he had witnessed that morning. The blows on his body mattered little. What he couldn't forget was the fear in the eyes of the crowd as they watched the humiliation of the two men. He, for one, did not intend to live in such fear. He would not be a citizen of a country where his dignity and safety would be constantly called into question. "Russification," that policy begun fifty years ago under Czar Nicholas I in an attempt to have the Republic of Great Russia dominate the other republics, especially those of White Russia and the Ukraine, was worsening. And the power of the Russian Orthodox Church grew in proportion to the success of Russification, as everyone, Jews, Roman Catholics, Lutherans and Moslems, faced discrimination if they didn't convert. Couldn't his father see what was coming? The restrictions grew every day. Live here, don't go to that school, no university for you—the Jew quota is full.

He had watched a scattering of dry leaves blow along the street and thought of how those leaves were like his family, at the mercy of whatever political wind was blowing. If only they could see that.

Suddenly he had looked up to see four white horses and a carriage headed right at him. He recalled that he had jumped to one side as the gilded carriage tore around the corner and disappeared. He had felt a rush of rage that he had almost been run over by one of the czar's mad relatives, a minor prince or princess, who lived in lavish palaces outside St. Petersburg and roamed the streets in jeweled coaches while people were staggering in those same streets from hunger and others were being beaten because of the faith they chose to practice.

Well, what was he, Wolf Luminov, going to do about it? So his father was stubborn and couldn't, or wouldn't, see how fragile his place in this country was. Wolf had known he wasn't his father's charge any longer. At his bar mitzvah three years before, hadn't Wolf heard his father say the traditional Prayer of Release: "Blessed be He who has freed me from being responsible for this young man's conduct." So now Wolf was a man and responsible for his own life. He knew what had to be done, and if his father couldn't see, that still should not deter Wolf as a man from doing what he believed.

He remembered returning to the house and letting himself in quietly. Nobody saw him come in, nor did anyone see him leave a short time later. He carried with him a shopping bag, such as the servants used, in which were several changes of clothes. He also had two small paintings by Claude Monet and one by Edgar Degas which he had stripped from their frames and carefully rolled.

By late that afternoon he had sold the three impressionist paintings and with part of the money bought a train ticket for Vilna. In the middle of the empty frame where the painting of Monet's water lilies had been, he had scrawled a note to his father, explaining why he had done what he had done. As he had written the note, he had promised himself he would get his parents out of St. Petersburg and to Vienna, no matter what. He remembered his resolve.

Now after last night and the three weeks on the ship, it felt good to walk in New York. He had spent the night on the cold, barren floor in the main processing room at Castle Garden. How he had hated being herded like an animal with the hundreds of other immigrants. He had watched them cling to their pitiful bundles of rags and felt sad for their children wailing in the night as they scratched and dug at the fleas and vermin that were rife in the huge, crowded room.

Now that he was out on the streets, he felt truly a free man, suffused with exhilaration, eager to join into the life awakening around him. He walked quickly and confidently, a man with a purpose.

Along the water's edge were warehouses already teeming with activity as men hauled barrels and crates from ship to pier and back again. The sight of the men working and calling to each other in various languages buoyed him all the more. He recognized fragments of Polish, Russian and English, all languages among the six his father had insisted he be tutored in. Here in

America there was room for all, he said to himself. Here he would make something of himself.

He turned and went up Catherine Street as the muscle and jocularity of the docks gave way to a different tempo. He was used to cities, and although St. Petersburg was not as large as this one, still he felt comfortable with the idea of being in one. Yet, he noticed, the sidewalks were covered with garbage and filth, not like in St. Petersburg where they were washed and scrubbed every day. Nor did he see buildings in the French or Italian style, as those in St. Petersburg, in bright, cheerful colors. The buildings were mostly of grey stone or brick, and although not as pretty, they were taller, some even six or seven stories high.

At the corner of East Broadway he turned right onto a wide boulevard lined with more grey buildings. On Essex Street he found a room as a boarder with a large noisy family originally from Lithuania. It cost him seventy-five cents a week for his room, which included laundry and a mug of coffee in the morning.

Eager to be outside again, he followed the flow of people who had started to throng the streets. He didn't have the name of a particular street he wanted; he knew that where there were lots of people, there was likely to be a chance for work of some kind. Caught up in the current of the crowd at Ludlow Street, he was pressed left to Orchard.

Here he found himself in the middle of a tumult. His nose wrinkled at the variety of smells assaulting him in the open-air market. Fumes of garlic and onions mingled with live roosters, pigeons, canaries, dogs, tangerines, cheese, butter, prunes, plums. Everything, it seemed, was for sale here: breads, vegetables, potatoes in large sacks, meal, eggs, ropes of onions, glassware, matches, candles, breeches, shirts, old coats, wine, fans, copper pots, baby rattles, dishpans.

What looked like hundreds of wooden pushcarts had jammed into the street and were competing with the stalls and peddlers for his attention. Each seller had his own particular tune for selling his wares and sung it out in a shrill, nasal voice. The noise was almost painful. Wolf felt it like a jolt through his body, but at the same time it made him ready, eager to test his wits in this sweating cauldron of humanity.

He pushed his way through to Hester Street and found more of the same. Signs in Yiddish, English and even Russian beckoned him here to eat *gribenes*, pieces of chicken crackling, and over there to sip coffee. Boys dashed through the street hawking newspapers or offering to black his boots. Some clanked along under wreaths of tinware, their shoulders draped with scissors, cups, plates, pails. Men dressed in long, black caftans and hats hurried past. Others wore yarmulkes and had trailing white beards. The city was at the same time both familiar, with its cries and signs in languages he could understand, and yet unmistakably foreign. He saw Negroes, Chinese, Italians, nationalities he had never seen before, only read about. Nor had he seen so many women with their hair flying loose for everyone to see. In Russia it was the custom for all women, Jew and Gentile, to cover their heads. Men dressed informally, many without hats, their shirt sleeves rolled up, cigarettes dangling from their mouths. Yet the men and women were dressed better than most of the people he had seen in the market place in St. Petersburg.

To one side of Ludlow Street, he saw knots of men clustered about, all immigrants. He recognized the place as the "Pig Market," spoken of by the men on the boat as the place where a newcomer might find employers looking for workers. He stood to one side and watched a short, fat man make his way through the crowd of men, calling out for cutters and seamers. Here was someone looking for cheap help in the needles trade, Wolf said to himself. From all he had heard of the wages and conditions, this was the last thing he wanted to do. He hadn't uprooted himself from family and home to end up hunched over a sewing machine or sweating in front of a pressing board. Poor bastards, he thought, as a handful of men detached themselves from the group. They fell in behind the fat man, who had already started to sweat and was mopping his broad forehead—a sign, thought Wolf, of what's to come for these unlucky fellows.

No thanks, he didn't want to work in a sweatshop, and he had no intention of turning to peddling either, as so many of the other new arrivals did. He wanted something different. For another hour he stood watching the ebb and flow of would-be workers and would-be bosses. None of the jobs sounded like anything he wanted.

As the hour grew later, Wolf realized the crowd was thinning and fewer and fewer men came to yell out opportunities for work.

Behind him a voice called, "Delivery boy, delivery boy."

Wolf thought quickly. Not ideal, but it would give him a chance to learn the city. He could be out meeting people, making contacts. Where there were goods to deliver, there were bound to be other possibilities, a chance to produce, improve or manage them.

He raised his arm and yelled out to the man who continued to make his way along the street. Wolf's voice was almost drowned out by the calls of two other men also responding to the cry for a delivery boy.

The man stopped and turned. He was of medium height, with a gaunt, sallow face and a bony chest that was more skeleton than skin giving him the aspect of a cadaver. "Hey ho, me lads! What have we here? Some takers, do we?" He rubbed his hands together like sticks and sized up the three men standing before him.

Although each was dressed in a different garb, each was clearly a new arrival. "You," said the cadaver, jabbing a finger at a middle-aged man to Wolf's left with a worried look on his face. "How's your back? Strong as a stallion? In faith, I need a strong man."

Just one man? The three immigrants darted furtive looks at each other out of the corners of their eyes.

"You," the man said, coming within inches of Wolf's face to glare into his eyes, "can you lift two hundred pounds of dead weight?" He laughed loudly as if he had said something clever.

Wolf glared back. He didn't know how much 200 pounds was, or even one pound, but he was sure he could lift it.

Before he could answer, the man waved his finger at the three of them and said, "It's tonight you'll be starting."

The middle-aged man was clearly upset. This evening was the beginning of the Sabbath. Couldn't he begin the next night?

The Irishman looked as if he had been personally affronted by the suggestion. "You want to work, you work. You want the weekend off, you'd best become a banker, me boy. You're wasting me time."

He spat on the ground and scowled, then focused his attention on Wolf and the other man, a short, stocky fellow with a dark brown beard. "All right, you're on. Both of you. I'll be seeing you tonight at seven. The Fulton Ferry Building. That's on South Street. Just ask your way. A deal?" He stuck out his hand.

Wolf thought quickly. *Shabbas* began at sundown. But he needed a job, and this sounded like the best he'd heard of so far. Here in America, what came first was survival. He could keep the Sabbath in his heart instead. That was important, the feeling in the heart, he told himself, not the outward form. He put out his hand.

"You tell us what it is we deliver?" The other man's voice came out in a thick Italian accent.

"No time to be explaining all that now," said the man. "Besides, you'll be finding out soon enough. Just ask for Teddy tonight. That's me." He disappeared into the crowd with the hurried gait that Wolf was beginning to realize was typical of this city.

Now that he had a job, Wolf could afford to wander more slowly through the crowd and look at the faces and wares. He stopped in front of a thin-lipped old woman and asked the price of the alarm clocks piled in a bin at her stall. Already he sensed the clock was czar in this country. He knew better than to accept the price she quoted, and after a spirited exchange of numbers, he walked off with the clock at a third the original price.

As he was stuffing the clock into his bag, he looked up just in time to see a head of red hair disappear into the milling throng. His heart jumped and he had to catch his breath. Could it be Marya? He ran after her, but the crowd surged in his way. In a matter of seconds he had lost sight of the spot of red he had been following. Probably it wasn't her, anyway, he told himself. Besides, he couldn't be chasing after every auburn-haired young woman he saw. Still he had to admit that just a glimpse of reddish brown hair was enough to set his pulse racing. It was a reminder of how much he wanted to see her. Somehow he had to find her.

He searched for a quiet spot where he might sit and be alone with his thoughts of Marya. He walked a few more blocks and looked for a park but found nothing. Although every street was a little different, with neighborhoods of Russians giving way to Hungarians and then to Rumanians, all were swarming with adults and children busy walking, selling, playing ball, or just talking. Nowhere was there a chance for privacy or solitude.

Wolf felt a hard thud against his back. Almost simultaneously he heard something glassy fall at his heels and shatter. He spun quickly but saw nobody who appeared as if he might have hurled the bottle.

Loud laughter drifted down to him from a fire escape. "Hey, look at the greenhorn!" Three young men were looking down at him and pointing.

"And look at those boots," jeered one. "Must be

a Roosky. Hey, Roosky, why you wearing that short little dress over your pants?"

They laughed uproariously, and Wolf saw that a few people had stopped to watch. He looked down at the belted tunic he wore over his trousers. His skirt and pants were finely made and of excellent fabric, but they were nothing like what most of the men here wore. He had never thought much about his clothes, but now they suddenly seemed all wrong.

So this was how people saw him! Like all those others just off the boat, poor peasants and ignorant wretches straight from the *shtetl* or some mountain hamlet. He walked away briskly, fingering the last gold coin still sewn into the lining of his jacket. He would have to wait until he got his first pay. But as he walked, he studied the clothes of the people around him more closely and tried to see what they told him about the person wearing them.

"I'm Mario," said the Italian, holding out his hand. He and Wolf stood on the pier next to the Fulton Ferry Building, beneath the soaring spans of the new Brooklyn Bridge, and looked down at the small ferryboat bobbing just below.

Even in the waning light Wolf could see its paint was peeling and it was obviously in need of repairs. Teddy gestured to them to climb aboard.

Wolf stood alone in the prow as the boat made its way up the East River for the choppy waters of Long Island Sound. Yesterday, after weeks of being cramped in the hull of a ship, he had sworn he would never set foot on a boat again. But here, on the deck, with the salt spray hitting him in the face and the wind combing through his hair, it was a completely different experience than holing up in the steerage. If he could have sailed first class, he would have had more comfort, more fresh air, and that alone would have been worth the cost.

He remembered talking on board ship to an old

couple from Poland whose children, already living in
Cleveland, had worked and saved to send their parents
first-class tickets, having themselves already lived
through the horrors of crossing in steerage. But the
steamship agents in Hamburg insisted the tickets were
for steerage. What was the couple to do? They couldn't
read the English or the German printed on the ticket,
and had only the letter of their children to go on. This
freshness, this exhilaration is what the old couple
should have had. He promised himself he would travel
only first class from now on.

Less than a mile away, Wolf could see an area
dotted with occasional lights. It looked peaceful in the
twilight. "Brooklyn," Teddy called out.

Wolf looked back over his shoulder at the city
lighting up against the night, and he felt a sense of
completeness, of rightness. This was where he belonged. The swarms of people he had seen in the
streets, the animated selling and arguing, the horse
carts jammed at the intersections—all grabbed hold of
his senses and filled him with anticipation. There was a
dynamism here, a vitality. He could see it in the way
people walked and talked. Life was fast because everyone had someplace to go, something to do. He knew
that here he could do and be whatever he wanted,
businessman, teacher, doctor—he didn't know what
yet.

They continued past the northeastern edge of
Manhattan. Wolf saw open fields and wooded patches
of rough terrain. Teddy continued to call out the
names of the places they passed. "Ward Island.
Rikers," he intoned from the back of the boat. They
rounded a curve of land and came out into a large expanse of water, which Wolf thought must be Long Island Sound. Ahead was a long, low island. The boat
headed for its northern tip, and as they passed its
length, Wolf had an opportunity to survey its barren-
ness.

He wondered again what kind of delivery job this

was he had. He had seen the oblong wooden boxes of varying sizes piled in the bow of the boat when he boarded, but had no idea of what was in them. It was no use asking Teddy any more questions. He'd just have to wait and see. But he had a feeling he was going to like the job if it meant being out in the air on a boat. And while he wasn't crazy about working the night shift, he could work days eventually.

"Hart Island!" called the skipper as the island loomed large. They pulled alongside a creaking makeshift pier at the tip of the island.

"All right, you two!" yelled Teddy from the back of the boat. "Give a hand here."

Wolf and Mario grabbed hold of a wooden box, one at each end, and swung it up and over onto the wharf. They unloaded box after box until their arms began to ache and what seemed like hours must have passed. There must have been over a hundred of those boxes, figured Wolf.

From the pier they lugged them onto the sandy shore. A rich, rotten smell of swamp grass and weeds rose up and hit the two men in the face.

Teddy handed each of them a shovel with a long handle and pointed across a rutted dirt road to a jumble of underbrush. "There," he said, "there's where you'll want to be digging."

Wolf and Mario stopped walking. Had they heard right? Wolf knew he spoke for both of them. "This is supposed to be a delivery job. We unloaded your boxes for you. You never said anything about digging or shoveling."

Teddy cleared his throat and spat. "Just off the boat and you're getting in a mighty hurry already, just like everyone else. It seems you haven't finished making your deliveries yet, laddies."

"We'll make deliveries," said Wolf. "That's all."

Teddy's mouth tightened. "Now it's digging you'll be doing if you want your pay tonight."

Wolf's first impulse was to knock the bastard to

the ground and leave him there. But that wasn't how he wanted to start his first job here. There were bastards everywhere, he reminded himself. He'd bide his time. He picked up the shovel.

"That's what I like to see," said Teddy. "Good boys who know how to cooperate. You'll go far here, I can tell." He led them across the soft ground to a cleared area where the dirt had recently been upturned. "Here," he said. "Make the holes long enough to hold these coffins."

"Coffins!" Wolf exploded. "That's what your little deliveries are? Dead bodies?" He threw his shovel at Teddy's feet. "Why didn't you say so from the start!" He clenched his fists and started to charge at Teddy, who suddenly lost his cocky expression. At once he felt Mario's arms close on him from behind.

"We wait," whispered Mario. "Wait until good time. Better."

Teddy had regained his usual demeanor, and his voice dripped with menace. "Now listen to me, boys," he said, but he looked at Wolf alone. "There's only one way off this island, and that's the way you came—with me, unless you prove to be pretty powerful swimmers. And I haven't ever heard of any greenhorns who are." He took time to laugh. "So I'm recommending you just follow my advice which I'm passing on to you in a friendly, well-meaning way. Understand?" He turned to Wolf. *"Verstehen?"* And to Mario, *"Capice?"*

Wolf and Mario said nothing.

"What we have here is a potter's field. A burial ground for those who pass on without any family or friends or money. What we have in these boxes are dead bodies and sometimes pieces of arms and legs that the cops or somebody finds along the street or behind a building. We bring them here because they got to go in the ground somewhere. That's why you're here. To make sure those dead babies and bits of leg get a decent Christian burial."

Wolf wanted to laugh out loud, scream, do something. What a fool he'd been. He'd sold out! And for what? He knew that to get ahead he had to change some of the old ways, and so he had been willing to work on the Sabbath. But to work as a gravedigger in an abandoned field? That, he knew, was forbidden, dirty, unclean, and he recalled the words from Leviticus in the Torah about handling the dead. He could not stop himself from imagining the bits and pieces of human bodies stuffed in those oddly shaped caskets. The poor, the destitute, the luckless. He shuddered at the thought of them, and of the failure they represented to him. Better to be blown to bits in the heat of battle than to dwindle away unknown, unsung and a nobody without family or even a friend to claim you and wish your spirit well. He thought again of his family in St. Petersburg and felt an ache. He cringed to remember the pretty feelings he'd been allowing himself on the ferry ride just a few hours ago. This was it . . . this was reality. He grabbed the shovel and started digging furiously. All the anger he had toward Teddy, but most of all for himself for being such a schnook, for getting sucked in, went into digging the graves.

He continued to dig for the next few hours, saying nothing. Once or twice Mario tried to get him to loosen up and talk but gave up when he got no response. Finally his outrage subsided a little, and he became aware of Mario's steady breathing as he worked a few yards away. Poor sucker, he was in this too.

"Hey, Mario, where you from?"

"Sicily. Where you from?"

"St. Petersburg. That's a city in Russia."

"Oh, yeah?" Mario laughed. "You're the first person I ever met from Russia."

"Well, you're the first person I ever met from Italy."

"Sicily, not Italy. It's important."

"Sorry."

They talked a bit more, and Wolf learned Mario

was the oldest boy in a family of thirteen children. He and his father, Angelo, had come over together to find jobs six months before. Sicily was a poor area, Mario explained, and there were not enough jobs that paid a man anything he could raise a family on. His father had got a job on the docks here. And he, well, he had worked on the docks for a while but now wanted something different, something better. He snorted as he said that, aware of the irony in what he had ended up with tonight. But, he said, he and his father knew that if they worked hard and saved their money, they'd be able to bring over Antonio, the next eldest, in six months. One by one they planned to bring the boys over so they could earn money. Soon there would be enough to buy tickets for his mother and the girls, and then all the family would be together again.

Once more Wolf felt a pang at the mention of family. That afternoon he had mailed them a letter he had written on the boat, but it would be months before they got it, and still more months until he got a response. In it he had told them he was in America, not Vienna, and tried to explain the opportunities he felt awaited them all here, even more than in St. Petersburg.

As dawn was breaking, they walked back to the boat, arm in arm, each too tired to walk on his own. Strange, thought Wolf, this Sicilian was probably the closest thing he had to a friend in this whole country, unless he included Marya, and he had no idea where she was.

They threw themselves on the deck, too exhausted to move. As Wolf lay there listening to the slapping of the water against the side of the boat, he felt his hope returning. No, he wouldn't give up. He'd dump this job and find something better. There was always something better. Soothed by this thought, he dropped into a deep sleep which lasted only until the boat arrived back at the wharf.

Teddy doled out their pay: eighty cents. "When

you're ready to work again, be here any evening, seven sharp. The boat goes out every evening. Death takes no holiday," he added philosophically.

Wolf and Mario shook hands. "Good luck, Mario," he said. "Hope you get that family of yours here right away. There's nothing like family to keep you going," he added, more to himself than Mario.

One afternoon on Orchard Street looked like the next, Wolf noticed as he pushed his way through the ever present swarms of sellers and buyers the next day. He knew he had to look for work again. He refused to go back to hauling dead bodies and digging graves. Some delivery job that was. Never would his father learn his son had sunk to shoveling dirt in a pauper's graveyard in the Promised Land and on *Shabbas*.

He turned onto Delancey and followed it west toward Broadway. That's when he saw her. He just had time to catch a glimpse of her hair before she turned the corner onto Allen Street.

"Marya!" he yelled and started to run. He sped around the corner. "Marya!" He dodged his way through the crowd but wasn't able to get out of the way of a woman carrying three flats of eggs. His elbow caught hers, and the eggs spattered to the ground, leaving yellow streams of yolk dripping down the woman's skirt and across her shoes.

"Klutz!" she screamed. "So watch where you're going! Such a hurry you're in and now look at me. Covered with *schmutz* from head to toe."

Wolf had no choice but to stop. He apologized and pulled out his handkerchief to dab at her long apron as quickly as he could.

Not bothering to look at him but addressing the passersby instead, she increased the volume of her wail. "Why should this happen to me? What to sell now? All mine eggs, gone, running in the dirt. How to live?"

He craned his head, trying to keep an eye on

Marya while he pulled from his pocket a fistful of coins. "I'll pay, I'll pay," he said. "How much?"

The woman abruptly broke off her lament and studied the coins in his hand. "Such fine eggs they were, the best quality."

"Quickly!" he urged. "Tell me how much." He could see Marya's head disappearing into the throng.

The woman looked up and gave him a hard appraising stare, taking in his long legs and broad chest. Then she sighed. "You give me thirty cents for the three dozen. The rest maybe I can forgive for an accident, such a nice looking man as you. Maybe you come to my house sometime and meet my daughter? A face like an angel, this girl."

But Wolf didn't hear. He had already stuffed the coins into her hands and was running up the street.

He caught up with her in the next block. "Marya," he started, "I can't believe it's. . . ."

She turned and looked at him. She saw a tall, dark-haired young man who looked as if he had been running for some distance. She liked what she saw and couldn't help it that she smiled. There hadn't been many appealing men in her life of late.

"Forgive me, miss," he said. "I—I thought you were someone else."

"You look so disappointed," she said, wistfully. "It almost makes me wish I was this . . . this . . . Marya did you call me?" She paused, wondering how she might keep the conversation going.

"Yes," he said. "Marya. Only now I can see I made a mistake and bothered you with—"

"Then I must look a little like her?" she asked.

He took a few steps back so that he might survey her the better. She was tall, he realized, taller than Marya. And she was a little more filled out. Her face wasn't as pretty, but she did have beautiful hair almost the same shade of red. "Well," he said, "there are some similarities."

She smiled. "Nice ones, I hope."

"Yes," he said and laughed. "Some nice ones." Some very nice ones indeed, he thought. God, it felt good to be talking to a friendly soul and actually to be laughing. He had missed having someone to talk with. He realized now it had been months since he had felt carefree.

"How would you like to have a cup of tea with me?" he asked suddenly.

In the next hour he learned that her name was Etta, she had left Warsaw the year before with her husband and had arrived in America a widow, her husband having died of pneumonia on the voyage over. He also learned that she had a pretty smile and that she was lonely. But what the hell, he was too. So it didn't feel awkward when, seeing her to her dingy tenement building and then to the door of the single room she shared with three other immigrant women who also had the misfortune to be alone in this new country, he accepted her invitation to come see her again.

Chapter 4

"Your chest, so broad it is, you'll need your jacket custom-made," said the small, thin man, who was all elbows and angles. The rimless spectacles he wore gave him the appearance of an insect, but a very competent insect, as he held the tape measure around Wolf's chest, which was at his eye level. He squinted at the tape and announced, "Forty-six inches."

"I want it right away," Wolf said.

The tailor looked at him in disbelief. "Right away is not possible," he said. "But I will tell you what is possible. At least two weeks I'll need."

"One week or not at all," said Wolf.

The tailor sighed, shaking his head from side to side. "Such a hurry," he said. "Everybody who comes in here is in a rush, in a sweat, having an emergency, going to a funeral, in a wedding, late for a bar mitzvah." He fidgeted with the account book that lay open on the desk. "I'll tell you what you can get in a week. Maybe a vest, maybe a matching handkerchief."

Wolf waited and said nothing.

"All right, all right," said the tailor finally. "So you get it in a week. It'll be fifteen dollars, and you give me a deposit of seven dollars now."

Wolf immediately pulled out the money, all fifteen dollars and laid it on the table. "You can have it all now if the suit's ready in three days."

The tailor eyed the cash. "Four days," he said.

"Three," said Wolf, and started to draw the bills back.

The tailor's hand quickly moved out to cover the other half of the dollar bills. "A work of art takes more than three days. It took God seven days to make the earth."

"Six, Mr. Zeidenbaum. He rested on the seventh. And I'm not asking for creation, just a suit."

They exchanged long looks.

"Mazel tov," said the tailor and scooped up the money. "Congratulations! In three days you'll have a new suit."

Wolf left the tailor and returned to the Pig Market, where he had spent the morning to no avail. Again he became part of the gathering of immmigrants, one of whom, to the eyes of a native-born American, could be changed for the other, so alike were they in their "foreignness," even though to their own eyes they were all dressed in varying styles and spoke and carried themselves as Galicians, Litvaks, Rumanians, regions unknown to American ears. One hour passed, then two, then three as the only employers looking for workers were those in the garment trade, and Wolf was still set against working in one of the infamous sweatshops. At a certain point in midmorning he had seen Teddy passing through, calling for more "delivery boys." Wolf fought a strong urge to yell back and tell anyone who would listen that they'd soon be up to their knees in remnants of human flesh if they followed this skeleton of a man. He knew that Teddy had caught sight of him because his face suddenly closed and he veered sharply in the opposite direction. Let him go, Wolf thought, one day he'd get his chance with Teddy.

As the time passed with no offers of work that

Wolf deemed suitable, he began to realize this day would bring him no work worth having at all. For his new suit he had paid out almost the last of his money, and he had only forty cents left in his pocket. He knew he needed to find some kind of work. He wrestled with himself as he determined that a job in the garment business would at least give him enough money to pay for his board and contribute to meals. But no, he decided, he couldn't do it. He would come back tomorrow and look for work again.

The next morning and the next he went through the same routine. He stood in the Pig Market in the morning, and then went to places of business in the afternoon.

On the third day he returned to the market and took a job as a baster for a subcontractor that made men's coats. He was given the address of Abe Detweiler, where he was told to come the next morning. For a short while he could stand it, Wolf told himself. But he vowed he wouldn't get caught in it longer than three weeks, and every chance he got he would look for more work.

Wearing his new suit, the next morning he appeared at the address on Baxter Street and was let in by a ferret-like man who looked at him in astonishment. The man, who introduced himself as Sol, led him into the basement room where about ten or twelve workers, their shirt sleeves rolled, were hunched over machines or standing over pressing boards. Like Sol, they all stared at him, observing the cut and fabric of his obviously custom-made jacket and trousers, but saying nothing.

For his part, Wolf was appalled by the closeness of the room and the clutter everywhere. Below street level, the room was already hot, although it was only six o'clock in the morning. The gasoline heaters on the pressers gave off an odor that mixed with the body odor of the workers who were already suffering from the heat. It was a smell so permeating, Wolf suspected, that it did not go away during the night when the room was not in use. Being in the rear of the building next to garbage and manure bins in the alley, the room received an additional influx of stench from outside.

Next to the window sat the three machine operators, with bins attached to their machines so they might immediately push the completed garments away. To one side were the two pressers and one finisher. In the middle, on high stools, sat two basters next to tables piled high with fabric. Everywhere the floor was littered with half-sewn garments.

Wolf was shown to a spot next to the other two basters, who had to move their stools to make room for him, and was told to watch what they did. They each gave him a sidelong glance that clearly told him they did not trust him, dressed as he was and obviously not one of them, neither in appearance nor spirit. Wolf had to watch only a short while to see the repetitious nature of what basting consisted of. The men would quickly stitch together the pre-cut garments that the contractor delivered at various times throughout the day. The basted garments would then be thrown into the pile for the machine operators to sew together. No skill was required, only endurance and the ability to work full out, as the peak of one's energy from daybreak to nine or ten in the evening, often seven days a week.

It would be just for a short time, Wolf told himself as he set to work. As he basted, he took time to study the other people in the room. All spoke in Yiddish, he noticed; all had recently come over. He couldn't help but wonder how the slight, older woman managed to lift the twenty-five pound pressing iron hour after hour. He also wondered if the flush on her face came from the heat or from what the immigrants called the white plague—tuberculosis, the scourge of the East Side. She kept up a continual coughing, as did one of the machine operators.

Wolf suddenly realized that the hum in the already tense room had intensified. He looked up to see a large, pot-bellied man with a cigar who was dressed in a suit and standing in the doorway.

"Everybody is to keep working," he was forced to bellow over the stepped-up noise of the machines, "while I remind you of the rules."

Wolf figured this must be Abe Detweiler, the owner. The machines kept whirring and the pressing irons thumping as the man stomped about the room yelling at the top of his voice in badly accented Yiddish.

"Anyone of you who is late will lose half a day's pay. Anyone who leaves early will also lose half a day's pay, and quitting time doesn't come until ten. There's to be no smoking or you'll be fined twenty cents. And don't think you can smoke in the restroom; that's an unentitled rest period and gets a twenty cent fine too. If you faint on the job, you also loose half a day's pay." His list continued, and it consisted entirely of what they couldn't do and what they'd be fined if they did. When he was finished, he gave a blast on his cigar and went out, muttering about the heat and the smell.

After he left, Wolf noticed that nobody looked up from his work. As if inspired, or intimidated, by the boss, all continued to work just as fast as when he had been in the room. Nor did anyone say anything. Wolf didn't know about the others, but he knew that Detweiler was the kind of man he could easily have a tangle with, and he wondered how long it would take.

Wolf had planned to see Etta that evening after work, but he was so tired he could only drag himself to his room that he shared with five other men and throw himself down on his mattress, which lay on the floor.

It seemed like only minutes later that his alarm clock was screaming in his ear again that it was five in the morning.

Every muscle in his body ached, and he knew he was not rested. He reminded himself he would have to eat more today, to take better care of himself. He dressed in his same suit and got to the shop early. No one was there yet but Detweiler, a cigar already between his lips. As Wolf came in the door, Detweiler gave him a sidelong glance while he eyed his clothes. Wolf was surprised when Detweiler started talking to him, especially when he didn't look at Wolf but buried his attention in sorting through the armful of garment pieces he had just dumped on the table.

"Those sons of bitches at the manufacturer's say there isn't enough work to go 'round. The only way I could get us anything at all was to underbid the other shops. But I promise my people they won't make less money. You'll still make the same amount, you'll just have to make one more coat today than yesterday."

"Thirteen coats, instead of twelve," said Wolf out loud, to make sure he had heard correctly.

"That's right."

"Sounds like a cut in pay to me," Wolf said slowly.

Detweiler looked up and gave Wolf a long, cool appraisal. Then he said, "I never cut my workers' pay. And making thirteen coats in one day is a hell of a lot better than having no coats and no pay, like at some of the other shops."

The two men glared at one another until Detweiler's attention was drawn by two more of the workers coming into the room. Three more came in and then three more and suddenly the room was awhir with activity again. The male presser and one of the women who operated the sewing machines came to the door a few minutes behind the others. Detweiler spun at them and said, "That's it! You're ten minutes late. You forfeit half your pay today."

The two workers started to remonstrate, but Detweiler waved them away. "You know the rules, everyone knows the rules. I go over them every day with you for just this reason. I'll have no slackers here." He noticed that Wolf and a few of the other workers had stopped and were staring at him. "Back to work," he shouted, "or I'll fine you too!"

Wolf was immediately suspicious. It hadn't seemed like the two who were fined had come in ten minutes late, or even five. But what could he prove? He only knew that he liked this Detweiler less and less.

That night when he left work, Wolf met Etta for a cup of tea. He had wanted to go to her room again, as he had the other night, but she had told him that the two other women who lived in the one-room apartment with her would be home, and he thought he detected a note of relief in her voice. He thought back to how she had fixed them a simple supper of chopped herring, rye bread and pickle that evening, and of how they had talked quietly as they sat at the small table in the corner of the room. She had seemed a little nervous that night, torn between her desire to have some privacy with this extremely attractive man, privacy being so cherished on the Lower East Side, and the impropriety of having a man alone in her room with her.

As Wolf looked at her over the rim of his cup, he couldn't help thinking again of Marya. Etta's hair was the only real resemblance; her other features and personality were completely different. Where Etta sat quietly sipping her tea and nibbling on a piece of kuchen as she waited to see what he wanted to talk about, Marya would have been jumping into the conversation, laughing, teasing, challenging. Then it dawned on him that the only reason he was seeing Etta again was that he was trying to recapture Marya in her. He wouldn't see her anymore after this, he told himself.

Six months passed with Wolf following much the same routine. Work from sunup to just before midnight. On the rare occasions when he had to work only six days, he would see Etta, and each time he felt guilty, driven to it by a desire for Marya.

He had looked hard for Marya, giving up his evening meal to walk through the night schools where new arrivals were learning English, and haunting the open-air markets whenever he had a break, always hoping he would find her in the midst of doing her daily shopping. At home, if he had been searching for someone, he would have started with the shul, the synagogue, which was the center of community life. But here in New York there were hundreds of shuls, little congregations tucked into stores and tenement flats. He could scarcely find, much less visit, every one, and even if he could have, he had no certainty of finding her, for religion did not play such a big role for the newcomer as it had at home. Here it was often equated with the roughness, squalor and ignorance of the world people had fled and no longer wanted to be associated with.

He had not counted on having so little free time, and virtually no time during business hours when he might look for another job. The seven dollars he made at Detweiler's shop each week barely covered his room and board. He had time in the morning for only a cup of coffee, and the meal he ate at the end of the day was soggy and overcooked from sitting on the stove several hours past the hour when the family had its supper. Like the other workers in the garment shop, he was eating too little and sleeping too little, and it was only from sheer determination that he did not collapse like many of them did from the heat, from sickness, or from exhaustion. Still, the unvarying cycle wore on him, and he felt he was not as strong as he was used to being.

He also didn't like it that he had received no word from his family. Although he had sent them three more letters, he had yet to get a response. A month before he had written to some of their close friends and even the rabbi. Still he heard nothing.

Then the previous evening, on the way home from work, he had run into a group of German boys who were roving the streets. He had heard of the German and Irish gangs that would often prey on Jewish immigrants on the East Side, and knew that they would be spoiling for a brawl. Had they caught sight of him dressed in his custom-tailored suit, they would have passed him by. But the night was dark, and they only saw a tall, broad-shouldered man coming at them, the kind who would probably be some sport and put up a bit of a fight and whom they'd be able to overcome by their greater numbers. They set upon Wolf with glee, but were surprised when he proved to be more of a fighter than they had expected. Had he been in his usual condition, Wolf knew he would have had the best of them, but weakened by the long hours of work, they succeeded in getting in a lot of punches. They finally left him bruised and bleeding, although still on his feet.

The next morning he ached all over and barely managed to pull himself from bed. Rather than arrive early as he usually did, he came in the door right at six, the starting time.

"You're fined! You lose half a day's pay," Detweiler announced as Wolf entered the room.

He could hear the gloating in Detweiler's voice as he stood glaring at him. Wolf knew that everything about him, the way he dressed, the way he carried himself, both of which were unlike the ways of the other immigrants, annoyed Detweiler. Wolf glared back at him. "What's this about a fine?" he said. "I'm not late." As he had passed the bank just minutes before, he had noticed the clock at ten to six.

But Detweiler was poking his finger toward the clock on the shop wall, which read 6:20. "That's not what this clock tells us."

"Then that clock is wrong," said Wolf.

The room was perfectly quiet. No one was sewing or ironing. All waited to hear what Detweiler would say.

"Listen, fella. It's the clock we go by, for starting and quitting. If it's a minute or two fast, that just means you get off a minute or two sooner than you would by another clock."

"Then I'll work till 10:20," said Wolf, "and you'll have your same number of hours."

"Doesn't work that way. Next thing you know I'll have you people straggling in here an hour or two late thinking you can stay later and make it up. Sorry. Nobody can run a business that way. You were late. That's all." He turned his back on Wolf as if he had finished what he had to say on the subject. Then he angrily added over his shoulder, "Let me give you some advice, buddy. If you weren't so busy with making yourself out to be something you're not, you'd get along a lot better in this business."

Wolf gave up his lunch that day and instead used the time to buy a pocket watch. It took all the money he had been planning to pay for rent and food that week. Then he carefully set the watch to the clock in Detweiler's shop.

That afternoon the atmosphere in the shop was somehow different where Wolf was concerned. The other workers seemed more accepting of him and even proud of his having stood up to Detweiler. It was clear they all hated their jobs and by extension hated Detweiler too.

A few hours after he had come back from buying the watch, Sol, who operated the sewing machines right next to him said, "You can't trust these *Yekkes*, you know. They've got control of this business, and they'll get away with anything they can to make another buck."

"Yeah, Germans," said Wolf. He didn't look up from the panel he was working on.

"Sure, they may be Jewish but I'd never trust one any more than a goy, less even. They're embarrassed by us newcomers, you know."

Sure, Wolf thought, that made sense. Everything about Detweiler shouted out the scorn he had for this roomful of "old country." He had seen how Detweiler cast narrow looks at their clothes, their gestures when they spoke, their ignorance of American customs.

"But at the same time," Sol continued, "he's not too crazy about you either, even though you don't look or act like the rest of us. You dress too much like him, so you're too dangerous. After all, it's our old country ways, which he despises so much, that help him keep us in our place and make him rich.

"Those people came over here from Germany about fifty or more years ago," Sol went on. The more he talked, the madder he got and the faster he peddled the machine's foot treadle. "There weren't so many of them, and they managed to blend in. Now they're afraid we're going to give Jews a bad name. They really wish we'd just go back to Poland and Russia and Hungary where we came from."

Sol's words rankled Wolf. He thought about the irony of what Sol was saying. Jews were leaving eastern Europe in droves to get away from their oppressors, only to find themselves enslaved in a sweatshop in the land of freedom and tyrannized over by a fellow Jew, almost always a German, who considered himself superior. His thoughts on the subject were interrupted by a loud thump.

The consumptive looking woman who was one of the pressers had almost lost control of the heavy iron, and it had half fallen from her hand to the pressing board with more than its customary speed. Wolf could see her face was even brighter than usual and her eyes glittered. He got up and suggested they change jobs for a while. After all, it wasn't as if either of them did work that required any special training, and she clearly was on the verge of fainting.

A short time later Detweiler came in and announced it was time for a five minute rest period. Wolf looked at his watch; it said 6:35. They all hurried out into the comparatively fresh air of the alleyway, glad to be out of the confines of the close room. Just as Wolf was going out the door, Detweiler stopped him. "You were hired as a baster. I don't want you pressing."

The woman Wolf had exchanged jobs with overheard Detweiler's comment and lingered nearby. Suddenly Detweiler looked calculatingly from Wolf to the woman and back to Wolf. "Listen, she's not sick, is she? That wouldn't be what's behind your Good Samaritan act, would it?"

What did Detweiler think, Wolf said to himself. Who wouldn't be sick standing over a pressing board and lifting a heavy iron sixteen hours a day? Sure she was sick; even a child could look at her and see that. They were all sick, sick from the heat and the hours and the lack of ventilation. But Wolf knew he couldn't tell the truth or she'd be fired. "We wanted a change in routine, nothing more."

Detweiler put his cigar in his mouth and blew a blast right at Wolf. "Well, I don't like changes I haven't approved, see?"

It was all Wolf could do to keep from hitting him, but he had to keep his head for the sake of the woman. Without another word, he spun, took her by the elbow and led her outside.

When they returned with the others a few minutes later, Wolf noticed that the clocks in Detweiler's shop now read 6:00. Wolf's reaction was immediate. He grabbed Detweiler by the collar and spoke in a low voice between clenched teeth. "I know what you're up to, Detweiler. We're not supposed to notice that you're playing with the clocks here."

"Get your hands off me," Detweiler growled. Like Wolf, he was a large man, and he wasn't afraid of a fight, if it came to that.

Wolf tightened his grip. "Never cut your workers' pay, do you? You just require more work each day and then fiddle with the clocks. I call that cutting pay; it's just worded a little more underhandedly, that's all."

"Get your hands off me, you Russian kike," snarled Detweiler. He swung his right arm at Wolf's head, but Wolf ducked and came back at him with a blinding left hook to the temple. The big German staggered backward and fell to the floor in a sprawl.

The room was deadly silent.

As Detweiler shook off the effects of the blow, Wolf turned to get his jacket. Crawling on the floor like a crab, Detweiler was suddenly up and lunging toward him. As Detweiler threw his weight into the small of Wolf's back, they both fell and crashed into one of the basting tables, scattering scissors, threads and fabric across the room. They grappled with each other on the floor, rolling from left to right as each tried to gain the superior position.

The other workers were on their feet now and had cleared a spot as they tried to get out of the way of the two big men. They watched as Wolf got on top of Detweiler and proceeded to hit him twice in the jaw.

Detweiler temporarily subdued, Wolf dusted himself off and reached for his jacket which Sol had rescued from the floor when Detweiler had come at him from behind. As he was putting his arms into the sleeves, one of the other workers yelled, "Watch out!" Wolf spun just in time to see Detweiler let go of a still-hot pressing iron, hurtling it toward Wolf's head. He dodged to one side, and the iron crashed through the dirty, fly-specked window and clattered into the alley beyond.

"Good idea!" yelled Wolf. "Let's clear the air here," and he snatched up his basting stool and hurled it through the shattered window after the iron.

At once Sol was on his feet, tipping his machine on end till he had hoisted it through the window after Wolf's work stool. Chaos erupted as worker after worker joined in the melee and tossed machines, stools, tables and piles of unfinished garments out the window and into the alley.

"You're fired!" screamed Detweiler, now on his feet but standing helpless by the door. "You're all fired!"

But no one cared. They were all out of a job, but this was the happiest any of them ever had been in that miserable little room.

Wolf grabbed his jacket and the other pressing iron. As he went out the door, he flourished the iron in Detweiler's face. "Consider this my pay for the week," he said. Then he was out in the fresh air, away from the fumes and the stench and the sweat.

Behind him streamed the others, laughing and joking, glad to be free of Detweiler and his system of fines, even though deep down they knew that because they had to eat, tomorrow they'd be back in another sweatshop, perhaps just as bad as Detweiler's. Once out on the street, still laughing, they all shook hands, wished each other luck, and promised to keep in touch. Then, not knowing what else to do, they turned and all went their separate ways.

"Wolf!"

It was Sol, who had hurried after him. He pressed into Wolf's hand a slip of paper. "Here's my address. If you ever need someone to work for you, you'll know where I am." Then he reached out his hand, pumped Wolf's again vigorously, and was gone.

Wolf had to laugh. Work for him? He didn't even have a job himself. And now that the exhilaration of the moment was waning, he realized how shaky from fatigue his legs were. His head ached, and his skin was hot and dry. He walked for hours as the shadows of the afternoon blurred into evening, paying little attention to where he was. Finally, when it was completely dark outside, he looked up to see that he was on the street where Etta lived. He dragged himself up the three flights to her flat and knocked. It had been more than a month since he had last seen her, and he wondered if she were still living there.

Etta herself opened the door. "Wolf?" As the weeks had slipped by, she had not been sure if she would ever see him again. "Is it really you?" Her welcome was careful and hesitant, the tone of a woman who doesn't want to hope for too much.

He leaned against the doorjamb and looked past her to see if they were alone.

She could see that he was pale, perhaps sick, and there were beads of moisture above his lip. "Come in," she said at last, and reached out for his hand. "I'll fix you something hot to drink. Are you hungry?"

He let himself be led into the room, and at the touch of a warm, sympathetic hand, he suddenly reached out for her and drew her into his arms. Quickly, almost desperately, he pulled the combs from her hair and let it fall down over her shoulders.

She hadn't been with a man for over a year, and her desire was more than she could bear. Her reluctance fell away and she responded to his need without shame. Hurriedly she pulled at her clothes and his and drew him down on the small bed that also served as a sofa. He buried his face in her red hair and pressed his body into hers. Then, he quickly entered her and as he gave vent to the urgency that was driving him, he saw Marya's face flash before him and he cried out her name.

Afterward, Etta was very quiet. Without looking at Wolf or meeting his eyes, she quickly put her clothes back on. When she finally did look at him, her eyes were veiled and withdrawn.

He knew he had hurt her. All he could say was he was sorry, but that seemed so inadequate. He knew he could not give her the reassurance she wanted.

"I think we'd better not see each other again," he said.

His words unleashed the anger that she had been burying. "Get out," she said in a low voice that was beginning to crescendo. When he didn't move immediately, she said again, this time louder, "I said, 'Get out!'" Suddenly tears were streaming down her face, and she was reaching wildly for anything she could get her hands on, a book, a plate. . . .

"Etta," he said, and tried to get hold of her hand.

She pulled her hand back and grabbed at her shoe. As he stood up to leave, she hurled it at him with all her might. Wolf let himself out the door, and the shoe thudded against the wall, leaving a mark that wouldn't go away.

The gaslights along East Broadway were circled in rainbow hues, and the buildings had become fuzzy. His legs felt shackled, so heavy were they. He didn't know how long it was since he'd left Etta's, but he felt like he'd been walking for hours. He found it hard to admit, but he was sick. His forehead was burning, and his eyes wouldn't focus right. One moment he was so hot he wanted to tear off his jacket and shirt; the next he was trembling with cold. Worst of all, his legs would carry him where he willed only if he used the utmost of concentration. And it was hard to concentrate on walking at all because what had just happened with Etta kept replaying in his brain and made him feel even sicker.

He vaguely wondered where he was now, but of more concern was the pain that had begun to stab at the base of his skull. Could that be what was making it so hard for him to see, he wondered. He turned down a side street and from that one onto another and then another. He had no idea of how to get back to his lodgings on Essex Street.

As he wandered, the sky gradually grew lighter and the gaslights of the city went out. One by one the stores in the bottom of the tenements began to open their doors, and the owners busied themselves with makeshift brooms as they raked and swept the street in front of their doorways. Outside of one shop a short, round man with a severely receding hairline was washing the dust off the windows of his store, and behind him Wolf could dimly see what looked like an assortment of vials and cannisters. He stood and tried to make out the sign on the storefront, but the letters wouldn't stop moving in front of his eyes. After he studied the writing for a while, he finally read what looked to be Vertov's Herbs and Apothecaries.

He must go in and ask for something that could

help him, he told himself, but his legs refused to go any further. His head was reeling as he somehow half pushed, half stumbled his way through the door. Big blotches of blackness were intruding on his vision now, covering up more and more of what he could see.

Behind the counter was a woman whose face was pale and distressed, and who was reaching out her hands toward him. Just before the blackness took over completely, he could dimly see, as if underwater, tendrils of her long red hair. He wondered what Etta was doing there.

Chapter 5

Wolf suddenly opened his eyes. The room was unnaturally quiet. Where were the others, Itzak the peddler and Karl the handyman? Had their Lithuanian landlady finally kicked them out, or had they gone of their own accord? Itzak had felt she always watched him as he sugared his coffee, begrudging of each spoonful he took. Maybe he had finally gotten tired enough of feeling he was always being watched and had taken off and found a new place to board.

As Wolf's vision cleared, it dawned on him this was not the room where he lived. No mattresses were scattered on the floor; the furniture and windows were completely different, and he was actually lying in a bed. Outside he heard horses and peddlers' cries that told him the windows of this room faced the street. He got up to investigate, but as he stepped from the bed, his legs would not support him, and he abruptly had to sit down.

In a haze it now came back to him: his fight with Detweiler, his last conversation with Sol, Etta's hair undone, his wandering the streets and then his collapse. Even now his head felt light, and he had to lie back down. He wondered how long he had been here and what day it was. Then he fell back into a deep sleep, and it was some time before he heard the voices.

"Don't you think we should wake him?" said the man. He sounded restless.

"Shhh. No," said the woman. "Let him sleep. His body is mending itself."

Then the door quietly opened and shut, and Wolf sensed only one person in the room now.

He opened his eyes and then immediately closed them again. He must still be dreaming. Slowly, carefully, he edged them open again and tried to see clearly.

"Hello, Zavel."

He must be careful. He must not say the wrong name this time, but he felt so confused and his head was still splitting.

She looked at him, his big body overwhelming the narrow bed, his coloring still strong even in sickness. Should she help him with his struggle to place her? After all, he was obviously still sick, and despite the attentive care she had given him these last seven days, he was not yet himself, nor ready to get up.

"Don't go away," she teased, knowing full well he could scarcely stand, and she left the room. A few minutes later she returned with a steaming bowl of soup.

He still could not get over her. He watched as she pulled a chair alongside the bed. Then she sat down and ordered him to open his mouth so she could spoon the hot chicken broth into it. While he obediently sipped the soup, his eyes drank in the sight of her, from her small waist and the curve of her breast under the thin white blouse to the slim, aristocratic nose and brilliant green eyes and red hair.

He finally said her name. "Marya."

She smiled and nodded. "What I want to know now is, am I dreaming or are you? You were supposed to be in Vienna."

"I knew that you were here, not in Vienna."

"You knew that I was here? You changed your plans, just like that? How did you even know I wanted to see you again?"

"I wanted to see you, that's all."

She was amazed by his confidence and secretly pleased.

"I knew you were for me from the very start," he said. "Even in that little room in Vilna, I wanted to bash in the head of that agent who was running his eyes over you."

"You took such a risk in coming here, Zavel."

He reached for her hand. "Too much of a risk?"

She met his gaze. "I don't know," she said slowly. "It's just that I was so afraid of you, afraid of every man. You must have seen that. You had no reason to think I'd be any different here." She paused a moment, then asked, "And what of your family?"

He wasn't ready to speak of other things yet. "Is that why you shied away from me that night in the barn? Because of your fear of men? You wouldn't even let me help you."

"I told you I was frightened. I . . . I. . . ." She heeded her vow not to talk about her past in Russia. That was all done, all ashes. "I had had a hard time already, traveling alone, and—"

"Why were you traveling alone? Where was your family?"

"I . . . they—"

The door opened and into the bedroom came a short, balding man who Wolf thought looked dimly familiar.

"This is Lubish Vertov," Marya said at once, glad to be able to change the subject. "He's my cousin, two times removed. It's his shop you came into before the pneumonia you were walking around with knocked you down. We had to call the doctor to help get you back together."

Then Wolf recognized the man in front of him as the man who had been sprinkling water on the street that morning he had stood outside and tried to make the letters on the sign come into focus. His face was pear-shaped, with the sides round and full, the forehead narrow. He looked to be in his mid-thirties, and his face already bore lines from worry.

His small, round eyes glanced at Wolf, then back to Marya. An indefinable emotion flickered across his face and was immediately gone. "We need your help in the kitchen," he said. Addressing Wolf, he said, "You will excuse me, but we're preparing this morning for tonight's *Shabbas* meal." Then he added, almost as an afterthought, "Perhaps when you're well enough, you'll be able to join us. I hope that will be soon."

Wolf fell back into a light sleep, a sleep punctuated with vague, disjointed dreams. At one point he saw a procession of the women in his life he had felt passion for. Among them was Vida, who had cast smoldering black eyes at him from behind her fan in Madam Navowski's salon when he was barely thirteen and she was the same. He reached for her in his dream, surprising her from behind, and when she turned in his arms to face him, it was Marya he held.

Then came Kayla, whom he had held hands with in his father's library when he was a little older. As she had stood on tiptoe and reached for a book high above her head, his eyes followed the smoothness of her arm into the elbow length sleeve, and he was held captive by the curve of her bodice as it rose and fell, rose and fell, in response to her futile efforts to reach the book. He easily extended his arm over her head for the volume and when he handed it to her, it was Marya who smiled back at him.

And finally there was Shosha, who was probably the one he had spent the most time with and who was the one who had chased him the most. In his dream, he saw again a picnic in the woods with both their families. Shosha stood a little apart, back behind a tree where no one could see her but he. She beckoned to him to come take a walk. He slowly sauntered away from the picnic, but in a different direction. Then when he got where no one could see him, he circled back and met her. She pulled him to her at once, and he could feel her breasts firm and high pushing into his chest through their thin summer shirts. She took his hand and guided it to her breast, and he didn't know what would have happened if they hadn't both heard a noise, a twig snapping. They jumped back from each other, and each went in a separate direction, circling back to the clearing where the picnic was. His blood was pounding in his head. All he could think about was her. But he knew he didn't love her; she was a flirt, a tease. In the dream they had stolen a moment alone at a soiree in her parents' summer home, and as he at last pulled her against him and held her tightly, it was Marya who returned his kisses so ardently.

Wolf woke hot and flushed, and when Marya came in the room to check on him, his eyes soaked up every inch of her. He wanted to pull her to him as he had done in the dream and feel her breasts taut against his body.

Marya looked into the blackness of his eyes and felt she was falling. It was like falling down a well that had no bottom, and the feeling both thrilled and terrified her. She wanted to mask her feelings from him, not sure if he felt as intensely as she, but didn't know how.

As he sat up, she put her hand on his forehead. "You have a fever," she managed to say. "Your head is burning hot."

She returned immediately with a bowl of water and a cloth and began to wash the water over his forehead.

"Your cool compresses won't take away my fever, Marya."

"No?" she said, her heart pounding loudly. "Is it that stubborn and vicious a fever?"

"Vicious? Not at all. It's not from my illness. It's

from you." He paused. "Don't you have a touch of it, too?"

She held her breath. She had known what he was going to say. The feeling was so strong it permeated the air they breathed and was all around her, all around both of them.

She wanted to look at him but felt that if she did, she would be hopelessly lost and under his power. "I think so, Zavel," she said, and studied a crack in the wall. She feared losing herself in the emotions that welled up in her. Their intensity and the nature of the events she had witnessed in her parents' house in Russia and again in the streets of Petrovichi were somehow linked, and one part of her, a very powerful part, pulled back.

"And your fears of me, you left those behind in Russia?"

She couldn't say anything but tried to smile.

He touched her cheek, and as their bodies made contact, suddenly the feeling between them became stronger than her fears. Their faces moved of one accord toward each other. Wolf encircled her with his arm and pulled her lips against his.

Later she wondered how long Lubish had been calling her before either she or Wolf heard him. She had had to pull herself from Wolf's kiss and hurry to the shop below, her face flushed with emotion.

In the weeks that passed, Wolf grew stronger under Marya's care. Any spare moments she could steal from her work in Lubish's shop, she would spend with Wolf. Often she would appear with a strangely colored liquid, sometimes hot, sometimes cold. "Drink," she would insist, and he would have to hold his breath as he downed the ill-smelling potion, but always he'd comply. Fate had seen fit to deliver him into her hands, and his only inclination was to surrender totally. So he obediently swallowed the peculiar ground herbs she brought and drank of the unusual teas.

"What is this drek?" he occasionally asked after swallowing a particularly noxious mouthful.

"I can't tell you that," she laughed. "The mystery is part of the cure. If you knew what you were drinking, it might not work."

So he learned not to ask and to trust her completely.

Once or twice in the evening he thought he heard other voices in the flat, but always she came to say good night before she went to sleep and never did she mention anyone but Lubish. Their times together he liked best were those minutes early in the morning, before the shop opened and while the day was still quiet. She would sit by his bed, and they would talk of those matters closest to their hearts. At such times she was most relaxed, fresh and optimistic.

He told her about his family in St. Petersburg and of how none of his letters had been answered.

"Yes," she said, "not knowing is hard." She involuntarily thought of her own hundred days of searching and waiting for David.

He wanted to know about her family, and about Lubish.

"When I first came, I went to a home for young women," said Marya, reluctantly. She was not used to talking about herself much, and it made her distinctly uncomfortable. "It was a kind of settlement house operated by wives of wealthy German Jews. My first day there, after I was introduced at the dinner table as Marya Vertov, a woman came up to me and asked if I were related to the people who run Vertov's apothecary shop. I said I didn't know and found out from her where it was.

"The next day I went into the shop and asked for the owner. Out came Lubish. I didn't recognize him. I hadn't seen him in eight years. In Russia he had lived in Mstislav, another town not too far from mine, and I had been only eight, just a girl, the last time we saw each other. He had come to help my father with his"—she hurried along now, not wanting to say too much or think about her family. "Well, anyway, it had been a long time, and our families had lost touch. We didn't know each other at first. He just stared at me and stared. Finally he started to shake me and kept saying some kind of foolish things about what a woman I'd become. Then he insisted I come to stay with him and his wife—"

"He has a wife?" Wolf hadn't seen or heard another woman there.

"She's confined to bed. She was stricken about a year ago and she hasn't been able to do much for herself ever since." Marya recalled the look Alma had given her when Lubish had taken her up the narrow stairs in the back of the shop that led to their four-room flat, luxurious by the standards of the other immigrants and the result of a bustling business in medicines, an ongoing preoccupation of the Lower East Siders. Marya had seen a pale, thin face on the pillow, and her impression was that the woman had no body under those blankets, so little were the bedclothes lifted or disturbed. Most of all, she noticed Alma's eyes, like huge black holes, that stared at her with a mixture of interest and fear. Here was another woman who could keep her company and talk to her, and here was a potential danger to her marriage.

Wolf was surprised to learn there was someone else there who also needed tending.

"Bedridden? Is she so old?"

"No, but her life has been very difficult, and she and Lubish had such a hard time when they first came here. The business now does well. That's why they can live in this tenement flat that has two bedrooms."

"Two? I must be in your room then. Where do you sleep?"

"On the sofa in the front room."

"Where everyone can see you?" His voice betrayed his feeling that she was his, and not to be casually ogled or desired.

"Who's everyone, Zavel? There's only Lubish and his wife, Alma."

"I thought I heard another voice, another man."

"Only the four of us are here, you and me, Alma and Lubish," Marya said, then added, "Sometimes friends come to visit. Perhaps that's who you're hearing," and she began to speak of how Lubish had insisted she come to stay with them.

" 'It is a sin against God for a beautiful young woman such as yourself to be on her own,' Lubish said to me. 'The streets are full of unscrupulous men who prey on naive young women fresh from the old country. You can see what becomes of such girls if you, God forbid, just go down to Allen Street any night. There you can see eighteen-year-old girls who have already become hardened women for whom life holds no wonder anymore—'

" 'Hush, Lubish,' Alma said. 'You make too much of such things.' "

Ultimately it was Alma who had suggested that Marya could help take her place in the shop and take over some of the cooking and other household chores. "So," said Wolf, "it's from working in Lubish and Alma's shop that you have learned so much about herbs and can work your magical cure on me."

"Yes, I've learned a lot. This is not what I want to do all my life, I know. But it is good for now, and it lets me earn my way so I'm not a drain on Lubish. Then in the evening I have time to sketch or read. What I want to start doing soon, though, is going to night school again. I want to improve my English more."

"But your English is good, especially for someone who's been here barely a year."

"I know I have a very noticeable accent, and I hate it. I want no traces of the old country in me."

"Marya," he half teased her, "why would you throw out everything that has made you who you are?"

But she took his question seriously and sat without answering.

"Someday I would like to go back to St. Petersburg for a visit, but that would be after the pogroms cease, maybe in a few years."

"Tell me about your family," she said, wanting to keep the conversation off of her and on a subject that was dear to him.

"There are eight children in the Luminov family," he explained eagerly. "Six boys: Tobiah, Joshua, Dziga, Micah and Shachna, and just two girls, Zelda, who's two years older than me, and Tamara, who's eight. I wish you could meet them all, but especially my sister, Tamara."

"It must be fun to have a sister," she said, inadvertently revealing something of herself. "I never had a sister or brother."

"That's unusual. It seems like almost every Russian Jewish family had at least nine or ten children. Were you ever lonely?"

A veil appeared to drop over her features. "There were always so many other children around." Her fingers fidgeted, making little pleats with the fabric of her skirt. Always when he tried to get her to talk of her past, she grew remote, reluctant.

"I want to have a big family," said Wolf, "like the one I grew up in." He looked at her sitting on the edge of the wooden chair, lit by the morning sun, the embodiment of health and radiance. She would bear him fine sons, he said to himself.

"Yes," said Marya, her eyes distant. "That would be nice." With all this talk of family, Marya felt hollow and cold inside, and she was sorry she had brought up the subject. A cold, dreary wind blew over the emptiness of her past. Talk of family seemed futile. If you care too deeply, she thought, it could all be blown away from you tomorrow.

"What about you?" Wolf was asking. He took her

hand again. "Wouldn't you like to have lots of children, in the Russian tradition?"

As always, when he touched her, she felt her skin catch fire. She could think only of her hand enclosed in his and of the nearness of him. She could feel the strong throbbing of a pulse—was it hers or was it his? Their hands were one.

She was too distracted to answer at once. "What, Zavel? A family? Yes, big families must be nice," she said vaguely.

"But would you like to have one?"

"Oh, Zavel, I don't know. I haven't thought about it lately."

"Marya," Lubish called from the other room. "I need your help now."

At once Marya was on her feet and out of the sunlight.

"He always needs your help at a crucial moment," Wolf observed, as Marya hurried out the door.

She was half thankful that Lubish had called her just then. She felt so confused when Zavel spoke that way to her, and his voice was so intense. She wished she could marry him, and have a big family, but always a reluctance held her back.

It did seem, too, to be more than coincidence that now Lubish was always calling her or coming to check on her whenever she had been in Wolf's room more than a few minutes. She suspected he felt protective, especially now that Wolf was getting visibly stronger every day. Lubish had also taken to staring at her of late, as if he were trying to read her thoughts.

Having left Russia only four years before, after the first of the bloody pogroms stirred up by the assassination of Czar Alexander II, Lubish Vertov had become surprisingly successful in a short time. A combination of good timing, hard work and an unrelenting business acumen had got him where he was. Unlike the huge majority of the other immigrants, he had been able to parlay his modest livelihood in a small Russian town into an even bigger livelihood in New York City. He and his father had operated a small apothecary shop in Mstislav, and when his father died in 1880 and the pograms began in 1881, he recognized it as a good point in his life to make a big change. Before he left the old country, he had deliberately married a woman for whom he felt no passion but who had a reputation as an untiring worker and who brought with her a sizable dowry, sizable for Mstislav, at any rate. What Lubish prized above all was hard work and money, so he had found his dream woman.

Like many driven and unyielding men, he had a sentimental weakness, which he had just recently discovered. It wasn't animals, or alcohol or children; it was his newly arrived young cousin. He had decided a few weeks ago that if he couldn't keep her for himself, and he knew his wife Alma would never accept Marya's being there permanently, the next best thing would be to arrange a match of his choice for her— one that might bring him some business advantage along the way. So it was with serious misgivings he allowed her to tend this penniless *landsman* who was becoming stronger and more aggressive every day and who Lubish feared could thwart all that he had in mind for Marya.

That night Marya did not come to sit with Wolf. Only a few other times had she not come until much later, and he could have sworn he heard the voice of another man, a voice he didn't know.

A week later he heard the same voice again. He was well enough by this time to stand up, so he made his way to the door and opened it slightly. The voices wafted in, and now he could hear the man clearly.

"Wasn't that a good play? We'll have to see another of Goldfaden's dramas again. Maybe one night this week?" asked the man. His voice was smooth and confident.

"Oh, I'd love to! He's my favorite!" It was Marya.

* * *

Wolf closed the door. What a schlemiel he'd been. There was another man. That was what explained Marya's occasional absences. That was what explained her sudden reticence when he brought up certain subjects like having a family. He had taken her for granted. Of course she was seeing someone else. A woman as compelling as Marya could not go unnoticed and unsought after. He determined to find out how far things had gone.

His legs still unsteady after his weeks in bed, he change into the pants he had been wearing when he'd arrived. Then he walked down the hall and into the main room.

Marya was sitting on the sofa, and the man had pulled his chair immediately adjacent to her. He appeared to be of medium height, with a full head of light brown hair and a thin, angular face. Wolf noted he was well dressed in a suit that had obviously been custom tailored. His hat, of brushed felt, had been carefully placed on another chair, along with a paper sack of what Wolf guessed was candy.

He walked right up to the man. "Wolf Luminov," he said, extending his hand.

The man was taken aback by this stranger who had appeared seemingly out of nowhere and suddenly dominated the room. "Nate Wysinski," he said, rising to take Wolf's hand.

Marya was looking at Wolf, her eyes wide in anticipation, and she looked uncomfortable. Then she turned to Nate. "Haven't I told you about our patient?"

"No," said Nate. "He looks fairly hale and hearty to me." There was no warmth in his voice.

"Thanks to Marya, I am," said Wolf.

"The doctor said it was pneumonia," Marya explained.

"Yes," Nate said, nodding his head. "It seems to strike almost all the greenhorns. That or consumption and of course just general breakdown from the conditions those poor people are forced to live and work under. Too bad, though Lubish tells me that's why his business is thriving and he's not one of them. And I must say, what's good for Lubish's business is equally good for mine." He laughed and rubbed his hands together.

Marya interpreted for Wolf. "Nate has a pharmaceutical supply business. He's Lubish's main source for supplies."

Wolf only nodded. He couldn't help but be reminded of his father's prospering pharmaceutical business, the biggest house in St. Petersburg.

"Proverty is a dreadful thing," Nate continued, "and I should think you're very lucky you found Lubish, Marya, so you didn't have to be undergo its indignity."

Wolf stretched out his long legs and waited.

Nate continued to make small talk for a while, some more about the theater, about the best bakery to buy a *challah* if you weren't lucky enough to know someone who could provide you with a homemade one. Here he winked at Wolf as he made mock eyes at Marya. But Wolf said nothing, nor did Marya, and Nate's fingers eventually began to drum on the arm of the chair. He talked about *The Commercial Advertiser* and *The Evening Post*, which he said he always liked to read. He much preferred the English newspapers to the Yiddish penny papers, didn't they? On and on he talked.

Wolf wondered what Marya saw in him. That man tried to be an authority on everything. Surely she wasn't taken in by his slick suit and patter about the latest trends. She seemed to be paying Nate only polite attention, he observed. But then she wasn't paying any more attention to him, either. Her face was vacant, and she appeared to be somewhere far away.

Neither man would give up and be the first to leave. Finally Marya broke into Nate's explanation of how an investment in tenement flats was the smartest way for a newcomer to go once he saved a minimum down payment and found a partner he could trust. "I'm afraid I have to get up at dawn tomorrow."

Nate immediately picked up the cue and pulled out a pocket watch that was attached to his trousers by a slim gold chain. He flipped open the cover and said, "I suppose the hour must be getting late for our patient here, too."

Wolf lifted Nate's hat from the chair. "Yours, I believe?" he said, handing it to him.

Nate glared at Wolf a second, then turned to Marya. "Well," he said, "will my new fiancée walk me to the door?" He shot Wolf a glance.

Wolf did not blink an eye. So that's how it was, he thought. Still, he did not get up or show any signs of leaving, forcing Marya and Nate to bid their farewells with him there. Awkwardly they said good-bye to each other, and as Nate made a move to kiss Marya good night, she turned her head at the last moment and offered him the side of her face.

As soon as the door had shut behind Nate, Wolf was on his feet and had enfolded Marya in his arms. She tried to fight him, and he pulled back just long enough to say, "You may be engaged, Marya, but you're not married. And until you're actually wed to someone else, you're a single woman, as far as I'm concerned." Then he pressed his mouth against hers until she no longer resisted and parted her lips slightly to receive his tongue.

The next day Wolf told Marya and Lubish he felt well enough to leave. He also said to Marya, within earshot of Lubish, that he would like her to go for a walk with him that afternoon. Marya's eyes lit up, and she agreed, while another furrow appeared on Lubish's brow.

Early that afternoon, Lubish found reason to

draw Marya aside. He led her to the storeroom in the back of the shop and pointed out a high mound of cartons. "I just received those boxes of chamomile and borage we ordered," he said, "and I'd like you to inventory them and have them put away before *Shabbas* begins at sundown."

Marya's eyes met his. There was no way she could finish the work before sundown, even if she gave up the walk. "You don't want me to go, do you." It was more a statement than a question.

He busied himself with dusting the tops of the cartons. "Go where?"

"With Wolf. You heard him ask me to go for a walk this afternoon."

Lubish sighed. "I simply think you're about to make a mistake, Marya. You're spending more time with Wolf than you do with Nate. After all, he's your fiancé, not Wolf."

Marya cringed to hear him use the term fiancé. It was true that a month ago she had agreed to marry Nate, and because it was Lubish who had introduced him to her, the plan had Lubish and Alma's blessing. It was Alma who had seemed especially pleased with the plan, she noted. And Marya had acknowledged she couldn't stay a single woman indefinitely. Life was too hard on a woman alone. But somehow, practical as the decision to marry was, she couldn't imagine herself going through with it. "I just can't," one part of her whispered. "But you must, for your own good," returned a louder part. The battle had raged on in her until a few weeks ago. Since the day Wolf had come into her life again, she had put it from her mind. Now Lubish was trying to bring it all back to her, but she was still unwilling to think about it.

Lubish looked at her sharply. He could tell she hadn't been listening. He put his hand on hers. "Listen, Marya, I just said you're a very desirable young woman, and you acted like you didn't even hear me." He said again, "Very desirable," and started to stammer. "You must be careful not to throw yourself away."

She noticed he stood very close to her now, closer than she found comfortable.

He took hold of a strand of her hair. "It is a pleasure, I think, to see how you young women wear your hair in this country. So loose and free." He sifted her hair through his fingers.

She felt trapped. A familiar panic began to build in her. Her urge was to slap him across the face and bolt. But she knew she couldn't do that. Lubish had been too good to her. She would endure—as she always had—she told herself, and clenched her teeth tightly.

"Not like in the old country," Lubish was saying in slow, dreaming tones, "where never did we see a woman's hair flowing unbound like this."

"Lubish, I must get started on those boxes," Marya said sharply, her mind suddenly made up. "Otherwise I won't have time to walk with Wolf. I'll only have time to do half before he comes anyway." There, she had said it. Surely he would leave her alone now.

Her rebuke snapped him out of his trance. He dropped her hair at once. "What should I tell Nate, should he come looking for you?" There was a hint of sarcasm in his voice.

"Tell him I'm with a friend," said Marya, and began to hum as she ripped into the first of the boxes on the floor.

Wolf had first gone to find another room, this one on Stanton Street, and talked the landlady into waiting a couple days for her week's rent, then he had found a job for the next day doing road repairs. He had told Marya he would come by at four o'clock, and when he hadn't come by a quarter to five, she began to wonder if he were truly coming. At five o'clock she looked up to see Wolf filling the doorway.

He grabbed her by the hand. "Let's go," he said.

"There's something I want to show you." Before she could put her pen down, he had pulled her out the door and was leading her up Monroe Street toward Corlears Hook Park. When they came to the corner of Montgomery, he led her into an old wooden building on the corner and up three flights of stairs. They stopped in front of a door, a door like all the others they'd passed in the building, and Wolf magically produced a key. As Marya stepped into the room, she saw a pool of sunshine that fell on the floor from the window on the small side. Otherwise the room was stark and plain, with grease stained walls and uneven flooring. It led to another room that looked just the same.

Marya went to stand in the warm circle of light and turned to Wolf, a quizzical look on her face.

He looked at her with the sunlight beating on her hair and knew he had done the right thing.

"This is where we'll live," he said, "if you say you'll marry me."

Her body strained toward him with all its might, but inside she was afraid, afraid of a man's passion, and of her own, and afraid of losing it once she admitted to herself she wanted it.

"Marya, say, 'Yes.'" He put his mouth on hers and kissed her long and slowly.

She felt his body large and strong against her and his arms encircling her. She noticed her breathing was throaty and audible. She struggled to control the voice of fear that was rising inside her. She wanted him to keep touching her, but always there came to her the memory of passion run awry.

He kissed her again and again, until the frightening memories started to fade and she scarcely realized she was murmuring, "Yes, Zavel. Yes, yes, yes."

Chapter 6

"What do you want with a penniless suitor?" Lubish demanded. It was the first time she had seen him angry. "He's a *griner tukes*," he said, although he had to admit to himself that Wolf certainly did not have the distinguishing characteristics of the usual greenhorn. In fact, he had more confidence and know-how than most native-born Americans seemed to. But he was not about to acknowledge anything at all positive about Wolf in front of Marya. "And even his health is not so good," he continued. "Here you have Nate, who has everything: he's got a successful business started, he knows his way around the city and how to act here, he's generous, he treats you like a princess. What more could you want?"

"I want a man I love."

Lubish snorted. "Love! Here in America everybody suddenly wants to marry the person they love, but in Russia you love the person you marry. That's an important difference. What does a girl know of love?"

Marya didn't reply. She too had her doubts, but they were far from what Lubish was talking about. What did she know of love? She had grown to love her first husband, in the old country manner, just because he was her husband and he was kind to her. But she had never felt the physical stirrings or longings for him that she felt for Wolf. Their lovemaking had been soft and quiet, performed in the dark. Gershon was gentle but awkward. Still, she had never known any other touch until now. At what point might the current of such strong feelings swell up and run raging beyond control? At what point might they transform themselves into the grunts and snorts she had heard as she held her hands over David's ears that bloody afternoon? Did these longings she felt for Wolf, to be near him, to touch him, have anything to do with love? She didn't know, but she felt she would do anything to feel his lips on hers again.

"I can't let you jeopardize your future with Nate. You must think what a future it would be. You would live in a beautiful home, like this maybe." He waved his hand toward the floor, the walls, the ceiling of the main room where they were standing. "To eat, you would have the best, always the finest meats: brisket, veal, lamb. And fish: herring, flounder, cod. And clothes! *Oy*, think of what to wear! Just imagine the dresses and the little blouses and the shoes of leather so soft you could wear it on your hands, just like the wives of the *knokers* wear on Fifth Avenue." He paused, then suddenly, "Listen, Marya, how long have you been here?"

"About a year."

"And this makes you an expert on how it is in America? Listen to me. You don't know how hard it can be. You were lucky. You came to this house to live right away. You haven't known of the filth and the grime not fit for animals even."

His voice took a quick turn, becoming soft and tremulous. "I just can't let you make this mistake. You're like a daughter to me, or even a. . . ."

"I'm too old to be your daughter," disagreed Marya. Her voice was sharp.

Some of the dreaminess left him. "I'm the only

family you have now. And I can't give you permission."

Marya considered her plight. Her first marriage had been arranged by her parents, but that was the custom in Russia. And yet that custom was still so ingrained in her and almost everyone else from the *shtetl* who got off the boat from eastern Europe. Families still gave their blessing to their children's choice of mate, or made the choice for them. This tradition was what allowed Lubish to enter into this parental role so freely, and it was what held her in the role of obedient daughter, even though they were now in America where one might marry for love. And the immigrants were not insensitive to that lure either. Lubish nevertheless remained firm in his opposition to Wolf, and Marya, caught between two traditions, did not outwardly oppose him. Also, Marya felt too much gratitude and even fondness for Lubish and Alma to walk off in anger and abandon him, which she knew she was free to do.

And what could she do if she did leave? Wolf could not support her yet, and her English wasn't good enough for her to get the kind of job that would pay a living wage. She would end up like the other luckless immigrants, chained to someone's kitchen table constructing bow ties or making lace in a passementerie factory. Wolf had told her what she could expect of work in a sweatshop, and she had no inclination to disbelieve him.

Yet, she didn't see how she could give up seeing Wolf.

"Marya, what do you know of selecting a husband. You have never been married before; you're but a girl."

Marya caught her breath. She had not been able to bring herself to talk about her marriage to Gershon, nor about David, even though she felt she should. It was part of that vast wound she could not bear to touch for the pain was still too great. The more time that passed without her saying anything about it, the more difficult it became for her to bring it up. Lubish had never learned of her marriage or child, and one day she realized it was unlikely that there was anyone who could tell him.

She had gone back to her father's name, and there was no one who knew Lubish who would have any cause to link her to the town of Petrovichi or to the Bonarsky family, which had virtually disappeared off the earth. Ultimately she renewed her vow to say nothing at all, to Lubish or anyone ever, of that life she had renounced.

"You must look for qualities that will endure, that will make your union a fruitful and happy one." Lubish was warming to his role of parent.

"Yes, Lubish, I know that."

He stood looking at her, taking all of her in, and she could see he was going into one of his trancelike states again. "With your kind of beauty, Marya, there isn't anyone you couldn't have. Your eyes are like green fire, your skin like golden honey, your breasts like two little lambs nestling—"

"Please, Lubish!" Marya interrupted.

He regained his composure. "Well, at any rate, you must not throw yourself away. Making a good marriage is like making a smart business deal. You must know your worth."

Marya realized that Lubish, in spite of his tendency to grow romantic and sentimental, was a hard-headed realist and one who liked to drive a shrewd bargain. And what threw off those who did business with him was that he could quickly change from one to the other. But she didn't care about this talk of business and getting your money's worth in marriage. It had nothing to do with how she felt. She found a way to excuse herself and go to her room.

But that was not to be the end of their discussion. In the next week Lubish found ample opportunity to plunge in again. One day he said, "I knew I shouldn't have let him come to stay here that day he collapsed in the shop. This is all my fault. I am to blame for this folly that has seized you."

"It's not folly, Lubish. And you mustn't blame yourself. You were doing what was right and kind. It was a mitzvah, a good deed. Besides, what else could you have done? I was pleading with you and told you how he had saved my life in helping me get out of Russia."

"I should have seen what was coming. I'm older, more experienced in these matters."

Marya smiled to herself. Lubish always overindulged whatever emotion he was feeling at the moment. She felt some of her fondness for him returning, a fondness that had been strained this past week. She laughed to herself that he always thought her so naive, completely at the mercy of anyone with nefarious intentions.

But in spite of the fondness between them, Lubish continued to say no. "You cannot marry him, Marya. He is not worthy of you," he reiterated. Then one day soon after he added, "Nor can I permit you to see him anymore. It's clear the more you see him, the more determined you appear to become, and the more you cling to your impossible and destructive desires."

Marya wanted to run to him and tear at his skin with her nails. Not see Wolf anymore? It was unthinkable. But she didn't run at Lubish. Instead she kept her anger and fierce resentment inside. She did not see Wolf for five days. She waited for him to come, but Lubish always intercepted him, or perhaps he didn't come at all; she wasn't sure which.

By the fifth night she could no longer stand the thought of not seeing Wolf. After she heard the door to Alma and Lubish's room shut, she got up and dressed without a sound. Carefully she turned the doorknob to her room. The door wouldn't open. When she realized Lubish had locked her in, she began to beat on the door with her fists.

"Lubish! Lubish!" Her voice rose in hysteria.

But the door remained locked. Nor was it opened the next morning.

"May this silence bring you wisdom," said Lubish through the closed door on the second day. Then she heard footsteps as he hurried away before she could say a word.

On the seventh day she woke with a sore throat. By midday she had a burning fever, and her legs refused to hold her. Every time she moved, her head felt as if a searing iron were being held to her scalp. Every bone, every fiber in her body hurt, and by evening she was so miserable that she thought what a relief it would be to die. Then came the delirium, when she no longer knew where she was or what was happening to her.

That night Lubish gave her teas made of skullcap and Saint-John's-wort to try to control the fever. But when the fever raged on, he became frightened and called for the doctor. He was a very good doctor, Lubish assured her the next morning, and he had come from his office uptown where he had many important patients.

But she barely heard him.

Dr. Addison was a tall, thin man with stooped shoulders. Except for his highly starched and very clean white shirt, he was dressed all in black. With his sunken chest and grave mien, he would have appeared the very harbinger of bad news but for the redeeming sparkle in his eyes that revealed he had learned more of the human condition than mere medical texts could teach. He removed his rimless spectacles from his long, down-turned nose and folded them slowly. It was never easy to deliver bad news, but it pained him even more when the patient was one so young and was looking at him with large, clouded eyes. "Scarlet fever," he said, and rested his hand lightly on Marya's shoulder.

In her delirious state, she heard his words, but

their significance was too much for her to think about. What struck her fevered mind most at that moment were the doctor's cuffs, incredibly white and stiff, which protruded from the blackness of his sleeve and swooped close to her face like sparkling white birds.

All the color drained from Lubish's face as he heard the doctor's diagnosis from where he leaned against the wall on the other side of the room. His mind came to a halt while conflicting emotions warred with one another. The fact that his Marya had been felled by a serious disease was matched against his growing realization that now he had another burden, another charge to look after and care for as best he could.

Day after day Marya lay in the bed. One day she would sleep fitfully, as if her illness were a physical presence she was literally struggling to wrestle down; the next she would appear to sleep soundly, having come to some kind of terms with the demon. From time to time the white birds would come back and flutter about her, then disappear again.

Lubish could not bring himself to tell Wolf that Marya was ill. Wolf only knew that whenever he came to the shop, Lubish told him Marya was out shopping or Marya was with her fiancé, and then finally, because Lubish didn't know what to say anymore, he said Marya didn't want to see him anymore; would he please go away?

Lubish would look in on Marya as often as he could, but it was difficult for him now that he was the only person in the shop and had both Alma and Marya to feed and tend.

One afternoon, Marya had a moment of lucidity. She opened her eyes to see Lubish sitting next to her, his face lost in worry. She put out her hand, which was hot and damp. "Poor Lubish," she said. "I'm adding lines to your forehead, aren't I?"

He was startled to hear her addressing him so clearly. He looked at her face, though it pained him to see it thin and pale, and shook his head. "No," he said. "I know you're getting better. The doctor says we must be patient."

"And the shop? How's it coming without me?"

He released the breath he had unconsciously been holding. "Today I hired a young man to help me."

"Wolf? You hired Wolf?" But she knew he would not have.

He shook his head from side to side. He couldn't tell her of the mixed thoughts he was having now that he had gone over the account books again, thoughts he was ashamed of. He wanted to take her in his arms, and at the same time he wanted to make sure she did not become a financial drain on him. He wanted her to stay forever, and then he wanted her wed and gone.

Chapter 7

In the third week of her fever, Marya awoke and began to scream. She screamed and screamed, a scream so deep down from within that no sound would come out. Scattered over her pillow and the head of the bed lay strands and strands of her long red hair.

The next day and the next her hair continued to fall, until finally there was no more left to come out.

Dr. Addison was summoned, and even he was startled to see his patient. "It sometimes happens when the fever is very bad," he said, and shook his head.

"Will it grow back?" Marya asked him, her voice a whisper from her dry screams.

He sat down beside her on the narrow bed and took her hand in his. "I don't know. There's a chance."

"How much of a chance?"

"In half the cases, the hair grows back just as thick, occasionally thicker than ever."

"And in the other cases?"

"Well, it never really does come back, only a light down, very soft and fine."

Marya swallowed, but she refused to let her voice tremble as she asked, "When will I know?"

The doctor looked at her eyes, still bright with fever and all the larger in her face now without the familiar fullness of her hair. "It's hard to say," he said and faltered as he felt the greenness of her eyes burning into him. "Each body has its own rhythm, its own timetable for healing. It could take two weeks before you start to see signs of growth; it could take two months, or even longer, maybe even years, and," he added, wanting to keep her hopes realistic, "that's if you fall into the fifty per cent who eventually regain their hair."

For the next two weeks Marya chose a time each day, when the sun was at its brightest, to sit by the light from the window and carefully examine herself in a small hand mirror to see if there were signs of her hair regrowing. But each day she was disappointed.

One day, weeks after Marya's hair had all fallen out onto the pillow, Lubish unlocked the shop early in the morning, as was his practice, and stepped outside to begin his usual raking and sprinkling of the street. Suddenly he felt a large hand on his shoulder and turned slowly, as if he already knew, to see who was there.

"Good morning," said Wolf.

Lubish jumped. "Hello, Wolf," he replied. His eyes darted away quickly, and he busied himself with picking up first a crushed carton, then a sheet of yellowed newsprint that littered the area in front of the shop.

"How's Marya?"

Lubish kept his head to the ground. "She's fine," he said sullenly.

"Why didn't you tell me?"

Lubish said nothing. He continued to fill his arms with the random pieces of trash that were strewn on the ground.

Wolf took him by the arm. "We'd better talk."

Lubish had no choice but to drop the rubbish in a heap at his feet and accompany Wolf down the street. The tearooms and cafés were still closed at this hour, and they had to walk several blocks before they found a shop that was just opening on Hester Street.

Wolf made an effort to control the anger he felt. "As I see it, you're in a difficult position," said Wolf, the steam from their tall glasses of tea rising between them and putting them slightly out of focus to each other.

Even through the steam Lubish could see Wolf's eyes were steely and narrowed. He stared into his glass and didn't respond.

Wolf waited.

"I suppose you think you can have whatever you want," Lubish suddenly spit out. "She's already engaged to be married. And to a very successful man. Doesn't that mean anything to you?"

Wolf suddenly moved his glass to one side, and the steam cleared. "She's not married. That's what means something to me. She's not anyone's wife, and you can seriously ask yourself if she ever will be."

"Wh-What do you mean?" Lubish asked, but he knew. A month had gone by, but there was yet no sign of Marya's hair coming back. He had taken Dr. Addison aside the day before to question him more closely about the after effects of the fever and the chances of Marya's hair growing again soon.

But Dr. Addison had been elusive, pointing out the medical pros and cons, and finally remaining noncommittal. "Each patient responds a little differently, and it would be neither helpful nor ethical of me to lead you to expect results which I can only surmise," he concluded, and indicated to Lubish that their discussion of Marya's case had come to an end. So Lubish was left with no indication of when the situation would change, if ever.

The steam blurred Lubish's mouth, Wolf saw, giving it a twisted, helpless quality. "You have a reputation for being a good businessman," he said. "I have a proposition I think will interest you."

Lubish looked up at once.

"Marya has no other suitors."

"I told you, she's engaged, and going to be married just as soon as—"

Wolf broke in impatiently. "Marya could be living with you the rest of your life, Lubish. We both know that."

Lubish tried to interrupt but couldn't.

"And we both know that Nate Wysinsky hasn't been seen or heard from in weeks, not since he heard from you what happened to Marya and then paid her a visit." Wolf refused to let go of Lubish's gaze. "Nate Wysinsky has been in the company of three other young women these last two weeks, once in Sach's café, twice in—"

"What do you want?" Lubish broke in. His face was tired and bloodless. He had no reason not to believe that what Wolf was telling him was true. He had seen Nate as he was leaving Marya's bedside that afternoon he had finally come to see her. Nate's eyes were like distant tunnels, and Lubish had known instantly that things were different. "Just tell me what you want," he said to Wolf.

"I want Marya for my wife."

Lubish nodded his head slowly up and down.

"And I want part ownership in the shop—"

"What!" Lubish began to sputter. "What did you say? *Meshuggener*, you are crazy? You're a robber, *ganef*, a thief!" In his agitation, he knocked over his glass and sent the hot liquid streaming over the edge of the small table and onto the floor.

"That you can give Marya as part of her dowry."

The waiter, a small, wiry man of indeterminate age, appeared and began to wipe the puddles of tea with great energy.

"No, never!" Lubish said. He was almost shouting. "You're an unscrupulous swine." He pounded the table with his fist.

The waiter's head jerked up and his eyes widened.

He looked from Wolf to Lubish and back to Wolf again.

Wolf took his time in replying. "She's part of your family, Lubish, and like a daughter. You would provide for her in some way, I'm sure." He waited.

Lubish was quickly trying to juggle all the odds: the chance of Marya's hair growing back, the chances of her getting other suitors if it didn't, the likelihood of his having her living in their home forever, what Alma would say if she learned he passed up this offer, what Wolf's next move would be if he were to refuse.

"I figure a small percentage, say one third of the business, would be appropriate," Wolf said. "And Marya could continue to work there after the wedding, if she wanted."

"Thirty-three per cent is unthinkable!" Lubish could not believe the effrontery of the man.

"You could have the option of buying us out, if you chose," Wolf countered.

Lubish fidgeted and said nothing.

"Of course," Wolf said finally, "you could always wait for a better arrangement, although I frankly don't know what that would be."

Lubish thought of Alma at home, Alma complaining about having another woman in the house, and a young and beautiful one at that. He thought of the little privacy they had had in the last year. He thought too of the advantages of having Marya there, but he kept coming back to the realization that he might very well have an unmarriageable woman on his hands who, according to the customs with which he had been raised, would not cease to be his responsibility until she had a husband or other family member to provide for her. And that wasn't likely. True, she could help out in the shop, but what if she should fall in ill health again? Her fever might come back or she might even end up an invalid like Alma and end up unable to work, unable to contribute.

Lubish threw up his hands. "Take her. She's yours."

"And the shop?" Wolf pressed.

"I can't go more than a one-fourth share," he said. "One third is impossible."

From the pocket of his jacket Wolf pulled a sheet of folded white paper. As he carefully smoothed it out, Lubish could see it was blank. Wolf began to write the terms of the agreement, just as they had discussed them. Then he signed his name and pushed the paper across the table to Lubish. He held out the pen and Lubish slowly took it and even more slowly wrote his name across the bottom.

Wolf refolded the paper and returned it to his pocket. Then he stood up and held out his hand to Lubish. "Mazel tov, we're now business partners."

"All I ask is that you let me tell her the news myself," said Lubish. "I'm afraid she isn't yet up to the kind of excitement your presence would create." But more important, thought Lubish, he wanted to make sure that the story Marya got of how he had changed his mind and of how her dowry came about was the one he wanted her to hear, not Wolf's.

"Of course," said Wolf, "whatever you want." But he had no intention of not being the one to break his news to Marya.

Marya automatically reached her fingers back to run them through her hair, only to find nothing there. It was the ageless gesture of the beautiful woman who unconsciously knows the primeval lure of a thick toss of hair. She tried to break herself of the habit, but it was a reflex, a motion she had performed unthinkingly since she had been a small child. Her head felt light-weight, like it would float away without her hair to tie her to the earth.

Now the fever was completely gone, and she could take over the running of the household while Lubish devoted all his energies to the shop below. She had spent two frustrating afternoons tying scarves onto her head in an effort to find an arrangement that pleased her. Finally she found a style that she could bear looking at herself in, and she ventured out of the tenement and onto the streets. She had returned to her Russian heritage in spite of herself, she realized bitterly. As she made her way along Forsyth Street, she appeared every bit the immigrant woman she was. She found a shop that sold *sheitels*, the wigs worn by religious Jewish women.

Once she was home again, she unwrapped the package, and set the wig atop her head. Then she started to cry. She didn't know what she hated most. Was it the way the wig looked on her with its dark brown hair that looked so strange and harsh against her skin? Was it the construction that allowed the netting underneath to show through? Or was it the memory of Russia it brought back to her? She carefully rewrapped the wig, set it on the floor at the back of the wardrobe, and went back to wearing the cotton scarves.

The next morning as she was standing over the hearth stirring a pot of sweet tsimmes, she sensed the room had gotten slightly darker, and she felt a presence behind her. She turned slowly to see Wolf standing in the doorway. It was the first time she had seen him in over two months. She instinctively put her hand to the bright scarf tied about her head. If only she had known he were coming, she said to herself, she could have . . . could have . . . could have what? What could she have done to make her appearance different from the way it was?

Wolf gazed at her, at her head, at her lips, at her eyes big and luminous. "You look like a Gypsy now," he said softly, continuing to stare at her.

She waited, scarcely daring to breathe. She was waiting for some sign, some indication of how he felt, seeing her this way. Her heart was pounding wildly, and as she timidly looked back at him, the longing she had felt for him these last two months only intensified. As the light struck the angular planes of his face, emphasizing the straightness of his nose, the deepness of his eyes, he appeared to her more handsome than ever.

Suddenly there was a big smile on his face as he started to pull her into his arms. Wolf was kissing her hungrily.

She found herself sobbing as the emotions of the last months spilled over. "Oh Wolf, you know I haven't been well. I wanted you so badly. You have no idea of the thoughts that ran through my mind as I lay there for weeks, hoping you would come. At the same time I hoped you wouldn't. I was afraid you would see me like this and . . . and. . . ."

His kisses stopped her words for a long time. His voice was husky with emotion when he said, "It doesn't matter. It doesn't matter."

"You always told me you loved my hair. You made me promise never to cut it, never to change it in any way."

"Marya, darling, it's you I love. It's the essence of you that counts. That will never change." He pressed her against him, and for several minutes neither of them spoke. Wolf felt her trembling in his arms.

As he tightened his hold on her, Marya felt a desire for him to look at her again, to reassure her with his eyes that his love for her was unchanged. She pulled herself back and looked at him full face. "Since I look like a Gypsy, shall I tell your fortune?" she said with an attempt at her former playfulness. "I can see the future for you."

"Yes, your 'pictures' are always right," he said, and smiled, remembering how she had told him in the Polish border town that she would see him again someday.

She felt disappointed when he pulled her to him again, seemingly out of his view, even though he began to whisper in her ear. "But this time I shall tell your fortune. You shall marry a tall, dark man who has come from a faraway country to seek you, and you shall have armloads of babies and be very happy together."

"Wolf! Is it true? Say it's true," she cried. "We will be married after all?"

"Now, remember, you already said yes, you would marry me, some months ago. All that remained was for me to carry you off in the night, or to get Lubish to agree."

She remembered that this was the point at which she began to feel the first signs of the fever, the sore throat that had presaged her weeks of agony that winter, and she felt a nervous tremor just at the thought of it.

"I've spoken with him. Lubish will not stand in our way now."

"One month," she asked for when Wolf gave her the news of Lubish's assent to their bethrothal. "Let's wait a month until the wedding." She was buying time. She had every hope that her hair would have begun to grow again by then. She could not stand to think that she might go to her wedding appearing the way she did.

They had made light of Marya's catastrophe. Wolf seemed as attentive as ever, although she wasn't sure if his eyes lit up the same way when he saw her, and she longed to catch him staring at her the way she remembered. But then, she wondered, perhaps her doubts were in her imagination only. Still, she realized that dressed in her scarves, she now looked every bit the old country woman, one of the illiterate horde that Wolf was loath to associate himself with. She knew he was unable to forget that he had come from a family whose position commanded respect and automatically conferred status on its children, and here it rankled him daily that he was just another member of the masses, grouped in with all the other immigrants without distinction. And now, with her at his side, he appeared unmistakably foreign.

As the day of their wedding neared, Marya renewed her resolve not to think or speak of her past again. As far as she was concerned, this was her first marriage and the only one that counted. Before, she had been almost a child, too young to understand what was happening to her. The choice had been made for her. This time the choice was hers. She remembered Lubish's face as he had come into her room to tell her the news.

"I have been reconsidering," he began, "your desire to see this green friend of yours."

She listened to him warily and continued to jab the needle into the piece of embroidery she was working on. Ever since the night before the fever began, the night Lubish locked her in her room, she no longer trusted him. She was sure Lubish didn't know Wolf had already been to see her. And if Lubish said he had been reconsidering, something had happened that he probably wasn't going to admit, something that had forced him to reconsider, and that he most likely would present in a self-flattering light.

"You mean Wolf." She rankled at his refusal to use his name.

"Yes." He swallowed, and attempted a smile. "I have been unnecessarily harsh. Perhaps it is better if you follow your heart."

She waited to hear what he would say next.

"After all," he continued, "it is you who must live with whomever you choose, and therefore you probably should have some say in the matter. Still, I would urge you not to abandon Nate altogether and to keep an open mind."

Marya almost laughed out loud. "You know very well I haven't seen Nate in weeks. Now that he can no longer parade me through the cafés, he's not interested. He's a . . . what's the expression here? a fair weather friend. He would be the last man I would want."

Lubish stared at her, still lovely and enchanting, her dark-fringed eyes dominating her face, the patterned scarf tied to one side of her head giving her an exotic air. He was sorry for the bad feelings that had come between them, but it couldn't be helped, he supposed. He was just trying to do what he thought best, and he couldn't help it that she was so headstrong in opposing him that she had made herself sick. Now she seemed stronger than ever, and somehow changed, more confident perhaps, although in a strange way, and more determined. He doubted he could have held her away from Wolf anyway. He wished, though, there were something more he could say to gain back her friendship, but nothing occurred to him.

"Besides," she said, "I'm going to marry Wolf."

"You've seen him then, I take it," Lubish said. "Against my will."

"Against your will? You just now said it was all right and that I should follow my heart."

"Well, yes, it is all right, of course." He realized he had spoken too hastily and out of anger, but he deeply resented that Wolf had spoken to her before he had, and felt like a fool that all along she had known where the conversation was headed. He felt his attempt at peacemaking was not going well.

"Then I suppose he told you of the dowry I offered?" He hoped to see a smile light up her face.

She looked at him, surprised, and he saw that Wolf hadn't said anything about it yet. "Of course, I couldn't do less for my own blood, Marya." He looked at the incredulous expression on her face, and felt again a stab of anger that Wolf had broken the news of the marriage before he himself could, and somehow he couldn't resist adding, "It certainly made the whole idea of marriage more enticing to Wolf. Now he's on his way to a respectable future."

If his words affected her, he didn't know. She immediately lowered her head and resumed her stitching. She didn't even thank him, Lubish noticed.

But his words stayed with her. In the four weeks before the first of May, the day she had chosen for the wedding, his words managed to worm their way into her thoughts more than once as she wondered if Lubish's offer of a dowry had been the reason Wolf was willing to take on a wife who was now a little odd looking without her hair. She believed he loved her, but still. . . .

The first of May finally arrived, and Marya and Wolf stood together under the *chuppah,* the velvet wedding canopy edged with gold lace. She had allowed Lubish to bring her to the canopy, symbolic of the bride and groom's new home together, and the rabbi said the words of thousands of years. They were handed a single glass of wine from which they both drank, to represent, according to the custom, their partnership. Then, after Wolf placed the ring on her finger, he crushed under his heel the empty wine glass. At once there were shouts of mazel tov, and Wolf embraced Marya for so long that one of Lubish's friends began to whistle and stomp his feet and Lubish also laughed loudly.

That night they spent in their two-room flat, furnished with only a bed, the flat that Wolf had shown to Marya that day almost three months before. He lifted Marya over the threshold, then went back into the hall for the cardboard box that held in it all her wordly belongings, virtually the same belongings she had brought with her out of Russia close to two years ago.

He carried her into the bedroom and set her gently on the bed. She looked at him, and she was torn between desire and dread, now that he would see her for what she was, completely stripped of any decoration, any softening scarves or clothing.

Carefully he lifted the layers of white veils and pulled them slowly from her head. She trembled slightly as she felt the protective layers leave her. Her head felt at once light and dizzy. She felt the air, cool about her neck, her ears, and then she was exposed.

He gazed at her and smiled. Indulgently, he ran his fingers through the loose red ringlets that had just begun to grow back. "You're beautiful, Marya," he said, and pulled her head to his lips. He seemed to plant kisses in every curl as he slowly made his way forward to her ears and face. Then, he took her chin in his hand and lifted her head, finally kissing her lips.

At first Marya was shy and unsure, and her fear made her seem a blushing virgin. And she really did feel a virgin. She had determined in advance to pretend, if need be, for the sake of her future, for the sake of everyone, to be a virgin, but it was a pretense she did not have to make, beset as she was by fear of passion, fear of losing herself, fear of going beyond control.

It didn't cross Wolf's mind that Marya might not be a virgin. Her hesitancy, her unsureness, told him all he needed to know. Slowly, they undressed each other, admiring, stroking, teasing, until they could no longer stay ununited. Then they reached for each other, and as Marya learned what it was to unleash her passion and follow it as far as it could go, Wolf found he entered her with surprising ease. Then all thoughts vanished in their mutual ecstasy as over and over she and Wolf called each other's name.

Marya felt they were melding into one another, bodies and souls merged into one, so that neither knew where one's body left off and the other's began.

Now she knew what love between a man and a woman was, and she knew she had forever found her mate. Early that morning, as they finally tired and began to drowse into sleep, she envisioned their love as an indestructible thread, shimmering with light, binding their bodies together tightly for the rest of their lives. "I love you," she said, and never before had she understood or felt those words so completely. "I love you, and you are the only man I have ever said that to."

They slept pressed together, their bodies still damp with desire, and as Wolf slipped into sleep, he knew that never before had he loved a woman like this, with every fiber of his being.

Chapter 8

"I think we should sell our share in the shop," Wolf said, three days after they were married. He had awakened that morning with a plan. The only things he liked about the plan were the end result and that the plan was workable. The steps along the way were just something he would endure to get him where he wanted to be.

"What? We just got it. We haven't even had a chance to see if it's going to be lucrative for us or not," protested Marya. The arrangement, according to the terms of Wolf and Lubish's contract, was for her to continue to work in the shop during the day. She started there each morning at seven, and stayed till after six, except on Fridays when she could leave at three for *Shabbas*.

She felt herself resisting this proposed turn of events that had sprung up so suddenly. It was not that she had any attachment to the apothecary shop—she certainly didn't and would have liked to leave it in good time—and it wasn't that she had much of an attachment to Lubish any longer, in spite of his sudden announcement the month before that he was presenting a share of the business to her as her dowry. She looked on the gift of the dowry as his attempt to expiate his guilt, and not for one moment did she consider it an act of pure generosity or concern for her future welfare. She was well aware of what he really thought of Wolf and knew that he would most likely wish hard times upon them so he could feel smug that he had accurately assessed Wolf and his potential.

"Why so suddenly, Wolf?" she asked to his abrupt suggestion.

"Because we need the money for an investment."

"An investment? What are you talking about?" She had the feeling she was not being consulted so much as informed, and for just a moment a spark of her earlier doubt about why Wolf had married her flamed up.

"I want us to start our own business."

"Doing what? What do we know how to do?"

"It's what I know how to do. We'll capitalize on my biggest failure. We'll start our own manufacturing business."

"Failure? What are you talking about? Manufacturing what?"

"Clothes."

"You mean a sweatshop? It's bad enough people have to go to work in them, but you want to create one voluntarily?"

"Listen, Marya. You know what that Detweiler was doing? He was getting coats, already cut from the manufacturers for pennies and sewing them together, for less than ninety cents. He was nothing but a contractor, a middleman, and he made a lot of money doing it."

"But you just got out of a sweatshop, and now you would go right back in?"

"It makes all the difference when you're the boss, not the worker. I have no intention of working for someone else again. Anyway, I wouldn't run a hole of filth like his. Our factory would be a place where a worker could have a sense of dignity."

Marya could see that he was determined. He had thought this through without her, and it was what he wanted to do. But she still didn't see how it could be done.

"We don't need a lot of capital," he told her. "We can do it for sixty-five dollars."

"Sixty-five dollars? That will mean almost our entire share of the shop. And that's assuming Lubish will even want to buy our share, or be able to."

"He'll buy. He doesn't want us as partners any more than we want him."

She did not press him on that. She knew what he said about Lubish was true, although she wasn't aware before this that Wolf had been so attuned to Lubish's real feelings about him.

"But, Wolf?"

"Yes?"

She didn't know what to say. She just had a vague sense of not wanting to rush into this, of wanting to stop and mull it over first. But that was her nature, and, she realized, it very definitely was not his.

"Oh, I don't know. Are you sure this is what you want? Why don't you try some other type of work first, to see if you might prefer it?" But even as she was talking she knew it was of no use. His mind was made up.

He didn't tell her that he had tried other jobs. It was more than his pride could bear to tell her he had dug graves. He also remembered how he had left Lubish's tenement flat that first morning, his legs still wobbly under him, but his resolve firm that he was no longer going to be taken care of. He had dressed in his oldest clothes that morning, ones he had brought over from Russia, and he had left early, without telling anyone good-bye. Three hours later, he was standing on Orchard Street, with a bin on each side. In one bin were shoelaces; in the other were bottles of seltzer. He had become a peddler. But he had had no intention of hawking his wares in the street. Being a peddler was an honorable enough form of work in Russia, albeit not one in which he would have found himself. When a peddler went into the countryside, people were glad to see him, and he was greeted with smiles and even hospitality. But he soon found that peddling in America did not at all match the tales of how it was in Russia.

Instead he would rely on his knowledge of languages and make his way through the neighborhoods, which changed from one nationality to another every few blocks. This was all for Marya, he told himself, so that he might earn enough for them to have a small apartment. For even then he was determined to have her.

As he had made his way down Cherry Street, a woman had called out to him from a fire escape four stories above.

"What are you selling, peddler?" she cried in a badly accented Yiddish.

When he held up his wares so that she might see, she called for him to come up.

The stairs that led to her fifth floor flat were narrow and dark, and at each landing a different smell met his nose—cabbage, stinking drains, a puzzling combination he didn't want to contemplate.

At the fifth floor, he was met at the landing by the woman who had called to him. She was middle-aged with fine light brown hair that hung in wisps to just below her ears. Her skirt was faded, slightly torn along the hem, and the white blouse she wore was stained with grease. She led him down the black hallway and into a room that was living room, kitchen and bedroom all in one. The odor of old garlic and onions hung in the air, seemingly oozing from the dirty walls and unswept floor since no food was at that moment on the fire. As soon as she was in the room, she shut the door and leaned her head back against it. Her right hand quickly undid the buttons on her blouse, revealing the pale skin of her breasts.

"Now I shall show you my wares," she said in a British accent, and began a deep, throaty laugh that ended in a racking cough. "Gawd, it's been a spell since I've laid eyes on the likes of you." She looked him up and down with the glittery eyes of desire. *"Mein mann,* 'ow do you like me Yiddish?" she laughed. "In this neighborhood, I can't 'elp but learn. And it can be useful, it can. It 'elps me get what I want." She looked at him pointedly, and her mouth parted slightly.

When he had picked her up bodily, she had let out a whoop. "Me gawds, I love a strong one, I do!" Her glee changed to chagrin as he immediately set her down across the room. Before she realized what had happened, he had unbolted the door and was on his way down the stairs.

Out on the street, he still had the fumes of onion and garlic with him. He looked at his watch. At this rate, he wasn't going to make the amount he had estimated. He moved to another block and began to go from door to door. His knowledge of most of the immigrants' languages finally served him well. When a frazzled Pole or Lithuanian opened the door and tried to talk to him in fractured and hesitant English, he was able to discern the accent of the speaker and switch to his native language. By midday he had made even more money than he had originally projected. And so it had continued. But the money wasn't enough to make up for the humiliation, the taunts, especially from the Irish, and the pranks children tried to play on him. Because of his size, he was luckier than most peddlers, and he was able to forestall problems a smaller man couldn't have. But his size also served to bring on some problems. He had turned the corner abruptly the second day to find four teenagers heading right for him.

"What a prize, eh?" one of them, tall and thin and covered in freckles, said. His hand darted out, and he helped himself to a bottle of seltzer as he came alongside Wolf. "Feeling right thirsty, I am."

His actions spurred the other three to try to do likewise. Wolf used the bins as a battering ram to push the first tough against the wall. He managed to keep that one pinned while he grabbed hold of another with his left hand. He closed his fingers around his windpipe and squeezed until the boy's face went red and he began to sputter for air.

"Get out of here, the lot of you," Wolf threatened, "or I'll squeeze his skinny neck until his eyes pop out like marbles."

They hesitated a moment until they saw their companion's eyes start to bulge from their sockets.

"C'mon, Jimmy," said the shortest one to the one who looked to be the ringleader. "He's crazy. He's gonna kill Fred."

"Let's go," snarled Jimmy when he realized there was little else he could do, and the three took off.

When Wolf was satisfied they were gone for good, he released his hold on the one called Fred, and shoved him to the ground with one hand. "Get the hell out of here," he said. "I see you around here again and I'll finish what I began."

Fred scrambled to his feet and took off so fast that he was half running, half stumbling down the street.

So, Wolf thought as he watched Marya pull her chemise down over her breasts as she began to dress herself, he had tried other lines of work. No, he needed something where he could use his brains, and where he would have people working for him. He had tried it the other way, and it hadn't worked.

"Let me talk to Lubish," Wolf said. "He'll come to see it our way about selling our share."

"No, Zavel. I should talk to Lubish. I know him well now and can anticipate the ins and outs of reasoning with him."

Wolf saw her thinking, although he was sure it wasn't reasoning that Lubish responded to most quickly. They discussed beforehand what would be the best approach for her to take. She would wait until that point in early morning when there was always a lull, after the emergency cases had hurried in and before the regular customers came.

The next morning Marya looked around the shop that had been her home for the last year. The walls were lined with shelves that held jars, some quite large, most smaller, filled with herbs and powders in varying hues—greens, yellows, browns, lavenders. In addition to the jars were assorted crocks and bottles. There was a single counter across the width of the shop at the back, and on it were more apothecary jars, a scale, and two large volumes bound in dark green leather with the word "Pharmacopoeia" embossed in gold letters. Behind the counter were two stools. She sat on one of them.

She would miss knowing that a part of this was hers. Never had she truly owned anything before that she had helped create or sustain. The shop and house that had come to her in Mogilyov and Petrovichi were nothing she felt she earned, and any pride of ownership she could have felt was tainted by the manner in which the property had come to her. Now her first real property was to be sold. But any misgivings she may have felt were lost in her adoration of Wolf and her desire to have him happy.

Lubish came into the shop from the upstairs and started to restock his bottle of laudanum. Marya joined him in the task of refilling the jars. For a while they worked side by side in silence.

"Lubish," Marya began, her voice breaking the quiet, "I would like to sell my share of the shop."

The jar top he had been holding in his left hand clattered to the counter top. "What?" he sputtered. His eyes were wide and hard with indignation.

"Yes," continued Marya, trying to keep her

breathing calm as she shook a sackful of powdered lupine seeds, known for their beneficial effect on women, into the jar in front of her. "We need the money."

"You must be crazy! The ink is hardly dry on the contract!"

"We'd like to offer the share to you first," said Marya, "before anyone else."

Lubish thought quickly. Sell it to someone else, perhaps a complete stranger? That would mean he could be forced into a partnership with someone he didn't know, maybe even someone he wouldn't like, or would like less than Wolf—at least Wolf he didn't have to work with directly. "This is blackmail," he finally managed to say. He wouldn't have been surprised if this had been Wolf's intention from the very start. He knew Wolf had never forgiven him for keeping Marya's illness a secret from him.

"No, Lubish, this is just business." She began to open a pouch of arnica, the dried yellow flower used to treat bruises and sprains. She was saying just what she and Wolf had planned for her to say, and she was pleased at how accurately they had anticipated Lubish's responses.

"I need to think it over," he said finally.

"Of course, Lubish. Take your time. Let us know in a week, if you wish."

"A week? You call that taking my time?"

"But you must understand. We are pressed. We have no choice." There, she had said it all. The atmosphere between her and Lubish crackled.

The week went by, and on the eighth morning, as Marya came into the shop, Lubish met her at the door. "I'm raising the money," he said, "to buy you out."

It was all going swiftly and just as Wolf had predicted. He had even estimated how long it would take Lubish to come up with the money. Four weeks later Lubish said he was ready.

That morning Marya had awakened with queasiness in her stomach. She attributed it to the fact that the day had finally arrived for them to complete the sale. Or maybe, she thought, it was the muggy summer heat that had just begun. But the queasiness was not gone the next morning or the morning after. She made herself cup after cup of chamomile tea in an effort to calm her nerves and her stomach, but it had no effect.

A week later Dr. Addison attributed the queasiness to another cause. "You're going to have a baby, Marya. You're suffering from nothing more than morning sickness."

All at once, in spite of the heat, her skin felt cold, and an image of David's face flashed in front of her. She felt dread of this experience which could bring back to her so swiftly all that she had tried to forget, and which could force her to risk the unthinkable. She had lost one child. She did not dare to chance another.

But as she sat in Dr. Addison's office, keenly aware of his staring at her and at the thick curls that had begun to make their way out of her bonnet and were already clinging to her cheek, she recalled Wolf's words the morning after their wedding night. He had awakened with a wish, which he voiced out loud. "I hope we have a son. It's time to begin our family."

Marya had said nothing, but her feelings were neither as clear nor as untangled as Wolf's. Then she brought herself to ask in a soft voice, "You want a baby right away?"

"Yes. The sooner the better."

It had taken him a while to express the terrible fear that had never ceased to gnaw at him, the fear of having lost his family in Russia. She knew he still hadn't heard from them, not a word. All his letters to them and to their friends had brought not a single line of comfort or even of information. He feared the worst, and she realized it was only natural that he was eager to build up around him a family to replace the one he feared he had lost.

Without analyzing why, he knew he wanted a line

of sons, sons as his father had had. Sons who could help him build the business he longed to start. Marya knew of his dreams to make a success of himself in this country, someone who would be respected as his father in St. Petersburg was, or had been. He did not want to let himself dwell on the many tragic circumstances that could have befallen his family and that were behind this ominous silence. But he knew as surely as if he had been told that something awful had happened, and that it was because they were Jews. It had happened as he had predicted, and he took no comfort from having seen it in advance.

"If only I had been able to make him see," he kept repeating to Marya. "I should have forced them to come with me. I should have. . . ."

"But what could you do," she reasoned, "short of tying him up in ropes? Besides, it would have been impossible to get someone across the border who didn't really want to go. A person must burn inside to leave or he will never be successful. There are too many hardships."

"I could have been more persuasive. I could have argued better. I could have taken him with me into the Jewish quarters so he could have seen firsthand, and I could have kept him from turning away his eyes. Now there are rumors that the czar may change the emigration policies. Russia is beginning to think she may be glad to let her undesirables get out of the country."

"Then, if that happens, your family might be safe, Zavel. They may be in Vienna, looking for you."

"But where are they now?" he had almost shouted. "The new policy is just talk. It's not in effect yet or even close to it. I want to know where they are now! I don't even know if they're in St. Petersburg any longer!"

She knew the general reports coming from Russia offered no hope, and who knew how much was rumor and how much was fact? The riots, the disturbances,

the pogroms were only worsening, and the flood of new
arrivals from Russia continued to swell.

Wolf's dream of starting a new family was now
coming true, she thought to herself.

Dr. Addison saw the tears in her eyes. "Those are
tears of joy, my dear."

For just a second Marya looked startled, found
out. Then she said, "Yes, Doctor. My husband will be
very happy."

He looked carefully at her. He had a great deal of
affection for this young woman in his charge. He
sensed there was much she wasn't saying, and that her
feelings were complex. "You are looking very pretty,
Marya, very healthy indeed," he said, changing the
subject. He did not want her to rush away. He wanted
to give her time, a chance to relax and unfold what
was on her mind.

He saw she had been watching the ceiling fan as it
turned lazily. She looked at him and smiled faintly.
"Thank you, Doctor. I have been lucky. I am no longer bald as an egg, although my hair grows very
slowly."

He laughed and removed a crisp, white hander-
chief from his breast pocket and used it to dab lightly
at his forehead. "Marya, I can assure you there never
was a prettier egg, as you call yourself. And your new
groom, how is he?"

Her face broke into a full smile. "He is fine, Doctor, he is very fine."

It was obvious to him that she adored her husband. Perhaps he had been wrong to think something
was bothering her. "With a first baby, like this," he
said, "we like to tell our mothers-to-be what to expect
from their bodies."

Marya listened politely as Dr. Addison discreetly
listed changes she could anticipate and explained the
stages of development the fetus would pass through.

He could see, though, that she was scarcely paying attention.

"Marya," he said suddenly, "do you want this baby?"

"Yes, Doctor, I do. It's only, only that . . . well, so soon after and . . ." She caught herself from saying what she was thinking, that it was so soon after losing her other.

"Of course," Dr. Addison was saying. "It is soon. Just a little over six weeks." He winked at her. "Wanted to prolong the honeymoon a little longer?"

"Yes, that's it," she said. How could she tell him she wasn't sure she wanted to be a mother again ever. She had lost one child and never did she want to risk such a loss again. She had kept her promise not to speak of what had happened in Russia. But she was unable to keep the past from invading her sleep or catching her thoughts unawares. And at those times what got through was David's face. More than once she had found herself staring at the faces of three and four-year-old boys, only to rebuke herself sharply and renew her pledge to put the past behind her. But she was still more sensitive than she wanted to be, still vulnerable, and the realization that she was pregnant brought it all crashing down on her. She also realized that there was no one in the world she could share these fears with.

"You come back in a month, and at that time we will examine you more completely, just to make sure everything is coming along as it's supposed to," said Dr. Addison.

His words made her blood run cold. She would be examined? Of course she'd be examined; that was standard procedure. He would be able to tell, she knew. He'd be able to tell she'd already had a baby.

"Now, you mustn't get nervous about it." He had seen the look that had fanned across her face. These young women from the *shtetl* were shy about such matters, he said to himself, and far more used to midwives to handle these things. He did his best to reassure her. "The nurse will be here, and everything will be quite modest. It's for your own well-being and that of your baby. And after all, it's not as if we haven't known each other before. Then we will have a midwife for the actual delivery. I'm sure you'd prefer it that way, and. . . ."

He went on, but she hardly heard what he was saying. She would never have come to see him if she had for one second thought she was pregnant. She had been so careful to put her past behind her, and now all might tumble out. She sat frozen in terror.

He got up from behind his desk and came to sit in the chair alongside hers. "Marya, all will be all right."

She turned a look of pure anguish on him. "Will it, Dr. Addison?"

And then the veil had immediately dropped over her expression, and again her face was closed.

After Marya had left his office, he was well aware that much more was troubling her than the unknown rigors of a first pregnancy.

"Zavel," she said that afternoon as Wolf reappeared in their workroom, followed by two boys carrying high stacks of yardage bolts in their outstretched arms. He made a sign that he would be there in just a minute, but a minute came and went, then ten and fifteen, and still he didn't come, lost in the details of arranging and cataloging the new supplies he had just received. He went out again and came back a couple hours later, and again Marya called to him.

He had a tape measure draped about his neck this time, and he was in an energetic discussion with Sol. "Just a moment," he called back, then promptly returned to the conversation.

An hour later she appeared in the doorway of the workroom. He noticed her face was pale, and she looked tired, as she had these last few weeks. "Zavel, there's something I'd like to talk to you about."

"I'll be right there," he promised, but he did not

foresee the dispute that would break out between a finisher and a sleeve feller over the pace of their work so that the afternoon and early evening slipped away from him.

Later that evening, as they ate their plain supper of lentil soup and kishke, Wolf noticed Marya seemed uncommonly quiet. Then he remembered she had been wanting to talk to him all day.

"What was it you wanted to talk to me about earlier? I got so busy I hardly had a moment's peace."

"I went to see Dr. Addison today."

He drew his breath in sharply and wondered how he could have let it slip his mind. This was what she had been so worried over. This was what she had wanted to talk to him about. "What did he say? What does he think is causing your tiredness?" he asked quickly.

She took a deep breath. "I guess we're going to have a baby."

"What!"

"A baby. We're going to have a baby, the doctor said." She looked down at her plate, but Wolf didn't notice. He jumped to his feet so suddenly that he knocked his bowl of soup onto the floor. He reached across the table and yanked her to her feet and into his arms.

"I can't believe it!" he cried. He covered her face with kisses, then yanked the scarf off her head and ran his fingers through her hair. "Tell me again," he said, and looked into her eyes with that longing of old.

Despite her misgivings about bearing another child, she felt herself responding to him, to his concentrated passion and energy, as she always did. She returned his look, her eyes aflame. "We're going to have our first child, Zavel. Dr. Addison has confirmed it." Then she leaned her head against his chest and felt the tears come, though whether from joy or fear she would not have been able to say.

Wolf was beside himself with a sense of satisfaction and achievement. In less than six weeks marriage was fulfilling some of his deepest desires. He had Marya as his very own; he had a nest egg with which to begin the business that was going to take him to the top, and he had his first son soon to be born.

The day Marya collected the money for their share of the apothecary shop from Lubish, Wolf had, that same day, taken it and invested in three treadle sewing machines, two long tables to use for cutting and basting, two pressing irons, and a number of chairs and stools. Overnight their small home was transformed into a miniature factory. Next to the windows were aligned the sewing machines, and taking up the middle of the room were the long tables. The table they had previously used for their meals and for Marya's sketching was relegated to the other small room that was their bedroom and that now also served as their entire home, the only place they could get away from the huge stacks of fabric on their way to becoming coats and in various stages of completion about the room.

The next morning, after Wolf had gotten up before dawn and left on an errand, Marya heard a knock at the door. She opened it to a small man with a sharp, pointed face who introduced himself as Sol Eliason and asked if this was where MW Enterprises was located.

"No," said Marya.

As she was about to shut the door she heard him ask, "Well, is Wolf Luminov here?"

She was startled to hear this mole of a man ask for Wolf by name. "No, this is his home, but he isn't here just now."

A perplexed look crossed the man's face. "Perhaps I could wait here for him. He told me he would be here."

Marya didn't know what to say, so she let the man in.

"There will be others," he said, and almost as

soon as the words were out of his mouth, there came another knock at the door, then another as one by one each visitor asked for MW Enterprises.

"If you would permit me," said Sol, and each time there was a knock at the door he now went to answer it. Within a matter of thirty minutes the room had filled with ten people, all of whom seemed to know one another already. They ran their hands through the piles of material and commented on the arrangement of the room. Marya was amazed and eager for Wolf to come back and take charge of this noisy collection of individuals. She had decided they must be people he had hired to work in the new business, which he had evidently already named on his own, but she didn't know how he had found them so fast and how it was they all seemed to know him, for his name drifted in and out of the buzz of conversation repeatedly.

At last Wolf had returned, and a big ruckus ensued, for all the world like a party. These were all workers who had been with Wolf at Detweiler's, she learned, and they were excited, every one of them, about the chance to work for Wolf Luminov. After another half hour of "So, how are you?" they were finally ready to start to work. Thus began Marya's introduction to the garment business and to Wolf's mode of operation.

Their days were taken with the typical duties of the contractor, for that is what Wolf had become. Each morning he would leave the tenement early to line up with the other contractors and bid on the completion price for the precut coats that were offered by the manufacturers.) Then he would pull back through the streets a rickety wooden wagon piled dangerously high with the coat parts he had managed to underbid the other contractors for. At various points during the day he might return to the mart to get more parts for his crew to work on. From the start Wolf prided himself on allowing his workers adequate rest periods and the best lighting and ventilation he could arrange. Never, he swore, would they find working for him to be the way it was in most garment businesses. The work was hard enough as it was.

Marya did her best to anticipate problems and keep the system flowing smoothly. The new business was, if not immediately prospering, at least surviving and earning them a living, although they did have a few difficult months in the beginning, the whole economy of the country having taken a downturn.

Although she was tired in the evenings, she wanted to attend night school, but Wolf insisted she stay home now that she was expecting the baby. So she would pass the time much as she had when she was living with Lubish and Alma. Her legs curled under her, she would sit with a piece of paper and idly sketch whatever was in front of her. When she grew tired of sketching the cookpots, the table, the chairs, the bouquet of daffodils that Wolf had brought her—though she didn't know how he afforded them, she turned her attention to images she carried in her mind and began to draw Wolf as he had caught her eye at various moments since she had known him.

Her memory held him struck in different moods and postures, almost as if he had been photographed and held still in time. She drew him as he had looked as he heard the news that she was expecting a baby, his head thrown back in a triumphant laugh, his hands in the air, lentil soup puddling on the floor. And she reproduced the look she remembered in his eyes as he had first brought her to see this room that he had somehow managed to rent—she never understood how he'd found it or paid for it. Scarcely realizing she was doing so, she began to sketch idly the silhouette of him as she had seen him in the night crossing the Russian stream with the child lifted onto his broad shoulders.

One day she made a discovery that improved her sketches immensely. She noticed that if she concentrated on what wasn't there in whatever object she was looking at, her drawings were much better. So she began to draw the spaces around the teapot. The empty spot in the handle was no longer nothing, it was something, and rather than focus her attention on the handle alone, she studied the form the absent part of the handle took. A void took on a shape. Her drawings became sharper, more precise, and Wolf, always attentive to the subject and style of her sketches, noticed the difference. When her time wasn't spent drawing, it was spent reading. She had discovered the newly established public lending library, where she could borrow books for no charge with just the signing of her name.

"Why, dear, you must read the classics of American literature, of course," had said the white-haired librarian with the tiny heart for a mouth and the spectacles that glinted in the light as she turned her head from side to side when she spoke. She was delighted that Marya, who was eager to soak up as much history and heritage as she could from her adopted country, had consulted her about what to read. So it was that she absorbed *The Scarlet Letter, The Deerslayer, Walden's Pond, The Adventures of Tom Sawyer,* and even *Moby Dick,* which she found to be the biggest challenge of all to her English skills. After a few months of direction from Mrs. Steinberg, the librarian, she began to wander through the stacks on her own, making numerous discoveries. She stumbled across the world of Henry James in *Century* magazine, which was serializing *The Bostonians,* and she was quickly caught up in the elegant and refined society he portrayed.

"To appreciate Henry James," the librarian had cautioned her with a wag of the finger, "you must be one on whom nothing is lost. He is a writer and an observer of human nature, certainly, on whom nothing is lost."

So Marya strove to be a reader on whom nothing was lost, alive to every nuance, the significance of every gesture, each utterance. Never had she been exposed to a world such as this, and she felt a feverish curiosity to know more. Such a life must have been Wolf's in St. Petersburg, she thought, and to better understand that fierce determination to raise himself back up to that level, which was so much a part of him, she threw herself into learning as much as she could. From the books about Boston society she ventured into New York society: the world of Fifth Avenue and its massive mansions, of the Astors, the Whitneys, and the Vanderbilts.

One Saturday afternoon she and Wolf had gone for a long walk uptown, and he had pointed out to her the mammoth residences of New York's very rich. On Fifth Avenue and Fifty-second Street rose an elegant and massive fortress of a building. It was four stories tall and had an elaborately decorated facade, which included a turret on one side.

"See that? It belongs to one man, William K. Vanderbilt." He had also pointed out the two Italianate palazzos to the left which he told her had been built by Vanderbilt's brothers-in-law, William Sloane and Elliot Shepard in a kind of family rivalry. Further to the left rose another imposing mansion, that of William H. Vanderbilt, now the senior member of the family.

She had been astonished to see that such grandeur, which in her mind was only associated with the czars, existed in this country. It seemed as if the characters from the novels she'd read were suddenly before her there on Fifth Avenue. She couldn't help but notice, too, the fashionably dressed women with their parasols and plumed bonnets as they paraded daintily down the avenue, accompanied by gentlemen in tall silk hats. As they had left the house, Wolf had told her how pretty she looked in her new bonnet, her hair now halfway to her shoulders and tucked up inside. But next to these elegant ladies in their new fall finery, she felt drab and insignificant, a mule among thoroughbreds.

She had tried to read the emotions on Wolf's face that afternoon as they stood and stared at the immense edifices before them and watched the stream of elegant passers-by, especially the ladies, but she saw that his expression was closed and careful and that it was impossible to know what he was really thinking.

Later that evening, she had started to read to him a passage from one of her novels. The excerpt was about a dinner party attended by a dozen or more from New York City's most elegant and important coterie at which the choicest dishes were being served and where the conversation was as sparkling as the wine.

In the midst of her reading aloud, Wolf slammed his hand down on the table.

She looked up from her book at once. "What's wrong?" she said, instantly alarmed by the angry set to his jaw.

He said nothing, and instead stood up and took his jacket from the peg by the door. Just before he went out he turned and said, "I'm just restless, that's all. I'm going for a walk."

Marya knew that his thoughts these days were always on the business, and she wondered if that was what was on his mind or something else, something that had to do with their walk that afternoon. She put away the novel, reading having suddenly lost its appeal for the time being, and tried to content herself with sketching. But the dinner party she'd been reading about was still in the back of her mind, and she found that she was creating a gown for each of the ladies to wear.

She busied herself with the series of drawings. She could see each of the women in her imagination, one wearing a dress of grass-green satin, with a slight bustle to accentuate her curves, bustles having recently come back in fashion; another wearing a dark blue dress of striped satin, as was still all the rage, with a high-necked bodice trimmed in a fichu of ecru net and with fitted sleeves stopping just below the elbow. The next

was gowned in a three piece dress which Marya sur-
feited with decoration, embroidered bands and ruffles
running down the arms. Suddenly she realized that this
gown was in the Russian style. She had inadvertently
drawn a wealthy woman dressed in the grand Russian
manner, strands of pearls running through her hair and
into her headdress and standing in an ornate salon typical, according to the way Wolf had once described it,
of the period, with its lavish use of gilt and massive
picture frames and rich upholstery. But this wouldn't
do in America, she decided, and crumpled up the
sketch sheets.

She ran her hands over her stomach. Her pregnancy was now in its fifth month, and her belly swelled
slightly. She shuddered as she recalled her visit back to
Dr. Addison for the thorough examination he had insisted on. After he had finished the check up, he said
nothing, but she thought she had detected a look in his
eye, but then she wasn't sure. She thought surely there
must be some way for him to tell that this baby was
not her first, but he said nothing to indicate he questioned her. She had to endure the uncertainty of not
knowing just how much he knew, or had surmised,
about her past.

Through these past months of her marriage, her
biggest source of comfort and strength had been Wolf.
Their passion had not cooled; rather it burned more
fiercely now than in the beginning. All these new un-
dertakings drew them closer together, and the words of
Lubish no longer came to her mind.

She saw that it was getting late. The clock on the
wall read ten-thirty, and she felt a longing for him, a
desire to know that his mood had passed and that he
was all right.

It was another hour before Wolf came home. His
face was drawn and tired, and he threw himself down
next to her on the small sofa in their bedroom and lay
with his head in her lap.

"What is it?" she said. "Is it the business?"

"There must be a way," he said. "There must be a way." He pounded his left fist into the palm of his right hand.

"But we're doing well, Zavel. We're making enough after we pay the workers for us to take good care of ourselves."

He sat up suddenly and turned to her. "But that's not the point. We're getting by. Fine, but we want to do more than just get by. We don't want to stay where we are now for the rest of our lives."

"The rest of our lives? It's only been five months that you've been a contractor. It's amazing, really, how well you have done. I've never had this much in my entire life. I feel very lucky."

He looked at her sharply. "Wouldn't you like to live in a bigger apartment? Wouldn't you like to wear pretty dresses like the ladies we saw on Fifth Avenue?"

She was aware he was watching her closely. "Yes, Zavel, of course, but it's not that import—"

"How do you think we're going to get anywhere in life if we just accept where we are?" He stood up and began to pace around the small room. "There must be a way," he kept repeating. "If I could just find a way to cut a little more off the cost, to give us more of an edge against the other contractors." But he knew there were certain things he couldn't do. He refused to act like Detweiler and ask his employees to up the number of coats they made while receiving the same amount of pay. And he refused to trick them into working longer hours than they realized or to institute a system of fines. Such actions he considered extortions, even though such practices were common in most work places.

Marya went to him and put her head against his chest. "Zavel, let's go to bed now. Something will occur to you. It always does."

He looked down at the printed babushka on her head, and suddenly he was reaching for it, yanking the ends where it was tied. "Why do you still wear this old thing?" he said. He grabbed it and threw it to the floor, and her hair tumbled loose, thick and glossy.

Marya looked up in surprise at the intensity in his voice. "It's not old. It's—" she started to say.

"Get rid of it. You don't need to hide behind it anymore. I don't want to see it on your head again."

Then hardly aware of what he was doing, he started to rip at the blouse she was wearing. "And this thing! Throw it out too." He took it by the collar and ripped it down the front, tearing her chemise at the same time so that she was standing before him with her breasts exposed. "These rags aren't you! Get rid of all of it!" he cried, and spun her around to undo her long skirt. Then, impatient with the fastening, he tore at it until the threads gave way. He gave a violent tug and the skirt, along with the remainder of her chemise, fell to the floor.

She stood before him naked, and he saw the rise and fall of her breasts in time with her breathing. His own breathing was ragged and loud from his exertion. He stared at her. Her face was flushed, and there was a faint smile on her lips. But it was the look in her eye that caught him. He saw there a softening, a letting go of some indefinable emotion that she had been holding back these last months.

She stepped toward him and raised her arm to his shoulders. He caught her to him tightly, and he could feel the points of her breasts pushing into his chest. As he felt the warmth of her body lengthwise against his, his passion for her, already sparked, now exploded. Feeling the intensity of his desire for her, she responded in kind. She led him to their bed and as she drew him to her, they once again renewed the physical surrender to one another of their wedding night.

"What have we here?" exclaimed Wolf the next morning as Marya came into the workroom before the employees had arrived. He had smoothed out on the table her crumpled sketches of the previous night and

was studying them intently. "Do I see a Russian grande
dame here?" He looked at her out of the corner of his
eye. "You're not getting lonesome for Mother Russia,
are you?"

Marya's eyes snapped. "Never."

Wolf encircled her in his arms and his voice was
full of controlled excitement. "This could be it, Marya.
This could be it."

She had only a vague idea what he was muttering
about, but wasn't ready to admit it by asking questions.
Yet, that morning, with Wolf's encouragement, she began a series of sketches of what were to be, according
to Wolf, what women might wear to an afternoon
party. Marya sketched for a while, then stepped back
to assess her work. "No, this is not it. These dresses
are too stiff, too artificial, not what a lady might actually wear," she said. "They look made up."

She began again, and after a number of hours, she
set the new sketches on the floor against the wall where
she might look at them critically. Still she was not
pleased. She stuffed her red curls, which were now at
ear-level, into a babushka, and hurried out of the
apartment. The afternoon was spent at the library,
where, with Mrs. Steinberg's assistance, she was
pleased to find exactly what she was looking for. She
had in her arms three novels of what Mrs. Steinberg
called the silver spoon set. For the next couple of
hours Marya read randomly in the books, soaking up
the atmosphere of people who went to such afternoon
parties. She knew she'd never been to an afternoon
party, although she'd certainly been to parties held in
the afternoon. But she knew somehow that wasn't the
same thing. Once steeped in the ambiance she wanted,
she returned home to pen and paper.

This time she felt she had it. She drew a day dress
of pale green gauze, to be printed in lines to give the
effect of watered silk. The skirt was ruched and
trimmed with a frill of green and white, and the fitted

sleeves were ruched from elbow to wrist to match the skirt. The next gown was of primrose-yellow silk with an underdress of fawn-colored taffeta and small puffs at the tops of the sleeves. She continued until she had completed six afternoon dresses that she could envision being worn to the gardens and summer homes described in the novels.

"These are beautiful," Wolf said when he saw them. "Women would pay lots of money to wear dresses like these."

She knew that where he came from he had had plenty of opportunity to see women in fashionable dresses, and that his eye could be trusted. "Most women couldn't afford to, though," she said.

Wolf continued to ponder the drawings. Suddenly his eyes lit up. "Do them again, Marya."

She looked at him in astonishment.

"But this time make them more simple. Make them more for a woman who wants to look like she's wealthy but isn't. Something for the average woman who doesn't want to look it."

Marya passed the evening working on the drawings. That night, before they went to bed, the sketches were finally completed, and she presented them to Wolf.

He saw that she had replaced the silks with cotton and muslin, and that the amount of fabric in the dresses had been lessened. There were other changes, subtler changes, that made a difference in the cost of the materials and the time required to assemble them. "These are perfect," he said and without further elaboration scooped her into his arms and carried her to bed.

The next morning he disappeared before Marya arose and took the sketches with him. He walked into the shop of Mr. Zeidenbaum, the tailor who had made his first American suit, the suit he was wearing at this moment.

"Mr. Luminov, such a pleasure it is," said the wizened tailor and put out his hand. As he pumped Wolf's arm, the tailor couldn't help eyeing him from head to toe. He took hold of Wolf's sleeve and rolled the fabric between his fingers. "Not bad," he said, "not bad. This fabric will last you thirty years, maybe longer if you're lucky. Another suit you should have, of this material. The finest brushed wool it is."

"I didn't come here for a suit." Wolf spread out the last set of sketches Marya had completed and waited for the tailor to comment.

"Very nice, but for what are you showing me this?"

"I want you to make me up one of each and—"

"Just a second, just a second. A tailor I am, not a dressmaker. You want this kind of work, you got to see a dressmaker."

Wolf removed from his pocket a wad of bills and peeled off twenty dollars. "You make these for me in the next three days, and you can have the twenty for your labor alone. The materials will be extra."

The tailor rolled his eyes upward. "Lord of the universe, why me? Why do you send me madmen in a hurry? Why do you make my life harder with requests for work I do not do?" He picked up the twenty as he continued his dirge. "Why do you tempt me this way, O Lord?"

Shaking his head from side to side, he turned his attention back to Wolf. "Now I ask you, why me?"

"You're fast, you're good, you want the money."

The tailor sighed. "Yes, that's true."

"And you can work miracles in three days."

The tailor sighed again. "Yes, that's true, too." He looked resigned. "Who should they fit?"

Wolf had completely forgotten about that, so intent had he been on having the dresses made up immediately. He left the shop and ran home to get Marya. He hurried her along the street with him, offering her no explanation of where they were going. Back at the tailor's, he said, "For her. Make the dresses to fit my wife."

Mr. Zeidenbaum took in Marya's swelling belly under her loose dress. "To fit her as she is she is now? They will be too small already by the time you pick them up in three days."

"No, make them to fit her as if she weren't pregnant. They're for her to wear later."

"Clothes to wear later? In maybe five or six months? And these are the dresses you have to have in three days?"

"Yes," said Wolf.

The tailor threw up his hands but said nothing, and Marya tried hard not to smile as Mr. Zeidenbaum set to work to measure her, muttering under his breath about having to subtract inches for the *kind* and about this not being his regular line of work, and questioning the heavens why was he given the opportunity to meet this *meshuggener* again.

When Wolf returned to Mr. Zeidenbaum's three days later, the dresses, perfectly fashioned, were hanging on a rack at the back of the shop. Wolf got from the tailor the exact amount it had cost him in fabric to make each dress, and the time each had taken. Averaging together the expenses, each dress had cost Mr. Zeidenbaum $2.30 in total. For an additional dollar Wolf also bought the pattern pieces that the tailor had devised.

He returned to his workshop and spread out the dresses on the table where Marya sat helping with the basting. "Here is our new line," he said, and waited for her reaction.

She looked at the greens and yellows and blues that had suddenly brightened up the table where she was accustomed to seeing the drab greys, greens or blacks for the coats. "New line?" She lifted her eyes to Wolf's. "You're sure?"

They were aware that the activity in the room had diminished, and the other workers were straining their ears to hear. Wolf pulled Marya from the stool and into the other room.

"Yes," he said, as soon as the door had shut behind them. "We're going to start manufacturing dresses for the ladies."

"What are you saying?" It seemed like a hundred of her thoughts were tumbling one over another at once. "Does . . . is . . . is that why you asked me to make those sketches?" she managed to say, her suspicions beginning to be confirmed.

He gathered her into his arms. "Marya, with your designs, we can move into a whole new area. We don't have to be mere contractors anymore, bidding on garments someone else has designed and cut. We don't have to be the middleman."

"How do you mean?"

"Cloth is cheap, nothing's cheaper. We can get it directly from the mills, and with the patterns Mr. Zeidenbaum makes, and with Sol's knowledge of tailoring—he's worked in almost every kind of shop there is and made almost any piece of clothing you can think of—we can do it all ourselves. We can cut it ourselves. Then we sew it up, just as we've been doing the coats."

"Do you really think we could do it? Do you think anyone would want my designs?"

"I'm sure of it. Those fancy gowns you drew the other night are what started it all. When I saw what you could do, I knew that other women would fight to get hold of those dresses."

Marya thought again about the six gowns in the other room strewn out on the worktable like giant flowers. It was possible, she thought, it was possible.

Within a matter of a week, Wolf had purchased two more machines. They were old and used, but they were cheap and they ran. There was no place for the new machines to fit but in the bedroom, an invasion of what little privacy she and Wolf had that Marya had not counted on. And with the machines had come more operators: more basters, more pressers, more finishers. Marya felt they were about to be squeezed out of what little living area they had left to them.

But Wolf had been right. It had been surprisingly easy for him to sell the finished dresses to the first store he showed them to. In the last seven days it seemed the only time they had alone together was when they slept. Mornings he was up even earlier than ever now, on his way to the textile manufacturers. During the day he was in and out, dropping off bolts of material, conferring hastily with Sol and sweeping up the finished garments to take to the shops.

Wolf was constantly in a state of optimistic excitement. With his coaching, Marya began to turn out more sketches, more designs for the woman who either couldn't afford a dressmaker or who preferred to buy her clothes ready-made. No sooner had the drawings left her hand, than Wolf would snatch them up and start them on the process to becoming actual dresses. His appetite for designs appeared insatiable, and Marya was completely occupied as she lost herself in ideas for day dresses, evening dresses, even wedding dresses and mourning dresses in everything from poplin and muslin to flannel and cotton and occasionally taffeta and satin. At those times when she got stuck for an idea, when she just couldn't seem to get the mood of the dress she wanted, she hurried to the library and buried herself in books that would help her create the right atmosphere, the right nuances.

At night, as they held each other in their arms, they were both very tired but very happy. Wolf had what he wanted: a business that appeared well on its way to becoming successful, the woman he loved, and a child soon to be. It was with considerable shock, then, that Marya woke him in the night two months after they had started the new line. In that faint light that came in from the window he could see her forehead glistening with sweat, and her hand felt hot and damp on his chest. The pains in her abdomen had become too much for her to bear, she told him, and asked him to call Dr. Addison.

Chapter 9

When labor began, Dr. Addison was called. The doctor did what he could, but there was no way he could help Marya other than by his presence. Marya's screams woke up half the tenement, and finally, five hours later, the baby, a boy, was born dead.

That morning Wolf posted a sign on the door that the shop was closed, but those workers who signed in would still be paid. Then he spent the rest of the day with Marya, amid the machines and bolts of fabric piled high on one side of their room and their living space squeezed into the other half. Marya did not awaken once that day, so he had plenty of time to sit and think. He left her for only a brief period that afternoon, and when he returned, he had managed to rent another flat one story below their present one, and identical in layout. The next morning, he moved the ladies' line out of their bedroom and to the new apartment, where it seemed to mushroom to take up both rooms. Then he threw himself into his work with even greater intensity than he had before.

No one could reach Marya for a long time. She had sunk way down inside herself, where she wanted no one to find her. No one knew her loss was for two sons, and both bore David's face. All her defenses, all her vows not to think of the past were for naught. She no longer had the strength to withstand the assault of her memories. She could not erase the image of his terror stricken expression as she had last glimpsed it in the streets of Petrovichi, his arms outstretched toward her as the old woman appeared from behind and picked him up. Now she had lost him not once but twice.

Wolf tried everything he could think of to break through to her. He took time out from the demands of their shop to visit the library and, under Mrs. Steinberg's tutelage, he selected books for Marya to read. He encouraged her to accompany him on walks uptown or along the river. He brought her choice slices of strudel and honey cake. He bought her expensive new sketching papers with the hopes she might begin to draw again. But most of all he tried to get her to talk. To everything, her response was tepid and listless.

Dr. Addison came to visit every week. In the beginning he would sit by the bed and talk to her about how much stronger she was getting. After the second month his voice and manner changed.

"There's nothing more I can do for you, Marya."

She was sitting in a chair near the window. Her eyes looked tired as she looked up at him. He could hear the whirring of the machines in the next room where the coats were still being made.

"You are the only one that can make you feel better now. It's your will that is keeping you from going forward, from continuing to live."

She said nothing.

He continued. "You will feel better, happier again, when you decide that is what you want to do. Losing a child"—he hesitated only a moment—"or children—is part of the natural rhythm of life, the sorrow that goes with the joy."

She turned back to him and her eyes were filled with tears, the first he had seen her cry. "What do you know of losing children?" she cried, and as her breath came out in big sobs, she ran to him and beat her fists on his chest.

He held her against him and let her cry. It seemed the more she cried, the more there was still to come. "You're healing yourself now, Marya. You are your own physician. I want you to know you are always welcome at my office. I would always want to see you. Please come."

Three months later Marya was indeed sitting in Dr. Addison's office. He had just finished examining her, and he was smiling. He took her by the hand. "This is good news, Marya. You are expecting a baby."

That night, even though she hadn't sorted out her own feelings, she asked Wolf if he would forgo his plan to comb through the account books for the business as he usually did in the evenings. She had something she wanted to talk to him about. Because it had been so long since she had initiated any kind of talk other than about the most mundane of their daily activities, such as pertained to the running of their household, Wolf agreed at once.

"I went to see Dr. Addison today," she began.

Wolf watched her carefully, sensing that what she was going to say was crucial to their lives together.

"He told me I'm going to have . . . I'm going to have a baby." She paused, then suddenly her words were tumbling one over the other in her haste to let out what she had pushed down inside these past months. "Wolf, how can this be happening? How can we do this again? I don't know if I can go through it another time. I don't know if I can put you through it again. I know I've been far away from you these last six months. They couldn't have been easy for you, seeing me so distant, so unreachable, locked into my misery. You, too, have been hurt and needed comfort. But I took it all for myself. I don't know what to do. I can't bear the thought that I might bring more disappointment, that I might lose another—"

"We will have the baby. Of course we will." He seized her by the wrists. "Where is my woman of the *shtetl*? Where is my woman of the old country, where husbands and wives knew they could lose more children than would live?"

"No!" Marya cried, and tried to put her hands over her ears. "Don't talk to me about the *shtetl*. Don't talk to me about Russia."

"Marya, the blood in your veins, in the veins of everyone who made it here, is blood that has the will and the means to survive. You made it out of Russia, you left it all behind you, family and friends. That means you can make it through anything, and you can make it through this. You—we—must take a chance. We must take a chance that the baby will be born and that our new family will begin."

His grip on her wrist was hurting her, and she could feel her heart pounding in her chest. She knew he was right. They would have to take a chance.

Eight months later a healthy baby was born. During the time she was carrying it, Marya had done everything she could to make it a girl. "It will be a girl, it will be a girl," she had said over and over to herself. She knew she could not face the prospect of another dead son, no matter how strong she was. Nor did she want a son to remind her as he grew up of David and how he had looked at each age, or to make her think of how he would have looked had she been able to see him through all his growing years. It would be better to have a girl, to begin truly anew. And so she had, for the first time in her life, set her mind on seeing if she could, through her ability to see glimpses of the future, her pictures as she thought of them, have any influence on what might happen. Make the baby a girl, she had wished ardently, a girl.

And so the baby that was born to Wolf and

Marya, on March 29, 1887, was named Elke, after Marya's mother.

Wolf had stared at the naked child as it was held aloft by the midwife assisting Dr. Addison. Even through the glistening wetness and blood still covering it, he could see it was not a boy.

From where she lay in the bed, Marya thought she saw a strange look flicker across his face, lasting no more than a second, but she was never able to be sure. Almost at once he was kneeling by the bed. She held out her hand and immediately he seized it and pressed it to his lips.

"She's fine!" he kept saying. "She's a beautiful girl. She's alive, and she's fine."

No sooner had he said that than the midwife, a squat, middle-aged woman with lemon-colored hair, administered a swift spank to the newborn, and robust squalls filled the room as if in confirmation of his words.

"And her hair? Does she have any?"

He looked at her strangely, but he thought he understood. "It's . . . it's . . . well, there isn't much yet, just a little black fuzz here and there," he admitted.

He couldn't tell if she was satisfied with his response, but he saw that with the infant in her arms a few minutes later, she easily fell into a sound sleep.

In the next months, while Marya was occupied with Elke, Wolf was occupied with the demands of the business. The ladies' line, in particular, called for an increasing amount of his attention and time. The depression of 1886 and 1887 was beginning to lift, and sales had gone up thirty per cent in the last month. As Wolf would tally the accounts at the end of each day, Marya no longer peered over his shoulder out of curiosity nor did she keep mental tabs on their earnings.

"More and more women must be forsaking their dressmakers," said Wolf, one evening three months after Elke was born. He was sitting at the round wooden table next to their bed, the table that served as their desk, drafting board and kitchen table in one. In front of him were random bits of paper on which he had jotted income and expenses incurred during the course of the day. He was entering them in the ledger book and his face wore an expression of supreme satisfaction. "The ladies are opening their purses again, and what they're buying are our dresses."

Marya was lying on her side on the bed, and Elke was lying in front of her, nursing at her breast. Marya was studying Elke's head and was pleased to see the black down had finally given way to fine red strands.

For a moment he studied the serene picture the two of them made before him, then said, "It's time for us to move, Marya. We need a bigger place now with Elke, and we can afford it."

Marya looked up suddenly. "I don't know, Zavel. Perhaps we should wait a little longer, until we're sure of our new earnings. Maybe this improvement in the economy is just temporary. Better to save the money, or put in into more machines instead. We must be practical."

In the months that followed, Wolf would occasionally mention their need for a larger flat, and Marya would quietly demur.

"First let's make sure we have a firm foundation under us," she said. "Let's see what happens with the business." She was wary of the ups and downs the country's economy was going through, and didn't want to relive the rigors and uncertainties of their first year with the shop. Starting a new business during a depression had been madness, now that she looked back on it, even though they had managed to make it work after all. Still, this was no time to pursue luxuries, she said to herself.

Elke now absorbed most of her attention. It had been right to have a girl, thought Marya. The unrestrained love she might have had difficulty unloosing on another son flowed freely to this daughter. She was relieved to see Elke's red hair was growing fast now, and she was becoming prettier almost each day. Marya spent hours marveling at the exquisiteness of her daughter's tiny features and perfectly formed limbs. She loved to sew little dresses, bonnets and blankets for her. As she held the baby to her breast, she felt a bond developing between them stronger than she would ever have felt possible. This girl would be very special, she thought, very special indeed.

Wolf never tired of the bustle of the streets. At almost any time between six in the morning and ten at night the streets of the Lower East Side were lined on both sides with wagons and pushcarts, and minding the carts and bins and oaken barrels were women of all ages in their long skirts, aprons and shawls. Old men with flowing white beards, young boys in knickers, men in knee-length jackets and bowlers, all had a purpose, a mission and were hurriedly on their way somewhere. From Hester Street he turned left onto Orchard and passed through Essex Market Place. He made his way through the usual crowd in front of the Essex Market Police Court, where residents waiting to have their cases heard mingled with the pupils from P.S. 137, just across the street and with shoppers and sellers from the street market.

At Delancey he slipped into a narrow doorway and climbed to the fourth floor. He stopped in front of the door to the right, and it was opened almost immediately by a stocky man of medium height who was dressed in a long black jacket with matching trousers and a plain white shirt. He had a square black beard and closely cut hair, except for the long forelocks hanging from next to his ears. Outside the trousers and below the shirt hung the long fringes of his religious undergarment. Wolf recognized him at once as a member of the Chassidim, a singularly religious sect.

"Wolf Luminov," he said, putting out his hand.

The man blinked slowly, than extended his own hand. "Jacob Molnar," he murmured in a broadly

Hungarian-accented voice that was to Russian ears almost humorous, and he led Wolf to a wooden table draped in black velvet next to the window. On the far side of the room were two other men, dressed in a garb identical to that of Jacob. One was sitting at a workbench, engrossed in some detailed work that Wolf couldn't see, and the other was bent over what looked to be a lathe. Neither looked up when Wolf came in.

Jacob motioned Wolf to sit in one of the two chairs next to the table, and he took the other. Methodically, he began to take from his pockets little pieces of paper folded into small squares no bigger than an inch or two in width. He arranged the papers, which looked exactly like miniature envelopes, in an even pattern across the table, then began to unfold the one closest to him. His fingers, lightly tufted with dark brown hair, were short and stubby, but they worked deftly. Inside the square of waxy paper lay a diamond, and when it was unwrapped, the light from the window struck it and seemed to give it life as it instantly became a blaze of color. One by one he continued to unfold the squares until the table was a rainbow of sparkle.

Wolf looked at the table and waited.

Jacob also waited.

Finally Wolf pointed to one of the stones.

"That's a top wesselton, a 1.25 from the Kimberley Mines. Note the white-white color," said Jacob in Yiddish. He held up a small magnifying glass. "Look at it through this loop. You will see that it has no haze, or snow, as we call it. Nor does it have any black dots, which indicate carbon. A very fine stone." Wolf pointed to another, of the same size but a bluer color.

"Also a 1.25 from the same mine. A rare blue. It's called a river. Your eye is good."

Wolf continued to indicate the stones that interested him and Jacob responded with the size, origin and any other pertinent information. At Jacob's direction, he peered through the loop and began to learn the difference between a river, a top wesselton, a wesselton and a diamond with a slight yellow tinge.

"And this one?" Wolf pointed to a medium-sized stone with a fiery red cast to it and a high degree of transparency.

"That one is an old stone, from India most likely. See how it is cut in an old fashion. That was a style done in the seventeenth century in Amsterdam, before the center for diamonds shifted to Antwerp. Most likely this diamond was brought to England by the British East India Company and from there taken to Amsterdam for cutting."

After another thirty minutes of discussion, the man who had been hunched over the workbench rose and approached the table where Wolf and Jacob sat.

"You would like to take some tea with us?" he asked Wolf.

The discussion of the diamonds stopped completely as the four of them halted their work to drink their tea. No one spoke during that time and the diamonds continued to glisten on the table. As they sipped their hot tea from their glasses, Wolf had an opportunity to study Jacob in more detail. He was a young man, about the same age as Wolf, although his manner of dress made him appear older. He had a square, pleasant face, of which the most prominent feature was his light grey eyes that were alive to the smallest movement about him. He gave the impression of being able to look at two things at once, and his eyes seldom seemed to be still. What might have been termed shiftiness in another man was in him alertness and curiosity.

As Wolf looked about the room, he realized the man who had been at the workbench had most likely been setting a diamond, and the other man cutting or polishing one.

The glasses at last empty, all returned to their original tasks, and the leisurely bargaining between Wolf and Jacob resumed.

"This one," said Jacob, "is worth twice what that one is." He indicated another diamond Wolf had been asking about. "For that price you offer it is not possible. It is a perfect half-carat. Still, it is not flawless." He put out his hand for the loop Wolf was holding and exchanged it for a different one. As Wolf gazed through the stronger glass at the diamond, Jacob added, "You will see this diamond has a tiny speck of snow, detectable with a very strong loop, but never visible to the bare eye."

"Then a tiny speck lowers its cost a tiny bit," said Wolf.

Jacob nodded slightly.

Wolf had to respect this wily diamond merchant's manner of doing business. It was slow, it was careful, and it was unfailingly polite. Another hour passed, and both had what they wanted: Wolf the diamond with the fiery center, and Jacob a goodly sum of Wolf's money.

As they parted, Wolf said, "I plan to see you again. Soon."

"That is good," said Jacob, and smiled. "You will find your purchase will last forever. It is indestructible."

Marya knew he was standing behind her. As always she could sense when he was near. He said nothing. Slowly she turned to face him and smiled.

"Zavel! How long have you been standing there?" She knew very well how long he had been there but at his unexpected presence found herself babbling whatever came into her head.

He could not help but be struck by her beauty. He looked at her seated in front of her drawing table, her hair now fuller and richer than ever, spilling over her shoulders, and her hand with the pen just lifted from the sketch she was working on held poised in the air as she looked at him. He knew that he wanted her very much. If he did what he wanted, he would yank her from that table and pull her into his arms. He couldn't help it that she still affected him this way.

Instead he reached into his pocket and drew out the small box. He felt like a little boy as he held it toward her. Words usually came to him when he needed them, but none was coming now. He tried to hide the slight trembling of his hands.

Marya looked puzzled for a moment. Then she slowly reached out and took the box. She lifted its velvet top and saw the ring. It was a diamond, lightly tinged with red and set in platinum. She stared at it and tried to sort out her mixed feelings.

"Oh, Zavel. It's . . . it's beautiful!" She looked up at him. "But how . . ."

"Put it on," he said. His voice sounded hoarse in his ears.

She slipped the ring on and as Wolf looked at it on her long, slim finger, he was suffused with a feeling of accomplishment greater than he had felt since coming to this country. This was how he wanted to see Marya. This was how he wanted his wife to look. He wanted to cover her beautiful hands with diamonds, emeralds and rubies and hang them from her ears, wrists, neck. The endless hours in the sewing rooms, the insults in the street, the meager meals he ate—they were all worth it for this moment.

"Hold it to the light," he said.

Marya went to the window and held the ring up. The sunshine cast a prism of red and white that glanced off it and across her face, her hair, her body and across the room.

"See how it sparkles, Marya." He saw there were tears in her eyes.

"But, Zavel," she whispered, "how could this be? Where did you get it?"

He yearned to cry out that he wanted to cover her in jewels from head to toe. She was a queen. What did it matter how he got it or where it came from? She deserved it, that was all.

Marya tried to laugh through her tears. "Oh, Zavel, you give me a diamond as if I'm royalty." She smiled at him again, with just a hint of sadness. "Don't give me jewels . . . give me buildings, give me tenements, for both of us."

Tenements? Surely she was joking. "For you a tenement building isn't good enough, Marya. A tenement we already have." He ran his eyes over the cracked yellow walls of their two room home and over the stains in the floor that no amount of Marya's scrubbing had been able to take out. "I want beautiful things for you. Not ugly. Beautiful for beautiful."

Marya laughed gently. "But with tenements we will have beautiful things later. If we continue to save our money now, live carefully. . . ." She broke off and waved her hand toward the black treadle machines lined up against the wall. "We could use more sewing machines."

"Yes, we can always use more machines. We can use more of everything. More machines, more rooms, more furniture, more workers."

"If we start small now and save our money for a building, then we can live in it free and collect the rents to make the payment, and we can. . . ."

Wolf could not hear her words. He could only see the ring sparkling on her finger. Marya had hands like his mother's, hands meant to wear rings. He remembered how he would watch his mother as a child, her hands gracefully tracing arcs through the air as she talked. Whatever she said was punctuated by the flash of her rings. His father had marked every birthday, every holy day with another jeweled creation, each more delicate, more beautiful than the last. His mother had worn them with belief in her husband, pride in this material symbol of his love, pride in his success as a man. This is what he wanted for Marya and him. He would set off her beauty with precious stones, a sign of the love they had together. He wanted everyone to look, to know that here was a woman who was loved, a woman from a family that was something in this land.

Wolf watched the fire from the ring dance and grow and with it grew his desire for her. It grew and grew, so great it overwhelmed him. He gathered her in his arms as she was still talking.

The current that was always between them swept through her and stopped her words.

He picked her up and carried her to the bedroom. Marya could not help herself. She responded to him hungrily. The moment pushed away thoughts of all else, thoughts of their hard work, long hours and even of the diamond ring—all disappeared in their need for each other.

Two days later Marya pawned the ring, receiving four hundred dollars in cash. She said nothing to Wolf and hid the money.

Six months later Wolf presented Marya with another ring, this one a ruby. He stood watching expectantly as she opened the box.

As she slipped the ring over her finger, she said, "Zavel, it's very beautiful. You're so good to me. But"—she looked up to see his face begin to cloud at her words, yet she couldn't stop—"can we afford it?"

"Yes."

"It's just that we need other things so much more. Jewels, rings—these should be for later."

She thought she detected a strain in his voice as he answered, "There's no reason we can't have it all, Marya. No reason we can't start to live the way we want to even now."

"We could take this money, the money for the ring, and start to save for our own tenement. We could even find someone else to go in with, a partner. It wouldn't take long that way. Then later, when we're more certain of our money, we could . . ."

It seemed to Wolf he heard the echo of her former suitor in her words, of Nate's talk about tenements being the smartest way for the newcomer to go.

Interrupting the flow of her words with an angry wave of his hand, he seized her hand with the ring on it and held it up for them both to see. His tone suddenly became quiet and intense. "I want you to have the best. I want you to look like a queen."

Marya snatched her hand away. "That's just it. I feel like some kind of demented, antique Russian princess with these jewels. I feel like—"

"What is this hatred you have of Russia? Everything that seems the least bit Russian to you, you turn your back on. I don't understand this immense, one-sided—"

"I don't expect you to understand. I don't expect you to understand at all." She looked away from him.

On the other side of the room the baby began to cry softly.

"It was my country too," Wolf argued. "But I don't feel the way you do. It's like you become a different person whenever the word Russia is spoken. You get hard. I feel your resistance like a wall of iron."

She made a great effort to keep her voice calm. "Russia is no longer my country. When I made the decision to leave, I also made the decision to put all that behind me. I said good-bye to all the empty traditions and practices that do more harm than good. It is a country of superstitions and evil policies and—"

"Superstitions? You talk about putting superstitions behind you? What about all these pictures you say you see? These feelings and hunches you get that you cling to as tightly as any peasant clings to his icons?"

She put her hands over her ears. "Stop! You don't know what you're saying! Stop!"

"What's the difference between you and the old yenta of the *shtetl* who puts ash on a pretty girl's forehead to mar her beauty so she'll be safe from the evil eye? Isn't it all imaginings, inventions in the air?"

Her eyes were aflame as she turned and flung her words at him. "How dare you talk to me this way! As if I were some, some child or worker you could brow-beat!"

Elke had begun to cry with full force.

His back stiffened. "I don't, as you say, browbeat my workers. Nor do I make it a practice of brow-beating children."

"Well, you're doing it to me." She snatched up the wailing child along with all the blankets in her crib, then grabbed her coat from the peg on the back of the door.

"Where are you going?" he demanded.

She didn't answer and slammed the door hard be-hind her.

She turned east, toward the river, and as she walked, she cradled Elke in her left arm and held out her right hand in front of her where she could see the ruby ring. The sunlight penetrated into the center of the stone, deepening its richness. It was lovely, she said to herself, but it was too soon. It wasn't that she didn't want beautiful things; in fact, she wanted them very much. She didn't like their tiny apartment any more than Wolf did, nor did she like the plain clothes she wore. She planned to do something about it, and soon, but it was important that they not act too fast or they could risk everything they'd worked for. They had other things more fundamental, more basic to plan for just now. She just had to make him see that. The first opportunity she got she would pawn the ring as she had the first. The cash would be more valuable to them some day.

As the slamming door reverberated in his ears, Wolf was left to confront certain thoughts he had tried to ignore. Now he knew why he had never seen her wear the diamond he had given her. It reminded her of her past life, for which she had such an unreasoning repulsion. All right, then, he wouldn't push her on that for the time being. But he had no intention of giving up his plan to bestow jewels on his wife. Eventually, these fears of hers would surely lessen, and he would continue with his schedule of giving her two precious stones each year. In time she would see it his way.

Marya had been gone a little over an hour when he heard a light knock on the door. He opened it, prepared to take her in his arms, anxious about their squabble and eager to exchange reassurances and renew the bond between them.

"Hello, Wolf," she said quietly.

He stared at her. Her face was sallow and drawn and her hair was pulled back in a tight bun at the nape of her neck. She was dressed all in black and her eyes were rimmed with red. His eyes moved down her body to the small child that stood alongside her, his head scarcely as high as her knees.

"Etta!"

"May I come in?" Her voice was low and soft.

He led her into the workroom and moved one of the operator's chairs over for her to sit on. She pulled the child onto her lap. He took a stool for himself.

She slowly ran her eyes over him. "These last two years have been generous to you, Wolf. You look good."

He could not return the compliment. He said instead, "And how about you? What has happened for you?"

She glanced at him quickly. "Since I last saw you? I met a man, also from Warsaw."

He glanced at the child. "And you married?"

She appeared withdrawn and there was no joy in her voice. "Yes. He is very kind to me."

"Then things are going well for you?"

"More or less. Moses—his name is Moses—works as a peddler. In just one day he climbs sometimes four hundred sets of stairs. He has to, to make any money. It is such hard work, Wolf." She turned her eyes upward, beseechingly.

"Yes, I know," he said, remembering the degradation. He wondered if that was why her eyes were red, from worry for her husband.

"He sells tinware from door to door. That's how I met him. He came to our door. I bought a dishpan." She smiled faintly and stirred in her chair, then looked toward the window. "But things are not easy for Moses. He is not happy here. He talks constantly of Warsaw. He misses the old country and the friends he left behind. There he was a cabinetmaker. He had a skill he could be proud of. But here he has none of the special tools a cabinetmaker needs."

"You are saving, then? For his tools?"

"It is not easy to save, with my child." She looked down at the dark-haired boy who was kicking his heels in her lap.

"He's a fine looking boy. What's his name?"

She let out her breath slowly. "His . . . his name is Zavel. I named him for you."

Wolf stared at her. He wanted to ask her why she had come, but he thought he was beginning to know. "How did you find me?" he asked suddenly. He could feel his heart pounding.

"It wasn't easy. It took a long time. I asked a lot of questions. And I knew the name of your wife, you'll recall. That helped too."

She set the boy down on the floor between them. They sat in silence and gave him their full attention. The boy toddled to Wolf's trouser leg, then sat abruptly and began to untie Wolf's shoelaces.

"He looks like you a little," she said.

The sinking feeling that Wolf had been feeling hit bottom. "Not like Moses?"

"Oh no, how could he? I was already pregnant with Zavel when Moses and I met." She raised her eyes to Wolf's and held his gaze. "That is what I mean about how kind he has been to me. He is a good man and he truly loves me. He still was willing to marry me, even though I was carrying"—she paused as the words caught in her throat—"another man's baby. I just want him to be happy, the way he says he was in the old country."

Wolf stood up. His hands were damp and he was suddenly tired. "Then you must get him the right tools." He reached into his pocket and pulled out a roll of bills. "I will make you a loan."

"No, no. I couldn't. You mustn't." She shook her head vaguely from side to side.

He knew her protestations were to save what remained of her pride. "I insist," he said. "I won't let you leave without taking this money." He held out a handful of bills to her. "Take it. It's forty dollars. That should be enough."

She gasped. It was more than Moses made in two months. "No, Wolf. I can't. I shouldn't."

"It's merely a loan. You can pay me back."

"But I have no way to pay you back," she moaned. "Can't you see?"

"I'm in no hurry," he said. As he looked at the black-eyed boy scuttling about the room, half walking, half crawling, he felt his heart was going to explode. It pulled him in one direction one moment, the opposite direction the next. At the same time, he realized Marya would be home any minute. She had already stayed away longer than she ever had before. He didn't want Etta and the boy here when Marya came back.

Etta finally reached for the money. "I don't know how I will pay you back, but I will." She dabbed at her eyes with a handkerchief she had pulled from her small shopping bag. "I promise."

Etta was slipping the bills into her bag when the door opened, and Marya came in. Her face was flushed from all the walking she had done, and Elke was asleep in her arms. She looked quickly from Wolf to Etta and back to Wolf, a question on her face.

"This is my wife, Marya," Wolf said, not looking at Etta. His eyes found Marya's, and he tried to read the expression there. "This is Etta, Etta. . . ." He realized he didn't know her married name.

"Etta Salenski," she said, finishing for him as her eyes went from Marya to the infant in her arms. Etta's face had gone white, and she started to fidget with her sleeve. "I've heard nice things about you," she started to mumble to Marya, then looked down at the floor.

Suddenly she convulsed into motion. "Where's Za—where's my son? We'd best be going." She flew to one corner of the room where the boy was engrossed in playing with a spool of thread. She scooped him up and headed for the door, throwing her shawl over her shoulder with one hand as she hurried by. "Thank you very much. Thank you for taking time to talk to me," she was saying, not looking at either of them. Then she was out the door, the boy Zavel with her.

"What a nervous young woman," Marya said as soon as the door was shut. "Who is she?" Her voice was neutral, with no traces of her earlier anger. But she had seen Wolf watching the woman's little boy out of the corner of his eye and she felt a sudden pang as it brought back to her his yearning for a son.

Wolf avoided her face. "Oh, just someone looking for work."

"Did you hire her?" she asked over her shoulder as she went into the other room to lay Elke in her crib.

Wolf followed her into their living room and bedroom. He watched the curve of her hip as she leaned over the small crib. "No."

"Such a *shayne punim,* her son," Marya said, thinking of how cute the baby was.

Wolf made no reply.

She arranged the blankets around the sleeping baby and leaned over to kiss her softly on the head. Then she became aware that he had been looking at her.

"Marya," he said, and there was that light in his eyes that told her he wanted her.

She put out her hand, and he came to her, needing the comfort and reassurances their lovemaking brought. She put her arms around him and pulled him tightly against her. She leaned her head against his chest, and she could hear the beating of his heart. "I'm sorry," she whispered. "I got too angry." He picked her up in his arms and set her on the bed. Her eyes closed as his hand touched her breast.

Nine months later to the day, Marya gave birth to a son. Wolf was by her side during the eighteen hours of labor and throughout the ministrations of Dr. Addison and the lemon-haired midwife, the same one who had delivered Elke.

"My father's name is David," said Wolf immediately after the birth, "so we'll use the first letter of his name and call our son Daniel."

Marya glanced up at him with a quick intake of her breath. It was not the custom to name babies after the living.

His jaw was set and he did not meet her gaze. "It's been a long time," he said. "I don't want to go on believing in the impossible." He looked at his son where he lay cradled in Marya's arm and ran his hand alongside the newborn's face. "Now my family is here. We will have many more sons."

Marya did not reply but stared at the stain on the wall. Shortly after Daniel's birth, Wolf presented her with another jewel, this one an emerald, set in gold and suspended from a long chain. This time Marya knew better than to argue. She admired it profusely. The following week, when she was strong again and able to walk, she sold it, just as she had the ones before it.

Wolf noticed that Marya wore not one of the jewels he'd given her. But he was too busy to argue with her about it. The women's line had continued to grow, from thirty-two per cent in the first year to fifty per cent in the second, with a promise of an even higher percentage this year.

From the very beginning Wolf was devoted to Daniel and appeared eager to begin grooming him for the role he envisaged him as eventually playing in the business. Carrying the infant in his arms, he toured him through the workrooms, showing him to each of the workers. "When his time comes, my son will be a wizard in this business," he said more than once. In the evenings he would hold him on his lap and read to him from the children's stories Marya brought home from the library. He was never so busy that he couldn't find time to attend to Daniel's needs when Marya was occupied with Elke and would gladly bathe him and comb the soft brown curls so different from his own hair.

After the birth of Daniel, Marya had started to sketch again. In the beginning she had let her imagination wander freely and busied herself with designing dresses for herself, dresses she had no plans ever to have made up. She made evening dresses, day dresses, walking dresses, traveling suits, a yachting costume, even a hunting dress and a riding habit, although she didn't even know how to ride, nor had she any interest in learning.

One day Wolf suggested she design another line of dresses for their business. That put an end to her desultory and random creations for a time and took several weeks of concentrated work. As soon as she was finished, he had patterns made from her designs. Two weeks later those same designs were already being cut in pieces and readied for sewing at MW Enterprises on the floor below. That accomplished, Marya returned to her dallyings with the sketch pad, amusing herself for hours with the fashions she copied and sometimes created.

Wolf came into their room by surprise late one morning and found Marya standing in front of the long mirror she'd recently insisted on buying. It was so seldom that she wanted to spend money that he had readily agreed. She was holding several yards of a mulberry-red fabric, which wasn't in their inventory, and was experimenting with draping it around her body in various arrangements. She hummed as she held the

"Where did that yardage come from?" he asked.

fabric one way and then the other.

"I bought it. It's for a dress I decided to make for

myself." For the rest of that day and most of the next, she draped and cut and pinned and basted and finally stitched, and when she was done, she pressed it herself. Then she put it on and assessed herself in the mirror. She saw a slim, well-proportioned young woman in a stunning red wool suit. The jacket had a stand-up military collar and was trimmed down the front and along the sleeves with black satin braid and jet bead decoration. The underskirt was edged in a pleated ruffle, and the overskirt rose in the back to a bustle made of deep box pleats.

"That is a suit worthy of Fifth Avenue," said Wolf when he saw her.

She was keenly aware that he was used to fashionable women and that in St. Petersburg he had been acquainted with some of the most beautiful.

"It can stand with the finest." He looked at her thoughtfully. "Where are you going to wear it?"

"I don't know. I'll find a place I suppose. I just wanted to see what it looked like made up."

As soon as Marya had finished the red suit, she began another project. This one was a figured silk evening dress in a pale yellow-green trimmed with a brilliant orange velvet ribbon. When it was finished, she immediately threw herself into sewing another one of her creations. Beginning with a piece of flannel in a pinky-fawn tartan, she fashioned a winter dress with a slight fullness in the top of the sleeves. She finished the dress with bronze gilt beads and a bronze-colored silk ribbon for a sash.

The next afternoon she put on the new tartan dress, piled her hair on top of her head in the style she had seen the ladies along Fifth Avenue wear and asked Wolf if she could leave the babies with him for a couple hours while she went to the lending library. Then she set out for a long walk. She didn't tell him that the library she was going to was the Lenox Library on Fifth Avenue between Seventieth and Seventy-first Streets. She had heard from Mrs. Steinberg of the library, now about thirteen years old, with its fine collection of books left to the city by James Lenox, along with the land, and she wished to see it for herself. But by the time she reached Washington Square, she had begun to tire. As she passed under the Fifth Avenue marble arch surmounted by a statue of George Washington, she signaled for a horse-drawn cab that was in front of the old red brick mansions on the square's north side. The rest of the way to Seventieth Street she bounced along over the narrow cobbled streets, carefree and happy, and felt very much the lady with this unaccustomed comfort.

At Madison Square Park she passed the arm and torch from the Statue of Liberty which Wolf had told her had been brought from the Centennial Exposition in Philadelphia and set up in the park to appeal for funds so that the rest of the statue might be cast. North of the square old brownstones eventually gave way to the fashionable display windows of jewelers, art dealers and dressmakers. She passed Delmonico's fashionable restaurant with its striped awnings on the corner of Twenty-sixth Street and the equally fashionable Brunswick Hotel, and a little further north the four-storied marble mansion of A.T. Stewart, touted as one of the world's most successful merchants and one of New York City's largest property owners. As she peered still further up the street, she saw on her left in the distance the spires of three churches, then a little later the neo-Gothic St. Patrick's Cathedral. She passed again the Vanderbilt's Italianate palazzo and then later on at Sixty-fifth Street, the white Renaissance palace of Mrs. William Astor, rumored to have cost two million dollars to build.

Stepping from the cab, she saw the dignified facade of the library at Seventieth Street. It was as beautiful as Mrs. Steinberg had told her it was. She went up the steps and rang to enter.

The large door was opened by an old, white-haired gentleman dressed entirely in black. "Good afternoon, madam," he said and nodded his head slightly.

"Good afternoon," she replied. "I've come to use the library."

His face looked puzzled. "I beg your pardon, madam?"

"I've come to use the library."

"Yes, surely," he said, but his face still looked perplexed. "What did you say your name was?"

"I didn't. But it's Mrs. Luminov, Mrs. Zavel Luminov." She could see him staring at her as if he were trying to figure out the answer to a question and she wondered why he didn't show her in right away.

"One moment, Mrs. . . . ." he began.

"Luminov. Mrs. Zavel Luminov. I'm Marya Luminov."

His voice was kindly. "Thank you, Mrs. Luminov. Could you wait here just one moment, please."

She waited on the steps for several minutes, listening to the clatter of the passing carriages on the rough paving stones and wondering why he was being so formal. She had never had to wait to get in a library before.

The man reappeared in the doorway, and his face bore a contrite expression. "Mrs. Luminov, I'm terribly sorry, but this is a library reserved for the use of scholars exclusively. I checked our records of visiting scholars who have made appointments, and I did not find your name among them."

Marya felt her cheeks flame red. Suddenly she felt like a fraud in her elegant dress, standing on the steps of this institution that would not let her in. No doubt the doorkeeper had been able to see right through her, she said to herself. He had heard her accent and knew her almost instantly for what she was, someone who didn't belong in this section of town. Without making him a reply, she turned and fled down the steps. Her earlier mood of gaiety and self-confidence had evaporated, and as she made her way down Fifth Avenue, she felt no inclination to take a carriage this time. She would just have to walk the long way home the best she could.

She walked past the handsome buildings with their graceful iron fences and stair rails, past the elegant lampposts, past the hotels and restaurants and refused to look to the left or right of her. After she had just passed Twenty-sixth Street and Delmonico's, she felt someone lightly touch her arm. She looked over her shoulder to see a middle-aged woman, nicely dressed in a plain fashion, who was smiling at her.

"Beggin' your pardon, miss," said the woman with a slight Irish lilt. "My name is Mrs. O'Shaugnessey, and I work for Mrs. Stuart Worthington. That's her carriage over there," she said, and pointed to a red carriage with shiny brass fittings and two men in beige livery standing next to it. "We were passin' down the roadway when Mrs. Worthington saw you coming along the sidewalk. She stopped the carriage on the very spot and bid me to ask you, if I would, if you would be so kind as to divulge the name of the person who designed the dress you be wearin'. Mrs. Worthington values sartorial splendor over all else and she greatly admires what you are wearing. So if it wouldn't be too bold, miss?"

Marya held herself tall and looked at Mrs. O'Shaugnessey in astonishment. "I have no dressmaker or designer."

"Then, if I'm not being too saucy, miss, how did you get the likes of this dress? For surely such a dress did not come ready-made."

"I designed this dress myself."

"Aye," said Mrs. O'Shaugnessey in sudden comprehension. "Then it's a designer you are. Well, what good news this is! Mrs. Worthington will want to employ your services straight-away, I'm quite sure of it. Would you take the trouble to step over to the carriage so that Mrs. Worthington might make your acquaintance?"

Marya stood for a moment and thought. Was she a designer? she asked herself. All she had done was to entertain herself by drawing some clothes that she liked and then stitched them up. But to call herself a designer?

Mrs. O'Shaugnessey had already taken her by the elbow and was propelling her across the cobblestones to the opposite side of the street. As they neared the carriage, one of the liveried gentlemen sprung into action, opened the door and a long arm gloved in pale pink kid extended from the opening. "Mrs. Worthington," piped up Mrs. O'Shaugnessey, "we have the designer herself right here. This is . . ." she looked quickly at Marya, realizing she hadn't yet gotten her name.

"Mrs. Luminov," said Marya, "Mrs. Zavel Luminov." She was not unmindful that she had just gone through this ritual further up the avenue, and she was wary.

"This is Mrs. Stuart Worthington," continued the Irish woman.

Resting against the velvet cushions of the carriage sat one of the most elegant women Marya had ever seen. Around her shoulders was wrapped a silvery grey fur and on her head was a black silk bonnet dotted in small pearls. Her pale and flawless skin was stretched over high cheekbones and Marya could not begin to tell her age. She had an ageless beauty.

Her voice was low and musical. "I hope you can come at once, Mrs. Luminov. If your other designs are at all like the one you are wearing, then you are a very talented young woman indeed." She turned her eyes to her employee. "Mrs. O'Shaugnessey, please be good enough to give my calling card to Mrs. Luminov."

As Mrs. O'Shaughnessey poked in her bag for the card, she continued, "Tomorrow afternoon at three would be very convenient. I do hope you can come then."

"Yes, of course," said Marya, hardly knowing what she was saying. "Yes, I can be there at three."

"That's delightful," said Mrs. Worthington, and she smiled at Marya and extended her hand again. "It has been a pleasure meeting you, Mrs. Luminov."

Mrs. O'Shaughnessey handed her a small engraved card on ivory vellum, then climbed into the carriage across from her employer. "Good-bye, my dear," she called out to Marya as the red carriage rolled away.

"So that's why I need to find someone to watch Elke and Daniel while I'm gone," Marya said to Wolf later that evening.

He had waited two hours past when she had said she would be home and had begun to worry. In his mind were thieves and con men such as frequented Sixth Avenue near Broadway and Thirty-third, or Mullin's Alley, or not too far away, Mulberry Street. He had feared that something had befallen her, and for that reason he was not in a genial mood, or at least he told himself that was the reason he was not as enthusiastic as she probably would have liked about her plans to see Mrs. Stuart Worthington the next afternoon.

"Zavel, you should have seen her carriage. It was beautiful, just like—"

"Like the Russian nobility?" he said, a little more harshly than he had intended.

"Of course not. It wasn't vulgar or ostentatious," she said, equally harsh. Then her tone softened. "What I was going to say was that it was just like in the books I've been reading."

They were standing in the workroom, and Wolf was sorting through a bin of felled sleeves, examining the work that had been done on them. "Where does she live?" he asked, seemingly giving more of his attention to the garment pieces before him than to her.

She withdrew the vellum card from her bag. The

faint scent of perfume wafted into the room. "It says 518 Fifth Avenue."

"That's near Fiftieth Street," he said. "You can take the horse-car out there, but the elevated would be faster."

"And the children?"

"Just this once, we can get Mrs. Abrahms to watch them. I'm sure she'll be glad to exchange a couple of hours of pressing for a couple of hours tending infants."

The next afternoon Marya had a hard time restraining her excitement, but she tried to cover it the best she could, sensing it wasn't shared by Wolf. She dressed in the red woolen suit with the black trim and drew her hair up and back in a series of ascending waves. Then she boarded the el for the clanking ride to Fiftieth Street. It was the first time she had ever been on one of these noisy, smoke-belching machines, and as she looked over the edge at the people below, she couldn't help but feel sorry for them at the oil, water and ashes she knew the train was flinging down on them. She had heard of accidents and runaway trains, and even now she could see a horse rearing up at the explosions the engine was making as it puffed its way down the track. Still, she had to admit the el afforded her some views of the city she had never seen and she liked the way she could see the East River the one minute, the Hudson the next, and into someone's bedroom the very next as the train curved its way north.

She stood in front of the elegant four-storied building that spelled out "Five Hundred Eighteen" in an elaborate script on the brass plate alongside the door. She took a deep breath and pulled on the bell. Immediately she was shown into the salon by a tall, thin butler whose distinguishing characteristic was the perfect blandness of everything about him, from his skin, to his tone of voice, to his mannerisms. She was left alone there to await the arrival of Mrs. Worthington, which the butler had promised her would be "imminent."

Never had Marya seen a room as ornate as this one. She was sure it must rival the grand salons of the Russian aristocracy for sheer opulence. There appeared to be not a foot of undecorated space anywhere in the room. Every surface had been gilded, bronzed, lacquered or upholstered. The walls were bronzed and strung with elaborate flora. The French furniture was carved, gilded and covered in embroidered silk brocades, and she counted four massive arrangements of freshly cut flowers on the table tops. Three splendorous glass vitrines, or cabinets, displayed an array of curios, bibelots, crystal goblets and Oriental and French porcelains. In the salon's four upper corners hung shields draped with jeweled beads and the ceiling was swirled with rococo moldings of gold gilt, formed in the shape of flowers, scrolls and shells. Marya felt dizzy just trying to look at it all.

"Mrs. Luminov," purred a voice behind her, and she turned to see Mrs. Stuart Worthington sweeping toward her, enveloped in white chiffon and trailing a boa of ostrich feathers. Her practiced eye quickly took in Marya's new red suit and Marya thought she detected a look of approval. "Seated in this room, you complete what is a very charming tableau, Mrs. Luminov," she said.

Marya wasn't sure what she was talking about.

"The name Luminov, Luminov, let's see, although the accent doesn't seem exactly true, you must be Russian."

Marya stiffened, at both the reference to her accent and to her being Russian. "I was," she emphasized.

Mrs. Worthington placed herself on the very edge of one of her French chairs and arranged her folds of chiffon about her. "Well, yes, I suppose you're an American now." She laughed lightly. "But blood always tells eventually, doesn't it?"

Her remark was made rhetorically and thus demanded no answer, for which Marya was glad because she didn't know what to say.

They spent the next hour looking at the sketches Marya had brought with her and discussing fabrics and finishing details. The meeting ended with their making another appointment to meet three days later, at which time Marya would bring the samples of fabric with her.

That evening Marya couldn't stop talking about the grand home she had spent the afternoon in until Wolf was moved to interrupt. "I certainly never expected your head to be turned so easily, Marya. It wouldn't hurt to keep your perspective on these people. I am sure they and their world are very beautiful and even enticing, especially to one who has never been exposed to anything remotely resembling that before."

"I am keeping my perspective, Zavel. I just think how they live, the way it's so different from everyone else, is interesting, that's all."

"The tone of your voice makes it sound like you think it's more than interesting. You sound like you've been enchanted," he said, unable to hide the annoyance he felt. "Remember, to those people you're a little above a dressmaker, no matter what pretty compliments they may be filling your head with. And a Jewish one at that."

"Zavel!" she cried, wanting to stop the barrage of his words. "This is an opportunity for us. If my designs catch on with Mrs. Worthington, no telling where I might be able to go from here."

He slammed his hand down on the account books spread out on the table before him. "You don't have to go anywhere, Marya. My wife doesn't have to hire out. We're having our best year yet. We're ready to expand into a bigger place. Then MW Enterprises will really take off. It'll be bigger than ever. You don't have to work at all."

"It's not work, Zavel. It's more like play. And I really like doing it."

When she was shown into the drawing room three days later, Marya saw that they were not to be alone. Next to Mrs. Worthington sat another woman, of a full and voluptuous figure and with a mound of black hair settled on top of her head.

"This is Mrs. Claudia Carter, wife of Mr. Leonard Carter of the Carter Bank," said Mrs. Worthington, indicating her companion.

"Natalie," said Mrs. Carter in a low, honeyed voice and looking fondly at Mrs. Worthington, "tells me you are a costumer of rare *mérite*. I told her I simply wouldn't let her alone until she promised to share her *trésor*, her marvelous find, with me."

Marya looked at Mrs. Worthington, but her face was expressionless and she made no response.

"Thank you for the compliment, Mrs. Carter, but I've yet to complete a gown for Mrs. Worthington," she said.

"But you've made the one you have on, and it is *tout à fait sensationnelle, merveilleuse*."

Marya glanced at Mrs. Worthington and caught on her face an expression that quickly disappeared as soon as she realized Marya was looking at her. "Well, Mrs. Luminov," said Mrs. Worthington as she stood up suddenly, "shall we start to work?"

After much discussion among the three women, Mrs. Worthington settled on a fur-trimmed gown in Venetian red with silk embroidery and a matching velvet toque topped with two tiny birds in red and grey. Mrs. Carter chose a white flannel yachting costume with blue braid and motifs and a cap in white cloth and leather.

In the next six months, Marya continued to see Mrs. Worthington almost every week, and more often than not, Mrs. Carter was there with her. Both women ordered freely from Marya, and expense never seemed to be a consideration. Mrs. Carter, in particular, complimented her lavishly.

"Your gowns are *très populaires*," she assured Marya. "Everyone wants to know who you are. But we're keeping you all to ourselves for just a little while longer."

Chapter 10

A crowd had started to gather on lower Park Avenue near Mulberry where the two men were wrestling on the rough and uneven paving stones. It was a noisy crowd as partisans for each of the two called out hoarse encouragement for their favorite and disparaging epithets for the other. From where he stood along the sidelines, Wolf caught a glimpse of the fighters over the shoulders of the crowd. Both were streaked with dirt and their clothing was torn. Evidently the fight had been going on for some time.

Suddenly the spectators parted as the fighters rolled in a new direction and now Wolf had an unobstructed view. The two men appeared to be in their midtwenties. Each was powerfully built with broad shoulders and a stocky, muscular frame, making them well-matched for their violent contest. By now the two had pulled apart and were standing again, hunched over and circling each other slowly, warily, each calculating the best second to lash out at the other. Wolf's attention was drawn by the shorter of the two men. Something about him looked familiar, although he couldn't say just what. The man reminded him of someone he had met somewhere, sometime, but his memory refused to jog and identify him.

The men were on the ground again and this time the shorter man had moved into a position of dominance. From where he sat on top of the other's chest, he was raining blows on his face.

"Stop! *Basta!*" cried someone in the crowd, and as others picked up and repeated it, three men moved in to pull the winner off the other fighter, who now lay completely motionless on the ground. The three men then picked up the loser by the shoulders and began to drag him away as the friends of the winner closed in around him, slapping him on the back and laughing loudly. The crowd parted again as the winner began to walk toward the ramshackle wooden tavern on the opposite corner of the street, his friends trailing with him.

Suddenly he looked at Wolf and stopped. He stared, open-mouthed, for a couple of seconds without saying a word. Then his face broke into an enormous smile and he began to exclaim without stopping. " 'Ey! Wolf! *Buon amico*! My friend! Long time, long time." He threw his arms about Wolf's chest and pounded him on the back.

"Mario!" Wolf returned. "You're kidding! Mario! Is it you?" It had to be, he decided, although Mario was considerably heavier and more filled out. The lines on his face showed these last years had not been easy for him.

"You come with us. Have some vino with us," Mario said.

Wolf allowed himself to be pulled along to the café, the infamous Black Horse Tavern, and once inside seated next to ten or eleven other men, all of whom, it turned out, were relatives.

"You remember I tell you of my family?" His face was beaming as he waved his hand at the assortment of faces around the table. "I want you to meet my brothers," he said, singling out six of the men. "The rest are all cousins. We're all here in America now, the whole family," he said, and the table gave a cheer.

They spent the rest of the afternoon and into the evening drinking wine at the tavern. Finally Mario said, "You come with me again. I want you to meet the rest of my family."

They left the camaraderie of the tavern and emerged into Mulberry Street, alive with its own brand of excitement. Along the streets of this Italian section of the city's Lower East Side stood groups of boys and men, laughing and talking with animation. Mario led him down the street, past the wooden buildings still typical in this old part of the city and considered a fire hazard by all. The romantic sounds of a mandolin drifted from one of the open windows they passed.

A few blocks later Mario turned left into a narrow stairway that led to a second-story flat. "Talk loud when you meet my mother," he said. "She don't hear so good now." He opened the door and they stepped into a small but cheerful apartment. The only people there were two young women, both around sixteen or seventeen, who were engaged in a heated argument.

"But you know Papa will say no, Lucia! He will kill you if he finds out," the more slender and animated of the two said.

The other was replying with calm, sulky assurance, "I don't care. And besides, he won't—" when she looked up and saw her brother standing in the doorway with a tall, handsome man she didn't know.

"These are my sisters." Mario nodded toward the two women who sat looking round-eyed at the stranger in their midst. He motioned toward the slender one. "This is Angelica."

She looked from her brother to Wolf and broke into a big smile, which enhanced her already pretty face with its straight, narrow nose and large, round eyes.

"And this is Lucia," he indicated the other of the two. She was shorter than Angelica, and rounder, with a body that was full and voluptuous. Of the two she appeared to be the older, so Wolf was surprised when Mario added, "She's the bambino of the family."

A hint of a smile played about her lips as she looked at Wolf. "Hello," she finally said. "It is a pleasure to meet my brother's friend."

"Mama? Papa? Where are they?" Mario asked.

"To the rosary. They went to the rosary tonight for Mr. Genco," volunteered Angelica.

"That is too bad," said Mario, turning to Wolf. "You must come another time then. To meet my parents."

"Yes, I'd like to," said Wolf.

"You should come for Sunday dinner," piped up Angelica. "It's always the best, and everyone is here."

"Thank you very much," said Wolf. "But I'm not sure I can do that. I have my own family I must be with." He saw the look of disappointment that flashed across her face. "But I promise I will come another day."

When he and Mario were out on the street, Wolf asked, "Where are you working now?"

"I've ended up in a garment shop." He didn't sound too happy.

"What's your job?"

"A little of everything. Mostly I'm the muscle man. I carry heavy stuff around."

"How's the money?"

"That's the worst part. Maybe I make five dollars in a good week." As they walked, he stared glumly at the pavement. "What are you doing?"

"I started my own garment business."

Mario's head jerked up. "You're kidding!" He started to laugh. "You're one of the bosses now, eh?"

"That's right. Listen, how'd you like to come work for me, Mario? Whatever they're paying you at this other place, I'll beat it by half again."

Mario stopped walking. "You serious? You want me to come work for you?"

Wolf shrugged. "Why not? That's one of the advantages of being a boss, isn't it? You can choose the people you want around you."

They walked on for a while more, and finally Mario asked, "What would I do?" His voice became wistful. "I'd sure like to get away from all this muscle work for a change."

"Talk to Sol. He runs the shop. Used to be a tailor in Lithuania. He knows everything there is to know about manufacturing clothes and keeping the workers happy, which is as important to me as the clothes. Come. I think you'll like MW Enterprises."

Mario looked incredulous. "MW Enterprises? I've heard of it. 'Ey, you really have done all right for yourself, haven't you?"

Wolf laughed. "It's been a lot of late hours and long work."

"Give me your address. I'll be there tomorrow morning at six."

"Seven's good enough," Wolf laughed.

Claudia herself opened the door. She was wearing the green linen suit Marya had designed for her last year. Marya could see that Claudia had gained weight, for the blouse was stretched snugly over her ample breasts and the fabric was pulled too tightly against the curve of her hips. She made a mental note that she would find a way to suggest tactfully that Claudia allow her to alter the garment. It wouldn't do for her clients to wear her creations if they didn't fit properly. The clothes had to hang the way they were designed, with the cut and fall of the fabric working in conjunction with the woman's body. It would be bad for business otherwise.

"Marya! How good to see you again, and how delightful of you to come yourself!" She greeted Marya warmly and Marya saw that Claudia was made up as if she were going out. Her black hair, perfectly groomed, was pulled back in a large glossy bun at the nape of her neck. Her wide mouth had been rouged in a deep red.

She took Marya's hand in both of hers and led her from the reception hall up the curving staircase and into the luxurious sitting room, decorated in shades of white, the only spot of color being the deep blue Oriental rug in the middle. She leaned forward to greet Marya with a kiss and as Marya touched her lips to Claudia's cheek, she caught the sweet scent of flowers, which kind she wasn't sure.

Claudia was laughing and talking at the same time. "No Marya, dear, not on the cheek. We'll get our lip rouge on each other." She brushed Marya lightly on the lips and continued talking, leading her toward the hallway.

This was the first time Marya had seen Claudia's home. Her other contacts with her for showings and fittings had always been at Natalie Worthington's palatial residence on Fifth Avenue. Claudia lived in the new, smart West End, above Seventy-second Street on West End Avenue itself, in a handsome new home of creamy white brick fashioned without the traditional high stoop of the earlier brownstones of the area. Marya was curious to see the interior of Claudia's home and she tried to imagine from what she saw there—the furniture, the paintings on the walls, the arrangements of freshly cut flowers—the kind of life Claudia and her husband—a banker, wasn't he?—led. Always she was eager to know more about this world of power and money, whose inhabitants were so completely at ease wherever they took themselves. She could always pick them out, just entering or leaving imposing stone buildings, stepping from carriages, going into the theater or a fashionable restaurant like Sherry's or the Brunswick Hotel. They seemed confident, poised, never doubting that they belonged, that the whole country lay before them.

Claudia looked at the satchel in Marya's hands.

"Let's see. We need a place to spread out the sketches, don't we? And of course a mirror."

Whenever Marya had seen Claudia, she always seemed full of easy laughter and gaiety, with a way about her so light and charming that Marya couldn't help but be caught up in her playful mood. As Claudia led her down the hallway, walking as fast as she was talking, the colorful paintings on the wall caught Marya's eye, but she was walking too fast to get a good look. She made a note to herself to ask Claudia if she might study them after the fitting. The color combinations might give her an idea about a design for Claudia sometime.

The hallway opened into a large master bedroom. Marya drank in the details: the dark polished wood, the bed covered with an ivory satin spread, the oval mirrors set in mahogany frames and arranged in a semicircle next to two tall armoires.

"Marya, darling, we can work here," said Claudia, pointing to a carved table inlaid with pieces of malachite and lapis lazuli.

Marya arranged her three latest sketches on the table. She explained the types of fabric that each would require and the special detailing. From her satchel she pulled out sample swatches of the material and began to drape them over Claudia as she stood before the mirror.

"See how the peach-colored silk heightens the natural color in your face," Marya said, "not at all like the navy blue. It's too drab for you." She artfully arranged the folds of silk around Claudia's torso.

"Ah yes, Marya," Claudia said. "*C'est vrai,* I can see you're quite right. As always, *toujours*." She sighed and smiled at her.

"Good. Then you will trust me," laughed Marya, "when I tell you I can do something to that green linen suit you're wearing to make it even better on you."

Claudia willingly slipped out of the blouse and skirt and handed them to her. Marya began to rip out the seam in the skirt at once. When she looked up, she saw that Claudia had slipped out of her undergarments as well and stood completely naked before her. She tried not to stare at her full breasts and incredibly white, flawless skin.

Claudia giggled. "Marya, darling, you should see the expression on your face! Your beautiful coloring for once has gone quite pale. Now, dear, bring me the silk again. I want to see it against me another time to get a better idea of how it will hang. It was so hard to tell anything with all those layers from my suit underneath, don't you agree?"

Marya could say nothing. She picked up the swatch of silk again and started to drape it around Claudia.

"No, I changed my mind. Let's try the yellow georgette first." After Marya had arranged it about her, Claudia asked, "Well? What do you think?" She smiled.

Marya tried to appraise the golden form in the mirror. "This, too, is good. But the peach is better," she said slowly.

Claudia let the georgette fall in a puddle of gold at her feet. "Now the silk. Hold it against me again, Marya."

Trying not to stare unnecessarily, Marya lifted the fabric up to her. Claudia's body felt warm under the silk, and the fragrance of crushed flowers was growing stronger. As Marya dutifully studied Claudia's reflection again in the mirror, she saw Claudia's chest rise as she lifted her arms to her head. In a second she had pulled the pins from her bun, and with a flick of her head her hair fell loose and fanned out across her shoulders.

She gave a light laugh and looked down at Marya's hand where it held the material in place against her hip. She drew Marya's hand away, and as the silk started to unwind from her body and fall along the carpet, she led her to the edge of the bed.

"Sit down, Marya," she said. "I have something I want to ask you."

Claudia had a tight grasp on her hand. Marya found the smell of the flowers—gardenias?—overbearing now. She felt lightheaded and had the vague feeling that something was getting beyond her control. From where she sat on the bed she could see their images in the mirror, herself slim in the smart new suit she had just made, her hair piled high on her head, and Claudia next to her, pink and white against the satin coverlet.

"You must tell me, Marya, if you will make me a suit just like the one you have on." She took her other hand and ran it lightly over Marya's body, touching her breast, her hip, her thigh. "You are beautiful in it, *très, très belle.*"

Marya's head was whirling. Surely this elegant woman wasn't, didn't . . . she didn't know what to think. She felt Claudia stroke her hand back up to her blouse. This time her touch was firmer, surer. "This blouse is exquisite." Quickly she reached for Marya's other hand and drew it toward her.

Marya felt a rush of warmth come over her. She tried to fight through the webs in her mind. With a great burst of determination, she pulled herself from Claudia's hold and stood up.

She heard herself start to talk, but she scarcely knew what she was saying. She was sure she must be prattling. "I . . . I must go now. My husband is waiting for me. I'm sorry to have to leave so fast. Do please excuse me, I have to hurry . . . I should have told you from the beginning, I suppose, that I have another appointment. The green suit will be ready for you in no time, you can count on that." While she talked, she was stuffing the silk and georgette into her bag. She picked up the designs and jammed them in too.

Claudia lay stretched out on the bed. She was propped on one elbow and still smiling at her. "Why,

Marya, you actually seem nervous. But, of course, darling, we have time to meet again." She watched Marya cramming the sketches into the satchel. "We can take all the time we need at our next fitting. I do trust your judgments, Marya."

Did she, Marya wondered. Marya trusted them too, and they were telling her she had to get out into the air as quickly as possible and away from the heavy fragrance of gardenias, away from the thick carpets and rich woods.

The cool afternoon air stung her face, but she liked it. She tried to make sense of her feelings. She could ill afford to insult Mrs. Claudia Carter, certainly not just when her designs were catching on with such elite and powerful women. She wanted their business and was determined to have it. But she had to admit she didn't really know what went on in their world, nor was she sure she was ready to.

It was with relief that Marya opened the door to MW Enterprises and let herself in. She had had time to think as she bounced along in the dilapidated horse-drawn omnibus, clinging to a strap along with the other rush-hour passengers, most of whom were on their way out of the city and returning to their homes across the river. Perhaps Wolf was right. She didn't know these circles of women for whom she was now spending so much of her time designing. "You're just hired help," he had said to her more than once. "Don't forget it." She wondered if Claudia had expected her to respond differently, as part of her hired role.

As soon as she got home, she checked on Elke and Daniel and relieved Mrs. Abrahms, who, it turned out, had begun to spend as much time watching the children as she did working in the shop. Then Marya made a cool compress for her head and went into the bedroom to lie down. After a while, she heard the outside door open and close, and through the bedroom door, slightly ajar, she could hear Wolf's voice. He was talking to the new Italian hand he had hired and she could hear their loud laughter.

Her first reaction was that she was pleased to hear Wolf laughing, but at the same time she was mildly annoyed. In this last year, as both had been caught up with their separate circles of demands—he with the garment making, she with her designs for her circle of wealthy clients—they were making more money than they ever had before, but a remoteness had grown between them.

The door opened and Wolf came into the room. He saw her lying on the bed. "So, you're home. Elke and Daniel have been crying for you."

She didn't look up, but continued to lie with the compress on her head. "They were in good hands. Mrs. Abrahms is sweet and motherly."

"She practically is their mother, Marya, for all the time she spends with them."

She sat up and glared at him. "It's no more than a few hours a week, Zavel. The way you exaggerate you'd think I'd abandoned my children, my husband and my home completely. In fact, I'm here more than you. You're either downstairs in the shop or with your friends."

He ignored her reference to the frequent evenings he now spent socializing with Mario and kept the discussion on her. "Face it, Marya. Every week you're gone more and more. What are you doing this for? We don't need the money. MW Enterprises is bringing in more money than ever." His voice had turned icy cold. "I suspect this dress designing of yours has become more than just a little business."

"What are you talking about, Zavel?"

"Since when did you start lunching in Fifth Avenue restaurants?"

She looked up sharply. "A client took me there. It was all part of business."

"And the dandies you meet in those places? That's all part of business too."

"I didn't meet any dandies, as you call them. I was just there with Mrs. Worthington and a few of her friends."

"I don't like you going to those places. Remember what I told you about those people, Marya. I know them well. You'll think they're your friends. But they'll never stand by you. You're just a plaything to them, an entertainment. They look at you just like they might a performance by a musician or dancer they hired for the evening. You'll always be an outsider."

"For God's sake, they were just some of her friends who had admired my creations. She wanted them to meet me." She felt the anger starting to get the better of her. "What were you doing, Zavel, spying on me?"

He turned and walked out of the room, slamming the door behind him. A few moments later she heard the sound of loud laughter, his and Mario's, and then the slamming of the outside door, followed by silence.

Marya went into the children's room. Elke and Daniel were still napping. Then she wandered back out to the parlor and stood by the window. She watched the people hurrying through the streets, dark silhouettes barely illuminated by gaslight, their shabbiness softened by the night. As she followed the movements of these poorly fed, poorly housed immigrants, Wolf's word "dandy" was pulsing a counterpoint rhythm in her head. Were the two gentlemen, friends of Mrs. Worthington, seated at the next table that afternoon at Delmonico's, in fact dandies?

She had been aware of them staring at her throughout the lavish luncheon. Finally one of them had gotten up and made his way to Mrs. Worthington to whisper something in her ear. Natalie's mouth had parted in a brilliant smile as the man, who was of medium height with thick sandy hair, had continued to whisper to her. "Yes, yes, Gregory, I promise," she had laughed. "I will, you have my word." Then the man had returned to his seat, pausing slightly to smile at Marya as he passed by.

They had come to the last course of what for Marya had been the richest meal of her life, and as they took their coffee and chocolates, Natalie would occasionally give her a knowing look and then a cryptic smile.

When they were ready to leave, Natalie seized Marya by the hand. "Darling," she purred, "you must meet two charming and handsome friends of mine. And they are just beside themselves to meet you."

She had steered Marya to the table, and both of the gentlemen had immediately gotten to their feet. Natalie nodded toward the man who had come to their table earlier. "Marya, I would like you to meet Mr. Gregory Keller."

Claudia Carter, who was standing behind her, whispered over her shoulder, "Marya, dear, he is a horseman par excellence and *sans pareil*. A marvelous seat. Indeed, a memorable seat without peer."

"And this is Mr. Andrew Markingham," Natalie continued, indicating his companion, also of medium height and with a thick shock of blond curls. He appeared to be in his early thirties and had a compact, athletic frame.

"He has one of the finest legal minds in the city," again whispered Claudia. *"Très intelligent."*

Marya saw him looking at her quietly with his piercing blue eyes as if assessing her. His manner seemed amiable but reserved, that of a man not given to quick or facile judgments.

His friend, Gregory Keller, drew her attention back to him when he said, "Madam, it is a pleasure to meet you. You are an uncommonly beautiful woman. I . . . we . . . could not take our eyes from you. You must pardon us if we were too bold."

Her duty done, Natalie Worthington then drew her party of elegant ladies together, and sailing before them like the masthead of a ship, swept them from the restaurant, leaving a sea of turned heads in their wake.

Now, wondered Marya, were those gentlemen dandies? Dandies to her meant men overly given to cutting a fine figure in their elegant clothes, men to whom appearances meant everything. Neither of them seemed to be what she would call a dandy, especially not Andrew Markingham. And she had to admit it was a pleasure to be so openly admired. It felt good to have a man devour her with his eyes the way she wished that Wolf still did.

The whole family barely fit around the three tables that had been pushed together to make one, then draped with a blue and white oilcloth. Hot platters of chicken, spaghetti and vegetables sent up columns of savory steam and somehow even more dishes kept mysteriously appearing from the tiny kitchen.

"Mama!" roared Mario, seated next to Wolf, "this spaghetti is your best ever!"

His mother put her hand to her ear for just a second, then beamed at him.

" 'Ey, Angelica," he continued, "you keep practicing, maybe someday you can cook this good. Maybe fifty years from now."

Angelica shook her head. "Not for you I won't. I'll cook for someone who appreciates me. I'll cook for my husband."

"He better be practicing on shoe leather now," threw in Tuleo, another brother, a little younger than Mario, "so's his teeth get good and strong."

"What husband?" put in Antonio, still another brother. "She'll never get a husband. Already eighteen and not married. She's too old now."

Angelica darted a withering look Antonio's way. "It's not the fashion in America to marry so early," she announced. "I'm not worried."

"Me either," said her father and he smiled at her across the table.

Seeing the huge family crowded around the table, Wolf was reminded of his own brothers and sisters seated around the long mahogany table in their elaborate dining room in St. Petersburg. Although mealtime conversations had not been as lively, especially when his father was present, the easy banter back and forth among the children made him reminiscent. He was lost in his own thoughts when he became aware that he was being stared at by two sets of eyes. From far down at the other end of the table, Lucia was watching him with a burning gaze, while across from him Angelica was smiling sweetly and also staring.

After the meal was over and the dishes had been cleared, Mario announced that he and Wolf were going for a walk.

"I want to go for a walk, too," said Angelica. "I never get to go out in the evening."

"That's because it's too dangerous," said Mario.

"So take me with you. Let me have a chance to see what the streets are like after dark."

"You don't want to know," Mario said.

"Just this once." She took hold of his hand and pressed a kiss into it.

"All right, all right. Just this once."

Instantly Lucia was on his other side. "Me, too," she said in her low voice. "I want to go too."

Mario threw up his hands. "Okay, both of you, this one time, and then no more."

Out on the streets, the sisters stayed close to the two men. Wolf noticed that Lucia leaned against him slightly and whenever the opportunity presented itself brushed against him with her breast. It seemed that whenever he looked down, she was looking up, her eyes sultry and inviting.

From time to time Angelica would glance at her sister and then up at Wolf. Finally she repositioned herself so that she was on one side of him while Lucia was on the other.

After they had walked for a while, Wolf suggested

they go to a café. The two sisters looked at each other quickly in surprise, and then at Mario, who to their relief nodded his head yes. Never before had they been out at night, unless it was to accompany their parents to church or a rosary. Now to a café—they were tasting of two forbidden fruits at once.

The café Mario led them to was full of men mostly, with a sprinkling of women, some accompanying their husbands, some plying their trade, a scene being enacted in cafés throughout the city, the only difference being the language in which the bargain was struck and the cost. They found a table in the smoky room and the young women ordered tea, the men wine.

"Hey, there's Adrianna," said Mario suddenly and pointed to a woman who was engaged in a lively conversation with three men. Her dark hair was swept back off her face in a large bun and her skin was a dark, smooth peach. Her eyes and nose were large, making the overall impression she created a dramatic one.

"Adrianna!" Mario called.

She looked up when she heard her name and instantly broke into a huge smile. She said something to the men next to her, then rose and made her way to their table.

Mario pulled up a chair for her. "Wolf," he said, "This is Adrianna Sabatini, a friend of mine." He smiled at Adrianna and then at Wolf. "Adrianna, this is Wolf Luminov, my first friend in this country. And these are my sisters, Angelica and Lucia."

The woman turned her large, expressive eyes on each person as Mario said the name and put out her hand. Then her gaze came back to Wolf, who was returning hers.

He saw that she was tall, taller than was usual for an Italian woman, and that she carried herself with confidence. Her voice was husky and poised when she said, "Yes, thank you. I will join you."

Angelica and Lucia, who had been chattering in

their excitement at being in a café for the first time, now fell silent. Lucia in particular looked at the older woman with sulky dislike. The more the woman threw back her head and laughed in that low, deep way of hers at what Wolf and Mario were saying, the more the two sisters disliked her. They disliked it even more when Wolf and Mario threw back their heads and laughed at what she was saying. At last, after what seemed like unbearable hours to the two young women, it was time to go.

"I do hope we will meet again," Adrianna said to Wolf and leaned forward to brush him lightly on the cheek with her fingertip. "I am here often. You must come back."

"Yes," Wolf heard himself saying. "I would like that too."

"Tell me when," she said and smiled from beneath her lashes.

"Tomorrow," Wolf said, and was astonished that he had said it.

As she turned and slowly made her way back to her table, her hips rolling slightly as she walked, Mario turned and said to Wolf, "Adrianna, she's very choosy. It's a good sign that she likes you. I think you will like her a lot."

Later that evening, when Wolf returned with Mario, Marya caught the faint smell of alcohol on their breaths. They had come into the parlor and Wolf had announced he wanted to show his son to Mario.

"Look at my boy," said Wolf, taking him from where he lay sleeping in Marya's arms and holding him up to eye level so that Mario might see him.

"For two years old he's a big one," said Mario.

"Oh, he's going to be big, really big."

Mario slapped Wolf on the back. "Like his old man, eh?"

Wolf gazed at the boy with unabashed tenderness. "Maybe bigger."

Elke lay sleeping on the sofa on the other side of

Marya, who struggled to keep her face from revealing her feelings. Always it was Daniel that Wolf turned to first, always Daniel that he wanted to show off.

Mario noticed the other child curled up next to Marya. "And this must be Elke," he said. "A sleeping angel."

"Yes," said Wolf, as if noticing the child on the sofa for the first time. "She's only three and already you can tell she's going to be beautiful."

"Like her mother," said Mario, and smiled at Marya.

She returned his smile weakly. She hadn't made up her mind how she felt about this new friend of Wolf's. He was unfailingly polite to her and always friendly. He showed a willingness to get to know her better, but for some reason which she didn't have the energy to fathom, she resisted. As he continued to gaze at her, she looked away.

"Daniel's learning to talk," said Wolf. "Listen to this." He motioned for Mario to follow him to the kitchen table, where he set Daniel down. "Tell your father," said Wolf, "where were you born?"

"Please, Zavel, don't," interrupted Marya from where she stood across the room. She had heard the recital too many times before and it had begun to pain her.

Wolf acted as if he had not heard. "Come on, tell your father."

Daniel stood on the table, dressed in his new leather shoes and a pair of miniature wool knickers Wolf had had especially tailored for him. His infant face grew serious. "A-mer-ca," he said, exaggerating each syllable.

Mario started to express his surprise, but before he could, Wolf asked Daniel another question. "Where was your father born?"

"Rush-sha," Daniel blurted at once.

Marya had moved closer. "Zavel, please don't take him through this again."

"And who's the czar of Russia, Daniel?"

"Al-x-zan-ner!" cried Daniel, holding up three fingers and starting to jump up and down.

"And what do we think of Czar Alexander III?"

"Feh!" cried Daniel, and screwed up his face. "Feh, feh!"

Mario looked at Wolf in amazement as he scooped Daniel up off the table and held him in the crook of his arm. "Now tell me, Daniel, what are you going to be when you grow up?"

Daniel's eyes were open wide as Wolf held him near. "Prez-dent," he said, more subdued now.

"President of what?"

"Prez-dent of this comp-nee," he said, and threw back his head and giggled, knowing he had performed as his father wanted him to.

After Mario had gone, they did not speak to each other. Wolf lay in bed and watched Marya undress. She stepped out of her smart, fashionable dress and stood in her chemise. Even her undergarments were elegant now, he noticed, as he saw the delicate eyelet trim and satin ribbon ties. She was more beautiful than ever. But it wasn't just the clothes she wore. She had always been poised and radiant, but now there was an added confidence, an assurance that showed in how she carried herself and in how she looked at him.

She pulled the long pins from her hair and shook it loose down her back. He felt stirrings of his longing for her and rolled onto his side, turning his back to her. He didn't want to look at her anymore. It made the ache too great. He felt she was slipping away from him, bewitched by the false allure of aristocratic New York, of these fast new circles in which she was spending more and more time.

He considered the irony of it: he had feared just a few years ago she was clinging to her dowdy babushka and plain dresses. He had wanted her to be more fashionable, more involved in what was going on around her, especially after the death of their first son. Now she was too involved. Now she seemed detached from him, not needing him. As far as he could see, she needed neither his companionship, his money, his success and growing status in the business world, nor his jewels which to him symbolized his love for her and which she never wore.

Marya saw Wolf's turned back and sighed. More and more he was sleeping with his back to her, a sign, she thought, of his growing remoteness. She yearned to have him turn toward her again and pull her to him the way he used to. With his growing aloofness, her old fears had come back. She questioned again why he had married her, and Lubish's words still rankled. Yes, there was no doubt the offer of the dowry had sweetened the possibility of marriage. She knew he was consumed with the need to succeed and build up a flourishing business just as his father had done. So the opportunity to gain a share in an already surviving business would have been too tempting to resist. Why else could he have married her, bizarre looking as she had been?

The next morning Wolf opened his eyes with the dim memory of having promised to see the woman he had met in the café earlier the previous evening. She was very attractive, very lovely, but he wouldn't do it, he decided. He was a married man and the woman he loved was here. He'd find a way, somehow, to get through to Marya again.

Marya was already up and he could hear her in the kitchen with the children. He stood in the doorway and surveyed the scene. Marya, her hair streaming down her back, looked wild and enticingly disheveled, as she sat with Daniel on her lap, Elke across from her in a chair, and attempted to spoon feed both children at the same time.

"Where's the elegant Fifth Avenue designer of ladies' gowns and dresses?" he asked. "I see a wild woman of the woods before me and her wild brood."

Marya made no reply.

"Motherhood becomes you, you know." He tried to keep from sounding flippant: he sincerely meant what he said. An image of how it would have been for them if they were in Russia flashed through his mind. But here in America, along with the freedom of education, politics and religion, came a freedom from the old ways prescribed for men and women to act. Here there was a greater freedom to grow apart from their need for each other.

She kept spooning the cereal into Elke's mouth and didn't look up. "I should think you'd be proud of me, Zavel, for having caught on with the city's rich ladies. Isn't that what you want, for me to be among the appropriately fashionable, as is fitting for a successful businessman's wife?"

"What I want is for you to be here more, for your family."

Why can't he say it, she said to herself. Why can't he say he wants me to be here for him? It would make all the difference if he said it that way.

"What are you going to do when you have another baby?"

She looked up quickly, then back down to the children. "I'd like to borrow Mrs. Abrahms around midafternoon today," she said, changing the subject.

"You going out again? You've been out every afternoon lately."

"This is just for tea. Mrs. Worthington insisted I meet her. She's my biggest patron, so I didn't see how I could say no."

"Say no? You never say no. You've no idea how."

Her voice was calm and remote. "No, Zavel, it's that I have no idea why I should say it." Then she looked up suddenly, and her eyes were full of anguish. "Oh, Zavel, please, let's stop this petty. . . ."

But he didn't hear her. He had already turned and

left the kitchen and Marya did not see him for the rest of the morning or afternoon.

"Dear Marya," Natalie Worthington said as she joined Marya where she had been waiting in the lobby of the Brunswick Hotel, "I do hope you won't mind that I've invited a third person to join our little tea party."

She was wearing a walking suit of pale pink flannel that Marya had designed for her the previous month when Natalie let fall an idle remark about needing something to wear when she went out shopping, which she virtually never did, such matters being attended to by the servants. Still, it would be fun to have a dress that allowed one to stretch the legs a little when walking, and that didn't encumber one with yards of fabric.

Marya looked at her creation approvingly. "Of course, Mrs. Worthington," she said to her remark about another person joining them for tea. She knew this was how Natalie Worthington liked to introduce her to new clients, and she was pleased and curious to see who this latest in a trail of fashion-conscious women would be.

As they were seated, Mrs. Worthington cried out, "Oh, there's Andrew!" and lightly waved her beige glove in his direction.

Marya looked in the direction of the glove to see one of the men she had met the afternoon of the luncheon at Delmonico's. He was walking confidently toward them, and as he drew near, Mrs. Worthington said, "You remember Andrew Markingham, don't you?"

"Of course," Marya said, recalling that he had been the quieter of the two and had not been as fawning as the other man toward her.

"Good afternoon, Mrs. Luminov," he said, taking her hand.

As he sat down, Marya realized that their small

tea party, as Mrs. Worthington called it, would actually have four people at it. But as the time passed and no one else came to join them, it dawned on her that Andrew Markingham was the third person that Mrs. Worthington had meant all along. The conversation was dominated by Mrs. Worthington and Marya was glad, for she wasn't sure she would know what to say to this man if she had been required to keep up the small talk.

From time to time their eyes would meet and he would smile at her, but they exchanged no dialogue. Marya thought it odd that Mrs. Worthington had invited a man rather than a potential client, but then thought that he might very well have a wife who would be interested in her work. But on second thought she decided this notion didn't please her very much either.

After less than half an hour, he looked at Marya and said, "It was a distinct pleasure seeing you again, Mrs. Luminov," and gave a cryptic smile. As he stood up, Marya offered him her hand. He took it in his and she was surprised by the warmth of his skin. Still holding Marya's hand, he turned to Natalie Worthington and kissed her lightly on the cheek. Then he was gone.

"Well, my dear," said Mrs. Worthington, her eyes shining brightly, "what do you think?"

"I think he's a very amiable gentleman," she said, not sure of what Mrs. Worthington was after.

"Don't you think he's wonderfully brilliant?"

"Yes, he seemed very intelligent," she replied, although in truth she hadn't had much opportunity to find out since Mrs. Worthington had done most of the talking.

"And very handsome, don't you think?"

"Yes," she said reluctantly. "He's a fine looking gentleman." She had found him very good looking indeed and was not unaware of the effect his piercing blue eyes had on her. But she was not about to tell Mrs. Worthington that. She wondered why he had been invited to join them, but did not have the kind of relationship with her employer that would allow her to ask.

As if reading her mind, Mrs. Worthington said, "I hope you didn't mind my inviting him to our little tea party."

Marya took advantage of the opportunity to say, "I was surprised to see him, I must confess."

"You must know, Marya, that I took a little liberty, I'm afraid, in inviting him." She looked at Marya over her fan. "But then I had a hunch he wouldn't refuse." She smiled knowingly.

Marya was aware that something was going on behind her back, and Wolf's words came back to her. "What those people like most is intrigues, especially amorous intrigues, and the more illicit the better. They have nothing better to do with themselves."

She returned home late that afternoon and looked for Wolf, but he wasn't there. That wasn't unusual, she told herself, he was often in and out. She felt a need to make some kind of contact with him, to break through the barrier that had formed between them.

By early evening he still had not returned. She put Daniel to bed and sat Elke next to her and began to read out loud. "And so the prince and the princess were married and lived happily ever after," she said, and closed the book.

"Mommy, are you and Daddy married?" asked Elke, her green eyes large as she tried to figure out something that was puzzling her.

"Of course, Elke. We've been married almost five years."

"Are you 'happy ever after,' like in the story?"

Elke's question caught her unawares. "Yes, darling, of course," she said quickly. She stopped and asked herself, was she? She didn't know the answer.

By the time Wolf finally came home, Marya had long been asleep. For hours he had been on a lengthy walk, along the piers of South Street, then around Battery Park on the south tip of Manhattan and up along the Hudson. He had known that if he went to the café,

Adrianna would be awaiting him there. But the comforts of a woman he barely knew were not what he wanted. What he wanted was his Marya of old, as she had been before she got caught up in her separate life.

At last he had turned eastward, inland from the Hudson and walked along Canal Street. He paid little attention to where he was going, until finally he was standing across the street from the café where he had been the night before and where Adrianna was now waiting for him. Through the windows he could see a blur of faces engaged in lively talk.

He stood there and thought of Marya, gone in the afternoons, leaving the children in the care of Mrs. Abrahms; Marya, spending more and more time in Fifth Avenue eateries fashionable with the horse-and-carriage set; Marya, who never wore any of the jewels he had given her.

Then he shrugged his shoulders and went in.

Chapter 11

All were gathered around the dinner table again, but something wasn't the same, Wolf noticed. Lucia kept her eyes turned down toward her plate during the entire meal, and Angelica looked everywhere and at everyone except him. After dinner, Lucia helped her mother with the dishes while Mario and his father went to the flat below to talk to someone in the building who was attempting to organize a petition to the landlord for lighted hallways. The other family members one by one went their separate ways until just Angelica and Wolf were left alone in the main room.

"How have you been, Angelica?" Wolf asked, hoping to calm her down and get her to stand still long enough to look at him. "It's been a few weeks since I've seen you."

She said nothing, but hurried around the room straightening the bright drawings of the Virgin Mary and various saints which were tacked to the walls and were already straight.

He continued. "It was when we were all last at the café together, wasn't it?"

She sniffed the air loudly.

"What's the matter? Didn't you like the café? I thought we all had a good time, the four of us."

She devoted herself to unpinning one of the drawings and dusting it thoroughly. "You had a good time maybe. You and Mario and that woman. It was fine when there were just four of us, before she came."

He was surprised at the intensity of the anger in her voice. "You mean Adrianna?"

She still hadn't looked at him. "I didn't like her one bit," she said. "Neither did Lucia."

Suddenly she spun and glared at him. "A woman like that, I hope you never see her again." She couldn't resist adding, "Did you?" She waited for his reply.

He picked up his hat and threw it at her. "You've certainly become nosy about other people's business, haven't you?"

Her black eyes were snapping. "It's not other people's business. It's my business too. And I know what kind of woman she is. I can tell by looking at her. She's the kind that think all the men are watching her, and—"

He could see that she was just getting wound up, so he stood up and called loudly, "Signora Verdi, Signora Verdi."

Mario's mother appeared in the doorway, a dish towel in one hand and a large platter in the other. "Ah, Wolf," she said, and smiled.

"*Grazie, grazie*, for another delicious dinner. *Eccellente! Delizioso!*"

She beamed at him and set the platter down on the sofa, then held out her hands. "*Grazie,* my son. Come again. You are always welcome in this house," she answered him in Italian.

Wolf had picked up enough Italian in the last month to have a good idea of what she was saying, and he smiled in return and gave her a warm hug. Over her shoulder in the kitchen he could see Lucia leaning back against the table, staring at him sullenly, her eyes dark and narrow.

"Good-bye, Lucia," he called, and he thought he saw her make a perfunctory wave of her hand. He turned to her sister standing behind him. "Good-bye, Angelica."

"*Arrivederci*," she said without looking at him, her tone wistful.

"Come," Jacob Molnar said to Wolf, and led him into the other room. "You are a connoisseur of beauty. I have something I think you might like to see." In the last six years since he had begun buying jewels from this Chassidic Jew, Jacob's fortunes had prospered along with Wolf's. From the small single room that was both home and workshop for three people—Jacob and the two men who were his stone polisher and setter—they had moved to a two room place then a three room place and now into one of the newer, more livable tenements, with two bedrooms, a parlor and a kitchen.

At the same time, the friendship between the two men had slowly grown as they'd spent long hours discussing the merits of Jacob's stones and then gradually ventured a little about their own histories.

Jacob had left the Austro-Hungarian Empire about the same time Wolf had left St. Petersburg. Like Wolf, he was from a large cosmopolitan city—Budapest—where for the last century his family had worked as jewelers.

"You see, the family fortunes have taken a turn for the worse," he had told Wolf some three years earlier, when they had first become more than business associates to each other. Jacob had pointed to the small room in which they were sitting and shrugged his shoulders.

Wolf was surprised and flattered that he had earned Jacob's confidence and trust enough for him to speak of his personal life. Jacob's Chassidism would have been, in most cases, a stumbling block between them, a difference in religion so great, despite the fact that they both were Jews, that the relationship would have always been a business one only. But over the course of three years of doing business together, they had managed to get beyond that difference, and had earned each other's respect and trust. From that had developed a curiosity about each other, which they took their time in satisfying.

Jacob had gone on that day to say, "Just now the wheel of fortune is at its nadir, its lowest point. But it will reach its zenith again. There is a rhythm to the Molnar family's fortunes." He looked away for a moment, then resumed. "My father's great great grandfather and their grandfathers before them were moneylenders." Again he shrugged. "What else was there for them to do? Jews were not allowed to own land."

Wolf nodded. In Russia Jews were not only prohibited from owning land, they could not even reside on it, being forbidden to live in rural areas and confined to the small towns and cities in the area in western Russia set aside for them, the Pale of Settlement.

"As moneylenders, they had a pawn shop, and because they often received jewelry in pawn, they had to learn to repair and assess it. In time they came to deal more and more in jewelry and eventually had their own shop for just that. It was my father's grandfather who was the first to become a purveyor of precious stones. There was a big demand for diamonds and other precious stones throughout the courts of central and eastern Europe, and he became active in filling that need." He sighed, and that was all he had said on the subject at the time. Wolf still had not learned how and why it was that Jacob had left the family business and made his way to this country. But he knew that in Jacob's own time he would know.

Now Jacob led Wolf into the room that served as his bedroom and unlocked a large trunk covered in old leather. From the trunk he withdrew a box of sturdy metal that looked to be fireproof, and from that he removed a stack of large envelopes, each approximately twelve by fifteen inches. He set the envelopes on the small wooden table, the same table where they had consummated the purchase of Wolf's first diamond. From the first of the envelopes he extracted a sheath of tissue paper, placed it on the table and began slowly to unwrap it. Wolf caught a glimpse of brilliant color, then he saw what looked like an ornate document consisting of a single page, heavily illustrated and illuminated. In the center of the document, he saw a block of writing in Hebrew and Aramaic.

"This is an old *kesubah*," explained Jacob. "It's a wedding contract. From the time of the Babylonian exile there have been these formal contracts drawn up to set forth the bridegroom's duties to his bride."

Wolf had heard of these elaborate contracts but had never seen one. He knew they were a custom mostly of the early Jews and then of the Sephardic Jews who had settled along the Mediterranean, or who had dispersed to places like Holland, Germany, or even England after they were expelled from Spain at the end of the fifteenth century.

Jacob turned the *kesubah* so that it might catch the light from the small window and show the vivid colors to better advantage. "Such a document was a confirmation of wedlock, and thus a means of safeguarding a woman's position. If her husband happened to die, or to divorce her, the *kesubah* would establish her legal right to a claim in his property. All this was so that, as in the words from the Gemara, 'He should not deem it an easy thing to send her away.'"

Wolf ran his finger by the length of the document, taking care not to touch it. "You can see it's old from the quality of the parchment and also from the Hebrew and Aramaic script in which it is written."

"This one dates from the seventeen hundreds and is from Venice. Note the bright flowers and exotic birds painted around the border. As was often the custom, Biblical scenes from the namesake of the groom or bride were worked into the ornamental framework. Here you see scenes from the life of Abraham because in this case the bridegroom's name was Abraham. The artwork on the *kesubos* from Italy is, I think, the most beautiful of all."

He set it to one side and began to unwrap another. "This one is from Amsterdam. Notice the difference. It's engraved in black and white, showing the influence of the art of etching that was flourishing in Holland. Also, the top of the parchment isn't cut in an undulating line like on the one from Venice."

Jacob unwrapped another, this one from Isfahan, Persia and embellished with bright peacocks, cypresses and flowers, giving it a condensed richness similar to that of a Persian carpet. He unwrapped another and then another until the table was covered with artwork.

Wolf looked at Jacob and saw that his face was beaming and that his eyes had a dreamy quality as he gently rewrapped the contracts. "You may wonder what I am doing with so many of these *kesubos*. How my collection—for that's what it's become even though I have never thought of myself as the collecting type—got started was completely by accident. In Budapest, a client of mine, a very aristocratic Jew, had become enchanted with a particular pearl I possessed. Legend had it that the pearl had once belonged to Maria Theresa of Austria. So enamored of this stone was this patron and so determined to have it, that when his family lost a large sum of money, so much that it made it unfeasible for him to go ahead with his purchase of the pearl, he insisted I take an ancient and particularly valuable *kesubah* in trade. I had no desire to have a *kesubah,* but God had a different opinion about the matter, I suppose, for here you see years later I have a goodly number. God often signals us what he really wants us to do, doesn't he? That is how I knew I should come to America." He was suddenly conscious of how much he had been talking. "But that is another story," he added hastily.

His face lost its dreamy quality and resumed the expression it bore in their usual encounters. "I continued to add to my collection until the time I left Budapest. Then I was no longer able to buy more. But I did promise myself that no matter how bad things became for me in my new country, I would not sell the *kesubos*. Once gone, I know I would never get them back again, for they are priceless."

He began to slip the contracts back into their sheaths, then placed the envelopes back into the heavy metal box. "I must put them away now," he explained. "I can look at their beauty only rarely. They cannot survive out in the air where everyone can see them." As he returned the padlock to the leather trunk, he added, "But then that is how it sometimes is with certain things of great beauty, isn't it? Like a beautiful woman, perhaps? They should not be for everyone to gawk at freely."

Wolf said nothing, his feelings about Marya being too confused to agree or disagree with what Jacob was saying.

He made his way up the dark street and climbed the stairs to the second story, then rapped softly. Adrianna opened the door. He saw that she was wearing a tight-fitting dress in dark green.

Her voice was breathless as she said, "Wolf! I was hoping you would come."

As he entered the small room, he saw that another woman was there. She appeared to be of early middle age and was sitting in a wooden chair by the window, holding a hat in her lap.

Adrianna saw him looking at her. "That's my sister," she said by way of explanation. "She was just leaving."

As if on cue, the woman stood up and held out her hand. "I'm pleased to meet you. My name is Rosa." She was not as tall as Adrianna, but had the same round, womanly body, perhaps a little plumper.

She smiled at Wolf, then was quietly out the door without a word more.

Adrianna shut the door behind Rosa and leaned against it. Then she threw her arms around his neck and pressed the length of her body into him. "I needed to see you these last few days so much. When I go even two days without seeing you, it is more than I can stand. Oh, Wolf, hold me close to you."

Her words were like nectar to him, and he found himself responding to her passion. He pulled her so tightly against him that he could feel the pounding of her heart through the fabric of her dress. If only it were someone else crying out to him like that, he thought in spite of himself. If only it were Marya. But it wasn't and couldn't be, he said, determined not to long anymore for what couldn't be, and pulled her even tighter, feeling the soft mounds of her breasts melt into him.

She pulled away and reached up her hand to undo one by one the buttons of her bodice. As he saw the roundness of her bare breast, he picked her up and carried her to the single bed, placed against the wall. Then he gave in to his need for a woman's passion completely and lost himself in her soft flesh.

Marya waited in the drawing room of the Gregory Keller residence. The Kellers, a family that had distinguished itself by erecting a number of lavish and popular hotels, lived in one of the new apartments that had just been built and which were the subject of much dispute among the circle of Marya's clients. "What? Live on a shelf with other people and share a common roof?" one particularly outraged member of New York's Four Hundred was heard to remark. Still, the apartments, as they were called, had become fashionable as more and more of the young elegant set opted for their smart locations and convenience, and to a family that had made its fortune in the hotel business, the idea of sharing a common roof did not seem such a déclassé arrangement at all.

She was waiting for the appearance of Mrs. Keller, who had asked through Mrs. Worthington if she might avail herself of Marya's services and talent. Mrs. Worthington had made all the arrangements, and as usual before she met a new patron for the first time, Marya was curious.

She was surprised to see that the person who finally came into the room was not Mrs. Keller but Mr. Keller, one of the two men who had eyed her so openly in Delmonico's a year ago. She was even more surprised when he came up to her and took her hand, fervently pressing it to his lips.

"Come into Marion's sitting room with me, Marya," he said.

Marya was used to holding sessions with her patrons in their dressing rooms, and until her experience with Claudia Carter, whom, she was thankful, she had not had an occasion to see since that last time, she had preferred the coziness of the boudoir sessions to those held in the salons and drawing rooms, where the atmosphere was always excessively formal.

As he led her through the apartment, she saw that the Kellers, unlike the Worthingtons, had embraced the modern look in furnishings. The sitting room was draped in red silk like a Turkish tent, and underneath was a divan strewn with colorful cushions. On the wall hung an arrangement of scimitars and spears. As she looked past the sitting room to the attached bedroom, Marya saw that the modern look extended to the Keller's twin beds, now the latest innovation in modern bedrooms and the subject of hot controversy.

Gregory Keller stopped and boldly looked Marya over from head to toe, then motioned her toward the plush divan.

Marya did not see Mrs. Keller in this room or the next, but she did see the expectant look on Gregory Keller's face.

"I cannot tell you how delighted I was," he said, "when Natalie Worthington told me you had agreed to come today."

Marya thought it strange that a husband would be taking that much interest in his wife's wardrobe that he would even be present for the consultation. "I am very much looking forward to meeting Mrs. Keller," she said. "Mrs. Worthington has spoken so highly of her."

"Yes, of course, she is a marvelous woman," he said, "none better," and stepped very close to Marya. She caught the faint scent of pipe tobacco from his clothes. "But what to talk about now is us."

"Us, Mr. Keller?"

"Us, Marya," he said as he put his arms around her and kissed her.

Immediately she pushed away from him. "Aren't you getting ahead of yourself, Mr. Keller?" She wondered how he dared to take such liberties with his wife due to come into the room at any moment.

"Marya," he said patiently, "you need not play the coy maiden with me. After all, you agreed to come here today."

"I agreed to meet with Mrs. Keller, nothing more."

"I find your naiveté in this matter more than a little annoying, Marya," he said and roughly pulled her to him again.

She again pushed him away and in spite of her resolve to tolerate the not inconsiderable foibles of her patrons, slapped him soundly.

He instantly put his hand to the red welt across his left cheek. "I certainly didn't deserve that, certainly not under the circumstances of your having accepted my invitation to come here."

Marya felt no need to reply. She had by this time figured out that Mrs. Worthington had deliberately misled her about the nature of this visit to the Keller residence today. It wasn't Mrs. Keller who had asked for her; it was Mr. Keller, and most likely Mrs. Keller didn't even know of her existence. She recalled now that, in fact, Mrs. Worthington had never actually said Mrs. Keller, rather she had implied that the meeting was to be a fashion consultation, and Marya had had no reason to expect that her meeting was to be with anyone but Mrs. Keller. Although she didn't condone Gregory Keller's willingness to have a romance with her, she now at least understood the puzzled look that had crossed his face when she had mentioned his wife as soon as they had come into the bedroom.

"I'm afraid there's been an unfortunate misunderstanding, Mr. Keller, both yours and mine," she said. Then she found her way back to the front door and let herself out.

"Don't be a ninny, Marya," Mrs. Worthington said to her the next time they met. "Gregory Keller is one of the most dashing men in this city, and if he takes an interest in you, you'd be well advised to make the most of it. You can admit, can't you, Marya, that it was a wee bit entertaining to have an adoring man waiting for you instead of Mrs. Keller." She laughed. "Darling, you have no idea how very boring La Keller can be, how very seriously she takes herself."

Marya pondered Mrs. Worthington's use of the word entertaining. What did it matter to her whether Marya had been made to feel a fool, or whether her friend Gregory Keller had also been made to feel uncomfortable? What was important was whether she had had an "experience," whether she had been entertained, and even more crucially, whether Mrs. Worthington herself had been entertained. Clearly the right or wrong of her manipulation was not a consideration.

Mrs. Worthington was now studying her intently. "Tell me again, Marya, what is your nationality? By that I mean, your blood origins? Russian, didn't you say?"

"Yes."

"Would you by any chance be, *Oriental,* dear?" She continued to peer at Marya.

"Oriental?"

She saw that she needed to be more direct. "Oriental is a polite way of saying Jewish. Are you Jewish?"

Marya now returned Mrs. Worthington's bold stare. "Yes, I am."

Mrs. Worthington nodded her head as if an intuition had just been confirmed. "Ah, well yes, that explains a lot, I believe."

Marya was becoming angry with Mrs. Worthington's condescending tone. "What exactly does it explain?"

Natalie Worthington ignored the temper she heard rising in Marya's voice and tried a different tack. "Marya, dear," she said with as much sincerity as she ever mustered, "you must reconsider your opportunities with Mr. Keller. Really, dear, he is a very charming gentleman. Many highly placed ladies can attest to that. And he can be most generous. Also, he is someone you would never want for an enemy, and some ladies can attest to that as well. Incidentally, I certainly hope that you're not letting the fact that you have a husband somewhere in the background deter you from a chance that could open many doors for you."

Husband in the background? thought Marya. Yes, that's what she had now, just a husband in the background, just someone who was there. This husband had cautioned her how easy it was to become just a plaything of the beautiful and fashionable and rich. She couldn't see how what Natalie Worthington was coaching her to do would open any doors, other than bedroom doors. She had heard the thinly disguised contempt in her voice when she had said the word Oriental, and she realized enough to know that as a newcomer, and especially as a Jew, she would not be allowed any but the most temporary and useful of niches in this elegant world.

"Your husband," Mrs. Worthington pursued, "what did you say his name was? Something unusual, as I recall, rather foreign."

"His name is Zavel. That means Wolf in Hebrew," she said evenly.

"Yes, yes. That was it. I knew it had something to do with an animal. He is Oriental too, I imagine."

Suddenly Marya felt an overwhelming need to be with Wolf and away from Mrs. Worthington. His words echoed in her ears. "You will always be nothing but a servant to them. Especially because you are Jewish." She had somehow excused herself from her meeting with Mrs. Worthington and hurried home on the el. There was a chill in the air, and no matter how tightly she pulled her cloak, she couldn't get warm.

As Marya drew close to Chatham Street, she smelled smoke in the air. Another of the many old and hazardous wooden structures that lined the street had caught fire, she said to herself, and she shuddered involuntarily at the thought of the wooden building where their own home and business were located. Perhaps Wolf was right; it was time to find another place, maybe in one of the newer, fireproof buildings.

As she turned the corner, she saw a crowd gathered in the middle of the street in front of her building. Then she saw the flames. They were shooting up against the black sky, their orange hue eerily brilliant against the early evening. She started to run. As she drew near to her building, the crowd in the street grew more congested and everywhere there was pandemonium as passers-by and spectators mingled with the frantic dislodged inhabitants of the building. Another ripple of excitement ran through the crowd as they heard the familiar clanging of the fire wagon and then the thunderous pounding of the horses' hooves as they drew near.

She pushed her way through the crowd. A few times she heard someone call her name, but she didn't bother to look at any of the people huddled in front of the burning building. All she could think about were her children and Wolf. She was surprised at how calm and clear her mind actually was. She knew exactly what she was going to do.

She fought her way to the front of the crowd. At the entrance to the building a large, burly man was barring the way. She marched up to him and started to push past.

"Beggin' your pardon, ma'am, but no one goes in."

"My babies are there. I'm going to get them."

He stepped directly in front of her. "Sorry, ma'am, orders is orders."

Suddenly the calm and sureness that Marya had felt vanished. She began to beat on his chest with her fists. "You can't stop me. I've got to get in." She reached for his face with her nails and tried to kick at his shins.

He grabbed her wrists and held them firmly in one hand. "Now, now, lady, just wait. We got eight men in there and they're getting everyone out of the building. I reckon those babies of yours are already out and safe."

His words had no effect on her. She twisted and turned in his grasp and tried to get loose. When he refused to let go his hold on her, she started to sob. "Don't you understand? My children are there, my babies! Elke!" she cried. "Daniel! My babies!"

The more she writhed, the tighter he held her. Suddenly it was the Cossack in Petrovichi all over again, and she began to scream, no longer aware of what she was crying out. "David!" she screamed. "David!" She screamed so hard and so completely that she doubled over.

As she started to collapse, another man appeared in the doorway, one of the fire fighters, who had just come down the stairs and was carrying a wizened old man in his arms. The man who had been barring the door signaled to him for help. The firefighter carried the old man to a safe spot, then returned and swooped Marya up in his arms. As he headed for the knot of spectators, the crowd opened up and made a pathway for him. He carried her to the stoop of the building across the street.

"Make way, make way," he said to four boys who were using the stoop as their vantage point from which to watch the fire. The youths immediately jumped from the stoop and stood below to watch the fire fighter and the woman they assumed he had just rescued from the building that was now sending up tunnels of thick, grey smoke. As soon as he set her down in a sitting position, Marya curled up, placing her head in her lap and sobbed.

"Marya!"

She heard Wolf's voice and felt his hand on her head. She looked up and there he stood, holding in his arms Elke and Daniel.

It took her a few moments to realize what she was seeing. She started to laugh, but all that came out were more tears. "Thank God, thank God," she cried and tried to put her arms around all three of them at once. Wolf handed her Elke, and she pressed the girl so tightly to her that Elke at one point complained that Mommy was hurting her. Wolf had Daniel in his one arm, the other around Marya's shoulders. They stood that way, facing the now severely damaged building for a long time.

That night they spent in a settlement house, a five story building opened the year before with funds from German Jews to help new immigrants better assimilate American customs and to refine what they saw as the unfortunate old country rawness that still clung to these lower orders from the *shtetl*.

"We can't stay here," Wolf announced almost as soon as they walked through the doors.

Marya knew that it rankled him to accept any form of charity, especially that of German Jews. "It's just for one night, Zavel. It's too late now for us to look for another place. The children are frightened and tired."

He knew what she said was true. Daniel even now was trembling in his arms, unaccustomed to the strange people—others made homeless by the fire—and all this commotion at an hour of the evening when he was usually asleep. Elke whimpered softly in Marya's arms. He realized he had no choice but to keep his family here. But it would be for just this one night. As he looked at the other victims of the fire beginning to bed down on the sofas, chairs, wherever they could find a place, he was reminded of the indignities of Castle Garden where he'd gone through immigration upon his arrival in America. He had been glad when the large circular building had been torn down and replaced with a new hotellike structure on Ellis Island, although he had already heard rumors that it was just as bad.

It was ironically fitting, he thought, that they should be reduced to looking like Castle Garden arrivals again. Once again they were homeless, back where they started, back to beginning anew.

He put his arm around Marya and pulled her close. She leaned her head against his shoulder. He wanted to tell her how much he loved her. Instead he kissed her forehead softly. Then he slept on one sofa with Daniel cradled in his arms and Marya slept on another with Elke in hers.

Wolf's kiss had been enough for Marya to know that he wanted her again, but despite this comforting knowledge, she slept badly. She dreamt of the fire and of Petrovichi. In the flames she kept seeing the face of a young boy, now eleven years old, with hauntingly green eyes. "David," she cried, unsure if she were dreaming or awake.

The next morning Marya handed a wad of bills to

Wolf. "This is money I had in my purse. It's quite a lot because I was just paid for one of my commissions."

He took it and she hoped he accepted the lie. She could not tell him where the money had really come from, that it was some of the money she had received from the sale of the jewels he had given her and that she always carried in a hidden compartment she had fashioned in her handbag.

He counted it. "It's almost two hundred," he said with surprise and looked at her.

"Yes." She also did not tell him there was even more. She knew he would have been suspicious, not believing her commissions could have brought her that much money, and she knew his pride would be wounded to take so much from her, even though she was accustomed already to turning over her money to their common fund. But at this particular moment, she sensed it would be especially hard for him to be rescued by money from any pocket but his own.

"Who's David?" he asked suddenly.

Marya gave a start. "David?" she said.

"Yes, David. Who is he?"

"Someone I knew a long time ago. A boy." She saw that Wolf was waiting, looking at her closely. "He was killed," she added. She hated the lie as she said it. Never had she been able to believe that David was dead and it seemed bad luck to say he was when she didn't really believe it. Wolf had seemed satisfied with her explanation, but still she felt relieved when he left. He went to find a new place for them to live.

While he was gone, she studied the people who were now starting to come into the settlement house. The staff assured those of them that had spent the night there that they were free to mingle with the regulars coming in the door, for everyone was welcome there. The settlement house was open each day from nine in the morning to ten at night. Immigrants of all ages came to learn English, use the library or gymnasium and perhaps take a free bath or shower or maybe enjoy the roof garden. Since the goal of the settlement house was to accustom the newcomers to everything American, no Yiddish was allowed to be spoken, and classes were held in civics, American literature and American history.

By noon Wolf had returned. "Come," he said. "I want to see if you like this place I found on Cherry Street." His tone was light and half teasing. "Considering how completely you settle in once you move into a place, I want to make sure it's somewhere you'll like. We must be the only East Side family not to have moved at least three times a year since getting here."

She thought it a good sign that he was cheerful, but then having a course of action to follow usually did put him in a good mood. "And what about the business?" she ventured.

"It was time we moved it to a new location anyway. But this time we'll spread out a little and have our shop in a separate building from where we live."

"Yes, that would be better."

"Then if there were to be another fire, we wouldn't lose everything at once, like this time." A sigh escaped his lips, the first sign she'd seen from him that the calamity had affected him.

"I've also been thinking," he said, "that we should abandon our line of coats." Then they both started to laugh in comic relief as they realized there was no longer any line for them to abandon.

As they walked out of the settlement house and into the streets, Wolf explained to her his plan to have just the line of women's dresses. While it was true the sewing machine had changed the making of clothing in the last fifty years, it was not true of all forms of clothing. Most women's clothing continued to be stitched by hand, usually by dressmakers.

"That has to change," Wolf explained. "There's no reason that women's clothing won't all be made by machine as well. And when that happens, there will be an enormous upsurge in the purchase of our line of clothing. I want us to be in a position to take advantage of that inevitable increased demand. Our women's line before was just small herring, just a little fish compared to what I want to build now."

Yes, thought Marya, he was probably right. In the last couple of years, since the turn of the decade, she had noticed a change in how active everyone had become and the popularity of outdoor activities, with bicycling in particular becoming a major pastime, as upper class ladies led the trend. This greater amount of activity and freedom called for a greater range of clothing and already ladies were sporting loose undertrousers tied at the ankle called bloomers after Mrs. Amelia Bloomer, the feminist. Marya knew that this call for clothes that allowed more freedom of movement combined with Wolf's insistence that women would continue to wear more and more machine-stitched clothing meant that maybe, just maybe, if nothing went wrong, they could be very rich, very soon.

Marya noticed right away that the building Wolf had found was all brick. The flat he wanted her to see was on the third floor and was built in the "dumbbell" style that had mushroomed throughout the Lower East Side in the last fourteen years since the designer, James Ware, had won a competition sponsored for a tenement that would best blend low cost to the builder with safety and convenience for the tenant. The rooms of the flat were laid out in a straight line, with the living room in the middle, a parlor to its right and a bedroom to its left. Each room was a little over ten feet wide, necessarily small since the competition had required that the building be designed to fit a lot 100 feet by 25 feet. As usual, the toilet and spigots for water were outside on the landing and shared with the three other flats on that same level.

Marya was disappointed that the flat did not get more light and ventilation, but she knew they were not likely to do any better since so many of the tenements were built to this same floor plan. It had more rooms than their old flat, but other than that Marya couldn't see any other advantages.

Wolf read the look on her face. "We don't have to stay here long, if you don't want. Just long enough to get ourselves established again. With the money you gave me this morning, we should have ourselves a new work place with all new equipment by the end of the week. We'll soon be making money again, and we'll be able to afford something better."

How like him, she thought. Always he was full of optimism and ready to throw himself into work. She looked at the children already playing on the floor. "This will be fine, Zavel. We can be happy here." She looked up at him and smiled. "Remember when you practically dragged me through the streets to show me our first place before you had even asked me to marry you? You were so excited."

He returned her smile and came to embrace her. "We must remember that no matter what happens around us, we still have each other to count on."

They kissed for a long time. Then Marya said, half laughing, half crying, "I feel like a bride again, Zavel, as though we're starting over in more ways than one."

"We are," he said, and pulled her back out into the hallway. He scooped her into his arms and carried her over the threshold.

Wolf was as good as his word as he threw himself into the myriad of details that starting the business again required. Marya made another set of sketches for the new line, all designed for the active woman of the nineties. She created bicycling skirts, yachting costumes, and skirts and jackets suitable for wearing on long walks in the country. Once again Wolf took the designs to the tailor, Mr. Zeidenbaum, who as usual complained, but also as usual quickly made up the patterns, which Wolf then passed on to Sol. He knew that most likely Sol could have made the patterns himself, expert in tailoring that he was, but Sol was more needed to help him with the endless details of setting up the shop and organizing the workers, all of whom had followed him to his new location on Greene Street.

"Mario," Wolf said during that same week, "I need an assistant production manager. How would you like to be it?"

Mario's face lit up instantly. "Just tell me what I do, I'll do it."

In the next two months everyone worked longer hours for Wolf than they ever had before, especially Mario, but all felt it was worth it. All wanted to see not only their own livelihoods assured, but their employer, whom they trusted, restored to a position of success, because Wolf belonged to this newest wave of immigrants rather than to those who had come over from Germany in the early part of the century. He was one of them and his success gave them some vindication for the humiliating conditions under which they lived and the low esteem in which they were held.

Ever since the night of the fire and the visit to their new set of rooms the next morning, the stalemate between Marya and Wolf had been broken and they were close again. He had felt no need for Adrianna's embraces and in the last two months had not been to see her once. From his renewed passion and intimacy with Marya, he had hoped to hear that she was pregnant again, but she said nothing.

Marya had been kept so busy with her designs for the ladies' line that she had not had time to accept any more commissions from her Fifth Avenue patrons and once again spent all of her time on the Lower East Side. One day after they had been in the new flat for about a month, she had received a small envelope embellished with an elaborate seal on the back. The note inside, written in an elegant script, was short.

"Do not be away from us too long, Marya," it said, and nothing more.

Chapter 12

"You come to our house soon," said Mario. "My mother, she asks, 'Where's your friend Wolf? How come I don't see Wolf here in such a long time?' I say, 'Mama, be patient. This is a hard time for Wolf, now that his home burnt, and his wife and children have to have a new place to live.' 'His children!' she cries. 'You never tell me he has *bambinos!*' Then she started in on me: 'When you gonna have bambinos? When you gonna find a nice Sicilian girl? You're not gonna find her in these cafés you go to every night. These bars where no decent girl can be seen for blocks.' "

Wolf smiled. It was true about the hard work. Setting up the new shop had taken so much of his time that he had not seen anyone but his workers and family for weeks. Nor had he had any time or desire to start frequenting the cafés again.

Mario threw up his hands, still not finished with his tale. "Then my sisters join in. 'Wolf has a wife?' screams Angelica. And she starts beating on my arm. 'How come you didn't tell us? We never knew all this time.' So then I said, 'He told you himself he had a family.' Then Angelica said, 'Well, you have a family too, but that doesn't mean a wife or children. We thought he meant his parents.' " Mario looked at Wolf. "I can't see what difference it all makes, can you?"

Wolf didn't see how he could say to Mario, if he hadn't noticed yet, that his sisters had more than a polite interest in him as their brother's friend. To imagine that his sisters might be interested in a man who wasn't Italian and who was also their brother's employer was apparently more than Mario could manage.

"It's not as if you're her boyfriend. So why should she care? And Lucia, she comes to stand behind Angelica. And such looks she shoots me. Her eyes look like a gun, and I can tell she's even madder than Angelica." He looked at Wolf sharply. "What did I do, anyway, to get my sisters so mad." He shook his head. "I don't understand it. That's what I tell them, too. 'I don't undertsand it. I didn't tell you because I didn't know it was important.' Then the two of them go sit at the table together, and I can hear them whispering to themselves about it. Now I can hear them mention Adrianna's name. They're both still real mad, I can tell. My mother comes into the room again, and hears my sisters saying your name, only she hasn't heard all the other things they've been saying, so she claps her hands and says to me, 'Mario, you invite them all to eat. Invite the whole family, Mrs. Wolf and bambinos too.' My sisters get quiet and don't say a word." With a flourish of his hand, he began to wind up his story. "So Wolf, later today I'm going to ask Marya if she'd like to come to our house and see what it's like to eat the Sicilian way. What do you think?"

"Sure, Mario. It sounds like a good idea," said Wolf. Truthfully, though, he didn't look forward to the prospect of sitting at the table again with Angelica and Lucia poring over not only him but this time Marya as well. Nor did he know if Marya would feel comfortable with this family of outgoing, exuberant Sicilians who spoke more often in Italian than they did in English and probably had no more knowledge or understanding of a Jewish woman from Russia who had turned herself into a fashionable lady worthy of Fifth Avenue than Marya would have of a family of Catholic Sicilians on Mulberry Bend.

When Mario, with Wolf's permission, went to see Marya later that afternoon, he found himself looking at her and feeling slightly tongue-tied. With her long hair and delicate features, he saw in her something of the madonna, and he could not get from his mind the memory of how she had looked, so soft and loving, that evening he had been at their place many months ago when she sat with Elke curled in sleep next to her on the sofa.

"Wolf told me I might find you home now," he began as he stood in the doorway. He was careful to make no move to go in.

Her eyes widened slightly with curiosity. "Yes?"

He could see Daniel and Elke playing on the floor behind her. "My mother, she would like me to tell you that you should come to our place for dinner with the bambinos. She says Wolf is like a son now to her and she wants to meet his beautiful wife."

She tried not to blink as he slightly emphasized the word beautiful.

"Maybe you could come Sunday next?"

Marya could feel his eyes roaming over her as she answered. "That is very kind of your mother. Next Sunday? I . . . I think it will be good, but let me talk to my husband to make sure, and he can let you know tomorrow, if that is all right with you." She always felt a little uneasy with Mario, and the way he was looking at her did not help matters.

"It would be an honor for us, signora."

He smiled broadly at her and she forced herself to hold his gaze until it seemed the decent thing to do was bid him good-bye and shut the door.

Lucia pulled her cloak tighter around her and paused just a second. Angelica would kill her, she was sure, when she found out. And of course she'd find out because Lucia herself planned to tell her.

She almost faltered. Then her resolve renewed and she knocked on the door. A beautiful woman with a mass of reddish-brown hair piled on her head opened it. For a moment Lucia stood and stared. So this was Wolf's wife. She wasn't sure why, but she hadn't been expecting someone this beautiful.

"Mrs. Luminov?" she said.

Marya was surprised to hear a young woman with a heavy Italian accent asking for her. She supposed she had something to do with their shop and that Wolf had sent her. "Yes?" she said.

"My name is Lucia Verdi. Mario, who works for your husband, is my brother."

"Oh, yes." Marya smiled and opened the door further. "He was here earlier this afternoon. Please come in."

Lucia quickly looked around the apartment that was only slightly bigger than theirs, but somehow seemed much finer, perhaps because only four people lived here rather than eleven. Her eyes came to rest again on Marya. Although she knew that Wolf owned the business where Mario worked, she hadn't been prepared to see a lady so pretty and stylish that she could have belonged on Fifth Avenue. For just a flicker, her resolve wavered again, but then she gained hold of herself.

Marya was waiting expectantly. She noticed that the girl had one of those expressions that was a perpetual pout, but at the same time she seemed unsure of herself.

"Mrs. Luminov," Lucia began hesitantly, then gained confidence, "there's something I think you ought to know."

Marya was still waiting.

"It's about your husband."

"Yes?" Marya's hand went instantly to her heart. "Did something happen at the shop?"

"No, nothing like that." She took a deep breath. "I just think you should know, Mrs. Luminov, that he sees another woman."

"What!" Marya's heart began to pound wildly in her chest. What was this young woman saying? Was she mad? Why was she telling her this awful thing and could it be true? "What are you talking about?"

Now that she had said it, Lucia felt calm, even chatty. "He has a girlfriend and her name is Adrianna."

Marya struggled not to betray the feelings that were rising in her. "Why are you telling me this?"

"I just think you should know. This Adrianna is not a good person. And your husband is not as good a husband as you think."

Marya wanted to put her hands up to her ears to stop the words she was hearing. Instead she managed to say, "I see. Thank you. You can leave now."

"Yes, I wasn't going to stay any longer," said Lucia, insulted. She turned and let herself out the door.

Marya heard the sound of Lucia's shoes as she made her way down the staircase. The tapping of those heels as they became progressively fainter was the only thing that kept her from thinking that she may have imagined the whole scene that had just taken place. She hurried to the window in the parlor but was unable to see which of the many dark shapes below might have been the vicious young woman who had just visited her.

Marya felt numb. Splashing water in her face didn't help. She thought how flimsy and fleeting her newfound happiness with Wolf really had been. She had thought that their love and passion had renewed itself. Now she questioned whether there had ever been any true love in the first place. The Italian girl's words were a confirmation of her deepest fears, fears she had pushed far down inside and convinced herself were unfounded. Now they all came back to her, larger than ever. He had never loved her. He had wanted her only for the dowry. He had been willing to take her on so that he could make a good business move. That was the most important thing to him, clawing his way up to a position equal to that of his father. She had been a weak fool to have ever believed otherwise.

Lucia walked as quickly as she could along the unfamiliar streets. She had seldom on her own ventured much further than the few blocks around Mulberry Bend, so she had to pay special attention. Still she had no fear of getting lost because she knew that the Hudson River was to the west and the East River on the other side, so even if she did make a wrong turn, eventually she could find the right way. She could hardly wait to get home and talk to Angelica. After Angelica got over being mad, she would probably come to see this Lucia's way. All Lucia knew was that she had never had feelings for a man the way she did for Wolf. She had had so many dreams about him that she'd lost count. He was in her mind all the time and it had made her feel dizzy just to think about his being near her, or it had until the night at the café.

She could not forgive him that he had so obviously preferred the company of that woman Adrianna when she had sat down at their table. She had felt so grown up herself that night and she knew that she had looked good. She thought she had seen him looking at her earlier in the way men looked at women. Then she had hated the way Mario got that knowing smirk on his face when he told Wolf how nice it would be for him to see Adrianna again. How could Wolf turn from her, and Angelica also, to that woman who wore make-up and who had almost eaten Wolf up with her eyes in front of everybody? After that, the fact that he had a wife and children came to her as another betrayal, but after the other, it was not as public or personal or embittering.

As soon as Wolf looked at Marya that evening he could see something was wrong. He put his arms around her, but she pulled away, saying she had to tend to Elke and Daniel. That day had been a particularly hectic one for him: a large delivery of yardage that was already late was sent to the wrong address; tempers had flared between two workers and the argument had grown to the point that Wolf had to be the final arbiter; the newest group of patterns had gotten lost and they had to delay cutting while they searched for them; on top of it all, three workers were out sick. What Wolf most wanted just now was to hold Marya next to him and talk over the frustrations of what had happened that day.

He watched her cutting up bits of fish for Daniel, carefully removing the bones.

She seemed to be taking an interminable amount of time tonight, or maybe it was just that he especially needed to have some time himself with her. He saw that her jaw was set and her eyes were veiled.

"Three of our crew were out sick today," he said, as she continued to work meticulously on the fish.

"Mmmm."

"You can imagine the headaches that created for Sol. And when Sol has a headache, it's not long until I have one too." He expected her to make some kind of reply, at least give a sign she had heard him. Silence.

Elke and Daniel, aware that something was wrong with their mother, also sat uncustomarily silent. Elke stared at her plate as she slowly chewed her supper. Daniel looked up at his father, hoping to catch his eye but sensing, from the looks on their faces, something important was going on between his parents.

Wolf continued. "That was just to start the day. You wouldn't believe what happened from there." He saw she hardly seemed to be paying attention.

"I guess you must have had a pretty hard day yourself here. You seem pretty tired."

"Yes, that's what I am, tired," she said suddenly, her voice harsh in a way he hadn't heard it before.

He stood behind her and ran his fingers lightly

along her neck. "After the children are in bed, we can make it nice for each other."

He saw his son looking up at him with wide, uncomprehending eyes. When she didn't say anything, he added, "Come on, let me finish feeding Daniel. You put Elke to bed and then go rest."

"That's all right," she said in a monotone. "I'll finish feeding him myself. He's almost done anyway." When Wolf continued to leave his hand resting against her shoulder, she slammed the knife down on the table, splattering bits of fish and bone through the air.

Elke burst into tears.

Wolf had never seen Marya like this before and wondered what had upset her so much. Wanting to be helpful, he picked up Elke and carried her into the parlor, which Marya had turned into a bedroom for Daniel and Elke since it got the best ventilation of any room in the flat. As he sat her down on the bed, he was surprised to see how much she had grown. She had stopped crying and was looking at him expectantly. She wasn't ready to go to bed yet and lifted her arms high, trying to put them back around his neck, delighted at this attention from her father.

"Hold me, Papa. Hold me, Papa," she chanted, her sad mood having vanished, and danced her feet up and down on the soft bed.

He noticed how much she looked like Marya. Mario had been right. He just hadn't noticed how strong the resemblance was before this. It was more than just her hair, long and the same unique color of red. Already she had the same oval face with the promise of high cheekbones, and her eyes were large and green. He recalled how Mario had said to him later, "I sure wouldn't mind seeing her by the time she's twenty-four or twenty-five!"

"Twenty-five," Wolf mused. That was Marya's age now. She was at the prime of her beauty. And he felt he loved her more each day. He wondered what had made her so tired and withdrawn today. Now that she was no longer making daily trips uptown, she seemed to him to have even more energy. He had been pleased to see that she seemed quietly contented, peaceful in her activities for their home and the new women's line. Today was the first day that she had said she was tired, or that she hadn't greeted him at the door with a warm embrace. He would have to remember to ask her about her day when they got in bed.

Marya continued to be busy about the house for the rest of the evening. Wolf ended up eating supper alone because she was up and down so much as she fussed with putting Daniel to bed, checking on Elke and completing an assortment of small tasks. Then, after supper, she sat at the table, her papers for sketching in front of her. Thus passed a few more hours. Wolf made several attempts to talk to her, but she seemed preoccupied.

Finally he stood in the doorway. "Let's go to bed."

She was engrossed in her drawing and didn't look up. "I'm not ready," she said and continued to sketch.

He sat down at the table across from her. "Marya, is something wrong? Tell me."

"I have some new plans I'm working on."

He saw that he couldn't draw her out, so he got up and went to bed. He lay a long time alone in the dark, waiting for her, but still she didn't come.

Marya had made up her mind that she would say nothing to Wolf about Lucia's visit. What good would it do to confront him, she asked herself. But she also knew she would not be able to respond to his lovemaking the way she had before. She thought back to Elke's question the night she had read her the fairy tale. Now she knew the answer. No, she wasn't married happily ever after.

The next morning she went down into the street and surveyed the stream of passing boys. Some were laden down with piles of coats which they were probably taking from a sweatshop somewhere to the manufacturer. Some were draped in tinware which they were energetically peddling. Others were hawking penny newspapers. And still others were hurrying along, obviously pell mell on completing some kind of errand.

"Errand boy," she called. "Errand boy! I need an errand boy."

After a few false starts, she found a boy who was willing to take the el to the north side of town.

"Be sure you take this to the right address," she cautioned the boy, who looked to be about eleven years old and was covered in pale freckles. She handed him a small envelope. "The number is five-eighteen."

"Right," said the boy, obviously eager to be off.

"Now tell me again," she said. "What's the number?"

"Five-eighteen on Fifth Avenue," he recited.

"Good," she said, and as she pushed a nickel into his hand, he was off and running. "Bring me a reply," she called after him, "and you'll have another nickel."

A couple of hours later, she heard someone calling her name outside in the street. She hurried down the stairs to see the freckle-faced boy standing out front with a cream-colored envelope resting on his outstretched palm.

She traded him five cents for the envelope. His face broke into a big grin when he received the nickel, revealing a missing front tooth. Marya tore open the envelope and read the short note on the spot. As the boy turned to dash off to find his next adventure, Marya stopped him.

"What's your name, boy?"

"Moishe."

"I have another errand for you, Moishe. I want you to go to Cherry Street, to MW Enterprises. Go upstairs and find Mrs. Abrahms. You got that? Mrs. Abrahms at MW Enterprises. Tell her Mrs. Luminov needs her this afternoon at two to watch the children.

You don't have to talk to anyone else. Do you have all that, Moishe?"

The boy nodded vigorously and repeated what she had said word for word in a breathless stream. When he saw her nod in approval, he was once again off running. She watched him darting and threading past the other people on the street until he disappeared around the corner, and then she went back upstairs.

She took extra care in selecting the dress she wanted to wear, finally choosing a long green walking dress that matched the color of her eyes and was cut with the new full leg-of-mutton sleeves.

"How clever of you to have thought of designing me an ensemble just for bicycling," Natalie Worthington said as she sifted through the pile of sketches Marya had spread out on the table before her. "Now I will be able to take on Central Park in style. You have heard, I imagine, that unfortunately, some dreadful elements have started to cycle as well." Her frown of disapproval changed to a smile as she saw one of the sketches she particularly liked. Then she resumed her frown. "That musical comedy actress, Lillian Russell, has been seen on a simply garish bicycle, completely gold-plated with jewels set in the spokes and the handlebars made out of mother-of-pearl."

Marya started to laugh.

"Yes, dear, it is ludicrous, isn't it. You do very well to laugh. Everyone says it must have been a gift from that garish Diamond Jim Brady. He's a friend of hers, you know. Ah, this is the one," she said suddenly, pointing to a tightly cinched jacket with wide lapels and leg-of-mutton sleeves shown over a tailored midcalf skirt and a mannish shirt.

"I've got it!" She clapped her hands. "We'll put together a bicycling party. Tell me, Marya, would you like to come along on this outing? It would be loads of fun and good for your business. There are some people who have been asking after you, not having seen you in ever so long. Where were you, anyway?"

Marya started to say that she'd been home with her "Oriental" husband and to tell her about the fire and their struggle to start the ladies' line anew, then changed her mind and said, "I was busy doing some other designs for another client."

"Oh, who?"

"MW Enterprises."

"Never heard of them. Ready-to-wear?" she asked idly.

"Yes."

"Oh," she replied, her voice dropping with lack of interest. Then she went back to planning her bicycle tour.

"But I don't know how to ride one of those things," said Marya, who had little enthusiasm for this outing.

"Oh, it's easy," Natalie had assured her. "You'll catch right on."

The bicycling tour was scheduled for two Sundays from then. Marya did not tell Wolf that she had started designing original dresses again for "the Four Hundred" as New York's fashionable circle of "those that mattered" was dubbed. Nor did she tell him she had been invited to go bicycling. She quietly made arrangements for Mrs. Abrahms to watch the children, although she knew that it was just a matter of time before Sol or Mario mentioned to him where Mrs. Abrahms was starting to spend her afternoons again.

This time Mrs. Worthington had made no secret of the fact that she was inviting gentlemen to their little affair as well. Among those she was inviting, she told Marya, was Andrew Markingham because he had asked about her the most often.

What difference did it make, thought Marya. She barely knew him. Nevertheless, in the next two weeks, she did find herself thinking of him from time to time and wondering if they would have more of a chance to talk than they'd had last time, and if they did have more of a chance, she wasn't sure what she would have to say anyway.

That Sunday, while Wolf was at the shop, she dressed in the new cycling skirt she had fashioned for herself, having taken care not to make it too much like that of Natalie Worthington's, and placed on her head one of the latest stylish boaters. The effect, she decided as she assessed herself in the mirror, was just right.

The plan was for the group, which was made up of about twenty of Natalie Worthington's friends, to ride through Central Park, then continue on Riverside Drive to the site of Grant's Memorial. They would have an early supper at the Claremont Inn nearby, where they would be able to sit outdoors in the garden festooned with colorful Japanese lanterns. Then they would return home, retracing their way along Riverside Drive.

Marya did not find cycling nearly as easy as Natalie had promised. Because she felt she might fall at any moment, she was afraid to go very fast, and her bicycle wobbled unsteadily.

"You have to maintain a certain speed," explained Andrew Markingham, who had lingered in the back of the group with her, "just to keep your balance." He had been unable to keep his eyes off her from the moment she had arrived, and he was glad to have this excuse to stay by her side. He continued to offer her tips and encouragement, and would steady her bicycle with his own hand when it looked like she might be losing control.

Gradually she started to feel that she was learning the secret to keeping the bicycle from wobbling. "This is beginning to be fun," she said at one point after she had had no close calls for the last fifteen minutes. It gratified her, too, to see that there were lots of other novices here and there peddling tentatively along.

She was surprised at how kind and attentive Andrew Markingham continued to be throughout the afternoon. She would often look over at him, confidently cycling next to her, and find his intense blue eyes looking at her. She was surprised by how easily conversation had come between them and remembered how she had once thought she wouldn't know what to say to him.

"You're from Russia, aren't you," he asked her at one point.

"Yes."

"From what part?"

"A very small town in the Smolensk Guberniya, which means in the district of Smolensk," she added, translating the unfamiliar term for him. "That's in the republic called Great Russia, not too far from the upper Dnieper River."

"I've heard of it," he said. "The city of Smolensk and of course the Dnieper River. It's very famous."

"I'm surprised. Most Americans know almost nothing about any place outside of this country unless it's one of the major capitals like London or Paris."

"Some of us have had an opportunity to read more than others," he said and smiled.

She noticed that when he smiled, small lines formed by his eyes that made him look slightly older, just as she would expect someone who had read a lot to look.

During dinner he made sure he sat next to her and again they talked. She found him to be not at all like the other members of Natalie Worthington's set. He appeared to measure his words before he spoke and he was always able to see both sides of a controversial topic of discussion, so that while he did have his own opinions, he was not so intransigent as to be unable to concede some points to the opposite side.

By the time they rode back home under the trees of Riverside Drive, it was twilight and the lights from the other bicycles glimmered in the dusk. By the time they reached Central Park again, the members of the party were now dark shapes situated above a flicker of light.

"I had no idea we would be returning so late and after dark," Marya said. "I have to get home at once." She knew Wolf would be worried about her and she had no idea what she was going to tell him about what had kept her so late.

"The fastest and most comfortable way for you to get anywhere you're going in this city, Mrs. Luminov, is still by carriage," said Andrew Markingham. "You must permit me to offer you mine."

"That's very kind, Mr. Markingham, but I couldn't."

"No, you must," he countered gently. "I insist." Then, sensing her reluctance might be because of where she lived or the fact that she was married, he added, "I can drop you at any point you wish. And I can assure you that if you must get home quickly, this is the best way."

Marya thought for a moment, then said hastily, "Very well, you might take me to Corlear's Park." From there she figured she would be able to walk home in a short time.

Andrew raised his eyebrows at the mention of Corlear's Park but said nothing. He led her to his carriage, a dark brown sedan with a collapsible top, and sporting the fashionable new rubber wheels. His driver had been waiting nearby all this time and now sprung to open the door for his employer, then climbed to his high seat in the front.

Inside Marya sat back carefully against the plush cushions. Andrew Markingham placed himself next to her, leaving a respectable distance between them.

The ride was surprisingly smooth and the usual clatter from the paving stones was muted by the rubber of the wheels. As they crossed under the clanking Ninth Street el, Marya was glad to be in the quiet luxury of the landau.

They rode for a while in silence until Andrew Markingham broke it. "You're very easy on the spirit,

Marya. You don't mind if I use your first name, do you? I'd like you to call me by mine."

"Not at all, Andrew. Please do."

"There's a gentleness about you, combined with hardheadedness. That's a blend I find very engaging."

"Thank you, Andrew," she said. She was acutely aware of feeling two sensations at once. On the one hand she wanted him to stop, as she feared that he might say something to which she wouldn't know how to respond. On the other hand, his words were soft and kind and it pleased her that a person of Andrew Markingham's caliber foud more than her beauty appealing and wanted to say these things to her.

Suddenly she felt his hand move on the seat to cover hers. "I hope there will be occasion for us to see each other again."

"Perhaps." She felt his eyes boring into her and had to turn her face the other way.

They were passing through the infamous Tenderloin District with its bright saloons and dance halls and prostitutes who stood openly on the roadways. The streets were thronged in her area of the city as well, but it was by and large with a different kind of person.

To her surprise, Andrew signaled the driver to stop. Then he stepped out and said something to him she couldn't hear. The driver returned a few minutes later with a large bouquet of long-stemmed, deep red roses.

As Andrew handed them to her he said, "These are our new American Beauty roses. I am giving them to a woman who has truly become a new American Beauty."

As she held them in her arms, the wonderfully sweet scent wafted upward. No man but Wolf had ever given her flowers, and red ones at that. She knew that yellow flowers stood for friendship, red flowers for love. She wondered if Andrew, as an American, was aware of this old country significance to the color of the flowers he had given her.

By now they had ridden over via Broadway to the area south of Fourteenth Street. Out the window she now saw the familiar mixture of her streets. There were signs in Russian and Yiddish, scholarly looking old men in long caftans, plump women covered in folds of fabric from head to toe, men and women whose faces were drawn with fatigue carrying home their dinner of pumpernickel bread or a half-rotting fish wrapped in coarse brown paper or dropped into a frayed shopping bag.

Andrew too had been looking out the window and observing the change in scenery. "This is another country down here, almost another world," he said almost under his breath.

Marya knew that he did not mean his words to be unkind, yet she felt herself wince.

He turned to her again. "Please, Marya, let me take you a little farther. Corlear's Park is notoriously dangerous. There have been reports of an unscrupulous gang that congregates there. I couldn't think of abandoning you at that place."

She told him he might take her to East Broadway where she would feel quite safe. On no account did she want him to take her to where she lived.

"East Broadway," he called to his driver. Immediately he turned back to her. "Marya, this is ridiculous. Let me take you directly to your building. It's the safest and quickest way."

She shook her head resolutely. "East Broadway will be quite fine." She could take no chance of having Wolf see her step from an elegant carriage, and even worse yet, catching a glimpse of the handsome gentleman inside.

As they entered the broad boulevard, Andrew again put his hand on hers. Before he could say anything, she quickly said, "Thank you, Mr. Mar— Andrew. Without your help today I would have surely landed on my face more than once. Thanks to your patient assistance, I now know how to ride one of those things." She felt him staring at her again.

"It's because of you that the bicycle tour was so marvelous today, Marya."

Before she realized what was happening, he leaned very close to her and gently kissed her on the lips.

During the duration of the kiss, everything crystalized for Marya. She longed to give in to his embrace and this slow and tender kiss, but felt herself standing on a tightrope. With this kiss, she knew she was capable of forever changing the nature of her marriage. To allow Andrew Markingham to kiss her again would be to give her assent to seeing him again and to a romance. She would become his mistress. His lips were soft and inviting. It would be so easy and such a pleasurable decision to make. But despite Wolf's betrayal of her, she wasn't ready somehow to do the same to him.

She pulled away from the warmth of his body. "Thank you, Andrew," she said, and didn't know what else to say.

"I'm confident we will see each other again soon." He leaned forward and rapped on the landau's front as a signal to the driver.

The carriage came to a stop. "East Broadway it is, sir," called the driver. He held the door open so that Andrew and Marya could exit. As they stepped from the carriage, Marya was aware of the stares they were receiving from the people passing by. Clearly Andrew Markingham and his elegant landau were not from this part of town, and dressed as she was in her fashionably short bicycling skirt, neither did she appear to be. She smiled to herself as she realized that passers-by thought of her as one of the Four Hundred.

Wolf was still sitting in the chair he had been in when it still had been light outside. It was dark now, and he hadn't bothered to light the gas lamp. When he had gotten home a few hours ago, he had been surprised to see that Mrs. Abrahms was still there and Marya wasn't. Mrs. Abrahms had told him Elke and Daniel were hungry and he had done his best to find them something to eat. Then he had sat in the chair, where he still was, and let them have the run of the flat. He kept going over the details of the last two weeks: Marya's sudden coldness to him, precipitated as far as he could tell by nothing. She had taken to coming to bed later than he and rising earlier. It seemed he could never manage to get her alone. Always she was with Elke or Daniel and too engrossed in what she was doing to give him her attention. The attempts he had made to get her to talk had failed. He had learned today that Mrs. Abrahms had resumed her frequent babysitting and that told him that Marya had resumed her trips uptown. Now she was out later than she ever had been before.

The door opened and Marya came in. Wolf jumped to his feet. "Where have you been?"

Marya saw him survey the way she was dressed. "I've been with Natalie Worthington."

"You've been with Natalie Worthington, dressed like that?"

"Yes. She invited me to go bicycling."

"Why would Natalie Worthington invite her hired help to go bicycling?"

Marya bristled at the rancor in his voice. "I designed a bicycling costume for her. She thought it might help my business if I were to join her and be seen. And I resent this interrogation. You make me sound like a criminal."

"You belong at home making dinner for your family. I can't believe that all these hours you spend out of the house are just to further your business. It makes me wonder just what your business is."

Before she realized what had happened, she had slapped him across the face. The anger she had been holding in these past two weeks came flooding out of her. "How dare you! How dare you question my business when, until our tenement burned to the ground, you were the one out night after night. And I'm sure you weren't just with that Sicilian friend in all those low-life cafés!"

She felt herself getting dangerously close to saying something she didn't want to say, to something once said would change their marriage forever. It took all she had to rein herself in. She abruptly stopped talking, and she and Wolf stared at each other for a moment in open hostility, until she broke the impasse and ran into the other room.

She snatched the straw boater from her head and threw it on the bed. Maybe she should have let Andrew Markingham make love to her, she thought. Maybe she should have made more definite plans to see him again, as he so clearly wanted her to do. All that Wolf cared about was having her home to take care of the children and his meals. And his enormous pride, his colossal arrogance, was wounded to think she might prefer some other company to his, even though he had so clearly and so recently preferred other company to hers.

She heard the outside door slam and then heavy footsteps in the hallway. She knew where he was going, but she wouldn't think about it. Instead she would think about tomorrow. She had an appointment to see Natalie Worthington at the new Waldorf Hotel for lunching out, which, with that hotel's famous cuisine and luxury, had suddenly become fashionable as the place to be seen. She promised herself she would dress very, very carefully for just perhaps she would encounter Andrew Markingham there.

She was fast asleep by the time Wolf finished his walk up and down South Street and let himself in.

The next afternoon as Wolf climbed the two flights of stairs that led to MW Enterprises on the second floor of a twenty-year-old brick building, his mind was on two things at once: the outstanding progress the women's line was starting to show again, and Marya's return to hiring herself out to the fashionable circles uptown. He preferred to think about the business, for that, at least, was good news. It had taken three months, but they had started to make their first profits. At this very moment he owned all the machines and other equipment outright as well as a sizable inventory of cloth. He was enough ahead to have the pay for the crew for the next two weeks, as well as the rent on both the workshop and the flat, with still a modest amount left over to re-invest in more inventory, and he felt very satisfied that at least the business was going well, even if its two namesakes weren't.

The woman standing in the corner at the top of the second landing had to call more than once to break through his thoughts.

"Wolf!"

He looked up and even in the dim light he could see clearly one of the last persons he would have expected to see.

"Etta? What are you doing here?" Foolish question, he said to himself. She was waiting for him, it was obvious. He saw at once that the boy wasn't with her.

"I have to talk to you." Her voice was low and urgent.

Inside he could hear the hum of the machines and the thump of the pressing irons. "We can talk better here than in there," he said, nodding toward the door where MW Enterprises was stenciled in neat red letters.

"It's about Zavel," she whispered. "He's sick."

"What is it?" He knew his voice sounded controlled, even indifferent, but inside his pulse was racing.

"I don't know. He just lies in the bed and cries and he's hot all over."

"Did the doctor come? What did he say?"

She looked at the floor and he could see she was on the verge of crying. "I haven't gone to get him yet.

It's been hard, Wolf, so hard. . . ." Her voice trailed off as her sobs overcame her.

He put his arm around her shoulder to steady her.

She began anew. "If you only knew how unhappy Moses has been. All he says, over and over, is how he wants to go back to the old country. He isn't happy here in America. He doesn't work; his wares, all those pots and dishpans, just sit in the corner of our room gathering dust. I have to beg him to work when there's no more food in the place and no money to buy any. Then he goes out for a little while, just long enough to bring back some money so we can eat for another day or two." She looked up at him, and standing so close to her, he was shocked to see how much older she looked. He could now see the fatigue lines etched in her face and the puffiness under her eyes.

"I know he would never run away and leave me like so many men do."

Wolf thought of the many advertisements he had seen in the Yiddish papers for missing husbands on the Lower East Side who had abandoned their families and the squalor of their lives in what was supposed to be the country with streets paved with gold.

"But I'm afraid of something worse." Her voice was barely audible. "I'm afraid he might kill himself."

"He talks about it then?" Wolf asked quietly.

"Yes. Sometimes. But most of the time he talks about how he wants to go back to Warsaw." The desperation in her voice turned to extreme fatigue. "Now with Zavel sick, I don't know what I'm going to do. I thought maybe I could get some kind of work again, nothing too hard because I still have Zavel to take care of. But Moses could help take care of him during the day while I'm working. He loves him like a—"

Her words were interrupted by Wolf pulling from his pocket a wad of bills. He pressed the money into her hand. "This is for the doctor. You must get a doctor right away for Zavel. I insist."

"But this is too much. I need only a dollar for the

doctor, or just half a dollar if instead I take Zavel to his office."

"Get the doctor to come to your place, as often as you need him."

"This is still too much, Wolf." She attempted to place half the money back in his hands.

He resisted her. "Keep it."

He saw her body tense. "No, Wolf! It is too much. You cannot. I will not accept it." She stepped back in indignation. "The money to pay the doctor for Zavel, yes, that I'll take. The rest, no."

"You have no right to say no. Think of Zavel. It is all for him. You will take this money and buy three tickets that will take you to Hamburg. From Hamburg you will be able to get a train that will take you back to Warsaw, just the way you both probably came."

She shook her head and started to cry again.

"It is a loan, Etta, nothing more. A loan for Zavel."

Her voice trembled as she said, "But I haven't even paid you back for the other loan you gave us. And this one is for so much more."

"You can pay me back when you're all back in Warsaw and things are going well for you again."

"I don't know what to tell Moses. He'll want to know where I got all this money."

"Just present him the tickets, already paid for. He won't ask too many questions. If he does, you can tell him it was money you earned as a surprise for him by doing sewing work while he was out on the streets. Make it a gift."

"I—I don't know."

But Wolf knew. He knew Moses was too defeated to ask too many questions once he saw the actual tickets right in front of him.

As she turned to leave, Wolf stopped her and took her chin in his hand. "You must let me hear about you, about you and the boy. Every two years you must send me word here at the shop."

She managed a smile. "Yes, Wolf. I promise. And I promise to pay you back too. I really will."

"I'm in no hurry," he said. Then, while he listened to her footsteps as she hurried down the stairs, he began to think about where he would get the money for the upcoming rent on both the flat and MW Enterprises and another source of inventory.

Marya held her chin high as she walked the three hundred feet of Peacock's Alley, the nickname given to the Waldorf's wide corridor of honey-colored marble. Heads turned to watch prominent and fashionable women promenade through the hotel.

She was to meet Natalie at one o'clock in the Palm Garden. She heard Natalie's familiar dulcet tones call to her as she neared the end of the corridor. She and Natalie were lightly bussing each other on the cheek when a masculine voice sounded behind them.

"Ah, Mrs. Worthington! What a pleasure indeed!"

Marya turned to see a tall, dignified looking man on the portly side who hurried forward and greeted Natalie effusively.

"Mrs. Luminov," Natalie said as she turned back to Marya, "this is Oscar, the maitre d'hotel. He will be a positive genius at suggesting the very best plates for us."

As they made their entrance and continued past the sea of tables, Marya was aware of all the eyes on them. Except for one pair of eyes, all else was a blur to her on this her first visit to this famous room that had become all the vogue of Fifth Avenue. The eyes, which were a deep green, belonged to a boy, almost a young man, of twelve or thirteen.

Something about them disturbed her so much she lost all realization of where she was.

PART II

"Sharper than a serpent's tooth . . ."
from *King Lear*

1900-1913

Chapter 13

"Wait here. I'll be back in a few minutes," his father had said to him. So Daniel was waiting as he had been told. He sat on the edge of his bed and studied himself in the mirror. He saw black eyes that stared back at him from a face that was wide and open, with high cheekbones and a strong jaw. He had neither his father's nor his mother's hair for his was a mass of unruly brown curls, but he did have his father's eyes and frame, and of that he was very proud. The expression on his face was calm, even controlled, and not unlike that of his father, as people often pointed out. Of that similarity too, he was proud.

But today his outward appearance belied the excitement he felt inside. This was the day it seemed like he had been waiting for his entire life. Now he was thirteen years old, a man. How many times had his father said to him, "I am doing this all for you. One day this will all be yours," and he would wave his hand in a circle over his head to indicate first the small workroom where MW Enterprises started out, then the larger workrooms in an East Side tenement on Greene Street and more lately the small factory on Broadway that the business had now grown into, taking its place alongside the rows of bigger factories.

"When you grow up, when you become a man," his father would always say when Daniel would ask him when the time would come that they could be partners. For that is what Daniel had been promised, to be partners first, and then one day when his father retired, he would become the sole manager, the sole owner of whatever his father and he had acquired. To that end, Daniel had consecrated his entire life. Whatever his father had asked of him, he had done, and more. Now the day had finally come when he could stand alongside his father as a man in his own right.

He thought of how beautiful Elke and his mother had looked when he sat next to them on the way to his bar mitzvah. The ceremony had been everything that he could have dreamed of. The temple had been full of well-wishers, and he had practiced in advance the section of the Torah that he was to read, and worked especially hard on the chant for the selection from the Prophets so that he was able to perform without a flaw. He had seen his father looking at him proudly, and although he couldn't see his mother and Elke where they sat in the women's section, he knew they too were proud of him. He knew his mother hadn't cared whether he made his bar mitzvah or not, but his father had been adamant that he would, and Daniel was thankful she hadn't stood in his way.

He heard his father's footsteps in the hallway, then the door opened and Wolf filled the doorway.

"Get your jacket, son," he said. "I want to take you somewhere."

Daniel hurried to get his coat, then stood next to his father.

They were now almost of the same height, and Wolf realized it was likely that Daniel would eventually be even taller. He knew this was an important day for his son and he hoped what he had planned would make it even more memorable. He put his arms on

Daniel's shoulders. "You're a man now, Daniel. I'm very proud of you. The vow of manhood you took today, and the Prayer of Release I said are just one part of your step into your new life. I want you to take the rest of the step."

Daniel tried to keep his excitement from showing as his father led him down the stairs and into the streets. He couldn't help but wonder if they were going to the factory. Perhaps his father was going to show him the papers that said half the business was his, or perhaps he was going to make his statement there, amid the machines and the yardage, where it would be especially significant.

As the carriage Wolf had hired turned west onto Forty-second Street, Daniel realized they weren't going to the factory, for it lay in the other direction, further down Broadway. His father signaled for the driver to stop, and they stepped out of the carriage into the animation and agitation of the Tenderloin District.

Running from Madison Square to Forty-eighth Street, between Fifth and Ninth Avenues was a "village" devoted to the pursuit of pleasure and crowded with dance halls, saloons, brothels, disreputable hotels and gambling houses. Daniel had never been in this area of town before, although he had heard of it. He saw a sign over a door that read "Haymarket," and he recognized it as the name of that lurid dance hall which was also a restaurant and variety show. It was the place where rumor had it that even Diamond Jim Brady, when he visited there, left his jewels at home and where the women were as gaudy and loud as the variety shows. They turned into a darkly lit street and went behind one of the many improvised wooden fences erected in front of various houses on that particular street.

Wolf sounded the brass knocker and almost immediately an incredibly beautiful woman opened the door. Daniel stared at her. His mother and sister were beautiful, but they did not look like this woman. She had long blonde hair that fell in ringlets down her shoulders and she was wearing a tight red and white striped dress made of satin and velvet, and the top was cut so low that Daniel couldn't help but focus his eyes on the swell of her breasts. He was surprised to see the look she gave his father and even more surprised when she then turned and looked at him the same way. When they followed her into the house and up the stairs, they came out into a large room full of well-dressed gentlemen and beautiful women. A petite dark-haired woman swooped toward them and Wolf put out his hand to greet her. She shook it daintily, then looked at Daniel questioningly.

"This is my son, Daniel. Today he is thirteen years old. He's become a man," Wolf said.

The woman's eyebrows lifted slightly as she appreciated the significance of what Wolf was saying. Then her face broke into a big smile and she extended her hand. "How do you do, Daniel? I am Madame Dubeau. It is a pleasure to have you with us on such a momentous occasion. We will do our very best to make it a day you will never forget." Her voice was as thick as honey and she was still holding on to Daniel's hand when she turned back to Wolf. "I have someone very special in mind for Daniel. Leave it to me."

Daniel realized what kind of place he was in, even though he had never been to one before and had only heard stories. Now he knew that this was part of what his father meant by entering into manhood and he was overwhelmed by the thought. He couldn't help but be excited and nervous about what his father had in mind for him and what was about to take place. His palms were sweaty. He hoped that whatever happened, his father would be pleased with him. At the same time he couldn't get out of his mind his anticipation about going to the factory. His father must be planning to take him afterward, he told himself, but he would rather have gone there first, in spite of the excitement that was growing in him as he looked at the enticing array of women before him. Daniel watched as Madame Dubeau went up to a woman whom he could only see from the back. She had extremely long dark black hair, long enough for her to be able to sit on, and she appeared to be very slim. As soon as she turned, Daniel saw at once that she was Chinese, very pretty and not much older than he. He had not seen many Chinese girls before. Whenever he went into the neighborhood between Pell and Mott Streets known as Chinatown, he saw mostly men with pigtails dressed all alike in Chinese costume, but few women, especially young, pretty ones like this girl.

Madame Dubeau took the girl by the hand and led her to where Wolf and Daniel were waiting. "This is Sue Fen," she made the introductions. "Sue Fen, this is Wolf and his son, Daniel."

"I approve." Wolf laughed as he looked at Madame Dubeau.

The girl's eyes widened slightly as she looked from father to son, both of whom were handsome men, and then she bowed gracefully. She took Daniel by the hand and led him upstairs.

The room they went into was small but ornate. The walls were papered in peach-colored velvet and the bed was draped in a velvet coverlet of the same color. From the moment they entered the room Daniel could not take his eyes from the bed. He scarcely looked at Sue Fen until she sat down directly in front of him on its edge. Slowly, without taking her eyes from him, she began to unfasten the top buttons on her dress. She let the edges of her bodice fall and Daniel could see the curve of her bare breasts. She beckoned for him to unbutton the rest.

He sat beside her on the bed and his fingers felt frozen. With difficulty, he managed to undo the remaining buttons until the top of her dress was completely open. Lifting her long hair behind her head, she turned so that he could release the buttons that held her skirt. Then she stood and stepped from the dress,

now clad only in a thin, sheer petticoat under which he
could see she was wearing nothing. He had never seen
a naked woman before and he found himself staring at
the dark triangle between her legs. With an almost imperceptible flick of her hand the petticoat was undone
and it fell to her feet. She stood before him completely
naked and he couldn't take his eyes from the curves of
her womanly beauty. She stepped toward him and began to help him from his clothes. Then she pulled him
toward her onto the soft bed.

She took his right hand and placed it on her
breast. Daniel thought he had never felt anything that
soft before and quickly put his free hand on her other
breast. Still holding onto his hand, she moved it gently
in circles around and around her breasts until he was
surprised to see the skin of her nipples dimple and feel
them harden under his palms. Then she moved his
hand down her smooth belly and brushed it between
her legs and as she did so, she drew in her breath and
moaned softly.

Daniel felt stirrings in him that pushed from his
mind all the eagerness he had felt to go to the factory
and instead replaced it with total surrender to the incredible sensations that were building within him at
this moment. With her other hand, Sue Fen began to
stroke his body, moving slowly from his chest down
across his waist and then finally to his groin. Daniel
had begun to quiver all over as he felt himself stiffen
and become harder than his imagination had ever before been able to make him.

She put her mouth against his and as she felt him
respond to her kiss, she started to tease his mouth with
her tongue. His longing for her began to build itself
into an ache and then an overpowering urge so that he
slipped his hands beneath the skin of her buttocks,
smooth as satin, and pulled her urgently against him.
Rhythmically, she began to undulate her hips against
his, as she all the time continued to stroke his groin
and tease him with her tongue. She guided his hand

again between her legs and pushed him to explore there. As he touched the sweet wetness of her, her moaning became louder and he felt he was going to explode. Quickening the undulations of her body, Sue Fen parted her legs to receive him, and he moved toward her in the full throes of his passion. And then, before he could climax within her, he felt himself exploding everywhere, his desire already driven to its ultimate.

As they walked back along the streets, Wolf noticed that his son didn't look happy. "Is something wrong, Daniel?"

"No," he said, trying to mask his voice. He knew he could never tell his father of the sickening feeling he had inside him. How could he tell his father that he had failed him, that he had been unable to perform like a man with Sue Fen? His father would never understand, for Daniel was sure such a thing had never happened to him, even once. Sue Fen had been very understanding and reassuring, but that had only made him feel worse. She had waited a period of time, then began to caress him again, and although her touch had felt good, he had not become aroused a second time.

His thoughts of the factory and what was awaiting him there were no longer held at bay and they had crowded in on him, filling him with anxiety. He hadn't seen how he could have explained any of that to Sue Fen, so he had said nothing. She probably didn't even speak English, he had told himself, since she had only smiled at him, never once saying a word. Now all Daniel wanted was to get to the factory as soon as possible. That was all he had wanted in the first place, and that had been the problem. He had been unable to get from his mind the thought of him and his father alone in the factory. There his father finally would present him the legal documents that would acknowledge him as his partner in the business and thereby as a worthy man. Sue Fen was beautiful, but Daniel had not just then, on that all important day, wanted a woman. It was his father's recognition he wanted. Now he could hardly wait to get to the factory, where he knew he would be able to put aside the memory of what had just transpired.

They walked from Seventh Avenue to Thirty-fourth Street and then over to Sixth. At Sixth Avenue when Wolf turned left, Daniel was so astonished he stopped cold. "But the factory's this way!" he blurted out before he could stop himself.

"The factory? Why would we want to go to the factory at this time of night?" Wolf said and kept walking. "What you need now is to get some sleep. You've had enough excitement for one day."

"But today was my bar mitzvah. I'm a man now. You said so yourself." He stopped. He saw that his father didn't have the slightest idea of what he was intimating. Daniel just stood there and couldn't move.

"That's why I took you to Madame Dubeau. You've entered your thirteenth year in a style any young man would envy. Now come on. Let's go." He looked at Daniel who was still standing in the same spot, his face visibly white even in the dimness of the gaslight on the corner. "What's the matter? You're certainly not acting like a fellow who just had his bar mitzvah and his first woman. Are you coming down with something?"

It took everything Daniel had to get himself to start walking again. So it was not to be. So his father wasn't going to present him with his share of the business after all. So his father was not yet ready to recognize him as an equal. He didn't know in what way he had failed him, but he must have.

His father's voice cut through his thoughts. "What would you want to go to the factory for tonight?"

"You promised me."

"I promised you what?" Wolf looked genuinely perplexed.

Daniel saw no choice but to spill out what had

preoccupied him completely this last year. "You said that when I became a man, I would be your partner. I would have a share of the business."

Wolf started to laugh, then stopped. "So that's it. That's what's behind your long face."

Daniel's pulse was racing so loud he could swear his father could hear it from where he stood a few feet away. He told himself he was too old to cry.

"You thought I would take you to the factory and have some kind of small ceremony where I made you my official partner? Is that it?" Wolf asked with an incredulous tone that was slowly changing to one of comprehension.

David swallowed hard and nodded his head yes.

Wolf put his hand on Daniel's shoulder. "My son, I never intended to do that tonight. I never intended to take you to the factory or to present you with legal documents as you hoped. You're not ready yet, Daniel. The time is coming," he repeated, "but you're not quite ready."

Daniel tried to keep his voice from wavering. "Why not? I'm a man now."

"There are many responsibilities that go with having a business."

"I know them already, Papa. I have been watching and learning everything you do for as long as I can remember. I can do anything. I can cut and baste and stitch and finish and press. I know everything that Sol knows and even Mario. I—"

Wolf silenced him. "There are still more things you don't know, Daniel. There will come a time when you'll be ready, but that time isn't now."

Daniel stared at Wolf, his eyes open wide with some emotion Wolf couldn't read. Wolf felt it necessary to explain further. "Daniel, you must remember I always consider you my partner, even now though you aren't my legal partner. To me you are already official, and when the time is right, we will sign the formal papers. But for now, you must wait. Do you understand?"

"Yes," Daniel said glumly and fought back tears of disappointment.

Elke was sitting in a chair reading when Wolf and Daniel came in. At fourteen, she scarcely knew what to do with her long legs. It seemed that all her growth had taken place in her legs and nowadays when she sat down they were always getting in the way. This evening she had managed to reach a comfortable compromise with them by draping them over the edge of the chair and propping her book up against her thighs. She had been lost in Sir Walter Scott's *The Lady of the Lake* when she heard the footsteps of her father and brother on the porch outside.

She quickly glanced from one to the other. Her father appeared to be in a good mood, but she was surprised to see the expression on Daniel's face. Never had she seen Daniel anything but ecstatic in his father's presence.

"Hello, Elke," her father greeted. Daniel said nothing and didn't look up.

"Hello, Papa. Hello, Daniel."

Daniel still didn't respond and headed immediately for his room. Elke was doubly perplexed. Today being his bar mitzvah and his having just spent several hours with his father, she couldn't understand why he would look so disheartened. She looked at her father expectantly and hoped he would sit down and talk to her for a while.

"It was a beautiful ceremony this morning, Papa, didn't you think?"

"Yes." He went to the desk and picked up a stack of papers.

"It was one of the most beautiful I think I've ever seen."

"That it was, Elkeleh," he said absently.

She loved it when he called her Elkeleh, but still

she wished he would look at her. It seemed he almost never did anymore, not in the last two years anyway.

He took the sheaf of papers and sat in the other chair. She knew the papers were receipts and invoices from the business and that there would be little chance she could reach him once he started in on them. She went back to her reading but found that Sir Walter Scott couldn't compete with the thoughts that had begun to absorb her mind. She stared at her father where he sat under the pool of light from the new electric lamp. He always looked like the heroes in the stories she read—tall, broad-shouldered, with strong features and eyes that seemed to see everything.

She liked to think about one time recently when her mother had been lamenting about her as they all sat around the table. It wasn't her mother's complaint she liked to think about, though, it was her father's response. "Elke, you spend so much time with your books. You sit in your room all day reading so that we hardly know what you look like anymore. And if your family doesn't even know, how can you expect the young men in the neighborhood to have a chance to take notice?"

She had felt her father staring at her intently from her head down to her waist. "When Elke is ready, there is not a man in Manhattan who won't take notice, Marya."

She had blushed but was secretly pleased he had been looking at her. So many times it seemed he went out of his way not to look at her, and when their eyes did meet by accident, he quickly glanced away.

Another time, a few years ago, he had caught her slumped over at the dinner table. "Sit up," he ordered. "If you don't sit up straight, your chest won't develop right." It was a measure of how much she wanted his attention that even though his frank words had been mortifying, she had been glad he had noticed her.

Daniel was treated with more importance, of that she was well aware. She thought of the many times he had come home and asked first for Daniel, pulled Daniel to him for a kiss before he gave her one, and of the special outings he had taken Daniel on but not her.

Her mother had tried to explain. "There are certain things a father wants to do with his son, and certain other things he wants his daughter's company for." But Elke could tell from the look in her mother's eye that she didn't believe her own words. Elke had not been satisfied and was aware her mother had just been trying to reassure her. She couldn't for the life of her recall an occasion when her father had preferred her company to that of her brother.

"Your father adores you. He's so proud of how pretty and dainty you are," her mother had added. Elke had felt like a beautiful but useless doll when her mother had said that.

One of the things she remembered most of all about growing up was the look of adoration always on Daniel's face whenever he looked at his father. She wondered what expression her own face had carried and whether her father had looked past her red hair and green eyes so like her mother's. She remembered how when Daniel was still a small boy, he tried to imitate Papa's walk, his tone of voice and some of his expressions. Everyone always thought that was cute, everyone except her mother. Elke had noticed how her mother had found it hard to delight in Daniel's blind emulation of his father.

When she thought of her mother, Elke always felt warm inside. She knew that her mother loved her completely and unconditionally and wanted the best for her. The only problem was that her mother so often wasn't home and when she was, she was busy with her commissions from her shop and from her fancy patrons. So Elke had turned increasingly to her books, and it was they who spoke to her more than any person.

As if he had been reading her thoughts, she heard

her father say, "I wonder what's keeping your mother. She should have been home long ago."

Elke didn't know what to say. She tried to keep out of the arguments that developed between her parents. Still, she too wondered where her mother was.

She went back to her reading and Wolf to his papers, but both were aware of the clock ticking on the curio cabinet filled with the family's *chachkahs*. Finally they heard Marya's footsteps on the stoop. Elke saw at once that her mother looked radiant as she stepped through the doorway, and she couldn't help but feel a pang of jealousy. What had made her mother look that way was something other than her own family.

Marya saw Wolf look up, take note of what she was wearing and just as quickly look back down at his work, a frown on his face.

"You've been gone a long time, Marya."

"Have I?" she said lightly. She didn't sound at all disturbed by his tone. She came to Elke and planted a kiss on her cheek. "And what have you been doing all evening, my darling? Reading again?"

"Yes, Mama."

"Just take care not to wrinkle your brow when you read."

"No, Mama," she replied, and saw her mother leave the room, scarcely having looked at her father.

When Wolf opened their bedroom door a few minutes later, Marya was already completely undressed. At the sight of her body, the old feelings kindled in him anew, but he tried to fight them. At thirty-two, Marya was just as beautiful to him as she had always been. She had the fresh glow of a woman in her twenties, and it was hard for him to believe that she had two children almost fully grown. She still turned heads wherever she went, and he was just as proud as ever to have her on his arm. But now the occasion seldom arose.

"There's something I want to talk to you about," he said.

"Oh? What is it?" She tried not to be aware of his eyes moving up and down her as she reached for a negligee. "It's not about my work again, is it? Frankly, I don't think I can take another one of those discussions just now."

"No. Not that. I've given up on that, Marya. I know you'll do what you want and see whomever you want and call it whatever you want."

"I thought you said it wasn't going to be about that."

"It's not. It's about Daniel. I want to start sending him to the textile mills upstate in my place."

"What? He's only thirteen, still a child really."

"He doesn't look like a child. He's taller already than most grown men and he certainly doesn't carry himself like a child."

"No, he carries himself like you. But he isn't you, something I think it's hard for both of you to realize."

"Although he still has a lot to learn, he now knows enough about what's going on to be able to get the job done at the mills. Remember, I wasn't much older than he is when I left St. Petersburg on my own."

"You were four years older, which at that age is a lot, a fourth of your life. And I repeat, Daniel isn't you. He's still too young to be going upstate to the mills by himself."

"Someday this business will be his. I want him to know every aspect inside and out. Now that he's come of age, I'm going to give him even more responsibility."

"I know. First you'll make him a partner, then owner. You've filled his head with that since he was an infant and you put him to work before he was barely able to stand, as I recall."

"You're exaggerating again, Marya, something you seem to do more and more of. It must be the company you keep."

"Ah, now our discussion is back on familiar

ground. Am I to take it that you have nothing more to say about Daniel?"

"Why is it so hard for us to have even a simple discussion about something we have in common, namely our son?"

"Our son? He's more your son. Do what you want, Zavel." Even as she said the words she realized she didn't really mean them. She turned to face him again and her voice let go of its annoyed tone. "Please, Zavel, be careful, for your sake and Daniel's. Sometimes I feel he's too driven, too dedicated to pleasing you. Please don't push him too hard. He worships you, you must know that."

Before he left the room, Wolf said, "I'm doing the best with him I can. He's my only son, Marya, and you know how much he means to me." As he said those words, the image came to him unbidden of young Zavel, Etta's son, of whom he had received no news since one brief note six years ago telling him they'd all arrived safely back in Warsaw. But he had to banish that memory from his thoughts as Marya stood facing him, waiting to say still more about Daniel.

She did know what that meant to him, and for Daniel's sake, she tried to keep the resentment out of her reply and not think about Elke at that particular moment or the reproach that she had not been able to provide him the long line of sons he had wanted. "I don't know how to say this, Zavel, and have it sound right. I know it's natural for a boy to idolize his father. But you're his whole life, and I just hope—"

"You just hope I'm not disappointing him."

"Yes."

He looked at her standing there, her hair now loose and falling down her shoulders onto the ivory-colored negligee. He wanted to say, "Like I disappointed you?" but his pride stopped him. "Don't worry," he said. "I'm looking out for the boy."

Marya said nothing. She was afraid that continuing this discussion would thoroughly sap her of the ex-

hilaration that had swept her through the door. Their
conversation had seriously lessened it already, and she
wanted to cling to what was left. She had been forced
to stay late at her shop as she so often did these days.
Seldom did she mind working in the evening though.
Because it was her own shop, which she had managed
to put together with her own hard work and a little
help from Andrew, she threw herself into it eagerly.
Certainly there had been nothing but discouragement
from Wolf who still wasn't reconciled to her working
and who was even more horrified when she insisted she
was going to establish a little shop on Seventh Avenue.
Even though it was two years ago, she still shuddered
when she remembered their fight. That talk had taken
place in the bedroom too, just as their talk tonight,
only that one had ended on a very different note.

"Why would you want to do such a thing,
Marya?" Wolf had asked her with extreme patience in
his voice when she had first told him of her plan.
"What is behind this compulsion to be out of your
home? Now we have a nice house in a quiet neighborhood. What are you trying to do, make enough money
so you can move to Fifth Avenue with your friends?"

"I've told you and told you. They are my patrons,
not my friends."

"You spend enough time there for them to be
your friends," he had said with a sudden angry leer.
"So you're not gone enough already? Now you want to
be gone even more? To do what? Sit in a shop all
day?"

"It's not that I want to be gone. I want to feel I'm
contributing and that I could sustain us if anything
were to happen to you. I just think it's smart to grab
an opportunity when I see one, that's all."

He took hold of her arm. "Marya, I can grab
enough opportunities for the two of us." His grip
tightened.

She refused to look at him. "Let go, Zavel. You're
hurting me."

He started to release his hold on her, but before he did, he spun her around to face him. "I'd like to know what's behind this fierce push of yours? What happened to you in Russia before I met you? You still keep your lips primly shut whenever anyone asks you about your girlhood. I'd give a lot of money, Marya, to know what went on and what has made you so cold and resistant. One day I'll know."

Her eyes snapped with resentment. "How many times must I tell you. Nothing happened. Nothing at all. I was just left on my own after my family was killed in the pogrom, to take care of myself the best way I could."

"But you're not on your own anymore. You're my wife. You don't have to take care of yourself. What are you trying to do, make a fool out of me? Tell me why you can't be satisfied with being a wife and mother like your friend Leah?"

Marya thought of Leah who lived next door and wanted to laugh in Wolf's face. She and Leah had come from such different backgrounds. Yes, they were both Jews and they both had children, and they both had husbands who worked hard and wanted to make a mark for themselves. But Leah had been born here. Her parents had left Poland when Leah's mother was pregnant with her, and so what did Leah know of what it was like to be forced to survive entirely on her own wits, without husband or family, in a land that offered her no choice but to remarry anyone, it didn't matter whom, just to have a husband?

Marya knew Leah disapproved of how she led her life, although Leah was careful not to say so directly. But Leah was the kind of woman who was content to speak Yiddish to her children the rest of her life and to satisfy herself with running their lives. That was all fine for Leah, Marya thought, but not for her. Life was too full of chance for her ever to think she had found lasting security. Everything changed. A child disappeared;

another child died; a husband was killed; parents were killed; you came to a new country; a new husband came along; a new husband no longer loved you. At any time it could all be gone. She had to accomplish as much as possible while she could.

Wolf was still clenching her arm and his grip tightened yet again. "I've let things go entirely too far, Marya. I should have stopped all this a long time ago."

She drew in her breath and looked at him defiantly. "I don't know what you're talking about."

"Don't be coy, Marya. Of course you do. For years I've been telling you I don't want you to work, that I should be the one who works and that you should stay home where I want you and take care of our children."

Marya's voice began to rise. "I have stayed home and taken care of our family. I'm gone maybe two afternoons a week, Zavel, no more. You make it sound as though I've abandoned you all for the glamorous life of high society, as if you've even forgotten what I look like."

"Sure, you're here, but not in spirit. How many times do I find you with your patterns and designs spread all over the floor, paying more attention to that dressmaker you hired than to Elke and Daniel."

"Elke and Daniel aren't children anymore, and you know very well they don't require constant watching. Half the time they're outside with their friends."

"That's because your real interest is with those Fifth Avenue—"

"Now we're going in circles," Marya said wearily.

"I won't have it, Marya. I will not have my wife spending half her time on snooty Fifth Avenue and the other half in a wretched little shop."

"What do you care if it's wretched, as you call it? You won't have to be part of it."

"What do you mean I won't have to be part of it?

Don't you think everyone will know that my wife has started a seamstress shop, the poor thing? Don't you think that reflects publicly on my ability to succeed?"

Her tone was steady and calm. "I intend to do it, Zavel. I intend to have a shop of my own."

Wolf heard the resolution in her voice but was determined to stay in control. "There's only one way I will permit such a thing."

"Permit!" Marya was incredulous.

"These are the conditions: you may open a shop, but you give up these weekly visits to the homes of your Fifth Avenue friends."

She ignored his deliberate use of the word friends again. "Are you serious?"

"You haven't been the same woman since you became involved with them. And if they want your designs so much, they can come to you. They can find you in your little shop."

"They'll never do that, Zavel, and you know it."

"Then what good are they?" he spat out. "Why must my wife always go to them?" He continued. "My second condition—"

"I don't want to hear about your conditions!" Marya exploded. "I can't believe you're being this high-handed!" With a burst of strength she tore loose from his grip.

Wolf had suddenly turned and opened the door to her wardrobe. One after another he began to pull her gowns from their hangers and throw them on the floor.

"What are you doing!" she cried. "Have you gone crazy?"

Wolf was flinging her shoes and hats through the air. "All of this! It's nothing but an excuse to get away from me! Don't think I don't know it, Marya!"

Acting instinctively, she tried to grab him by the arm, the elbow, the hand, anywhere to stop him. As soon as he felt her touch him, he spun and grasped her arm again and held her even tighter than before. Without realizing that he was doing it, he picked her up and carried her to the bed.

"No, Zavel," Marya cried. "Wait! Not like this!"

But he scarcely heard what she said. He threw her down on the bed and without removing his clothes, he pulled up her negligee, thrust himself between her legs and spent his angry desire within her.

Afterward Marya lay very still. No tears came. She felt a dry emptiness inside and she was frightened. At last she saw the beast in Wolf that she had always feared. She also glimpsed his grim determination to have his way that she had first seen some sixteen years before when he had taken charge of their scraggly group at the border.

He pulled back and looked at her. Their eyes met and he saw in hers a look he had never seen before. He felt overwhelmed with guilt. "Marya, I'm sorry," he whispered hoarsely. "I'm sorry."

She turned her head away. At first she said nothing. thinking about the impasse they had come to. For years she had yearned to have him pull her to him with desire again, the way he used to, but now that it had happened, she felt cheated, as if it were only impersonal lust driving him, fueled by an angry need to dominate her rather than by real desire. She had an intimation that because of what had just happened between them, they would never make love again.

Finally she said softly, "I know how important it is to you that I do not go my separate way. And you must know how important it is to me to work and have something of my own. I can't explain to you why that is, it just is. I will give up my Fifth Avenue patrons, Zavel, but I want to have that shop. I think the best thing would be to affiliate the shop publicly with MW Enterprises. Privately, I'd be on my own. But publicly it should appear that my shop is an extension of MW Enterprises. That way it won't be openly known that your wife has gone into business for herself."

Wolf looked at her and again was overcome with a rush of remorse. "Yes. That would be the best way."

"I'm not asking for your assistance in any way. I'll run the shop on my own."

Marya had found herself turning to Andrew for help, for guidance more than anything else, in regard to the financial aspects of establishing her own shop. Wolf never asked her how she had learned what she needed to know and of course she'd never told him about Andrew's kindly intercession. To get started, she dipped into the box of jewels she still had hidden away. With the money she got from the sale of a ruby necklace and ring, she figured she had more than enough to see her through the first six months until she was established.

She had explained to Andrew what she envisioned. "I have in mind a small, intimate shop where women can come to consult with me and see my designs, where the dressmakers are right on the spot for fittings."

"Then you propose to lure the ladies of Fifth Avenue into your shop?" Andrew had asked with a skeptical lift of his brow that reminded her of Wolf's reaction.

"Maybe they wouldn't come. But I know there are other wealthy ladies, not as rich as those on Fifth Avenue, who would come. Besides, it would just be more convenient all the way around to have my own shop. Now my parlor is cluttered with all my sewing things and I have the dressmaker come there and do the work. It would be a relief to get all that out of my home and into a shop."

"It could be a good idea," Andrew agreed reluctantly.

She didn't tell him that the shop, if profitable, would allow her to provide her children with more advantages and that it would ensure her future should anything ever happen to Wolf. Nor did she tell him about her deal with Wolf and how she had bargained away her high society patrons for the sake of a shop of her own. At least, Marya noticed, Andrew didn't get upset with her the way Wolf had when she had first told him of her idea for the shop. Instead, although not strongly approving of her plan and cautioning her of all the hard work it would take to make a go of it—more work than designing for the socialites had been so far—he had offered to look over all the papers she had to sign and to advise her however he could.

Now, earlier this same evening, as she had sat at her desk in the back of the shop and looked at the racks where the sample designs were hung and at the sewing area to the right where the two dressmakers she had hired worked, she had allowed herself to have a sense of satisfaction in this solid little niche she had managed to carve out for herself.

After her conversation with Wolf this evening about Daniel, she was clinging to what vestiges of satisfaction she could and tried to keep all bitter thoughts away, particularly thoughts about Elke. When Wolf had brought up the subject of Daniel's future tonight, she had automatically thought about Elke's in contrast. Elke was one subject Wolf never brought up on his own. Marya wanted Elke to have the same opportunities she wanted for her son. This was America, wasn't it? With opportunity for all? There was even talk now about women getting the vote, and although it would probably take a long time to happen, it was a measure of the kind of country America was that it was even under consideration. She fervently hoped Elke would never have to experience the bleakness she herself had felt in Russia when she saw the future stretch out narrowly ahead of her with countless limitations on what she as a woman and a Jew would be allowed to do. As a result of her experiences, she wanted for Elke all she had wanted for herself and more. Elke could be a designer, a teacher, a businesswoman, perhaps something even more significant. In this sense, she thought perhaps ironically, what she wanted for Elke was not so far removed from what her husband wanted for Daniel.

Chapter 14

The next afternoon Daniel was at the factory as usual. He had not yet seen his father since their walk home last night and was anxious to see what kind of a mood he was in. He surveyed the rows of machines on this floor and felt a surge of pride in what his father had created, and that pride helped to relieve the sting he felt from his double failure of the night before.

On one side of the large loft were the sewing machines, all owned by MW Enterprises. Wolf did not hire operators with their own machines as many of the contractors and factories did. He reasoned that a man with his own machine was likely to leave sooner, always on the lookout for a few pennies more he might earn somewhere else. Wolf wanted his crew to stay and he offered them as much security as he could muster to ensure that they did. Even if a worker could earn more temporarily by traveling from place to place, in the long run he could earn more by staying with Wolf. To this end he extended the work season a little longer than anyone else so that he could give his crew more than just three months in the summer and three months in the winter.

On the other side of the room hung a fog of steam

from the pressers. Rubber cables and gas lines dangled from the ceiling and led to the pressing tables. Although Wolf had installed ceiling fans in an attempt to lessen the heat and humidity, the men were still stripped to the waist and worked with a fine film of sweat glistening on their bodies. Daniel knew his father had met many times with Sol, his production manager, and Mario, the foreman, in an effort to find some additional way of cooling the building and making conditions more comfortable for the workers, but the fans had been the best they had been able to do so far.

There were two other floors to the factory, but Daniel preferred this one because it was the heart of the whole business and he found the steady hum of its industry a reassuring sound. The floor immediately above was where the pattern graders, cutters and basters worked, and the floor above that was given to storage for the hundreds of bolts of yardage, the threads, storage racks, canvas pressing cloths, sponges and countless other supplies that were part of the production and finishing process.

At last Wolf came through the door, and Daniel could tell at once that he was in a bad mood. His eyes were hooded and his jaw set. Almost immediately his eyes found Daniel.

"Come," he stated tersely. "I want to talk to you." He led Daniel into his plain but functional office where the noise of the machines was muted by the glass windows through which they could still see the workers. "Sit down."

Daniel did as he was told. He didn't know what to expect and whether he should be glad or anxious. He wanted to say something to break the tension but was afraid whatever he might say would only make things worse.

"Damn troublemakers," Wolf muttered. "I could hardly get in the building."

He didn't know what his father was talking about. "Troublemakers? Who?" he ventured.

"Didn't you see them? Open your eyes, boy. Street is full of those union agitators. They've got the entrance to every contractor and factory on this street blocked. I had to come in through the back and take the freight elevator up."

"What do they want?"

"Haven't you been paying attention to what's going on in this city? What they want is what they've been wanting for years. Only now there are more of them, and they're getting pushier."

"Now there are more factories, too. More clothes are being made than ever," Daniel offered quietly.

Wolf looked sharply at his son. He knew that Daniel was echoing a statement he himself had made a number of times before and he was secretly pleased that the boy had remembered and was quoting him. He softened his tone a little. "Daniel, these people out there in the streets and in our own shop, I understand them. I've been where they are. I've worked under conditions that were both unsanitary and humiliating. I know what they want. They want a shorter work week, a wage they can live on, a healthier place to work with better ventilation, clean toilets and more precautions taken against fires. They want honest foremen to tally the number of garments they make and they want the work distributed evenly, with the foreman not giving extra to his favorites. Everyone should get a chance to earn the same amount." He looked intently at Daniel. "What do you think of those demands?"

Daniel's face was perplexed. "I don't understand what the fuss is about. That's what our workers already have."

"Our workers, yes. Other workers, no. There are sweatshops and subcontractors tucked into every nook and cranny of the Tenth Ward. There are things going on you wouldn't believe. People are treated like workhorses."

"So that's why the workers are trying to organize? Because of the bad employers?"

"That's right. But what I don't like is that they want to force every factory, every employer to have a union, even if he's already meeting the conditions they're demanding. And I'm opposed to that. It smells too much like the highhanded tactics I left Russia to get away from. Only there it was a different group in the driver's seat. It was the czar trying to make everyone into a member of the Russian Orthodox religion and discriminating against those who wouldn't go along. I'm against anything that's not a matter of free choice."

"Some of the garment places around here have closed up," Daniel observed.

"Yes, well, I don't feel for them, either. What's happened is that the radicals put pressure against some of the worst offenders. So now it looks like they're out of business, but they're not. They're just moving on to another city where there are a lot of immigrants from eastern Europe they can get to work for them, just as they did here. Those shops aren't out of business; they've just moved to Boston or Cleveland or Philadelphia. No," he shook his head, "I don't feel sorry for them at all. They're cockroaches and bloodsuckers. They're the ones who got us into all this in the first place." Wolf grew silent for a moment.

"But that wasn't the reason I called you in here. I just got a little carried away when I couldn't get in the door of my own business. I had something else I wanted to discuss with you."

Daniel held his breath. Here it comes, he thought. Now he would find out what he had done wrong, why he hadn't lived up to his father's expectations and hadn't received the bar mitzvah present he had been expecting. He was convinced it was his own fault that he hadn't yet earned the right to be his father's partner.

"You're familiar with the Hammond Mill upstate in Schenectady?"

Daniel nodded his head. He had been there on business trips with his father a number of times.

"I'm sending you up there at the end of the week to do our buying."

Daniel let out the breath he had been holding. So he wasn't being chastised. He was elated. He wanted to ask if he'd be making the trip all on his own but was afraid that his father might think he was questioning his decision.

"It's time you had more of a role in running this outfit, I think. And you can purchase our goods as easily as I can, I'm sure of it."

Daniel's heart leapt. The awful burden of failure that he had been carrying since last night had lifted with just a few words from his father. What his father was saying meant that he still had his approval. Why else would his father entrust him with even more work and a bigger job than he ever had before? Perhaps he had been wrong after all to think he had failed him. His father had his own timetable, and just because Daniel had wanted so terribly for the occasion of his bar mitzvah to be the day on which he could stand alongside him in the business, it didn't mean that his father had ever planned it that way. He would wait, Daniel told himself, until his father deemed him fit. After all, he was sure his father knew what would be best.

Daniel's spirits were sufficiently buoyed by what he saw as the renewal of his father's faith in him that he was ready to put into action a plan that had crossed his mind the night of his bar mitzvah while he lay in bed unable to sleep. When he got home later that afternoon, he went directly to his room and pulled out a cigar box from under his bed. He removed from the box a small wad of dollar bills and a random amount of change which constituted all his savings, money he'd received as bar mitzvah gifts and pay from his father's factory. He counted the money quickly, then put it back in the box and back under the bed. He sat for a few minutes and thought about whether it was enough.

He decided he would work just another couple of weeks, and when he added that additional pay to the contents of the box, it would surely be an adequate amount.

Almost a month later, he again removed the money from the box and stuffed it into the pocket of his best pair of pants. Then he carefully combed his hair, which he had already combed five times that evening, and left the house.

A half hour later he stood on the stoop of another house and sounded the bell. The woman who opened the door was not the same one who had opened it the last time. This one had curly brown hair, not unlike his own except that hers fell past her shoulders. She was wearing a white satin gown, almost like a bridal dress, and it clung to her so snugly Daniel could almost see the details of her anatomy through it. And unlike any bridal dress he had ever seen, it was cut amazingly low in front. She tossed him a saucy look, and having been here once before, he followed her up the stairs with a certain amount of confidence, enjoying the exaggerated swing of her hips.

Inside the scene was exactly as it had been the other time, as if time ceased to exist once a person climbed the stairs to this room. There was Madame Dubeau moving toward him just as she had moved toward him and his father over a month ago. She smiled at him and extended her hand, and he was left with the feeling that she recognized him and had been waiting for just this night. Whether in fact she did recognize him was another issue; in this world it was the feeling that was more important than anything else. He quickly surveyed the room and was pleased to see the Chinese girl sitting in the corner. He had feared she would already be taken for the evening and that he might have to return another night, for he was determined to have no one but her. When he pointed her out as the woman he wanted, Madame Dubeau beamed approvingly. "Yes, yes. I knew you would like her," she said. "She is a favorite."

Daniel wasn't sure he liked her last remark, but he didn't have time to give it any more thought because Sue Fen was already walking toward him. She was wearing an evening dress of peach silk, and as she walked, it shimmered in the gaslight of the room and accentuated the gentle roundness of her body. This time Daniel took his time and admired her, from the smoothness of her walk to the black glossiness of her hair. The last time he had been so overwhelmed with the occasion, of simply being there and with the glamour of the women that he had found it hard to appreciate it all, but this time was different. He was in control of what happened to him, he told himself, and he need not be in a hurry or feel anxious.

Sue Fen led him to the same peach-hued room they had been in before, for he had also insisted to Madame Dubeau that he wanted that particular room. As soon as Sue Fen had shut the door behind them, he picked her up and carried her to the bed. Quickly but deftly he removed her silk gown, then the chemise under which she was again perfectly naked. He did not need to be guided this time. He began to stroke her body, slowly and confidently, until she began to moan softly. Not until her moans had become sobs and they were both almost maddened by their mutual desire, not until then did he swiftly and explosively enter her, and they peaked together in a sudden and violent outburst.

Daniel spent the rest of the evening there in the peach room, lost in the silkiness of her dark peach skin, and they made love again and again. Over and over he practiced the art of waiting and self-control. Each time they drove themselves to the same point of frenzied and unconsummated desire, and each time it was not until Sue Fen cried out for him and he felt he was ready to burst, that he would enter her and release his passion into her.

The sky outside was beginning to grow light as

Daniel finally made his way home. As he passed
through the streets that were just starting to stir again
with life, he walked with a surer step and carried himself with greater confidence. He now saw that the key
to succeeding at anything was to be patient and bide
his time. If, in his effort to get whatever he wanted, he
could keep from rushing and maintain his control, he
would eventually get what he wanted. He was proud
that he had performed as a man, and he knew his father, had he known, would have been proud also.

Elke stood in front of the mirror in her parents'
room and took stock of herself. Until just a few months
ago, she had been one of the shortest girls in her class
at school. Now it seemed within a matter of only weeks
she had shot up and was on her way to being taller
than most of the others. She turned from one side to the
other, examining her profile. There wasn't much to
see, she concluded. She was still mostly planes and
sharp angles. She stepped closer to concentrate on her
face. She decided she was pleased with what she saw
there, on the whole. Her eyes were wide and bright
green, like her mother's everyone said, and her nose
was straight and not too long. Her best features,
though, were her thick red hair and pale skin. Some
days she hated her very fair skin, but other days she
changed her mind and felt it suited her just right. Today was one of those days. She stood back again to
take another look at her body's profile. She was all in a
straight line and had almost no breasts at all. Definitely
not encouraging, she decided. She took off her socks
and stuffed them down the front of her dress to see
how it looked to have breasts, even bumpy and uneven
ones. She was admiring herself that way when the bedroom door suddenly opened.

"Elke! What are you doing in here?" Marya
asked, then instantly regretted having questioned her.
It was only natural for a young girl to be curious about

her appearance, and clearly Elke had just come to use the mirror.

Elke quickly put her hands to her chest and hoped her mother had not seen the lumpy protuberances there.

"I think it's time we got you a mirror of your own. What do you think?"

Elke nodded her head. She felt too embarrassed at being found out to say anything. When she saw Marya turn her back to hang her jacket up, she quickly reached down the front of her dress and yanked out the socks. Then she headed for the door.

"Just a minute, Elke. I'd like to talk to you."

Elke felt her cheeks flush. She wasn't sure she wanted to hear what her mother was probably going to say, but she sat on the edge of the bed and waited obediently.

As Marya finished undressing, she felt Elke's eyes upon her, and she recalled how when she was ten or eleven, younger than Elke even, she had tried to catch glimpses of her mother's unclothed body in an attempt to gain some kind of preview of what she herself might look like as a woman some day. Of course, it had been difficult ever to see her mother wearing less than three or four layers of clothing in that drafty house, and given the careful sense of privacy both her parents had about their bodies. She wondered, in fact, if they had ever seen each other fully undressed. It was strange to think she had been raised to live that same life, and now the life she was living and the world she had entered were so completely different from anything they or she could have imagined even in their wildest flights of fancy. She and Wolf gave their children everything they could, but she felt an ache of regret that neither Elke nor Daniel could ever know those kind and simple, yet incredibly wise, people.

"I wish you could have known your grandmother," she grieved and was surprised to hear herself say that out loud. That wasn't what she had meant to talk to her about at all.

Elke was at once relieved to hear her mother was not going to talk about what had just happened. Maybe she hadn't seen the socks after all. She was astonished, though, to hear mention of her grandmother. Marya almost never talked about anything that happened before she came to America.

"Your grandmother was a person who talked a lot, but she didn't just rattle on without saying anything. She knew just what to say when someone was feeling bad. She had that ability you don't see too often of making other people feel better, just by being around them."

Elke sat very quietly. She didn't want to say a word or move even her little toe for fear her mother might get distracted and stop talking.

"Your grandmother wasn't at all like her mother, though." She added as an aside, "Just as we're not alike."

Elke hadn't heard her mother talk to her this way before. She was amazed. She was hungry to hear all the details she could of these mysterious people that were her relatives. The other girls who were her friends in the neighborhood and at school had huge, sprawling families, with both sets of grandmothers and grandfathers and all kinds of aunts and uncles and great aunts and great uncles and first and second cousins, so many that they had trouble keeping them all straight. She had often thought of how much fun it must be to have a big, noisy family like that. Then she'd always have someone to talk to. Now she didn't want her mother to stop for anything and was alert to her every word.

"Your great-grandmother was thought a bit strange by most people. She didn't have the way with people her daughter—your grandmother—did. But people listened when she talked, just the same. She had a way of seeing what was going to come in the future." Marya started to laugh a little. "Maybe that's what put her in such a bad mood all the time." She started to sit down on the bed and Elke quickly made room for her. "She was always having bad dreams and muttering about her 'pictures'—that's what she called her premonitions of what was going to happen." Marya's voice changed and she said almost under her breath, "Sometimes I wonder if I'm going to end up like her."

Elke didn't know what her mother was talking about. Did she have bad dreams about what was going to happen? She wondered if her mother had had any about her, and she shuddered slightly to think her mother might know something awful that was going to happen to her.

"What happened to my great-grandmother?" she asked.

"She just died of old age. She must have been over ninety years old. We never knew for sure. There wasn't much in the way of records in those days."

Elke didn't ask how her grandmother had died. She knew it was in a pogrom, but her mother never went into any detail.

As if sensing Elke might ask about that very thing next, Marya changed the subject. She had no intention of mentioning the sudden appearance and disappearance of Elke's bosom, but she knew Elke was worried she might. Instead she had something else on her mind.

"I've been giving some thought to opportunities for you, Elke."

"What kind of opportunities?"

"Have you given any thought to what you'd like to do with yourself later on?"

"Later on today?"

Marya laughed softly. "Later on in your life. I'd like to know what you'd like to work at."

Elke shrugged. "I don't know. I never thought about it, I guess."

"Well, it's time to think about it now."

She shrugged again. "I just thought I'd get married and have babies. I'd take care of my husband and children."

"What if something happens to your husband?"

"What do you mean?"

"Something could happen to your husband, Elke. He could have an accident at work, or be killed by a horse-cart or carriage out of control. He could get sick. He could be killed in a war. Then what would you do?"

"Nothing's happened to Papa."

Marya remembered her feelings when she had received the crisp, official letter announcing to her that Gershon had died. She had been just a little older than her daughter now was. But of course she could say nothing of that to Elke. "Things do happen, Elke, when you least expect them. Look around you. People get sick or have accidents every day, and for everyone that happens to, at least one other person has his or her life changed because of it. A woman needs something to fall back upon in case something happens to her husband."

Elke didn't want to think about what her mother was saying. She didn't want to think of people getting sick or dying. She just wanted to be married and take care of a big family and not have to worry about things like that. Then something occurred to her.

"Mama, is that why you work?" she asked suddenly. "Because you're afraid something might happen to Papa?"

Marya didn't know what to say. She didn't know how far to go in revealing herself to Elke. "I work because I love it. That's the main reason," she said slowly. "I like the satisfaction of creating something that I think is beautiful and having other people think it is beautiful too."

"But Papa must be a part of it, mustn't he? You're afraid something might happen to him?"

Marya let out a sigh. "Yes, that's part of it too.

Believe me, Elke, you never know what's going to happen to you. I started out my life in a small town somewhere between White Russia and Great Russia. I never dreamed I would be anywhere but there my entire life. And you see how my life took a completely different course?"

She felt a strong urge to get the conversation back onto Elke and her original intent. "That's why you must be prepared, Elke. That's why I want you to start thinking about what it is you would like to work at." She put up her hand to stop Elke's protest. "Just in case." She measured her words carefully. "For starters, you might consider whether you would like to do what I do. You already sew beautifully and I know you have a good eye. With training, you might find that dress designing is something that you could do well and enjoy."

Elke stared at her mother, her eyes wide. She had never had any desire to design clothes of any kind and had only learned how to sew because it was expected of her and so she would be able to make clothes for herself and her children. It had never seemed like anything she would want to do to earn money.

"I would like to be able to help you, Elke. If you decide this is what you want to do, I can get you started. I know a lot of people now, and so much of the way is paved for you already." She noticed Elke was looking down at the floor. She lifted Elke's chin with her hand and turned her head to face her. "Remember, you don't have to do the same work I do. I just want you to think about it, that's all. And if you decide there's something else you would rather do with your life, that's all right too. Really it is, Elke. I want you to know that. Tell me you do."

"Yes, Mama. I do. I know you want what is best for me."

"Then you'll think about what I've said?"

"Yes, Mama." Then on an impulse, she threw her

arms around Marya, squeezing her so tightly against her own body that Marya could scarcely breathe.

Andrew Markingham watched Marya walk toward him across the busy restaurant. She was wearing a fawn-colored skirt trimmed with emerald green piping and a matching jacket that nipped in at the waist, accentuating her small midriff and shapely hips. Her hair was dressed in the new style that allowed women to balance larger and larger hats on their heads. As always, he drew in his breath when he saw her. She was still as luminous and beautiful as the first time he'd laid eyes on her some eight years ago.

During that time he had managed to fall deeper and deeper in love with her to the point that even though she continually resisted his advances and had never become his mistress, he still pursued her. He had taken care not to move too quickly for fear he might scare her away, and it turned out that he, unlike so many men, was well suited to waiting. The forbearance, patience and attention to detail that had made him one of the city's most successful and wealthy attorneys was what made him able to wait so long for whatever it was he decided he wanted. And what he wanted was Marya. As a result of his patience, she had never cut him off completely, and for that he was extremely glad because he couldn't begin to think what it would be like not to see her again. He had even managed to make himself useful to her by helping her establish her shop, although he did not care for the idea of her becoming a kind of upper level shopgirl.

Their encounters had been limited to afternoon teas before or after her sessions with various patrons and to occasional walks in Central Park. Seldom would she let him take her in his carriage in the direction of where she lived, and never had she let him take her right to her home or even to her street. Where another man might have been daunted by her reluctance and extreme caution, Andrew found he was drawn to her all the more because of it. He was not a man who threw caution and restraint to the wind and he did not want a woman who did either. He wanted, besides a woman with extraordinary beauty, one whose judgment he could trust, and in Marya he believed he had found both. That combination, he knew, was worth waiting for.

As she threaded her way among the tables, he saw her eyes dart across the room as they did whenever he met her, as if they were looking for someone in particular, someone besides him.

"I'm sorry I'm late," she apologized, sinking into her chair. "The traffic on Fifth Avenue was impossible, and it took a while to find a carriage."

"There's something different about you today, Marya."

She looked a little surprised, then smiled at him. "Is there? Then it must be my new walking suit. I've made so many for my clients that I felt it was time to make one for myself. After all, I probably do more walking than all of them put together."

"No, that's not it. It's something else."

"What is it? How mean of you to tease me like this. Is it something good?"

"Very good, I would say. I hope you would too."

"Now I really am curious. What is it you're talking about? You must tell me."

"There's a new softness about you. I sensed it the moment I saw you today. In fact, I sensed it the last time we were together."

Marya knew what he was referring to. She marveled at how alert he was to everything about her. So he had been aware of how she had been feeling then.

"I sense a shift, a subtle shift, but a shift nevertheless. Am I right, Marya?"

She took her time in responding and he let her. She studied him for a moment. Over the last few years, she had begun to look forward to their meetings more and more. In that time, the years had been good to him. His thick blond curls were now streaked with touches of grey and the lines around his eyes had deepened slightly. He was still astonishingly fit and his athletic physique looked unchanged from when she had first seen him. What she liked best, though, were his eyes. It was more than their piercing blue intensity, it was another quality that attracted her—the kindness and compassion she saw there.

She didn't answer his question directly. "You've become such a part of my life now, Andrew."

"And you part of mine."

"I can't imagine what it would be like not to have you in it, not to be able to look forward to our times together. At first I feared you might be like Gregory Keller, so grasping and arrogant. I knew I couldn't bear to be around another man like him. But I've discovered you're not like him at all. It seems that all I've found out about you and am still finding out are only good things."

The waiter came, and while Andrew ordered their tea, Marya was silent. As soon as he left, she picked up where she had left off. "One of the things that means the most to me is that you are so sensitive to everything about me, to my moods, my reactions, my feelings."

"How can I not be, Marya? I have been in love with you for a long time."

She knew what he said was true, but this was the first time he had ever said it out loud. "And I like it that I have never had to spell things out for you," she said. "That you just know."

As they had their tea and pastries, their talk turned to other things, to Marya's patrons and the oddities of their behavior that still amazed her and to Andrew's business concerns, but the underlying current between them was unbroken. Finally Andrew called for the check, and after he settled the account, they walked outside together. He summoned his carriage and held the door for her. This time she got in without a word of protest.

Fifth Avenue was more crowded than ever as people began to leave their jobs and head for home. At times the carriage would come to a complete standstill for several minutes and they would hear a burst of shouting as the drivers of whichever vehicles had collided would vent their anger on one another. Neither of them minded the delays much. They talked a little and smiled at each other from time to time. It seemed like more than thirty minutes before the carriage came to a final stop and the horseman was holding the door open.

Marya stepped out in front of a house that was made of neat white brick and was trimmed in brass and black. She was glad to see that where he lived was not ostentatious like the homes of so many of her clients. "What part of town are we in?" she asked.

"This is Morningside Heights."

She noticed the tree-lined streets and the other houses, all quietly elegant. "It's lovely."

He led her up the stairs and into a modest hallway. Even from the decor of the hallway, she could tell she approved of his taste in furnishings. But then, she said to herself, she supposed she had always known she would.

He turned to her in the hallway and said, "We're quite alone. The servants have gone." Then suddenly he had picked her up in his arms and carried her into the sitting room. He sat her down on one of the divans.

They looked into each other's eyes, and without a word between them, they understood each other perfectly. Still looking into her eyes, Andrew began to loosen the buttons on her walking suit. He removed first her jacket, then her blouse and skirt. When he had her completely undressed, he stared at her.

"You're the most beautiful woman I've ever seen," he murmured, stroking his hand down her breasts and across her hips. "You're all circles. All curves and rounded, flowing lines."

She began to undress him just as slowly and carefully as he had undressed her. She was delighted to discover his broad chest was covered with a blend of dark brown and blond hair, and when he was totally unclothed, she said, "You're like the pictures I've seen of the statue of David in Italy. You're in perfect proportion."

They moved slowly from admiring to touching, and even more slowly to the final movements of lovemaking. They had waited eight years. They trusted each other fully, and they were in no hurry.

Afterward, as they lay with their bare legs entwined on the divan, Andrew began to question her gently. "Tell me about your husband, Marya. In all the time we've known each other, you've said very little about him."

Marya wondered at herself that she did not feel any guilt to hear her husband mentioned as she lay there with another man. "I don't have much to say. He has a strong personality, he's a hard worker and extremely intelligent," she said a little too hastily. "What else would you like to know?"

"I'd like to know how it is between you."

She sighed without realizing it. "It's how it is between most husbands and wives, I suppose."

"Then there is no great passion?"

She shook her head. It hurt her to have to acknowledge it, as if saying it out loud made it real.

"Have you ever thought that you might leave him?"

Marya looked at him sharply. "Leave him? What for?"

Andrew laughed. "You needn't look at me as if I just uttered blasphemy. It's done all the time." He chucked her lightly under the chin. "Women leave their husbands because they aren't happy with them, because they're mistreated or maybe just bored. Often they leave for another man." He paused.

"I've never thought about leaving my husband."

"You're in America now, Marya. You don't have to stay in a situation that doesn't provide you enough of what you want, be it love, sex, money. . . ." His voice trailed off as he left her to her thoughts, feeling no need to say too much to her about it just then.

Later that evening, as Marya rode home in the carriage he had summoned for her, she felt content and strangely at peace. She had been to bed with a man who wasn't her husband, she told herself, why was it that she didn't feel guilty? Instead she had a sense that things were right, that she had even done the best thing. Her love for Andrew was soft, deliberate and steady, and that was the way their lovemaking had been. Her love for Wolf—she admitted that she still loved him and always would no matter what happened between them—was wild and intense, just as their lovemaking had once been. But she and Wolf did not make love anymore, or even talk much. These last few years it had been Andrew who was always there waiting for her, eager to hear what she had to say and what was happening to her. Lately she had been able to count on Andrew more than Wolf. He was unfailingly gentle and loved her very much, and she knew that she needed and wanted that love.

As he had put her in the carriage this evening, Andrew had said, "I would like to see you again very soon, Marya. I would like to take you out someplace with me. Can you arrange that we could have an entire evening together?"

"I'll see what I can do. I'll let you know, Andrew." She didn't know how she would manage it, but she would find a way. The rest of the way home her mind was on Andrew—the look in his eyes as they had made love, the smoothness of his touch, the trust she felt in him. After the storms with Wolf, it was a luxury to bask in Andrew's sunny disposition and reassuring love. Perhaps Andrew's implication was right. She was still clinging blindly to the old world tradition by staying in a marriage that no longer brought her any happiness. Perhaps that was the true blasphemy. She thought she had carefully rooted out all of that old way of thinking, only to find that sixteen years later, she still had some discomforting remnants. In Russia, a marriage was virtually forever. But she was no longer a peasant girl, she reminded herself. And Andrew offered her the kind of love that would age well over the years.

Chapter 15

Daniel watched his mother as she rolled out the dough for *challah*, the ring of bread which Marya would bake with carrots in the Russian style for the holiday of Rosh Hashanah and which he and Elke always looked forward to dipping in honey. He felt a little awkward with just the two of them alone in the kitchen. Usually when he was in the same room with his mother, Elke was also there or sometimes his father. It hadn't been his idea to sit here but his mother had specifically asked him. He watched her as she sprinkled flour on the table and rolled out the dough a second time, then formed it into three large ropes and three small ones. He waited for her to say something.

"You haven't been seeing your friends as much, have you? It seems like we don't hear any more tales of what Jerry or Sheldon are doing."

"No. I don't see too much of them anymore."

"Why not? What have you been doing?"

"I've been busy at the factory. There's a lot to be done."

"Yes. I'm sure your papa sees to that." She had braided the three large ropes and was now joining their ends together to form a ring. "He has big plans for you."

"Yes. I suppose so."

"Suppose so? What? You have some doubt, Daniel?" She looked at her son, surprised at his response. Perhaps that was what the change in his demeanor lately was about. She had noticed that he had grown increasingly withdrawn in the last few months and she wanted to find out what was behind the change.

He watched her start to braid the three small ropes and form them in a ring. When she had finished, he still hadn't said anything.

"Daniel?" she prompted.

"Yes?" he said absently.

"I asked you if you had some doubt about your father's plans for you. I haven't heard your reply."

Daniel looked uneasy. "I don't know what to think," he said reluctantly. "He's always saying he wants me to have part of the business."

"Well, he does," she said as she took the remaining dough and formed it into a large coil and then a small coil. She placed the small coil on top of the larger one, covered both with a cloth and set them next to the stove. "Now, we'll let those rise for another hour until they've doubled in size," she said. "Then I'll brush them with egg yolk, sprinkle on some poppy seeds and they'll be ready to bake." She slapped the flour from her hands and sat down at the table across from him.

Now that she was sitting so close and looking right at him, he felt more uncomfortable than ever. It wasn't her presence that he found disturbing; that he always liked. What disturbed him was that she wanted him to talk. He knew that she loved him and wanted to help him, but he didn't know what to say to her. He always found it easier to talk to his father. There was always something to discuss about the workers at the factory or the orders or the production process.

His mother had always been a presence he depend-

ed on, for fixing his meals, for tending to him when
he was sick, for keeping track of where his father and
Elke were. But he had not thought of her as someone
to talk to. Her interest in the factory was minimal, and
he had to admit he had little knowledge or interest in
her designs that she was always working on for those
rich ladies on Fifth Avenue. Still, he thought she was
beautiful, more beautiful than any other mother he had
ever seen, and he liked to feel her hand on his brow
and the scent of her when she came near. But talk to
her about his father? He didn't think he could.

"You like working in the factory with your father,
don't you?" she said as if reading his mind.

"Yes."

"Is it the thing you like to do best in the world?"

"Yes."

"Then you're lucky. You're lucky that you've
found out so early in your life what it is that you're
happiest doing."

"Yes. I guess so."

She paused a few moments, then added, "But you
don't seem happy, Daniel."

He looked up quickly and his eyes met hers. He
wondered how she had been able to tell, and all of a
sudden he felt transparent, as if all his secrets were
open to anyone who cared to read them.

"It's just that you don't laugh as much as you
used to, and at the dinner table your eyes are so far
away now."

He swallowed. He hadn't known anyone was paying that much attention to him. "When is he going to
do it?" he blurted out all of a sudden.

"When is who going to do what?"

"When is Papa going to make me his partner like
he promised?"

She looked at her son. She saw so much of Wolf
in him—his big square shoulders, his black eyes, the
expressions on his face, and now his impatience. But
impatience in Wolf translated itself into impulsiveness,

and she had never considered Daniel to be impulsive. Instead, he turned his impatience inward where it gnawed at him and was now making him unhappy.

"I'm sure he'll do it just as soon as you're ready. You've still a lot to learn, I imagine, and he wants to make sure you've learned enough to take on that responsibility."

"But I *have*. I study everything at the factory, more than I ever study anything at school. I could run all the machines by the time I was seven years old. When I was ten I understood about cutting and tailoring. Last year, after I turned thirteen, he started sending me to the mills in his place to do the buying. I'm doing everything I can. I could do even more if I had more time." He hesitated a few seconds. Then his words came in a rush. "I don't want to go to school anymore. I want to spend all my time at the factory helping Papa."

She sat stunned. "Quit school?"

"What do I need with it anyway? I know what I'm going to be. It won't help me get a better job and I'm not going to be a doctor or rabbi, so what's the use?"

"How could you even think of such a thing? Quit school? Do you know how fortunate you are to be able to go to school at all, to get as much education as you want, and for free?"

"I've got all I want, Mama. Now I just want to work alongside Papa in the factory."

"Have you told your papa what you're saying to me?"

He knotted his hands together and let out his breath. "No."

"Why not?"

"I think he's mad at me."

"Why would he possibly be mad at you? This is the first I've heard of such a thing."

"He's gotta be mad at me. He hardly talks to me anymore. Nothing I do seems to please him."

"Maybe it's not you. Maybe he's got other things on his mind, that's all."

Daniel thought about what she said. It was true his father had seldom been there in the middle of the afternoon in the last six months. Daniel didn't know where he was, but when he came in later, he was always rushed and if anything having to do with the factory seemed to take too much time, he became irritable. Still, Daniel felt that part of his father's anger had to do with him and that it came from something—he didn't know what—he had done to displease him.

"Remember how he's always called me his wizard?" Daniel asked.

Marya nodded her head. "He thinks you can do anything, that you can work magic, that's why."

"Well, he doesn't call me that anymore. In this last year I've been anything but his wizard. Nothing I do seems to be good enough."

"Has he said that?"

"No. But I can tell from the look on his face. He just doesn't look at me in the same way."

Marya wanted to suggest to her son that perhaps it was all his imagination but something prevented her. She was afraid of stopping his words. This was the first time they had been able to sit down and talk, perhaps ever. But also, although she desperately wanted to believe it wasn't so, she wasn't totally sure that Daniel's fears were all in his imagination after all.

Daniel interrupted her thoughts. "That's the reason I want to quit school. If I spend more time at the factory and learn even more, maybe he won't be so displeased with me. I'll be able to do a better job and he'll act toward me like he used to."

Marya reached out her hand and gently touched Daniel on the cheek. "I understand why this is so important to you. But believe me, Daniel, dropping out of school is not the answer. You have to do the best you can with both school and work. You know how your father values education. I can assure you that if you were to quit school, he would be truly displeased with you, even more upset than you think he now is."

Daniel knew how important a good education was to his father. He had often heard him speak bitterly of the "Jew quota" in Russia that prohibited more than a certain small percentage of Jews from attending the university, no matter how qualified they were. Wolf had marveled at the system of free education in America, where anyone could learn as much as he wanted or aspire to whatever profession he wanted. He had pressed upon him and his sister the personal joys to be had from learning itself, not just to get a job later, but from learning for its own sake. He would tell them about the tradition of Jewish scholarship, where young men would devote their entire lives to studying in the *yeshiva* so that they might learn the holy Torah and the Talmud with all its interpretations and commentaries on the Torah.

"The love of study is part of the Hebraic tradition," he had said. "Not just study to lead to an end but knowledge for knowledge's sake. A life dedicated to learning is the most honorable life of all." And so Daniel knew that part of what his mother said was true. His father would never allow him to quit school. But what was he to do, then? How could he get back in his father's good graces? He knew he could never ask his father what he had done wrong. He did not have the heart to ask him such a direct question on such a delicate subject. But he also didn't know how long he could stand to live with his father's displeasure.

He realized his mother was still watching him and suddenly he put out his hand and laid it down over hers on the table. The warmth of it felt good underneath his, and he found her touch reassuring. How strange, he thought, to think that he came from the belly of this slim, pretty woman who sat across from him. She was so unlike the mothers of his friends, not just because of her beauty, but by her nature as well.

Who else had a mother who one afternoon sat and talked to her son with flour streaked on her face while she waited for the *challah* she was baking to rise, and who the next afternoon would be outfitted in the most fashionable ensemble in the city as she prepared to meet the wives of such illustrious names as Stuart Worthington and Gregory Keller? He hadn't thought about it before, but just now he could see how his father had fallen in love with her.

Wolf was hurrying through the crowds of Orchard Street the best he could. Columns of pushcarts lined both sides of the narrow street, pushcarts for shoes, pushcarts for pants, pushcarts for hats. Name it, he said to himself, and there was a pushcart for it. The roadway was crammed with shoppers, mostly immigrants and particularly Jews. But here and there was a smattering of Poles, Italians and even Irish, all attracted to the best bargains to be found in New York. At one particular pushcart, of the double-tiered sort such as fruit was often sold from, an especially large crowd had gathered. Wolf inadvertently jostled shoppers to his right and left as he tried to make his way through the impasse. Suddenly he felt someone tugging at his sleeve.

"Wolf," called a woman's voice behind him.

He turned and ran his eyes across the pool of nameless faces. Then he saw a young woman standing a little to one side and gazing at him intently. "Angelica!" he said. It was Mario's sister. He noticed at once how good she looked. Her black hair was swept up on her head and formed over pads in the fashion of the day, and she was wearing a light pink shirtwaist that brought out the pink flush in her cheeks.

He took her by the arm and lightly steered her to a small open area back closer to one of the buildings. "How have you been? It's been years since I've seen you."

"Not since my wedding, Wolf. That was five years ago."

"Was it? My God, five years is a long time. A lot can happen."

She looked down for a moment and made a motion with her shoe in the dirt. "Yes. It can."

"You must tell me how you've been. How is your husband? Gregorio, wasn't that his name?"

She was looking off to the side, Wolf noticed, not meeting his gaze. "He's doing fine. Same as before."

"Does he still work on the docks?"

"Yes, whenever he can."

"You must have many bambinos by now."

She looked up. "No. None. Not yet."

He tried to read the expression on her face but saw that it was uncustomarily closed. "Well, there's still plenty of time for that. Years and years."

"Yes, I suppose so."

"You're certainly looking very"—he wanted to say beautiful, but knew that even though he was a friend of the family, that statement would be too bold—"very healthy and fine," he uttered lamely.

She smiled at him but didn't reply.

"And Lucia, how's she? At your wedding I remember she was arm in arm with her husband the whole time and was soon to have her first baby."

"She has a big family already. Four babies now and another to come."

"Well, I'm happy for her and happy for your mother too. Now she must not be giving that die-hard bachelor Mario such a hard time about providing her with grandchildren."

She laughed lightly and for a moment he saw a flash of the girl he had known before. "Listen, Angelica," he said on an impulse, "do you have time to sit and have a cup of tea with me?" He motioned to a delicatessen nearby.

She looked in the direction he was pointing. "I don't know," she said tentatively.

"Come. Talk to an old family friend. It will be all right." He sensed she might be worried about the propriety of being seen with a man other than her husband. "No one knows you here. In fact, I'm surprised to see you here at all."

As he talked, she allowed herself to be led into the delicatessen. "I normally don't shop in this neighborhood. But I know that the prices are even better here than on Mulberry Bend. So sometimes, when I feel like a change, I take a little walk."

Wolf ordered their tea and two pieces of honey cake. He noted that she played with the strap of her shopping bag and he wondered whether it was he or something else that made her a little nervous. In an effort to relax her, he tried to ask her about her brothers besides Mario, whom he saw every day at his factory. But she seemed to have little enthusiasm for the drift of the conversation.

Suddenly she let go of the shopping bag's strap and planted her hands deliberately in front of her on the table. "Do you want to know why I really come shopping in this area?" she interrupted him in midsentence. "It's because I know your factory is not too far away. I come because sometimes I hope I will see you."

"Why do you want to see me?" he asked softly, surprised by this sudden outburst.

"I'm not sure I know. I just do. I start thinking about you, and then I want to see you. So I start walking."

He looked at her. She was more lovely by far at twenty-five than she had been at eighteen when he'd first met her. The angles of her face were more pronounced, less softened by vestiges of teenage roundness, and the change was for the better, giving her appearance more depth and drama.

"And now that you've seen me?" he continued.

She started to gather her shopping bag and parcels into her lap. "Now that I've seen you, I want to see you again," she said simply. "I want to talk to you."

He noticed her preparations to depart. "What's wrong with right now?"

"I can't, Wolf. I have been gone too long already." She looked up at him and he saw that her expression was earnest. "But I can come here again next week."

"I'll be here. Just tell me when," he agreed, mystified as to what she wanted to talk to him about. He wondered if it had to do with her family or with money problems, or with some difficulty she had gotten herself into, one she couldn't talk about to a member of her own family. At any rate, she was very pretty and she was still Mario's sister, even though she was married. He would gladly be there for her in whatever way he could.

She stood up. "At ten o'clock, outside by the door?"

"Yes." He knew she was still too much schooled in the ways of the old country to wait for him alone inside.

She extended her hand. "Good-bye, Wolf."

Her hand felt small and vulnerable inside his, and he was aware of how much larger, older and more experienced he was. Something in her made him feel very protective. "I'll see you next week, Angelica." He watched her walk away, the soft sway of her skirt drawing his attention to her hips. She was damned pretty, he said to himself.

The next week he was waiting in front of the delicatessen at the time they had set. His attention was drawn to a man walking down the middle of the street shouting loudly about a belt that would make the wearer invisible. Draped over his arm like serpents was an assortment of cheap looking belts that would have enough to do to hold up a pair of pants, much less make a person invisible. Nevertheless, heads turned to his cry for the magic belts, and a horde of boys danced around him, no doubt foreseeing the limitless quantities of sweets they would be able to steal from the candy pushcarts once they were invisible in their magic belts.

He made a note to himself that he would have to warn Daniel to be wary of such tomfoolery as belts that would make one invisible, but then he decided that Daniel was not so softheaded as to be taken in by such nonsense. He recalled the only time he had attempted to warn him of the perils of the streets. He had tried to make Daniel read a publication entitled *The Snares of New York, Or Tricks and Traps of the Great Metropolis,* which even though it had been written in 1879, still contained information about the kind of evils and misadventures the unwary could fall into on the streets. It covered everything from the pickpockets and beguiling ladies who would rob you, to the street merchandise like the teeth whitener that would strip the enamel from your teeth and rot them, to the book that showed you how to get a fowl to roast itself and to call on the spirits of the dead to bring you good fortune and luck.

"I know about most of that already," Daniel had said, and Wolf had felt Daniel had only opened the cover because he didn't want to offend him. He noticed that Daniel didn't bother to read it and decided that perhaps Daniel's education on the streets was already complete.

As Wolf watched the man with the magic belts disappear down the street toward the left, he heard Angelica greeting him from the other side. When he looked at her, he was struck again by how attractive she looked. Today she was wearing a summery gold dress fashioned in cotton and on her head was a matching gold bonnet. He was glad to see that she was smiling at him and he led her inside right away. As soon as they were seated, she began to talk, the words unleashed from her in a torrent.

"It's my husband, Gregorio. He works so hard every day. Every morning he gets up before it's light outside and he goes to the docks. It's dark already when he comes back and he's tired and his body is sore. It hurts him everywhere. Then the next morning he gets up and goes to the docks again and comes home again so tired he is almost sick. He works and works, and still it is not enough. The money is not enough for us to live on, Wolf. I tell Gregorio I want to go to work. But he says, 'No, never!' His wife will never go out to work. I say to him, 'What difference does it make? There are no children. Why should I stay home? To do what?' Then he just stops talking and stays quiet like that the rest of the night and won't look at me. I try to talk to him a little and get him to laugh, but still he just keeps to himself and doesn't say anything."

"It's not an easy thing for a man when he's doing the best he can and it's still not enough."

"That's why I want to help. I can work. I'm strong and I can work hard."

"What would you do?"

"I don't know. That's why I want to talk to you. I thought, maybe because you're a businessman, you would have some ideas."

"You're sure that you must work, Angelica?" He thought of the irony of the situation. Here he was, a man who did not want his own wife to work, advising the wife of another man, a man who clearly did not want his wife to work either, on how to go about getting a job.

"Yes," she said passionately. "Wolf, if I had children, then I would not. But, now, what difference does it make? None."

"It makes a difference to Gregorio."

"But we need the money. What is this thing about a man's pride if we don't have enough?"

"It's an important thing. Forgive me if I'm being too bold, but it could affect other areas of your marriage."

"Maybe it's too late for that anyway," she said with a touch of bitterness.

Wolf waited for her to explain, but almost instantly the bitterness was gone. She continued on the subject of work. "Wolf, there must be something I could do, some little thing that would help out. Maybe there's a way I could work and Gregorio wouldn't find out? Do you know of anything like that?"

"What do you mean? How could he not find out?"

"Maybe it would be something I could do just a few hours a day? Or a job I could do at home?"

Wolf knew immediately of a form of work that would meet those requirements, but he wasn't eager to see her become involved in what could end up being tedious, boring work for very little pay.

While he paused to think, she renewed her suit with even more fervor. "You are the only one I could come to, Wolf. I could never tell Mario or my other brothers. They wouldn't understand either, and they would tell Gregorio at once."

When Wolf still didn't say anything, she added, "I'm going to find a job, no matter what. I don't care what kind it is. So I can't read or write. I can still do things with my hands. I'll find something."

He saw her determination. "You could take in piecework," said Wolf slowly.

"What? Take in piecework? What does that mean?"

"Listen, Angelica. This kind of work is not easy. It can rob you of all your enthusiasm and energy for doing anything else. But it would allow you to work at home, if you found the right contractor."

"Contractor? I don't know what all this means. What does contractor mean? What is this piecework?"

"In the clothing business, there are people called contractors. What that means is they make a deal with the manufacturer of a piece of clothing to do part of the work on that piece of clothing for a certain amount of money. Then that contractor finds someone else, someone who is willing to do the same work for even less, and he has that person do it instead. Imagine if the manufacturer said, 'Okay, I've cut out all these pairs of pants. Now I need someone to sew them up and add buttons and buttonholes.'

"Then a fellow steps forward, a real go-getter eager to make a buck, and this fellow says, 'I can sew up those pants for thirty cents each.' But somewhere another go-getter shouts out, 'I can do it for twenty-five cents.' So the manufacturer gives the pants to the man who said he could do it for the lowest amount.

"Now what? Now that the go-getter who said he could do it for twenty-five cents has all these pants to sew up for the manufacturer, he looks around for someone who wants a job real bad, so bad that she's willing to sew up those pants for fifteen cents each. Then he dumps all the pants on her, and when they're done, that contractor's made ten cents on each pair. Do you see where you come into this chain?"

She nodded her head. "I'm the person who wants the job so bad I'm willing to sew up the pants for fifteen cents."

"Or less."

"Or less?" She looked dismayed.

"If you're hungry enough. And if there's another hungry person willing to do it for fourteen cents a pair, then you'll say you can do it for thirteen cents each. Not a very pretty system, is it, when you're talking about people desperate for a job and who have no other choices."

"But you can do it at home?"

"Sometimes. Most contractors want you to do it in their shops, which are usually in their homes. But some work you can do at your own home."

"Then that's the kind for me. Tell me, Wolf, how do I find one of these contractors?"

"You must be very careful. Some are completely dishonest, and others will talk roughly to you, whether they're pleased with your work or not. One thing I want to make very sure of, Angelica. You're absolutely sure you want to do this?"

"I'm sure of it."

He realized he needn't have asked. He could see the answer in her eyes. "Then I'll give you the names of a couple of contractors you can trust more than most."

She seized his hand where it lay on the table. "*Grazie, grazie*, Wolf." Tears filled her eyes. "You are a good friend."

"You must promise me you won't say anything to anyone. If Mario found out the kind of work you'll be doing, he'd be furious. He knows too much about the garment business not to be upset that his sister has become a part of it. I'm sure he wouldn't want it for you."

"I promise, Wolf. I do. Really I do."

In the next few weeks Wolf made good on his offer to provide Angelica with the names of contractors who would give her piecework she could do in her home. Almost immediately she had contracted with one to do nothing more than sew on buttons. It was one of the lowest paying jobs of all, but she was content because she could do it at home and without Gregorio realizing she was working.

"Doesn't Gregorio notice that his money all of a sudden buys more?" Wolf asked when they met again a couple months later.

"What does he know of how much food costs?" she replied. "Now I can buy better meat and fruit and sometimes a few sweets. He doesn't ask any questions. He just thinks I am very crafty at getting good bargains."

Wolf understood. He thought of Etta and how her husband Moses had willingly believed her story about where she got the money to return home. Sometimes, when the truth is too unpalatable, when it shatters an image we hold of ourselves, we can choose to believe blindly rather than examine the truth. He wondered if this had ever happened to him or ever would, and he hoped that his pride would not be so unyielding as to allow it.

He continued to see Angelica every couple of months to check her progress with the work. At one of their meetings after almost six months had passed, he said to her, "I'd like to see you move up and do some work that pays a little more."

"I don't mind sewing on buttons. It's a little boring, that's all, but it's easy."

"As long as you're going to be putting in the time, you might as well get more pay for the same amount of energy. I've made a few inquiries for you, and I have an arrangement that's much better. How would you like to start sewing trim on ladies' blouses and get twice what you're making now?"

"I don't know. Is it very complicated?"

"You could learn it in thirty minutes."

"Could I do it at home?"

"Of course."

"What's the name of the contractor?"

"Don't worry about his name. I'll get the materials for you and have a delivery boy bring them over tomorrow, if you say you're interested."

"Why not? It would be crazy to turn down twice the money for the same amount of work."

"That's what I think. So it's agreed. I'll send someone around tomorrow morning."

Daniel looked out the window of the train at the green countryside rolling past. This wasn't his first trip out of New York City, his father having taken him along on summer trips to the mills since he was seven years old. But always it was exciting to be going somewhere, and to see the grimy brick buildings of the city gradually give way to trees and green fields. Only a few times, though, had he been further east than New York State. Now it thrilled him to think he was soon going to be on his own in Massachusetts. He had been twice to the mill town of Fall River with his father and once to New Bedford, both on Massachusetts' southern coast, but this would be his first time to the town of Lawrence, which was a center for worsteds located in the Merrimack River valley. He felt honored that his father was sending him to such an important mill, especially since he had never been to Lawrence before, even with Wolf.

Once there, he saw that the town was not unlike the other mill towns he had visited. The mill workers lived in squalid one room cottages or crowded together in one or two rooms of the many ramshackle tenements that stood four or five stories high. These buildings had stairways perched precariously on the outside and had been hastily built to accommodate the influx of new workers during the last fifteen years as the textile industry had expanded in response to the explosion in the garment business. But whereas the immigrant workers in the garment trade were primarily Jewish and Italian, the workers in the mill towns were largely from England and Ireland.

As early as 1875, families were lured by the possibility of turning the two hundred fifty dollars a year they might make in an English mill town to the four hundred seventy-five dollars they could earn in a Massachusetts mill. The heart of the town was the mill itself, an enormous brick building built over the river and at least as long as a city block. The overall effect was of a dilapidated and thoughtlessly planned settlement where the standard of living was only as high as it need be to keep the workers alive.

Daniel knew his father liked to buy in volume directly from the mills rather than from the warehouses and outlets in the city. Wolf always said he liked to eliminate the middleman whenever possible. He had often pointed out to Daniel that that was the practice he had followed since he had first arrived in this country, moving from baster, to subcontractor, to contractor, to manufacturer, and he still always thought it the wisest course to follow.

Once at the mill sites, Daniel went right away to the mill's warehouse. As always when he stepped into one of these huge cavernlike structures where bolt after bolt of fabric was stored, his eyes began to sting slightly from something in the air. He had never determined what it was. He passed rows of gabardine and serge and other worsteds, and each row was a different color. As he moved amid the fabrics, busily making notes in a small notebook he had brought with him, he became aware of another man not too far behind him who was going through the same process. Daniel wouldn't have noticed the man in the first place if it hadn't been that the man almost seemed to be following in his exact footsteps. Wherever Daniel stopped and made notes, it seemed that a minute later the man did too, as Daniel could see from his new position further down the row.

The man appeared quite a bit older than Daniel, maybe about his father's age or older, and was very well dressed in a suit made of brown-checked worsted. Daniel noticed the suit in particular because, although worsteds had been used for women's clothes for many decades, it was only more recently that they were used for men's. The suit fit him well, in spite of his potbelly and large frame, and even gave him a somewhat dapper demeanor. He had a large round face, slightly reddish, with a straight nose and prominent chin, and he was wearing a Homburg.

Daniel spent several more hours choosing the fabrics according to the guidelines Wolf had taught him. Then he approached the clerk at the long counter in the back of the warehouse.

The clerk was middle-aged, had a sharp, pointed nose and pale, worried eyes that went with his very businesslike manner. As he looked over Daniel's order, he began to make a column of hasty black scratchings on a pad. Then he cleared his throat and began to punch the numbers into a black adding machine with short stabs of his long fingers. "That will be four hundred and sixty-eight dollars," he announced briskly.

Daniel raised an eyebrow. "That's almost twenty per cent more than last time."

"Well, yes. Prices are going up everywhere. Haven't you heard?" the clerk replied, slightly annoyed.

"Five per cent, maybe eight. Not fifteen."

"You're behind the times, sonny. These are the new prices, just posted this week. Now do you want this order or not?"

Daniel calculated quickly. He would be returning to MW Enterprises with much less inventory than his father was expecting. Still, if those were the prices, he saw that he had little choice.

The clerk cleared his throat to signal his impatience.

"I'll take them," said Daniel, and wished he could be pleased with his decision.

As he was leaving the counter, the clerk looked up to see the large potbellied man in the worsted suit approaching him. At once he went into a sequence of bowing and scraping. "Ah, Mr. Detweiler," he exclaimed. "One of our very favorite customers!" He ran around from behind the counter, and began to pump the man's hand furiously. Daniel repeated the name Detweiler to himself a couple times and wondered who the man was.

The next morning, as Daniel stood at the train station awaiting the train back to New York City, he saw the same man he had seen following behind him at the mill. He had to struggle for a moment to recall his name. Then he remembered it was Detweiler. The man was standing not too far from Daniel on the platform and was busy unwrapping a large cigar which he had taken from his breast pocket. Daniel noticed Detweiler had manicured fingernails which made him wonder more about the man. Everything about his attire was well turned. Only the big cigar and red face contrasted with the aura of elegance he reflected. As he lit the cigar, he looked up and saw Daniel watching him and smiled politely, then averted his gaze as he puffed a cloud of ill-smelling smoke into the morning air.

"Detweiler," Daniel repeated to himself. The name was beginning to sound familiar, but he didn't know why.

Then he forgot about the man as the train steamed into the station. On the trip back to New York, he didn't look out the window once. Instead, his thoughts were on the rising costs of worsteds, what his father's reaction might be, and what he could do about it.

"Four hundred and sixty-eight dollars for how many bolts?" Wolf's voice rose registering his astonishment.

"That's what the prices are now. They've gone up again." Daniel did not like the role of delivering his father bad news, especially when he had a plan he hoped his father would heed.

Before Daniel could say anything more, Wolf banged his fist down on the desk. "That's outrageous!" he shouted.

Daniel was determined to stay calm. "You're right. And it's not going to get better."

"You're telling me? Well, I won't stand for it," he announced. "I'll think of some way around all this. You can count on that." He slammed the accounts book closed.

"I think I already know a way," ventured Daniel.

Wolf looked at him sharply. "Yeah? What is it?" He had noticed lately that Daniel was speaking with more confidence and authority all the time. He didn't know how he felt about that. He was glad the boy was turning out to have some fire to him, but on the other hand, he didn't like the possibility of anyone running things but himself, not yet anyway. The day when he would have to step down would come soon enough.

Daniel sensed he had to move carefully. "Well,

actually, it's something I'd guess you've already thought of."

"What's that?"

"We both know the prices in the mills are going up all the time. And, no matter what, we need fabrics."

"Yeah, so, get to the point. What was my idea?"

"You're always saying to me, 'Cut out the middleman.' That's how you got MW Enterprises to where it is today. Well, that's what I think we ought to do. Cut out the middleman and buy our own textile mill."

Wolf stared at him, then finally spoke in slow, measured tones. "Sounds like a lot of work. And there aren't any textile mills in New York City, which is where I'm needed."

"You don't have to run it. You can send Mario up there. As a bachelor, he won't mind leaving his family. Or you could send me."

Wolf looked at him and Daniel could tell his father was sizing him up. He slowly lifted his chest and stood up taller, taller even than Wolf.

"Sit down," Wolf said suddenly, "so we can talk more comfortably." He felt a lot better when he could look the boy directly in the eye.

"I think you're doing a fine job, here," Wolf began.

"I could do a good job with whatever you give me," Daniel professed.

"Yes, in time you probably could."

Daniel tried not to bristle at his father's use of the term *in time*. So far, *in time* seemed to be what everything came down to between him and Wolf.

"In time," Wolf repeated, "you could do anything you put your mind to. I've no doubt of that. But right now I think you're a little young for such a responsibility as running a textile mill. You don't know a thing about mills."

Daniel thought, *No less than you do,* but he kept it to himself. "I know about business though, just as you do. I know about systems and procedures and managing. I could run MW Enterprises and I could run a textile mill."

"I think you're getting ahead of yourself, boy. Although I do think the idea about buying a textile mill has possibilities."

Wolf finally agreed to consider Daniel's idea and during the next few months he thought a lot. He had to admit his son had made a good suggestion. If MW Enterprises could control its own mill, it would be able to get its own fabrics at cost, and the mill would still be able to charge whatever the market would bear to the other manufacturers. That would put MW Enterprises that much ahead of the competition. The best thing to do, he decided, would be to make a scouting trip to upstate New York. If he could find something closer to home than Massachusetts, perhaps in one of the cities on the Hudson's east bank, say Troy or Schenectady, then he just might be on to something.

It was ten o'clock in the morning and Wolf's usual delivery boy had not yet come in. Wolf went down in the street to see if he could tag someone looking for some quick money. Normally he would have sent Mario or one of the workers on this kind of errand, but under the circumstances he knew he couldn't. Once on the streets, his arms laden with the bodices and trim, he thought, What the hell. He'd take the work over to Angelica himself.

"Wolf!" she exclaimed when she opened the door. She hastily pulled her robe more tightly closed and smoothed her hand over her hair, which was loose over her shoulders. "Please excuse me. I forgot this morning was when the new materials were coming." She paused a moment, then added, "I never expected you to be the delivery boy."

He could see she didn't know whether to be pleased or embarrassed that he had found her half-dressed, and although he tried not to look at her too intently, he still noticed she looked tired and her eyes had dark circles around them. "I had business over in this area anyway. I decided I might as well drop the work off myself."

She showed him to the sole table in the middle of the room that was living room, bedroom and kitchen all in one. He spread the materials out and spent the next twenty minutes showing her what needed to be done with the garment tops and answering her questions. She had so many questions that he began to feel she was trying to delay him.

"When I am ready, then shall I take them to the contractor? I think I can be finished by the day after tomorrow."

She was looking up at him, and he noticed how petite and fragile she was next to him. Again he felt a surge of protectiveness toward her, a desire to shield her from anything ugly, harsh or difficult.

"That won't be necessary, Angelica. Someone can come by to pick them up."

"The contractor will do that?"

He nodded his head.

"Thank you again, Wolf. You've been so good, like a . . . like a godfather to me." She reached out and touched his arm. She was trembling.

"Angelica?" he said softly. Suddenly she started to cry. "Come," he said at once and led her to the make-shift sofa that served at night as a bed. He sat down next to her. "Tell me, Angelica. Why are you sad?"

At his question she shook her head vigorously from side to side and her crying deepened into sobs. He pulled her against his chest and held her there in his arms. As he felt her shake and tremble against his body, she reminded him of a small puppy.

Finally she managed, "I can't tell you, Wolf. I can't tell anybody."

"It would make you feel better to talk to someone about it." He took out his handkerchief and tried to dab at the tears that had streaked the side of her face, but she clung to him and refused to sit back.

"Please," she whispered, "just hold me."

He held her as she had asked, and in spite of his concern for her unhappiness, he had to admit he enjoyed the feel of her, so small and obviously needing him, as she nestled in his arms. They sat that way, his arms enfolding her, for what seemed to be a long time. Later, he couldn't remember who it was who started it, but suddenly their lips were touching and then the robe was falling from her body and she was murmuring to him.

"Wolf, hold me tighter," she whispered. He held her tightly as she asked and caressed her soothingly. When the robe fell from her shoulders, he felt her bare skin underneath his hand. She was soft and warm and trembling slightly.

"I want you to do something for me, Wolf," she said in his ear. "I want you to make love to me."

He held her away from his chest and looked at her, seeing first the look in her eyes and then the bareness of her body. He gave in to the desire that he had been holding in check and as they began to make love, her tears finally stopped.

Afterward Wolf was determined to know what it was that had made her so unhappy. When she resisted his probings, he insisted. "Angelica, this is nonsense. You start to cry in front of me, then you tell me you can't say what you're crying about. If we know each other well enough to have made love just now, you can tell me."

"It's so hard for me to say this, Wolf, because Gregorio . . ." She paused and he feared she was going to start crying again. Then her words came out in a rush. "He doesn't want to touch me. When I come close and start to kiss him, he always tells me he's too tired. Wolf, he's tired all the time, even on Sunday when he doesn't have to go to the docks. That's why we have no bambinos, and we never will." She sat dry-eyed and shrugged lightly as she looked at him. "So I try to tell myself, maybe if you work hard and make a little money, Gregorio won't be so worried about money all the time and he won't have to work so hard. Then he won't be so tired always, and maybe we can have a baby."

"I can make sure, Angelica, that you always have work. You can count on that."

"Wolf, there is more. I am sometimes afraid that I don't want Gregorio anymore either. I'm afraid that if he starts to want me again, I may not want him to make love to me. I'm afraid that when he touches me I will think of you and wish it were you that were touching me."

Wolf pulled her to him. "Angelica, we must not worry too much about things that might never happen. You must give Gregorio more of a chance. Five years is not a long time, although I'm sure it seems like that to you. You married him because you loved him. It's that you must remember. So what if you don't have a whole household full of children. You still have each other." He couldn't help but be aware of the irony of his advice, advice that he might just as well have given to himself in his own marriage. He took her gently in his arms. "Besides, you know we cannot meet like this again."

Her mouth dropped open in a pout, but she said nothing.

"It wouldn't be wise, you can see that, I'm sure. It isn't that I don't care for you. What we have just shared is very special to me, just as you have always been, and I would do anything I could to help you. You must believe that. But I have a wife and you have a husband."

"That didn't seem to stop you just now." She glared at him defiantly.

He forced a halfhearted smile and chucked her under the chin. "Such outrage, Angelica." He sighed, and his face became serious. "But it has always been my wife that I cared most about and really wanted to be with." As he said this, he felt a sickness in the pit of his stomach.

"Then why weren't you ever with her. Why did you come to our house all the time and talk to me and Lucia?"

"I came to your house because Mario was my friend, and because my wife was always busy with her own work at home." He tugged on a lock of her hair, somewhat amused at her strange reasoning. "And if I remember right, it was always you who were talking to me, rather than the other way around. I can't continue to see you because it would hurt your husband very much if he found out, and it would hurt my wife." Wolf felt the irony of these words too, for deep in his heart he wasn't sure Marya would even care any longer. He wasn't sure it mattered to her what he did anymore.

"But you did see that whore Adrianna," Angelica insisted stubbornly. "I don't see why you can't see me now."

Wolf thought back on that scene in the café with Mario and Lucia so long ago. Before he could reply, Angelica began again.

"And your wife, was she mad with you when she found out about Adrianna?"

Wolf stared intently at her. "She never found out."

"But she did," Angelica countered, impassioned. "Because Lucia told her that. . . ." A wild look in his eyes made her break off in midsentence.

He grabbed her by the shoulders. "What did you say?"

"I . . . I. . . ." Angelica was unable to finish her sentence.

He tightened his grip. "You just said that Lucia told my wife something, didn't you? Are you telling me that Lucia told my wife I had seen another woman?" He looked at her fiercely.

"Yes," she said in a small voice, afraid to say anything else.

He let his hands drop and his voice was quiet. "When did this happen?"

"It was years ago, before Lucia and I married, when Lucia . . . when we were both so much in love with you. You shouldn't have gone with that whore Adrianna, Wolf," she looked up, slowly regaining her composure.

"I can't believe she's known all this time," Wolf groaned, half to himself, half aloud, ignoring the reproach that had crept back into her voice.

She heard him. "If your wife never said anything to you, then maybe she doesn't care," she suggested with a mixture of anger, hope and a trace of compassion.

Wolf looked right through her, having completely forgotten his present predicament. His thoughts were all on Marya. Maybe Angelica was right. Maybe Marya didn't care. It was astounding to think that all this time she had said nothing to him. The more he thought, the better he was able to pinpoint the time when this must have occurred. He remembered his and Marya's renewed closeness after the fire and then how it had abruptly ended and he had no longer been able to reach her. Their marriage had suddenly turned cold again and he had not known why. Now he recalled that shortly after that, she had renewed her sketching and begun to visit those Fifth Avenue patrons that she had given up during the period when they were close and passionate with each other.

It cut him to the quick to think he had created all the distance that had grown between them in these past years.

Chapter 16

Marya felt an extra excitement as she waited downstairs in Andrew's drawing room. Tonight he had told her he wanted to take her to Richard Canfield's famous casino. She had dressed in a gown of black lace as fine as cobwebs over yellow silk taffeta, and trimmed in black satin ribbon. The bodice was cut in a moderately low circle and its slightly pouched front accentuated her small waist. She had wanted to look especially good tonight, for it was the first time she had ever dared to meet Andrew at night and the first time he would be taking her out among his friends.

It had been surprisingly easy for her to get away from the house tonight after all because Wolf had decided to take Daniel and Elke to one of the new nickelodeon houses that were all the rage and she had no interest in going. She knew they would be out late, and that she would be able to slip away for a few hours with Andrew.

She also knew that what she was doing represented a further step in her romance with Andrew. This was the first chance she had taken that was truly risky. Although there was no risk that she would run into Wolf, what she was doing was admitting in certain

circles that she was seeing Andrew Markingham more
than as a casual acquaintance. She well knew that such
a liaison did not, in Andrew's circles, make her a
woman of questionable repute, but it did in her own
mind. Yet, she insisted to herself in a state of annoyance, she should shake these last vestiges of those old,
empty values she had tried to leave behind her in the
land of the czars. Still, she hadn't been as successful at
leaving behind as much of those early teachings as she
had tried. As a result, there were just certain things she
preferred not to think too much about, and this was
one of them. Wolf was no longer her lover and she
needed a man's love, she told herself. There was certainly nothing wrong with that.

Canfield's Casino was reputedly the most exclu-
sive and elegant gambling resort in the country, if not
the world. It was the casino of the Four Hundred, New
York's cream of society, and was impeccably run by
Richard Canfield, the extent of whose own gambling
was limited to following inside tips on the stock market
provided him by his wealthy patrons. Marya had heard
her clients talk of it for years, and although she largely
kept a realistic head about the great wealth and fashionable surroundings she found herself amidst, her
curiosity had been piqued by the discussions of Canfield's Casino and of the man himself.

He was reputed almost never to come into the
gambling rooms or supper club of his casino. His main
interests in life were his magnificent art collection, said
to be one of the most impressive private collections in
the country, and in literature, which he pursued by
amassing an equally impressive library collection. And
yet, it was whispered, he was a common hoodlum who
had even served time in jail for his activities some
years before. Such talk had fired Marya's imagination
and so it was that she eagerly looked forward to a
glimpse, if not of the enigmatic man himself, at least of
his palatial casino.

Andrew was suddenly standing before her.

"My God, Marya, I've never seen you look more beautiful. You'll turn every head in the casino tonight." He continued to stare at her until she blocked his vision by kissing him lightly on the lips. Then he helped her on with her cape and they went outside to the waiting carriage.

A while later, as they stood in a small corridor between two locked doors, unable to proceed into the casino, Marya was mystified. She looked to Andrew for an explanation for why they couldn't enter at once.

"Don't worry, my darling," Andrew reassured her as he put his arm around her. "We're just being examined by Canfield's employees through peepholes this very minute to make sure we are who we say we are."

"Why is that?"

"Rumor has it that the prince of gamblers, as he is called, will admit only those patrons who he is sure are financially sound enough to sustain large losses at the gambling tables."

"Then the odds are that much against the patrons?"

"Indeed. Canfield always cautions people that it is unavoidable that they will eventually lose, and they must not be given false confidence by any short term winnings."

"And yet the people still come?"

"Such is human nature. You've heard the expression 'Hope springs eternal'? Just like the attitude many have toward death, although it is inevitable, each thinks he might beat the system."

As soon as one door was unlocked by a special mechanism, they found they had come to another which also required unlocking. Having passed successfully through the series of doors, they emerged into an exquisitely decorated reception room. From there they ascended to the second story where the gaming rooms were. As Andrew escorted her from room to room, Marya saw that there were no more than five or six people in each.

"You see, Marya, it is just as I predicted. You all but stop the gaming in each room that you enter."

"Then that is another reason people come here. Not just to gamble but to be seen."

"Always, my dear. The pursuit of beauty is one of the cornerstones upon which high society is built."

"If that is one of the cornerstones, then another must surely be pleasure."

"Add to those two cornerstones status through money and then power, and you have the foundation for the whole edifice. Of course, less flattering, and perhaps more realistic names for the cornerstones might be greed, fear and insecurity."

"And the fourth?"

"In place of the pursuit of beauty, there would be the pursuit of superficial gloss. Remember, Marya, to be successful in society, one must always elevate style over substance. One must never become confused about that and mistakenly think that the substance of something, its meaning, is more important than the form it is delivered in, its style. Form is always more important than content."

"Now you sound cynical, Andrew."

"Not really. I just know my people, that's all. I've lived in this world all my life, so I have had over forty years to study the denizens of these lofty climes as a naturalist might study life in the jungles of the Amazon, the bowerbirds of New Guinea or the aborigines of the Australian outback." He steered her into a room that was more crowded than the others. At the long table sat elegant women draped in more diamonds than Marya had ever thought one person could own. Because her dealings with the rich had been limited to afternoon meetings and teas, she had never seen the glitter of the night life in full regalia. The gentlemen were dressed in dark evening attire with crisp white shirts and many of them also sported enormous diamonds on their fingers.

"This is the roulette table," explained Andrew. "Shall we see if luck is smiling on us?"

"Of course," Marya agreed and wondered why it was that so many things Andrew said often seemed to have an added significance. He made it sound like he was talking about more than just their luck at the table.

The croupier looked up from the table and saw them. "Good evening, Mr. M.," he nodded.

Andrew returned the croupier's greeting. "Good evening, Frederic. I'd like you to meet Mrs. L." Andrew turned to Marya. "Only the initials of a patron's last name are used here," he whispered, "to maintain a facade of privacy."

"But everyone knows who everyone is," protested Marya, incredulous.

"Of course."

She also realized he must come here fairly regularly if he was known by the staff, and she was aware of how little they really knew of their lives apart from each other.

He handed her a marker. "Place it on any number you wish. If your number comes up on the roulette wheel, you'll win seventeen times the amount the marker is worth."

Marya noticed that some players had straddled numbers with their markers and asked Andrew what that meant.

"Should either of the two numbers that their markers are straddling come up, they will win eight times the amount of that marker's value. See how there is a marker straddling four numbers at the end of the board? It's covering numbers twenty-nine, thirty, thirty-two and thirty-three. If the roulette ball should stop on any one of those numbers, the payoff is four to one. You have other choices, too. You can bet two to one that the number the ball settles on will be black or red—that's the safest bet of all—or you can play 'thirds.' That means you bet the ball will fall on a number located on the first third of the board, the second third or the last. So, Marya, now you have the full range of bets possible, from the most to the least safe. Which will you play?"

Without hesitating, she put her marker on number eighteen, that representing the number of years she had been in America. The croupier spun the wheel in one direction with his right hand and the smaller circumference of numbers in the other direction with his left hand. All heads watched the silver ball spinning in circles, completely under its hypnotic allure until it came to a stop on number nineteen.

Immediately the croupier set an ornament, an eagle formed out of solid gold, onto the winning number. Then he raked from the table all markers that had not won.

Marya watched her marker being swept away. "Oh," she sighed in disappointment. Then she remembered that the number of years she had been here was nineteen. She should have bet nineteen after all, and she would have won.

Andrew was handing her another marker. "Place another one. And remember, you don't have to play the highest odds."

This time she placed the marker on number nineteen. Andrew raised his eyebrows. "Are you sure you want to play that same number, Marya? It's highly unlikely it would come up two times in a row, and you are playing the greatest odds."

"Yes. It's the number I should have played in the first place."

The look in her eyes caused Andrew to shrug his shoulders. His tone changed to one of amusement. "But then I never like to hamper a lady's hunches. They're what most luck is made of."

The croupier spun the wheels and the silver ball clattered as all eyes tried to follow the blur of its motion. Then the ball came into focus as it slowed down and rolled past fifteen, ten, three, one, starting again at thirty-six, thirty, twenty, nineteen, eighteen, and around one more time, seeming to take forever in the minds of those who watched it, until it rolled more and more slowly and finally stopped on number nineteen.

The crowd gasped. Everyone looked at Marya as the croupier announced, "Number nineteen," and smiled at her. All heads turned her way as the golden eagle was placed on her number. Then her winnings—seventeen more markers—were spilled alongside her original marker. Again the croupier quickly raked away all markers that hadn't won. Marya felt a thrill run through her. She had never gambled before and she experienced a jolt of excitement to see the pile of markers she had garnered.

The crowd around the table had grown. Many people were just watching rather than playing, their attention riveted by the pile of markers in front of the beautiful red-haired woman in the black lace dress. Andrew heard the undercurrent of voices around the table and he knew they were asking who this thrice-blessed woman was, blessed with luck, beauty and one of the most influential men in the city.

"You are indeed a lucky lady," said Andrew with admiration. "I see I must always keep you by my side. You appear to be very good with games of chance."

Marya looked at the markers with astonishment. How easy it had all been, she remarked to herself. The crowd was still staring at her but she wasn't at all aware of it.

Andrew's voice cut through the dreamlike state she felt herself in. "Do you wish to place another bet, Marya?"

She shook herself lightly and suddenly said no in a very determined voice.

Andrew took her by the arm. "Come, let's get something to eat. The supper room on the basement floor is magnificent, and the cuisine as good as that of Delmonico's or Sherry's." He took from his pocket a velvet bag and began to scoop the markers into it. On the first floor he stopped at the cashier's to redeem the markers for cash.

Marya's eyes widened in disbelief as she saw the amount of money the cashier was laying on the counter. She saw hundred dollar bill after hundred dollar bill set down before her until by her impromptu reckonings the total must have come to over eight thousand dollars. Never in her life had she seen that much money in cash, and her knees felt weak to think of how far that money would go on the Lower East Side where ten dollars a week was not an uncommon wage.

Andrew pushed the bills into the small velvet bag, and as they walked away from the cashier, he put the bag in her hand. "Your winnings, my dear."

"You aren't serious, are you?" She came to an abrupt stop.

"I certainly am. This is what you won. Take it."

"But it was just a game. I wasn't even using my own money. It was yours."

"And you are my guest. So you are entitled to take whatever you earned."

Marya knew money was something never to be discussed among the very rich and that it was bad form for her to press the issue, but she couldn't help herself. "Andrew, I didn't earn it, as you say. And what I won was done without a cent of my own money or even my intelligence. I simply can't accept the money. I don't even understand how it could have amounted to such an astronomical sum."

"It's not a gift, I assure you. I would be highly offended, Marya, if you didn't accept your earnings. I certainly don't need it and besides, although the sum may seem incredibly high to you, I can tell you that by the standards of Canfield's Casino it isn't unreasonable or unheard of. In fact, it's the standard win when you play roulette at such high odds and have a bit of luck. You must be able to figure out that the winnings would be high when the minimum bet here is five hundred dollars."

Marya gasped in spite of herself. She had no idea that the marker had stood for five hundred dollars or that so many people had that kind of money with which to play nonchalantly. She looked at Andrew standing there very determined and weighed what he had said. Finally she saw she had no choice but to take the money.

As they crossed the reception room toward the staircase, a new group of people was coming in, having just passed through the system of locked doors. The group was small, with three gentlemen and an older woman, all wearing extravagant evening dress. Their eyes couldn't help but be drawn to Marya and Andrew as they came into the room for they made a very striking couple. Marya was aware of the woman assessing her with a cool detachment while the three men gazed in open admiration. Something about one of the men in particular made her return his gaze a little more than she normally would have. He was considerably younger than the other two men, of moderate height, with a thick shock of brown hair that had glints of reddish gold highlights. He had broad, squared off shoulders and what looked to be the gait of a sportsman, which contrasted with the midnight blue tailcoat, matching trousers trimmed with braid down the side and his white piqué shirt, all of which he wore with white kid gloves and patent leather shoes. In his hands he carried a black silk opera hat. But it was his eyes, a deep green, that startled her. They made her think at once of the boy she had seen in the Palm Garden of the Waldorf some ten years ago and whom she was constantly on the lookout for whenever she went into a public place, although she was never sure why. She was still looking in the direction of this well-dressed young man as he disappeared with his party up the staircase.

Andrew noticed right away that she had been distracted by the foursome that had just come in. "Did you see someone you know?" he asked.

"What?" returned Marya absent-mindedly, before she recovered her presence of mind. "No," she added hastily, "I thought for a moment I did, but, no, I don't think so at all."

Later that evening as Marya rode home in Andrew's carriage, she thought of the two remarkable events of the evening. She was still stunned to have tucked into her purse over eight thousand dollars. Once she'd gotten over the shock of receiving that much money—she still couldn't bring herself to say she'd earned it—she'd begun to plan with great satisfaction what she would be able to do with it. Now she would be able to give piano and dancing lessons to Elke without asking Wolf, and even some art instruction just in case Elke decided she wanted to become a couturiere. It would be good to have a little extra and this way she wouldn't have to touch the remaining jewels, which she wanted to keep in case of emergency. Although the shop was doing well, she remembered what it was like to have nothing and always felt better having a cushion.

But, strangely enough to her, overshadowing the impact of having become a rich woman within a matter of minutes at a gaming table was the sight of the young man with the green eyes. Even now as she thought about him, she tried to shake the cobwebs from her mind so that she might be very clear about her thoughts. In spite of what she had told Andrew, no matter how clearly she tried to think she kept coming back to her first impression, which was that he bore a strong resemblance to the young man she had seen in the Waldorf so many years before. Somehow she was sure it was the same boy, despite the fleeting glimpses she had caught of him on both occasions.

Her preoccupation with this trivial coincidence bothered her. What was it about this young man that so intrigued her? How could she be positive it was even the same person? But somehow she just knew. She thought of her pictures, as she called them, and guessed that this was another of those unexplainable notions. She knew by now not to question these pictures or hunches, for they defied all logic and reason. Marya therefore resolved silently to discover what it was about this young man that so intrigued and disturbed her. Something inside her, though, warned that this was a task better kept to herself, so she said nothing to Andrew or anybody else. She promised she would put herself in a position to find out, so that at the very least, the matter might finally be laid to rest and stop disturbing her.

Wolf sat at his desk in the empty factory and looked at his watch. It was the Sabbath, the workers were gone, and he was expecting Daniel to arrive at any time. He had asked Daniel to come to the office because he wanted to tell him about the Arawanee Mill in Troy for which he had begun negotiations. Now he scratched rows of figures on a blank pad of paper as he prepared what he was going to tell Daniel. Arawanee was a mill that met his specifications. It was within the state of New York, so he would be able to get to it quickly and fairly easily in the event of pressing business or emergencies. It was small but had the possibility of expanding and it was moderately profitable. Also, it manufactured worsteds exclusively, which were always in great demand by the clothing manufacturers.

He hadn't yet told Daniel of his trips to look at the mill because he preferred to investigate the matter on his own and then inform Daniel once he was close to a final decision. It was good for the boy to come up with suggestions like buying a mill, but he feared Daniel might have such an attachment to his own suggestion and to Lawrence where he'd first had the idea, that he might find it hard to be objective. Wolf knew he himself was the best judge about the matter and didn't want anyone else's opinion to obscure or hinder his conclusions.

He heard footsteps on the far side of the huge loftlike room, which, because of the emptiness of the building, resounded loudly. He continued writing figures on the pad and looked up only when the door opened. He was surprised to see it wasn't Daniel who stood in the doorway.

"Hey, Mario! What are you doing here? You're supposed to be chasing women today." He stood up and started to walk around to the front of the desk to shake Mario's hand. He stopped when he saw the expression on Mario's face.

"You son of a bitch," Mario hissed. "What do you think you're doing?"

Wolf stuck his arm out and put his hand on Mario's chest to slow him down. "Wait a minute, Mario. What's going on here? I don't know what you're talking about."

His face was dark with anger. "I'm talking about you and Angelica, that's what I'm talking about." Wolf put up both hands and tried to take Mario by the shoulder. Although Mario was considerably shorter, he was built like a bull and just kept coming. Wolf hoped to calm him down. "Now just a second. Let's sit down and talk."

"There's nothing to talk about." Mario pulled back his right arm, then swung it at Wolf as hard as he could.

Wolf saw it coming and at the last minute angled to the side. "For God's sake, Mario, stop it! I don't want to fight you!"

"I want to fight you, you son of a bitch. C'mon. Let's go."

He swung again, and again Wolf turned to one side. He had tried to stop Mario, but it hadn't worked. Now he was beginning to get angry. Mario swung again, now with his left and this time the blow connected. Wolf staggered back a few steps, then suddenly he lost his temper. Thoughts of Daniel's imminent arrival flew from his head. Enraged, he threw himself at Mario and they both crashed to the floor. They continued to punch at each other as they half-crawled, half-rolled across the office.

For the better part of the next fifteen minutes, they wrestled and pummeled one another. The longer they fought, the slower and heavier their motions became until they were both swinging as if they were drunk. Finally Mario rolled to one side, and trying to sit up, fell back against the wall.

When he began to talk, his words were slurred. "What the hell you doing to Angelica? I thought you was my brother."

Wolf hadn't planned to admit that anything was going on between him and Angelica, but now he was too exhausted to see what difference it made. If Mario wanted to know, he'd tell him. He braced himself against the opposite wall and stared back at him. His words were as slurred as Mario's.

"Yeah, I've seen her. So what?"

"So what?" Mario growled with what little energy was still in him. "That's all you have to say, 'so what'?"

"Yeah, that's all I have to say. So what? No, I have one more thing to say. What are you going to do about it?"

Mario tried to straighten up but collapsed instead. He lay flat on his back and stared at the ceiling. "How could you do it?"

"It was easy," Wolf finally said. "She asked me."

"Hah! She asked you to give her a job as a subcontractor? How could she? She didn't even know the word. It was impossible she could ask you for such a thing."

Wolf stared at Mario, but Mario was still contemplating the ceiling. He sunk down onto one elbow and rested his chin on his hand. "What did you just say?"

"How did she even get the idea to do piecework?"

Mario stressed each word. "It had to come from you."
He stopped looking at the ceiling and turned his gaze
on Wolf.

Wolf found it hard to believe what he was hearing. Did Mario know the whole story about him and
Angelica, or did he just know that he had been giving
her jobs so she could earn a little extra money? He
concluded that Mario must only know about the garment work.

"How could you do that to my own sister? Isn't
she like your sister, too? How could you get her started
in this rotten business—and at the lowest level of it?"

Wolf, a little stronger now, was able to sit up.
"Look, Mario. She was desperate. She needed money
and she didn't want to hurt her husband's pride. So she
came to me and asked if I knew of something she
could do."

"Gregorio would kill you if he found out. All he
has to do is to come home sometime in the middle of
the day. That's what I did . . . dropped by because I
was making a delivery in the area. She opens the door
and right away I can tell something's wrong because
she's not at all happy to see me. She just stands in the
doorway and acts real nervous. For one second, to tell
you the truth, I think maybe she's got some guy there
or something. Can you imagine? I thought that of my
own sister. That's how guilty she was acting. Then I
pushed by her to see what was up in her place. That's
when I see the table and the floor under it all covered
with piles of sleeves. I look at those sleeves, and I say,
'Hey, I recognize those sleeves. I see the rest of those
dresses every day at work.'"

"So she told you?"

"Yeah."

"Anything else?" Wolf asked noncommittally.

"Yeah. She said you got her a manufacturer that
pays real good, more than anyone else. So I tell her
what a kid she is. That manufacturer is you."

"You told her that?"

"Yeah. I also told her I didn't want her to be doing that kind of work anymore. She needs money, she can come to me. I don't have any wife or kids, so I got a little extra to help her out with. I help my parents too, but what the hell, I got enough left over."

"So it's settled."

"No. She tells me she doesn't want anybody else's money. She says she likes doing that kind of work. Can you imagine? You and I and everybody else can't wait to get on to something better. But she likes it."

"It's only because she doesn't have to make her living that way. It gives her something to do until the babies come."

"That's what she said. I still don't like it though. It's not right for a lady."

"What's the difference if she's happy, Mario?" Wolf stood up with an effort.

Mario got to his feet and threw his arms around Wolf. "Hey, brother," he grinned. "Let's just forget it, okay?"

Wolf laughed and shook Mario's hand. "That's fine with me. You're a hell of a fighter." He couldn't help but wonder how their fight would have gone had Mario known about the rest of the story.

They were standing like that, their clothes in tatters and traces of blood on their hands and faces, when Daniel opened the door. "Hey, bambino," Mario cried when he saw him. "You come with us. We're just now going to celebrate with a little wine."

Wolf saw Daniel looking at him with an expression of utter bewilderment, and he nodded his head yes. Then the three of them clambered down the stairs together, heading for a café.

Daniel watched for the next two hours as Mario and his father celebrated. He sipped at his wine and didn't feel particularly jubilant. He had been looking

forward to hearing what it was his father had called
him to the factory for that morning and was disappointed to find that their talk was delayed.

Although his father seldom drank, when he did it
usually was with Mario and it was liable to go on for
some time. It wasn't until many drinks later that Daniel
was able to piece together part of what must have happened between the two men. It had been apparent from
the moment he opened the door that they must have
had some kind of scuffle and he learned it had something to do with Mario's sister doing piecework. But
since he had never met Mario's sister to his recollec-
tion, it was difficult for him to have any real interest
in their disjointed references to the incident.

"Daniel, listen to this," his father said, one arm
around Mario's shoulder. He took out his keys and
sounded them on his wine glass. "Attention, Mario.
Attention, Daniel. I want you to hear this. It concerns
you both."

Mario put down his glass, and Daniel sat waiting
expectantly.

"I want you to know MW Enterprises is expanding. I'm in the process of buying a textile mill."

Daniel gave a slight start, but waited for his father
to finish. Suddenly he felt hopeful, although he told
himself to expect nothing. He had been disappointed
too many times before.

"And if all goes well, as I expect it will, then I
will be selecting a new manager for the mill."

Mario nodded appreciatively. "You're doing it,
Wolf. You're doing what you came here to this country
to do. One day you're going to be one of the biggest
men in this city." He laughed, sizing Wolf up. "Maybe
you already are."

Daniel held his breath and waited. He wanted his
father to continue.

"Where's the mill?" Mario asked.

Daniel fidgeted with the stem of his wine glass.

"It's in Troy. About one hundred and fifty miles

from here. You'd be able to make it back here to see your ladies in no time."

Daniel's heart fell. He knew what his father was saying.

Mario looked perplexed. "What do you mean?" He started to laugh as it dawned on him.

"That's right, Mario. As manager of the new mill, we might not see as much of you. You'd have to confine your romancing to the ladies of the east Hudson."

Mario was beside himself. "You're quite a man, Wolf. I've never known anyone else like you. Quite a man," he kept saying in almost boyish admiration.

Daniel stared into his wine glass until finally Mario spoke to him. "What's the matter, bambino? Aren't you going to congratulate me? I just got a promotion."

"Sure," Daniel tried to muster some enthusiasm. He raised his glass to Mario. "Mazel tov." Then he downed the rest of the wine in a single gulp and got up, preparing to leave the café.

"Where are you going?" Wolf asked.

"For a walk. I don't like the air in here."

"Wait a minute." Wolf got up. "I'll come with you." He bid Mario good-bye, then father and son stepped out into the cold, sobering air.

They walked along South Street where a strong breeze was blowing across the East River. Daniel set a brisk pace.

"You're upset," Wolf began.

"I guess you could say that."

"Listen, Daniel. You're my son, and one day everything will be yours."

Daniel stopped and faced Wolf. "You're always saying that. But when?"

"When you're ready. You're only—"

"What difference does my age make? What should matter is what I know. I've spent more years in that factory than almost anyone."

"Not more than I have and not more than Mario.

I still know what's best for MW Enterprises." He caught himself and changed his tone to a more conciliatory one. "Look, Daniel. I know you wanted to manage the mill. But it's too soon for you to be that far away from home."

"I'm almost the age you were when you left home."

"Almost. But you're still younger. And things are different now. This isn't Russia."

"No, this is America, the golden land. Where it's safe for us to live and we are supposedly free to do anything we wish. No, it definitely isn't Russia. You're always telling me life is easier here. So the fact that I'm younger than you were when you left home shouldn't matter."

Wolf was beginning to lose his patience. "Will you stop interrupting me? Just listen."

Daniel stopped talking and stared off in the distance at the long rows of ships, lined up prow after prow all the length of South Street and on out into the mistiness of the afternoon.

"You know I've been working ever since I came to this country to build a business my children and wife could be proud of. That's what my father did for his children, and that's what I expect you'll do for your children. But you haven't even finished high school yet. You just have to trust me when I tell you that the time is coming when it will all be yours." He waited a moment, and when Daniel didn't say anything, he asked, "Do you?"

"Do I what?"

"Do you believe me?"

"I guess so," Daniel said without enthusiasm.

Several months passed before Marya had an opportunity to suggest to Andrew that she would like to go to Canfield's Casino again. "Ah, so the bug has bitten you," he teased. But he eagerly agreed that they should go as soon as Marya could find a night free. He had even acquiesced to her request that she be allowed to use her own money for gambling since she could certainly afford it.

"Whether she can afford it or not," Andrew replied somewhat coolly when she mentioned it, "a lady is always a gentleman's guest."

But Marya persisted, and sensing it was the only way he might be able to have her company at all, he reluctantly agreed. But he could have no way of knowing that what was most on Marya's mind was not the gambling at all. She was staking her hopes on getting another chance to see the green-eyed young man who had intrigued her so.

So totally were her thoughts on the likelihood of again encountering the young man that she hardly was aware of what she put on for the evening. She was surprised, therefore, at Andrew's long and enthusiastic appreciation of her appearance when they met at the Brunswick Hotel for an early supper before going to Canfield's. But distracted as she was, she still noticed he was even more attentive than usual, more alert to her every emotion and need. As usual, she found such attention flattering, and couldn't help but think briefly and with a touch of bitterness about how different his concern for her was from Wolf's. Once at the gambling casino, Marya couldn't keep her eyes from roaming the faces there, searching for a glimpse of the young man. Andrew took her immediately to the roulette table, and she was disappointed to see there were just a few people around it and they were older gentlemen. Their eyes lit up to see the likes of Marya grace their table and they looked at Andrew with unconcealed envy.

As they were preparing to place their bets, their attention was drawn by the appearance of the reclusive proprietor, Richard Canfield. He was tall, heavyset and immaculately and elegantly dressed. Immediately his eyes went from Andrew to Marya, and then after a very long gaze, back to Andrew again.

"Mr. M., it is always a pleasure to have you as

our guest." Canfield welcomed them genially and extended his hand to Andrew. Then he turned his attention to Marya.

"This is Mrs. L.," Andrew presented Marya.

"Ah, yes," Mr. Canfield said at once, "a very lucky lady, I have heard."

Marya smiled and looked surprised that he would have heard of her.

"News of winnings travels fast," he explained, "and when the winnings are made by a beautiful woman, the news travels even faster."

"Thank you, sir, for the compliment."

"I don't give compliments, Mrs. L. It is simply a statement of fact, such as I might make about a magnificent painting or bust in my collection or," he paused slightly, "about one which I wish to acquire. You see, I am a connoisseur of beauty and have devoted my life to its attainment in every form."

"That is evident by your impressive casino," Marya said.

"The finest in the world," Andrew agreed.

"I see that my friend Mr. M. also has an eye for beauty," Canfield glanced at Marya. "Therefore, perhaps the two of you would do me the honor of visiting my personal apartment on the fourth floor. I would like to share with you the pleasures of my art collection."

Although sorry to leave the public rooms where she might have a chance to look for the young man who had gained such a hold on her thoughts, Marya looked forward to finding out more about their mysterious host. She was stunned by the luxury and taste of Richard Canfield's private quarters. He guided them from room to room, pointing out various paintings.

Marya spotted a portrait of Canfield himself and noted it was titled "His Reverence." When he saw her studying it, he remarked, "That was painted by my close friend James McNeill Whistler. Quite a remarkable artist, isn't he?"

Wanting to show them more of Whistler's works,

he then ushered them below to the casino's third floor. It was the floor, Andrew had told her, where there were private rooms for those players who wished to exceed the official limits of the house. Those limits, he added, were already higher than those of any other gambling resort in the world. As they came into one of the private rooms, Marya suddenly felt clammy all over and her knees were weak. Directly in front of her, talking to another gentleman, was the young man who had so obsessed her. At once he stepped forward and he and Canfield greeted each other.

Canfield turned to Marya and Andrew. "Mr. M. and Mrs. L., I'd like you to meet Mr. S."

"Mr. S. did you say?" Marya asked breathlessly, very disappointed that she was not to learn his full name quite yet.

"Yes. That's correct." The young man smiled at her peculiarly.

Canfield looked at her. "I think, Mrs. L., you and Mr. S. will find you have something in common, for he too is one of our exceedingly lucky patrons."

Marya stared deep into her young acquaintance's eyes as if she could read there some answer to her eternal question. He looked back at her admiringly, not at all displeased to have such a breathtaking and sophisticated woman looking at him so intently. Finally his attention was called away by Canfield addressing him.

"I hadn't expected to see you so soon after your spill in Central Park."

"I was fortunate indeed to be up on my feet again a few days later." He turned to Andrew and Marya. "I was the innocent victim of some out-of-control bicyclists last week," he explained in apparent good humor. "Novices, you know."

Richard Canfield took up the story. "I was passing by in my carriage at that precise moment and happened to witness the collision. Fortunately I was able to take Mr. S. home in my carriage. But from the looks of him that day, I never expected him to be up on his feet again so soon. And not only on his feet again, but on his bicycle. This fresh air enthusiast has already returned to his Sunday bicycle tours through the park, ready to trust his limbs and sanity to chance."

"But you must admit, more often than not chance has been very generous to me."

"So it has," agreed Canfield.

When he resumed his tour, Marya had no choice but to pull her attention away from this Mr. S. Just before she turned to go, she suddenly extended her hand toward the young man. "It was indeed a pleasure meeting you, sir. I hope we will have the opportunity to see each other again."

He took her hand and bent over it, kissing it lightly. "I'm sure we will."

"And you must take care in the park," she added, and then felt embarrassed because it had been such an obviously motherly thing to say. She was also aware Andrew was scrutinizing her every move. It wasn't like her to speak so boldly to a gentleman she had just met and one who was obviously her junior. From the look he shot her, he was clearly intrigued by her uncharacteristic behavior. She was relieved when he kept his reservations to himself and didn't question her about it. She was hardly aware of what Canfield said to her during the rest of the tour through his art collection, although she vaguely realized he was looking at her a great deal. She turned her thoughts about Mr. S. over and over in her mind and couldn't stop herself from thinking all kinds of ridiculous things, even though she cautioned herself it was all rather bizarre.

Later that evening as they bounced along in Andrew's carriage toward Marya's home, he suddenly seized her hand. "I want you to listen very carefully to what I'm going to say, Marya. Please don't interrupt me until I'm through."

She broke out of her thoughts about the enigma of Mr. S. with a twinge of dread. She was afraid he was going to talk about her inappropriate friendliness toward the young man earlier that evening.

"We've known each other for almost nine years, and during that time I have ceased to look upon you with anything but increasing admiration. I think seeing you that day in Delmonico's was the closest thing I've come to love at first sight and I've never stopped feeling that way. You have everything I want a woman to have. You are beautiful, you are intelligent, you are talented, and you are charming. When our friendship deepened into a love affair, I waited to see if I could still trust my feelings. I thought perhaps my enchantment with your physical allure was clouding my mind. But now, a year later, I still feel the same. I want you more than I've ever wanted a woman before in my life, and I want you in every sense. I'm not used to making declarations like this, so please bear with me. I tell you all this not to make you uncomfortable but to press upon you how much thought I have given to what I'm about to say. Marya, what I want, in short, is for you to leave your husband."

"I couldn't possibly do that," Marya looked at him, startled. This speech was not at all what she had steeled herself to hear, and it found her totally unprepared.

"I want you to let me finish, as I requested at the beginning. Now, what I was going to say is that I want you to leave your husband and—"

"I'm sorry, Andrew," she broke in again. "I know what you're going to say. And I just couldn't live in your keep as your mistress."

"Marya, will you listen to me? I didn't say anything about establishing you in a townhouse somewhere so that I could visit you just when I needed a convenient bit of physical or emotional solace and then carry on with the other parts of my social life as usual." He took her by the shoulders and looked her square in the face. "Will you just listen to me long enough so I can ask you to marry me?"

Marya stared at him and tried to gather her wits. "Marry you?"

"Yes. Marry me."

"Andrew, I couldn't possibly do that."

"Why not?"

"I . . . I . . . I just couldn't. I. . . ."

"You couldn't leave your husband?"

She looked down at her lap. "Yes."

"You've said little about your husband in these last few years, but I've been able to surmise certain things. One is that your circumstances are what I would term modest, although to you perhaps they seem quite good. But more important is that the romance between you is over. Am I right?"

It took her a while to answer. "Yes, I suppose so."

"I want you to think of what I can offer you. You will never want. You will live in an elegant house, wherever you choose, and your children will be well provided for. We can travel. We can entertain. You will have a husband who adores you."

His last statement stung. She thought of Wolf who so plainly did not adore her, who was busier with his business and his son than with her or his daughter. Still, she started to shake her head. "Andrew, I just can't."

"You're a beautiful woman," he broke in passionately. "You can't just throw your life away in a dead-end marriage. This isn't Russia and you're not the woman you were. I'm offering you something that can endure, that isn't just the product of overactive glands."

She was shocked by his frank language and her face registered it.

"You must pardon my directness, Marya, but I want you to consider all facets of what I'm offering you, and I want you to consider it from the viewpoint of a sophisticated woman in her thirties, not from that of the teenage girl you were when you left the old country."

She started to say something, but he put up his hand. "Marya, look at me. I want to say something that I think is important you hear. I have told you that you are a very beautiful woman, and I'm sure you can see it not only in my eyes but in the eyes of every man you pass. But I don't think you understand the nature of your beauty. It is an exquisiteness that is beyond . . . race. In short, Marya my dear, what I am trying to tell you is that with your fair skin, green eyes and rich red hair, and with the slight bit of accent you still retain—please don't be embarrassed to hear me speak this way—you can easily leave behind you all those distasteful memories of your past. There is no reason to consider yourself Russian or Jewish. Your accent is so minor. It doesn't scream out that you are from any particular country or religious background. All it does is add charm. I am telling you this so that you can capitalize on all of it. Americans adore accents, and they adore mystery, and they adore beauty. You have all three. They also adore money, and as my wife, you will have more of that than you can imagine. You need not tie yourself to your Jewish past. You left all that behind you years ago. If you just reach for it, Marya, you can have the promise of America, all of it. You can have the mansion on Fifth Avenue. You can lead the life that your beauty and intelligence have clearly destined you to lead. Isn't that what you came to this country for? To find a new life and a better one?"

"Yes, Andrew," she conceded, "but. . . ."

He pulled her to him and brushed her lips with his. "I don't want you to say yes or no. All I want is for you to think about it. Will you do that for me? I think that after our years of friendship I deserve at least that. Then, when the time is appropriate, we will talk about it again. We have time, Marya." He continued to kiss her until she felt the stirrings of desire for him once again.

"All right. I'll think about it," she murmured between kisses.

And she did think about it. Upon returning to the stultifying silences that always marked the occasions when she and Wolf were in the house together, she couldn't help but think about how, with just one word, her life could be so completely different. She watched herself, like someone watching a character on a stage, to see which way her heart would direct her.

Chapter 17

Marya stood at the foot of the Central Park reservoir, her eyes on the endless circle of bicyclists. She told herself she was behaving foolishly, but no matter how strongly she admonished herself, she couldn't stop herself. She had been standing there for over an hour and had already seen the actress Lillian Russell make two tours around the reservoir in the company of a florid and exceedingly flashy man. From his many rings dancing in the sunlight, Marya guessed he was the famous Diamond Jim Brady.

After another hour of standing, she decided she'd better walk or the pigeons would think she was a statue and start to roost on her. As she strolled, she was careful to scrutinize the face of each passer-by. All of a sudden she heard the screeching sound of bicycle brakes behind her and she whirled around to see a bicycle skidding toward her. At the last minute the driver swerved to avoid her and in so doing, lost control and slammed to the ground.

Marya was horrified. She had recognized the fallen bicyclist as the very person she had been seeking.

"David!" she cried as she ran to where he lay entangled with his bicycle on the dusty roadway. "Are you all right?"

He looked up at the woman standing over him and rubbed his eyes. He recognized her at once, but it took him a moment to realize where he had seen her before.

"Are you all right?" she repeated, her tone betraying her worry.

"I think so," he answered shakily. "Let me check myself over." He gingerly lifted up and freed his left leg from where it had been pinned underneath the trunk of his body. Then he took his right arm from between the wheel and the handlebars, and taking hold of the bicycle, raised it up off him. "Everything seems to be in working order so far," he grinned at her. He slapped his right hand against his leg to get the dust off, then offered it to her. "By the way, how is it you know my first name? I know you only as Mrs. L., I'm afraid," he laughed.

"I'm Marya Luminov. But I believe you're mistaken. I know you only as Mr. S."

"Sheffield. David Sheffield." He took a long look at her. "Strange, when I fell I thought you yelled my first name. Well, perhaps I hit my head too hard!" He noted she was wearing one of the new tailored suits. It was made of blue serge, featured a bolero over the skirt and was trimmed with black satin. At her throat was a black silk bow and on her head was a straw sailor hat circled with a black satin band. Most of her red hair was swept up under her hat, and as he looked at her, he remembered one of the things that had first struck him in Canfield's Casino was the incredible richness of her hair. All in all, she was a very fine specimen of a woman, he decided.

"Do you mind if we walk a bit?" he proposed. "I want to make sure no stiffness sets in and I'd deem it a delight to have your company."

Marya wasted no time in accepting his offer. As they continued through the park, she was overwhelmed by strange thoughts and sensations but still managed to exchange small talk as they made each other's acquaintance. They were walking past the lake, which was dotted with graceful gondolas and an occasional launch propelled by oar. On the opposite bank they could see the white wooden boathouse standing out sharply against the dark trees.

"Isn't New York beautiful," David nodded his head in the direction of the lake.

"Have you lived all of your life in New York?" Marya asked.

"Not really, but it surely seems it. I've been here almost as long as I can remember. Why do you ask?"

"I don't know. I just thought perhaps you reminded me of someone I once knew long ago."

"Well, I certainly hope he was someone you have fond memories of. Then you see, we should get along very well together. Because I already have good memories of you, just from the short time I've known you."

Marya was flattered and a little amused. Was it possible, she asked herself, that he was beginning to flirt with her? She looked at him out of the corner of her eye and saw that he was watching her intently. "How are you feeling from your spill now? Are you all right?" she asked.

"Yes, I'm perfectly fine. Say, I've an idea. Let's hire a bicycle for you and then we can ride together. Can you ride?"

Marya looked at him in astonishment. She had been waiting in this park for hours hoping to get a glimpse of him and somehow a word or two. Quite by chance things had turned out better than she could have planned and it seemed it was he who was eager to prolong their time together. He was doing all the pursuing for her. "I can probably ride better than you," she rejoined and began to tease him. "At least I haven't had any spills yet. As I recall Mr. Canfield mentioning, you've had more than one lately."

They rented a bicycle for Marya and as the two of them rode side by side through the park, Marya tried to study him whenever she could. It was preposterous, she told herself, even to be spending her time with this young man.

Her thoughts were interrupted by a young child who was running alongside their bicycles yelling something. She glanced down at the boy and then up into David Sheffield's smiling face at her side and involuntarily shuddered. But his grin was infectious and she found herself beaming back at him. Finally she decided that she liked this David Sheffield, whoever he was. He was a charming and friendly young man who carried himself well and was handsome. If she were his age, she might even fall in love with him, she giggled to herself, feeling suddenly very happy.

"Why are you laughing?" he asked.

"Nothing," she replied. "Just a foolish notion I had, the kind that would sound even more foolish if I were to say it out loud."

"I like to see you laugh. You're even more beautiful when you do."

Marya looked at him sharply. "Young man, I do believe you're flirting with me."

"No," he said. "I'm very serious. I'm serious, too, when I say I'd like to see you again. What do you think about meeting here again next week for another wholesome turn or two around the park?"

Marya did not need even a second to think about it. She agreed at once.

Their second meeting was marked by the same easy bantering that had marked their first. Marya wondered why she had taken such pains to look good for a young man who was obviously destined to be more a friend than anything else. After much indecision, she had finally selected an emerald green suit that matched her eyes and had a trim, relatively short skirt that made it ideal to wear bicycling.

David was unable to keep his eyes off her. Again

and again he stared at her and told her how lovely she looked.

"You mustn't flatter me so," she finally stopped him, laughing.

"I do it to hear you laugh and to hear you get angry with me," he teased. "When you get even the least bit excited, your accent starts to come out."

Marya looked at him indignantly. "It does not. I scarcely have any accent at all anymore."

"Where did you come here from?"

"From Russia. Many years ago. But still, I admit it, I have traces of the old country in my talk."

"Russia? That's where I came from too. I was born Russian, not American. But since I grew up here, I don't have any accent at all. In fact, I don't even know a word of the language. My parents do though."

Marya's heart had begun to beat wildly. "You're from Russia? Are you sure? Of course you're sure, I mean, how do you know, no, I mean, how did you get here?"

David laughed at Marya's tongue-tied outburst. "My parents brought me. I don't remember anything. I was just a baby."

"So your parents, they must speak Russian?"

"Oh yes, they're a very Russian couple, but they only speak it between themselves. And of course, we have certain Russian things in our house, like the eternal samovar for tea. I suppose you do too?"

"No. Nothing Russian anymore."

"That's a surprise. Well, we do. We have Russian food all the time. *Smetana* and *borscht* and marinated *maslyata*—mushrooms, you know, with vodka. And my parents still attend the Russian Orthodox Church. But they've insisted I be brought up completely American. Life would be easier for me, they said, if I forgot the past. And since I remember almost nothing from those first years in Russia, in a way I'm not really Russian at all."

Marya felt a jumble of emotions. It was incredible

to her that David was from Russia. But she also was aware that he kept speaking of his parents, who, he'd said, were Russian Orthodox. She felt excited that he was at least from Russia and inexplicably discouraged at the same time, as he spoke of his parents.

"But Sheffield? That's not a Russian name. It's British," she ventured.

"My parents went from St. Petersburg across the Baltic and the North Sea to England. We stayed with an aunt who lived in London and when we came through customs, my father said Sheflesky, but the customs agent heard something closer to Sheffield. And so Sheffields we became to the English speaking countries."

Marya considered the name Sheflesky. She'd never heard it before. It meant nothing to her. Her sense of disappointment grew.

She continued to see David however. She accepted his request to join him for tea and continued to bicycle with him on Sundays. She realized she was becoming careless in the alacrity with which she allowed herself to be seen publicly with him, but she was driven by something too strong to resist. She knew that they were turning heads when they lingered too long over the luncheon table at the Waldorf-Astoria, and that people were beginning to talk. But still she didn't care. She was always hoping to hear just one more clue drop into their conversations. All she wanted was some one sure thing that would put to rest finally the confusion she felt more strongly than ever about him.

It should not have come as a shock to her when Andrew finally brought up the subject of David Sheffield a few months later. "You and young Sheffield certainly seem to get on well together," he commented as they sat in his drawing room one evening. He wasn't looking at her but instead had pulled a small wooden pipe from his pocket and began to tamp tobacco into it.

Marya sensed immediately where the conversation

was heading. "I didn't know you smoked!" she exclaimed, to gain time.

"I imagine there are a number of things we still don't know about each other even after almost ten years. Now, what's this about young Sheffield?"

"He's a fine person," she said guardedly, "and we enjoy teasing each other."

"You know the rumors are flying?"

"Rumors always fly, whether there's cause or not. They don't mean anything. Coming from those circles, you of all people should know that."

"Would you like to hear what's being said?"

"Certainly not. I'm sure it's outrageously off the mark."

"They say he hangs on your every word and has eyes only for you."

"He's courteously attentive. It's amazing how things get distorted."

"They say he's in love with you."

"Certainly not! He enjoys the attentions of an older woman, nothing more. Truly, Andrew, I don't want to hear any more of this."

He took her by the chin and looked into her eyes. "You must tell me. Are you in love with him?"

She returned his stare incredulously. "I am not."

"But there is something about him?"

"I don't know. I keep thinking he reminds me of someone I once knew, long ago. I see glimpses of another person in him. Perhaps I am trying to get this other person back by being in his company."

"Did he tell you he's from Russia? Did you know him before?"

She weighed her words carefully. "Yes, he told me. I don't see how I could have known him before. He's much younger than I am and apparently came from St. Petersburg. I never was in St. Petersburg in my life, or even near there."

Andrew said nothing but just looked at her as he drew on his pipe. Even though he had asked her if she were in love with David, he sensed that indeed she was not, even before she answered. There was something else besides romantic love that propelled her toward this young man. He wondered what it could be. He puffed thoughtfully on his pipe. The lawyer in him had been alerted to certain clues. Perhaps it warranted a bit of investigation, he decided after a little more contemplation.

In the last three years since his thirteenth birthday, Daniel had devoted almost all his time to his father's business. He had been excited to see the factory expand into the building next door and then the textile mill added to MW Enterprises' holdings, and he felt he had played some important part in that expansion. Every afternoon when school was out, he would run to catch the el so that he might get to Broadway as soon as possible.

"Why don't you stay around and play some ball with us?" one of the boys in his class had asked a couple times.

He'd replied that he couldn't, that he had a job to do in his father's factory. "Some day I'll be the owner so I have to learn everything I can," he'd explained, and he had felt pleased to see the awed look that crossed the boy's face. After that the boy no longer bothered to ask Daniel to play ball and Daniel was glad.

Once he'd overheard his mother say to his father, "Daniel spends all his time in that factory. What kind of life can that be for a boy? He no longer has any friends. He should be spending time with his friends from school and from the neighborhood." But Daniel didn't care at all that he had no friends his age. His friends were at the factory. They were Mario and Sol and some of the pressers who would call out to him and tease him as he went by.

"Hey, boss boy," one of them named Mendel would yell to him. "You want to work your way to the top? Strip off your clothes and come take my place in this jungle of steam and hoses." Daniel liked it that he was teased that way. It showed that they all recognized that he would one day be completely in charge of this business with its factory that was sprawling larger and larger.

The only thing he didn't like about his life was that he didn't know when he would officially become his father's partner. Each year he had expected to be the year, particularly since his father now sent him not only to their mill in Troy, but even farther away to all the big mill towns of Massachusetts where he would buy the nonwoolen fabrics that the business required. He knew that it was a mark of his father's trust and confidence in him to send him that far. But if his father thought that much of his ability, why didn't he go ahead and make him a legal partner as promised? Now that Wolf had followed some of his suggestions for the business, why didn't he go all the way and make the partnership legal? He knew his father now was waiting until he finished high school. Once Wolf had mentioned that possibility, Daniel embraced it so fervently that it became almost a sure thing in his mind. He had only to wait for the day, and now that he had a certain day in mind, the waiting was more tolerable.

That afternoon he and his sister Elke were to join his father on a trip uptown. For years he had heard Wolf speak of Jacob Molnar, the Chassid who dealt in jewels, particularly diamonds. He knew that this was the man Wolf had gotten the jewels from that he had given his mother.

Daniel was waiting in the living room when Elke finally came down the stairs. He felt proud to have her as a sister. She had filled out and gotten even prettier and more like his mother in the last few years. Like Marya, she was slim. But Elke was taller than her mother and where Marya's body was well rounded, Elke's verged on voluptuous. Her reddish brown hair was thick and wavy, and she wore it pulled back from her head in a large bun from which curly wisps always escaped, giving her a softer, less severe look than that of most girls. She had her mother's brilliant green eyes and fair complexion, and when Daniel looked at her, he thought she couldn't be prettier. It was sometimes confusing for him to look at her though, because although she appeared to be completely a woman, there were aspects of her personality that were still very girlish.

"Where is he?" Elke asked expectantly.

"He said he'd be here at three. He might be a few minutes late if the traffic is heavy."

"Who would want one of those noisy dirty things, anyway?" said Elke. She wrinkled her nose in mock disgust.

"They're no worse than a horse," Daniel maintained. He could see Elke was in high spirits, and he knew that it had to do with the fact that their father had invited the two of them to accompany him.

"You're so lucky," Elke announced, sitting down next to him. "You get to go places with Papa all the time."

"I do?" Daniel didn't feel it was as often as Elke was making it out to be.

"Sure. You've been to Coney Island and to Central Park and to all the farms on the north end of Manhattan and even out of the state to the other mills."

"Well, all that's just because he sees so much of me. I'm almost always right there at the factory and handy for him to ask along."

"Do you think that's it?" Elke asked wistfully.

"Sure. What else could it be?"

"Sometimes I think he hardly remembers I'm here. Then when he does see me, he acts like I'm some kind of china doll that might break. He's so careful around me."

"It doesn't mean anything," Daniel tried to reassure her although he felt at a loss. "It's just his way."

He was relieved when a few seconds later Wolf

came through the door. Wolf looked at his son and then Elke. His glance lingered. "How grown-up you're getting, Elke. I almost thought you were your mother standing there, except that you're much taller. Come, give me a kiss."

Elke stood on tiptoe and threw her arms around his neck.

Wolf grabbed hold of her wrists and backed away slightly. "Not too tightly, Elke. You'll wrinkle your dress." He glanced quickly at the front of her pale green shirtwaist.

Elke obeyed immediately and pecked him circumspectly on the cheek. Then without meeting her eyes again, Wolf hurried them out the door.

A small woman dressed in black, from the sensible shoes on her feet to the scarf covering her hair, opened the door of Jacob Molnar's flat. They were shown into a comfortable parlor, decorated in mahogany furniture. In the corner was a spinet piano and on the sideboard was a seven-branched candlestick ornately fashioned in silver. As they sat listening to the ticking of the grandfather clock in the corner, they were all lost in their own thoughts. Elke ran her eyes over the polished wood and warmly upholstered chairs and tried to imagine what it would be like to be in charge of a big house like this.

Daniel was more conscious of his father's presence than his surroundings. He glanced at his father who appeared lost in his own thoughts. Daniel had no way of knowing that the ticking of the clock had transported Wolf back to his father's home in St. Petersburg. For the last fifteen years Wolf had succeeded almost completely in blocking from his mind all thoughts of his parents and brothers and sisters. It had been one of the harshest realities of his life that he had never learned for sure what had happened to them. During his first five years in America he had carefully questioned anyone he met from St. Petersburg. But many of those immigrants were poor people who had never even heard of Luminov Pharmaceuticals. Those who had come from more prosperous circumstances sometimes had, but they were not well enough acquainted with the company to know what had become of it or its owner. The ticking of the pendulum grew louder and louder in his ears, reminding him that one day he would have to risk returning to Russia. He would have to know what had happened to them.

His train of thought was broken when Jacob entered the room. Wolf hadn't seen Jacob in the last few years, and during that time, he noticed, Jacob had become downright prosperous. He carried more weight and his face was ruddy with health and contentment. He spread his arms out wide as if to embrace all three of them at once.

"Ah, I see Mrs. Chotzinoff, my housekeeper, showed you in and got you settled." He waved his hand to indicate the room they were in. "You see, now that I have this Russian Jewess managing my household, all is the utmost in efficiency. You Russians are like that, true workhorses."

Wolf laughed as he stood up, and the two men embraced. Then Jacob looked at Daniel and Elke and beamed. "So. You have finally made good on your promise to let me meet your children."

As Wolf introduced them, Jacob looked them over and made approving comments. Then he looked back to Wolf. "You told me your family was a pleasure to you. But you didn't tell me your son was so handsome or your daughter so beautiful. I can imagine from looking at her how her mother must look."

Daniel laughed lightly at this unaccustomed attention and Elke blushed. But their discomfort was only momentary as they were caught up in the warmth and vibrancy of Jacob's personality. He led them into another room almost identical to the one they had been in except for the table against the far wall, and motioned for them to sit. Then, as he had done so many times before for Wolf, he covered the table with a black velvet cloth and began slowly and deliberately to unfold the small waxy envelopes that each contained a single jewel.

Wolf's eye by now was practiced and he studied the jewels knowingly. Jacob turned to Daniel. "Your father is one of my finest customers. And he is one of my most discerning." He directed his question to Wolf. "What, may I ask, is the occasion of your purchase this time?"

"It's for my wife, to celebrate the seventeenth anniversary of the birth of our first child. It marks the start of the Luminov family in America."

Elke realized that the birth her father was speaking of was hers, and she was flushed with emotion. She looked up to see Jacob staring at her.

"Now she turns pink," he commented. "She looks like a rose."

Elke smiled, then looked back down at once and stared at the brilliant drops of color arranged in a neat pattern across the table top.

Wolf finally settled on a particularly fine top wesselton diamond of one carat, and he and Jacob began the negotiations over the price, negotiations which had by now become a ritual. After much give and take, a price they could both live with was reached. Jacob clapped his hands and announced it was time for tea.

As they sat with the tall, steaming glasses cupped in their hands, Jacob suddenly addressed Daniel. "Seeing you, my boy, in the flush of your youth, reminds me of when I was close to your age, or perhaps a little older. You know, we can be very young when the course of our lives is suddenly and irreversibly changed."

Daniel and Elke looked intently at Jacob and waited to hear what he was going to say.

"My father, God rest his soul, was a very prominent jewel merchant who provided the finest jewels to the courts of Europe. Our family had been living in

Budapest for several generations, but we also kept a home in Vienna where my father made frequent trips. This was in the time of the Emperor Franz Josef, and in his court there was a particular woman who was in love with my father. She was a lady-in-waiting to the Empress, and very beautiful. Although," he added, "not as beautiful as your sister here." He looked at Elke, and she again blushed.

"She found occasion to see him saying she wanted to examine his assortment of jewels, but in truth what she wanted was to be alone with him. My father had not yet married at the time, and as a bachelor, he was free to accept this lady's advances. But always he was most careful to keep his distance. He recognized how dangerous it would be for him as an outsider—and a Jew, at that—to establish a liaison with one of the women of the court." Jacob stopped and sighed, then continued. "The more he pulled back, the more she moved forward, until finally she was driven nearly mad. Shortly thereafter my father married my mother, and when this woman learned of it, she swore revenge, even though she and my father had never been lovers." He paused to take another sip from his tea, then suddenly looked up at Daniel and Elke. "My story is not too long?"

They instantly assured him it wasn't.

"Very well then, I shall finish it but as briefly as I can. As I was saying, when I was about your age, Daniel, my life changed completely. At nineteen I began to make many of the business rounds for my father. The jewelry business was my whole life and I was eager to throw myself into a world that seemed so exotic to me. In particular, my father sent me to the court in Vienna, feeling himself too old to travel such a great distance from Budapest, although I think it was that he didn't want to see the lady-in-waiting who had become so obsessed with him.

"I entered this same court that he used to frequent and there I met a lovely young woman who begged me to show her my collection of stones. She showered me with attention, and, being very young, I fell in love with her and thought that she was in love with me. She was—I could have no way of knowing this—the daughter of that same woman who had once been driven mad by my father.

"Finally, after a number of visits to the court over the space of eighteen months, I arrived one day to find myself enmeshed in a scandal. The young woman swore I had tried to take physical advantage of her, and that it was only thanks to her screams, which had alerted a nearby palace guard, that I was pulled naked from her knees." He sighed again and took a long drink from his glass. "It was, of course, completely a fabrication, but she was even able to produce a man she claimed was the guard who had pulled the lascivious Jew off her. I knew little in those days, but I knew enough to know I had to escape at once.

"I fled the palace immediately and hurried to the barge that would take me along the Danube to Budapest. In my parents' house I was ashamed to speak of what had happened, but I knew I needed their advice. When I finished telling the story, my father shook his head sadly and said, 'All these years and she has not forgotten.' 'What is this you are talking about?' asked my mother, alarmed. 'Who is this woman?' 'This is my fault,' said my father. 'I should have known. I should have warned you.' My mother cried out, 'Of what are you speaking? Will someone please tell me?' 'You must leave tonight,' my father told me. 'A woman so highly connected and with hate that can last all these years, to the point of bending her own daughter to her poisonous will, she will have you followed. You must go.' My mother began to weep and my father said, 'Hush now, we must pack as well. It is not safe to be here. She will follow the son to find the father. This is all my fault,' and he began to beat his breast. He bade me take the purse of jewels that I still had upon me from my visit to the court. 'You can begin again,' he said. 'But it must be in a place where as a Jew you will be safe. You must go to America.' I was frightened to think of going so far from home to this place that meant nothing to me, but I did as my father instructed me. I came to America, and instead of a jewel merchant to the courts of Europe, I was a very little merchant who lived in a single room with two other bachelors and knew nobody."

"What happened to your father?" Daniel asked. "Did the woman find him?"

"She did not. But to save his life, my father had to give up his entire business. Now that her intent for revenge was out in the open, and now that she had lost not only the father but the son, he knew she would hound him from the courts. He opened a small pawnshop in Belgrade—at least there he still had the Danube—and he found himself back at the same level as my great-great-grandfather had been many years before. He died a year later and my mother died two weeks after him."

There was a long silence until finally Jacob himself broke it. "Why do I tell you this story? Certainly it isn't a cheerful one. I think it's because you are the treasured children of my good friend here," he gestured toward Wolf. "And I want you to know how important it is that you not become too complacent. We Jews must always remember by what a thin thread our happiness dangles, and we must be always watchful of forces that can turn swiftly against us."

A short while later when Jacob bid them all good-bye, he took hold of Daniel by one hand and Elke by the other. "Now that we have met, please know that you can come to see me any time you wish. It would always be my pleasure."

As they took the el back home, Daniel and Elke talked about Jacob. They decided that they both liked him, and that he was a man that they could trust. Although she didn't say it out loud, Elke also thought he was like what she would imagine a kindly uncle to be. Because she did not have any uncles, she did not have anyone to compare Jacob to. But she liked his warmth almost like a father should be.

Chapter 18

As Elke walked up Fifth Avenue, she felt small next to the large buildings, but she enjoyed that feeling. As a tall young woman, it was not a feeling she often had. She passed rows of elegant stores, mostly dress shops for women, and as she looked at the gowns displayed in the windows, she noticed that for elegance and style, none of them could touch what her mother created. She glanced idly at the facades of the fashionable restaurants and thought of what the people must be like who frequented them. It was strange to think that her mother had had as her patrons perhaps some of these same people she saw entering these Fifth Avenue shops and eateries.

She stopped in front of one of the shops to look more carefully at a rose silk dress with crocheted lace across the bodice and a matching lace bonnet. She knew from all the hours she had seen the dressmakers working on her mother's designs how long it took to make lace like that or to add the special finishing touches, such as the inverted box pleats and the bishop's sleeves that set the dress apart from ready-to-wear.

As she studied the dress, she became aware of her

own reflection in the glass. She saw a young woman with large eyes and an ample figure dressed in a tailored suit of brown wool, finished with a black velvet collar and cuffs. People often told her she was pretty, as her father's friend the diamond merchant had said a few months ago when they had visited him, and men always looked at her when she passed by, but then she thought they looked at every woman the same way. She thought she was a little on the plain side, with her pale skin and straight, ordinary nose. Maybe, she concluded, people just said things like that to young women because they didn't know what else to say. She certainly didn't look the way the heroines in her books were described. They always had perfect teeth and perfect hair and perfectly formed noses. She continued along the street, observing everything she could. Seldom did she come to this part of the city.

As she passed by the window of a small, fashionable restaurant, a certain color of hair caught her eye. She stopped and glanced in. It was just as she had thought—there was her mother, talking to a man. She could only see the back of his head, but she figured he must be one of the wholesalers her mother had to deal with. She decided to go in and say hello.

Marya looked up to see Elke standing in front of her, an expectant look on her face. "Why, Elke!" she exclaimed. "I'm so surprised to see you here." She gestured toward the man with whom she was sitting. "David, this is my daughter Elke. You've heard me talk of her."

Elke turned her attention to the man her mother indicated who was already looking at her and smiling. She was surprised to see that he was young, not too much older than she, and was what she would call rather pleasant looking.

"I'm David Sheffield. Delighted to meet you, Miss Luminov. Perhaps you could join us?" David invited.

Elke looked to her mother for approval. Marya nodded her head. She suddenly felt very happy at the thought of being able to contemplate both Elke and David together.

"Very well," Elke said shyly. "But just for a moment."

David noticed the books in her arms. "Are you still in school?"

"This is my last year," Elke explained, feeling self-conscious about her height. Did he think she was too old to be a schoolgirl because of that? Then she remembered her books. "These aren't books from school. I was just now on my way to the main library."

"Elke is a constant reader," Marya smiled. "Her nose is always tucked into a book."

"Then the daughter must get it from the mother," David remarked. "Didn't you tell me, Marya, that one of the things that helped you adjust to America when you first got here was all the books by American authors that you read?" He turned his head sideways and tried to read the titles on the spines of Elke's books. "I used to read all the time too when I was in school. What do you have here?"

Elke responded a little stiffly. "I just finished a couple books by Sir Walter Scott, and one by Mark Twain and—"

David's face broke into a grin. "Twain? He used to be my favorite. Have you read *Pudd'nghead Wilson*?

Elke began to feel a little more relaxed. "Oh yes. I read *Innocents Abroad* and then went on to *Life on the Mississippi*." She looked toward Marya. "My mother sometimes makes suggestions and I find I always like whatever she recommends."

"I find I always like what your mother recommends too." David smiled at Marya. "Be it food, or books, or clothes, or even a course of action. She has excellent taste."

"Now you two, stop it," said Marya. "Such flattery is too heady for me. It will make it hard for me to go back to work."

"Must you?" sighed David, looking disappointed. "I thought we would have a little longer to visit."

"I have a patron coming in at five o'clock. I believe you know Mrs. Williston, David?"

He looked down and grimaced. "No wonder you must get back." He explained to Elke. "Mrs. Williston is known for her self-dramatizing tirades. Once she even backed A.T. Stewart, head of New York's finest and most lucrative department store, against the wall with her tongue."

Elke started to laugh. Mr. Sheffield was, she decided, more than just pleasant looking as she had first thought. He was actually a bit handsome.

"But your mother handles her effortlessly," David added.

Marya laughed. "It just seems effortless," she said, standing up.

As they prepared to leave, David turned to Elke. "Perhaps I could walk with you toward the library? I was going that way."

Elke agreed and after they waved good-bye to Marya, they continued along Fifth Avenue, talking all the while.

Later that evening, Elke was waiting for Marya when she came in the door. She followed her into her bedroom and sat on the bed. She watched as Marya changed her clothes.

"What is it, Elke? You've been dogging my steps like a puppy since I got in."

Elke saw her image in the mirror and quickly raised her hand to tuck in the strands of hair that had strayed from her bun. "Your friend Mr. Sheffield is a very nice man," Elke started tentatively. She hoped her mother would take the cue and tell her more about him.

Marya had sat down at her dressing table and was now removing the pins from her hair. "Yes," she said through closed teeth as she placed a pin in her mouth.

"I always enjoy seeing him. What did the two of you talk about on the way to the library?"

Elke looked down at the bed's coverlet and idly ran a forefinger along a seam. "Oh, lots of different things."

Now that all the pins were out, Marya shook her head and her hair tumbled down her back. "Like what?"

"Like what we like to do on Sundays, and what some of our favorite foods are and some more about what we like to read. The things he likes to eat, well, I'd never even heard of half of them! Where do you know him from anyway? I thought he was a salesman, but he just laughed when I said that and said he worked in a bank."

"Oh, we just ran into each other," Marya answered vaguely, smiling to herself to think how true her words were of their meeting in Central Park.

"I guess it was through your Fifth Avenue patrons?" Elke asked. She had noticed that David too seemed reluctant to talk about how he and Marya had met, and that hesitation made Elke even more curious.

"I seldom see them anymore, unless they come to the shop. But, yes, you might say it was through them. Through a friend of a friend. You know, one of those things." She wished to shift the subject slightly. "So tell me, what did you and David tell each other you like to do on Sundays?"

"Well, I just like to read, I told him. But he said that was fine for every other day of the week but not for Sunday. He said that bicycling was the best thing for someone who had sat inside all week reading the way I do." She added quietly, "He says he wants to teach me how."

Marya inadvertently let go of the pins she was holding in her mouth, and they clattered to the dressing table's glass top. "What did you say?" Marya tried to keep her tone casual as she hastily swept the pins across the glass and into her hands.

"He said he wants me to go riding with him next Sunday," Elke continued as if she hadn't heard the question.

Marya caught the slightly dreamy tone in Elke's voice and tried to get a look at her face in the mirror to see if the dreaminess was just her imagination. But Elke was lying on her back, holding her hands up in the air and studying them. Her position made it impossible for Marya to see the look on her face.

"Well, Elke, that could be fun." She added, "If you take it the right way."

Elke sat up. "The right way? What do you mean?"

"Probably he's just being courteous. Perhaps you made your enthusiasm so apparent that he had no choice but to ask you."

Marya saw the hurt look that crossed her daughter's face but she couldn't stop herself. Instigated by the languor of Elke's voice just now, there had flashed before her a picture of Elke and David together as lovers. Marya felt slightly ill at the thought.

"But I wasn't acting overly interested. Honest, Mama. I wasn't even acting interested at all. It never occurred to me that he might even care about whether I was interested in bicycling or not."

Marya turned on the swivel stool and looked right at Elke. "What did you tell him?"

"I told him yes, of course. Wouldn't you? I mean, he is so nice, and he's your friend, so I know you approve of him. And then, he's really kind of handsome too, don't you think?"

"Yes, Elke, I do. But I'm just not sure it's a good idea to think too much about him. He comes from a very different background than you."

"You mean because he isn't Jewish? That's never meant anything to you before." Her voice had just a trace of defiance.

"By different background, I mean that he was raised in a different part of society than you, and it's one I know fairly well, and believe me, things like this invitation to go bicycling will mean something different to him than it does to you."

"Like what?" Elke said a little too harshly.

"It's hard to explain these things to you, Elke. It's just a sense I've developed. And that sense tells me that it would be best for you to think of him as just an older friend, more like my age really."

Marya left it at that, even though she knew she had not given Elke a very good explanation of why she should not entertain any notions about David. Still, she resolved to speak to David as soon as possible to deter him as well from any plans to see much of Elke. She wasn't sure just what she would tell him, but she'd think of something. She laughed to herself at how quickly her happiness at seeing Elke and David together had turned to fear. She had never foreseen that they might be interested in each other.

Elke found it impossible to heed her mother's words. Since she had parted from him at the library steps, she had thought of no one and nothing else but him. She took some comfort from the fact that her mother had not expressly said she couldn't go on Sunday, so she continued to plan what she would wear and to spin fantasies about what it would be like to spend a whole afternoon together.

When Sunday came, Marya watched Elke leave the house with a strong sense of foreboding. This time it was Marya who was waiting for Elke when she came through the door late that afternoon. Elke's face was radiant and Marya was struck by how beautiful her daughter looked.

"Well?" Marya said. "Can you now ride a bicycle?"

"No," Elke laughed. "We didn't ride bicycles after all. He said his leg was bothering him from a fall he took last week and that he didn't want to chance riding again so soon. From what he says, he certainly seems to have a lot of accidents." She laughed again.

Marya didn't laugh and stood waiting. "So what have you been doing the last four hours?"

"Just riding around and around," Elke said. "He had his landau at the park and asked me if I would like to go for a ride in the country."

Marya was feeling increasingly uncomfortable. "All that time? You just were riding in his carriage? Where did you go?"

"We went as far as we could toward the northern tip of Manhattan. Then when the terrain got too rough to go any farther by carriage, we got out and walked about a little bit."

"Where was the driver all this time?"

"Oh," Elke said airily, "David dismissed him for the day and did the driving himself."

"Elke," Marya said suddenly and in a stony voice, "I simply cannot allow this."

"Cannot allow what, Mama? It was all perfectly harmless. All we did was laugh and have a good time."

"What I cannot allow is that you see this young man anymore."

"This young man? You talk about him as if he were a stranger instead of someone who is a good friend of yours."

"I know more about him than you do, Elke. He is a fine young man, indeed. But I just sense he isn't the young man for you."

"But Mama, he's like a prince to me!"

"Elke, how can you say that? You hardly know him."

"I just know it. You're always talking about how you just know certain things, how you see them in your mind. Why can't I know some things too?"

Marya sighed. "Maybe you can, Elke. But I just don't think this is one of them. You're not even talking realistically. A prince!"

"You've always said you wanted me to aspire for

more. Well, I am. I'm aspiring for him. He's a prince to me because he's smarter and has seen a lot more than I have and done a lot more."

"Elke, stop this talk. You're sounding like some weepy heroine from one of your books with all this talk of handsome princes."

"But, Mama, I love him!" As soon as the words were out of her mouth, Elke was sorry. She saw the shocked look that covered her mother's face and she sensed that her admission held even more significance to Marya than it did to her, although she couldn't imagine why.

"Go to your room at once, Elke," Marya managed to say. "We will talk of this later and get it settled once and for all." She watched as Elke stomped up the stairs, the sound of her footsteps conveying the anger she dared not display to her mother in words.

Marya looked in the door of Elke's room a few hours later. Elke was wearing a pink negligee and was curled up on her bed reading. For a moment Marya had a very confused sensation that she was seeing herself some twenty years before sitting there on the bed. The hair, the shape of the face, the eyes, her posture as she read with her arms folded and hugged in against the top of her body, all this reminded Marya of herself.

Elke looked up as Marya entered. Before her mother could say anything, her anger, which now could no longer be contained, gushed out. She stood up so quickly that the book clattered to the floor, but she was oblivious to its fall. "You don't know what it's like anymore! You once told me that cousin Lubish tried to keep you and Papa from seeing each other, and he locked you away in a room so long that you got sick. Now you want to do the same thing to me!"

"Hush, Elke, that isn't true. No one's locking you in your bedroom."

She began to wave her arms and her voice rose. "But what you're doing is the same thing. You're telling me I can't have the man I want. Don't you remember how you felt? Didn't you hate cousin Lubish for doing that to you? How can you do this to me? You see? History does repeat itself in families. You're making the same awful thing happen."

"It isn't the same thing at all. I had known your father much longer, we had risked our lives together crossing the border, I had nursed him when he was sick. You can't equate the two situations." But Marya was shaken more by Elke's words than her expression or voice revealed. Under no circumstances did she want to put Elke through what she had been through. But if there was a romance blossoming between Elke and David, her instincts told her it was a dangerous thing. There was the chance that this romance was all in Elke's imagination. Perhaps Elke had made a romance out of something that was only fondness or friendship on David's part. She resolved that she would ask him as soon as possible.

"Your daughter Elke is every bit as enchanting as you," David burst out next time Marya saw him. They were again having afternoon tea at the Waldorf, a practice that was becoming a weekly ritual with them. "Truly I think I could fall in love with her, wishing of course, that it were you. But all my attentions to you, Marya, have been met with the utmost propriety on your part."

Marya was tempted to reply that she was old enough to be his mother but thought better of it. "You turn my head with such elaborate compliments, David. I never know if you're serious or joking. Now it's more of the same. I don't know if what you're telling me about Elke is sincere or not."

He took hold of her hand. "I'm perfectly sincere with you always," he said. "You know the old saying, 'truth in jest'? It's just that I sometimes don't know how to say these things without sounding melodramatic, so I feel I have to add a light, humorous touch. If I didn't, I might make you and myself too uncomfortable."

"Now, at this very moment, I believe you. I think you are being totally sincere."

"I always mean what I say."

"Then you meant what you said about Elke?" She watched him carefully.

"Yes. I find Elke refreshing and unspoiled. And believe it or not, we have quite a few things in common. I would like to see her again, with your permission."

Marya smiled halfheartedly. "It seems you have already seen her without asking my permission."

"That was a whim, born of the moment and the circumstances. Had you been there, I can assure you I would have asked you before proceeding."

"Then you do definitely want to see Elke again?"

"Yes. There's something about her. There was an affinity between us almost instantly, just as there was between you and me."

"David . . ." Marya hesitated. "I don't know how to say this, but I just don't think, I mean, it's really not such a good idea, after all."

He saw that she was serious. "Why not?"

"Because, I don't know, I just would feel awkward, that's all."

"What? Could it finally be that you're just a little bit jealous? I've been trying to no avail to make you jealous for months."

"David, be serious."

"I am serious. I'm looking for some good reason why you might not want me to see Elke. All I come up with is the possibility that you might be jealous. And since that doesn't seem at all like you, I can't help but wonder what your real concern is."

She had been unable to give David an answer that satisfied him, and after their conversation, she felt even more disquieted than she had before. Elke and David were on her mind almost constantly as she considered over and over again possible courses of action.

Early the next evening, she was still working in the shop when Andrew entered unexpectedly. She wondered what had brought him there since he had been there just once before and only at her invitation. She was glad she had sent the dressmakers and their assistants home early.

Andrew saw at once that they were alone and took advantage of the situation to pull her into his arms and kiss her passionately.

"You look marvelous, as always, Marya. I know this is sudden, but nothing would make me happier than having you tell me yes, you will drop everything and join me for supper."

Marya was surprised at the suddenness of his invitation but welcomed his company. He would provide a distraction to her obsessive thoughts of the last few days about Elke and David. No matter what she had been doing—talking to patrons, sketching or conducting business with salesmen—just below the surface was the nagging question of what she was going to do about the problem. She looked at her watch and smiled at him. "How easy it is to make you happy, Andrew. Yes, I can join you, but just for a little while." More and more lately she had been working past the dinner hour, and although Wolf glowered at her, he had said nothing. Elke had been delighted to take charge of planning the suppers and running the house in Marya's absence, so there had been virtually no disruption in routine on the occasions when Marya came home late.

Andrew took her to a small French café not too far from her shop. The café specialized in the cooking of Provence, and they enjoyed a simple but exquisitely flavored meal spiced with plenty of garlic, oil and tomatoes. All during the meal, Marya expected to find out what the occasion was for Andrew's impromptu appearance. He was a man of habits, and this wasn't at all like him. They talked about Marya's shop in detail, a little about Andrew's practice and a little about the people they both knew. Their conversation was light and easy, but contained nothing out of the ordinary.

When they were finished eating, Andrew suggested they take a short ride along the Hudson River in his carriage. Marya was beginning to think she should return home, but something in his voice made her decide to accompany him.

The night was calm and the moon illuminated the water with a golden swath. Across the river she could see the lights of New Jersey. She felt a reassurance at the order and peacefulness of the scene. It was the first time she had been able to relax and think about anything other than her past and future conversations with Elke and David.

Andrew took his pipe from his mouth. "You're still seeing quite a bit of young Sheffield, I hear."

Marya felt as if he had been reading her thoughts and gave a slight start. She felt Andrew watching her intently. "No more than usual," she said casually.

"I've sensed this young man is important to you, Marya."

She started to say something, but he wouldn't let her.

"I know you're not in love with him. I'm not worried about that. But you do have more than a usual interest in him, do you not?"

Marya's heart fluttered wildly. "I told you before that he reminds me of someone."

"Yes. I remember very well." He put his pipe back in his mouth and took a long draw on it. "That's why I began to make investigations into his background."

Marya looked at him wildly. "Investigations? What kind of investigations?"

"I wanted to find out more about his family and the circumstances of his coming to this country." He paused.

"And?" she prompted.

"And I learned that his parents were moderately successful shopkeepers in St. Petersburg where they came from three generations of shopkeepers. A dry goods store, it was."

Marya started to breathe a little more easily. All of this she knew already.

"His parents are quite old, perhaps too old, I thought, to have a child as young as he is. I discovered that they are not his real parents."

The relaxation she had started to feel was gone. David was adopted? Her throat suddenly felt dry and her palms moist. "Then who are his real parents?" she managed to ask more calmly than she felt.

"I thought perhaps you might have some idea, Marya."

"What do you mean?" Her voice was rising. "How could I possibly know? I told you, didn't I, that I've never been in St. Petersburg."

"His parents, or I should say adoptive parents, got him from the father's sister who didn't live in St. Petersburg."

"Where then?" Marya asked too quickly.

"Some smaller town some distance away. Some area in White Russia."

"What was the name of the town?"

"They didn't say."

Marya stared at him dumbfounded. How could they not say? How could they tell him just this much and then stop. He could be withholding the rest on purpose, to see what she would say. And if he knew this much, then most likely he knew everything. Or did he? She mustered as much control as she could. "How strange that you didn't learn the name of the village or town."

"Why would you like to know, Marya?"

"I didn't say I did. I just think it curious that your investigations went so far and no farther. I think it even more curious that you would bother to look into the matter in the first place." Her fear was starting to subside and a new emotion to take its place.

"This man has some kind of hold on you, Marya. You are the woman I love. Never have I felt about another woman the way I feel about you. I want to know what it is that has caught your attention this way. From the moment you saw him that first time in Canfield's Casino I was aware of something there. At first I thought it might be a romantic attachment, but as I watched you, I knew that there was something else involved here. I already knew enough about Sheffield to know that a common link you had was your Russian heritage, and it was that aspect I resolved to pursue. I hired investigators, and they set to work."

"Is that all you've learned so far?"

"The investigations are still in progress. I expect to know the rest shortly. But on the basis of what I've learned, I've been able to draw some conclusions."

"What are they, Andrew?" She was beginning to feel impatient with the way in which he was analyzing her as if she were one of his legal cases.

"This young man has played some part in your life. There is nothing else to explain the way you have reacted to him and even the way you have just now reacted to this information. You can't imagine, Marya, the emotions that have crossed your face in the course of our conversation."

Again she started to say something, and again he stopped her. "I know you're becoming angry with me at this minute. But I want you to bear with me and hear me out. I know you refuse to talk about your life in Russia. You must know that such secrecy exacts a price, and the price is that people gossip about your remote past or suppose whatever they will. Quite naturally they invent romantic and exotic stories for you, reasoning those would be the kind most likely to have compelled you to silence. Perhaps you enjoy the aura of mystery that envelops you. More likely you are oblivious to it.

"But I am not immune to the very human trait of curiosity and I too have had my wild imaginings. At first I thought perhaps Sheffield was a relative, even a brother. But he's too young to be your brother. I now suspect that he was the son of someone you once loved, of a man you were very much in love with perhaps, and that is why you are obsessed with this boy. He reminds you of his father."

"The son of a man I was in love with?" Marya repeated, astounded.

"Yes. You were in love with David Sheffield's real father. That is what I think at this point in my investigation."

When he paused for a moment, Marya burst in, the emotion having built to a point she could no longer keep silent. "I resent all of this! I find it offensive the way you have pried into my life, for that is what you have done, Andrew, pried into *my* life, not David's. You want to see if there are some skeletons in my past that might be embarrassing if I were your wife. What you were really looking for was information about me, whatever nasty little secrets you could find—"

"Marya, that isn't true." He tried to grab her hand but she wrenched it free.

"Don't, Andrew. I'm not finished. I see now what was behind your unheralded appearance in my shop this evening, and what was behind the passionate embrace and compliments. You've taken me out tonight for the express purpose of cross-examining me, just as if I were a criminal on the witness stand. You were feeding me information, just to see how I would react. Well, you're getting your reaction. I don't like this whole process, and I won't go along with it. I won't stand for it!"

Andrew's face looked truly distressed. "You must believe me. This is not what I intended."

"Then what did you intend? What was the purpose of this examination?"

"I'm not examining you, can't you see? I'm

merely reporting to you the results of an investigation I made on your behalf. The information I find will mean much more to you, Marya, than it will to me. You can see that, can't you? This is all for you."

She looked out the carriage window and said nothing.

"Don't you want to know whether in fact this young man is who you think him to be?"

She didn't know what to say. She'd been teasing herself with thoughts of David since she'd first caught sight of him, but now there seemed to be hard evidence for the idea. And what Andrew was suggesting rang true as well. But her life in Russia was behind her, done with. She didn't want to open old wounds. Yet once having thought it, she couldn't escape it. Who this young man reminded her of was Gershon, the man she had married when she was fourteen.

And then another thought forced itself upon her, one that made her both ill and terrified at the same time. She tried not to let herself think it, but to no avail. The body, she whispered to herself, they had never found the boy's body. The words started to pulse in her head. Was there any chance in the world that. . . . No, there couldn't be. Her son was dead and that was it. She had believed that for almost twenty years. She couldn't question it now or she'd go crazy. Still, she had never been absolutely certain that the battered and bloated body the townspeople had brought to her that day was David. Her suppositions soared wildly. What if . . . what if her David had somehow survived, been raised by someone else, and like so many Russians, ended up in this country? Although she continued to resist it, the possibility was firmly planting itself in her imagination. She'd had a tormenting dream the night before. In the dream, the face of David Sheffield had been superimposed over the face of young David her son, and he was reaching out his hands toward her, just as her son had done when she had last glimpsed him in the streets of Petrovichi. She had awakened from the dream with a start.

As if from far away, Andrew's words managed to come through to her. "I said, Marya, can you look at me and say you know for certain who David Sheffield is?"

Marya was still in the dream as she turned to face him. "No," she said evenly, but she was frantic and torn with doubt inside.

Andrew's tone was conciliatory. "Wouldn't you like to know, Marya? Isn't it eating at you? You must spend a lot of your energy and time thinking about it."

"Andrew, I'd like to go home," Marya said. "I'd just like to go home. I told you that I don't want to cooperate in this interrogation and invasion into my past. This much I can tell you: what happened to me in my town in Russia was horrible, although, in truth, it was not necessarily any more horrible than what happened to any other Jew."

"Marya, stop. I asked you a question. You haven't answered it, and I think it's important. Don't you want to know one way or the other whether David Sheffield is who you think he is?"

She looked at him. At this point his conclusions about David's significance to her were completely wrong. But if he continued his investigative work, he might unearth David's real significance to her. And what if he did, she asked herself. As her friend and her lover, would he not safeguard the information, telling no one but her? And, as he had pointed out to her, wouldn't she then know for sure? She wondered if knowing were worth the risk. She took a deep breath.

"Yes, Andrew, you are right. I would like to know for certain." She leaned back against the seat and felt suddenly drained.

"Then it's true," Andrew said quietly. "He is the son of someone you loved." When she didn't reply, he ordered the driver to take them toward Marya's home.

* * *

Elke was lying on her bed reading when she heard footsteps in the hallway, followed by a rapping on her bedroom door. Almost immediately it opened and Wolf came in. She could see that he was upset and she was aware of his eyes flicking lightly over her. She sat up at once and pulled the edges of her robe closer together, conscious of her old nightgown underneath that fit too snugly and revealed too much of her. She saw his eyes follow her hands as she smoothed the folds in the robe and rearranged the way she was sitting to a more modest position.

"I'd like to talk to you, Elke," he said.

She felt excited and hopeful to think that her father had sought her out and actually wanted to talk to her about something. At the same time she wondered what it could be to make him change his customary behavior this way and she wondered about the expression on his face. She looked at him standing there as if waiting for her reply, something obviously on his mind. "Of course, Papa," she said, and patted the foot of the bed.

Wolf sat down and reached into his pocket. He removed a small box and handed it to her. "This is for you."

Elke took the box and opened it. Inside was a diamond set in a platinum ring. She recognized it as the one her father had purchased for her mother that day he had taken her and Daniel to Jacob Molnar's house. She looked at her father, a question on her face. "I don't understand," she said.

"It's for you. A gift."

"But I thought it was for Mama. For your twentieth wedding anniversary."

He ignored her implied question. "It's for you, Elke. You heard me tell Mr. Molnar that I wanted to celebrate the birth of our first child. That's why it's for you." He lifted the box from her hands and took the ring out. Then he picked up her right hand and slipped the ring over her finger.

Tears welled up in Elke's eyes. If she had planned such a scene, it couldn't have matched what was actually taking place. Her father was proud of her. He wanted to recognize her importance in the family and the fact that she was the first. All her life where her father was concerned, she had never felt first, never felt she was anything more important than a pretty decoration to sit on his knee. More recently she had not even felt that because he almost seemed to go out of his way to avoid her.

"Papa, it's beautiful," she said amid her tears. She waved her hand, and laughed out loud to see the diamond sparkle. It made her feel like an adult to have such a valuable and beautiful ring like this. The motion of her hand reminded her a little of her mother as she had been when Elke was still very small and her father had presented her with jewels.

Even though she had been very young, she remembered the expression on both of their faces, her mother looking a little worried one moment, happy the next, her father always completely proud and smiling.

She looked up at him now, still sitting woodenly on the foot of her bed and, she wondered why he didn't look happy. Why wasn't this a happy occasion for him the way it was for her?

"Papa?" she asked. "Is something wrong?"

"Not at all, Elke," he said right away. "To the contrary. I'm pleased to see you happy."

"Oh, Papa, and I am happy. I don't know how to tell you how much." She held the ring up again and admired it as the light danced off its surfaces. She wished she could dare tell him how close she felt to him just now. Inside she felt a soft glow because he was finally recognizing her and taking the time to talk to and look at her. "I thought you were choosing this stone for Mama," she said suddenly.

Wolf didn't reply. Instead he continued to look at her and then look away whenever their eyes met. He couldn't believe she hadn't heard the argument downstairs just a few minutes ago between him and Marya, but then Marya had always told him how Elke could lose herself in her books.

"Speaking of your mother, there's something else I'd like to tell you," he finally said.

Elke looked at him expectantly.

"Your mother tells me you have been seeing a young man."

Elke's eyes flew open. She never had dreamed her mother might tell her father about David. "A couple times," she admitted reluctantly.

"It's time for you to be taking an interest in young fellows. You're that age now. We realize it." He paused.

Elke was alarmed by the way he had said, "We realize it." It told her that her father and mother had probably been talking about her a great deal.

"Your mother tells me that he's a fine person."

"Oh, yes. He's wonderful," she spilled out, in spite of a warning voice that told her to wait and see where this discussion was leading.

"His name is David?"

"Yes."

"David. That's a good name, a good solid name from the Bible," he observed. "What's his last name?"

"Sheffield."

"Sheffield?" He repeated the name and paused. "That doesn't sound Jewish," he said finally. "Is it?"

"I don't know." Elke remained evasive.

"How can you not know, Elkeleh? You tell me he's a fine man, and yet you don't know enough about him to know what faith he practices?"

"No. It just never came up." She lifted her head and looked in her father's eyes. "I suppose it never came up because it doesn't matter to me."

"Now you sound like your mother! Elke, I know that these things are not important to your mother. She looks at everything that has to do with her past as an unwelcome burden. She must feel that if she were to acknowledge it, it would suck her back into the pain it brought her. But you know I don't see things that way. It's true that I don't practice my faith the same way I did in Russia when I was a boy. But deep down, I still believe. And I think it's important that you eventually find a boy with a background as much like yours as you can. You want one who is almost like a brother, who shares your Jewish faith and heritage. It may not seem to matter to you now, Elke, but it will someday, I can promise you. One of these days you will marry one of these young men, and marriage is hard enough, and the differences between a man and woman great enough, without your adding more."

"But Papa, I want a man I love. That's the most important thing to me. To love him and take care of him and to have children together." She looked at him so intently that for a moment something in her voice and her eyes reminded him of Marya when he'd first met her.

"What I want to tell you, Elke, is that I don't want you to see this David Sheffield anymore. I believe you when you say he's a good man and perhaps one you could love. But I can't permit you to see him."

Elke was sitting perfectly still without blinking or moving her eyes. Nothing about her gave him any indication that she had heard what he had said. "Do you understand?" he asked, to make sure she was listening.

"Yes," she said in a dull voice. As he stood up to leave the room, the excitement and sense of importance she had felt just a short time before when he had given her the diamond disappeared. She wondered why he had bothered to come. Was the diamond just a way of sweetening the message that had more than likely been his main purpose for coming to talk to her at all? The warm glow was replaced with a bitter dread. She was afraid of the forces in herself that were so strong and unpredictable. She dreaded what such forces might make her do.

She looked at the diamond ring again. It no longer seemed to sparkle as brightly as she had first thought.

Wolf left Elke's room upset with what had just taken place between them. It had been so easy to see her exhilaration slide into sadness as he had told her she could not see David Sheffield anymore. Elke was not like her brother Daniel. Her feelings were inscribed on her face and easy to see for anyone who cared to look. But he was convinced he had done the right thing. It was best to stop her at once from seeing any young man who wasn't Jewish, and to let her know what he expected from her. Marya had done the right thing in telling him, even though a problem with Elke was the last thing he had wanted to think about at that exact moment. The argument he had had with Marya before he'd come to Elke's room still made him feel bad.

When Marya had returned home after her carriage ride with Andrew, Wolf had been waiting for her. It was a struggle to have to think about anything else but her conversation with Andrew. As they had ridden to her street in silence, she had been obsessed with finding a solution to the problem of Elke and David. It was an obsession that in truth sickened her, for she recognized that she would have to put an end to their friendship, and that meant she would have to manipulate their lives in a way that repulsed her. She had always prided herself on avoiding such interference. She had never considered herself a manipulative woman. The good things that had happened to her had resulted from hard work, timing and a bit of luck. She hadn't juggled other people's lives or tried to play their emotions against them. But that was what she needed to do now. She was going to find a way to stop Elke and David from seeing each other again, no matter what.

Meanwhile, the look on Wolf's face told her immediately that he was angry, and exhausted as she was, she had to brace herself for a confrontation.

"Where have you been?" he demanded.

"I stayed late at the shop, then had supper with a business friend," she said dully and started to walk past him toward the dining room, but he barred her way.

"I suppose you were seeing one of your Fifth Avenue friends again," he accused in a way that demanded a reply. "I know you haven't kept your promise to me."

The sternness of his tone jolted Marya back into the present. "I don't know what you're talking about, Zavel," she said.

"Oh hell, Marya, what I'm really talking about is that you're gone more and more. You're not here when Daniel or Elke comes home, and you're certainly not here when I come home. I wish I knew what is really going on inside your head. It seems we have less and less to do with each other each month."

"What are you trying to say, Zavel?" She was puzzled. She hadn't been expecting such an outburst. Since she had started the shop, he had seemed quite content to let her set her own hours, and he had stopped questioning her years ago. Now, when she was virtually crazed with her thoughts about David and just as pressing, her thoughts about David with Elke, Wolf had to become angry. She could scarcely attend to what he was questioning her about. Instead, underlying her responses to him, she was thinking of the problem over and over, desperate to find some kind of solution. Then an idea occurred to her.

"Well," she said quite suddenly, "I was with someone from that circle."

Wolf stared at her. He had not been expecting an admission, and in fact he had not really been concerned that she was with those people. He had assumed she was doing nothing more than working late in the shop, and it was only out of frustration at her apparent independence from him that he had ventured to open an old wound.

"A young man stopped by to see me," she said.

She observed herself detachedly, and she noted she had reached the point where she was ready to lie. She saw that he was watching her intently, and although she wasn't sure whether her sudden plan would work, she plunged on blindly. "He's someone I know through my business with the high society ladies," she explained, thinking to herself that in a sense her statement was true. It was because of the clothes she designed that she had ever been in a position to meet David Sheffield in the first place. Then she wondered why it should matter to her whether what she said were true. What mattered was that she get the results she wanted.

Wolf was waiting for her to continue.

"He's someone that Elke met through me, quite by accident." She affected an idle tone. "I had no idea they would have an interest in each other, but then one can't always predict the whims of one's children. I do think he's a fine young man, which is a relief because they, to my surprise, have started seeing each other."

"What do you mean, seeing each other?" Wolf asked.

"Going places together, cafés and parks. According to what Elke tells me, they're getting serious quite fast." She knew this was only partially true—probably the actual seriousness at this point was just on Elke's part—but she felt it was necessary to say. She could take no chance on its developing beyond this point. "For all I know, I may have to be designing a bridal gown," she added.

She had seen Wolf blink rapidly. She knew this was coming as a total surprise to him. To their knowledge, Elke had never gone out with a young man before or even had a crush on one. Now Marya was speaking casually of Elke's getting married.

"I wonder if I should think in terms of a temple wedding or a church wedding," she continued.

"Is this fellow Jewish?" Wolf asked suddenly.

"I don't know. I doubt it. He has sandy brown hair and green eyes."

"That doesn't mean anything," Wolf said with exasperation. "You have red hair and green eyes. You sound like a goy, Marya. You know as well as I there's no standard look."

"Somehow I just don't think he's Jewish. But what does it matter? It certainly doesn't to me."

"I know well enough how you feel about all that," Wolf cut in. "But I don't want to get into that right now."

"Well, if you want to know so badly, why don't you ask her?" said Marya.

As Wolf had left the room, the awful feeling inside her intensified. She knew she had set him up to question Elke about whether or not David was Jewish, and it both satisfied and sickened her that he had taken her bait.

The sickening feeling had deepened when she went into the dining room and saw on the table a poppyseed cake. The cake was untouched and had obviously been placed there for a celebration of some kind. To the left of it was a bottle of schnapps and two glasses. Marya had the awful feeling she had forgotten some important occasion, but as she mentally ran through the dates of her anniversary and everyone's birthday, she couldn't think of anything.

Wolf had left his conversation with Marya having more than David Sheffield on his mind. He had not told her the real reason he was so upset when she came home so late. He had planned for the three of them—Elke, Marya, and himself—to have a small celebration as he presented Marya with the diamond ring that marked the beginning of their family. Ever since his conversation with Angelica, he had been looking for some way in which he could reach out to Marya again and maybe bridge the gap that had grown between them. When Marya had not come home, he had paced impatiently, and as he waited, he had become increasingly angry. As the hour grew later, he finally decided to hell with it. Maybe it was too late to change things between them. Maybe he and Marya were simply out of time.

He would not give the diamond to Marya after all; it would go to Elke instead. Now, as he left Elke's room, his intention realized, he thought again of Marya, and of the seemingly hopeless stalemate their marriage had become.

Chapter 19

For courage, Elke looked at the diamond flashing on her finger, then knocked on the door. The same wizened lady who had come to the door the first time opened it again.

"Hello, Mrs. Chotzinoff," Elke said. "I've come to see Mr. Molnar."

The old woman recognized her and smiled a wide grin that revealed a missing tooth in the front of her mouth. With great energy and enthusiasm, she showed Elke into the parlor she had been in a few months before with her brother and father. Then the housekeeper set about building a fire. As Elke settled into a comfortable armchair near the fireplace, she hoped she had done the right thing in coming here. She didn't have long to ponder the wisdom of her decision for Mrs. Chotzinoff had a fire burning within a matter of two minutes and had scuffled out of the room to find Mr. Molnar.

Almost at once he was bursting into the room and taking her hand into both of his. "What a delight this is, Elke. You don't mind if I use your first name, do you?"

"No, Mr. Molnar." He was so ebullient and warm that she quickly felt at ease.

"Ah! And you must call me Jacob in return. Or better yet, call me Jake. That is more American and you younger people are more used to the American names anyway." He motioned for her to sit back down and drew a matching chair close to hers.

Conscious of his gaze, Elke looked down at her hands in her lap, then back up at him. "You're probably wondering why I came here."

"I am, of course, but I'm just glad you came. Never do I receive visits from ladies as pretty as you. And I do remember extending an invitation to you and your brother to come visit me any time."

She hadn't planned to smile in response to his compliment but she did anyway. "I just thought it might be nice to see you again."

His eyes went to her lap where she was turning the diamond ring round and round with her left hand. "I see you are wearing one of my diamonds. Did your mother give the ring to you?"

She responded slowly. "No. My father did."

Jacob raised a quizzical eyebrow. "Then he surprised you, I'm sure. He led us all to believe the stone was for your mother the day he bought it." He chuckled and added, "Your father is clever, very clever, and a good man."

"Yes."

"Come now, *maidele*. That was such a brief answer. I suspect you and your father might be having a problem."

Elke nodded her head abruptly.

"Would you like to tell me about it? I promise you, I can keep a secret better than anyone you've ever met. Better than a clam even."

She smiled at him, then took a deep breath. "He is very strict," she began tentatively.

"Ah yes," he nodded. "Well, that can be good. It all depends. What is he strict about?"

"He wants me only to be around men who are Jewish."

"And is that such a horrible thing? Are Jewish men so distasteful to you?"

"Oh no. That's not what I meant at all." She shook her head vigorously. "It's just that I don't know any."

"I should think we're all around you, my dear. There's your father and your brother, and I imagine a goodly number of your neighbors and the fellows in your class at school. And at this very moment, there's me."

She looked at him and laughed. "I know. But there aren't any that I'm interested in."

He mocked being wounded. "Elkeleh," he gasped. "The things from your mouth, they cut me like swords."

She laughed again and leaned forward to shake his arm. "No, that's not what I mean either. Why is it so hard for me to explain?"

He grew more serious. "I do know what you are saying, Elke. You are telling me that you would like to talk to and go places with young men who aren't Jewish."

"Well, it doesn't matter if they are Jewish. I just want it not to matter either way. But to my father, it does."

"And to your mother?"

"She doesn't care about such things either."

He looked thoughtful. "That is unusual in a Jewish mother."

"She says in America such things are not important. She says the sooner we look at ourselves as Americans, the better for us and everyone else."

"I see. And that's what you believe, too?"

"I don't see what difference it makes which religion a person practices or whether he calls himself a Jew or a Methodist or a Russian Orthodox."

"I agree. In terms of determining his value as a

human being, it doesn't matter at all. But when we speak of marrying that person, that's another matter."

"But I'm not talking about marrying. Just going places and having fun."

He leaned forward and took her hands in his again, the way he had when he had first come into the room. "Elkeleh, would you be very offended and stop coming to visit me if I told you I agree with your father?"

Something about the earnest way he looked into her eyes reassured her and made her laugh. "No, I wouldn't."

"Do you promise?"

"Yes, I promise." There was something about him, she decided, that made it easy for her to accept what he said and not feel upset about it.

"Very well, then, I shall give you my opinion. Human nature is such that if we spend a lot of time with a person, we can easily come to love that person. It doesn't matter whether we are just having fun, as you call it. And many times, when we love someone, we want to be with that person all the time and share everything in our lives together. So what do we do? We marry. And if we marry someone who comes from a different background, we can have many problems because we are used to doing things differently. So what your father wants for you, Elke, is to be happy and not have many problems. Your father doesn't mean that a Gentile boy is not as good as a Jewish boy. It doesn't mean anything like that at all."

She nodded and didn't say anything. She still didn't think she agreed. It seemed to her that falling in love was a question of choice. You didn't have to fall in love with someone just because you spent a lot of time together. And whether or not you were happy when you married and let differences become problems also was a matter of choice. But even though she didn't agree with him, she felt good to have him take her seriously. He held her hand to show he cared.

"So tell me," he pressed. "Who is this boy you have been seeing? For you to be so unhappy with what your father said, there must be someone in particular."

"There isn't one." That was a true statement, she said to herself, because she hadn't seen David Sheffield in over a month now, ever since her father had come into her room to give her the diamond.

At first Jacob just looked at her and was silent. Then he exclaimed, "Well, then, I am lucky."

Elke looked at him surprised, and the expression on her face told him she didn't know what he meant.

"I'm lucky," he explained, "because that means you'll have more free time to come visit me like you have today."

Elke laughed. She reflected on how comfortable it was sitting here like this by the fire and talking to someone who seemed to have all the time in the world for her. It dawned on her that talking with Jacob was even better than reading a book.

"I will come visit you again, you'll see," she promised suddenly. "I'll come so often you'll wish you'd never invited me."

"You must be a woman of your word, Elke," he teased.

Elke kept her word. She paid several more visits to Jacob in the following weeks and looked forward to each more than the last. And after each visit, she felt blissfully content and shored up against her troubles. Problems that had seemed serious now didn't seem so important. The fact that her mother and father didn't have time to talk to her didn't seem so unbearable now that she had Jacob. And little by little, her thoughts of David Sheffield grew less painful.

It was always a source of wonder to her how easy it was to talk to Jacob. He was patient and concerned and always friendly, almost like a father, or the way she wished her father was. At the same time, he was so easy to talk to that she forgot all about his being a lot older than she and talked as freely as if he were her own age.

Almost two months went by before Marya heard from Andrew again. She had felt no inclination to contact him. She knew he was continuing his investigation into David Sheffield's background, and she knew he would get in touch with her as soon as he learned something substantial. She hadn't allowed herself to see David either. Her thoughts were too intense for her to be in his company without alarming him.

In a way, she was glad to have a period of time in which she didn't see Andrew because it gave her a chance to take stock of their friendship and to see how much she missed him. If her affair with him was to terminate, this is how her life would be, she told herself. Weeks without Andrew. Weeks without anyone showing concern or wanting to enfold her in his arms. Except that the weeks would become months and then years. It was too much for her to contemplate, and besides, she told herself, she loved Andrew and had no intention of not seeing him. But at the same time she wondered how long he would wait for her. It had been a long time ago, when he had asked her to marry him. He had told her he was a slow, measured man, and she should take her time in making her decision. But she suspected that if she didn't give him an answer soon, he would become discouraged and leave her for someone else. And was she clinging to him as the one source of love in her life—other than Elke and Daniel—that had prevailed the longest, that had not been lost to her or forsaken her?

And then yesterday the new telephone in the shop had rung, and she had heard Andrew's voice.

"How good it is to hear from you, Andrew," she blurted out, then wished she had not been so obvious in how much she had missed him.

"How about dinner tonight?" he suggested.

She thought quickly. She remembered Wolf's anger the last time she had missed dinner. Since then she had tried to be there for the evening meal any time she knew that Wolf didn't have to work late. But in a way she had felt resentment that it was she who had yielded. It was that resentment that suddenly made up her mind for her. "Of course, Andrew. It sounds splendid." Wolf would just have to accept the fact that sometimes she would not be home early.

She took a carriage to the Hotel Brunswick, and as she met Andrew outside the dining room, she was surprised to see how he had changed. He looked tired and older and he had lost weight. But his smile as he greeted her was unchanged. "Marya, you're as luminous and radiant as ever."

She laughed. "You know that's why I keep seeing you, Andrew, to hear you flatter me that way."

"And why do you think I keep seeing you?"

"I don't know. Force of habit?" she offered.

"Because I love you, you silly woman. Can't you keep that in your head?"

"No. I need to be told over and over . . . at least twice a day."

They continued to laugh and joke as they dined on a sumptuous meal of roast lamb served English style with a zesty onion sauce. After dinner, Andrew suddenly became more serious.

"You are probably wondering how the investigations are going."

"Yes." Marya also became more serious. "I've thought of you often during these last weeks."

"Thought of me or thought of the investigations?" he asked in a voice that made her look at him sharply.

"Why, both, of course."

Andrew put his pipe in his mouth. "At any rate, we've had a hard time of it. Suddenly everyone's clammed up. At first the family was willing to talk, were perhaps even flattered to be questioned. Now, they've become suspicious. They want to know why we're so intent on finding out David's origins. I think they expect scandal, so of course they don't want to cooperate in any way."

"Of course," agreed Marya, but she was disappointed. She had hoped that one of the reasons Andrew had asked her to have dinner with him was because he had found out at least some bit of new information. Some tiny piece that meant nothing to Andrew and his investigators at this point might mean everything to her.

"So I have nothing more to report."

"Nothing?" she echoed.

"It looks like we may have gone as far as we can. The thing to do, of course, is to continue the investigations in Russia. But as you know, the country is in the midst of upheaval."

"Yes," she nodded. The papers had been full of it. And Wolf had insisted on telling her, even though she didn't want to hear it, of how the Social Revolutionary Party was proposing that the land be given to those people who actually worked it. Russian workers, further disillusioned with the czarist government because of its losses in the war with Japan, had even gone on strike in industrial cities like Moscow and Vilna. When the czar's troops had fired on a peaceful procession of strikers in St. Petersburg, who were on their way to present a petition to the czar, political murders and disorder broke out throughout the Russian empire, and the day had been dubbed Red Sunday for the bloodshed that ensued.

Andrew drew to a conclusion. "So it's quite out of the question that we can pursue it there. We wouldn't even be able to get into the country in the first place, much less travel freely from place to place and ask questions. The railways are operating under martial law, the universities have been closed, and in the rural areas, wandering bands of peasants are said to be pillaging and burning the estates of the aristocrats and the wealthy. We would surely be thought suspicious and shot by one side or the other for being sympathizers with the enemy. The truth about our reasons for being there would never sound plausible."

"Yes, of course." She tried to keep the tremendous letdown she was feeling out of her voice. She had allowed herself to hope. She had to admit that what she had hoped Andrew had discovered was that David Sheffield was nothing more than an extremely bright and genial young man from the hinterlands of Russia who, by accident and good fortune, was adopted into a Russian Orthodox family that then emigrated.

And if David weren't her son—she shuddered to think of what she had done to poor Elke. Her breakup of their romance had not rested lightly on her, and it was only justified in her mind if David were in fact Elke's half brother. Sometimes she wondered how much longer she could live with the uncertainty of it all.

Andrew saw her shudder. "Are you cold, Marya?"

"No, I was just thinking of something."

"I have been thinking of something, too."

"What is it?" she asked with a certain amount of dread sparked by the way he had said it.

"It's about us. I know it's been a while since I asked you to marry me, and I want to renew my proposal. I don't want to rush you. But if you know your decision already, I would like to know. You see, if you were to become my wife, if you wished I would gladly make arrangements to pursue the investigation into Russia, despite the impossible odds. For the right amount of money, almost anything is possible. I would do it because I would want my wife to be happy, no matter the cost."

Marya thought of the irony of his words "no matter the cost." "It isn't the financial cost I'm weighing, Andrew."

"Of course not, Marya. I know that. But I do want you to take into consideration all possibilities when you make your decision. I want you to know what you would be getting into, taking me as your husband who would support you in every way. Every way," he emphasized.

And what, she wondered, would he be getting as a wife? He might find that he was marrying a woman who had buried another life and identity in Russia, with a husband and child. She thought of his expression again, "no matter the cost." What would be the costs to her if she were not to marry Andrew? She would continue to live with a stern and forbidding husband who clearly did not love her; she would surrender the emotional and physical support Andrew had never ceased to offer her lovingly; she would not be able to enter into what the newspapers called high society other than as the hired employee she had always been; and she would probably never know any more than she did at this moment regarding David Sheffield's real identity.

And if she were to marry him? She would have to let go of any troubling vestiges of distaste for divorce, for try as she might, she found she still had a great deal of the old country's attitude about the permanence of marriage. She would have to surrender any small part of her that might still identify itself as Jewish, for Andrew had hinted more than once that as his wife, she would have no trouble "passing." And she would have to take the chance that it might all end in disgrace if he learned the truth about her life in Russia, and the lie that she'd been living. So the ultimate cost was unknown.

"I need more time, Andrew."

One afternoon a few weeks later Marya came home and found Wolf waiting for her, pacing anxiously. Marya dreaded the thought of another argument about her work or her hours, although she happened to be arriving home a little earlier than usual this particular evening.

"Do you know where Elke is?" Wolf asked, obviously trying to keep his self-control.

Something in his tone frightened her. "No. Should I? Has something happened?"

"It's after dark and she's not home."

"She's not in her room?"

"That's the first place I looked. I had hoped she was with you."

Marya shook her head. "I'll check with Leah next door. Maybe she's there. She sometimes goes there in the afternoons to help her with the children."

When Marya returned a few moments later, Wolf could tell from her face that Elke wasn't there.

"Maybe she stayed late at the library or is visiting one of her friends," Marya suggested without conviction. But she knew it wasn't like Elke to forget the time and stay out past dark.

Because neither of them wanted to be the first to suggest foul play, each continued to suggest other possibilities for her whereabouts, possibilities which the other one would immediately argue down. Finally Marya said, "We can't go on making ourselves scared like this. She's probably some very safe place and will be in contact with us as soon as she realizes how late it is. I suggest we just relax and wait."

But as she sat curled up in a chair in the living room, Marya found she wasn't able to concentrate on the book she was trying to read. She glanced at Wolf and saw that he too was watching the clock.

When he saw that she was looking at him, he stood up and announced, "I'm going to start making some telephone calls."

Elke snuggled further down into the chair. She was warm and comfortable, and she couldn't remember ever being so content. In the corner the clock was ticking, and its rhythmic sound lulled her back to sleep. She was still fast asleep when the front door opened.

"Elke! You are still here? What happened to you?"

Elke rubbed her eyes and sat up slowly. "Jake?" It took her a moment to realize where she was. "I guess I fell asleep. It was so warm and peaceful here by the fire, and after you left I thought I would just stay a little while longer."

He sat down across from her and took her hands in his. "How warm they are," he squeezed them lightly.

"I love being here, Jake. It doesn't surprise me that I fell asleep so easily. It's because I'm so relaxed here. I've never been anywhere before where I felt so much at home, not even in my own house."

"It makes me feel good to hear you say that, Elkeleh. It's a good sign that you are so happy in this little corner of the world I've created for myself."

"Everything is perfect." She stretched her arms high over her head and arched her back. "I could stay here forever."

Jacob watched her long body and couldn't help but admire its full curves. "What a pretty picture you make, Elkeleh, stretching in front of my fire like a cat." Then, suddenly conscious that he might be embarrassing her, he pulled his eyes away from her and hastily added, "But, to me, my home is not quite perfect."

She looked at him and saw in his eyes a look she had begun to catch every so often, and lately more and more. It was a warmer, softer look that she saw there and one she decided she liked. It made her feel like the world's most important person and its most beautiful woman.

"But it is perfect, Jake! What more could you want?"

"Sitting there like that, with the firelight flickering over you, it's you that makes it perfect. It's you that completes the picture for me."

Elke looked at him and smiled. Suddenly she was

kneeling in front of him. "Oh Jake, do you really mean that? Do I really mean that much to you?"

His face was very solemn. "This house without you, Elkeleh, is like a fine, well-wrought setting for a ring without the most important part, its precious stone that belongs in the center. When you come in the door, my home begins to sparkle. It's you who is the diamond in my life."

"Jake," she began, and then couldn't say any more. She had always wanted to feel this important in someone's life. She didn't want to cry and was embarrassed to feel tears starting to roll down her cheeks.

"Elke, you mustn't cry." He pulled her onto his lap and took from his pocket a linen handkerchief that he used to wipe her face. He carefully patted it dry.

And then it was if they were both simultaneously aware of the contact of their bodies and the warmth that passed between them. Elke put her arms around Jacob's shoulders and then suddenly she found her lips on his. They kissed one another slowly and gently at first. Then they kissed again and again, each time with increasing passion.

Finally Jacob managed to pull himself from her, and he took her by the chin and looked into her eyes. "Now I don't see how I can ever let you leave."

"I don't want to," Elke murmured. "I don't think I ever wanted to leave, even from the first time I came here."

"Then we will be married." He pressed her close to him again. "I will speak to your father."

"My father?" Elke's eyes flew open and she was immediately on her feet. "I completely forgot! I should have telephoned them! They have no idea where I am."

Jacob led her into the room he used as his office. "Sit here," he pointed to his desk chair. "They'll be very worried about you. I think I should call them for you and explain. Especially," he added with a twinkle in his eye, "because there is now so much to explain."

Elke sat in the chair and hugged her legs close to her. So it would soon be settled; she was going to be married. She marveled at how completely safe and content she felt. When Jake had encircled her in his arms and held her against his big, rounded chest, she had never felt so completely loved and taken care of as at that particular moment.

As he dialed the number, she asked, "And we will have babies?"

Jacob laughed. "As many babies as you want, Elkeleh. You can have anything you want."

"Now stand still, Elke," Marya said, her mouth full of pins. She deftly slid three more into the pattern fabric to hold it in place, then stepped back to survey her work.

She started to laugh. "You don't have to hold that still. You look like a statue. Relax a little so I can see how the dress will hang on you when you're being yourself."

Elke sighed and wriggled her shoulders to loosen up. She wanted to look at herself, but there was no mirror in the back room of Marya's shop. She would have to wait until she got a chance to go into the front. Then at Marya's direction, she began to walk around the room.

Marya surveyed her daughter with pride. Even clad in the mockup gown of plain fabric, Elke managed to look regal. In the finished dress she would be stunning. She stood tall and her mass of reddish brown hair was at the moment uncharacteristically loose and trailing down her back to below her waist. It gave Marya a sense of satisfaction just to look at it.

Elke felt Marya's gaze lingering on her. She loved the attention she was receiving from her mother. Ever since that night at Jacob's, she had been the center of everyone's attention. Her mother had taken a considerable amount of time away from her regular business at the shop to design Elke's wedding gown and then plan the details of the wedding, which Jacob had insisted be conducted in the Chassidic fashion. Her father looked at her a little more often now, and when he did, he often seemed to be lost in thought, as if he were finally acknowledging her as a woman. Even Daniel seemed to see her as more of a person now that she was about to become a married woman.

They had set the wedding for six months away, only because Marya had insisted. If Elke had had her way, she would have been married that night in front of the fire when Jacob first asked her. Now it was sweetly excruciating to be together because her longing for him was so intense. She had wanted to take off her clothes for him in front of the fireplace that same night so that he might see the firelight that he loved flickering all over her bare body, but Jacob had said that although he would like nothing better, they must wait until their wedding night. Only three more months, Elke told herself.

Marya beckoned Elke to stand in front of her again so she could adjust the pattern dress. "Elke," Marya said in a tone that let her daughter know she was about to discuss something serious, "there's something I've been wanting to talk to you about."

"Yes, Mama?"

"You are quite certain you are ready to get married?"

Elke looked at Marya in astonishment and put her hands on her hips. "Of course, Mama. I can't wait."

"Elke, please stand still as I asked you." Elke immediately put her arms down, and Marya continued to adjust the dress. "You feel, then, that Jacob is definitely the one for you?"

Elke stood perfectly motionless but her response was full of passion. "He's so good and kind and warm. I wish you knew him the way I do. Then you would see why I love him, and you would love him too."

Marya knew it was true that she scarcely knew Jacob Molnar, and perhaps judged him too harshly, partly because of his age and partly because she had had little to say in the matter of whether this marriage was to be or not. "I know you love him, Elke. And your father has always spoken highly of him. It's just that I wouldn't want you to turn too quickly to someone who might really be the wrong person."

Elke automatically put her hands on her hips again, then just as quickly put them down. "But why would I do that?"

"Well, because you were lonely or maybe to help you forget," she hesitated just a second, "to help you forget someone else." Marya told herself she was a hypocrite for not having said David's name, but she just couldn't bring herself to. Still, she wondered how much her having driven Elke and David apart had to do with Elke's sudden romance with Jacob Molnar.

"There is no one else, Mama. And never was. At least not like Jake. I've never known a man like him. He's completely a man and not at all a boy. That's one of the things I like so much about him. He's a little bit like Papa, and a little bit like the heroes in my books, and a little bit like nobody else I've ever met—just himself."

Marya wished she could have smiled. She recognized in Elke's voice some of the same single-mindedness that she had felt so many years ago toward Wolf. Nobody could have talked her out of marrying Wolf or made her reconsider, no matter what. But even though she could identify somewhat with Elke's feelings, she couldn't give her wholehearted approval to the marriage. She had tried hard not to let Elke know that, partly out of guilt for having interfered in her romance with David. And because she had gotten Wolf to forbid Elke from seeing David on the grounds of his not being Jewish—and felt like a hypocrite for doing so—she didn't see how she could object to Jacob Molnar, who so totally was. And for that reason she had more than ever thrown herself into the wedding preparations.

She considered the gown she had designed to be

one of her best. It was to be made of cream silk and embroidered with beads of the same color and tiny pearls. The sleeves would fit tightly from the wrist to the elbow and would puff fashionably large at the top. Behind would flow a train of long folds. The wedding dress was to be topped with a matching silk jacket, also of cream silk, trimmed with swans-down and graced with large silk ribbon bows that draped over the shoulders. She knew that Elke was pleased with the design, and she hoped that with the gown, at least, she could in some small way make up to her for having sent David away.

"You will look luminous in this dress," Marya said as she assessed the way the fold of the train fell. "Hold your hair up, Elke, so I can see the line of the back."

Elke seized her hair up with both hands and twisted it into a knot on top of her head. "It won't be long before I can say good-bye to all this," she said.

"All what?" Marya asked, as she made a few more adjustments in the pattern.

"All this hair."

"What are you talking about, Elke?"

"Jake wants me to shave my head. He wants me to follow the old custom." No sooner were the words out of her mouth than she screamed. "Ouch! Mama! You just stuck me with the pin!"

Marya stopped what she was doing and stared at her daughter. "I'm sorry I stuck you, Elke, but your words startled me." She kept staring at Elke. "You can't be serious."

"About what?" Elke saw that her mother's face was ashen. She knew something was very wrong.

Marya's voice was practically a whisper. "About what you just said. About shaving off all your hair."

Elke tried to make light of the situation. "Mama, if that's what Jake wants, I'll do it. I just want him to be happy. Besides, it's a custom."

Marya groped for the words to express herself.

"Yes, I'm well aware it's a custom. But it's just not done anymore. This is America, Elke. You needn't live the way our ancestors did just because they didn't have any other choices."

Elke appeared calm. "This is my choice. I'm not doing it because I have to. I want to."

Marya was too upset to continue working on the wedding dress. She set down the pins and tailor's chalk. "Elke, let's sit down. I think we should talk more about this."

Elke took a chair across from her, and Marya suddenly could tell from the serene expression on her face that her words would be wasted, that nothing would get through to her. But she still felt she had to try.

"Elke, I don't want to tell you what to do. But I think I have a certain perspective that may be helpful to you. Because you are marrying a man quite a bit older than you, and with different religious beliefs than you were raised with, your life as a married woman could be extremely different than it is now. You will have less freedom and you will find that your husband—"

"It's Jake. You can say his name, Mama."

Marya nodded. "You will find that Jake, because of his background and his beliefs, will be much stricter than your father is."

"I don't care about any of that. It's not important to me. I just want to be with him."

"Elke, you're so young to be making such an important decision by yourself."

"I'll be nineteen by the time I get married. You were eighteen when you married my father."

"Those were different times. We were both new to this country. We needed each other to make a life here."

"But you loved each other, I know. You used to tell me that."

"That's true. But Elke—" Her voice broke, and

she leaned forward and grabbed a handful of Elke's long hair. "To cut off all your thick beautiful hair? It would break my heart." Neither she nor Wolf had ever said a word to the children or to anyone else about her having lost all her hair just before they were married. She had never been able to bring herself to say anything about it to Elke and she knew she still couldn't. The horror of it and how she had looked to herself all those long months as it had slowly grown back in and how it was linked in her mind to her loss of Wolf's love—all that was still deep inside her. Now it was simply too much for her to contemplate that her daughter would voluntarily go to her own wedding night with a shaven head. She buried her face in the hank of Elke's hair she was still holding and began to cry.

Elke didn't move but sat perfectly still. This was the first time in her life she had ever seen her mother cry. She reached out and put her arms around Marya's shoulders. "Please, Mama. Don't be sad for me. I don't mind about losing my hair at all. Sometimes it's just a big bother anyway. It won't be so bad. You'll see. For me, it will be a joyous thing to cut off my hair, a gift I can give my husband. You've probably just never seen a woman without any hair before. And besides, I'll be wearing a *sheitel* so it'll look like I still have hair. It just won't be my real color, that's all, and there won't be as much of it. You'll get used to it. You'll see."

Feeling restless and introspective, Daniel decided to go for a walk. All afternoon thoughts of his father, of Elke's impending marriage and of his own future had been swirling in his head. Now, he told himself, he just had to think of something else. On an impulse, he took a horse-car to the Lower East Side and then walked in the direction of Greene Street and the neighborhood where he and his family used to live. Although they had moved uptown almost ten years ago, he still remembered this area vividly and every corner recalled scenes from his boyhood. That had been a time when he didn't work at the factory as much as he did now. More significant in his father's eyes had been his regular attendance at school. In the afternoons he still had time to run the streets with the other boys his age, teasing the pushcart peddlers on Hester Street or sometimes getting into fights with the Irish boys south of Cherry Street or the Italian boys west of the Bowery in which both sides would hurl dried horse droppings enthusiastically at each other and sometimes, in a pinch, not so dried ones. Sometimes they would discover a piece of ice to suck on, fallen from the ice truck, or a piece of candy near the newsstands. Other times, when the weather was muggy, they would cavort half naked in the fountain at Rutgers Square, or dive off the docks into the East River, where they would emerge covered with a film of oil.

The streets of the Lower East Side had changed only slightly since his boyhood. They were now better paved and almost all of the three and four-story wooden buildings such as used to line Hester Street had been replaced with fireproof brick tenements of six or seven stories whose fronts were bedecked with iron fire escapes, which served in the summer as alfresco bedrooms for the inhabitants. But the signs in four or five languages, the women with their oilskin shopping bags in which were indiscriminately dumped all their vegetables for *tsimmes*, the scholarly looking men in black caftans with long beards, the boys hawking Yiddish news sheets for a penny each—those aspects seemed frozen in time, not subject to change.

As he turned the corner onto Cherry Street, he came across a gathering on the sidewalk of young people, some of whom looked to be about his age, many a few years older. They were laughing and making jokes, and only half listening to a young man who appeared to be standing on an upturned milk box and was addressing them. After the young man, a thin, angular fellow with a slight Russian accent, stepped down, some members of the crowd applauded apathetically. Daniel had only heard enough to get a general idea of the speech, which had been about the advantages of socialism. Not being particularly interested in politics, Daniel was ready to move on. His attention was arrested by the next speaker to take the makeshift podium. It was a young woman who couldn't have been any older than he. She was dressed in a plain black skirt with an equally plain shirtwaist over it. She was small-framed and blonde and even atop the box she rose such a little distance over the heads of her audience that someone hastily provided her with a second box to lift her even higher. She began to speak in a lilting but insistent voice about the necessity of establishing a Jewish homeland.

"The time is now!" she concluded, and shook her fist. Her speech over, some of the crowd again broke into applause, this time only slightly more enthusiastic. Then the crowd parted and the young woman began to make her way through it, coming right toward him.

"That was a wonderful speech," Daniel surprised himself by saying when she got close.

She looked up at the tall young man directly in front of her and smiled. "It was my first and I was shaking all over. But if you think that was good, you should come with me now. I'll really show you good."

He decided he liked the pert way she handled herself, and because he had nothing better to do, he walked alongside her. "Where are we going?" he asked.

"You'll see."

To his surprise she led him into the same building in which he used to live and began to climb the stairs.

"I used to live in this building," he said. "Is this where you live?"

"You wouldn't believe where I live," she laughed. "The answer is no."

Together they climbed the full six stories, then another story to the roof. As they stepped out onto the top of the building, Daniel was surprised to see the number of young people congregated there. There were four or five separate groups, with an enclave claiming each corner, and one group in the middle where someone was playing Russian folk tunes.

There was a burst of loud laughter from one corner. "You can always count on finding someone who'd like to be the country's next vaudeville star up here. It's easy to find a receptive audience."

There was another burst of laughter, and Daniel saw her wrinkle her nose.

"Come over here," she nodded her head in the direction of a gathering in the opposite corner. As they neared the group, Daniel could hear a spirited discussion in progress. A number of the young people seemed to be voicing opinions, but the main participants were a young woman with dark curly hair and a man about the same age with pale red hair and freckled skin. They argued vociferously on the subject of labor conditions in the garment industry and the need for some kind of regulatory control.

"If the employers aren't going to do it voluntarily," said the woman, "then I say let's unionize."

"You'll never get the workers to unionize," put in the freckle-faced boy. "The turnover is too great and most of the workers have no energy left over for fighting with the bosses."

"And," added one of the others, "most of the workers are women. You'll never get them to organize."

"That's right," picked up the freckled fellow. "They see the jobs as temporary anyway. They know they'll soon be married and having children, so what difference does it make to them?" Daniel sighed. He had heard both sides of the argument before. His father had made him aware of the demands of many of the workers and he knew a certain amount just from talking to the workers in their factory. He looked down at the young woman standing next to him and as he did so, she happened to be looking up at him.

"What's your name?" she asked.

"Daniel. Daniel Luminov. What's yours?"

"I'm Alma. Hey, would you like to go get some tea or something? I can tell you're not exactly crazy over listening to any more of this."

Daniel laughed. "How did you know?"

"I can just tell, even though it's not easy to see your face from here because you're so tall."

"Well, it's pretty easy to see yours," he smiled. "And, yes, let's get some tea."

"Great. I know a café not far from here, over near Rutgers Square. Have you ever been to the Zum Essex?"

Daniel had only planned to spend an hour or so at the café, but the hour turned into two, then three, then four, as he and Alma managed to talk about almost everything that had happened to them since babyhood. She talked easily and laughed even more easily, so that he began to think her one of the most intriguing persons to be around whom he had ever met.

Once they were sitting across from each other, he could get a better look at her. She had bright brown eyes, an oval face and a small upturned nose. Her skin was remarkably fine and clear, and next to her eyes, it was the most arresting thing about her. Over all she didn't have the looks or bearing that most people would call beautiful, but Daniel thought she definitely had something that made her very pleasing to the eye. "I just can't believe that your family owns a dressmaking factory, too," she commented as she sipped what Daniel figured must have been their eighth cup of tea that evening.

"I've worked there ever since I was big enough to walk and follow directions."

"That's incredible. Daddy hasn't let me near our place other than for a couple tours. I once said I wanted a job as a baster and he got furious. Said it was a job for greenhorns from Russia and—" She saw the expression that crossed Daniel's face. "Oh, I didn't mean it like that. Those are my father's feelings, defi-

nitely not mine. He and I don't seem to agree on anything anymore, only he doesn't know that because I've
learned to save my real opinions for the friends I've
met down here. Anyway, as a result of Daddy's attitude about letting me near the factory, I feel like a
tourist when I go there, gawking at the spectacle of the
sweating workers."

"That's all I've done with my life, it seems, is
work in the factory. Half the time I'm one of those
sweating workers."

"Then you know about the conditions firsthand.
It's pretty awful, isn't it. That's what I've learned from
some of the soapbox speeches I've heard." She stirred
another spoonful of sugar into her glass.

Daniel raised his eyebrows and replied in a careful, measured tone. "It can be. In fact, in most places it
is. My father has told me some terrible stories of when
he was just starting out and working for other people.
He's sworn he'll never do that again. And that's why
he's tried to make our factory a better place to work."

She set down her glass and looked thoughtful.
"Your father sounds like one of the few enlightened
ones. I suspect my father is just the opposite. But as I
said, he never lets me close enough to check on what
it's really like."

"That's probably just as well," Daniel reflected.

"See? You're admitting that conditions aren't so
good."

"No. I just think there are probably better places
for you to be if you don't have to work there."

"But what about you? You said you're in your father's factory almost every day. Why do you do that?"

Before he could reply, she supplied her own answer. "It must be because one day you'll take over for
your father? Is that right?"

"Yes." Daniel's voice betrayed more emotion than
he had intended. His inclination was to ask her a question quickly so that he could mask his feelings and
change the subject. Then he thought better of it and

decided he would tell her what he was thinking about. "I have a feeling about you. I feel I can tell you what I really think and you won't laugh at me or tell me I'm crazy."

She grew serious. "I'm glad you feel that way about me, Daniel, because that's the way I feel about you. I know we haven't known each other more than a couple hours, but there's just something about you I liked and trusted almost from the very beginning. I guess it was when you were willing to come up those stairs with me, not even knowing where we were going. So I want you to know you can tell me anything you want. There's nothing about you I'm not interested in."

Her impromptu speech swept away the rest of his hesitation. "What I want to tell you about me is that the most important thing in my life is becoming my father's partner in the business."

"I don't think that's crazy at all. I think you're lucky you know what you want to do. So many men don't, like," she hesitated, "like my brother. But I'm sure you would be a fair and honest owner, just like your father."

At her mention of his father, he seized her hand. "You should know my father, Alma. He's a good man and he's smart. He's built up this whole factory from nothing. That's what he had when he got here, nothing. And now the business is getting bigger all the time."

"When will you become his partner?"

"He said it wouldn't be until I finish high school. This next year will be my last, so I expect it will be sometime soon."

She squeezed his hand tightly. "I'm so happy for you. You'll have to let me know when that happens so we can celebrate."

"That's what I've been trying to get to. When can I see you again?"

"I hope it's tomorrow."

Daniel laughed. "Then it will be. And you can tell me more about this Palestine thing. Now tell me where you live."

"I live on the West Side, but promise me you won't tell anyone down here that. They probably wouldn't let me come to their meetings if they knew my father was a big factory owner. And Daddy would lock me up if he knew I was coming down here among the eastern European workers to attend meetings on establishing a Jewish homeland in Palestine." She wrinkled her nose in mock disgust.

"What's the name of your factory?"

"You mean *his* factory. It's New Day. It isn't one of the large ones, but it's growing all the time. Have you heard of it?"

"I think I have, but I don't remember anything about it. I'll ask my father. I'm sure he has."

He walked her to the el and waited with her until it came. As it clanged to a stop alongside them, puffing steam into the air, he gave her a quick kiss on the cheek and bid her good-bye.

Just before she jumped on the train, she turned back toward him. Her words tumbled over each other in her haste to say everything she wanted before the train left. "You're awfully good looking, you know." She started laughing. "There! I said it. I've been wanting to say that to you all evening, but I didn't want to embarrass you." She pecked him on the cheek, then without looking back again, jumped into the waiting car.

He laughed out loud and started to say something, but it was too late. The doors had shut. As he watched the train pull away, he realized he had been so busy talking that he hadn't even got around to finding out her last name. But there'd be plenty of time for that tomorrow, he said to himself. He knew they'd be seeing a lot of each other.

Chapter 20

From her place in the temple's balcony, Marya looked
down at Elke as she stood under the marriage canopy,
beautiful in the silk bridal gown, her head covered with
a veil. Next to her stood Jacob, wearing the *kittel*, a
white robe, his face beaming. The blessing had just
been made over the wine and Jacob turned toward
Elke with the ring. Even from where she sat, Marya
could dimly see Elke's face through the veil as he
slipped the plain, unornamented band symbolizing a
smooth and unbroken marriage on to the forefinger of
her right hand. Marya had never seen her daughter
look so happy.

As Jacob put the ring on her finger, he began to
intone the ancient vow: *"Harey at mekudeshet li beta-
baat zu kedat Mosheh ve'Yisrael"*—"You are hereby
bethrothed to me by token of this ring in accordance
with the law of Moses and Israel."

She saw that tears of joy had flushed Elke's
cheeks when Jacob lifted the veil. As the rabbi began
to read the *kesubah*, the marriage contract which Jacob
had insisted be decorated and illuminated in the fashion of the ancient contracts from the late Middle Ages,
Marya wished she herself felt more joyful. Her

thoughts kept going back to the previous morning as she had helped Elke get ready for the *mikvah*, the ritual bath and purification ceremony that was supposed to take place at the bathhouse within twenty-four hours before the wedding.

Elke had been so excited she was unable to finish a single sentence and instead jumped breathlessly from topic to topic, one minute Jacob and how much she loved him, the next minute Jacob's house and what decorating changes she planned to make in it, and the next minute her complexion and why it had to get a tiny blemish on one of the most important days of her life. Elke had struggled with the long length of hair, trying to get all the strands to lie smoothly so she could sweep it up onto her head in a knot. She flung her head down so that her hair flipped forward and hung to the floor.

"Here," Marya took the brush, "let me brush it out for you. You're too excited to concentrate on what you're doing."

As she had brushed the long strands into a single, enormous hank, she again felt a profound ache to think that in less than an hour all this hair would be lying in a pile on the floor. She refused to let her daughter see the tears that had rolled down her cheek and onto the long strands of hair she kept brushing over and over, as if lost in a trance, until finally Elke had pulled her head away laughing, saying that her hair was supposed to be shorn at the ceremony, not brushed out of her head beforehand.

The fact that Elke was willingly divesting herself of this very visible aspect of her beauty bothered Marya enormously and somehow represented to her all that was wrong with this marriage. Jacob was simply too old for Elke—she would be a widow before her time, and Marya knew what that was like. He was also too conservative. As far as Marya could tell, he lived as if he thought he were still in the old country, following the ancient customs, and he would insist his wife do the same. She thought again of the jewels Wolf had given her and of how it was those stones that were to blame for all this. If Wolf hadn't been so driven with proving himself worthy to be his father's son, he would not have tried to turn her into his father's wife, festooning her with glittery stones like a Russian aristocrat. Then Elke and Jacob would never have met.

Nor did Marya herself feel blameless. She wondered why it was so many of the crucial decisions in her life had been double-edged. Why wasn't life ever a clear-cut choice between good and evil? Instead, it was a choice between two difficult ways to go, both laced with good and bad. When you tried to make a good decision, you were bound to hurt someone, no matter which way you went. She had done what she thought best when she interrupted Elke and David's romance, and in trying to do Elke good, she had unknowingly propelled her along another course that, as far as she could see, wasn't good for Elke either. And to make matters worse, she'd lost David too. She suspected he knew she had come between him and Elke in some way, for he had now started to avoid her.

Marya's attention was brought back to the moment as the rabbi began to read the first of the seven blessings. As she listened to his low, rich voice, she thought of her own wedding and glanced at Wolf, down below in the main section of the temple. How handsome he still was, she thought just a little wistfully. His large physique was as trim as ever, and the frockcoat with its satin-faced lapels made him look imposing and distinguished. He would have been proud to hear her thoughts, she realized, for he had often spoken of his father as a distinguished looking man, and his greatest ambition seemed to have been to emulate him in every way. She recalled how, like Elke, she had been so happy that day of her wedding. She'd had no way of foreseeing the cold rift that would come between her and Wolf. How she now wished it hadn't happened. And she hoped that at least Elke would be spared that sorrow.

The rabbi finished reading the first blessing and immediately the cantor picked up the same refrain and began to chant it in a high, melodic voice. When the rabbi finished the second blessing, the cantor again chanted it a cappella in a haunting melody. They continued to interweave the blessings, with the rabbi reciting in Hebrew, the cantor echoing in song. The effect was so beautiful it made goose bumps stand out on Marya's arms, and she was surprised and a little displeased that anything connected with the old customs had managed to affect her that way.

And then the wine glass was placed under Jacob's heel, and with one hearty stomp, he shattered it into a hundred tiny pieces.

"Theirs will be a happy and fruitful marriage," whispered a woman behind Marya, and then the wedding ceremony was over.

The reception was one of the most joyous Marya or Wolf had ever seen. The room was crowded with dozens of Jacob's Chassidic friends and it sounded as if six or seven different languages were being spoken at once. The men danced with great exuberance and sang until Marya thought surely their voices would go hoarse. Then everyone, men and women, feasted on roast chicken, potatoes, gefilte fish, cabbage and sweetened carrots, and the celebration went on twice as long as Marya had anticipated. Every time she looked at Elke, her head veiled, she saw that her eyes were still moist with happiness. Very well, thought Marya, at least let her have that. She has no way of knowing how bittersweet her life with Jacob might be.

"Zavel," Marya said a few months later, venturing one of their rare discussions about the children, "have you noticed that Daniel seems so quiet lately? He only talks if I ask him a question, and then it's a one-word answer. I expected that now that he's out of school, he'd be happier, having that much more time to do what he likes best, which is work in the factory. He never was very interested in school anyway."

They were eating dinner alone for once, Daniel having gone to Alma's house to eat.

Wolf sighed. "He takes himself too seriously, that's all."

"What do you mean?"

"I know what's wrong with him, Marya. He told me."

She looked at him surprised and waited for him to continue. Although she knew that Daniel idolized his father, she also knew he was not inclined to confide in him.

"He's upset because I haven't made him a partner in the business yet."

"Well, you can't blame him," she tried to point out tactfully. "After all, you've been telling him practically since the day he was born that you were just waiting until he became a man. Now that he's finished high school—and has to lower his head to look you in the eye—I don't think you can very well deny he's grown up."

Wolf didn't particularly like her observation about Daniel's height, but decided that to say anything direct about it would be a prelude to a fight. It had been so long since he and Marya had been alone and just talked that he wanted to avoid a confrontation if he could. "He may be physically big, but that doesn't mean his time has come."

"Perhaps the problem, Zavel, is that your time hasn't come."

He looked at her sharply. "What do you mean?"

"Just that you might not be ready to let go of your control."

"I'll be ready to let go of my control when I think he's ready to handle it as well as I do."

"Zavel," she said gently, "you know in your heart that you'll never think he can do it as well as you. The question is, could he do an adequate job right now? He doesn't have to be great, you know. Just competent. Can he handle it?"

"I don't know."

She put her hand on his. "Honestly?"

He was beginning to get annoyed with the turn the conversation had taken. "We're supposed to be talking about Daniel. All of a sudden, it's me and my motives we're looking at." He pulled his hand back.

Her expression gave no sign that she had noticed he had moved away from her. "He is your son, and almost everything either of you does is interlocked."

He looked her in the eye. "Marya, he's just not ready. You've got to believe me."

She met his gaze. "If you say so, Zavel." Then she added, "I just hope you're not expecting too much of him."

"He's doing all right. He's just got to relax about taking over his share of the factory."

"He's like you in a lot of ways. He keeps so much inside of him that I get fearful sometimes."

Wolf laughed. "What's there to be scared about?"

"I don't know. It's just a feeling I get."

"At first I thought you were going to say it was one of your pictures. Except it's been a long time since I've heard you say anything about them."

She looked at him quickly. She wasn't sure if he was being sarcastic or not. It had certainly been a long time since his voice had had that soft teasing quality when he spoke to her. "It's not that," she dismissed the notion. "I just worry sometimes that he might let this desire to work side by side on an equal basis with you get all out of proportion. Like you, he takes his work very seriously, and he's strong-willed and impulsive."

"I know. That's the very reason I've got to watch him. I can't let him take over too soon. It could spell the downfall of everything I've struggled for for the last twenty years."

Marya looked surprised. "Certainly we've raised

him with more levelheadedness than that. Zavel, can't
you see that he's also got your intelligence and common sense and dedication? What you're saying just
isn't possible."

"You don't see it in your pictures, eh?"

"Now you are being sarcastic. I wasn't sure the
first time."

"Let's not fight, Marya. Let's talk about something happier."

Marya looked down at her lap and tried to get
control of her feelings. Finally she said, "Well, I do
have some news for you. Elke's going to have a baby."

"What!" He almost jumped from his chair. "Already?"

"It doesn't take long to get pregnant, Zavel. Or
have you forgotten?" As soon as she said it, she was
sorry. She hadn't wanted to return his sarcasm, especially not on a topic that was so sensitive between
them. She had been trying to break their stalemate.

Marya wasn't the only one to notice that Daniel
seemed preoccupied.

"Daniel," Alma approached him one day, sum-
moning up her courage, "I have something to ask you,
and you have to tell me the truth."

"Sure. You know I always tell you the truth." He
wondered what she could possibly be going to say.
They were walking down Cherry Street on their way to
another rooftop meeting that Alma had insisted on taking him to. It seemed her involvement in what was
happening in Palestine was even greater than he had at
first realized.

She took a deep breath before asking her question. "Are you getting tired of my company?" she
blurted out much more impatiently than she had
wanted to.

He stopped walking. "Are you crazy? What would
I be doing with you if that were so?"

"Then why are you so quiet lately? You don't

seem to laugh as much as you used to, and lots of times you seem to be lost in your own thoughts."

He looked away quickly. "Well, I suppose I am. I've got a lot on my mind."

"What is it?"

"I don't want to get you involved in this, Alma. Honestly, you're not the reason I haven't been in such a good mood lately. It doesn't have anything to do with you."

"It does if it affects how you act when you're around me."

He looked back at her. She was standing there in her dark blue wool skirt and jacket with a matching hat tilted to one side on her head. With her pale blonde hair and large brown eyes, she was the picture of freshness. "I guess I could tell you," he began hesitantly. "I've always said I trusted you."

"I care about you, Daniel. I want to know what it is that's taken your thoughts away from me like this." She took him by the hand and pulled. "Come on. We don't have to go to that meeting tonight. Let's go someplace where we can talk."

He let her lead him to the Café Royale on Second Avenue. Even at that early hour of the evening there was already a considerable hubbub of activity as workers and residents from the area sat curled over their tea glasses and schnapps bottles at the round wooden tables. Some were lost in animated conversation while others sat alone and read newspapers as they poured their tea into saucers to cool it.

They chose a spot near the wall in the back where there were fewer people. As soon as they sat down, Alma reached out across the oak table and took his hands in hers. "Now tell me, Daniel."

"It's my father." His words were slow and careful, and as he listened to himself, he was surprised at how much anger was underlying them. "He hasn't kept his word to me."

"You mean about giving you an equal share in the business?"

He nodded.

"He said that he would make you his partner when you finished high school?"

"It seems like he's been saying it all my life. It's always just ahead. 'Just a little while, son.' Only that day never comes."

"We're only nineteen, Daniel. That's not very old, when you think about it. Maybe you need a couple more years to be ready."

He cast her an angry look. "That's what he says. But I'm ready. I've been ready for years. You can't know what it's like, Alma, because you're a daughter, not a son. All my life I've heard this stuff from him about how important it is to him to be able to pass on a legacy to his sons. I know it disappointed him that he didn't have five more boys, but at least he's got one."

"He's lucky. My father would love to have a son like you." But even as she said that a strange look appeared in her eyes for just a second, then quickly disappeared.

Daniel was surprised. "I thought you said you have a brother."

"I do. Or did. We never talk about him anymore."

"Then he's dead?"

"No. We don't know where he is. He ran away. My father wanted him to follow in his footsteps and take over the business. He was pushing it on him. My brother didn't want any part of it. He said he wasn't interested in the rag business and just wanted to be left alone. When my father kept after him about it, he just disappeared. Once a year we get a note from him telling us he's okay. He never gives us an address and every year the postmark's from a different place. He doesn't want my father to find him."

Daniel brought his fist down on the table so hard the glasses jumped.

Alma looked at him, startled. His face was contorted in anger.

"What is this thing about fathers and sons? It seems the wrong sons get the wrong fathers. Here your brother is content to let your father run everything, and I'm not. Your father is anxious to have his son take over, and mine isn't. Why can't we work it out?"

"I don't know," Alma looked into her tea. "I don't understand it either, but I think you have to give your father more time. He's not an old man. He's not ready to retire yet."

Daniel leaned forward and hissed through clenched teeth, "But he never said anything about waiting till he retired! He talked about us working alongside each other, equal partners, not just in blood and in spirit, but in law. Now all I want is for him to keep his promise."

She took his hand again. It was hot with the intensity of his emotion. "Have you talked to him about it?"

"Not in the last year."

"Maybe you should again. It might help to get things out in the open."

"I don't know." He looked away. "He's not an easy person to talk to." But even as he protested, he knew Alma's advice was right. He would have to talk to his father again. How he dreaded it. It seemed they had one of those conversations every couple of years and the results were always the same. Nothing changed.

"Alma, when am I ever going to meet your father?" asked Daniel many months later. "I've been seeing you for over a year now and I've yet to lay eyes on him. Are you sure you have one?"

Alma laughed. "Of course. It's just that he's always working. That's how it's always been with him as long as I can remember. He's either at the shop or on the road traveling."

"I guess that's how my sister must have thought of my father too," Daniel became suddenly thoughtful. "I was almost always with him in the factory so I never thought about his not being at home. She must have missed him."

They were sitting in the kitchen of Alma's house where their maid, a thin, good-natured woman of middle age, was rolling out dough for the *kreplach* that were to be part of the evening meal. Every few minutes Daniel's fingers would attempt a foray to snatch a tiny piece of dough. But Mrs. Mueller's fingers were just as fast. Fingers and rolling pin would collide at the same time as Mrs. Mueller exclaimed, "Ganef! Thief!" and chortled gleefully at having once again successfully fought off the marauder.

Daniel and Alma had spent many afternoons sitting in this same kitchen as Mrs. Mueller bustled about making preparations for supper. During that time he had been able to sample bits of homemade potato pancakes, or *latkes* as Mrs. Mueller called them, *kishka*, gefilte fish, and what had to be the world's tenderest sauerbraten. He had seen Mrs. Mueller in a tizzy of excitement as she prepared special dishes for the Passover Seder, the ritual dinner commemorating the passage of the ancient Jews out of slavery in Egypt.

Although his mother was a good cook, every bit as good as Mrs. Mueller when she put her mind to it, she hadn't cooked much these last few years, preferring to leave it to Elke. Luckily Elke had liked being in the kitchen, but although she had entered into her new responsibility enthusiastically, she was still a beginner, without her mother's more experienced touch. But Daniel had rarely seen Marya prepare a meal in honor of Passover, or Purim or Chanukah or Rosh Hashanah, or even Yom Kippur, the day when it was the custom in many households for parents to give their children a blessing. He remembered that once his parents had even fought over it. His father had asked his mother, just once, to fix a special meal in honor of Passover.

But she had refused, saying she had done with all that a long time ago. What had made the biggest impression on him was the expression on her face as she had said that. It had been a strange one, half hard and half fearful at the same time, and he had wondered what had made her feel so strongly. It was just a meal and a few prayers, after all.

"Does your family observe all the holidays?" he asked Alma.

"Of course. And we all go off to Temple Emanuel on Saturday mornings." Daniel recognized the temple as one frequented by the German Jews. But his parents never went to any temple. Once or twice he had heard his father talk about the religion he was raised with, but it seemed that when he had gotten to this country, there had been no time to practice the old beliefs. Now he sensed his father was more inclined to slow down and resurrect some of the practices that the practicalities of earning a living had forced him to abandon earlier. Still, his mother would have none of it.

"You are Americans all the way through," she had said to him and Elke more than once. "Never forget that."

Alma, still talking of the temple, broke into his thoughts. "But, just between you and me, I would rather—"

She was cut short by the back door of the kitchen suddenly opening. Into the room came a large, well-dressed man with a beefy red face.

"Daddy!" she cried and sprung to her feet. Her father immediately drew her into his arms and she put her arms around his immense body as best she could.

"How's my little sprite?" the man asked in a smooth voice that didn't seem to match the ruddiness of his face.

When Alma had stood, so had Daniel. He instantly recognized Alma's father as the man who had been in the textile mill at Lawrence the same time he had been. When Alma had told him the first day he had come to her house that her last name was Detweiler, it had sounded familiar to him, but he had had no reason to connect it with the man whose name he had overheard in the mill that day.

Alma introduced him. "Daddy, this is my friend Daniel. You've heard me talk about him."

"All the time," put in Mrs. Mueller in the background and Alma and Daniel laughed.

Daniel noticed Alma's father was staring strangely at him, almost as if he knew him, and Daniel thought about mentioning that he had seen him in the mills. But for some reason he thought better of it.

"What's your family name, young man?" Alma's father asked in a not unkindly tone as he shook Daniel's hand.

"Luminov, sir," replied Daniel.

"Luminov?" he repeated. "Isn't that Russian?"

"Yes," Daniel said.

He looked at Daniel again with that quizzical look in his eye. Daniel thought he saw a flicker of annoyance. Then Mr. Detweiler shook his head and laughed. "For a moment I thought you looked familiar, but I don't recollect hearing that name before." He smiled at Daniel. "Well, welcome to our household, young Daniel, although from what my daughter tells me you're hardly a stranger here."

"Thank you, sir," Daniel smiled. He was pleased to find that Alma's father wasn't as fierce as he'd first looked to be, his elegant attire notwithstanding, and that he wasn't going to banish him for being of eastern European stock.

"Daniel's father is in the garment business, too," said Alma, obviously trying to provide some common ground for the two of them.

"Is that right?" replied Mr. Detweiler. "What's he do?"

"He owns MW Enterprises. We make ladies' dresses." It felt good for him to say "we."

Alma's father raised his eyebrow. "MW Enterprises, eh? I've heard of them. Doing very well, I'd say. Just beat me out a year ago in an effort to buy the Arawanee mill up in Troy."

Daniel was surprised. His father had told him there was another bidder on the mill that he was worried about coming in with a lower price than his. What a coincidence that person should be Alma's father, Daniel thought.

Mr. Detweiler patted him on the shoulder. "Well, you two. I've got some work to do, so if you'll excuse me." Before he left, he gave Alma a buss on the cheek, then smiled and shook Daniel's hand.

Daniel was also relieved to see that apparently Mr. Detweiler bore no ill feelings over the matter of the mill. "Your father seems like a pretty nice man," Daniel remarked as soon as he was out of the room.

"He is, most of the time, and especially to me and my mother. His home is sacred to him. But he's famous for his temper. That's why I feel sorry for the people at his factory. Because when it goes, there's no stopping him."

"Well, he sure didn't seem that way just now. He seemed as relaxed as they come."

"That's because he's not at work," Alma rejoined. "Now, come on. Would you like to walk me to my German class? It's at Mozart Hall on Eighty-sixth Street between Second and Third, and it starts at four o'clock. So I'll miss it if I don't get going. And Daddy wouldn't be too happy about that. He's sending me three times a week to learn German so I'll know something about my heritage."

"You're just going to have to admit you're not here enough to keep up with this house," Wolf said to her one afternoon.

Whenever they'd had this discussion before, Marya always had replied that she didn't want a stranger running her house.

"The stranger, as you call her, will only be a

stranger the first day. After that she'll become like one of the family," Wolf had always answered, impatient with her reluctance to hire the assistance the house so obviously demanded. He was disappointed with her decision to turn down his offer of a servant, and tried to share with her some of the fond memories he had of servants his parents had had when he was a child. "You will be surprised, Marya, how soon you will grow accustomed to having someone take over those chores that cannot be pleasant to you anymore."

"I just wouldn't feel comfortable having some other person in the house all the time."

"Marya, I have never found fault with your housekeeping. When you were here and when you put in the time, there wasn't a household that sparkled more. But you recall that even then I wanted you to have help."

"And I refused."

"You said you could do a better job than any hired help who wouldn't really care as much. Elke willingly took up the running of the house when she was here, but now that she's gone, there just is no way you can do it, or really even want to do it all yourself. Now I am insisting that we have a housekeeper."

"And I'm insisting we don't."

To her surprise, Wolf had let the subject drop more quickly than usual. Two days later Marya came home unexpectedly in the middle of the day to find the house filled with the heavenly smell of challah baking in the oven, and a small, carrot-haired woman sitting at the kitchen table with her feet propped up on a chair as she sipped a cup of tea.

"Who are you?" Marya burst out, surprised to see this woman making herself so obviously at home in her kitchen.

The woman, who appeared to be somewhere in her late fifties and had a small freckled face with a sharp, pointed nose, kept her feet where they were and was apparently not at all concerned. "I'm Mrs. Sanders, the housekeeper. And who are you?"

"This is my house," Marya informed her, getting angry. "How did you get in?"

Mrs. Sanders slowly lowered her feet to the floor and stood up. "You must be Mrs. Luminov," she smiled. "You mean your husband didn't tell you? He hired me yesterday."

Marya didn't return the smile. "No, he didn't say anything about it."

"Most likely, then, he meant it as a surprise," decided Mrs. Sanders pleasantly, not at all nonplused. "It wouldn't be your birthday, would it? Or wedding anniversary?"

Marya stared at the woman and hesitated between ordering her out of the house at once and asking her to explain again. Not having been raised with household help, it embarrassed her to think this older woman would be scrubbing and scraping and rinsing on her behalf. It wasn't a question of the money. And she had been around servants when she had gone to the houses of her wealthy and fashionable patrons. But she had never had one of her own on a full-time basis.

Mrs. Sanders had broken into her thoughts. "I know what you're probably thinking. But you'll get used to having me around in no time. You'll see. Now, what would you like me to fix you for lunch?"

She hadn't been able to bring herself to ask Mrs. Sanders to fix her anything, and had instead left the house immediately and skipped lunch that day. The rest of the afternoon, as she was busy consulting with patrons at her shop and discussing her designs with the dressmakers, in the back of her mind was the question of what to do about Mrs. Sanders. She had opened the front door that evening to the transporting aroma of pot roast, and as she looked around the living room, she saw that it was polished, gleaming and spotless. She sighed and walked into the kitchen.

"Ah, Mrs. Luminov! How are you?" beamed

Mrs. Sanders as soon as she saw Marya. "Now what can I get you? A bit of tea to soothe you after a busy day of work? Here," she pulled out a chiar, "sit down and rest yourself. You deserve it, dear."

"Now, see here," Marya began, as Mrs. Sanders guided her by the elbow into the chair.

"With a sugar cube, sweetie?" the housekeeper interrupted. "Oh, but excuse me. You were saying something."

Marya sighed again. "Oh nothing, really nothing." She started to laugh to herself. She who had left Russia alone at age sixteen was feeling overwhelmed by this orange-headed little woman.

Mrs. Sanders had set a piece of paper in front of her. "Now, Mrs. Luminov, when you're feeling good and rested, I'd like you to take a look at this menu I planned out for the rest of the week. But take your time. No need to do it just now."

And so Mrs. Sanders had come to stay. A month later she began to prepare Sabbath dinners for them, and when Marya questioned her, Mrs. Sanders said she was merely following Mr. Luminov's orders. Marya had not been pleased, but rather than cause a scene she had acquiesced to the lit candles, special white cloth and best china. As long as it went no further than this, she told herself, she would make this concession to her husband's Jewishness, even though it alarmed her.

Now Mrs. Sanders was putting the finishing touches on the special dinner that Marya had asked her to fix this evening.

More than a year had gone by since Daniel had been seeing Alma, but there had not yet been a chance to introduce her to his parents. He had told them of the pert little blonde he found such good company, and Marya had followed with interest Daniel's accounts of what she saw as a deepening romance over the course of the last year. She had more than once told Daniel she would like to meet Alma and had suggested he invite her to dinner some evening. Finally they had found an evening that all four of them could make.

Marya heard voices in the living room and went out to investigate. Daniel had come in and next to him was standing a petite young woman with shining brown eyes and a big smile..

"This is Alma Detweiler," Daniel presented her. He looked her over as he introduced her and he felt that in her new pink wool suit she looked the prettiest he had ever seen her.

Marya could hear the pride in his voice and she did her best to make the girl feel welcome. "Hello, Alma. It's a pleasure to meet you. I'm afraid Daniel's father hasn't come home yet, so we'll have to wait a little while to eat. But that will give us a chance to talk some."

Daniel was chagrined to hear his father hadn't come home on time, tonight of all nights.

The three of them took up positions in the living room and found they were able to have an easy conversation. Alma asked Marya question after question about her business, showing obvious admiration, and then chatted readily about her school activities and German lessons.

After a half hour, Marya found she had already grown fond of the young woman. As discreetly as possible, she eyed the clock on the mantlepiece and wished Wolf would come home so they could begin the meal. When he still hadn't come fifteen minutes later, she decided they should begin without him.

"Something important must have come up to detain him," she explained, outwardly calm and inwardly seething, "so unless we want everything to be cold and, worse yet, Mrs. Sanders to be peeved at us, we'd best go ahead."

Daniel looked at Alma, but as far as he could see, her face was as sunny as ever. She knew nothing of his agitation, of the growing feeling in the pit of his stomach because of his father's absence. He knew his mother was trying to keep the atmosphere light, but that didn't stop the sinking feeling he had.

Mrs. Sanders served them a hearty meal of borscht, blintzes, brisket and compote, all prepared in the Russian style. The talk continued among them with no trouble, but Marya and Daniel were becoming uneasy with Wolf's absence. Daniel in particular felt let down since it had taken so long to arrange this occasion in the first place. He couldn't imagine what could be keeping his father so long and wouldn't allow himself to think that he might have forgotten the reason for tonight's dinner.

Finally they heard his footsteps on the stoop. The door opened and Wolf entered.

"Sorry I'm late," he said. "A problem came up at the last minute."

Daniel wanted to say that he could have at least phoned but didn't want to say it in front of Alma. He watched his father shake the snow off his winter jacket, then come to the table. He saw him catch sight of Alma and smiled at her. "Zavel, this is Daniel's friend Alma. Alma Detweiler," Marya began.

The smile on Wolf's face vanished. "Sorry. I didn't get your last name."

"Detweiler," Alma said. "It's German."

"Father in the garment business?" he asked shortly.

"Yes," said Alma, "isn't that a coincidence, Mr. Luminov?"

Wolf stared at her as he sat down in his chair. "Yes," he replied curtly.

Daniel was worried by his father's behavior. Wolf concentrated on serving his plate and didn't bother to make any conversation. Alma noticed too and tried to spark some dialog by asking Wolf questions about his business. Wolf's responses were always brief and without elaboration, until finally Alma's questions grew less enthusiastic and then stopped. Daniel wondered again what could have happened at the factory to put his father into such a black mood, and he regretted that it had to be this night, the night when Alma was seeing him for the first time. He hated to think what her impression of his father must be.

Wolf's presence and obvious preoccupation with his own thoughts cast a slight pall over the dinner, but somehow they managed to get through it. Mrs. Sanders brought out an elaborate Napoleon cake, full of whipped cream and jam, which brightened everyone's spirits momentarily. But after they had eaten it, the slight chill in the air returned.

Finally Alma cleared her throat lightly to make an announcement. "I have to go home now because I still have some studying to do for the test we're having in my German class tomorrow. But I want to thank you for a delicious dinner." She turned to Marya. "Mrs. Luminov, it's really been a pleasure meeting you. And you too, Mr. Luminov," she added. "I hope that problem at your factory wasn't too serious."

Marya and Wolf stood up to bid her good-bye, and Daniel noticed that only his mother walked her to the door.

"I'm taking the el with Alma and walking her home. Be back in a little while," Daniel announced hastily to his mother. Behind her he could still see his father's face, and it was dark and brooding.

When Daniel returned a couple hours later, Wolf was waiting for him. He saw at once that he was still in a bad mood.

"Sit down, Daniel. I want to talk to you."

Daniel did as he was told, choosing the spot in the living room as far from his father as he could get without appearing obvious.

"It's about this girl you're seeing."

"You mean Alma?" Daniel said right away. He took it as a bad sign that his father wouldn't even say her name.

"Yes. This Miss Detweiler." He emphasized the last name.

Daniel noticed his father pause, and he sat waiting to hear what he would say next. He couldn't imagine that his father could have much to say about her at all. He'd hardly looked at her all evening.

"I want you to stop seeing her."

Daniel's mouth flew open. "What! Stop seeing Alma?"

"That's right."

"But why?" Suddenly his hands were moist and sweaty, and he felt like he was hearing this from a long way away.

"Because her father is one of the biggest bastards in the business—"

Daniel cut in. His tone was harsh and accusatory. "How do you know? And even if it's true, that's her father—not her."

"Daniel, I've told you what it was like for me in this business when I was just a little younger than you and just starting out. You have no way of knowing this. But her father was the most dishonest, treacherous bloodsucker of them all. I'm not the only one he cheated and lied to. Talk to Sol."

"Sol?" Daniel was astonished.

"Talk to Mrs. Abrahms."

"Mrs. Abrahms?" Daniel echoed, picturing the frail and kindly grey-haired woman who did filing and other odd jobs in the office and who had taken care of him so often as a child.

"She wasn't always a clerk. She started out as a presser in a stinking little alley room owned and exploited by Detweiler. It made her so sick she got tuberculosis.

"You can talk to about six other of the old timers, the ones who've been with me since before you were born. You want to know what Detweiler is like? Ask them. They'll tell you. Why do you think they're so loyal to MW Enterprises?"

Daniel knew it wasn't just MW Enterprises that held their loyalty. It was Wolf himself. It was a sign of the intensity of his own unquestioning worship of Wolf that he had just accepted their fierce loyalty as his father's due.

"We all had a falling out. A violent one. I know I've never told you about it and I don't care to go into the details of it. Once was enough."

Daniel stared at his father and tried to square this account with what he had observed of Alma's father. The man he had met was unfailingly polite and amiable, although he remembered Alma had said he was different with his workers.

"I've met him and—"

"I don't want to hear it, Daniel. I can't stand to think you were in that cutthroat's house, accepting his food and drink."

Daniel glared at Wolf. "This has nothing to do with Alma. She can't help it if her father abused you twenty years ago. She wasn't even born."

"Of course it's not her fault. I'm not saying it was. She's probably a perfectly sweet child. But her goodness or lack of it isn't the point. I just can't have you associating with her anymore. That's the point."

Daniel heard his voice beginning to rise. "I don't believe I'm hearing this!"

Wolf stood and looked down at his son. "I know you're fond of her, Daniel. But you're just going to have to accept it. Give her up. I can assure you, coming from the family she does, no good would come of it in the long run anyway."

"But you don't know her. She's the nicest person I've ever met."

"Give her up. I have better in mind for you."

"What are you talking about? I don't want to meet anyone else."

"I'm not talking about a woman. I'm talking about giving you your share of the business."

Daniel sat there and didn't know what to think. Had he heard his father correctly? Had the day finally come, after all these years?

"You mean, you're going to make me your partner? Legally?" Daniel asked in a hushed voice.

"All I'm waiting for is for you to get married. I want to know that you're settled, and that you're not going to take up with some gold-digging woman who'll try to take you for your money. Because although we've made a lot, what with the success of the factory and now the mill, we're going to have a hell of a lot more. More than I think you have any idea of."

"Alma's not like that," Daniel protested quietly. "She doesn't need to marry for money."

"We're not talking about Alma at this moment. Do you understand? There's no way I could give you permission to marry her, Daniel. And I had no idea things between the two of you had come to that point. But since they evidently have, I know that this is hard for you to hear. I don't want to upset you. But there are certain situations I would find intolerable. I can tell you in no uncertain terms that marriage to a young woman who wasn't Jewish—"

"But Alma is. More Jewish than anyone in this family is."

"Or to a woman from a family I felt was without morals, completely beneath you. This I would oppose with every fiber of my being," his father continued.

A chill ran up Daniel's back. He knew his father could be single-minded to the point of obsesssion. His heart felt heavy as he thought of not seeing Alma again. How would he tell her? How could he possibly explain it to her? But his father had made a definite promise to him. He must marry and have sons. Then and only then would he be worthy of half of MW Enterprises.

"You have understood what I've said to you?" Wolf was asking him.

"Yes." Daniel's voice betrayed the heaviness that was weighing on him.

"Repeat it back to me so I'll know."

"You want me to stop seeing Alma. Then you

want me to get married to someone you approve of. Then you say I will become your partner, officially and legally," Daniel droned without enthusiasm.

"Do you promise you will no longer see this girl? One thing is contingent on the other, you understand."

Daniel saw no hope for it. All his life he had been groomed to be an owner of the family business. He couldn't walk away from that now. It was the most important thing in the world to him.

"Then you promise?" his father repeated.

"If you promise, I'll promise," said Daniel suddenly.

Wolf did not like this tack. "Promise what?" he said, annoyed.

"I'm making a formal pledge. I want you to make one. I want you to promise you will present me with the papers, completely drawn up and ready for signing, as soon as I marry."

"And have your first son," corrected Wolf.

Daniel repeated firmly. "And have my first son."

"I don't know why you want me to repeat my promise. I already promised that to you," Wolf grumbled.

"If I pledged formally, so can you."

"All right, if it pleases you. I promise."

Chapter 21

Marya had to admit that Elke was born to be a mother. She was sitting on the sofa of her living room with her legs tucked under her, her breast bared as she nursed her second child, Zosa, a girl, born the year after her first, and she was obviously contented. Her face bore the dreamy look of a nursing mother. The first child, Adam Dov, was at the moment leaning somewhat wobbily against Elke's knee, having just learned to stand, and was watching his mother feed his sister. Elke felt the baby put her tiny hands on her large milk-filled breast and pull at it with her mouth. She looked down at Adam and smiled.

"And Adam," Marya asked. "How does he react to having a little sister?"

"From the very first he's loved her as if she were his. Whenever I hold her, he stands next to me and wants to hold her too. He watches her all the time, as if she were a fascinating new toy that's come into his life."

"Then it's good you're not having a problem with his feeling left out."

Elke shook her head. "No. We are lucky." She added, laughing, "If I have a problem at all it's that he always wants to be next to her and gets in my way as he tries to help."

Marya looked at the two healthy babies. Adam Dov had his father's dark hair and dark eyes, but from Elke's side of the family he had inherited his size, because already at sixteen months he was larger than average. He was a lively child and highly curious, with the ability to concentrate on something for surprisingly long periods of time.

"Sometimes I find him staring for over half an hour at some toy I place in his crib. He looks at it so hard, it's as if he's trying to figure out how it's made," Elke had told her mother on one of her frequent visits to the house of late. She had noticed that after each baby was born, Marya had been there to help, and to Elke's surprise, her mother took many hours from the shop to be with her and the children.

As Elke removed Zosa from her breast, Marya reached out for her. "Let me hold her for a while, Elke." Full and content, the baby nestled in her arms, and after blinking her black eyes a few times, fell fast asleep. "She will have our hair." Marya ran her fingers through the strands of red hair that were beginning to show. Just as she had been with each of her own children, Marya was preoccupied with the growth of each baby's hair. It disturbed her to see the nearly bald heads of most infants, and she was haunted with fear until she saw that each of her children and grandchildren would have hair that was thick and richly colored. Over Adam Dov in particular she had worried as week after week went by without any sign of hair other than a few random strands of indeterminate color.

She had even fretted out loud, until finally Elke had tried to calm her. "Please, Mama, stop worrying about it. He'll eventually have hair. No one goes through life bald from birth."

Still, it wasn't until he was nearly six months old that he began to have what could really be considered hair at all, and when he did, Marya was delighted to see that it was wonderfully thick and curled just slightly.

Marya looked up to see Elke watching her, a faint smile on her lips. Today she was wearing a *tichel* or kerchief on her head instead of her usual wig, and what amount of hair she still had under it, Marya couldn't tell. In spite of what Elke had told her before the wedding, she still had not gotten used to seeing her without her customary masses of red-brown hair, and it was still painful for her to see the kerchief. But of course she could tell Elke none of this.

Elke watched her mother playing with Zosa's hair and shifted uneasily. All her life she had noticed what she thought to be Marya's excessive attention to hair, both her own and that of others, and wondered why it should mean so much to her. She knew her mother had been horrified when she had shorn her locks for her wedding, but she had felt it an honor to make the sacrifice. To her the most important thing in the world was her marriage and her family.

"A *mitzvah*," Jacob called it, "a religious commandment." Not to marry and bear fruit, in his eyes, made a person's spirituality suspect. Elke had not thought of it in those words, not having been raised religiously, but what he explained to her coincided with her own beliefs about family, beliefs she held intuitively. And so it was with great joy that they had set about their spiritual duty to propogate the earth, and Elke had been willing to sacrifice herself for the sake of something larger.

But even though she had no doubts about having shaven her hair and having wholeheartedly embraced Jacob's form of religion, it still made her uncomfortable to have her mother look at her. She knew her mother tried to hide it, but it was right there in her eyes that her daughter's appearance was too matronly and too reminiscent of the old country for her to accept.

"How is Daniel?" Elke asked, wishing to change what she suspected were her mother's thoughts.

"I worry about him. He's quiet and withdrawn, and when he gets that way, it always means there's something wrong."

"What do you think it could be?"

"He no longer sees Alma. I don't know what happened there, but they just don't see each other anymore, which is funny after how they saw each other practically daily for almost two years."

"But you say you don't know what caused them to split up?"

"No. Strange, but I dreamt about her the other night. In my dream, she was ice-skating in the park. She was dressed all in white, and in the dream her hair was the same color of white, not blonde like it really is. She was at one end of the pond and a young man, someone I didn't recognize, was at the other end, dressed completely in black. Each began to skate toward the other with breathtaking speed, and neither saw the other coming directly in the same line. They skated faster and faster, each unmindful that the other was there and they were about to collide. They slammed into each other with terrifying force and exploded together up into the air, merged into one as an exquisite bird. The bird began an elaborate dance in the air over the pond, and as it dipped and flapped its wings, it was one moment black, the next white, then black again, then white."

Elke looked at her mother. "That's beautiful but, you're right, strange. What do you make of it?" She remembered how her mother often had premonitions and wondered if this dream could be pointing to something.

"I don't know," Marya mused. "Perhaps it's just a dream, nothing more."

"And Papa? He's okay?"

Marya felt uncomfortable. It was always hard for her to talk about Wolf in front of her children. She supposed that was because so many of her thoughts were confused and she didn't know what she really thought about him half the time. "He's well. You know how your father always is. He's happy when he's working. And what with the new mill, he's working more than ever now. We see even less of each other than before."

"When is he going to make room for Daniel?" Elke pressed.

Marya wasn't used to such directness from her daughter, but marriage had given her a new confidence. Nor had Marya known that Elke realized there was a problem in this area, but she could tell from the way Elke phrased the question that she did. She sighed. "I ask myself that all the time. He says he wants your brother officially to become his business partner, but he keeps pushing back the date when that will happen."

"Papa will never voluntarily step down," Elke stated.

Marya looked quickly at her daughter. "I fear you're right. And I hate to think of the consequences for Daniel."

Daniel was waiting on the corner of Sixth Avenue at Eighth Street. His attention was drawn by a speaker standing on a soapbox not too far from him. The man, who was middle-aged and tall and thin, with stooped posture that made him look like a question mark, had managed to gather about him a small, fairly sympathetic crowd. Every now and then Daniel would catch several sentences.

"We must unite! We must stand together against the dishonest bosses," he heard, and "Our strength is in our numbers. If we stand together, we can bring every factory in this city to a standstill. But we must stand united!"

In the last couple of years Daniel had heard more and more of such talk. Across the nation workers were becoming increasingly conscious of their power and were raising their voices in an effort to change the conditions of the shops and factories in which they spent more than fifty-five hours a week. Daniel had even overheard some of the employees at MW Enterprises talking about the need to stand together to get what they wanted. When he had reported such rumblings to his father, Wolf had not seemed at all concerned. He was confident he was doing right by his workers. "They have a good deal here and they know it," Wolf had reassured him. "It's just a few radicals from the ILGWU that are shouting the loudest and making it seem like there are a lot more union members than there are."

So Daniel tried to put out of his mind the solicitations and protest he heard all around him, on the streets, in cafés, in the newspapers, especially ones like *The Forward*, and the *Frei Arbeiter Stimme*. Still, he was left with an uneasy feeling when he saw the amount of attention speakers like this one drew, and the expressions on the upturned faces of the workers as they listened to what he was urging. He hoped his father knew what he was talking about, because to gauge from the faces of these men and women, the words they were hearing over and over were a ray of hope that they might be able to better the conditions of poverty and exhaustion under which they struggled.

Now he looked past their faces for another face, the one he was waiting for. Then he spotted her.

"Alma!" he shouted and began to wave his arms.

She heard her name being called and turned in his direction. Then she saw him and began to hurry his way, her expression all smiles. When she got near enough, he reached out his arms and yanked her to him, then picked her up under the arms and spun her around.

"Alma," he breathed when he set her back down. "My God, it's good to see you. And you look as beautiful as always!" She was wearing a suit of deep gold wool and it featured one of the newer, shorter, "rainy-daisy" skirts that was short enough to keep from dragging on the wet sidewalk when it rained. The color of the suit highlighted her blonde hair and lit up her face. "You look aglow." He pulled her to him again to kiss her, even though they were still standing on the street corner where anyone who cared to could see them.

Alma looked surprised. "Daniel, we must be careful." But he noticed she didn't pull back from his embrace.

They selected a nearby café and chose a spot in the back, the way they used to, so they could talk without other people distracting them or gawking their way.

"Alma, you can't believe how I've missed you," Daniel said as soon as they sat down. "I'm so glad you wrote me that note."

"I know we shouldn't be meeting like this. Your father would kill you and my father would banish me to my room forever. But surely this once can't hurt. I've been miserable without you. The first three months I thought I was going to die. To tell you the truth, the whole last year has been awful. I've never gotten used to it."

"I woke up in the middle of every night thinking about you. I still do."

The words spilled out of them. It was as if one could not tell the other fast enough or often enough of how much they had missed each other.

Daniel felt the happiest he had in the last eighteen months since he had seen her. He reached out and seized her hand. "You must tell me everything you've been doing. Are you working?"

"No," she answered. "Daddy won't hear of it. He says no woman in his family has to work. He wants me to do charity work."

Daniel laughed, then quickly said, "I'm not laughing because I think there's anything wrong with charity work. I think working for a good cause, one you think is important, is a good thing to do. Maybe it's the most valuable thing a person could do with his life, if that's what he believes in."

"Daddy points out how I could work for the Hebrew Immigrant Aid Society or The United Hebrew Charities, the way my mother does."

"He doesn't know you very well, even if he is your father. That would never be enough for you."

"No, I'm afraid you're right. He doesn't know me very well at all. He just has preconceived ideas of what girls and women are like, and that's how he assumes I must be. I don't think he really sees me or hears me."

"Now you sound like my sister Elke when she would sometimes talk to me about my father."

"How is she? Is her little boy okay? Wasn't his name Adam?"

Daniel laughed. "You wouldn't believe how big Adam Dov is already, and how cute. He's so curious about everything in the world, and he's already walking all over the place and getting into everything. And you don't even know about Zosa, I bet."

"Zosa? No. Who's that?"

"That's Elke's new little girl."

Alma laughed. "She and Jacob didn't waste any time, did they?" She repeated the name. "Zosa. Zosa. "What does it mean?"

"It's Hebrew for sweet."

"It's pretty. I like it."

"And Elke's pregnant again, if you can believe that."

"You're kidding! She must really be happy."

He cleared his throat. "But I want to hear more about you." He hadn't planned to ask her this, but now that he had her right in front of him, he just had to know. "I suppose you have a boyfriend now?" He watched her carefully.

She shook her head. "Not really."

"What does not really mean?" He hadn't meant to ask her that either, but it had come out anyway.

"It means there's no one special." She paused. "No one like you."

He felt relieved, although he told himself it was silly to hold on to something that just couldn't be.

"And you?" she asked.

"No one either."

Neither of them spoke for a few moments. Daniel wished there were something he could say about how his father had changed his mind. He had gone ahead that night that was so fixed in his memory and told her everything, of what his father had said about not trusting or liking her father, of how he wasn't permitted to see her anymore. He hadn't wanted to hurt her by telling her what his father had said of hers, but at the same time he wanted even less for her to think that the reason he could no longer see her had something to do with her personally. She had not defended her father and she received Wolf's decision quietly, as if she understood at once the inevitability of it. And she had done her best to abide by Daniel's decision, until one night last week when she could stand it no longer. Then she had quickly scrawled him a letter and just as quickly mailed it to his home without a return address on the envelope before she lost her nerve.

"I just had to see you one more time," she explained after they had talked a while more. "I miss you, Daniel."

"I miss you too." As he said the words, he felt an enormous tide of guilt wash over him. He looked at her sitting there before him, and for the first time he questioned whether he was doing the right thing. For just a moment a doubt crept in and made him ask himself if anything in the world were really worth giving up someone like Alma.

"It's probably no use," she sighed as if she were able to read his thoughts. "We'd practically have to leave the country to get beyond your father and mine."

Daniel didn't laugh. "That's true. My father would never let us see each other, even if we weren't getting serious." He hesitated. "We were getting serious, weren't we?"

Alma swallowed hard and her eyes were open wide as she answered. "Yes, Daniel. We were."

Then it was time to go. They left the café and walked a few more blocks together, until they came to the spot where Alma was catching the horse-car. Reluctant to say good-bye to each other, they lingered a while longer, finding excuses to keep each other talking, neither wanting to be the one to pull away first.

The afternoon was crowded with the usual shoppers and people getting off work as Wolf made his way along Eighth Street and turned north onto lower Fifth Avenue. He was on his way to visit one of his distributors. The streams of people passing by were a blur to him, until suddenly he thought he caught a flash of someone who looked familiar. It was a young blonde woman in a gold-colored wool suit. He glanced her way again. This time he studied her a little more. He wondered where he had seen her before. Then he recognized her as the young woman his son had brought home to dinner almost two years ago. The Detweiler girl, he reminded himself. He couldn't remember her first name. As he looked at her a third time, he was shocked to see that he also recognized the person standing next to her. It was Daniel.

Wolf's mind began to race. So the boy was seeing that girl again. So he'd gone against his word, in flagrant disrespect for what his father's wishes in the matter were. In a matter of seconds, Wolf was beside himself with anger. He could take no chances, he told himself, that Daniel might marry that girl. And if he was seeing her again, there was every chance that Daniel would want to.

"The distributor can wait," he muttered and immediately turned and began to walk in the opposite direction. He crossed Washington Square Park and hailed a carriage. The carriage took him eastward toward Second Avenue, then south to Houston and over to Allen Street, where he signaled to the driver to let him off. He walked down this street, which more than any other in the area held the mystery of the Orient, with its drifting sounds of Arabic, Syrian and Greek music, and its stores like eastern bazaars with copperware dangling from strings, samovars, candlesticks, aromatic spices and teas, and here and there men smoking hookahs. He passed Hungarian and Rumanian restaurants that served heavy, well-seasoned dishes and restaurants run by Greeks and Arabs, and coffee houses where belly dancers were known to wriggle artfully. Had he wanted, he could have had his future told by a Gypsy or bought dates and sesame seeds and figs from the outdoor bins or a few minutes of love from one of the sidewalk prostitutes. He passed it all by with detachment as he read the signs of the stores, written in at least three different alphabets and even more languages. He had something else on his mind.

He stopped when he found what he was looking for. "Shadchen" read a small sign that had once been neatly lettered but now was beginning to peel. Underneath that had been hastily appended, "also translating and letter writing." He went through the door below the sign and came to a narrow flight of stairs. He climbed the stairs to the second landing where he saw a smaller version of the sign outside affixed to one of the doors. The hall was dark and musty with a slight smell of cinnamon and coffee.

He knocked on the door and waited for almost a minute. When no one came, he knocked again. This time he heard the shuffling of feet from inside, then the door was opened by a very short, very fat woman with bits of grey-black hair peeping out from under a black kerchief.

"I'm looking for the marriage broker," Wolf explained.

The woman squinted up at Wolf in the half-light of the hallway. "So you've found her." She held the door open for him to enter. "Come in, come in. I'm Mrs. Kreutzberg, the *shadchen*, and you are a lucky man."

She had a broad yellow face with a tiny puckered mouth, and had taken care to perfume herself lavishly and hang gold earrings from her ears. She led him to an oak table on which were two boxes filled with envelopes. One box was marked "*maidchen*" and the other, considerably less full, "*herren*." She lowered her bulk into a chair and motioned for him to sit down in the other chair.

"I have such a beautiful girl for you, you wouldn't believe," she said, setting right to work. She began to thumb through the box of envelopes marked "ladies." She pulled out four envelopes, setting three to one side. From the fourth she took out a photograph. "This is the lovely Miss Lensky." She laid the photograph in front of Wolf so he might inspect it.

Wolf saw a woman with small intense eyes, high cheekbones and no trace of a smile on her broad Slavic face. She appeared to be about forty years old.

As he looked at the picture, Mrs. Kreutzberg explained. "Miss Lensky is one of my best girls, and a very *frume* young lady, I can personally attest to that. You are a religious man, aren't you?"

Wolf ignored her question. "I'd like to see someone much younger. This woman is practically my age."

"Of course," said Mrs. Kreutzberg and blinked rapidly. "This is no problem. I understand. Many men do prefer the more mature ladies though. They already have all the housekeeping skills down pat. No burnt brisket from them." As she put the photo back in its envelope, she murmured, "And Miss Lensky is one of the best. Makes strudel fit to serve Franz Josef himself. Almost as good as mine."

She opened the other three envelopes and lined up the photographs for Wolf. "I think you will find this quite a breathtaking gallery," she boasted.

Wolf looked at the brown and yellow pictures of

the three young women. Their faces were such as he passed by the dozens on the street or who might be found working in his factory—girls whose very youthfulness made them pretty.

Mrs. Kreutzberg pointed to the first. It was a photo of a pleasant looking young woman with straight dark hair and a face as severe as that of the older woman.

"It would be nice to see one a little happier looking," commented Wolf.

"Of course, of course. This is no problem. Look right here at the next, Sonia Klein." The woman she indicated was indeed smiling.

"Miss Klein, you say?" Wolf looked more closely. The young woman was lightly freckled and appeared to have some personality. "And is she a girl of good character? That is more important than her looks."

Mrs. Kreutzberg drew herself up. "Mein herr, absolutely all my ladies are just as if they came from the old country. In fact, many of them did. Simple, virtuous girls with the old values."

"I see," Wolf considered. "And Miss Klein's family?"

"Such a nice German family."

"That won't do," Wolf refused flatly.

"Of course. I understand," Mrs. Kreutzberg said instantly, picking up the photo from the line-up. "This is no problem. You must now examine Miss Kayla Fenster."

As Wolf looked at the last picture, he saw a young woman with dark eyes and dark hair with her hands clasped to her heart and looking up to the ceiling with a dreamy expression on her face. "I don't think so," he decided, thinking she didn't seem the type to make a good, robust mother. "Have you no more?"

Mrs. Kreutzberg smiled a crooked smile and laughed. "Of course. This is no problem. There are always more. Why there's even me, if you were so inclined for a more mature woman instead of a girl." She laughed lightly. "Perhaps you do not know that I am a widow? My poor husband, God rest his soul."

When Wolf didn't say anything, she sighed. "But as you were asking, beautiful and good girls are no problem. I have so many. The problem is the men. Not often do I get one as fine looking as yourself. Obviously you are a gentleman." She smoothly looked Wolf up and down. "So for you, what we need is my finest, a true gentlewoman."

"You understand this bride is not for me," Wolf corrected her.

"No?" said Mrs. Kreutzberg, looking disappointed.

"But you are right in assuming I am looking for a woman of high standing. She should be from a family of some merit and she should be capable of bearing sons . . . many children right away."

"Of course. I understand. That is no problem." She returned to her file and skimmed through the envelopes. She selected two and withdrawing the photographs, placed them in front of Wolf for his inspection.

"This one on the left," she pointed with a gnarled finger on which flashed a ruby ring, "she is Rachel Miller. A very sweet and proper young lady."

Wolf saw in the photograph a dark-haired woman with a heart-shaped face and equally dark eyes.

Mrs. Kreutzberg indicated the photo on the right. "This is Bluma Kaganovitch, my other prized girl. You understand these are my very best."

This one was small featured, with a straight nose and light blonde hair. She appeared to be in her mid-twenties.

"Have you ever seen such beauties?" asked the marriage broker.

"And their families? Where do these two girls come from?"

"Miss Miller is the daughter of Moishe Miller, who owns a delicatessen on Orchard Street and another on Eighth. Her father and mother came over from Cracow ten years ago. They have not done too bad for themselves in that time, as you can see."

"And the other one?"

"Bluma's father owns a large shoe factory. His name is Herschel, and he came from Vilna almost twenty years ago. Such an amibitious man, you wouldn't believe. And very successful."

Wolf reviewed the two photographs again. "This one interests me," he said, pointing to the one on the right.

"Ah, you have made an excellent choice," Mrs. Kreutzberg exclaimed. She added, dropping her voice, "Such a girl from such a family, she will bring a big dowry. My fee is always ten per cent of the dowry, so I must tell you, she commands my highest fee."

"Of course. I understand," Wolf employed her phrase and smiled for the first time since he had been there. "That's no problem."

"I think you'll find she has lots of everything a man could want. And all in the right places," giggled Mrs. Kreutzberg as she looked at him slyly out of the corner of her eye. "Now, mein herr, I was hoping I could take your picture."

"Mine?" Wolf stood up and shook his head. "What for? I already have a wife."

"But, sir, is she in good health? In these winter months, one never knows. And you're such a fine looking man."

"I've wife enough," Wolf started to laugh.

"Maybe, then, you would like a letter written or a little translating into Yiddish or English? Business is not so good these days, you see. All the young people are caught up with this fad called love and making their own foolish choices."

As Wolf left the *shadchen*, he thought about his choice. The girl was pretty and with her blonde hair and small features, she didn't look too much different from this Alma Detweiler that Daniel seemed so attached to. So he shouldn't have too hard a time getting to like her. What was her name? Oh, yes, Bluma. He tried it for the sound of it: Bluma Luminov. Yes, it was okay.

Almost a month had gone by since Daniel had seen Alma. He told himself it was useless to keep thinking about her, but the memory of her face had a habit of popping up when he least expected it. Tonight, as he hurried to the factory to meet his father, his thoughts of her were interrupted by another street corner speech. It seemed they were growing in number and intensity. Alma had told him how the organizers were becoming increasingly dedicated and fevered, so it didn't surprise him that the talk of unions and strikes was everywhere in the air around him.

"But," he said aloud, "I mustn't think about the workers and their demands, nor about Alma." His father had again assured him that at MW Enterprises they had nothing to worry about. He turned off Broadway into an alleyway, slipped in through a delivery door and took the freight elevator to Wolf's office, wondering again what his father wanted to see him for tonight.

He could see Wolf through the glass windows of the office, bent over the papers on his desk. How many times over the years had he seen his father like that? He often worked late into the night, which Daniel well knew because most of those times he was there with him. But no matter how hard he pushed himself, Wolf always looked the same. As far as Daniel could see, he hadn't aged at all in the last ten years. He stood as tall as ever, and his hair was still jet black, untouched with grey. If his father had changed in any way, it was in his growing desire to reach out and embrace some of the rituals of his Jewish past. But other than his having asked Mrs. Sanders to do something so they might observe some of the holidays, there had been no other apparent changes in him.

Wolf looked up when Daniel came in. "Good. I'm

glad you could get here when I asked. I realize I didn't
give you much advance warning."

"It was no problem. I was planning to come down
here tonight anyway and do a little work." Daniel let
himself down into a chair across from his father.

Wolf cleared his throat and folded his hands on
top of the papers in front of him. "You're twenty-one,
Daniel, almost twenty-two. You're no longer a boy."

Daniel's heart leapt. At the same time he was
afraid to allow himself to hope. "I realize you still have
much to learn. Nevertheless, you're not a child and can
be expected to assume your place in the world."

Daniel held his breath. He was afraid to move lest
he miss a single word his father was saying. Was his father finally going to recognize him as a man, ready to
be his equal in the business, even though he hadn't
married and had a son as he had been directed to do?

"It's time, Daniel, that you took on other responsibilities."

Daniel nodded his head.

"I've seen our attorney and had a number of
documents drawn up," Wolf indicated the papers on
the desk before him. "I think their contents will interest you." He handed the papers to Daniel.

Daniel's hands were moist with excitement and
anticipation as he took the documents. He was almost
too overcome to read them, but he forced himself to
make out the words.

"Memorandum of Agreement," he read at the top
of the heavy paper. He moved his eyes quickly down
the page. He saw his name and his father's name and
the rest was a blur of long sentences in legal jargon.

He looked up at his father, who had stood up
while Daniel was reading the document and had begun
to pace behind his desk. He held in his hand the cord
from the venetion blinds, which he was idly twisting
into a series of small nooses.

"Does this mean?" Daniel began. He couldn't believe he actually had the papers in his hands after all these years.

"You're to be part owner with me of all that we have, all that MW Enterprises has become, the factory as well as the mill. Providing, of course, that I deem you ready."

"What does that mean?" Daniel burst out, none too gently. As far as he could see, he had been ready for years.

Wolf's voice grew sterner. "As you know, you have not yet assumed all the duties of a man, Daniel. It's time you started a family of your own. In short, Daniel, it's time you marry."

Daniel was puzzled. "You've told me this already. But you know I have no wife."

"Nor a son."

He stared at his father as he tried to make sense of what was happening. "And," his father continued, "your wife must be someone I approve of."

Daniel struggled to keep his voice from rising. He reminded himself that when dealing with his father, he must keep his self-control. That was imperative. "You mean, you went to the trouble of getting these papers drawn up, called me down here as if there was a do-or-die emergency, just to tell me that?"

"You'll notice the date is left blank."

Daniel looked again at the papers still in his hands. There, where the date should have been filled in, was nothing. "I don't believe this," Daniel said as he continued to stare at the empty line for the date, scarcely realizing he was talking out loud.

"You can sign those papers tonight, if you want, Daniel," Wolf said.

He looked up. "What are you talking about?"

"If you are ready to marry, you can sign the papers tonight. I am prepared to waive my original requirement that you have a son before you can assume any share of the business whatsoever. We can do this in installments. You can have ten per cent of the business now, starting tonight, with the other forty per cent transferred to your name the day your first son is born."

Daniel just stared at his father. Finally he said, "How can that be? How can I get married tonight?"

"There's no way, of course, you can get married tonight. I'm not suggesting that. But you can give your consent to meet a young woman I think you'll like. And if you do, I'll know you're acting in good faith."

Daniel was still staring.

"You're looking at me as if I were mad. You must know, Daniel, that there's nothing unusual about what I'm suggesting. It's done all the time in Europe, and even sometimes here. Parents arrange for the lifetime well-being of their children by looking for young men or women, as the case may be, who will be suitable matches and who will bring not only honor to the family, but happiness and fruitfulness to the son or daughter. It's an old and honorable custom."

"Your father didn't choose a wife for you," Daniel pointed out. As soon as he had said the words, he regretted them. He had never talked about the subject of his grandfather unless his father had first brought it up. He knew it was painful for his father.

"He would have if I hadn't left Russia, I can tell you that," Wolf said quietly.

Daniel tried to make sense of it all. His father was actually trying to choose a bride for him. He didn't need his father to explain the custom to him. He had heard of it over the years from snatches of conversation around him and from having seen the *Shadchen* advertisements in the Yiddish newspapers. He also knew the custom as the occasional butt of jokes he heard in the theaters and in the streets. But he had never dreamed a *shadchen* would be part of his life, for clearly his father had visited a local marriage broker. He could just picture him in some airless office with the files spread out before him as he outlined what he wanted. But he was an American, not a European,

didn't his father see? He didn't even know how to
speak Russian and his Yiddish was rough. This was
twentieth-century America.

Wolf was removing a yellowed photograph from a
brown envelope. He handed it to Daniel without explanation.

When Daniel first looked at the picture, he felt a
pain in his heart. For a fleeting second he thought it
was a picture of Alma his father was handing him.
Looking back at him from the picture was a woman
who appeared to be a few years older than he and
who, at least in the photo, was pleasant enough looking.

"Well?" Wolf asked.

Daniel continued to stare at the photograph in his
left hand. He felt cornered. Here it was, what he
wanted, so close at hand. The papers were actually
here. He still held them in his right hand, and if he had
not read them all the way through, he had at least
skimmed them. But to sign those papers would mean
he would have to say good-bye to Alma for good. This
time there would be no hope. Both hands felt over-
whelmingly heavy.

As if he were reading Daniel's mind, Wolf spoke
up. "I know you have broken your word to me, Daniel.
I know you have been seeing the Detweiler girl."

"Just once."

"I don't care how many times. It only takes once
to break your vow. And you have to know I consider
that a sign of contempt toward me, knowing as you do
my feelings toward her family."

Daniel swallowed and looked at his father. "I
don't mean it that way. She has nothing to do with
you."

"She most certainly does. But that's not what
we're here to discuss tonight. I have nothing more to
say about that. What I do want to discuss is where you
want to go from here. What should we do about
Bluma?"

Daniel looked at the photograph again. He felt as if he were falling down a long narrow well, but he had to have a legal share of that business. Something told him the chance wouldn't come again.

"All right," he agreed at last, "I'll meet her, but I don't want to sign the papers until I find out if I like her." He decided he must see Alma one more time.

Wolf smiled. "That sounds like a wise decision, Daniel. Although I think you're going to be pleasantly surprised. I've already met Bluma Kaganovitch and her family. They're fine people and she is a charming young lady. She'll make you a good wife, I'm sure."

That same night Daniel allowed himself to be taken to the house of Bluma Kaganovitch, also located uptown not too many blocks from his own. The meeting was stiff and formal, with Bluma and her mother and father sitting on one side of the room, and he and his father on the other. In between them and to the side was a Russian stove, which at the moment was making the room unbearably hot, and on the low table between them a samovar bubbled.

He and Bluma did not speak to each other directly, but instead listened to their parents talk and answered any questions directed their way, polite and perfunctory questions about where they had gone to school and how they each liked to spend their time. Daniel was thankful he was not expected to say much and he took advantage of his subdued role to take a good look at Bluma Kaganovitch.

He was surprised to see that she was nicer looking than her picture. It was just that a real live person was more animated than a photograph, he decided. She was short, with a small oval face, but when she laughed, her oval face became a round one and her eyes squeezed shut into little slits. Her nose was straight and not very long and her cheeks were slightly dimpled. If in the picture she had borne a resemblance to Alma, in person she did not, for the fineness of her face belied the solidity of the rest of her. The trunk of her body was broad and somewhat square, and she had a generous bust and bottom, both of which were clearly outlined despite the folds of her skirt and draped bodice. Two or three times as he looked at her, he caught her also looking at him and he had the feeling that she liked him. For some reason he found that pleasing, although he couldn't have said why.

It was hard for him to imagine what it would be like having her parents as part of his life. The mother, built even more squarely and closer to the ground than her daughter, controlled the conversation like a little general, maintaining eye contact with each person as she talked so that no one could look away for long. Her conversation was full of little expressions such as "God bless" and "It shouldn't happen to a dog" and "I should live so long," and she clearly enjoyed talking. The father was quiet and somewhat scholarly looking, with spectacles and a sharply pointed beard. He clearly appreciated his wife's conversation, for he laughed a lot at her turns of phrase, stroking his beard. Daniel found it hard to imagine him being the owner of a successful shoe factory. He looked like he should be studying the Talmud all day. Like their daughter, both parents managed to get in a number of long, assessing looks at Daniel and both seemed to approve.

The visit was mercifully a short one and it was decided at the end that Bluma should come to the Luminov household for dinner next Wednesday. As they parted, Daniel shook hands with Bluma, and he was surprised to find that her touch was much friendlier than he had thought it would be.

"What is this?" Marya looked at Daniel again and took her reading glasses off her nose. "You want to bring a lady friend home to meet me?"

Wolf was standing in the doorway between the living room and dining room, listening. "He's finally met someone he likes."

"What's her name?"

Daniel paused. He was conscious of standing awkwardly in front of his mother and father as if he were a little boy. "Bluma. Bluma Kaganovitch."

"Oh," said Marya. "How long have you known her?"

Daniel looked uneasy. "I just met her."

"Well, by all means, you're welcome to bring her here."

Satisfied with her response, Wolf left the room and went upstairs.

Daniel also turned to go when Marya stopped him. "I was beginning to wonder when you might find another girl you liked well enough to see more than two times," Marya smiled.

She shut her book and Daniel could see she wanted to talk. He felt uneasy and wished there were some way he could leave.

Marya studied her son as he sat down in the chair across from her. She saw much of Wolf in him, from the way he walked to the way he held his mouth when he was angry or disappointed. In spite of the physical similarities to his father, she knew he was very different. He was more sentimental, more vulnerable, and more in need of a woman's warmth and assurance. Or maybe, she said to herself, Wolf was that way too but just hid it better.

Daniel studied the pattern in the blue and rose carpet. Marya knew he didn't want to talk, but she also knew this was when he needed to talk most. "Daniel, I think you should tell me what's on your mind," she began.

"Nothing's on my mind. I just wanted to make sure it was all right to bring Bluma home for dinner." He stood up and headed for the door. "That's all."

Marya saw that there was no reaching him and picked up her book again. She sensed something was deeply wrong but evidently this was not going to be the time for her to find out. "Of course, it's all right, Daniel," she soothed. "It's always all right. Why wouldn't it be? When have we ever disapproved of any of your young ladies?"

She saw Daniel shoot her a strange look just before he left the room. A few minutes later she heard his footsteps coming down the stairs and then the slamming of the back door.

When Daniel had telephoned Alma's house, he'd made sure he did it in the afternoon before her father would be home. He was glad when Alma herself picked up the phone.

"I've got to talk to you," he stated without preamble.

She immediately knew who it was and heard the urgency in his voice. "Tell me where and when."

"Madison Square, on the northwest corner. Can you be there in an hour?"

"Of course."

He was there twenty minutes early. As he waited for her, he tried to compose his thoughts, but it was no use. Finally he saw her hurrying across the square and he ran to meet her halfway.

"You look beautiful." He spoke almost sadly. She was wearing a tailored suit of blue broadcloth with a black velvet collar and cuffs and a jacket that cinched in tightly at her small waist. On her head was a matching blue felt hat, tilted rakishly to one side. At once he felt a pang of longing. Why couldn't they be together? If only she weren't Detweiler's daughter, then he could have everything—the business he loved and the woman he loved.

As if she knew what he was thinking, she said, "Let's go somewhere more private. I don't want Daddy to see us."

"My father saw us last time," he said quietly.

She drew her breath in. "He did? What did he say?"

"He yelled at me for showing disrespect for him and told me it could never be for you and me." He saw tears welling in Alma's eyes as they turned down a secluded alleyway. They stood facing each other on the grey cobblestones.

"Daniel, I don't know how our fathers can do this to us. They just can't understand how much we've meant to each other, how hard it's been for us not to see each other." Alma began to cry, pressing her face against his chest.

Daniel looked down at her, struggling with his own emotions. He wrapped his arms around her. "Your father as well, Alma?"

"Yes. He didn't approve of you from the beginning, but he didn't tell me for a while. But he didn't want me seeing you even though I tried to tell him you were from a good family."

"He couldn't have remembered my father, could he—" He stopped as the realization struck him. "It's because I'm Russian, isn't it? Is that it?"

She nodded her head slowly. "Whenever I told him how ridiculous he was being, he would just send me away. Oh Daniel, how can they be so blind? We can't let them come between us. We just can't." She looked up at him. "I'll fight them if you will."

Alma's words jolted him. How could he tell her it was now out of his hands, that in order to receive his partnership in his father's business, he would have to marry Bluma. If he were to defy Wolf, he would be left with nothing.

He knew he had to tell her something to convince her as he had been forced to convince himself that this would be the last time they would be able to see each other. Never in his life had he felt so confused and at such a loss for words.

"Alma, it . . . it just can't be. Our fathers would never allow it, and we could never make it without them. Besides. . . ."

She was staring at him, her eyes red from crying. "Besides what?"

"I . . . I. . . . There's someone else. Since we last saw each other I've met someone who . . ." He faltered. He despised himself for these false words, but he knew it was the only way to resolve the situation. Before Daniel could say anything more, Alma broke from his embrace and ran away without looking back.

Chapter 22

Three months later, in the summer of 1910, Daniel took Bluma for his wife and they went to live in a small house in Brooklyn. Daniel had finally signed the papers in Wolf's office and now he owned ten per cent of the business, with the other forty per cent coming to him upon the birth of his first son, as Wolf had originally outlined that evening in his office. In their first year together, Daniel was to find out quickly just what kind of woman he had married, and she what kind of man.

Bluma turned out to be a true housewife, the kind of woman who makes cooking and cleaning her career and whose house constantly sparkles to the extent that a surprise visit at any time would never catch her unprepared. She was an excellent and thrifty shopper, not that with Daniel's considerable earnings she had to watch their money that carefully, but she truly enjoyed striking a good bargain and it was almost a game with her to see how much she could save. She fixed delicious meals of *flanken*, or veal or fish and even made *farfel*, which were ricelike noodles, and *kashe* soup, and took time to bake her own *challah*, pound cake and *kichel*, or crisp cinnamon pastries. Then she sat back and waited for the compliments and waited for the babies, the next thing she needed besides a husband to make her life complete.

But neither came. Daniel knew that Bluma was a good housekeeper, the kind that most men would have felt blessed to have. But when he was growing up, Daniel had always taken the running of a household for granted. First of all, he was seldom there, spending all his time at the factory or school. And in the earlier years, although his mother was often sketching and consulting with the dressmakers, spreading her materials over every room of the house, she still found time to have dinner ready for him. And when he came home, that was all that was important to him. After his mother opened her shop, his sister Elke took over the cooking and cleaning, and after her the housekeeper Mrs. Sanders. So Daniel had always taken such responsibilities as the running of the house as a matter of course. Now when Bluma looked to him for praise, she got only perfunctory comments.

"That's a good looking piece of fish," he would say, or "Somebody did a nice job of ironing my shirt."

Actually he was more interested in telling her about the threats of strikes that were taking place almost everywhere in the garment industry. Not long after they were married, a local of the ILGWU struck the Triangle Shirtwaist Factory, and he told her in detail of how a pitched battle had been fought between the police, who were stationed at the entrance to the factory, and the pickets. In response to that battle, other locals struck, and within a matter of days, a general strike of the ILGWU resulted, which spread as far as Philadelphia and was called the "uprising of the 20,000." Luckily the workers at MW Enterprises had not been affected, only a handful having joined the union.

"The strike has exposed the sweatshop and tenement conditions to the public," said Daniel. "Everyone is appalled. Now that the strikers have the public on their side, there's going to be no stopping them. My father is confident the end result will be scattered though. He points out that the strikers' attempts to make a general settlement were weakened because so many of the little shops went ahead and settled earlier. He says the other big factories have stood firm against giving recognition to the union and he plans to stand with them. I think he may be right for now, but in the long run, I'm not so sure."

"*Nu*, that's very interesting," said Bluma, when he spoke of such events, but it was hard for her to mean what she said. What she really wanted to hear about were matters closer to home, about what would make Daniel happier with their home life and her. But Daniel always seemed to want to talk about politics and business, which didn't concern her. To make matters worse, during these dinner time talks, Daniel did not eat hearty portions of the meals she so painstakingly prepared, but instead picked at his food with disinterest.

But the worst thing of all was their love life. It had gone from shaky to complete collapse in a matter of months. Whenever Daniel thought back on his wedding night, he winced. Weren't wedding nights supposed to be a time of joy, a physical enactment of a couple's emotional and spiritual commitment to each other? Daniel felt anything but joy. Bluma undressed in the bathroom and sprinkled her body with perfume. As she stood before him in the dim light of the bedroom, he was aroused by the generous and ample curves of her womanly body. But as he pulled her down to the bed and began to make love to her, suddenly her blonde hair and small face in the hazy light reminded him of Alma. Then, in spite of his best intentions, he realized what was going to happen. He could no longer maintain the self-control he had prided himself on developing so many years ago with the Chinese girl at Madame Dubeau's, and he found himself reaching the climax of his passion almost instantly, even before he entered her.

It took another two weeks of trying before their marriage was consummated, and during this period Daniel felt the despair that he experienced on the night he signed the papers in his father's office to be growing. By the sixth month of their marriage, Daniel could no longer perform sexually with Bluma. He wasn't even aroused.

So as Daniel's despair grew, so did Bluma's. She looked at her pretty house, which was perfectly in order and cozily decorated in floral patterns and soft, warm colors, and wondered where she had gone wrong. When she did not see the answer, she took off all her clothes and stood naked in front of the mirror, assessing herself through Daniel's eyes the best she could. What she saw there was a round and luscious woman, one that could be called voluptuous, with a pleasant enough face, even pretty to some people. She had done her best to please Daniel. She had done everything she knew how to do. Why had he agreed to marry her if he didn't want to touch her and caress her? It hurt her that she did not excite him.

As they ceased to make love completely, he ate less and less of her cooking and he began to lose weight. And as he lost weight, she gained. She began to fill herself on the tempting dishes that she had originally fixed so lovingly for her husband. Now it was herself she was feeding, as if the rich food could satisfy all her appetites. Plump to begin with, she grew even plumper and wider, until she almost appeared as broad across as she was tall. Now, a year after their marriage, as she again looked at herself in the mirror, she was able to provide herself a reason why her husband didn't desire her. She was too fat.

Neither of them knew where the babies were going to come from. After a year of marriage, they were both embarrassed that the new Mrs. Luminov wasn't pregnant. Perhaps if she just lost weight again, it would be different. But both needed the baby to justify their existence in their own eyes. To Bluma, it was no good just to be the world's best housekeeper; the picture required a baby to justify its existence. To Daniel, the baby could mean that his father would finally have to recognize that he had become a man and all that implied for their personal and business relationships.

On this particular day, in the summer of 1910, Daniel was on his way from a supply house near Madison Square. As he passed the Victoria Hotel at Twenty-third Street and Fifth Avenue, he saw a large group of people milling around in front. He remembered this was where the cloakmakers' strike committee had set up its headquarters. In the last two years, union leaders like Meyer London and Abraham Rosenberg had begun a massive campaign to improve the working conditions and wages of employees in the garment business. Mendel told him of the many meetings that had taken place and of the union's struggle to build up the strike fund. Although they were urging a huge general strike, the treasury held no more than seventy dollars. Daniel also heard the accounts of how the strike fund had been built up to one hundred twenty-six dollars a few months after that, and how an intensive membership drive was taking place as the union tried to sign up everyone—buttonholers, pressers, basters, fellers. New members joined from the United Hebrew Trades, the Joint Board, and the Cutters Local, causing the membership to swell. Mendel had shown him a copy of the *New Post* put out by the Joint Board and a copy of *The Ladies Garment Worker*, printed in Italian, English and Yiddish. Both newspapers gave their full coverage to just one story, the plans for the general strike. He had been quick to show copies of the papers to his father.

Wolf had glanced at the stories, then put the papers down. "Yes, I know. But this shouldn't affect us."

Daniel thought then that his tone had been a little less confident this time, but it was hard to tell.

Only a few weeks ago, Mendel told him of the test meeting that had taken place in Madison Square

Garden, this very place where Daniel was now walking. Daniel was curious to see how much support there was for the strike. Mendel also told him that Samuel Gompers had spoken at the meeting, and thousands of workers had been turned away for lack of room.

The strike had started on July 7 with a massive parade of workers swarming all the streets from Thirty-eighth Street down and from one side of the island to the other. Now, several weeks later, the strike was still on. He knew what the workers wanted were not only better wages, shorter hours and safer working conditions, but also recognition of the union by the employers and their acceptance of a closed-shop form of hiring.

Daniel saw pickets roaming the streets as they went from one shop to the other to help the striking workers keep up their morale. As he passed through this area, he found himself keeping an eye out for a small blonde. He hoped to run into Alma. He thought he should stop thinking about her. Still, his heart lurched whenever he saw a young woman with small features and a brisk, lively way of moving or talking. It was most likely that Alma might be down here. She wouldn't stay away from the tumult of the events unfolding almost by the minute. Daniel imagined that Alma would be conferring with her friends from the Cherry Street rooftops. He realized he missed her dragging him to meetings and giving him impassioned speeches about the workers' rights, the benefits of socialism and the need for a Jewish homeland. Certainly Bluma had no desire to talk or read about such things. In fact, Bluma didn't read any newspaper as far as he could see or discuss anything outside of their domestic surroundings.

He saw no sign of the blonde head he was looking for and continued on reluctantly up Fifth Avenue. He was on his way to Elke's house. With all the demands of the factory, and now the attention he was giving to the strike efforts in the garment business, he had little opportunity to visit his sister and her family.

A short time later, Mrs. Chotzinoff led him into the playroom where Elke sat on the floor with her skirts mushroomed out around her, reading aloud to the three children who were positioned on the folds of her skirt as if they were at a picnic.

"After all these years, you still have your nose in a book, Elke?" he teased as he walked toward her.

The three children sprung from their places and threw themselves on him. "Uncle Dan! Uncle Dan!" they screamed in paroxysms of delight. Sadie, the youngest at two years, was trying to hug his calf. Zosa, age three and Adam, now four, were holding hands and trying to leap up to his waist.

"Well, I see that at least the children haven't forgotten what you look like," Elke chided. "But where's your broken leg? It's been so long since I saw you that I thought your leg was in a cast. I didn't know what else would make you stay away so long."

Daniel laughed. "You have turned into a real Jewish mother, haven't you. But I admit, it has been a while."

He was pleased to see his sister was looking good. Despite the three babies, her figure was still trim in the right spots, and if anything, even more voluptuous. "Well, are you only good at sarcasm, or are you going to impress me with how well you can make tea?"

He was surprised when she led him to the bubbling samovar in the other room. "When did you start this?" He gestured toward the graceful silver urn for making tea. "We never had one of these at home and I know Jacob isn't Russian."

"It's just something I wanted to have." Elke placed a small dish of sliced lemons and another of sugar cubes next to the tea glasses. "I always thought they were pretty and practical. Even when I was a girl I wanted one, but I knew Mama would have been terribly upset if I had ever suggested such a thing."

As they sat to drink their tea, the children swarmed in on them. Elke sent them to the other side of the room so they could sip their tea in peace and hear what each had to say. As they talked, Daniel noticed she kept one eye on the children and one on him, but he supposed that was the way it was with all mothers. Probably Bluma would be the same way, if they ever had a baby.

As if she knew what he was thinking, Elke turned the conversation toward Daniel and his marriage. "Yes, I'm happy. But are you?"

"Happy?" Daniel wasn't used to thinking in those terms. "Well, I'm working hard and the business is picking up and the country's pulling out of the slow down we've had the last four or five years."

"Does that mean you're happy?" Elke persisted. "You're talking about the business instead of yourself."

He shifted in his seat. "Am I? Well then, let's see." He shifted again. "Uh, what was the question?"

"I asked if you're happy." She saw that he just looked at her, not replying. "Daniel, would you and Bluma like to have a baby?"

"Of course. In time." It was hard enough for him to admit to himself the growing desperation he felt in his situation with Bluma, much less to someone else. He felt not even the slightest bit of desire for her and nothing seemed to arouse him. He didn't see how he would ever be able to father a child for them. And without a son, his life would be meaningless in his father's eyes.

When she saw he wasn't going to say any more, she too became silent, allowing an awkward gap to form between them. She busied herself pouring more tea for both of them. Daniel looked over at the children playing across the room. Adam and Zosa were crouched with their arms interlocked as they faced each other, each trying to wrestle the other to the floor. Sadie sat off to one side, watching them, a pile of blocks between her legs.

"I can't believe how well Adam and Zosa get along together," Daniel remarked, finally breaking the silence between them. "They're so close they're almost like twins."

"Daniel, you're going to have to stand up to him one day."

He looked at her quickly. "What did you say?"

"You heard me and you know what I'm talking about. You can't go on like this, letting your desire to please him take over your life."

"I know," he admitted quietly.

"You let him talk you into marrying Bluma, right?"

"How did you know?"

"Because he once tried to interfere with my life. He drove me away from seeing someone he didn't approve of."

Daniel looked at his sister in surprise. "Why didn't you ever tell me this?" But he knew the answer. It was because they weren't always able to talk as freely as they could now.

She put another sugar cube in her mouth to sip the tea through. "You wouldn't have thought it especially significant at the time, idolizing him as you did. And probably still do," she added.

He laughed bitterly and she knew she was right. He still did worship his father and found it hard to find fault with him, even when he had pressured him into a marriage that was making him miserable.

After Daniel left, Elke was left to her own thoughts. Although she mentioned to Daniel the incident with David that had taken place almost five years ago, she didn't tell him of the small white envelope a messenger had delivered to the door just a few weeks ago. She had opened it to find a letter which left her stunned:

My dearest Elke,
    Please do not destroy this letter as you

probably will want to do. For the sake of what was once between us, please read on and hear me out. I know that you have married, and that you have no desire or need to have contact with me in any way. But I must talk to you, at least one more time. It doesn't have to be in person. It could even be behind the less personal and yet still private facade of the telephone. Here is my number at the bank. . . .

The moment she had read the number, she crushed the letter in her hand with great force, hoping at the same time to squeeze the number from her memory. She threw the envelope into the fire and watched the flames curl its edges. They consumed it in a matter of seconds. Her marriage with Jacob was the happiest and most perfect thing in her life, and next came her children. She wanted nothing more to do with David Sheffield and just wanted to forget the telephone number that she had read in the note.

Now when everything in her life was perfect, she didn't want thoughts of David haunting her.

Bluma was becoming obsessed with the desire to have a baby. But how could that ever happen if her husband never came near her? After she made herself another thirty pounds heavier, she decided she would have to seek help. She took the ferry to Manhattan. She had in her purse the name of the doctor that her mother-in-law told her had delivered Elke and Daniel and who had been their family doctor for years. She knew Marya must have wondered if her daughter-in-law were pregnant and that was the reason she was asking for the doctor's name and address. Bluma let her think that because she didn't see how she could have told Marya she had something to consult a doctor about that she was too ashamed to tell her parents' doctor.

When she was shown into his office, she found a tall, stooped man with a mane of greyish white hair. Perhaps it was his scholarly appearance or the sparkle in his eyes, which reminded her of her father, that helped put her at ease.

"Ah, so you are the young Mrs. Luminov." He took her by the elbow and ushered her to a chair across from his desk. Then he took his own seat. "I have known your husband's family for many years. But I'm sure you know that."

"Yes, Dr. Addison." She looked down at her lap and wondered how she was going to explain the reason she had come. She decided the best course was to plunge right in. "I don't know how to say this, but I have a problem of an embarrassing nature."

Dr. Addison looked at her kindly. "That's quite all right, my dear. You must understand that nothing is embarrassing to a physician. Please feel comfortable to speak freely."

"You see, it's a problem between me and my husband." She realized she was twisting the handles of her purse. She set it on the floor so that she would not be able to fidget with it and sat with her hands folded in her lap.

Dr. Addison helped her out. "Something of a sexual nature, you are saying?"

"Yes." She paused and took a deep breath. "It seems, you see, that we will never have babies. Because you see, we have a problem with. . . ." She did not go on.

Dr. Addison waited a moment for her to finish her sentence and when she did not, he said, "Your lovemaking."

"Yes. That's it." She felt tears welling up in her eyes and swallowed hard to keep them away. "You see, my husband does not want me . . . that way."

"You feel your husband does not respond to you sexually? He does not become aroused?"

She nodded.

"Your husband, then, is unable to perform sexually," he repeated, wanting to make sure he had it right.

"That's right." She felt a little stronger now that she had said it out loud to someone.

"Your husband suffers from impotency, then?" Before she could question the term, he continued. "Impotency refers to a condition in which the male is incapable of sexual intercourse."

"Yes, that is our problem. That is why I don't know how we will ever have a family. How can we when he doesn't even want to touch me?"

"Have you and your husband ever made love?"

"Yes."

Dr. Addison leaned forward earnestly. "Mrs. Luminov, you must understand that impotency is not a permanent condition. Many men suffer from impotency at one time or another during their lives. It can be the result of many causes, some psychological, some physical. In fact, many medical conditions are linked to impotency. It can affect a man during a period of his life when there are many pressures on him, pressures from his job or from some situation in his environment. Let's start there. Does Daniel seem preoccupied with his work?"

Bluma sighed. "That's all he seems to want to talk about anymore." Maybe, she thought, that's all he ever did talk about, even before their marriage.

"Well, you see? That alone might be the cause. It's impossible for me to say for sure, of course, not having examined or spoken with Daniel lately. But what I want you to understand is that because your husband was once able to perform sexually with you, there's every chance he will be able to again. I know what you must be thinking and it's natural for a woman to doubt her appeal in a situation like this. But since you cannot say you know the cause of your husband's impotency, you simply cannot feel that you are the cause. You just don't know that to be true. Now what I would recommend is that you ask Daniel to come and see me."

She was filled with alarm. "I couldn't do that, Dr. Addison. I couldn't tell Daniel I was here talking with you about him."

"Of course you can. You must find a way. It's for the sake of your marital happiness, Bluma—you don't mind if I use your first name, do you? You both want babies, don't you? You can't go on ignoring the situation. That will only make it worse."

Dr. Addison continued to press upon her the importance of her coaxing Daniel to visit him. Bluma wanted to take comfort from the words he offered her about the possible cause of Daniel's impotency. Maybe, just maybe, it was the situation at work. She was not unaware of the dominating personality of his father and of the relentless control that Wolf wanted to exercise over every facet of MW Enterprises. But deep down she couldn't stop thinking that the problem was really her. Daniel just wasn't attracted to her, that was all. But she had promised Dr. Addison she would find a tactful way to suggest to Daniel that he pay the doctor a visit, and she would. Dr. Addison told her that once he got Daniel in his office, he would take the situation from there.

It was with these thoughts that she returned to her house late that afternoon. Her visit to the doctor's office and trips across the East River on the ferry took her longer than she had planned. Daniel might already be home and she hadn't even started supper. She saw from outside that there was a light in the upstairs of the house. Daniel must already be home. And here she was without his evening meal. What kind of housekeeper would he think she was?

She let herself in and went straight to the kitchen. "Daniel?" she called. When she didn't see him, she looked in the parlor and other rooms downstairs, then climbed the stairs.

"Daniel?" she called again as she opened the door

of the bedroom. Daniel was standing naked in front of the bed. Before him, spread out on the bed, were a number of photographs of women, their breasts bare and their bodies arched in provocative poses. She saw that he was standing there in a state of sexual arousal, and instantly she understood the purpose of the pictures.

She slammed the door shut and ran down the stairs, back to the kitchen. Her emotions tumbled over each other and she could scarcely think. But certain things were very clear to her. Daniel wasn't impotent at all! It was just with her he didn't become aroused! It was just with her that he couldn't perform! Dr. Addison's kind words were all wrong. It wouldn't do any good for her to try to get Daniel to Dr. Addison. It wasn't Daniel's worry about the strikes or his father that were causing his impotence. It was her, and nothing else. She put her head down in her arms and sobbed.

As soon as the door was shut, Daniel exploded in anger, anger directed at himself. He felt ashamed and degraded, and suddenly he could see himself for what he had become. He turned and caught a glimpse of himself in the mirror and what he saw sickened him. He wasn't a man. What he saw was a slave to someone else's desires. All his life he had dedicated himself to pleasing his father. All he had ever wanted was his father's approval and acknowledgment, and to that end he had sacrificed everything—his freedom, his happiness, Alma. But no matter what he did and how hard he tried, he hadn't been able to please that man.

As he stared at himself in the mirror, he saw a giant boy, a boy who had made a humiliating mess of his own life and had willingly sacrificed the happiness of the two women who had loved him. He thought of Alma and how she'd looked when they'd said their final good-bye, and he thought of Bluma and the expression on her face in these unhappy years of their fruitless marriage. Poor Bluma, she deserved better than this. He knew how he must have hurt her by his unwillingness to accept her and by his lack of attention. She deserved a real man, one who could love and appreciate her and provide her with children, not this giant boy looking back at him in torment from the mirror. He picked up a stool and hurled it at the image and the boy fractured into large ugly splinters and fell to the floor.

From upstairs Bluma heard the sound of crashing and then the cracking of wood. She heard Daniel yelling in anger and there was a tone in it that frightened her. She sat where she was at the kitchen table and the tears continued to roll down her cheeks as she listened to the angry violence coming from above. Then she heard Daniel's heavy footsteps on the stairs and moving down the hallway. He called her name, but she didn't answer. He called her again and she could hear him going from room to room. She knew she didn't want to see him. She got up quickly and hid herself in the pantry. He kept calling her name. She knew he would be in the kitchen in another second. She didn't dare to breathe. He stormed into the kitchen and when he didn't see her, he went out again.

The front door slammed, and then the house was silent.

Daniel walked out into the brisk evening air. His thoughts were full of self-loathing. He was full of regret for the pain he had caused his wife. His resistance to her, his marrying her without love just to curry favor with his father, his abandonment of Alma—all that he now saw as immoral. He now saw clearly what a complete toady he had been to his father. And once he saw it, he knew there was no turning back.

Chapter 23

Daniel thought about how strange it was for him to be sitting in this plush office in an imposing granite building on Wall Street. He assessed the man sitting across from him. He appeared to be in his forties and was amazingly fit. His hair was a sandy blend of grey and dark blond, and he had an open, honest face. Daniel decided that he liked this Andrew Markingham.

He chose Markingham after recognizing his name as one of his mother's business associates. They were going step by step over the details of his business relationship with his father as it had unfolded over the years. Andrew Markingham listened thoughtfully as he puffed on his pipe and said little. Only now and then did he ask a question to clarify for himself the sequence of certain events or to prompt Daniel to recall other relevant episodes. Only when Daniel finished his lengthy account did the attorney appear ready to talk.

Andrew tried to disregard that the young man sitting before him was Marya's son. He didn't know for sure how he had gotten his name, but surmised it must have come from Marya in some way. It felt strange to him to hear this young man speak so dispassionately about the deeds of a man who happened to be the husband of the woman for whom he would do anything in the world. He did his best to put these thoughts out of his mind and attend to the details of the suit.

He cleared his throat. "You have a case, of that I have no doubt. First of all, there was the oral contract, for which there is sufficient reiteration over the years and witnesses for substantiation. The oral agreement was that the business would become yours when you reached manhood. Now, we could expect to be contested on just when the point of manhood is. We would argue, however, that, given your religious and cultural background, the age of manhood is thirteen, the day on which you were publicly recognized to have become a man and when you assumed your place as a peer in the community, both religious and secular. You understand, of course, that your father would argue otherwise."

Daniel swallowed, but his voice was firm and clear. "Of course."

Markingham struck a match and held it to the bowl of the pipe as he drew on the stem. When the tobacco lit, he waved the match to put out the flame and said through clenched teeth, "His contention will be that manhood is not reached until a certain level of emotional maturity is acquired. With that would go an ability to handle responsibility. He would probably say that at age thirteen, you were old enough to judge right from wrong, but that did not mean you were able to deal responsibly with sophisticated business matters. If he were to fight us, he would try to demonstrate that you did not have that level of maturity at age thirteen."

Daniel added coolly, "And not when I was eighteen, or twenty-one or when I married, or even now at twenty-six." How ironic, he said to himself. Here he was twenty-six, twice thirteen, twice a man even by his father's own standards, if he could admit the truth. And still his son did not have what was rightfully his, that which had been promised him from infancy.

"But of course, the fact that he sent you in his stead from the age of fourteen and older to conduct business for him, both within and without the state of New York, that evidence would argue for our side. It's an indication that he did in fact think you had the maturity—intellectual, emotional, and moral—to make decisions of a business or financial nature."

"And the Memorandum of Agreement that I signed? Would that complicate matters?"

"It shouldn't. It's really more substantiation for us. It's proof of his intent. There may be some argument that you accepted his revised terms when you signed it, but we should be able to show that your signing was done under duress."

Daniel thought about how odd it was to hear someone use the word "us" in reference to his conflict with his father. He was so used to thinking in the singular and feeling that his battle was one that he waged completely by himself. Now he would actually have someone on his side, someone who saw it his way, even if he was paid to do so.

Markingham took his pipe out of his mouth and started to say something, then hesitated. "There's only one thing here, Mr. Luminov, that I see as the crucial test."

He saw that the attorney was staring at him intently. "What's that?"

"Do you want to go ahead with this? Do you really want to sue your father? It could be very painful for all concerned." For Marya's sake, he had to say that. Yet he couldn't help but feel some satisfaction at what he knew his client's answer would be.

Daniel's answer was immediate. "Yes." Pain? he asked himself. He knew Andrew Markingham had no way of knowing how painful it had already been all these years, and what pain he felt at this particular moment as he forced himself to confront what he had done to himself and others, all for the sake of trying to gain his father's respect and approval.

Markingham began to make notes on the pad before him, then stopped and looked up. "We will need a couple of days to prepare the papers. Then we will begin the proceedings and serve the papers on him." He didn't look at Daniel as he said, "If, during that time, you change your mind, contact me at once." Then he stood up, offering his hand to Daniel.

Daniel shook it firmly. "Thank you for your counsel, Mr. Markingham." Then he turned and left.

As Andrew watched him go out the door, he marveled at how calm young Luminov had seemed. The only thing that belied the controlled and cold facade that he projected were the two damp spots Andrew had noticed on the knees of Daniel's pant legs. Each had borne the outline of a sweating hand.

Marya and Andrew sat across from each other at Delmonico's and Marya had the distinct impression that Andrew was fishing for some kind of information. He had been probing gently about each of her children and about Daniel in particular. She couldn't imagine why he should suddenly develop more of an interest in them than he usually had. It had always seemed before that he displayed what Marya thought to be just the right amount of concern. He wasn't overly solicitous about their welfare, as if he were trying to step in as a parent figure, but at the same time he always remembered to ask after them and showed the appropriate response to whatever little tale she might care to tell about either of them.

Andrew knew that Marya was curious about why he was asking more questions than usual. He warned himself to be careful. He knew he couldn't violate a client's confidence, even though the client was the son of the woman he loved.

He also had something more important he wanted to talk to her about. He gazed at her as she sat across from him, picking at the remains of her cassoulet. He never tired of looking at her. She was wearing a slate blue dress with a kimono bodice, and the skirt draped to an inverted V in the front to reveal her ankles. At forty-four she was as beautiful and fresh as she had been when he and Gregory Keller had first sighted her in this same restaurant many years ago.

"If you don't mind my changing the subject, Andrew, there's something else I've been wanting to talk to you about. It's about my business. I've decided I want to expand."

"Expand? Do you mean a bigger shop to house your work, or more customers?"

"Both."

A smile played about Andrew's lips. "What? Aren't you happy working ten hours a day? Now you want to work twelve?"

Marya laughed. "This time I don't plan to work any more than I'm already working. I want to hire more people to do the work for me."

"It's about time. That staff of six you have is completely inadequate. You could keep twice that many going."

She laughed again. "That's what I think too. Especially if I moved my shop to Fifth Avenue."

Andrew whistled lightly. "Step back, folks. This lady's on the march."

"Andrew, stop that. I'm serious. I want to know if you'll help me find a place. You have lots of contacts, and you hear of much more going on than I do. Tell me you'll help me."

"You know I will. I've already told you, I'll help you do anything you want." His manner turned more serious. "But there's something I've been wanting to discuss with you too," he said suddenly, "and in a way it's related to what we've been talking about."

"You mean something other than Daniel," she said, half-teasing.

He looked at her quickly. "Yes. Not the shop and not Daniel. Something even closer to home."

"Oh?" She sat smiling at him, twirling her wine glass in her fingers. "Well?"

"Marya, I don't know how to put this, but I'm not sure how much longer I can go on like this. I see you sitting across the table from me, looking more delectable every year, if I may put it in such a corny way, and then later in the evening you go home to another man."

Marya set her wine glass down and started to say something, but he stopped her.

"I know," he said, "that you could point out that nothing's changed. That's how it's been all along. But something has changed, and it is that each year I've fallen more in love with you. What was once in a sense tolerable no longer is. I can no longer bear the prospect of your leaving my arms to return to a man who clearly doesn't appreciate you and," he paused, "doesn't deserve you."

"Andrew, I—"

"Wait, Marya. Let me finish." He reached across the table for her hand. "I'm asking you to marry me again. And this time I would like an answer." His voice grew solemn. "Marya, will you be my wife?"

Marya was so stunned she overturned the wine glass she had been holding a few minutes before. Instantly the waiter was at her side, dabbing at the table with a napkin. Neither she nor Andrew said a word while the waiter solicitously cleaned up the wine and took an interminable time providing Marya with another glass.

"What is your answer?" Andrew asked when the waiter had at last gone.

She looked at him and sighed. What was waiting for her at home, she asked herself. Now that Elke and Daniel had left, what comfort did she find in that big house uptown? Wolf often worked late into the night, returning sometimes after she had gone to bed. Her

only company was Mrs. Sanders and even that was
only for the evening meal. There was nothing there for
her anymore. Although she and Wolf were stiffly polite
when they chanced to pass in the hall or both be home
for dinner, the truth was they managed to see surprisingly little of each other. And all this time, Andrew,
dear sweet Andrew, had been waiting patiently for her,
always at her side when she needed him, always ready
to put her first in his life. She couldn't imagine what
her world would have been like without him.

He was looking at her steadily, and only the soft
drumming of his fingertips on the tablecloth revealed
his nervousness.

"Yes," Marya finally said. "Yes, Andrew. I will
marry you."

His face lit up and he pressed her fingers to his
mouth. "My dearest Marya. You've no idea how happy
we will be together."

Marya felt tears come to her eyes. "Yes, Andrew,
I'm sure we will be. But you must give me more time."

He looked puzzled.

"I'm still a married woman. I have arrangements I
must make. The children must be told, and of course
my . . . my husband."

He squeezed her hand. "Of course, Marya. I understand. I've waited for you this long. I can wait a
while longer, especially now that I know you will soon
be my wife."

Daniel was not sleeping well. After tossing alone
in his bed for hours, his mind churning over and over
the arguments that Andrew Markingham had outlined
for him in his office a couple days before, he finally
gave it up and got dressed. Since that day with the attorney, he had slept more poorly than ever. Since the
incident—his term for what had happened with
Bluma—she had begun sleeping in the other bedroom,
the room that was once to have been the nursery. But
he knew it wasn't just what had happened with Bluma

and the way she had withdrawn both emotionally and physically that was troubling him. It was the suit against his father.

A constant refrain ran through his mind: How can I sue the man whom all my life I have only wanted to please? As angry as he was over what had happened, he wasn't sure he could go through with it. One moment he cursed himself for being a weak coward, still under his father's domination and lacking any real fire in his soul; the next moment he saw his reluctance to sue as enlightened and humane, a wise acknowledgment of the emotional bankruptcy of such an action. The gains he could make by winning his case would of course be bittersweet and without the same significance as they would have had if Wolf were to act voluntarily and recognize him as a worthy man, capable of making intelligent decisions and worthy of being his co-equal in business and before the world.

He stepped outside in the cold night air and began to walk. When he came to the ferry landing, he decided to take the ferryboat across the East River to Manhattan. It let him off at the Fulton Fish Market, and from there he wandered into the streets of the Lower East Side, streets he had known so thoroughly as a boy when MW Enterprises was still just a shop and still on Greene Street. He meandered from street to street, with no fixed destination in mind.

As he turned the corner onto Henry Street, he saw a light burning in a street-level room of an old tenement across from him. In the room a shape was hunched over a sewing machine, working by sputtering gaslight, just the way his father said he had once done, but that was many years ago before the advent of electrical lights. Poor wretch—having to work this late into the night just to earn enough to keep his family together. He had obviously brought home piecework to do in addition to his daytime work. As Daniel drew nearer the window, he was startled to recognize the person sitting there.

It was Mendel, the presser from his father's factory. Daniel was shocked to see someone he knew, after laboring all day, still working now, after midnight.

Just this morning Mendel had waved a handful of newspapers in his face and insisted on spreading them out in front of Daniel to show him the grisly pictures of the victims of the Triangle Shirtwaist Company. Daniel had already seen the pictures, for who had not heard of the deadly fire that had broken out just the week before in the ten-story building near Washington Square. It housed one of the city's biggest factories for ladies' dresses on its upper floors.

The story was that a man on his way to the toilet had dropped a match onto the cutting room floor and when it landed on scraps of fabric, a blaze had begun. The workers dashed into the hallway for the fire hose, but rotten with age, it broke into pieces. Within seconds the flames had reached inflammable cleaning fluids, and the fire quickly grew into a conflagration.

Panic-stricken girls, for the workers there were mostly young women, raced for the back exit, but every afternoon it was routinely locked by the bosses to prevent employees from pilfering as they left for home. Finding no way out but a lone ladder through a small door to the roof, some seventy girls managed to escape that way. The firemen's ladders reached only to the sixth floor, but the factory was on the seventh, eighth and ninth floors. One girl after another began to leap to her death from the burning building, the force of their falling bodies ripping through the firemen's nets. By the end, one hundred forty-six people had perished, most of them women.

Who had not been sickened by this disaster that so grimly pointed up the wretched safety conditions in the factories and shops? Daniel had been horrified and deeply shaken by the incident, but it was Mendel who had wept and who wrote poetry to express his grief, then pledged to redouble his activities on behalf of the union.

Now their conversations over the years came back to Daniel as he recalled how Mendel had suggested that the unions were the working man and woman's only salvation. It was Mendel more than anyone or anything else who had kept him informed about the typical sweatshop and factory conditions on the Lower East Side, of the work seven days a week and into the night, undertaken for just pennies an hour. But Daniel had never realized Mendel was speaking about his own life. It was Mendel who had talked to him about the economic struggle between the workers and the owners. But he had never realized Mendel had such a stake in what he was saying. He always thought of his father's workers as in a different category. He remembered how Mendel had often looked fatigued and drawn, but Daniel had put his appearance down to too many late hours in the cafés arguing politics, too much discussion in rooms filled with the smoke from Russian cigarettes, too much intellectualizing.

Now he knew what had been the real cause of those sunken cheeks and dark eyes.

He took care to stay in the shadows. If his friend saw him, he would have been embarrassed. He stood there a while longer, saddened by the reality of Mendel's life and probably the lives of all employees in his father's factory and other factories throughout the city. He was astounded by the injustice of it all. He well knew the kind of profits the manufacturers were making and the vast chasm that existed between their earnings and the earnings of the workers, even in a factory such as his father's where the workers, if they stayed for the entire season, could do better than elsewhere.

The longer he stood there watching Mendel toil by the flickering gaslight, the more a sense of outrage grew. Then Daniel had the beginnings of an idea. The idea grew and expanded as it became increasingly real to him. And with the idea came a sense of purpose, and this time the purpose felt right. He knew what he was going to do.

Daniel decided not to sue his father after all. He would do something that would benefit more than just himself and maybe, in some small way, would make up for the way in which he had hurt others around him. Tomorrow he would go to Mendel and tell him he wanted to offer his services to the union.

He abruptly turned and retraced his steps to the ferry landing. It was early morning by the time he reached home. He promptly fell into the soundest sleep he had experienced in a long time.

In the next few months, Daniel threw himself into attending countless rounds of meetings in underheated cafés and fiery speeches in overventilated lecture halls. He instructed Andrew to drop the suit against his father, and although he still went to the factory every day, his heart was no longer there in the same way. Now his energies went into the action committees and membership drives, and he had even encouraged Mendel to expand union membership at MW Enterprises. He obtained membership in the ILGWU, the Joint Board and the United Hebrew Trades. He began to donate a tenth of his salary to the unions' strike funds, then a fifth. He read *The Forward* and *The Day* religiously. He now felt more alive than he had at any period in his life. He had forgotten about his own concerns and was working for something bigger than himself and more important than himself.

The only thing he didn't feel good about was the situation with Bluma. The relationship between them was still strained. He wanted to talk to her but had to admit that he didn't know how. He didn't know where to begin. What could a man say to his wife when she had come upon him in the circumstances Bluma had? But did that happen to other men? And it wasn't even so much that she had walked in on him, it was the nature of their relationship leading up to that point that troubled him. Now her hurt had turned into bitterness and her tongue had become cruel and vindictive, making it all the harder for him to begin.

This evening, as he prepared to leave the house, he passed her sitting in the living room, pale and heavy under the lamplight as she read with her head bowed. He was on his way to another of his union meetings and he was buoyed by the thought that he would soon be amid the dynamic give and take of the union hall.

She glanced up as he drew near. "Going out again?"

"Yes." He tried to keep the eagerness out of his voice, but he knew he wasn't successful.

She returned to her reading without saying anything. At such times she reminded him of a lumpy sack of flour, and he knew he could never make love to a sack of flour again, not for his father's factory, not for the sake of his marriage, not for anything. Never again would he compromise himself. As he shut the door behind him, he felt a jolt of guilt at leaving her sitting there, but it soon disappeared in the exhilaration he felt as he made his way to the meeting place, feeling he was living his life as his own man.

Daniel stood against the wall and looked out over the hundreds of people gathered there, scrutinizing the faces of the other members of the audience as they listened to the speaker, Morris Hillquit, one of the labor movement's most articulate and persuasive orators. Hillquit leaned forward intently and lowered his voice. As his voice dropped, the audience all in a body leaned forward not to miss a word he was saying.

Hillquit raised his right arm. ". . . the gains of the cloakmakers' strike of 1910 are not enough. The Protocol of Peace is just a beginning. We have wrenched for ourselves not even the barest minimum: a fifty-hour week, a slight increase in our wages, the end to inside contracting. . . ."

Pride showed on the faces of the beleaguered workers to think that they had even achieved those meager victories that Hillquit was detailing. Daniel's eyes moved from face to face of the women and men who, after laboring all day, had given up their evening to be here, and he saw etched on their faces marks of toil and woe.

Suddenly his eyes riveted to one spot in particular. Gazing back at him was Alma. She smiled, then looked away. The rest of the meeting became a blur to him. He could not take his eyes from her. The moment the speech was over, he headed in her direction. She appeared to be there with a group of friends, and as they headed toward the exit arguing animatedly among themselves, she went with them. Daniel hurried up behind them.

"Alma!" he called. When she didn't stop, he called again a little louder.

This time she heard him and turned. When she saw him, she smiled again and put out her hand. "Daniel, what a surprise! What brings you here?"

He tried to keep his eyes from devouring her. The last few years had added a little fullness to her, but she was still petite and if anything, prettier and softer. He couldn't keep his eyes from straying to her hands to see if she were wearing a wedding ring, but his prying glances reaped no information. Her hands were gloved.

He tried to keep his voice calm. "I've been down here quite a bit lately what with helping with membership drives and distributing papers." When she gave him a quizzical look, he explained, "I joined the union."

This time she appeared even more puzzled. "You never were very interested in such things before, Daniel."

"A lot has happened."

"It must have." The look in her eye told him she was intrigued.

His heart leapt. He took it as a good sign, an indication that she at least still cared a little what happened to him. He wished he could ask her to go to a café with him and talk, but knew that he couldn't. He felt he had no right to ask that of her.

"How is your family . . . your mother and sister?" Alma asked, seeming to want to prolong their conversation.

Daniel laughed. "You wouldn't believe my sister. She's the mother of the world and happily spends all her time fussing over the three children and her husband. She keeps a kosher house and observes all the holidays. My mother never quite knows what to make of this daughter that she spawned. And what of your mother and Mrs. Mueller?"

"They're fine," she said.

He took a deep breath. They both were careful to avoid mention of their fathers, he noticed. Then before he realized he was saying it, the words were coming out. "I-I hope you're doing well. I think a lot about you."

Alma looked up at him under her lashes. "Even now?"

"Yes," he admitted.

"I'm okay. I think about you a lot, too." She paused. "But I'm trying to put all that behind me. It's for the best." She began to speak more rapidly. "I work a lot actually. I've become very active on behalf of establishing a Jewish homeland in Palestine."

"You were already working for that when we were—"

She cut him off from the painful reference he was about to make. "Yes, well now I'm completely dedicated. It's become the most important thing in the world to me. I feel the time is right. That's why I spend my time making speeches to youth groups about the necessities of Labor Zionism. It is my deepest wish to go to Palestine someday and be a part of all that is happening in the collective settlements that our people are struggling to establish there."

The more she talked, the more earnest she became. Her face shone with the ardor of her beliefs and she practically shook from the intensity of her feelings. Almost hypnotized by her enthusiasm, he couldn't pull his eyes from her. And he couldn't help but think with a heavy heart that this magnificent woman was what he had traded away . . . and for what?

A fellow from her circle of friends came up and tugged at her arm. "Let's go, Alma." He quickly sized Daniel up and cast him an unfriendly look as he said, "The others are waiting for us over at the Zum Essex Café. If we stay away any longer, they'll be wondering what hanky-panky the two of us are up to."

Daniel would have liked to smash him in the face for the implication in his remark. He had no choice but to watch helplessly as the other man led Alma away to the café where he and Alma had gone the first night they had met on Cherry Street. His only consolation as she was led away from him was that her eyes continued to hold his for a long time.

Chapter 24

Mendel was beckoning Daniel from across the factory. "Come here, *boychik*, and listen to this."

Daniel made his way among the dangling gas and steam lines to the high table where Mendel stood amidst piles of dresses waiting to be pressed.

Mendel waited until Daniel was standing directly in front of him so he could hear, and only then did he begin to talk. "You see, once there was this presser," he said and moved his eyes back and forth as he worked on the long skirt of the dress. "And once there was this baster." He set down the pressing iron and for a few seconds mimicked the motions of someone sewing. Then he returned to the role of the presser as he said in his thick Yiddish accent, "The presser looked at the sewer and said, '*Nu*, Max, so what did you do this weekend?'" Mendel returned to mimicking the stitching motions. "And Max says, 'This weekend? I went for a little hike.' 'That's very interesting,' says the presser. 'And where did you hike?' 'I hiked in the Himalayas.' The presser raised an eyebrow. 'The Himalayas, you say? And how high did you go?' 'To seven thousand feet. Then I fell.' The presser looked at Max, astonished. 'You fell seven thousand feet in the

Himalayas? According to that, you shouldn't even be alive.' It was Max's turn to raise an eyebrow. 'So you call this living?' "

Daniel grinned and shook his head. "Mendel, you're going to have to do better than that," he said affectionately. "That's not one of your best jokes."

Mendel picked up his iron again and immediately his bare torso was enveloped in steam. "So you think it's a joke? They'll be telling that seventy years from now and then it'll be a joke. But today it's no joke. But, even if you don't like my story, you've got to admit it sums up the situation in this business."

Daniel laughed again. "That may be." Then he turned serious. "Listen, Mendel. Is everything ready as we planned? Do all the workers know what's happening?"

"Don't worry. Everything's going to go just as you organized it."

The rest of the morning Daniel found himself watching the clock. He reviewed the steps he had taken. For the last nine months Mendel had been passing out union leaflets, inviting workers to attend union meetings, and arguing passionately the importance of everyone standing unified. He and Daniel had succeeded in registering almost seventy per cent of the workers in the ILGWU, and Daniel had begun contributing half his salary to build up a strike fund single-handedly, just in case. Two nights ago they had held a meeting of all the union members in his factory to go over the steps they had planned for today, the day they were going to present their demands for union recognition and a closed-shop method of hiring.

Daniel stood outside Wolf's office and looked at his watch again. Eleven o'clock. It was time. From across the floor he could see Mendel set down his pressing iron. Following the signal, men and women all the way down the row also set down theirs. Then the basters put down their needles and thread, and the stitchers stopped running their machines, leaving an eerie silence to prevail in the factory.

As planned, a delegation consisting of Mendel and two other union members approached Daniel where he still stood. They shook hands all the way around and together they went into Wolf's office.

Wolf looked up in surprise at his son and the four men as they marched in unannounced.

Daniel stood a little to one side as Mendel acted as spokesman.

"On behalf of the International Ladies Garment Workers Union," Mendel began, "I'd like to present this—"

"Get out," Wolf snapped. He looked from the three men to the idle workers he could see through the glass office window, all watching him, and then to his son.

Daniel met his father's gaze evenly. "I think they deserve to be heard."

Wolf glared at him. "What are you talking about? These are union troublemakers, and I won't have any part of it. The last thing we need in this factory is the union."

"That's one point of view," replied Daniel. "Besides, in case you haven't noticed, it's already here. I say we hear them out."

Wolf spun to face the three men. "I won't hear your demands. I'm the owner of this factory and I want you out of here." He pounded on the desk to underscore his remarks.

Daniel stepped in immediately. "As the other owner, I say you can present your list of demands to me." He reached out for the documents which Mendel was holding.

Wolf's voice was thunderous. "Daniel, I order you not to accept those papers."

But it was too late. Daniel took the documents from Mendel. The workers outside the office burst into applause. Then Mendel and the other two men filed out the door, leaving Daniel and Wolf alone.

Before Wolf could say anything, Daniel jumped in. "It's time to recognize certain realities—"

Wolf broke in, his voice harsh and angry. "Haven't you heard what I've been saying these last twenty years?" He pounded on the desk again for emphasis. "I don't want the union in here. We don't need them. This is my factory and I want to control things around here, not a bunch of—"

"This is our factory. And you can go on the rest of your life priding yourself on the fact that MW Enterprises pays a few more pennies than the sweatshops and gives *Shabbas* off. But it's factories like this one that are responsible for holding everybody down. Can't you see that?"

"I have struggled almost all my life and certainly all of yours to make something of this business that we could be proud of. I'm not about to give it away on a platter to a bunch of greedy and malcontent blockheads."

"You're always saying you know how the workers feel because you were once one of them. But I don't think you're that concerned for the workers at all. You give lip service and a few extra pennies, that's all."

"You don't know what you're talking about, Daniel. You're still wet behind the ears."

"I do know what I'm talking about. I know the only way to improve the lot of the workers is to build the union. As long as the big factories like ours hold out, that weakens the union, and the union is nothing more than the voice of the people who actually do the work."

"I won't have it here!"

"Open your eyes. It's already here. I brought it in."

Wolf gaped open-mouthed at his son. "You brought it in?" he repeated.

"It was on its way anyway, couldn't you see?

How long did you think you could pretend it doesn't exist?"

Wolf's tone was venomous. "I always knew you'd ruin this factory in one way or the other. I knew I couldn't let you have too much control."

"Ruin! Don't you see? This is the only way to save it in the long run. Have you forgotten what it's like to race from garment to garment all day, just to earn enough for some stinking fish at night and a one-room tenement? Have you forgotten what it's like to work with the sweat running down your back, day after day, even in the heat of summer? Don't you remember what it's like to—"

"Stop! I won't have you talk to me like this!"

"I'm just trying to get you to look at the justice of the situation. There's a moral issue here."

"I don't give a hang for the moral issue."

"You never did, did you? All you want is to maintain control over everything and everyone!"

"I've a good mind to fire you! Don't push me, Daniel."

But Daniel couldn't let up. "You can't trust anyone else to do anything. That's the way it's been between us all these years, hasn't it?"

"What are you talking about?"

"I'm talking about how it's been my whole life. I'm talking about how you always pretend you don't know what I'm talking about, how you've kept me under your thumb."

Wolf just stared at his son.

"I'm talking about how I was never good enough, never smart enough to measure up to you, or at least that's how you had me see it."

"That's not true."

"Yes, it is. Because that's what you yourself believed. And still do."

"Stop acting like a boy. You're making a fool of yourself."

"Because I question you, because I disagree with

you, I'm a boy? Don't you see how all my life I wanted to please you? And how all my life you kept me down, begging for whatever bits of approval and recognition I could get out of you? I was your good little boy as long as I did exactly what you said."

Wolf tried to say something, but Daniel wouldn't let him. Now the words came rushing out without control. "And what really gets me about all this is that I went along with it. I did everything you wanted, always looking for that pat on the head and the signal that you thought me a worthy son, good enough to share with what you had built."

"I've had enough of this, Daniel, son or no son. You can get out. I don't want to see you here again. You're fired."

"Fired? You can't fire me! I'm part owner. This is my factory too. You can't fire me any more than I can fire you, old man!"

Suddenly Daniel felt Wolf's hand across his face. At that instant like a reflex, his fist was drawn back and he was ready to spring. He poised, on the brink of letting go completely. From some place far away in his mind, he realized he was on the verge of hitting his father, and then, in what seemed like an agonizingly long time, he saw his fist go past his head and smash into his father's jaw.

Wolf staggered backward with the force of the blow and landed against the wall. In his eyes was a look that Daniel had never seen there before.

But Daniel didn't have time to dwell on it. He grabbed his jacket and was out of the room without another word. He charged down the stairs and rushed out to the street where he gulped in huge drafts of fresh air. He realized his mind was surprisingly clear, and then suddenly he knew what he wanted to do.

He had three stops to make. Two he was sure of, the third he wasn't. He walked briskly down Broadway in the direction of Wall Street. He was pleased to see Andrew Markingham was in his office, and he spent the next half hour with him, explaining what he had in mind. From there he took the ferry to Brooklyn, and then headed straight for his house.

He noticed the minute he got there that Bluma wasn't home. That was fine with him. He had nothing more to say to her anyway. He went upstairs, grabbed a suitcase and began to fill it with clothes. Then he slammed it shut and went back down the stairs. He slammed the front door behind him and continued on to the third thing he intended to accomplish.

Wolf sat alone in his office for a long while after Daniel left. He could hear the constant hum of the machines outside his door and through the window he could see the workers at their jobs. All appeared deeply absorbed in what they were doing. No one looked his way. No one came in to talk to him. It was if they all sensed what must have finally been said between father and son and they wanted no more involvement in it than they already had.

So Wolf was left by himself to think as hour after hour slipped by. When his private telephone rang, he answered it automatically, his response dazed and unthinking. "Mr. Luminov," said a smooth male voice on the other end, "I'm calling from the law firm of Markingham and Associates on behalf of your son Daniel Luminov."

"Yes?" said Wolf, becoming alert at the mention of Daniel's name.

"We would like to advise you, Mr. Luminov, of your son's wishes to transfer his share of MW Enterprises to Local 518 of the International Ladies Garment Workers Union. Ten per cent of the net earnings from the factory and the mill will henceforth be payable to the local chapter, which is, as I'm sure you are aware, located on the premises of MW Enterprises."

"That's outrageous!" Wolf yelled into the telephone. "I'll fight you every step of the way!"

"It is our client's instruction, Mr. Luminov, that

should you wish to do that, we will instead bring suit against you personally. On his behalf, we will sue you for the fifty per cent of the business that is our client's rightful share by virtue of your oral contract, a contract which, you will recall, has been renewed and witnessed many times over the past twenty-six years."

"What is this?" Wolf shouted. "You can't blackmail me like this!"

The voice on the other end of the line remained calm. "No one has even suggested such a thing, Mr. Luminov. What we are talking about is the law."

"I don't believe one bit of this!" Wolf hollered. "Show it to me in writing."

"That will be our pleasure, Mr. Luminov. Henceforth, you will hear from us by mail." As Andrew Markingham hung up the phone, he couldn't help but feel a certain satisfaction in having carried out Daniel's feverishly spelled out wishes.

The rest of the afternoon slipped away as Wolf still sat rooted to his chair. The hands of the clock on the far wall moved from five o'clock to six, to seven and finally eight. The factory was now empty. Finally he stood up and opened the door to his office. Before him were arrayed the rows and rows of machines, with stacks of garment pieces piled next to each one, waiting to be sewn. He walked through the empty factory from floor to floor, his footsteps the only sound. He surveyed his kingdom, all that he had built up from nothing since he had arrived on these shores almost thirty years ago. What had it all been for, he asked himself, if he had now lost the son for whom it was all meant?

He suddenly snatched up one of the basting stools and hurled it into the wall. "Daniel!" he yelled.

But the only response was the sound of his own labored breathing. "Daniel!" he called again, even though he knew it was no use. He leaned his head against the wall, where the plaster was now cracked and crumbling from the impact of the stool.

He was still leaning that way against the wall when the private telephone in his office began to ring again.

His voice was tentative as he hoped it might be Daniel. "Hello?"

"Luminov?" The angry voice on the other end blasted in his ear.

His response was equally harsh. "Yeah? Who is this?"

"Put Daniel Luminov on the phone."

"Anything you have to say to my son, you can say to me."

"Who the hell is this?"

"This is Wolf Luminov. You've got two seconds to improve your tone and tell me what you want or I'm going to hang up."

"Wolf, did you say?" The voice on the other end deepened in venom. "Wolf?"

"That's right. Who the hell are you?"

The voice paused, then it came on stronger than ever. "So you're behind this! I should have known all along, only I didn't recognize your last name. Probably never thought it was worth remembering. But I'd never forget your first name because it describes the conniving animal you are. What have you two done with my daughter Alma?"

The phone almost felt alive in Wolf's hand. "Detweiler? Is that who this is?" He gripped it tightly and started to laugh. "Detweiler, ey? So we meet again, after all these years."

"Listen, Luminov. Your son's got my daughter and I want her back. I know you're behind all this. You're still looking for some way to steal a little respectability for yourself, aren't you? Still aspiring to things beyond your station."

"Knock it off, Detweiler. I don't have your daughter. I never wanted anything of yours, anything. And I'm not responsible for my son. He's his own man." As Wolf said the word man, the irony of the situation didn't escape him. "And I have no idea where he is this minute or who he's with. Nor do I care. So I guess you'll just have to put your bloodhounds on them."

"You think this is funny, don't you, Luminov? But I can promise you, you won't think it so funny in the morning, in more ways than one. If you don't know where your son is, then that means you'll probably never see him again."

"What the hell you doing? Threatening me?"

"Look, Luminov. If you don't know where that kid of yours is this very minute, then it's already too late."

"What the hell are you talking about, Detweiler?"

"That means they're already on their way to Palestine, you bastard. And I don't believe for one minute that you don't already know all of this."

Wolf slammed down the telephone.

Palestine? His Daniel? And with Detweiler's kid? It couldn't be. He felt the blood drain from his face. Palestine, that was another land, weeks away by boat, maybe more. Palestine, wasn't that what Daniel had once said Alma was mixed up in? All this business of fighting for a homeland, as if she didn't have one here. He slumped back in his chair. This time he feared he'd lost Daniel for good.

Marya came home early that afternoon, one of the few times in the more than thirteen years she had been operating the shop. She still hadn't gotten around to telling Wolf about Andrew, and she had decided that tonight should be the night. When Wolf hadn't come home for dinner by seven o'clock, she was annoyed. She ate a solitary meal, then sent Mrs. Sanders home. It was almost nine o'clock when she finally heard Wolf's heavy footsteps on the stoop.

The moment he came through the door she could see that something was terribly wrong. In spite of herself, she felt concerned. There was, after all, no call to be unkind to him. "Zavel? Are you okay? You look awful. Are you coming down with something?"

Wolf shook his head. He started to say something but no words came out.

"Zavel, what is it?" she insisted.

A knock at the door stopped Wolf from having to say anything.

"I'll get it," Marya said.

"No, let me," Wolf said on an impulse and sprung up. He opened the front door, and suddenly the room filled up with three rough looking men. They were dressed in long black coats and felt hats. Two of them were stockily built with round, puffy faces, which bore the signs of recent scars. The third was taller and rawer looking with sharp, angular features, and wide, thin lips. "This is from an old friend of yours in the rag business," snarled the tallest one and let loose with an uppercut to Wolf's jaw.

Marya screamed and ran at them.

"Get out of here, lady, or you'll get hurt," one of the others growled. "This is just between us and the gentleman here." He stuck his arm out, and when Marya kept coming, he flung her across the room, where she stumbled and fell to the floor.

Wolf had staggered backward into the arms of the other thug. He spun Wolf around and hit him from the other side, propelling him back to the first guy.

Marya was on her feet at once and rushing at the attackers again. "Zavel!" she screamed. But her scream was cut short by the same man grabbing at her. He yanked her arm and pinned it behind her back. "Now do what I said, lady, and stay out of this." He shoved her down to the sofa and held her there while his two friends took turns punching Wolf.

Marya was forced to watch as the three of them took their time in working him over. Then when Wolf was covered with blood and looked as if he might be dead, they pushed him to the floor and left, leaving the front door open behind them.

The minute they were gone, Marya was on her feet and at Wolf's side. His eyes were closed, and as she touched his skin, it felt damp. "Zavel," she sobbed, then looked around wildly for the telephone. She immediately began to call the police, although what came later was to her all a blur.

Two months later Wolf was still in the hospital. He had damage to his kidneys, three broken ribs, a severe concussion and massive bruises and cuts. Every afternoon Marya dropped everything at the shop and spent the hours with Wolf. She hadn't spoken to Andrew since the night after the attack, when she had hastily told him over the phone that Wolf had had an accident and that she had to be with him. His voice had been distant but polite as he had told her he understood about family emergencies, but she could tell from the way he said it that this time he didn't. She knew it hurt him that she was avoiding him, but she felt compelled to be at the hospital with Wolf.

"Do you realize this is the most we've been together since the last time you were sick?" Marya pointed out one afternoon as she sat in the chair she had drawn up next to the hospital bed. In the last few days Wolf had looked better than ever. He had regained almost all the weight he had lost after the attack and most of the bruises and cuts had healed. As she looked Wolf up and down, she was conscious of him gazing back at her.

As if it had taken a few more seconds for her words to catch up with him, he said slowly, "You mean since I was in that God-awful bed at Lubish's?"

"Yes. That's how long it has been."

During the time Wolf had been in the hospital, they had started to talk again. It was as if they were trying to make up for all the years of silence between them. They had each spoken of their work, and Marya had even been able to tell Wolf about some of the funny things that had happened with her clients over the years. They talked about Jacob and Elke a great deal, and Marya revealed to him how hard she had found it to accept what Elke had done to her hair. The only thing they hadn't been able to talk about was Daniel. Neither of them had heard a word from him and each was careful not to bring his name up. Now they felt an ease with each other they hadn't experienced for over two decades.

Wolf reached his hand out toward her and he was pleased to see she took it. "I know it's not been easy on you giving up the time at your shop like this."

She smiled at him. "It's doing all right without me. And besides, you're more important to me. . . ." She paused.

He took up her thought. "I know. You were going to add 'right now.' "

She shook her head and looked serious. "No, Zavel, I wasn't. I wasn't thinking that at all. In fact, something quite the opposite."

He looked at her for a few moments and then tossed the bedsheet back and stood up.

Marya was alarmed at the suddenness of his move. "Zavel? What's wrong? What are you doing?"

"Get my things, Marya. I'm ready to go home."

His face was determined, but she felt she had to caution him. "The doctor says you need another week to recuperate."

"I can do it at home just as well as I can here. Besides, I'm much tougher than these doctors realize."

Later that evening, as Marya put away the few clothes Wolf had taken to the hospital, she was again aware of him watching her from the bed where he was lounging against the pillows. She felt a little nervous at the way he had been looking at her. She searched for something light to say. "It's not so bad having you around again, you know. You're not bad company when you're flat on your back."

"You're not so bad when you're flat on yours, either," he snapped back.

They both laughed.

"Come here, Marya." He held out his arms to her.

Marya approached the bed shyly. Why was it, she wondered, that she felt like an innocent girl again when Wolf looked at her this way, just as she had twenty-seven years ago?

He drew her down next to him and looked into her eyes.

She was aware of his hand still holding hers. She tried to fight the feelings that were building in her.

Before she realized it, he was pulling her mouth toward his, and in his eyes was the look she had not seen in a long time. As he kissed her, she felt a great warmth brush over her and she knew she could no longer fight the feelings that were sweeping her along.

"Marya," he murmured. "You don't know how many times I lay there next to you at night and wanted you. I wanted you so badly it made me ache. I couldn't bear it that you didn't want me."

"But I did want you, Wolf. I always wanted you. I thought that you didn't want me any longer, that you had stopped loving me."

He began to pull the pins from her hair until it fell, heavy and still rich with its red-brown color, over her shoulders and down her breasts. He buried his face against her as he said, "I never stopped loving you, Marya. I tried when I thought you no longer loved me. But I never could."

And then they lost themselves in each other and made love as passionately and wildly as they had when they were first married and their long love affair was just beginning.

Over the next few months Wolf and Marya drew even closer to each other, until they were completely in love again. Although he was well, Wolf delayed going back to the factory, leaving it in the hands of Sol. Marya herself went to her shop infrequently.

They held hands like teenagers and did everything

together. They went for long walks along the river, explored the rough terrain to the north of the island and even went bicycling one time, although that had not gone too well for Wolf, and Marya laughed until her sides ached. Marya took over the shopping from Mrs. Sanders, and Wolf insisted on going with her. Together they would have lengthy and intense discussions over matters no more momentous than which were the best tomatoes and whether it would be better to have carp or cod for the evening's supper.

One night, after an idyllic afternoon spent gliding together in the gondolas in Central Park, Marya cleared her throat to indicate to Wolf she wanted to make an announcement.

"Zavel, I don't want you to be the last to know, so there's something I think I should tell you."

Wolf smiled. "You seem so serious. Is it that you've decided that I'm too hopeless ever to learn to ride a bicycle?"

Marya laughed. "Well yes, it is hopeless between you and the bicycle. But that's not it. What I have to say falls into a different category of . . . of pleasure. You see," she hesitated just a moment, then plunged ahead blindly, thinking she would just have to be brave enough to accept his reaction, whatever it might be.

"You see, I'm going to have a baby."

PART III

"Trumpet the new moon"

1923-1935

Chapter 25

No sound had come from Sadie's bedroom for so long that Elke decided to unlock the door and see what Sadie was doing in there. Sadie at fifteen was no longer a child. In any case, she took the long key from the pocket of her dress and inserted it into the keyhole. As the lock clicked, she softly called Sadie's name. When there was no response, she said to herself that the girl was sulking, and pushed the door open.

The first thing she noticed was how cold the bedroom was and then she saw the curtain blowing in the breeze that was coming through the open window. "Sadie?" she called again. She knew Sadie was hiding under the bed or in the armoire and was doing this just to upset her. But Elke soon discovered Sadie was not in either of those places, and in fact she wasn't in the room at all. Within a matter of seconds it occurred to her that Sadie might have crawled out the second-story window of her bedroom and, using the sheet off her bed, lowered herself to the ground.

She tried not to panic as she thought about where Sadie could be now or how long she had been gone. Instead she went to the telephone. As she waited for the operator to make the connection, she leaned her head against the doorjamb and tried to be strong the way she knew her mother would be. She didn't need another one of Sadie's tricks just now. Her nerves were already strained from the note she had received from David Sheffield earlier that afternoon. This one had promptly been consigned to the flames, just as the other three had been. Still, it was harder each time, and Elke had begun asking herself if perhaps it would be better to meet with him just the one time he pleaded so that she could put a stop to these intrusions on her peace of mind for good.

She heard a click as the receiver on the other end was picked up, and she struggled to keep her voice calm. "Hello, Mama?"

In spite of Elke's efforts, Marya immediately detected the strain in her daughter's voice. "What is it, Elke?"

"It's Sadie again. She's gone," Elke burst out in spite of her resolve.

Marya's grip on the phone tightened. "Gone? What do you mean, gone?"

"She's not in the house. I had to lock her in her bedroom again after she started another fight with Adam and Zosa." Now, against her wishes, her voice started to tremble. "Mama, what am I going to do with her? She's too much for me. Why can't she be more like Adam and Zosa? Where did I go wrong with this one?"

"There's probably nothing wrong with what you have done, Elke. She's a bit high-spirited and mischievous, that's all. And she's probably just out roaming the neighborhood. When she gets tired, she'll be home. You'll see."

Elke wasn't reassured. "If she's like this now, I shudder to think what she'll be like by the time she's eighteen. She seems to be getting worse. I told you what she did last week, didn't I? She and her girlfriend Isabel had been in her room for some time. I could hear them giggling and talking and didn't think anything of it. When they finally came out and walked by me, I was nearly struck down by the fumes coming from them. They were out the door before I could realize that they had drunk a bottle of *Shabbas* wine between them. And you tell me she's nothing more than just a little mischievous! I didn't have the courage to tell Jake. You know how strict he is. He would have confined her to the house for three months. And now he's going to be home any minute and find her gone."

"Elke, you mustn't worry. I tell you, she'll show up within the hour."

Marya had no sooner hung up the phone than she heard a knock at the door. When she opened it, to her amazement she saw her granddaughter standing there. "Sadie!"

Sadie did not wait for Marya to say anything more. She opened the screen door and let herself in. For several silent moments, she and Marya stood facing each other in the hallway. Marya stared into a pair of black, intense eyes that reminded her so much of Wolf. Sadie was a vivacious girl, who was just now starting to blossom. She was on her way to being tall, like her mother, and had the same thick mane of red hair that Marya had, only hers had a slight wave to it, a trait from her father's side of the family. She had always been full of energy and enthusiasm, and in the last couple years that natural exuberance had started to take a turn toward wildness. But no matter how animated and extravagant Sadie became, Marya could always see the vulnerable little girl lurking just below the surface.

"Well?" Marya now said, breaking the silence, her hands on her hips expectantly.

"Bubbe!" cried Sadie and threw her arms around Marya.

Marya was not to be so easily won over. "Your mother is frantic over where you are. The first thing is to call her."

Tears sprung to Sadie's eyes. "Oh, please. Don't

do that. Let me stay here with you. I can't bear to go back there." She tightened her arms around Marya.

Marya had not been prepared for such a passionate response. As Sadie continued to hold her tightly, she absently began to stroke her long hair. "What is it, Sadie? How can you not want to go back to your home and your family that loves you?"

"But that's just it! They don't love me. They don't. I can tell."

Marya held Sadie a little distance away from her so she could engage her eyes. "That's not true, Sadie. You know that."

Sadie shook her head insistently and didn't blink. "It is true. You don't know. You don't have to live there. Please, *Bubbe,* let me stay here with you and *Zeyde* and Michael."

"Come into the drawing room with me, Sadie, and we'll talk about this some more."

As Sadie walked ahead of her down the hallway, Marya had a chance to see the way she was dressed. Sadie was sporting a lime green wool sweater-skirt with a lowered waistline and a hemline which, to what would have been the consternation of Jacob and Elke, dropped only a little past her knees. She obviously had decided a foundation garment was a useless encumbrance as the jiggling of her unfettered breasts demonstrated. On her very visible legs were blond stockings which she wore with a pair of brown leather ghillies.

Marya wanted to ask how Sadie had gotten out of the house dressed in that fashion, but she already knew—she had escaped out the window and Elke probably didn't have the faintest idea of the scandalous way in which her daughter was clad.

As they sat facing each other, Marya renewed her questioning. "Now what's this nonsense about not wanting to go home?"

"I don't know how to explain it, *Bubbe.* It's just a feeling I get when I'm there. I never feel like I'm important to anybody at home. I feel like I could disappear from right under their eyes and they wouldn't even notice."

"Well, you have disappeared, and they have noticed. Your mother is frantic over your whereabouts and has already called me. So you see, you're quite wrong about their not being aware of you. In fact, right now, I'd say they're all too aware of you."

Sadie's eyes grew darker and she seemed to sink back inside herself. "That's not what I'm talking about. It's . . . it's just so hard for me to put it in words. It's just something I know. Don't you ever just know things sometimes that you can't explain?"

Marya was about to say something when she heard the back door open. She knew Wolf had come home and she had to make a quick decision. "Here's what we're going to do. I'm going to call your mother first." She put up her hand to still Sadie when she saw her start to protest. "I will tell her you'll be spending the night here."

Relief spread across Sadie's face. "Oh, thank you, thank you. I knew you'd understand!"

As Marya spoke to her daughter a few minutes later, she could hear a sigh of relief from Elke, calmed to know where Sadie was.

"I swear, you're the only one who can manage her," Elke said with a trace of forlornness. "You and Papa."

"I'm not sure that's true," Marya said, but she suspected it was.

"Sometimes I think Sadie would be better off if she just went to live with you for a while."

"You're just saying that because you're upset," Marya soothed. She had to hang up then because Wolf had come into the room, and that meant any minute their son Michael would come running in too, and she wanted to be able to explain Sadie's unexpected visit.

The second Marya put down the phone, Michael came dashing into the room just as she'd expected and hurled himself first at his father, then at Sadie, overjoyed to see two of the people he loved the most in the same place together.

At ten years old, Michael was already tall for his age, although still with a boy's slim shoulders and hips. From Wolf he had inherited a broad face with a strong, straight nose, and from Marya his deep green eyes, fringed with lashes thick enough to make any woman envious. He was an outgoing child, easily given to laughter and to mischief, which Marya attributed to the more relaxed and permissive way in which she and Wolf had raised this child. Born in their middle years, he had always been a symbol to them of the renewed love that had flamed out between them after Wolf's accident, and Marya found she was able to love him with an abandon and openness that she hadn't been able to permit herself with Daniel.

Wolf was resting his arm on Michael's shoulder as they both talked to Sadie, and as Marya saw father and son standing there that way, obviously so much at ease with each other, she could not help but contrast their relationship with that of Wolf and Daniel. Neither she nor Wolf spoke of Daniel anymore, although Marya continued to receive a brief note from him each year, which he sent to her shop. He and Alma were living on a kibbutz on the south Judean plain, and were doing well.

Daniel had learned that even before he had fled to Palestine with Alma, Bluma had been investigating the possibility of a divorce. When she had gone through with it after his departure, he and Alma had quietly married on the kibbutz. Later that year they had been blessed with a son, Joshua, and now Daniel said he was the happiest he had ever been in his life. When Marya had told Wolf of Daniel's marriage to Alma and of their son, she had seen an expression cross his face that she had been unable to interpret. She hadn't known whether it was relief, pride, or hurt, but she knew the wound was still too raw for her to question him about it, and she returned to her practice of not discussing Daniel. But it was strange and painful for her to think she had a ten-year-old grandson, the same age as their son Michael, whom she had never seen. She knew Wolf must have had similar thoughts, but he shared them with no one.

As she looked at him now, standing there with his son and granddaughter, she felt an upsurge of pride. At fifty-six, he still stood tall and imposing, and had virtually the same robust stamina and energy he'd had almost forty years before. His black hair was laced with strands of white, which if anything made it look fuller and just as vigorous as ever. The main change the years had brought him was a certain softening in his expression, so that more often now he appeared happy and content and less fiercely in control, although that control was still very much a part of him, and his black eyes still shone fiercely, especially when he was angry. As Marya finally pulled her gaze away from her husband and son, she caught Sadie looking at her with a smile on her lips.

"*Bubbe*, you must help me," she said, laughing. "They're ganging up on me."

Marya was caught up in the mood of their teasing. "I'm sure whatever it is, Sadie, you can hold your own."

Michael took Sadie by the arm. "Come with me to my room. I want you to see my mahjong set."

"And what if I don't want to?" she retorted, although she was dying to learn how to play this ancient Chinese game that the whole country had developed a passion for.

Michael made his voice mock stern. "You have to. I'm your uncle, even if you are older than me, and you have to do what I say. All your life."

Sadie burst out laughing and allowed him to lead her from the room. Wolf watched them go, shaking his head, and Marya could see the delight on his face. "If Elke and Jacob ever don't want that child, we can always take her," he joked.

His words inadvertently brought to Marya's mind Elke's beleaguered plea earlier that afternoon. When Elke had first uttered it, Marya had not taken her seriously. But now, she was starting to think perhaps it wasn't such a far-fetched idea after all.

"You might want to think seriously about that, Zavel. Elke tells me we're the only ones Sadie seems to be able to get along with at all. Elke locked her in her bedroom today and—"

"She shouldn't be locking her up like a prisoner. I doubt Sadie could have done anything so bad as to warrant that."

"She was fighting with Adam Dov and Zosa again."

Wolf's brow furrowed as Marya mentioned his two oldest grandchildren. "I'd probably have fought with those two also if I were in her place."

"Well, they're getting kind of old for that. Furthermore, she's here visiting us today by virtue of climbing out of her second-story bedroom window after Elke locked her in." His expression changed. Her words appeared to be getting through to him. "So now I'm beginning to think there might be something to what Elke is suggesting," she continued. "It might not hurt for Sadie to spend a few months here with us. It might give her a chance to calm down some." She waited to see what Wolf's reaction would be.

He continued to stir his tea for a while before he spoke. "I think we should wait to see what happens. Perhaps she'll settle down after this escapade."

"Perhaps," Marya sighed. As she and Wolf sat across from each other, she continued to think about Sadie and the strange times they were all living in. The country had changed so much since she had arrived over thirty-five years ago and women had changed most of all: slight wonder Sadie baffled them all with her modern ways.

But then, neither she nor Wolf was the same person who had landed at Castle Garden with every world-

ly possession in a pack. So much had occurred that
they could never have foreseen. And it seemed that the
changes were coming even faster now. Marya wondered, did it just seem like they were coming faster because she was getting older? She thought of how much
had changed in their own lives just the last ten years,
since that horrible night when Daniel and Alma had
run away together and Wolf had been beset by Detweiler's thugs. And like all the significant changes in
her life, there was bad mixed with good. Her and
Wolf's refound love and its unexpected result, Michael,
was of course obviously the best thing. Neither of them
could have anticipated the joy brought by this child
who came so late into their lives.

Marya also treasured the increased contact she
and Wolf had in their work. And in a sense, it was because of that chatty little errand girl straight out of
London she had hired for her shop during the period
when she was spending so much time at the hospital,
and had to bring in extra help for her shop manager.

She recalled how Jane, the new girl, a plump
young woman with carrot-red curls and flawless white
skin, piped up one day when Marya happened to return there from the hospital for a few hours of work.
"Pardon me, mum, but if I appear to be snooping
around all the time, it's because you have so many new-
fangled gadgets in your dressmaking shops here and
lots of different ways of doing things. Of course, in
London I wasn't in a fancy designing shop like this
one. I was slaving in a bloody—er, pardon my language, mum—I was working in a frightful factory."

"How different could things be from one shop to
another?" Marya had asked. "It seems to me the only
difference is in the design."

"Well, mum. Here you take such pains to get the
dress to fit. I know of course that's why those ladies
that can afford it prefer to get their clothes from a
dressmaker rather than a factory. Those factory-made
ones never fit right. They're always too tight in the bust

and the hips, and then sometimes they're too snug in one place and too loose elsewhere, so you feel like a sausage below and a runny pudding on the top. It's fine if you're built in one of the three sizes they make the dresses in, but how many woman are?"

Marya asked the girl if she was exaggerating.

"As bad as it is now, my mum tells me it was worse before the war. Then the only inexpensive dresses came from home workshops and they were made just in one size. So at least the factories have improved things a wee bit. You might say the odds of getting a dress to fit you right are better."

The girl's observations had stuck in Marya's mind the rest of the day. She had heard that British ready-to-wear left much to be desired, but she hadn't realized that there were only three sizes and for a time only one. And she also was curious about just how adequate the sizing of American manufacturers was. She resolved to take up the question with Wolf that evening.

What she learned astounded her. "You mean," she said to Wolf after he explained the system used at MW Enterprises, "that's how sizing is handled? Obviously women don't come in just three standard sizes, and I think it's more realistic that you have at least five sizes, but I'm wondering if that's enough."

While Wolf hadn't shown a great deal of interest in the issue of sizing, seemingly content with the five sizes of each design that MW Enterprises was already producing, Marya had continued to be fascinated by the matter of whether the sizing at Wolf's factory was in fact taking into account how women were shaped. A few days later she had appeared unannounced at the door of Wolf's office, a string of women trailing behind her.

She enjoyed Wolf's astonishment when the fifteen women paraded into his office and circled around his desk. Wolf kept glancing from the women to Marya, back to the women and then back to Marya. He immediately noticed that each woman was wearing an MW dress.

"What's going on here, Marya? Why are you giving me a fashion show of my own line? I'm well enough familiar with it already."

"Don't you see?" she'd replied. "Look at the way these dresses fit. These are typical women with typical bodies." She had hired them off the street that morning, yanking them away from their shopping and morning errands. Now she gently propelled one of the women to the fore and slowly turned her around. The woman was wearing a poplin frock with sailor collar and cuffs and a hemline slightly above the ankles.

"This dress fits this woman, because she happens to be the only woman in the room who has the standard proportions of that size." She pulled two other women out of the group. "Now look what happens when you make the dress a size larger and a size smaller." She pointed to the way the dresses fit poorly at the waistline and bust. "Obviously what your pattern makers did is add an inch all the way around when they wanted to increase the dress by one size and subtract an inch all the way around when they wanted to make the dress in a smaller size." She then steered two more women to the front. One was a large woman and the other petite, and they were wearing the same style of dress, which fit neither of them well. "It's clear that the sizers are continuing to apply the same principle throughout the sizes, and so when we get to the far ends—the quite large woman and the quite small woman—the problem is twice as bad. The difficulty here is that women don't grow in convenient and neatly proportioned inches at all the critical points of fit. Women just aren't made that way."

Marya's live demonstration in his office got through to Wolf. As he appraised the dresses on the women encircling him, he had to admit that Marya had a point.

"But the situation's no better with any other manufacturer," he countered, "and to change our sizing methods would be costly."

"In the long run it will be even more costly not to," Marya argued. "Those women who went to work during the war are still in the work force. Many of them have discovered careers and will never return to the home. Others want to work in an office just for the novelty of it or the extra money. These women aren't going to have the time to spend getting fittings from dressmakers, or the money."

When he still looked skeptical, she argued passionately. "I can see it coming, Zavel."

He interrupted. "Pictures again?"

"Call it what you will, but those women are going to want easy, simple clothes to wear to work. Fewer women want to wear blouses and skirts, and the days of elaborate hand-sewn gowns are dying. Everyone wants light, easy-to-wear dresses—even the rich woman, unless it's for a fancy ball. This is the time when factory-made clothes can really sell—if you make them appealing and flattering. By flattering I mean they fit."

"Well, there's only one way I see this can be done," Wolf said suddenly. "And that's if you do it."

"*Me?*"

"You're the one who knows about sizing and fitting, after all. So why not you? Who better?" When Marya still didn't say anything, he added, "It seems to me in this fiery speech you just made about the future, you argued yourself right into a new business. If there's a change coming for me, there's certainly a change ahead for you too. What I'm proposing, Marya, is that now may be the time to join forces, to put our two operations together under one roof."

Marya had not been able to say yes or no at that particular moment, so stunned was she by the suggestion. But the more she thought about it, the sounder the idea appeared. She would be able to apply to the ready-to-wear line what she knew about sizing and detailing. And she would still have an opportunity to create new designs. At the same time, she also had to ask herself whether it would be a good move to give up her shop. If something should happen to Wolf, would she be able to carry on the joint business alone?

"Zavel, it's now my turn to make a proposal," she said a few days later.

They were sitting across from each other in the living room of their uptown home that they'd lived in for so many years. Wolf knew that she was talking about the business, and that the pros and cons of the merger must have been spinning in her head constantly the last few days. But if he had learned anything from these years with Marya, it was that she did not make her decisions quickly or impulsively the way he did, and that she always gave plenty of time to her conclusions. Once she did though, they were solid. "Yes?" he prompted.

"I think the idea of combining our two businesses is a good one. But there are some other changes, I think, that should go along with it. For one thing, if we're going to create a dress that really is ahead of its time, superior to those put out by the other manufacturers, then it seems to me it'd be smart to capitalize on our uniqueness."

"What do you have in mind?"

"Right now MW Enterprises is manufacturing the dresses and they're then bought up by a salesman who puts his own label in the dress and sells it to the shops and department stores. But why not put our own label in the dresses? If we designed an MW label and stitched it into each dress, and then hired our own salesmen to place those dresses in the stores, people would come to identify those well-fitting dresses with us. Believe me, once a woman begins to realize that she can count on a certain manufacturer for a good fit, she's going to start looking for that name in the stores. Right now there's no system to it, with salesmen buying garments from whichever manufacturer gives them the best price. A particular label offers no guarantee of consistency or quality. We'd be the first to do that, and that would give us a big advantage."

She paused, then added, "I wouldn't be surprised if the majority of the smaller dress stores find most of their time is being taken with doing alterations. They'll catch on fast that the line with the MW label is sized so that it needs less altering. If we have our salesmen publicize this advantage, those shops will want to buy our lines in larger quantity. They'll quickly be able to see how much money they'll save if they don't have to do so many alterations."

Wolf was looking at her with respect. "So far I like this proposal. What next?"

She took a deep breath. "I've been giving this some thought. What I think we ought to consider is expanding our production capacity to include an export line to Great Britain. I think there's a terrific market there just waiting to be tapped. As long as we're going to rethink our business, I think we've got to consider reaching the best markets we can."

Marya and Wolf went ahead with all of Marya's suggestions. They decided rght away that the amount of production they were now talking about required a bigger factory, and one modernized with the latest equipment. Wolf found a location on Seventh Avenue, not too far from Marya's present shop, and half again as large as their old place on Broadway. Then Marya threw herself into revamping MW's sizing techniques, introducing a systematic and detailed procedure. Wolf supervised the purchase and installation of power-operated sewing and cutting machines, and special machines for specific tasks such as hem-stitching, overlocking, button-sewing and felling. "It's time to go completely modern," he said.

The merger turned out to be the best thing that could have happened to both MW Enterprises, which had increased production to over eight thousand garments a week, and their marriage. The chief benefit was that they had more time at home with Michael. Then, as their export sales soared, they decided to leave their neighborhood, which was no longer a quiet village but had grown noisy and congested in the last few years. As they waited for the moving vans that were to take them to their fashionable new home on West End Avenue, Marya commented to Wolf, "Do you realize what typical New Yorkers we've become? The first of every October the streets of this city are filled with people moving. It's like a fever."

"That's a good sign," Wolf observed. "It shows the city's prospering and people are moving up."

Marya felt that this boom they were all experiencing had to end somewhere, but as far as she could see, no one else shared her view. The American spirit wanted everything to get forever bigger and better. Marya wasn't so sure.

Those cautious thoughts returned to Marya. The whole country was swept with every kind of mania, from fanaticism over sports, to dance marathons, flagpole sitting and other kinds of record-setting attempts, to crazes for celebrities and scandals, and anything sensational or titillating, be it axe murderers, spies or love triangles. It all seemed a little out of control. No wonder Sadie was the same way. "She's just an all-American girl," Marya said out loud as she came out of her reverie. "That's all."

Chapter 26

That night, as Sadie lay in the bed that had belonged to her mother when she was still a girl, she thought about this family into which she had been born. Maybe if she had been born first or second instead of third, things would have been different, she said to herself. Maybe then she would have been closer to Adam Dov or to Zosa, and it would have been one of them who was closed out.

She wondered if her mother cared about such things at all. Mostly what seemed to be important to her was keeping everything quiet and peaceful. Her mother hated arguments or even heated discussions and always cautioned her that she was behaving like "a savage" whenever she raised her voice, which seemed to be happening more and more lately, even though she honestly tried to stop it. All her mother seemed to want to do was keep a nice house for her father and have everything perfect and in order for him when he came home at night. Her father had the appearance of a big teddy bear, but his temperament was, in Sadie's mind, more like that of a grizzly bear. His word was law and his law was a strict one. She knew he must love her—fathers always loved their daughters, didn't they? But somehow she never felt it the way she wanted to.

She thought of the list she had made about a week ago of all the things she liked about her life and all the things she didn't like.

In the "Don't like" column, she had:
my brother and sister (too self-centered)
Shabbas dinner prayers (too predictable)
services at the temple (too long)
Father's job (takes too much time)
long skirts and long hair (old-fashioned)
having to stay in the house so much (boring)

In her column of "Like" were listed:
Mother's cooking (especially *kishke*)
Zeyde and *Bubbe*
Zeyde's factory (fun!!)
Uncle Michael (even though he's five years younger)
the new clothes I made myself (even though I'm not allowed to wear them)
the radio I got from *Zeyde* last Chanukah
Sunday drives in *Zeyde*'s Model T
stories like *The Primitive Lover* and *Indolent Kisses*
Rudolph Valentino in "The Sheik of Araby"

After she'd composed her list, she'd finally decided maybe it was a good sign she had more likes than dislikes in her life. But that was before her fight with Zosa.

Earlier that day she came into the living room just as Adam Dov, who was sitting on the sofa, was laughing out loud at the book he was reading. It seemed that Adam Dov and Zosa were always reading books. And it annoyed Sadie that day because her mother said in front of one of her friends, "Oh, Adam Dov and Zosa are just like me, always reading." Sadie liked to read too, but she preferred magazines, like *True Story, Life* and sometimes *The Saturday Evening Post*. Yet it seemed that everyone in their home scorned magazines as not being as important or as good as books.

When Sadie heard Adam Dov laughing out loud like that as he sat there alone, she gave in to an impulse to go sit next to him and see if she could find out what was so funny. To her surprise and delight, he responded to her question readily, and turned to explain the passage he'd been reading. When Sadie didn't immediately see the humor of it, he seized his book and began to read aloud to her. As he read, she began to laugh, and the more she laughed, the more he laughed, until they could barely hear what he was saying because he was laughing so hard. Sadie thought how strange and wonderful it was to be sharing something with Adam Dov.

They were laughing like that when Zosa appeared in the doorway, her dark eyes flashing. Everyone thought Zosa looked like a Gypsy, with her tangle of wild dark curls and dark eyes. Their mother had once even teased their father in front of them that he must have brought some Gypsy blood with him from Hungary that he had never told her about. When Zosa was angry, she looked more than ever like a wild-eyed woman, and her nostrils flared from the intensity of her emotion.

"What are you doing?" she hissed, looking at Sadie. Even though Zosa was just a year older than Sadie, she took it upon herself to order Sadie about whenever she could and now she saw an opportunity. "You leave Adam Dov alone when he's reading! He doesn't want you pestering him."

Sadie's response was shriller than she intended it to be. "I wasn't pestering him. Does it look like I'm pestering him? Since when does laughing look like pestering?" She looked to her brother for confirmation, but he stood up and was on his way out the door, clearly not wanting any part of the trouble he saw coming. As Sadie watched him go, she felt betrayed. She called after him. "Adam Dov, tell her. Tell her we were just having fun. And besides, it's none of her business!" But Adam Dov just walked away without even looking back.

Zosa had taken that as confirmation of her statement. "You see, he's trying to get away from you. He can't stand the way you're hanging on him."

Sadie's mouth flew open and she was on her feet. "Hanging on him? Me? You're the one who's always glued to his side! You're the one who's pestering him!"

Zosa flew at her and slapped her across the face. "How dare you talk to me like that!" she fumed and turned to leave the room, but not before Sadie had slapped her back. That stopped Zosa completely, and the two sisters had stared at each other venomously. Then it was Sadie who flounced from the room first, leaving Zosa speechless.

Afterward, Sadie was upset with herself. She and Zosa had fought before, but they had never resorted to hitting each other. Sadie wondered if this time she had pushed Zosa too far. She had known it would hurt Zosa if she said what she did. But at the same time, she couldn't stand the way Zosa acted like their brother was her own private property. The fight had taken place two days ago. Since then the tension between her and Zosa had been greater than ever before. It was made worse when Adam Dov continued to say nothing because his silence seemed to indicate he was siding with Zosa. It was after another one of their spats, still stemming from that original fight, that her mother finally locked her up in the bedroom. That's when Sadie made up her mind that she wasn't going to live there anymore, crawled out the window and determined to go to the only place in the world where she felt loved.

She liked the way *Zeyde, Bubbe* and Michael always included her in their conversations, and the way they all seemed to really like each other. She was especially happy tonight when she caught *Bubbe* looking at *Zeyde* as though he were the most handsome man in the world. She liked the way they would hug and kiss for no apparent reason, and she couldn't understand why her parents were always so careful not to touch each other, even a kiss, in front of their children. If she were ever to have a husband, she would want him to be romantic all the time like *Zeyde*—that much she knew.

Adam Dov felt guilty that he was slighting Sadie, but somehow he just couldn't bring himself to say anything before he fled the room, abandoning the two sisters to fight. He felt his behavior was despicable, but the only thing he could blame it on was the showdown he feared was coming between his father and him later that afternoon and that was monopolizing his thoughts. A few months ago, as they were on their way to the synagogue on Saturday morning, Jacob brought up the subject first.

"You have pleased me enormously, Adam Dov, with the progress you have made in your yeshiva studies. God has obviously given you a great gift, a great intelligence."

A wave of warmth rushed over him when he heard his father praise him that way, but his happiness was tempered by what he feared might be coming next.

"Because God, in His infinite wisdom, has seen fit to give you this fine brain, you must take care that you not abuse His generosity or His will. Indeed, the highest submission to His will and glorification of His name would be to embrace a life dedicated to reverence for Torah."

"I hope I have such a reverence," he replied uneasily.

"I would encourage you to take it even further. You could study for the rabbinate."

This was exactly what Adam Dov had feared. He knew that it made sense for his father to want him to become a rabbi. Certainly it would bring honor to their family and to pursue a scholarly life of that kind was, at least in the old world tradition, the highest good. But the truth was he had no desire to further his studies in that direction.

"Father, I do not feel I have the calling to pursue my religious studies. My interests are varied and broad—"

Jacob laughed. "What could be broader than the study of the infinite, Adam Dov?"

He felt his knees getting weak. "What I meant by broad were things having to do with the world beyond the spiritual."

His father spoke with the assurance of a man at peace as he made his way slowly down the street. "Beyond the spiritual, there is nothing."

Adam Dov was annoyed with himself that words, which usually came so easily to him, were failing him at this particular moment. Suddenly he seemed unable to express himself exactly. But he had to make his father see what he meant and perhaps the best route would be the most direct. "I want to further my education in secular studies, not religious studies. I want to attend the university."

"The university? Oh Adam Dov, I fear this is just a whim on your part. Your gift is too great to squander on the material world."

Adam Dov saw with a sinking heart that they'd arrived at the synagogue and there would be no more chance for discussion. His father turned to him just before they went up the steps and said, "I want you to pray for guidance. This is too important an issue to treat lightly. We will discuss it again soon."

Adam Dov was unable to let the matter rest. It dominated his thoughts to the point that he could no longer lose himself in his political science or history books, nor could he wait for his father to bring up the subject again. He became so tormented he decided to seek his father out and resolve the matter. He chose this day, the day Sadie and Zosa happened to fight in front of him, to talk to his father in his shop.

Jacob saw Adam Dov the moment he came in the door and came toward him. The shop on Canal Street had by now become a small factory, where Jacob had employed a staff of stone cutters, polishers and jewelers. Adam Dov, having little interest in gems or in working with his hands, seldom came here. He stood awkwardly, feeling like an interloper.

"Adam Dov, this is a pleasure," Jacob said and put his arm around him.

Adam Dov had to raise his voice over the noise of a nearby polishing machine. "Father, do you have time to stop for some tea? I would like to talk to you."

Jacob led him to the back of the shop, where the samovar Elke had insisted on providing him here was already bubbling. Jacob poured out two glasses and sat down across from his son.

"Father, today I received notice from New York University that I have been admitted for the fall semester."

Jacob looked up abruptly. "Then you went ahead and applied?"

"Yes."

Jacob concentrated on squeezing a piece of lemon into his tea. "Then you have made up your mind without me."

Adam Dov swallowed. "Yes."

Jacob sighed and didn't say anything for a few minutes. He looked into his tea glass and took small sips of the hot liquid. Finally he broke the silence. "If you should decide later on, say in a year or two, that you would like a change, that you have made a mistake, then you must not be ashamed to come to me."

Adam Dov was relieved. His father, it appeared, was not going to resist him as he had feared. "No, Father. I won't. But I don't think I'm making a mistake."

Suddenly his father looked very old to Adam Dov. Over the years Jacob had increased in girth, but for the first time Adam Dov noticed that his black hair and side curls had gone completely grey.

Jacob's face was solemn. "Perhaps you are not. Perhaps this is for the best. But I learned when I was about your age that sometimes God has something very different in mind for us from what we ourselves think. Sometimes the thing we think we are least going to do or least want to do with our lives is what we finally find ourselves doing and even, to our amazement, liking it. So I will not oppose your studying at New York University, although it would not be my choice for you, as you know. I have yet to see the value of a secular education for someone like you."

Adam Dov seized his father's hand and kissed it. "Yes, Father. I know that." He tried to keep from letting his happiness spill over too much and thereby grate on his father. But now, he kept telling himself, he would be able to pursue a course of study in political science and history, his first loves. And now he would be able to be more patient and civil to everyone, especially his younger sister.

Two mornings later, Sadie sat with elbows on the kitchen table, chin propped in her hands. Because she had come on a Friday, she had been allowed to stay at her grandparents' house over the weekend, with hopes she would cool down. Now she watched Wolf stir his tea as he told her about his boyhood in St. Petersburg. When he had finished describing his father, Sadie broke in. "Now describe your mother. Tell me everything. I want to know every little thing you remember."

Wolf painted a picture of his mother with words, the graceful aristocratic woman with pale skin and large brown eyes who'd had more patience than any other woman he had met. From there Sadie egged him on to describe each of his brothers and sisters, then his grandparents and aunts and uncles.

Finally Wolf set down his glass, which by now had grown cold. Sadie saw a sad look cross his face.

"Those people are gone, Sadie, and those are stories of a time that will never come again. Now, forty years later, they sound like make-believe stories, even to me. You have learned in school about what has been happening in Russia?"

Sadie nodded her head, although actually she had learned more from overhearing what Adam Dov had told Zosa about the revolutionary events in Russia than from school. She liked school in a way because it was fun to hear about new ideas, but she found that the teachers never discussed things in very much depth, not at all like Adam Dov, who was a lot younger than her teachers but who seemed to know a lot.

"I know that the czar was overthrown in March 1917, when the soldiers who were supposed to put down the strikers went over to their side instead."

"That's right. And then what happened?"

Sadie was herself surprised at how easily she recalled the things she had heard Adam Dov say. "Then, when the Duma, or parliament, also refused to obey the czar, they all formed a council or soviet to set up a new government. First it was headed by Prince George Lvov, but he got discouraged and resigned when the people became sick of war and wanted their soldiers to come home from the Great War, and when the new government couldn't agree on a program of reform. Then a man named Kerensky became the head, but he couldn't stop the activities of a radical group of socialists called Bolsheviks or Communists, which was led by Lenin and Trotsky. And the Bolsheviks were a very small group."

Marya had come into the kitchen during Sadie's recital and stood listening from the other side of the room.

Wolf pretended not to see her. "How did the Bolsheviks get control then?"

"They got into important positions on the

councils. Lenin promised 'Peace! Land! Bread!' The people wanted that because they were so tired of war and desperate for land and economic reforms."

Marya interrupted. "Zavel, you and Sadie are talking about events that are so far away. What good does it do to fill your heads with what's going on in a place you'll never see again."

No matter how many years went by, it seemed to Wolf this was still a topic that was sensitive between him and Marya, and which they couldn't agree on. But he couldn't stop himself from entering into an argument anyway. "These events in Russia do matter, Marya. They affect us in ways it sometimes takes years to realize. For one thing close at hand, the Russian Revolution certainly affected the course of the war in Europe."

"And besides," Sadie added cheerfully, "it's not a country we'll never see. I plan to go there someday."

Marya threw up her hands. "Still, why not talk about something closer at hand and more important to both of you, like the Sacco and Vanzetti case, or the Volstead Act that's made liquor illegal, or even talk about MW Enterprises."

Sadie's eyes lit up. "Yes, that's it. Let's talk about the factory. There's something I've been wanting to ask you about it anyway."

Wolf looked at her surprised. "What's that?"

Sadie picked up her spoon and began to play with it. "I was wondering if you would . . . if I could . . . what I wanted to know is if you'd hire me."

Wolf was astonished. "Hire you? To do what?"

"I wouldn't care. I can learn fast and there's lots of things I could do. It would just be for a little while after school every day."

Wolf looked at her very seriously. "You don't know what it's like to work there."

"Oh, but it would be exciting. I've always loved it when I came there to visit you."

"But working there every day isn't the same as

dropping by once a month. It's noisy, and can be very dirty and hot, and the workers are mostly new immigrants who chatter in Yiddish and Italian and who wouldn't feel friendly toward someone like you who was born here and who's had a lot of advantages in this country that they haven't. Believe me, I know what I'm talking about."

Sadie came to stand behind Wolf's chair and put her arms around his shoulders. "Just try me out. I could start with a little job in the office maybe, just helping you file away your papers and things. Maybe I could be an assistant to the office manager, Mrs. Abrahms, or to one of the secretaries. Please!"

Wolf looked at Marya, who was still standing by the kitchen counter and who had kept completely silent during this exchange. "See what we started, Marya?" he teased. "There's going to be no satisfying her."

"Not unless you say yes, I'm afraid," Marya chuckled.

Wolf reared back in his chair. "Ah, now I see. The ladies are in collusion."

Sadie was beside herself. "That's right! There's more of us than you. You have to say yes."

"Then we'll just have to wait until Michael gets here," Wolf jested, hoping to make light of the situation, "so I won't be outnumbered." As Marya replenished his tea from the bubbling samovar, he looked down into the hot amber liquid streaming into his glass and grew serious. "I don't know, Sadie, if it's really a good idea." He wanted to say that if anyone should be helping him down at the factory, it should be Michael, not her. After all, it would be Michael who might want to become involved in the business someday.

Marya knew exactly what Wolf was thinking. She suspected his hesitation was because, ever since what had happened with Daniel, he was reluctant to have another of his children, or in this case, grandchildren, working closely with him. She had observed in the last ten years how he had been so different with Michael from the way he had been with Daniel when he was a boy. Seldom did he try to push him to work with him at the factory or mills or say anything to Michael to indicate he expected him to take over some day. But Marya knew that deep down, Wolf did nurture a hope that Michael would want to emulate him and take over the far-flung business that MW Enterprises had become.

Sadie renewed her plea. "Oh, please, *Zeyde.*"

Wolf gently removed her arms from around his neck and pulled her around to face him. "I have to think about this for a while, Sadie. And I want you to think about it, too. It's not something I want you to rush into." He stood up and led her toward the door. "It's time now to take you home. Your mother and father will be jealous of all the hours we've had with you."

"But I don't want to go home," Sadie complained. "I want to stay here."

Wolf picked up his jacket and car keys. "You can come here any time you want, Sadie, but now I have to take you home. Besides, if you stay here any longer, people are going to start thinking you live here."

During the drive to her parents' house, Sadie decided the only thing that made the prospect of returning there bearable was that she was getting a chance to ride in her grandfather's Model T Ford. As they passed the horse-drawn carriages and rows of neatly painted houses, Sadie was thrilled to be moving so fast. She loved going places with her grandfather, but she could hardly wait to learn how to drive one of these horseless carriages herself.

Her lightheartedness disappeared the moment the car stopped in front of her home. She struggled to regain the feeling. Bouncing along in a tin lizzie with the breeze blowing through her hair, she had been her real self. That was her real life, she decided. She told herself that what lay inside her father's house was only temporary, and one day she would be free of it, free to drive through the wind and laugh and talk to whom-ever she wanted for as long as she wanted. If she could just hold on to that thought, maybe she could get through the rest of the time she had to live with her family the best she could.

It was with the memory of the wind blowing in her hair that Sadie passed through the next couple of weeks. She managed to ignore everyone else and stay busy with her magazines and radio and even schoolwork. One Sunday she went to a matinee of Clara Bow's new movie with Adam Dov and Zosa, but because they were in a movie palace, she didn't have to talk to them or pay them any attention so the after-noon turned out well, at least in the beginning. She lost herself in admiring Clara Bow's stylish clothes and styl-ish hair and stylish shape. She could certainly see why everyone called her the "It" girl and wished she hadn't gotten too big on top to look like her. Still, one day she would wear short, slinky dresses just like that and get rid of the petticoats and long skirts her mother insisted she wear.

On the way home from the Broadway movie palace, Sadie was annoyed that there wasn't room for all three of them to walk abreast down the sidewalk, and Zosa insisted on walking ahead of her, arm in arm with Adam Dov. She had no choice but to follow along behind like a little kid. She hated feeling that way. Then she reminded herself she was an "It" girl, just waiting for her day. She pretended, as she felt the breeze ruffle through her hair pulled up in a knot on her head, that she was riding in a tin lizzie with a boy who looked one minute dark and mysterious like Rudolph Valentino and the next athletic and graceful like Tom Mix.

Occasionally Adam Dov gave a quick glance be-hind to make sure that Sadie was still trailing them. But other than that, it seemed to Sadie that the two of them didn't know she was alive. When they turned into a soda shop, she hesitated about going in.

"C'mon," Adam Dov called. "What are you waiting for? It's too far and too dangerous for you to walk home by yourself." When he said that, she wished he wanted her company rather than just felt an obligation to take care of her.

Inside, Adam Dov and Zosa sat on one side of the table and Sadie sat on the other facing them. Adam Dov and Zosa began to discuss the movie they had just seen. They talked about it with great intensity and energy for what seemed like half an hour until Sadie finally interrupted them. "How can you enjoy it if you're so busy tearing it to pieces while you're watching it?"

Zosa looked exasperated. "That's what we like, seeing how all the parts come together so well. We like to look at the skill and craftsmanship."

"But it's just a movie," Sadie started to say, but Adam Dov had started a new conversation. He began to talk of the League of Nations and the Versailles Treaty and pointed out some of the issues he felt former President Wilson hadn't handled properly.

"But, of course, he had that unfortunate stroke right in the middle of his campaign to get the country to understand what the League was all about," Zosa observed.

"Of course," Adam Dov agreed and went on to present the tactics that President Harding's Secretary of State, Charles Evan Hughes, had used to gain Senate approval of the Versailles pact.

Sadie broke in. "I guess that after the war people were just tired of being involved in international politics. Just like I'm tired of it now." She felt the conversation had little interest for her, and she was no longer willing to be a silent audience.

Zosa looked at her scornfully. "What's the matter with you, Sadie? Don't you want to learn these important things? Don't you want to train your mind? Do you want to go through your whole life with a vapid girl's mind?"

Before she realized what she was doing, Sadie was

on her feet and running out of the soda shop. She
wasn't sure if she heard Adam Dov call after her or
not, but she was determined not to turn around and go
back to them. She had enough of their boring, dry talk.
She didn't care if it was too dangerous to walk home
by herself. She had no intention of being in their company one minute longer.

Sadie pulled her cape around her and walked
briskly, all the time Zosa's words echoing in her head:
vapid girl's mind. Sadie knew she didn't have a vapid
mind, far from it. It was just that she wasn't always interested in what they were talking about. She even got
the feeling sometimes that they did it on purpose and
enjoyed closing her out from their conversations, going
on and on about the things they read in their books
and newspapers.

When she got home, she was still angry. She
marched upstairs and faced herself in the mirror, staring deep into her eyes. They didn't look dumb to her.
They sparkled a lot and were alert. Maybe she didn't
like to talk about intellectual things constantly, she said
to herself, but what did it matter? She was a girl who
had "It" instead. What use had she for the way they
analyzed and criticized everything they read or saw or
thought.

As she gazed at herself, she suddenly decided to
get rid of the long plaid skirt she was wearing and the
silly blouse with puffy sleeves. She slipped into a
chemise she had secretly designed for herself, based on
one she had seen Clara Bow wear in a movie a few
months ago. Then she pulled the pins out of her hair
and combed it down over her shoulders to her waist.
She took the ends, and winding them around her hand,
tried to pin them, as best she could, up underneath her
hair next to her hairline. But it was hard for her to get
the effect she wanted just with pins.

She decided the only thing to do was to have the
real thing. She got out a pair of scissors and began to

cut. First she cut off twelve inches, but her hair was so long that didn't seem to make a lot of difference.

Then she cut off another six inches. This time her hair was definitely short; it hung just below her chin. Her hair was the length she wanted, but she had to admit it looked kind of uneven and didn't have the shape she was after. She parted it to one side and was ready to snip off some more, when the bedroom door suddenly flew open.

In just one second Elke was able to take in everything she needed to know. She saw the large pile of long red tendrils on the floor, and her heart lurched. Sadie had the effrontery, the disrespect, the cruelty even, to cut off her thick beautiful hair.

"How could you?" she cried in a dry whisper, so angry her voice failed her. "How could you cut off your hair like that? What are you trying to do? Look like a . . . a whore?" Elke didn't mean to use that word, but it was the one that first came to mind for what she was seeing before her.

Sadie found herself surprisingly calm. "It's just a bob. That's all. It's the look these days. I was sick of that long heavy stuff weighing me down, making me feel like I weighed three hundred pounds. I hate all that old-fashioned stuff."

Elke leaned her head against the doorjamb and told herself she must be steady and calm. As Sadie stood there before her, her head looking like a rag mop with its unruly tufts of short hair, Elke couldn't help but imagine in a far more visceral way than she had ever before been able, how her own mother must have felt when she first saw her sheared head just before her wedding to Jake. But at least that act had been part of a religious purification ritual and had some meaning. This act of Sadie's was nothing but an empty attempt to flaunt her disrespect for the values their family held dear.

"How dare you do this to yourself! Wait until

your father sees you. I can promise you he won't take
this lightly."

"I don't care," Sadie returned defiantly. "I look
the way I want to look."

Elke practically spat her words out. "You look
like one of those cheap loose women who drink and
smoke cigarettes, that's what you look like. That's what
everyone will take you for in a minute. I'm ashamed to
think my daughter wants to appear in public this way."

"Then maybe I'm not your daughter. Maybe I
shouldn't be part of this family anymore."

Elke tried to think what her mother would have
said in response to such a comment. She wanted to do
what was right and handle this in the best way. She
yearned to say something, but she couldn't think of
anything appropriate. Everything she really wanted to
say was bitter and vindictive, and she knew she
couldn't actually utter such thoughts out loud. She
would turn this over to her husband and her mother to
handle, she finally decided.

The next day Marya was seated in the barber-
shop, watching the barber as he smoothed out the
chopped bob Sadie had given herself and made it have
the sweep and turn the hairdo was supposed to. She
felt a pang as she gazed at Sadie, who despite the barber's best efforts still looked all out of proportion to
her. She found it hard to accustom herself to this new
hairstyle that so many of the young women were sporting these days. It seemed to her that, no matter what, a
woman was supposed to let her hair grow naturally,
and that there should be lots of it. She wondered if this
were another of those old country notions she had been
unable to shake off, or if it stemmed solely from the
horror she had felt at the loss of her hair during the fever. With this new generation, she was finding out all
the time she wasn't as modern as she had prided herself. At any rate, Sadie's lines simply didn't seem in

balance with such a short fringe of hair about her face and with no height on top.

The barber stepped back to examine his handiwork. He was a short man who walked like a penguin, and he had dark, hooded eyes. "Ooo la la," he said with a French accent. "She is perfect. Look how the waves mademoiselle was born with in her hair give her a natural marcel. Magnificent!" He turned to Marya for confirmation.

Marya stared bleakly back at him. "It's good luck if that's what Sadie wants. It will take some getting used to, I suppose."

"No, *Bubbe*. I love it already! It's just like Mr. Gaulois says—perfect." She held up the mirror he handed her and examined herself from all sides. She smiled to herself. She did rather look like Clara Bow now.

Marya was pleased to see Sadie smile, but what would Wolf say when he saw her? When she had received a stricken call the night before from Elke, she had resolved to say nothing to Wolf until after work the next day and until she saw the extent of the damage Sadie had inflicted on herself. Elke had been beside herself, contending that she just couldn't handle the girl any longer. Sadie seemed to resist or ridicule everything that she and Jacob held dear. She balked at going to temple; she read vulgar magazines; she complained incessantly about the clothes Elke made for her, calling them old-fashioned and uncomfortable; she complained about having to stay in the house and constantly made up stories about scandalous things she'd like to do someday when she was "free"; she talked about how she was never going to have babies and be some man's slave. And, finally, it seemed she just couldn't get along with her brother and sister for more than five minutes. Wouldn't Marya and Papa please take her for a while and see if they could calm her down?

For once, Sadie regretted that she was being kept home from school that day. She would have loved to

show the other kids her hairdo, which she knew
would look especially good if she wore her chemise and
rolled her stockings the way she'd seen some of the
girls on the Bowery do. But she had no choice but to
accompany her grandmother back to her house.

That evening Marya met Wolf at the door, eager
to get a moment alone before Sadie and Michael de-
scended on him. She outlined what Sadie had done, her
phone call with Elke, and then her talk with her when
she had gone to pick Sadie up.

Wolf sighed. "I suppose the time has come to talk
to Jacob. We could try it for a while and see how it
goes."

"It would be better for everyone than just letting
things go on the way they have."

Wolf gave Marya a searching look. "I can predict,
though, that Jacob's main concern is that we continue
to raise the girl with the same religious principles and
practices he and Elke have tried to instill in her."

Marya blinked rapidly. For some reason she
hadn't thought about that, but of course Wolf was
right. That would be the one condition under which
Jacob would let Sadie go.

Wolf could see her hesitate. He knew this was
hard for her and waited patiently for her reply.

Marya looked down at the floor and thought. Ultimately she saw there was no real choice. Something
had to be done about Sadie and her coming to live with
them temporarily was the logical solution. For Sadie's
sake, Marya told herself, whatever Jacob wanted would
be done. "I suppose you can give him that assurance,
can't you? After all, you have been taking up more of
the old ways each year, it seems."

Wolf put his arm around her. "It won't be as bad
as you think. And besides, we'll have the delight of
Sadie's company."

That's what Marya kept reminding herself. It
wouldn't be too bad. Between Wolf and Mrs. Sanders,

they were already observing *Shabbas* dinner of sorts, and Wolf himself could take her to temple on Saturdays and see to her religious instruction. Anyway, it was all a temporary arrangement in the first place.

Chapter 27

Zosa lay on the blanket that was spread on the sand, still glowing with the heat of the day, and listened to the crash of the waves. Overhead she could see the stars clearly and she thought how nice it was to be lying here in the dark, oblivious to all the thoughts that had been plaguing her earlier in the day. A light breeze was playing over her and she felt relaxed and peaceful.

She sensed someone bending over her and opened her eyes to see her brother silhouetted against the night sky. At nineteen, he now had a man's body, with a broad chest and muscular arms and legs. He took her hand, and she was reminded of how strong he was as he started to pull her to her feet.

"Come on," he urged. "We're all going in for a moonlight swim."

"But it's so comfortable here," she murmured, and didn't try to help him with his efforts to rouse her.

"You'd best come with me or the others will throw you in. One way or the other you're going in the water, so you might as well do it yourself."

She slowly came to a sitting position. "Adam Dov, you are always so logical, aren't you? Even at the beach."

He helped her to her feet, and before she had completely come to, she found herself stumbling along behind him to the water's edge. The sand was soft under her bare feet, and when she came to the water's edge, it grew damp and cool. The day had been so hot and muggy in the city that the coolness was a welcome feeling, one that made her feel refreshed and alive. She could see their friends Abe, Marty, Betty and Anne, who had already waded into the water as far as their knees. Marty, who was tall and lanky, always looked to Zosa like a cowboy instead of a second-year student in economics at New York University. She saw him gesturing for everyone to come hear something he wanted to say.

As Zosa waded toward him in the cool water, she marveled at the sensuous feel of the water and promised herself she would lie down in it later and let it wash completely over her, soothing her heat-jangled nerves with its freshness. Maybe she'd be able to persuade Adam Dov to try it too. Certainly this heat wave had made him even more short-tempered and irritable than it had her.

Now they all gathered near Marty and waited to hear what he had to say. Marty and Adam Dov were recognized as the leaders in their circle, which included another ten or twelve people in addition to the six of them who had decided to drive to this secluded bit of beach this evening. Where Adam Dov was indisputably the intellectual leader, Marty was often the social arbiter, setting the pace for what the circle considered smart or fashionable adventures to set themselves on, indicating which fads and trends had become embarrassingly passé.

"Look at us," Marty announced, disdain dripping from his voice. "Here we are on our own secluded beach and we're carrying on as if we were a bunch of *Yekkes* around the turn of the century." He put his hands on his hips and taking hold of his striped bathing shirt, yanked it over his head, revealing his broad, smooth chest. "We're all friends. What do we need with these symbols of bourgeois restraint?" He swung his shirt over his head and tossed it up on the beach.

Without hesitation the other two men had also stripped off their shirts and flung them onto the sand as well. The girls tried not to giggle in embarrassment and Zosa refused to stare at the men's bare torsos, although she was terribly curious to see how they looked unclothed and was not at all as blasé as she pretended. At the same time, she was aware, as were the others, of a heightened energy in the air, and she had to admit she liked this feeling of suddenly having all her senses awakened.

Then, to their astonishment, they saw that Marty was sliding his hands down his hips, pushing his bathing trunks down with them. He stepped out of the trunks and stood totally naked before them, as relaxed and unselfconscious as if they were all standing around his parents' living room in the clothes they wore to class. Within a matter of seconds the other men were just as naked.

Marty laughed and kicked a jet of water at Anne. "What are you staring at?"

Her usual self-reserve dropping from her in an instant, Anne screamed and splashed water back at him. An exuberant water fight broke out between the women, still clad in the new bathing costumes they had thought quite daring, and the unclad men, until all six of them were completely drenched and laughing. Through the ferocious spray of water, Zosa could see Adam Dov and realized that she never seen him naked before. But her contemplation was interrupted when Marty picked her up in his arms and started swinging her around in circles. When he finally let go of her, Zosa was so dizzy she could hardly stand. She put out her hand to support herself, but lost her balance and fell to her knees.

As the cool water rose up to her shoulders, she shuddered at its delicious, satiny smoothness. As if in a dream, she began to undo the belt of her bathing costume and allowed the water to balloon up under it. She decided how nice it would be to feel the water lapping against her breasts without any confines at all. She began to wriggle out of the bathing dress, until she was wearing just the matching underpanties, while the dress floated alongside her. She rose dreamily to her feet, and upon seeing her half-naked, the boys clapped their hands and stared in spite of themselves. The other girls also stared at Zosa's exposed breasts, then pulled off their own bathing dresses, including the matching underpanties, so that they were now completely naked just as the fellows were.

"C'mon, Zosa," Betty called to her, pointing at the panties Zosa still wore. "All the way."

Zosa shrugged and laughed, then pulled down the panties. As soon as they were all quite bare, the water fight broke out again, this time more animatedly than ever. They tried not to stare at one another's nakedness. It was for almost all of them the first time they had seen the opposite sex without clothes, other than in drawings or clandestine photographs. The water, lit by the moonlight, shone all the more as it sprayed through the air during their water battle, which raged on and on. Through the droplets, Zosa could see the round curves of the women's bodies and the hard lines of the men's, seemingly intertwining in a frenzied whirling motion, with no image remaining still for more than a second.

In the midst of it all, she felt someone grab hold of her wrist and pull her from the fray. It was Adam Dov and he was leading her up the beach, away from the water fight. When they had run perhaps five hundred yards and were no longer in clear sight of the others, he sank down into the sand and pulled her down with him. They lay side by side on their backs, panting from the exertion of the battle and their mad dash up the beach. For a few minutes neither of them spoke. Then Adam Dov rolled onto his side and raised up onto his elbow. "It's getting late. It's about time for us to start for home."

Zosa was keenly aware of Adam Dov facing her, and although her instinct was to raise her hands to cover herself, she forced herself not to. "Yes," she said, but she didn't make any move to get up.

Adam Dov couldn't keep his eyes from wandering over the roundness of his sister's body. He saw the fullness of her breasts, now flattened into soft mounds by the way she was lying and he could see her nipples, roughened to a point by the light wind that was blowing across them. He found that her skin was even creamier looking than he would have imagined as his eyes strayed down her torso to the tuft of dark hair between her thighs. She lay there beneath his gaze, perfectly still, as if she were willingly offering herself for his inspection. Then, as the silence between them mounted, Adam Dov felt he had to break it in some way.

He cleared his throat. "You are a beautiful woman, Zosa. I'm proud to have you as my sister."

He could see her smile in the moonlight. Then she slowly rolled over onto her stomach, came up onto her hands and knees, lingered just a second, then knelt facing him. "I couldn't imagine a more perfect brother. You are everything I want." She stood up and reached for his hand.

He gave it to her as he got to his feet, and they walked hand in hand back down the beach. They soon saw the others had come up out of the water and had put back on their bathing costumes.

Marty called out to them as they drew near. "What kind of water troops are you two, anyway? You gave up just as things started getting fierce. And for God's sake, put your clothes on. You look downright indecent."

Everyone laughed as Zosa and Adam Dov hastened back into their bathing suits. As they all walked back to Abe's new Chevrolet, a present from his father who owned a large department store on Broadway, Adam Dov declared, "This has been what I would call a perfect evening," his sister's word echoing in his mind.

Marty glanced his way. "The only thing missing was a little moonshine to go with the moonlight. Then it would have been really perfect."

Adam Dov didn't look at him. He caught Zosa's eye instead and the two of them smiled at each other.

"No, being together is elixir enough. It's perfect just as is," Zosa confirmed her brother's view.

In the next few days after the swimming party, Adam Dov and Zosa were careful to keep their conversation on a light level. They still talked as much as ever, but it was if each recognized that they had trespassed into some kind of dangerous territory that night at the beach, and they were both marked by it, although neither could admit it.

Adam was sitting at the dining room table, his books spread out in front of him. He was now in his third year of college, having been able to graduate from high school when he was just sixteen, and he spent more time than ever studying. Zosa sat across from him, her library books also spread out on the table. She considered the clutter scattered from one end of the table to the other. "I feel like we're two generals, staring at each other across the battlefield, and these books and papers are our dead soldiers."

Adam Dov lifted his head out of his book and smiled. "From your comment, you must be reading either history or political science right now, and I think it means you're ready for a break." He paused. "Have I told you how proud of you I am that you've kept up your studies since finishing high school, even though you're not in college?"

Zosa blushed, but was secretly pleased with her brother's compliment. She got up quickly, heading for the kitchen to get the tea they knew their mother had waiting for them.

Zosa returned with the tray of steaming glasses a few minutes later. "Even though it's been almost two years, it still seems strange not to have Sadie in the house anymore," she mused, putting the tray down in front of Adam Dov and remembering how they sometimes had been able to coax her into waiting on them when they were reading.

Her brother nodded. "She seems a lot happier where she is, though. But I do miss her a little."

"Sometimes I do too, although when she left I thought I never would miss her. Of course, who knew she'd be gone this long? It was just supposed to be for a few months and now it's two years already." She blew on her tea to cool it. "I guess she actually likes working afternoons in *Zeyde*'s drafty old factory. Can you imagine that?"

Adam Dov appeared thoughtful. "It's hard to. The only part that would appeal to me are the labor negotiations. But luckily for *Zeyde*, he was far-sighted enough to get most of that settled years ago. Knowing Sadie, I'm surprised she's stuck with the job this long. I don't remember her being able to concentrate on much of anything unless it was one of her magazine stories."

"I wonder what she'll do when she graduates from high school this year. Somehow I can't see her getting married right away." She sighed. "Even though that's what I know Mother and Father want for both of us."

"Oh, she'll probably calm down and get married within the next year or so. When she's out of high school and faced with working full time at the factory or some other grub job or doing charity work for some Hebrew organization all day, she'll come around fast. You can count on that."

They were both careful not to mention Zosa's own future.

It was Saturday afternoon and Sadie was lying on

the living room floor, her feet propped against the wall as she listened to the new radio. This one had a loudspeaker instead of earphones, and she liked that much better because this way the music could fill up the room.

Michael appeared in the doorway and right away started snapping his fingers and jumping around the room. "Look, Sadie! I'm doing the black bottom!"

Sadie sat up and watched him. Michael was almost thirteen, but he was still as lean as ever. So far he just kept getting taller, never broader. As he gyrated about the room, Sadie thought he looked like a mop handle having convulsions and she started to laugh. "That's not how you do it!" She jumped to her feet. "Watch me."

As she gracefully slipped into the motions of the dance, fitting her movements to the syncopated rhythm of the music, Michael came up alongside of her and tried to imitate her moves. Within a matter of minutes, he was able to perform a passable version of the black bottom.

Sadie watched him out of the corner of her eye and suddenly her face lit up. "Wait a minute! You've got the motions, but you don't have the look." She dragged him into the kitchen and forced him to bend over the sink while, despite his loud complaints, she poured a pitcher of cold water over his head. Then she pulled her hands firmly across his head, matting the hair down until he looked like a seal. Not until all his hair was completely slicked back was she satisfied.

"Now, little Uncle, come look at yourself in the mirror."

"Niece, don't call me little. I'm as tall as you."

She led him back into the living room and stood him in front of the ornately framed mirror that hung behind the sofa. "Now you're the kind of feller a girl like me would dance with. You look thoroughly modern." She leaned over and rolled her stockings to her knees, then she hitched up her skirt, which although short, was still not short enough for her taste. She threw back her head, grabbed him by the wrist and began to move them both around the room in a fox trot.

Michael barely managed to stumble through the dance. As their knees knocked together and he kept stepping on her toes, Sadie shook her head. "Better stick with the new dances, Uncle. You're out of touch on the fox trot. And you'd do lasting damage to your partner if you ever got into a marathon." She continued to dance him around the room the best she could, angling at the last minute to avoid delicate tables and forbidding armchairs.

They heard a loud cough from the doorway and turned to see Wolf peering at them. "Don't tell me the dance craze has invaded my own home? And here it is *Shabbas*."

Sadie shook her finger at him. "Well, don't just keep it to yourself, *Zeyde*. Tell us we're great. Tell us we're the bee's knees."

"And the cat's pajamas," put in Michael.

When Wolf didn't say anything, Sadie presumed, "It's probably just because you haven't seen our fancy stuff that you're not showering us with praise." She pushed Michael away from her and looked him in the eye. "Ready for the black bottom, Uncle?"

"Ready, Niece!"

Sadie and Michael threw themselves into a frenzy of motion before Wolf's startled eyes. "I don't think I can watch this," he finally decided before heading for the kitchen. "It still seems sacrilegious."

"Don't worry, Michael. We'll win him over yet," Sadie resolved and they danced on with just each other for an audience.

Wolf let Mrs. Sanders pour him a cup of tea. Her hair had now gone completely grey, but she was as energetic as she had been over fifteen years ago when he had first hired her.

"Sit, relax, enjoy," she urged as she set the samovar back down on the table and placed a plate of lemons and another sugar cube in front of him. "You look like you need a bit of a rest."

"I do," Wolf conceded. There was something he had to think about. It was the letter he'd received at the factory a few days ago, and which had been tormenting him ever since.

He pulled it from his pocket where it had been ever since he opened it, and went over the Polish words for what seemed like the hundredth time:

> Dear Mr. Luminov,
>   Allow me to introduce myself. My name is Zavel Salenski and I am writing you at the suggestion of your friend, Etta Salenski, who is my mother. I will have occasion to come to the United States sometime within the next year, and it is my hope that I will have an opportunity to meet you. I know that we met when I was a small boy, but of course I have no memory of that event. As your namesake I look forward to seeing you. I will contact you upon my arrival and perhaps then we can make arrangements to meet.
>   Sincerely,
>   Zavel Salenski

Wolf ran his hand through his hair and tried to sort out his feelings. So many years had passed since he had last seen Etta and her boy Zavel. Since he had not received any letters from Etta, other than the one many years ago telling him that the three of them had arrived in Warsaw safely, the boy and Etta had occupied less and less of his thoughts. Now, when he felt as if he were embarked upon his second family with twelve-year-old Michael and seventeen-year-old Sadie, he wondered why he had to be confronted by someone who was nothing more than a dim memory to him. He barely recalled a two-year-old boy playing on the floor of what served as MW Enterprises' first tiny workroom. He did remember how he had stared at the boy, afraid to let himself believe what Etta's words intimated, and then, although still not certain, feeling overwhelmed with guilt and responsibility. Now it was hard to imagine that two-year-old boy as a grown man. And why could the boy possibly want to see him? Did he want something from him? Had his mother told him of what had happened between them? Did he perhaps imagine he had some kind of share in MW Enterprises and was coming to put in a claim for it? What should he do when the boy appeared? He had no answers, only questions, and they swirled in his head during all the waking hours. They were mercifully interrupted now by Sadie and Michael coming into the room.

They sat down at the table on either side of him. *"Zeyde,"* Sadie began, "I have something I've been wanting to ask you about."

When he remained silent she demanded abruptly, "Are you happy with the work I'm doing in the factory?"

He set his glass down. "Yes. Don't I seem happy?"

"I guess I would say you don't seem *un*happy. But you are happy then?" She looked at him anxiously.

"Of course. I would let you know if I weren't. Now tell me, Sadie, what's behind this question?"

"I love working for you and I want you to know Mrs. Abrahms says she is pleased with everything I do."

"Yes, I have no doubt of that. She has sung your praises many a time."

"I wouldn't change anything . . . except maybe just one little thing—or maybe two." When she saw Wolf raise his eyebrows, she quickly added, "I would like to help you more directly. By that I mean I would like to take on a job with more responsibility than just filing and running errands. Don't get me wrong, I like what I'm doing. It's just that I think I could be more valuable to you in some other way. Almost anyone could do what I do. But I've kept my eyes open in the two years I've been there and I've learned a lot. You'd be surprised how much. I can"—she pretended not to see that Wolf was firmly shaking his head back and forth—"I can do almost all the jobs, and I've been looking over Mrs. Abrahms' shoulders at the books and I think I've a fair idea of how to—"

"Absolutely not."

Sadie stopped. For a couple seconds all she could do was stare in disbelief. Then she argued, "But there are improvements I could make, things that might make us even more profit."

Michael piped up. "Like what, Sadie?"

They all paused in their discussion a few moments as Marya came into the room.

Then, as if waiting for Michael's bit of encouragement, Sadie answered enthusiastically, directing her words at first to Michael, and then as the sound of her voice made her more confident, to Wolf: "Well, we could advertise, for one thing. I've seen advertisements for all kinds of things in magazines like *Collier's* and *Life* and *The American Mercury,* and even in the tabloids. They carry ads for everything from cigarettes to face soap and hosiery. Why not our dresses? Why not place an ad showing one of our designs in *Vogue*? And then," she continued without stopping for a reaction, "there's a really big step we could take to save money. I know this sounds a little crazy, but if you think about it, you'll see what a good idea it is. We could continue to do our own designs," she glanced quickly at Marya, "as we do now, and we could continue to design and special order the fabrics from our mills in the colors and patterns we want, just as we do now. We'd cut the fabrics and patterns we want, but then we would hire out the actual production to some other source. They'd return the finished dress to us, and that way we wouldn't have to worry about managing and financially maintaining a factory and—"

Wolf broke in vehemently. "That's enough, Sadie. You're absolutely right about one thing, this last idea of yours is crazy. How can you suggest eliminating the factory? As far as I'm concerned, the factory is what my whole life has been about. It's what I plan one day to turn over to my sons and grandsons. No, Sadie, I'm afraid I can't take any of these far-fetched suggestions of yours seriously. Especially the one about your continuing to work in the factory." He added scornfully, "The very factory you would abolish if you had your way."

Sadie was dumbfounded. "What do you mean? Why can't I work there anymore?"

Michael too looked surprised.

Wolf shook his head firmly. "Sadie, the factory is not the place for a young lady like you."

"But there are lots of women there. The whole place is mostly women."

"I said, 'for a young lady like you.' You don't belong there. I only let you work there because of your grandmother." His eyes met Marya's and the look she gave him tempered his response. "Your grandmother convinced me that you would be happier if you had an outlet for some of that energy of yours and also because I knew it would be temporary."

Marya was still staring at Wolf. "You might give the girl a chance, Zavel."

"Absolutely not." He struck the table for emphasis.

"But I finish high school this spring. I thought you'd want to take me on full time. I've been counting on it." Sadie's voice began to rise. "Now you tell me I don't belong. How can I not belong someplace where I've been very happy for two years? Tell me that!"

Wolf glanced at his son sitting on the other side of him. He asked himself how he could tell her that his dream was that it should be his son Michael or his grandson Adam Dov saying all this to him someday, not his granddaughter. Never once had he imagined

Sadie staying in that noisy, drafty factory more than as a part-time job, something to amuse her. She was a pretty, charming girl, if rather rambunctious, but she didn't have any idea how tiring and draining it could be to be tied to a job day in and day out. She'd be too exhausted to go out in the evenings with her friends and meet young men her age, and she certainly would never find any suitable ones there at the factory. Someday it would all be for Michael, if he wanted it. Wolf refused to push him the way he had Daniel, but if Michael would one day ask him if he might work there the way Sadie was doing now, it would all be his in a minute. The business was intended for his sons.

He saw she was round-eyed waiting for an answer and he tried to explain patiently. "You don't belong because you have so many other things you could do. The factory's no place for a young woman to spend her whole life."

"Lots of women do just that," Sadie retorted.

"It's because they have no choice. But you do."

Sadie's face was stubborn. "Like what?"

Michael could keep quiet no longer. "There's lots of things you could do, Sadie, if you wanted to. You could find some nice man and get married, and—"

Sadie turned on him. "You just said, 'if I wanted to.' Well, I don't want to. Married a woman can always get. I have the rest of my life to be married. Name something else for me."

Michael had a ready answer. "You can go to work."

Sadie looked exasperated. "That's just what I want to do."

"But at something else. Not the factory."

"Why not?"

Wolf broke in. "We just went through all that, Sadie. Now I suggest you think hard about what else it is you'd like to do after high school. I will help you in any way I can. But I simply can't go along with this notion of yours to work full time for MW Enterprises.

And," he added, winking at her, "don't shun the idea of marriage so quickly. You never know who might come along all of a sudden. Then you might have to eat your words."

Sadie glowered. She knew Wolf was laughing at her, thinking her idea was a ridiculous little girl's whim, thinking she would be swept off her feet by the first man who came along to make eyes at her. But she knew she wouldn't. She continued to contemplate what Wolf had said to her. She hadn't expected this kind of resistance. But now that he had spoken, she saw it was going to take more than her grandmother's intercession this time to get him to change his mind.

Marya looked pointedly at Wolf. "You said you will help Sadie do whatever she wants."

"Assuming it's nothing illegal or dangerous to her well-being, I give my word."

Marya turned to Sadie. "Then perhaps you might want to go to college, Sadie."

Michael's reaction was instantaneous. "College? For a girl?"

"Of course," Marya said. "Why not? Lots of girls go." She looked at Wolf's face to see what his reaction was. She was relieved that although his face was serious, he wasn't shaking his head this time. She addressed herself to Sadie again. "You would be the first woman in our family to go to college. It could be yours, but only if you really want it."

Wolf was silent. Now he addressed himself to Michael. "You can never underestimate the value of a college education for a man or a woman. One of the greatest riches my father gave me was an excellent education with the best scholars he could bring into our home."

He then looked at Sadie. "I don't expect you would have any interest in college. In no way do I mean to make light of your goals, but your fascinations have never seemed to be in the area of books."

"You're not like Adam Dov and Zosa," observed Michael, undiplomatically.

Wolf looked at him sharply. "This is between Sadie, your grandmother and me. Please reserve your opinion until later."

"I know that I'm not a bookworm. But I do like learning things. And if I can't work in the factory, then I certainly want to do something that is interesting and fun," Sadie responded.

Wolf spoke firmly. "College will be more than just fun. It's hard work, much more than you're doing in high school."

Marya put her hand on Sadie's shoulder. "First of all, you have to get in. Then if your grades are high enough to get in, you have to keep them high. We'll pay for your education, but only if we can see you're applying yourself."

"You'll pay my tuition?" Sadie was astounded. She certainly hadn't expected her grandparents to help her to that extent.

Now that the possibility of Sadie working full time at the factory had been squelched, Wolf was expansive. "Of course we'll pay. I told you I would stand behind you, didn't I? And, if you work hard and show promise during your first year, I'll make you a gift that should actually make your second year fun."

"A gift?" Maybe it wouldn't be so bad giving up the factory for a while.

Marya drew her back to the reality of the undertaking. "The first year would be the hardest. That's when you would have the biggest adjustment to make and that's when the temptations to play around would be the greatest."

Wolf couldn't keep still. "But if you keep high grades throughout your first year, I'll give you your own Model T to drive back to college for your sophomore year."

Sadie's mouth fell open and so did Michael's. "Did I hear you right?"

"Close your mouth, Niece," Michael quipped, recovering his presence of mind before Sadie. "Or he'll think you're dumb and you'll never get that tin lizzie."

For the next couple of days, Sadie floated in a bubble of excitement. She couldn't get over the fact that her grandfather had volunteered to pay for her college education and then to buy her a Model T for her second year. Her exhilaration left her completely unprepared for her father's reaction to the news that she was going to college.

It was the following Friday, and she was eating *Shabbas* dinner back at her family's house, one of the conditions under which Jacob had approved her temporary stay with her grandparents. On one side of the table sat Adam Dov and Zosa. Sadie sat on the other, next to her mother, and her father presided at the head.

When Sadie calmly announced her plans after high school to the family, Jacob put down his fork with a clatter. The sound caused everyone's head to jerk up and they all looked at him. Although he clearly worshipped his wife and would frequently defer to her decisions regarding the children and the house, such moments of acquiescence were done privately. In family gatherings such as this, he insisted on ruling with complete autocracy. Now he addressed his youngest daughter, who never ceased to amaze him with her presumptions and what his wife called cheek. She clearly needed to be reminded of her place. "Sadie, my dear daughter, would you please repeat what you just said?"

Sadie suddenly felt uneasy. She knew Adam Dov and Zosa were studying her intently from across the table and she figured they must enjoy seeing her put on the spot. They probably also thought she was too stupid to go to college. She cleared her throat lightly. "I said I've decided what I'd like to do after I finish high school. I'd like to start college."

"I see," Jacob said. "And are you asking me or informing me?"

Only Elke looked down at her plate and continued eating. The three children looked at their father with wide eyes.

"I . . . I . . . I don't know. I'm just telling you what I'd like to do."

Jacob picked up his fork and resumed eating. "Well, I see no point in it at all."

Sadie was still staring at him. Although her heart was now thumping wildly, she felt calm. "Why not?"

"Because there's no reason to send you to college. You'll never have a career, my dear, or be a scholar. The sensible thing for you to do is to get married as soon as possible." He laughed heartily. "You need a mensch who'll put a harness on you and curb that wild nature of yours. Someone who can control you."

Sadie's calm vanished and she heard her voice begin to rise the way it always did when she got angry. She tried hard to keep it from happening. It would only confirm their opinion of her as a wildcat. "I don't need to be controlled," she stated.

Her mother looked up. "Sadie dearest, don't you want someone to take care of you? A big handsome man to give you babies and buy you pretty dresses?"

Sadie happened to look at Zosa across the table. To her surprise, the expression on Zosa's face matched the emotion she felt her own must be registering. For just a second she wondered if Zosa could possibly have wanted to go to college too and had encountered resistance from their father when she suggested it. It was a sign of how distant she and Zosa were from each other that she had no idea. Then she turned back to her mother, who was still gazing at her, patiently awaiting an answer to her question.

Sadie forced herself to respond without anger this time. "I haven't thought much about it before, Mother.

I always figured a husband would be a long way off. I want to live a little before I get married."

"But college?" Elke sounded amazed. "Your father's right, dear. You've never been one much for studying."

Sadie felt a chill fall over her and she sensed she must appear slightly foolish. How, she wondered, could she have overlooked her father's adherence to his old-fashioned ideas? How could she have forgotten what he considered a woman's true role to be? She had just blindly assumed that with *Zeyde* behind her, everything would be all right. But if her father hadn't even allowed Zosa to go to college, and Zosa had always been more studious than she, then what chance did she have? But just as quickly it occurred to her that maybe Zosa had assumed his reaction and had never asked about college after all.

She was surprised when Adam Dov began to speak. "If you will permit me to offer an observation, I know that Sadie has not given promise of being a scholar. Certainly, even if she were a boy, she would not be marked for special training at the *yeshiva*. But I believe there is value to be had in a secular education, especially for a woman who will one day be the one entrusted with the upbringing of the children. The more of an understanding she has of her heritage, not just religious but secular as well, the better she will be able to prepare her children to take their places in society as informed and principled citizens."

He glanced at his father, and when Jacob showed no sign of countering him, he continued, his voice taking on more authority. He did not see Jacob glance quickly at Elke, although Sadie did, and she wondered what her mother was really thinking.

"Furthermore, many people are late bloomers. We already know Sadie is intelligent, but we have no idea what she might accomplish. I would say, give the girl an opportunity to do what's important to her. After all, times have changed. During the war, women took over for men, and they handled many jobs and activities just as well as men. They've earned the right to vote. What would it hurt to let Sadie have a chance at education?"

Sadie sat in amazement that Adam Dov had come to her defense. She even managed to screen out the pain and envy that flashed over Zosa's face. At the other end of the table her father was looking intently at Adam Dov and stroking his beard. Everyone waited to hear what Jacob would say. He looked briefly at Elke, then he moved his gaze to Sadie. She wasn't sure if it were just her imagination that her mother had seemed to give an almost imperceptible nod to her father.

"I believe if you really want to do this, Sadie, you will find a way. Therefore, if you go to college, I will not pay your tuition or contribute to your financial support. If God means your course of action to be thus, I believe you will find a way to get the money. I leave that up to you and God."

Sadie broke into a big smile. She knew this wasn't the time to tell him about *Zeyde's* offer. "Thank you, Father," she said loudly, and in her mind she added, Thank you, *Zeyde,* thank you, *Bubbe,* thank you, God. She glanced up at her brother, who happened to be looking at her. "Thank you, Adam Dov," she said. Although it had taken what seemed to Sadie almost all her life for him to see her side of any issue, she felt it had been worth the wait.

Chapter 28

Marya and Wolf were very proud that Sadie had been able to get into Radcliffe. Yet it was with a certain amount of sorrow that they'd packed her off that first year and after she was gone the house seemed unnaturally silent. Michael in particular was at a loss with himself.

At first the letters home, sometimes addressed to Michael, sometimes to Marya or Wolf, had come daily, so many that Marya was worried for Sadie. "If she writes us this often, when can she have time for study or the new friends she should be making?" Marya confided to Wolf. She enjoyed the letters, scrawled in a large hand with purple ink, but she couldn't help but wonder if the sheer volume of Sadie's correspondence was a good sign, especially since Sadie more than once wrote how different the girls were there. It wasn't so much a question of wealth as it was for many of them what Sadie called their country club backgrounds. Then after the first month, the letters came less and less often, until they slowed to a frequency of once a month, which to Marya seemed much more reasonable, making her feel more at ease.

One afternoon toward the end of Sadie's first semester, Marya had one of Sadie's letters in her purse when she decided to stop by Elke's house. Although she spoke to Elke on the telephone several times a week, she hadn't seen her in almost a month. Now she had a strong urge to pay her a visit.

Marya was surprised when Zosa rather than Mrs. Chotzinoff opened the door. She noticed Zosa looked tired and her eyes were red-rimmed, leaving Marya to wonder if she had been reading too much.

She gave her granddaughter a hug. "Where's Mrs. Chotzinoff? You must excuse me if I appeared a bit startled, but I haven't seen anyone but her open that door in the last twenty years." Then as soon as the words were spoken, she wondered if Zosa's red eyes had anything to do with the aged housekeeper.

"She's sick, *Bubbe*," Zosa half whispered, "very sick. Mother is with her now. She was going to call you to see if you could help. And now here you are, almost as if you knew."

Marya shuddered as Zosa led her into the cold parlor where Mrs. Chotzinoff's customary fire used to be burning and helped her off with her coat. "We don't know what's wrong, but she has chills and no matter what, she can't seem to get warm."

Marya followed Zosa to the back of the house to the room the housekeeper had occupied ever since Jacob, in his bachelor days, had brought her in to tend house for him. When Marya saw the old woman, her face as white as the pillow where her small head lay, she tried not to show her shock. On top of her minute frame were piled six or seven heavy blankets, but the old woman still trembled visibly from cold.

The moment Elke saw her mother enter the room she felt better. She always seemed to bring with her a calm and steadiness, and Elke was sure she would know what to do.

The first thing Marya did was place her hand on Mrs. Chotzinoff's forehead. Then she took the old woman's hands from under the blankets and held them in hers. They felt cold and dry. Marya rubbed them between hers to help their circulation. She asked Mrs. Chotzinoff for a description of her symptoms, and then she asked Elke what she had been able to do for the woman so far. After listening carefully to both of them, she asked for a piece of paper and wrote on it two long names. Then she handed it to Zosa.

"Take this to the pharmacy and ask the pharmacist for these herbs."

Elke reached for the slip of paper. "Let me do it, Mama. I know exactly where to take it. Zosa can stay here and help you with Mrs. Chotzinoff."

Almost as soon as Elke left the room, Mrs. Chotzinoff closed her eyes and fell into a sleep. Marya and Zosa kept watch at the foot of the bed and talked softly between themselves. Marya welcomed this opportunity to talk to this granddaughter she had never become as close to as Sadie. Where Sadie was an impetuous, outgoing girl, Zosa was more closed, her energies pointed in a different direction. Her source of solace and companionship appeared to be exclusively Adam Dov.

Zosa saw her grandmother looking at her and smiled shyly. "I could see Mother relax the minute you walked in, *Bubbe*. And I felt better too. She remembers how you were able to stop fevers and cure colds just by sprinkling a few herbs or powders in a glass of tea when we were all children."

"It's amazing how some of those old remedies work a lot faster than most of the new ones these doctors suggest." Marya laughed. "But listen to me, I'm talking like an old person. I don't know if I'm ready to do that yet."

Zosa laughed too and felt a little more at ease. As she looked at this pretty woman sitting across from her, it was hard for her to believe she was old enough to be her grandmother. She certainly didn't look like anyone else's grandmother she knew. She was still slim, and her hair was richly red, just as it had been when she was younger. She dressed elegantly and wore her thick hair in a full chignon at the nape of her neck, one of the styles now in vogue for those women who hadn't bobbed theirs off. As if her grandmother had known what she was thinking, she heard her say, "I'm pleased to see you still have your long pretty hair, Zosa."

Self-conscious, Zosa fluttered her hand to her head. "I'm afraid I couldn't bring myself to do what Sadie did. I don't have much desire to look like a flapper."

Marya smiled and snapped open her purse. "Speaking of Sadie, I have a letter here from her if you'd like to read it." She removed the heavily perfumed pink envelope and handed it to Zosa.

"Oh, no thank you, *Bubbe*. I'd just as soon hear it from you . . . if at all."

Marya was surprised by her indifference. "What is it, Zosa? Is something wrong?" She knew her granddaughters weren't close, but she hadn't imagined that Zosa would actually spurn news of her sister.

Zosa shrugged. "Sometimes these days it's hard for me to hear about Sadie. She's off in college and so is Adam Dov, and I sit here in the house all day, waiting for Adam Dov to come home so maybe we can go to a café or a movie house if he doesn't have to study."

"But aren't you staying home by choice?"

Zosa laughed bitterly. "I'm not sure how to answer that. You know how my father is."

"Zosa, these days a girl doesn't have to stay home until she gets married. If you're not happy, there are so many other things you could do."

"I'm not sure how to go about it. Sometimes there are advantages to being thoughtless like Sadie." When she heard Marya click her teeth lightly, she said quickly, "I mean she probably never gave it much thought that our father might turn down her plan to go to college. She just barged in and asked."

"If you wanted to go, why didn't you do the same thing?"

"I never dreamed he would say yes. I was afraid."

Marya saw that Zosa's lower lip was starting to quiver and she reached out and put her hand on her shoulder. "It's not too late now, you know. Why don't you talk to your father tonight?"

"You think he would let me?"

"Well, I doubt he would be overjoyed, but I don't see how he could say no to you when he said yes to Sadie."

"And the strange thing to me is that although Sadie got good grades in high school, she never seemed to care much about studying. And yet she's the one who's now in college."

Marya patted Zosa's hand. "You're just going to have to show a little gumption, child. If you see something you want, you have to go after it. No one else will do it for you. You don't see anyone else stepping forward to approach your father for you, do you?"

Zosa shook her head no. She resolved that she would do exactly what her grandmother suggested. She would talk to her father that night.

By the time Elke came back, Marya and Zosa had the hot water ready to make the herb medicine. Marya crushed the dark yellow flowers and leaves of the dried herb between her fingers and rolled the fragments in the palm of her hand. Then she measured three teaspoons of the powdery mixture into a pint of the hot water and stirred it until it was suffused with a deep yellow color. "Give her a large glass of this tea three times a day for the next two days. On the third change to this other herb." She opened the second package that Elke had brought home and smelled the dark green leaves to make sure they were what she had requested. "Give her two glasses a day of this one for the rest of the week."

Zosa was peering respectfully into the pot of yellow liquid. "What will happen when she drinks this?"

Marya explained as she poured out a tall glass of the tea. "Her chills should stop almost immediately.

Then little by little the aches in her bones will diminish and she'll regain her strength."

Elke had no reason to doubt it would unfold exactly as her mother had explained it. It had when she was a child and it had for her own children.

A couple of hours later, after Marya had left, Zosa suddenly asked her mother, "Did *Bubbe* learn about how to cure people when she was in Russia?"

Elke shook her head. "She told me she once worked in an apothecary shop before she and your grandfather married."

"The apothecary shop was here?"

"Yes. Your grandmother was very young when she left Russia, just sixteen, and she brought nothing with her. It must have been awful for her living there because she doesn't like to talk about it at all. Still, I like to pretend her knowledge of those natural medicines comes from the old country. Somehow it all seems so mysterious to me it's like it's part of the old ways. I know your grandmother wouldn't like to hear that. She's always wanted to be completely modern. And in truth, what she knows about curing aches and breaking fevers came from here in New York, on the Lower East Side where they first lived."

Zosa was thoughtful for a few moments. "It's strange to think *Bubbe* lived down there. She seems so . . . so different from the people down there. It's as if she lived on the West Side all her life. It's hard to imagine her struggling to make a living. She reminds me of a queen, someone who always had everything and who never went through any hardship or was ever poor or sad."

Elke looked sharply at her daughter, but her voice was kind. "Zosa, how can you say that? You've heard me say that when I was a baby, we all lived in one room with the sewing machines stitching away right in the next room. And then just when we got a little bit ahead, there was the fire and Mama and Papa had nothing again. Although they had been here five years, it was as if they had just gotten off the boat, and they had to start all over again."

"I know, but it's hard for me to believe all that when I look at them. They're both so proud and dignified, and they live in such a beautiful house and *Bubbe* doesn't even look like a grandmother. It's not easy to picture, that's all. It's hard for me to imagine Father living down there too. I feel he has lived here in this house all his life. I don't like to think that he was poor and like those people down there."

Elke was shocked. But she knew in a way what Zosa meant, not about the people on the Lower East Side but about how her father and mother seemed so far from all that turmoil. She knew it was sometimes hard for children to imagine their parents or grandparents as young people who had to make hard decisions and choices. And if they had meanwhile become successful, it was even harder to see them as they must have been before.

While her daughter and granddaughter were holding their discussion of her, Marya was on her way back to her shop in the carriage Wolf had insisted on buying for her shortly after Michael's birth. It was a smart cream-colored brougham with brass fittings and a dark blue trim. Marya knew Wolf would like to replace it now with a Model T or a Chevrolet, but she wanted nothing to do with one of those rattling noisemakers. She wondered if she was getting set in her ways. After all, she had always fervently embraced the modern and rejected the old. But lately she didn't seem to have such a strong compulsion to do that. It seemed infinitely preferable to her to have the kindly coachman in his blue livery handle the snarls of New York City traffic while she sat in cushioned comfort and looked out the window.

As the carriage slowed down and then came to a complete halt, Marya heard a lot of yelling and honking all around her. She craned her head out the window to see what the commotion was about, but all she saw was a sea of traffic—motorcars, carriages, horse-cars and jitneys jammed together in different directions completely filling the street. After fifteen minutes stuck in the same spot, the carriage began to inch forward until it came alongside a motorcar stalled in the middle of the road. This vehicle was the apparent cause of the tie-up.

They pulled next to the car, a sleek yellow and black thing Marya recognized as a 1921 Pierce-Arrow Runabout from the many pictures Michael had insisted on showing her of this vehicle he had dubbed his dream car. Marya did a double take as she looked at the driver, who was standing in front of the car and shaking his head. He was nattily dressed in a golf suit with plus fours of grey wool, a matching jacket and plaid woolen hose. The way he carried himself looked familiar to her. On the man's head was a beige felt hat, which completely obscured his face as he was bending over the front of the car. When Marya's carriage passed by, he looked up, and she was surprised to see that the man who was suavely dressed was Andrew.

"Driver!" she cried and knocked on the front wall of the carriage. The carriage stopped and she immediately called out.

When Andrew recognized the handsome woman who was calling to him from the passing carriage, his face lit up and he signaled for her to wait as he began to hurry forward.

She reached out a gloved hand and he took it in his. He gazed at her a few seconds without saying anything, and when he began to speak, the expression in his eyes belied the jovial heartiness in his voice. "My God, Marya, I don't believe it! It's been years. And like an angel of mercy you come along just when I'm needing a lift. Are you in a terrible hurry, or do you have time to drop me further uptown at the Plaza Hotel?"

"Of course I have time, Andrew." How strange it

was to see him again! She hoped everything would be all right between them. She instructed her driver to pull to the side of the road while Andrew busied himself with hiring two passing youths to push his car around the corner into an empty spot on another street. As she watched him through the carriage window, she noticed he was as tan and fit as always, and the grey of his hair accented the deep blue of his eyes more than ever. She felt an ache as she looked at him and thought of the last evening they had spent together more than thirteen years ago.

It had taken place soon after Detweiler's thugs had made their surprise attack on Wolf in their living room while she was forced to watch. Somehow Detweiler blamed Wolf for his daughter's elopement with their son Daniel, and although Wolf had told him he knew even less about it than Detweiler himself did, that didn't stop Detweiler from sending his goons to work Wolf over as a thank-you note. Marya shuddered to recall how bruised inside she had felt at having witnessed the attack. That Wolf had apparently also seriously injured two of his attackers was no consolation to her. She had spent the entire day at Wolf's bedside in the hospital and come home late that night to an empty and dark house. The telephone had rung just as she'd come in. When she'd answered it, Andrew had been on the other end.

For just one second she was startled that he had called her at her home. Always he made his calls to her shop. She suddenly remembered the long-standing plans they had made for that evening. It was Andrew's forty-eighth birthday and she had insisted she wanted to take him to dinner at the Waldorf's Palm Room. At the sound of his voice she felt physically ill as it all came back to her.

"I've been trying to get hold of you for the last two days," he said with an icy edge she'd never heard before.

She felt overwhelmed at the realization of how she

must have hurt him. "Andrew, I'm so sorry. I . . . Wolf . . . you see. . . ." She faltered, at a loss as to how to begin.

"Is Wolf there now?"

She wondered if he knew. "No." She tried to think clearly. "He's in the hospital."

"Good. That means he won't be home tonight. I'm coming over."

"Andrew, no, please. You can't. I—" But it was too late. He had already hung up.

As he stood under the lamplight on the front stoop, she noticed even in that imperfect light that his face was redder than she had seen it before and she could tell he had been drinking, although how much she wasn't sure. He still stood dignified and was impeccably dressed, but there was a glittery brilliance to his eyes and his gestures were a little more abandoned and free. Beyond him she could see his shiny new Oldsmobile parked out in the street. She had no choice but to let him in.

The moment they were both inside, he took hold of her arm. "Don't you know I've been driven nearly mad with worry? Where have you been?"

"Andrew, I'm sorry. There was an accident and Wolf's in the hospital. I've been there ever since."

"Couldn't you have sent a messenger or called me? The hospital would have let you use their telephone."

She shook her head. "Andrew, I'm so sorry."

"Will you please stop saying that? It doesn't make things any better. Now will you tell me why you didn't even try to get in touch with me? That's the least you could have done, if you cared."

She was stricken. "Andrew, I do care. I do. But you see, this accident . . . Wolf was seriously hurt. This is the first evening I've been home from the hospital." As she spoke, her voice trembled. The expression on Andrew's face as he listened to her made her knees feel weak.

When he spoke, his voice was sad. "The look in your eyes tells me more than your words do, Marya."

She felt dizzy and weak and held her breath in fear of something that she had just begun to realize and she knew that Andrew had too.

He spoke softly but with firmness. "You are still in love with your husband, Marya. It's all over your face and in your voice."

"Andrew, I. . . ." She wanted to shake her head, but she found she couldn't.

"It explains so much. I've just been so in love with you all these years that it's taken me a long time to see it. I understood when you asked for some time to notify your family and make arrangements to move out into your own place. I knew the divorce proceedings would take even more time, and that if I had waited over fifteen years for you, I could certainly wait a while longer." Suddenly his tone changed. "Let me ask you something. Did you ever tell your husband about us? About our plans?"

"No. I was waiting until—"

"Until never. In case you still can't see it, I'll tell you what that means. You never intended to marry me."

In spite of her best efforts to stop them, tears had begun to roll down Marya's cheeks. "No, this isn't so. What you are saying just isn't so. I did want to marry you."

"You see, Marya? You are using the past tense without even realizing it. But I understand, even if you don't, that although on the surface you may have thought you did want to marry me, deep down you were still in love with your husband."

Marya wanted to say that he was wrong, all wrong. But she couldn't. When the first attacker had swung his fist at Wolf's head that night, she had screamed with every fiber of her being, and in that scream was all the anger and hate at having seen her father and mother killed before her eyes, then her first

son disappear from her as she could only watch helplessly, caught in the Cossack's grip. The scream was
for her first husband, who went into the czar's army
and never came back, and for her second son, stillborn,
and for her son Daniel's disappearance. But most of
all, it was from the terrifying specter of now losing
Wolf, and it was a loss too horrible even to imagine,
the most empty and fearful blackness of all.

Andrew was still staring at her sadly. "I now can
see so clearly what for years and years I couldn't. It all
makes sense. The reason you never left your husband a
long time ago wasn't that you still had vestiges of your
old customs clinging to you, as I led myself to believe,
ever hopeful. It was because you still loved him and
couldn't leave him, even if he didn't love you." He
shook his head. "I was just too blind to see it. I suppose I didn't really want to see it. I couldn't bear the
thought of having to give you up. And now. . . ." His
voice trailed off.

Marya picked up his words. "And now?" She
made no effort to argue with him. The truth of his
words was too vivid to both of them. "I can't imagine
my life without you, Andrew."

He looked at her wildly. "Marya, now that we
both realize how it is, we can't go on in the same way
we have these past years."

"No. I suppose not." She was painfully aware of
the awful loss that was pending.

"I will always be here for you, Marya. I want you
to know that. But I cannot continue to see you. It
would be too painful, knowing I could never have you.
Before, even though I was sharing you with another
man, there was hope you would leave. Now I'm denied
even that sustaining hope." He turned and picked up
his hat from the marble-topped commode in the hallway and opened the front door for himself.

As he walked down the steps, Marya felt helpless
and torn. She wanted to run after him and tell him she
loved him. But she knew that for his sake, she couldn't

do that, even though she did love him. She couldn't prolong the pain for him any longer, and she knew, as he would too, the love she bore him was of a different kind than the love she bore Wolf. It was softer, gentler, perhaps just as lasting. But ultimately it didn't claim her.

And as she watched him go, she also realized how she had dimmed her chances of ever finding out for certain who David Sheffield was.

Now Marya was startled to see Andrew motioning toward a young woman who had been waiting on the curb and whom Marya hadn't noticed before. The woman was dressed in the lastest fashion—a frock that was elevated to the knee and was nothing more than a bare tube of beige cloth with a waistline dropped to the hips. As the young woman drew nearer, Andrew took her by the arm and guided her to the carriage. Marya watched while the girl's skirt rose even higher as she climbed up into the carriage, and when she settled onto the cushioned seat, it rose higher still, revealing the garters that held up her blond stockings.

"Marya, I'd like you to meet Miss Rita Chatham," Andrew said quickly as the young woman snuggled close to him and nestled against his arm.

For a moment Marya wondered if she had seen a look of embarrassment wash over Andrew's face or if she had just imagined it, or maybe she had even hoped for it. She tried not to stare at the woman, who appeared to be in her early twenties. Barely out of high school, Marya thought, and the excitement she had felt at suddenly seeing Andrew again now turned to dejection.

As the three of them rolled along in her carriage, Marya wondered if Andrew was thinking about that last painful evening together. She tried smiling at him and thought of how she might change the unspoken tension that hung in the air.

Andrew surprised her by speaking first. He talked generally of friends and acquaintances they had in common, of people Marya seldom thought of anymore. She learned that Gregory Keller, who had once made a pass at her, and Mrs. Keller had gotten a divorce. It appeared that Claudia Carter—she remembered the exotic Claudia—had developed an intense passion for horses, which had led her to being seen in Gregory Keller's company many times, raving about the "divine lines of the equine hindquarters." Claudia and Mrs. Worthington, Marya's first client, seemed to have had a falling out, something to do with a beautiful young masseuse from France they both had hired and whom each claimed to have discovered and insisted on having as a live-in.

As he spoke, Marya thought what a relief it was not to be caught up in that circle anymore. Not that she had truly been caught up in it, she told herself. It only looked that way to Wolf. But no matter how dazzling the mansion, and how exciting the amorous intrigues or how lavish the compliments and attention from both the women and men, she always felt she had at least one toe firmly planted on the ground. All along, all she really had wanted was recognition for her work and to build a firm financial base so that she might feel for once she had some control over her future.

As they spoke, Miss Chatham made a great display of opening her purse and extracting a compact and a tube of lipstick. She occupied herself with tracing a large red O around her lips with slow, loving strokes while she made mouths at herself in the mirror. Next she set about patting her face with a powder puff. In spite of herself, Marya was distracted, and finally could only stare at the young woman, having lost the drift of her and Andrew's strained conversation.

"I don't suppose you've had occasion to see David Sheffield, have you?" Andrew surprised her.

Marya shook her head, aware that Andrew, despite the casualness of his question, was now watching her as carefully as always. "No. We've fallen out of touch."

"You knew he was married, didn't you?"

She blinked quickly. "No, I didn't. To whom?" she asked trying to maintain an air of only casual interest.

The young woman popped up brightly. "Oh! David? Are you talking about David Sheffield? He married an Irish girl, Katie Flannagan."

Marya tried again to keep her tone casual as she addressed her question to Andrew, as if it were he who had just imparted this information to her. "Long ago?"

His eyes met hers and she searched them, hoping for some sign that would get the two of them beyond this awkwardness and back to the easy dialogue they once had.

"A few years back," he said. "They have a daughter. Lisa's her name."

Miss Chatham broke in again. "Quite a beauty, I hear, with David's red hair."

"Oh," breathed Marya, wondering how this woman knew David and thankful they had arrived at the Plaza Hotel because it would save her from having to keep up the pretense of nonchalance any longer.

As the carriage rolled to a stop, Andrew placed his hat back on his head and put his hand on the door pull. He gave Marya a long, hard look. "I hope you've been well."

"Yes, very well, Andrew," she answered, wishing she didn't sound so stiff.

He hesitated. "And your husband?" His eyes darted over the fine carriage and liveried coachman.

"He's fine. I don't know if you're aware we've had another son—Michael. He's already a teenager."

It was Andrew's turn to feign nonchalance. "Yes, I have heard you had another strapping lad. I'm very pleased you have a son." He carefully avoided mentioning Daniel and put out his hand.

Miss Chatham called to him from the curb, where she was hopping up and down with tiny steps. "C'mon, darling. It's cold."

Marya shook his hand. As he started away from the carriage, he hesitated again. "Remember, Marya, what I said to you the last time I saw you still goes. If you ever need me, you have only to call."

"Thank you, Andrew, and I have not forgotten that kindness."

She watched him moving deftly and gracefully through the door of the elegant hotel as Miss Chatham slipped her arm through his. Andrew had not changed in appearance, but she couldn't tell if he was still the same man underneath. She wondered if he had changed his feelings for her. For, she realized with a sudden sadness, she had not changed hers for him.

Wolf paced uneasily back and forth across the length of his office. He felt the same unnerving lack of control he had experienced the day Daniel had stalked out of his office and his life for good. He remembered, too, Daniel's subsequent bitter legal action. In the long run, Daniel's transference of his small percentage of MW Enterprises to the union coffers had little bearing on the day to day operations of the company. Wolf, however, always felt a combination of guilt and betrayal on those rare occasions when he was obligated to consult the union concerning a token corporate decision.

As he now awaited Etta's son Zavel Salenski's visit, he tried again to think clearly about how he would handle the boy, and he wished he could stop thinking of it as a confrontation. The truth was he had no idea what to expect. There was a light knock, and the secretary, a middle-aged woman whom Wolf had hired as much for her ability to speak the five main languages of his employees as for her efficiency, announced that Zavel Salenski was waiting in the outer office.

The man who walked into Wolf's office took him aback. Wolf had been expecting someone in his mid-twenties, about Daniel's age when he'd last seen him. The person in front of him looked to be in his forties. But what struck Wolf the most was the way he was dressed and how he held himself. This man was indistinguishable from any other of the thousands of newly arrived Jewish immigrants. He was clean but poorly dressed, and his eyes burned with a hunger to get on with the business of making a success of himself.

Was this truly his son, this tall, thin man with sharp features and black hair? His son—dressed like a greenhorn and looking like one of the masses? He tried to see himself in this person, but found the task distasteful. He represented all that Wolf no longer was, all that he had tried to put behind him as quickly as possible and for good.

He motioned the man toward a chair. "Please sit down," he said first in Yiddish and then in Polish.

The man replied in Yiddish. "I don't wish to take much of your time, sir. But you see, my mother has from time to time spoken of you and of your kindness toward our family."

"How is your mother?" Wolf asked politely. At the same time he wondered how much Etta had told him.

Zavel pulled from his worn billfold a photograph and handed it to Wolf. "Perhaps you would like to see this picture of her, taken a few years ago?"

A woman, her hair pulled tightly back in a bun, stared at him with round, watery eyes. She looked old and sad. He realized he wouldn't have recognized her if she had walked into the room.

"And your father?" he asked tentatively.

"Moses died when I was ten. He . . . he drank himself to death."

"You and Moses . . . you were close?" Wolf realized he was probing but couldn't stop himself. He noted that Zavel hadn't called Moses his father.

The man shrugged. "Not especially. We fought. You know how it is."

"And your mother? Someone takes care of her?"

"She works a little in a millinery shop, making hats. And I help her out with money. That's why I've come to America. To get a better job and send her money."

Wolf walked to the window and looked out on the bustle of activity in the street below. He saw young men laden with bundles of garment parts, others pushing racks of completed coats and dresses. "You would like a job here?" he asked. He noticed Zavel was fingering his cap nervously.

"If that would not be too much to ask."

Of course, Wolf thought, a job from one's father was not too much to ask. He ran his hand through his hair. But to see this man every day, this constant reminder of his long ago and ill-fated romance, if he could call it that, with Etta? This constant reminder that once again he had failed in his role of father? That he didn't want.

"If you are willing to leave New York, I can provide you with a job. Right now I need workers in my mills upstate. You can have a job there."

When Wolf saw the light that came into Zavel's eyes, he was embarrassed. The man was looking at him with total gratitude when he'd just given him no more than what he gave complete strangers almost daily. A job, nothing more. No welcoming embrace. No acknowledgment.

"Thank you, Mr. Luminov," the man kept saying.

"You can use my first name."

The man smiled. "Thank you, Zavel."

"Wolf," he said, firmly.

For a second the man looked perplexed. Then as he got up to leave, Wolf stopped him. "Why did you come to me? What did your mother tell you about me?"

Zavel looked down. "She had known you a long

time, she said. She had reason to believe you would help me." He stood up to leave.

"I hope you'll keep in touch," Wolf said, more out of a sense of obligation than anything else. And he thought of the irony of it all. He, who had come to this country with a dream of family, with the desire for a line of sons to whom he could entrust this huge conglomerate of MW Enterprises, seemed to find himself incapable of reaching out to those sons. Daniel had run away—or more accurately, been driven away; Michael showed little interest in the business the way Daniel had; Zavel was a stranger to him; and Adam Dov was clearly a scholar, a man of contemplation rather than a man of action that the business demanded.

Wolf knew he had been a success as a businessman. But as a father, so far the evidence didn't look reassuring.

Sadie ran her hands lovingly over the steering wheel of her tin lizzie and thrilled to think the car she was driving was actually her own. It didn't matter that it wasn't a new car and that her grandfather had passed it on to her when he had bought a new 1928 Packard for himself. She had ridden in this car many times before, and in a sense it had always been hers. As far as she was concerned, this car had captured her heart the first day her grandfather had taken her for a drive in it when she was just fourteen. Now at twenty, she felt like it was an old friend, and besides, she had earned it by keeping her grades high during her first year of college as she'd promised she would.

It was the end of summer vacation and she was on her way to Grand Central Station to pick up her friend Chris Hollington. They had met at the end of her freshman year at a Harvard fraternity party and during the last two weeks of the school year had managed to fit in three tennis matches and even a couple more parties. After the semester, as they both prepared to return to their families, they had promised to stay in touch. They had taken the train together as far as New York City and then Chris had gone south to his family in St. Augustine, Florida. Sadie had been delighted that he'd been true to his word and had in fact written her two letters. It was those letters that gave her the confidence to suggest in her last one to him in early August that she pick him up at the train station in New York on his way back to Harvard in September, and they could ride up to Cambridge together in her new car.

Inside, the station was its usual hubbub of local and long distance travelers. She stationed herself directly under the clock as they had arranged, and didn't have to wait long until she saw his blond head bobbing over the others in a knot of people surging in her direction. He broke loose from the crowd and headed toward her with long, confident strides, his face in a big grin.

Chris Hollington was, by anyone's standards, a good looking man. He was tall and athletic looking, with the slim-hipped and broad-shouldered physique of a swimmer. His blond hair was parted in the middle in the current fashion and slicked close to his head. He was wearing a large raccoon coat beneath which she could see the broad pant legs of his Oxford bags and the tips of his brown-and-white saddle shoes. He set down the two leather bags he was carrying, swooped her up under the arms and swung her around several times.

Passers-by turned to stare at the sight of this handsome "Sheik" and his squealing "Sheba," obviously college students and obviously "in the mode."

When he set her back down, he surveyed her boldly from head to toe. "Sadie, you look downright ritzy!" She was wearing a black cloth coat trimmed in curly black astrakhan, and a short pleated skirt with a beige crêpe de chine blouse with an ascot. A black felt cloche was pulled down almost over her eyes, rendering the edge of her red bob scarcely visible.

"It was a swell idea you had to drive us to Cambridge. Let's go, my dogs are killing me." She laughed and motioned him to follow her to the car. As Sadie pulled out into the traffic of Forty-second Street, Chris said, "I've never spent any time here in New York. It's always been just a place I changed trains. If you've no objections, can we drive about a bit in New York?"

"Sure," Sadie said and swung the car south toward lower Manhattan. "You're probably such an infant you've never seen South Street—that's the street of ships—or Wall Street or Broadway. I can even drive you past my grandfather's factory."

Chris leaned his head back and propped his feet up on the dash. "Whatever you say, Sadie. You're holding me captive. You can do with me as you wish. And, you're right, I am an infant. I've never seen any of those places."

Sadie drove down Seventh Street where she proudly pointed out MW Enterprises. The factory alone took up over half a block, having in the last fifteen years methodically proceeded to take over the adjacent factories, and it now employed well over a thousand people. As she drove past, Sadie hoped her grandfather wouldn't happen to be glancing out the window at that precise moment. Somehow it had seemed easier not to tell her grandparents she was picking a friend up at the station and instead to let them think she was on her way north from the time she left the house. She just wasn't ready to get into family introductions yet. It seemed the kind of thing some dumb Dora from the Midwest would do.

Chris whistled at the size of Wolf's factory. "Looks like your grandfather must be one busy man."

"He's even busier than you think, what with the mills to run too."

"Mills?"

"We have some mills in upstate New York. *Zeyde*—I mean my grandfather—has been thinking of selling them. He has a hunch hard times are ahead for the textile industries, but so far he hasn't done it." She laughed when Chris whistled again.

She turned left onto Division Street where they passed shop after shop of men's clothing, and where half the signs were written in Yiddish. Sadie had felt a little out of place the few previous times she had ventured south on Seventh past the factory. This time as she drove through the streets thronged with people from different countries was no exception. These people here all seemed so foreign.

The traffic was moving so slowly on Division Street she turned right onto another in an effort to move more quickly through this part of the city. This street proved to be even more congested than the other one. Pedestrians and peddlers threaded through the streets, in and out of the motorcars and carriages that had no choice but to inch along at a tedious rate.

Chris was shaking his head. "I've never seen anything like it," he marveled, his attention darting from the man who was banging on the side of the car, offering to sell him a chamber pot, to the old, bearded violinist on the corner playing Russian folk tunes, to the heavily shawled and kerchiefed woman behind a bin of apples who was proclaiming her product's virtues in a low, guttural chant.

"Have you ever seen so many foreigners?" he asked. "And they're almost all Jews, you know, streaming into this country every day by the hundreds."

Sadie found herself laughing shrilly. "These foreigners sure have strange ways of talking in loud voices. They are different," she added as they both laughed.

She was relieved when it was possible for her finally to turn onto South Street around the Brooklyn Bridge. She threw herself into pointing out the landmarks of the area—the Fulton Fish Market, Battery Park, the huge hotellike structure of Castle Garden across the river. She felt an odd twinge as she reeled off the names, names made familiar to her by her grandfather's stories of his early years in this country, and it felt even odder to think he was once just another face among the many yelling, laughing and crying faces they had just driven past.

She circled around the tip of Manhattan, then headed the car northward, eager to be out of the teeming Lower East Side. She drove fast toward the chic and exciting life that lay ahead of her in college and savored the fresh wind whipping across her face.

Chapter 29

As the four of them hurtled down the dark country road in Sadie's Model T, she tried not to think about the three tests she had just failed in history, biology and government. Three in a row, that was a new record for her, she told herself. As the road whizzed past faster and faster with Chris at the wheel, Sadie marveled at how her sophomore year seemed to be the inverse of her freshman year. In her first year of college she had studied a lot and socialized little until the very end. This year she was socializing a lot and leaving studying for the very end. It seemed that she and Chris and her roommate, Kathy Johnston, a tall, peroxided blonde from Connecticut, and her sometime boyfriend, Bob Wilson, could always think of something more clever and adventuresome than studying, and there were plenty of nights like tonight, spent roaming in her automobile.

She had put from her mind her father's reaction when he first learned Wolf had given her his motorcar to take back to college for her second year. "It's nothing but a wicked little room," her father had said, picking up the term of a current writer and commentator on the social scene, "a wicked room that can be conveniently moved to any dark, deserted road for any kind of unchaperoned and unlicensed behavior. The more you drive that car, the more your grades will fall," he had predicted, "and I shudder to think what else." Now as the memory of her recent test scores came to her unbidden, his words did too.

"It must be something in the id that's controlling us," Sadie suddenly said aloud, savoring the feel of the Freudian term on her tongue. She was sitting next to Chris, and in the back seat were Kathy and Bob who were laughing so much they hadn't heard her.

But Chris had. "The id? What are you talking about? What's that?" He pulled a small silver flask from his hip pocket and handed it to Sadie.

"Don't you remember? That's Sigmund Freud's term for part of our unconscious mind. It's our basic impulses that lead us toward fulfilling our instinctive needs." She took a swig from the flask and wondered how he always managed to keep it full.

Chris laughed knowingly. "Oh, that. All I can remember about Freud is all the writing he does about sex, how everything we do or think has to do with sex, one way or the other."

"Well, it does, you know. Just listen to how everyone talks these days. The popular girl is the fast-talking and fast-acting girl."

Chris glanced at her out of the corner of his eye. "What? Are you disapproving? You're not starting to think like one of those flat tires out of Iowa, are you? Of course sex is part of everything we do. That's what makes everything we do so much fun and worth doing."

By this time they had pulled up on the edge of a parking area in front of a long, low-slung building built a short distance back off the road. Around the building was arrayed a surprising number of other motorcars and even a few horse-drawn carriages. The sound of a jazz piano drifted into the night in stark contrast to the tall, silent pine trees that stretched forth into the woods around this noisy and unexpected outpost.

Inside, Sadie was startled at the number of people who had managed to squeeze themselves into a room so small. At first she had trouble getting a good look at them because of all the smoke. Every man and woman in the place seemed to have a cigarette dangling from the lips, and even the piano player was puffing away as he played, his eyes half-closed. The long tables, probably hewn from the same pines as stood guard outside, were covered with cocktail glasses and bottles of beer, scotch, rye and other illegal spirits. On the far wall behind which two particularly burly men stood guard was a door that Sadie imagined led to the private room of the roadhouse. She had heard stories of cocaine and marijuana dealers conducting business in such rooms and wondered, as her eyes surveyed the crowd, whether any of the patrons were "high" on those intoxicants.

She had never been to a roadhouse before, but of course she knew she couldn't tell the others that. When it came her turn, she asked for a glass of bourbon and water, a drink she had first tasted at a fraternity party a few months ago and that had become her drink ever since. Tonight what she had been drinking from Chris' flask was something he had identified merely as the water of life, which he explained he had learned in a literature class was what whiskey was originally called by the Irish. Now she was ready for a drink that was more familiar and more comforting.

The next three hours the four of them spent laughing, shouting witty remarks at one another over the din and pointing out unusual or unsavory characters among the patronage. They shared knowing winks over an aging prostitute, her bleached-blonde hair contrasting with her old-fashioned ankle-length dress. They laughed at the short, squat gentleman in a red vest who served as bartender, his bloodshot eyes and droopy mustache rising and falling in rhythm as he hurriedly juggled bottles and glasses in continuous motion. Every time the others had a drink, so did she, until the room and all its vivid characters began to blend into a kaleidoscopic blur. In her inebriated state, she saw only a dark pond of clinking glasses, with disembodied mouths that opened and shut in rubbery motions and watery eyes that leered and winked at no one in particular. She had been high a lot in the last few months, but never to this extent. Pretty soon she put her head down in her arms to shut out all those fishlike creatures and the opening and closing motions of their wet mouths.

"Time to go." Chris' voice sounded far away to her as though it were coming from the end of a tunnel. Sadie felt herself being lifted up in his arms, her ankles and arms dangling helplessly as he floated her away from the noise and the loud laughter.

The coolness of the night air started to bring her to her senses. She realized that Kathy and Bob had not come outside with them. Chris gently set her down on the seat, then climbed in next to her and held her in his arms. She felt the reassuring expanse of his chest and snuggled in closer. When she closed her eyes, the dreamlike sensation of floating on water came back to her. He began to kiss her forehead and her neck. She felt his lips, cool and wet, against her overly warm skin. On Chris' mouth she could taste the scotch he had been drinking, and she giggled. "I've decided," she said unsteadily, "that scotch is a tastier drink than bourbon and water. I think I'm going to switch."

But Chris didn't say anything. His breathing became louder and heavier, and the sound of it excited her. His hands began to move across her breasts and then down her thighs, feeling silky and warm. She saw no reason not to abandon herself completely to the feeling.

She opened her eyes once and was startled at how clear and still the stars overhead were. Then she closed them again and returned to the sensation that the whole world was swirling in circles. Chris lifted her skirt and began to pull off her panties, and as he did so, she felt she was whirling down into an endless vortex of pleasure. Only at a certain point some time later did she cry out in pain, and then the pain quickly vanished and she was crying out this time in ecstasy.

Only once did it occur to her that she might have preferred her first time to be some place more romantic than in a Model T.

Sadie's sense that she was swirling in a whirlpool of emotion continued beyond that night. The remaining months of the school year were a continuous round of parties. A party could spring up anytime and almost anywhere: at a fraternity house; at the home of an acquaintance who had vacationing parents; at the home of someone they had never met but whose party they had decided to crash, as was the fashionable practice; in speakeasies; in far-off roadhouses; even surreptitiously in their dormitory rooms. And always there was the taste of liquor and the promise of ready sex.

The day that Sadie opened the official looking envelope the college had sent her, she knew she had to find a way to break out of the circle. "I'm on probation for my grades," she told Chris later that evening, trying to affect a lighter tone than she actually felt.

Chris laughed. "Don't worry. You're smart. You can pull them up anytime you want. Besides, you don't want to be a grind, do you? This is the best time of our lives. Who wants to spend it in bed with a book?"

Sadie knew she was smart, smart enough, for one thing, to imagine what her grandparents and parents would say about her being on academic probation, not to mention what Adam Dov and Zosa would think. To Sadie's surprise, Zosa had decided to go to college after all. She was now enrolled at New York University. Sadie could imagine that Zosa's grades were excellent. Sadie pondered her academic predicament. She had to start studying hard at once to catch up. Otherwise, it would be too late and no amount of studying would be able to pull her out of trouble.

But then she would have to spend less time with Chris. He was so much fun and so unlike any man she had known before. The boys she had known in high school were either pimply-faced types who joined the science club and planned to be doctors when they grew up, or they were intense, religious types who bored her with their impassioned concerns for things she couldn't see had anything to do with her, things like Zionism and the labor movement and social welfare.

College had those same types and she could hear them arguing passionately about things like whether Sacco and Vanzetti, the self-avowed anarchists charged with the murder of two men during a payroll robbery, could have had a fair trial in a country scornful of Italian immigrants who couldn't speak English and of draft dodgers, and they were both. These college students were the same young men, sometimes accompanied by equally intense young women, who also argued about the social forces that had given rise to killers like Richard Loeb and Nathan Leopold Jr., the teenage sons of two successful and prominent Chicago families who had kidnapped and killed a fourteen-year-old boy just for the thrill of committing a perfect crime. Sadie shuddered whenever she overheard these conversations because they reminded her of Adam Dov and Zosa, and how concerned they always were with such matters that, as far as she was concerned, were out of their hands. She was thankful Chris wasn't at all like that.

A few days after she got the probation notice, she received an envelope addressed in a familiar hand. She was eager to rip open this letter from her grandmother, and at the same time she dreaded doing so. The mere presence of the letter served as an admonishment of her behavior. She opened it anyway and began to read, imagining she could hear Marya's faint Russian accent in the words:

My dearest Sadie,

You have been in my thoughts a great deal lately. I trust this second year of college has remained as intellectually stimulating as your first and that you are not falling victim to what I have heard referred to as sophomore slump. We here at home are extremely proud of you and I feel that in being the first woman from our family to go to college, you are showing tremendous foresight and wisdom. We miss you terribly of course, but are glad that you are doing what you really want to.

Michael has come up to my desk as I sit writing this letter and has asked me to tell you that he's thinking of coming up there and checking on you to make sure you're not turning into one of the flaming youth the radio broadcasters are always theorizing about. But, of course, you know he will do no such thing. He's too busy with his homework and has even started a business club in his high school. He always has his nose in some kind of financial publication and roams around dropping lines such as President Coolidge's, 'The business of America is business.' Lately he's started quoting some economist named Roger Babson saying sooner or later an end to this country's business boom is coming and the crash may be terrific. Your grandfather says that's foolish talk, but I'm not so sure. I don't know what Michael plans to do with all this business knowledge he's developing, but your grandfather and I imagine he will one day end up taking control of MW Enterprises. I was going to say it's tailormade for him to step into if he wants it, but it might be more appropriate to say it's ready-to-wear. He's finally starting to put on a little weight to go with all that height, and although he's still in that stage where he's neither a boy nor a man, I think you'll be surprised at the changes in him when you come home this summer.

As for your grandfather, he's as busy as ever. Sometimes I wonder if he's not pushing himself a little too hard because he occasionally looks a little tired and worn, but our business is having one of its best years yet. (Your grandfather is even talking about the possibility of MW going public and offering shares on the stock market, but so far it's all just talk.)

With all that's going on, can you believe your grandfather is urging us to move again? The old brownstones near the Queensboro Bridge between 57th and 59th Streets are being torn down and replaced with fashionable and elegant homes. The area's called Sutton Place, and there overlooking the East River is where your grandfather wants us to live. Park Place is too vulgar, he claims, and Fifth Avenue was never his style.

In parting, I just want you to know that I feel very close to you these days and miss you. Also, I want to drop a little hint that if you keep your grades high, your grandfather and I have a little surprise for you this summer.

We love you.

Your *Bubbe* and *Zeyde*

Sadie slid the letter back in its envelope. She wondered if her grandmother's concern for her meant she had been having dreams or pictures about her. Sometimes she felt as if she were transparent because her grandmother knew her so well. But she didn't want to think about that now.

She dropped the letter in the wastepaper basket and tried to think about how she was going to manage to lift her grades and still see Chris. She would just have to, that was all. But it seemed an overwhelming task. She was lost in a whirlwind of parties and drinking and the expectations of her equally fast-moving friends. She was left with a sense of impending doom.

During the next hour she found herself inadvertently glancing over at the trash basket until she could stand it no longer. She had to get up and retrieve the letter. It was almost as if her grandmother knew what she had done with it. As she glanced at the envelope again, she idly wondered what her grandparents could be planning to give her, providing she could salvage her grades? But somewhere deep inside her, she knew that didn't really matter. She had to improve her study habits, not for any kind of external reward, but because it was what she really wanted and had to do.

Wearing a peach-colored dress for the first time in years instead of one of her customary dark ones that Jacob preferred, Elke smoothed her hands over her hips and moistened her lips. She desperately wished it weren't so, but she was nervous. Then she saw him.

David spotted her at the same time she spotted him. She had been a little concerned that he might not recognize her after all these years and without her red hair visible. He had never seen her wearing the *sheitel*. But here he was walking up to her as if it were twenty years ago. She noticed that he had gained a little weight, but he didn't look as though he could be past forty. His skin was unlined and his hair still a red-brown not unlike her own had been. She wondered how old she must look to him, but she had no chance to think much about it because he was smiling at her and greeting her.

"Mrs. Molnar," he was careful to say just loud enough so the other people in the bank would think she was but another of the bank's customers, "how good it is to see you." He steered her gently by the elbow to his office and held out a chair for her.

She had finally agreed to see him, but only for a few minutes and only in the main office of the Metropolitan Bank, of which he was now president. The bank, she had decided, would be the safest and least conspicuous place and there she would feel less like she was having a rendezvous. She also knew she could end the meeting at any time without fear of a scene between them. But of course that was a silly precaution, she told herself. What kind of scene could there possibly be over someone she had long ago put behind her and who needed to be reminded of that?

David took his place behind the large desk of carved walnut. "Elke, you don't know what it means to me that you were willing to come here."

She sat very primly and erect. "I don't know what I'm doing here. I can't imagine why I agreed to come."

"I would like to think there's a good reason, the same reason that I haven't been able to get you out of my mind all these years."

"Stop, David. You mustn't talk like that." She looked down at her lap for a moment. "The only reason I came here today is that I wanted to discourage you from contacting me again. I thought that not answering your notes would do it. But it didn't. And I can't afford to have you continuing to try to get in touch with me. It's too . . . too disturbing."

She saw that he was staring at her intently with his very green eyes. "Disturbing? In what way, Elke?"

She also found the tone of his voice at this very minute disturbing, but she wasn't going to tell him that. "I'm very happy, David. I have a wonderful husband and three children that I'm very proud of. I wouldn't want to do anything to upset any of that."

"Would you expect that just seeing me once for old times' sake would upset it?"

"No, but—"

"Then, you see. You have done the right thing. No harm will come of this. I too have a family now."

She looked up quickly. "You do?" She hastily regained her composure. "But of course you do. You didn't seem the type to remain a bachelor. Do you have any children?"

"One. A daughter. Her name's Lisa and she's twelve years old now."

Elke suddenly felt sad. "Amazing, isn't it, how fast it all passes before we even get a chance to sort it out." Then, realizing she might have gone too far, she gathered up her handbag and glanced over her shoulder toward the doorway.

David saw that she was about to stand up so he began to speak hurriedly, "Elke, I know that you are very happy, and you must believe me when I say I respect your desire not to have me contact you in any way."

She was already on her feet and heading for the door.

His voice trailed after her. "I want you to feel you can always come here and just . . . just talk, if you wish," he concluded lamely.

She turned and looked at him. "Thank you, David. Your offer is really very kind. But you see, I just couldn't do that. It would be too. . . ." She faltered.

"Disturbing?" he asked softly, picking up her word for it.

"Yes. So I insist you don't contact me again." Then she fled out into the streets, glad to be able to lose herself in the anonymity of the crowd and realizing it had been a mistake to come here and stir up her buried feelings.

The small Greenwich Village café was dark and full of artists, writers and other intellectuals. On the dance floor a few couples clung indolently to each other. Many of the women wore batik blouses and smocks while the men wore baggy-legged pants. A number of eccentric characters, dressed in colorful, exotic garb, stood about, gesticulating grandly as they discussed issues of the day or examined more abstract matters on the nature of existence.

Zosa held on tightly to Adam Dov, who was leading her about the dance floor in time to the languorous music. His arms felt strong and protective and she liked the way he held her surely and firmly. When the song was over, they returned to their table where Marty and Abe had ordered them another round of coffee. As they sat down, Marty waved at two friends across the room and motioned for them to join his gathering.

He banged on his coffee cup with a spoon as they came up. "Quiet, everyone. I want you to meet Linda Barnes and Natasha Jakes." He proceeded to introduce each of the people seated at the table. Linda Barnes, standing to his right, was a tall, slender woman with dark, trailing hair. She had a look of perpetual disappointment about her, brought out by her pouting mouth and round, liquid eyes. The other woman was short, with hennaed red hair, and turned out to be wearing very little under her fur coat. Her thin, fashionable dress dipped low in the front and lifted high at the hemline. She sat next to Adam Dov, and Linda found a place near Marty.

Zosa noticed right away that Natasha wasn't the least bit shy. She quickly engaged Adam Dov in a conversation about a play put on by the Provincetown Players, one of the Village's new acting groups, and didn't bother to include Zosa in the conversation or glance at her more than once or twice. Abe moved over and sat down next to Zosa.

"Did you see that little bald man come in a while ago?" he ventured, obviously wanting to make conversation.

"No, I don't believe I did," Zosa returned absently. She was trying to listen in on what Adam Dov and Natasha were talking about.

Abe took her by the shoulder and turned her in the direction of a table full of professorial looking types. "Look over there. You'll see Joe Gould, the one with no hair and a small beard."

Zosa had no choice but to do as he directed, but she hadn't much interest in the person he was pointing out. She had heard of Joe Gould, who was supposed to be writing a long history or autobiography, she wasn't sure which, and was reputedly another genius, but then the Village was full of geniuses. She turned back around quickly and glanced in Adam Dov's direction. He was laughing loudly at something Natasha had said, but because of Abe talking in her ear, Zosa hadn't been able to hear what it was.

Suddenly Adam Dov stood up as Natasha, giggling and pleading, began pulling him toward the dance floor. Zosa watched as she leaned into Adam Dov and let him lead her into the dance. The girl was rubbing her body against his, and for once Zosa wished it were a Charleston or other fast piece of music the combo was playing rather than a slow ballad.

"They dance well together, don't they?" Abe observed over her shoulder.

Zosa glared at him. "I wouldn't dignify what they're doing by calling it dancing."

Something in Zosa's eye made Abe stop watching the two dancers and momentarily lapse into silence. Then he tried to start up another conversation with Zosa, this time choosing a safer topic.

The song had ended and another had begun. Adam Dov and Natasha were still on the dance floor. Zosa found it hard to attend to what Abe was saying, and her head had begun to throb. She tried to devote herself to Abe, but her attention kept being pulled back to the dance floor. She watched as Natasha, at the end of that song, stood up on tiptoe and kissed Adam Dov full on the lips. Such displays were common in the

Village, but what Zosa hadn't seen before was the expression on Adam Dov's face. His eyes were glittering and full of desire. He pulled Natasha to him again and this time they were pressed together tightly throughout the dance.

In midsentence of something Zosa hadn't been listening to, Abe changed his tone. "Zosa, are you all right? Your face has gone completely white." When she didn't answer, he began to shake her shoulder lightly.

She grabbed her coat and stood up, her face contorted with a strange look.

"Zosa, what is it?" Abe was now truly alarmed.

She spat the words out at him. "It's nothing. Just a headache. I'm leaving."

She headed for the door with her coffee cup. As she passed by the dance floor, Adam Dov chanced to look up at Zosa. As their eyes met, the sensual expression on his face dropped abruptly.

At almost the same moment, Adam Dov contracted his face and angled his body sharply, Natasha still enclosed in his arms. But he failed to avoid the cup of cold coffee that Zosa had hurled at him.

Zosa headed blindly for the front door. She yanked it open and ran headfirst into someone who was just coming in. Stunned by the force of the collision, she came to a sudden stop. The man she had collided with caught her in his arms and pulled her through the doorway and outside, where he held her a moment to steady her.

"I know you," he suddenly said. "I know you from someplace."

Zosa was panting breathlessly and she felt dizzy. She leaned against the wall of the building and looked at him. What she saw first were his dark brown eyes peering at her with concern. He had a thin, slightly down-turned nose, an angular chin and straight brown hair. The rest of him was obscured by a large, double-breasted coat.

She nodded her head. "Don't you go to NYU?" she managed to say.

He lit up with recognition. "That's it. You're in my economics class. Look, I hope you're okay. You were coming out of there in such a hurry I'm afraid you still might be a little woozy. You have to trust me in these matters. I'm going to be a doctor."

Zosa shrugged. To tell the truth, she didn't feel too sure of her balance yet. She knew that decency required her to make some kind of reply, but she was still so upset with what she had seen inside that she was trembling.

When she made no response, the man became more concerned. "I feel partly responsible for this. I was just barging in without looking. Why don't you let me take you someplace nearby where you can rest and get your bearings. It's not as if we're complete strangers, and I've been wanting to get to know you for some time, although I admit I wouldn't have picked this way."

Zosa couldn't get her thoughts off Adam Dov and the way he had acted like such a pushover with that girl who was dressed like a flapper, just the type he had always professed to scorn. Even now it was as if she could see them both naked before her very eyes. She looked at the young man wildly. All this time his face had borne the same concern. "Sure," she decided impetuously, thinking of Adam Dov and feeling betrayed. "Why not?" She startled the young man by suddenly putting her arm through his. "As you said, it's not as if we're strangers," her voice rose to a higher pitch than usual. "Where shall we go?"

He motioned her toward the street. "I have my roadster over here. We can go anywhere you want."

Zosa looked at the sleek car and wished Adam Dov could be here to see her ride off in it. She let him open the door for her and help her in. As he climbed in on the other side, she leaned over toward him and smiled unsteadily. "My name's Zosa. Zosa Molnar. What's yours?"

"Leonard Marston," he said and started the motor. "You . . . seem to be feeling a lot better."

"Oh yes, quite a bit." She smiled provocatively and tried to flirt. "It must be your bedside manner."

The car took off with a loud roar and lurched into the night.

Sadie stood next to Adam Dov on the pier and pulled her summer coat closer about her. For June it was surprisingly cool, or perhaps it was just the wind whipping off the water. She studied the massive ocean liner docked in front of her.

"It's hard to believe we'll be out at sea in just two more hours," she said half aloud to no one in particular.

"Isn't it exciting?" Adam Dov responded. "I can't believe *Zeyde* was willing to send all three of us to Europe this summer."

Although she didn't say so, Sadie couldn't believe it either. And she especially couldn't believe her last minute campaign to salvage her sinking grades had paid off, at least to the point where she had barely managed to pass all her courses. Her parents and grandparents had been considerably less impressed with this year's grades compared to last year's, and her grandmother in particular had given her a penetrating look and pursed her lips speculatively, but no one had suggested she not be allowed to accept Wolf's gift to the three grandchildren for having successfully completed the college year.

Adam Dov joined Sadie in appraising the ship. "It's too bad that Zosa won't be joining us, though."

Sadie heard the wistfulness in his voice and thought of the irony of it all. Zosa had startled everyone at the end of the school year with the sudden announcement that she was getting married. It had taken Sadie a long time for Zosa's plans to sink in. She hadn't known Zosa ever to spend much time with any man but Adam Dov, and since he too had so clearly preferred her companionship to that of any other woman, Sadie had somehow pictured the two of them remaining unwed, growing old and toothless together as the years passed. They would surely be like the old bachelor brothers and spinster sisters who ended up living together in their old age, fussing at each other just as if they were married.

Although also taken aback by the suddenness of Zosa's decision, her parents had been pleased. Sadie noticed that her father in particular seemed vindicated by Zosa's decision to abandon her college career for the wedded life. And the fact that her husband, Leonard Marston, was going to be a doctor also helped assuage any alarm they all may have felt over the haste with which the ceremony had taken place two weeks ago. When Wolf had learned of Zosa's plans to get married, he had generously included a steamship ticket for Leonard Marston, informing Zosa that it was his wedding gift to the two of them. As a result, Leonard and Zosa had sailed for Europe for their honeymoon three days after the wedding.

For once Sadie could have Adam Dov all to herself, but she would just as soon not. She watched him now pacing up and down the dock, observing the machinelike precision of the crew as they loaded the trunks and bags onto the ship. Ever since Wolf had announced his gift, Adam Dov had thrown himself into a frenzy of studying guide books and planning the itinerary for the three of them. Then, when Zosa's wedding plans had been revealed, the fire had gone out of him, and he no longer seemed interested in much of anything. Sadie knew he must be thinking of Zosa this very minute and she knew there was no way she could take her place. At the same time, she didn't care to. There were other things on her mind.

The sun had not yet come out today and the waters of the bay looked cold and gloomy. That meant the ocean would probably be choppy and a little rough. Sadie hated to think of bouncing around out there for two weeks until they arrived in Le Havre, France. She didn't feel well. In fact, her stomach was already queasy, even before she had set foot on the ship.

Another reason she wasn't looking forward to having Adam Dov all to herself for the next two months was that she would rather be with Chris Hollington. She knew Chris was right now still in New York, staying with a friend from college. He would be there another week and then he would be going home to St. Augustine, as he always did in the summer. She yearned to be with him, laughing at his light, easy banter and constant jokes. Adam Dov would only want to lecture her on western European history and such things as the aesthetic and sociological value of the sculptures adorning the facade of the cathedral of Chartres, or other things she already knew, even if shakily, from her classes.

Adam Dov motioned for her to follow him up the gangway into the ship. They easily found their cabin on the Lido Deck, where Wolf had bought them first-class tickets. Then they wandered back outside and hung over the railing, watching the other passengers board and the crew begin to make their final preparations. As she watched the people on the dock below, Sadie was glad that the family had elected not to see them off. Instead a farewell party had been thrown the night before at her grandfather's house, and all farewells had been made at that time. Everyone else, both those planning to sail and their visitors, looked so festive. On the deck below, the ship's band was playing a repertory of lively songs. Sadie decidedly didn't feel festive. It certainly would have been worse having to keep up pretenses in front of the family. As she glanced at Adam Dov out of the corner of her eye, she saw that he didn't look festive either. What a pair of flat tires, she thought, using one of Chris' favorite terms. Then she giggled out loud.

"What are you laughing about?" Adam Dov asked.

"Us," Sadie said.

"What's so funny?"

"Everything," she said cryptically, then turned away. "I'm going to our cabin."

Adam Dov was lost in his own thoughts and didn't say anything.

When Sadie returned to the cabin, she noticed that their baggage had arrived. She pulled hers over to the table and hefted it on top. She unzipped it and started removing her clothes. She took off her coat and spread it on the floor. Then she selected four light-weight dresses and threw them on top of the coat. She quickly rummaged through her suitcase and drew out a few more articles she deemed essential. These too she threw on top of the coat. Then she closed the suitcase, and getting down on her hands and knees, gathered the four corners of the coat together to form a giant, rather elegant knapsack.

She let herself out of the cabin, the knapsack slung over her shoulder.

Adam Dov heard someone calling his name. He looked to both sides of him. It sounded like Sadie, but where was she? She kept calling until finally he spotted her. To his amazement, she was standing down on the dock, waving at him frantically.

"Bon voyage!" she yelled. "Have a good trip!"

"Sadie! What are you doing down there? Get up here!"

The foghorns of the big ship began to sound, signaling its imminent departure. The band struck up a rousing tune as colorful streamers and confetti flew through the air.

"What? I can't hear you!" Sadie yelled back as she fought off a yellow streamer that was settling on her hand. The big horns continued to blow and the crew began to draw in the gangplank.

Adam Dov motioned wildly. "Get up here! We're

leaving!" As if to confirm his statement, the horns blasted the air again.

"I'm not coming!" Sadie yelled again. "I'm going to Florida. You'll have a much better time without me. Bye!" She blew him a kiss, and as he watched helplessly, she ran along the dock with her oversized knapsack, getting smaller and smaller until she was no bigger than a dot of confetti.

Chapter 30

Marya shuddered in her sleep and pulled the blankets tighter around her. She tried to break free from her dream, but it wouldn't let her go. A woman she didn't recognize was sitting in front of a large table filled with every kind of food imaginable—meats, vegetables, salads and desserts. She was stuffing food into her mouth as fast as she could, grabbing at it with her bare hands and cramming it all in indiscriminately, a fistful of chocolate cake followed by a fistful of gefilte fish followed by another of oily *chulent*. With each mouthful she grew visibly plumper, expanding like a balloon, becoming increasingly grotesque until finally, with one last dripping mouthful, she exploded. The explosion snapped Marya out of her dream, and she abruptly sat upright in the bed, thinking she heard a woman weeping.

Wolf stirred next to her. "Are you all right?" he mumbled, half asleep.

"Yes," she recovered herself, now wide awake and no longer hearing the weeping woman. "I was just dreaming. I'm sorry I woke you. Go back to sleep." He returned to sleep right away. When she lay back down, sleep wouldn't come. She kept staring at the ceiling and was filled with an uneasiness she could neither dismiss nor attribute to anything but the dream, which had disturbed her with its bizarreness. She had the impression she spent the rest of the night awake, and when the room finally started to grow light, she was drained but relieved.

The next morning as they were having breakfast, Wolf noticed that Marya looked tired and withdrawn. He was surprised when she suddenly spoke. "We got a letter from Sadie yesterday."

"How can that be? The boat shouldn't be in France yet."

Marya looked sad. "That's because the letter didn't come from France. It came from Florida. At the last minute Sadie changed her mind about going to Europe, it seems."

Wolf stared at her in disbelief as she handed him the letter. He grabbed it and read the familiar purple scrawl:

Dear *Bubbe* and *Zeyde,*

I know this is going to shock you, but I want to tell you right away not to worry and that I'm fine. You know how I sometimes make an impetuous decision. Well, I made one of those a few days ago as the ship was about to leave for Europe. I really wanted to go to Europe and I am very thankful for the gift. But I'm sure you're aware that my grades didn't really merit the gift as Adam Dov's and Zosa's did. Somehow I also couldn't bear the thought of being alone on that boat with Adam Dov when he would rather be with Zosa or alone. You know how different we are, and we would never want to go the same places or do the same things in Europe.

I decided to accept the invitation of a close friend from college (you don't know him yet, but you will) to visit his family in St. Augustine, Florida for a few weeks. I cashed in the ticket later that day, and will give you all the money back, even the money I took out for the train ticket to St. Augustine. I will be back in a few weeks, and then I'll tell you all about Florida. Of course this isn't the best time of year there and it's pretty hot.

With all my love,

Your granddaughter, Sadie.

P.S. It might be best if you didn't tell my mother and father. You know how stuffy and old-fashioned they always are about girls doing anything adventuresome on their own. I'll take the responsibility of telling them myself as soon as I get back. Love again, Sadie.

Wolf crumpled the letter and threw it on the floor. In a strained voice, he complained, "Stuffy and old-fashioned, that's what she calls anyone who doesn't see things her way."

Marya tried to read his expression, but his face was closed. She knew he had to be hurt by Sadie's blatant rejection of his generosity. "I'm afraid I feel stuffy and old-fashioned about this too," she offered.

"She's gone too far this time. The girl's too wild. It's as if she'd determined to be influenced by every crazy fad and irresponsible notion that comes along. And I was just starting to have some hope she was calming down. I don't think sending her to college was such a good idea after all. It has just encouraged her to soak up all kinds of nonsense that have nothing to do with her studies, as far as I can see. It's just not worth it to send her another year."

Marya was shaken. The possibility that the first daughter in the family to attend college—now with Zosa's marriage, the only daughter—might not finish was unthinkable. "Zavel, I agree that she's out of hand now. But why cut off the only thing in her life that has some meaning, some substance to it?"

"How can it have substance when she's not learning the material and doing the work? Why throw away our money and encourage frivolity? I'd rather hold on to it for Adam Dov and Michael. Perhaps Jacob was right, after all. Sadie needs a man who can control her."

Marya could not see the wisdom of continuing the discussion at that moment. Obviously Wolf was too upset. She decided to pursue the issue at a more judicious time.

Later that day as Wolf directed the annual inventory at the factory, he found his attention kept turning inward. There were three things on his mind, each more important to him at that moment than the inventory. Most disturbing was the cable he'd just received from Adam Dov, confirming Sadie's admission she was not on the Europe-bound ship. He knew that Marya always defended Sadie's behavior, and he had to admit that over the years he too had a tendency to regard it more lightly than either Jacob or Elke did, but this last escapade he couldn't excuse as youthful high jinks or boisterousness. It annoyed him that Sadie had so casually tossed off the gift he had carefully considered and planned, but it was just as unacceptable that she was staying at the home of a young man whose name they didn't even know. No matter what Marya said, the girl should be yanked out of college and provided with a husband as soon as possible.

Sadie lifted her hair off her neck with one hand and fanned herself with the other. "I can't believe how hot it is here," she fretted. "This weather makes a New York summer seem cool by comparison."

She and Chris were sitting on the wide porch of his parents' oceanfront home in St. Augustine. Chris was draped over a wicker chair, dressed all in white as if in the tropics, and Sadie sat in the porch's hanging swing, with one leg under her, the other dangling over the edge so she could idly rock herself in the hopes of creating a breeze of some kind.

Chris dabbed at his forehead with the linen handkerchief he took from his pocket, then picked up his iced drink for another sip. "You'll get used to it and then it won't seem so bad."

"Will I?" she asked without conviction. She took a big swallow of her drink and finished it.

As if the housekeeper had been waiting for that precise moment, she appeared on the porch with two more freshly made drinks.

"Ah, Mona, you must know magic and mind reading," Chris said to the old black housekeeper as he lifted a glass from the tray and gallantly handed it to Sadie, addressing her. "There isn't anything that misses this old woman's eye. She knows me better than anyone in this whole town and knows everyone else here just as well. If people in these parts have trouble, they always know they can come to Miss Mona. If she can't help them, she knows who can."

The housekeeper made clicking noises with her tongue. "Get on, now, Mr. Chris, with all that syrupy talk of yours." She went back inside and the porch grew silent again except for the tinkle of ice cubes shifting in the glasses as they melted.

For something to do, Sadie began to whistle snatches of "Ain't She Sweet," slightly off key.

Chris set down his glass loudly. "Sadie, I wish you would get the tune right. It goes like this," and he began to whistle a slightly improved version of the song.

Sadie laughed. "At least it's not too hot to whistle. That's about all I have the strength to do."

Chris broke off his whistling. "Will you stop complaining about the heat? That's all you've done since you got down here, Sadie. Complain about the heat, and how!" He then put on an exaggerated drawl, " 'Ah don't feel so good, Chrissy.' I swear, you outbelle the native girls when it comes to being delicate."

"Well, I'm not used to the climate here the way you are." She slapped at her arm. "And you have bugs here . . . that bite."

Chris rolled his eyes. "Just hold on until this evening. It'll be a lot cooler and we can go for a drive in my daddy's Buick. I'll show you some of these parts around here and you'll feel a whole lot snappier."

Sadie took another big sip of her drink. She doubted it would get any cooler. The nights didn't seem to be much better than the days. And no matter what she did, nothing seemed to make her feel any snappier.

That evening as they drove through the town in Mr. Hollington's white Buick, Chris pointed out some of the tourist sights of the area. He told her how Ralph Waldo Emerson had been among the many famous visitors who had started coming to St. Augustine decades ago for their health. Sadie thought it a strange place to come for health. But then she knew it must be a lot nicer any other time of the year. Ever since she'd arrived, all everyone seemed to talk about was real estate. People had for a while made a lot of money on the Florida land boom, buying building lots on a speculative basis and selling them for as much as seventy-five thousand dollars each. But that bubble had burst and now everyone was going on about how much prices had plummeted.

Chris pointed out the oldest house in the United States, a two-story Spanish style house surrounded by lots of foliage. They drove past the old part of town where the original schoolhouse still stood from the days when the British had briefly ruled the area after the French and Indian War in 1763 until the Spanish took over again twenty years later. They drove to a large imposing fort on the edge of the bay.

"That's the Castillo San Marcos." Chris pointed proudly at the fortress that shone white in the moonlight from the *tapia*, the mixture of seashell and sand mortar from which it was constructed.

"It's not exactly the Statue of Liberty, is it?" Sadie said, feeling suddenly lonesome for her native city. This place was pretty, but it was even smaller and quieter than the towns outside Boston. She wished she could lay eyes on a big skyscraper like the Woolworth Building that soared sixty stories above Broadway, intricately gilded and turreted. She was tired of looking at nothing but palmettos and low one and two-story buildings and feeling, everywhere and always and forever, the unrelenting heat.

Chris looked at her sharply. "What's the matter with you? You look pale. Are you going to be sick again?"

Sadie nodded. "I think so," she said feebly. She opened the car door and without getting out, leaned over and threw up over the running board.

"I swear, I never saw someone so sensitive to the heat as you," Chris shook his head sympathetically, handing Sadie his linen handkerchief to wipe her mouth.

"Oh Chris, it's not the heat." Sadie returned to an upright position.

"Well then, what is it?" he asked softly.

"I'm going to have a baby. That's what it is."

He stared at her in stunned silence. Then he pulled from his hip pocket the ever present silver flask and took a big swig. "You don't say. A baby." He contemplated his own words. Neither spoke for a few minutes.

Sadie stared out the window at the waters of the bay as she lifted the damp strands of hair off the nape of her neck. It was strange how, down here in Florida, being by the water brought no relief from the heat. If anything, it only made it worse.

"Is that why you invited yourself down here?" Chris finally quizzed. "Because you knew you were pregnant? Is that why you didn't stay on that boat for France?"

"Invited myself!" Sadie repeated indignantly.

"Ever since I met you, you've been going on about how you'd like me to come down South some time and see how lush and pretty everything is. Besides, I came here to be with you. I had no idea I was pregnant. It's only the last couple days I've started to figure out what might be wrong. Then I started to count up how long it's been since ... since ... you know."

"Yeah."

Even from here inside the car Sadie could hear the cacophony of chirps and cries coming from the insects in the nearby woods. If Chris didn't say anything in a minute, Sadie was going to break the silence between them.

"Chris, I—"

He overrode her. "Listen, Sadie, here's what I think we ought to do. You know I'm really fond of you, and I think you're still really fond of me ... you are, aren't you?"

She nodded her head and held her breath to hear what he was about to say.

"Well, then, it's clear to me the proper thing to do in this situation is to get married."

"Married?" Sadie echoed, partly to see how she liked the sound of the word. She had never really wanted to get married before she finished college, and had secretly scorned Zosa for doing so. Marriage always seemed like something that would come many years later, after college and after she'd done something with her education. But in the last couple of days, when it had begun to dawn on her that the reason she felt the way she did was because she was pregnant, she had started to imagine what it would be like. She could project only a fuzzy picture, but she finally decided that if she had to be married, it would be more fun to be married to Chris than to anyone else. At least he liked to laugh a lot, and he was definitely romantic.

Chris put his arm around her shoulder. "I don't see why I shouldn't do the gentlemanly thing for this lady in distress." He leaned over and kissed her. "We can start planning a wedding right away. You've already met my parents, but I don't know if there's a chance for me to meet yours now until just before the ceremony. We can have a big Presbyterian wedding. You did tell me your family was Presbyterian, the same as mine, didn't you?"

Sadie swallowed hard. "Yes. I did."

"And we can invite all the friends of the family. There are so many, you wouldn't believe. I don't know if we have time to get any of our friends from college down here on such short notice." He started to laugh. "But then they all love an adventure, so they'd probably break their necks trying. And anyway, we have to give your parents a chance to get down here and meet mine. So that'll take a few weeks right there. The way I figure it, we won't be able to have the wedding until another month or six weeks. Now how far along did you say you are?"

"Two months, I think." In spite of the heat, Sadie was aware of an icy sensation up the back of her spine.

Chris was smiling at her. "Well then, we have a little time. What do you think of those plans, missy?"

Sadie swallowed hard and clung to him. "Chris, do you love me? Do you really love me enough to marry me?"

"Yes, Sadie. I do love you." He pulled her to him and kissed her again, this time even longer and slower.

"I love you too. And since we're going to be married, there's something I want you to know about me. If you really love me, I know you'll understand."

Chris laughed. "You sound so serious. Is this going to be where Miss Lily confesses that she really has a dainty drop or two of Negro blood in her?"

Sadie blinked rapidly. "Would that be so awful?" she asked, not laughing.

He noticed her serious mood hadn't left. "All right. Go ahead, tell me what's on your mind."

"Well, you see, my family isn't really Presbyterian."

"They're not?" He thought a moment. "That's not so bad, really. Of course, my family would prefer they were. But I think we'll be able to talk our way around that one. But why did you tell me they were if they weren't? Did you think it really matters to me a whole lot? Because it doesn't."

"I guess I didn't want to tell you that they . . . I mean, we . . . are Jewish."

"Jewish?" He laughed. "You're kidding me. What are you really?"

"I'm really Jewish."

This time he stared at her before answering. "You are? Seriously?"

"Yes. Seriously."

He gave a long, low whistle. "Whew. This one will be a little harder to get out of." He grew silent again and took another drink from his hip flask. He offered it to Sadie, but she shook her head. "What I don't understand, though, is why you purposely misled me."

"I don't know. I guess I was ashamed. I thought you might not want me."

"Ashamed of what you are? That's crazy, Sadie. Everyone should be proud of what they are." He gulped another drink from the flask.

For the first time Sadie wished he wouldn't drink so much, especially at this particular moment. "I guess, too, that I've never felt very Jewish. I mean, I don't like to go to temple or pray. And although my parents are religious, I think I take after my grandmother more. She's not that way at all. You'd probably never know she was the least bit Jewish." She saw that he was looking at her intently. "What do you think your parents will say?"

He stretched out his legs the best he could within the confines of the car. "I think they'll say . . . no. Absolutely no."

The icy feeling returned to the back of Sadie's neck. "No?"

"You've got to understand what kind of people my parents are. They've lived down here all their lives in the oldest town in America, and they've done very well for themselves. Damn well. But they haven't been around much outside of Florida and maybe a few trips to Atlanta. They're educated people in some ways, but not, you see, in others. This part of the country has been so isolated until just recently. It's only in the last few years that different kinds of people have started to drift in from up North, wanting sunnier weather and nice views. To them Jews are still foreigners who practically have horns. It's not what their religion teaches them or anything. It's just something they've picked up out of—"

"Out of the air," Sadie finished for him, blotting the perspiration on her forehead with Chris' handkerchief, her voice considerably dulled.

"That's right," he said. "You understand now. So you see why it is we just can't get married."

Sadie's mouth fell open in surprise, but the surprise was quickly giving way to another emotion. "*Can't* get married? You mean you feel the same way they do? You'd let their attitude stop you?"

He took her in his arms again. "Of course I don't feel like they do, Sadie. You ought to know me well enough than to say a thing like that. It's just that I'm their son and they've put all their hopes in me. Everything they've worked so hard to amass here, they intend it for me. I'm all they've got. I don't see any way I could stab them in the heart by doing something that would wound them so deeply," he paused, "do you?"

"Let me make sure I've got this straight. You love me but you can't marry me because your parents, who hate Jews—"

"Now, Sadie, don't get ugly. I wouldn't go so far as to say 'hate.'"

"Doesn't it come down to the same thing if their feelings are so strong we can't get married because of it?"

Chris grasped the steering wheel with both hands. "I can see you don't understand after all. I can see that I've hurt you. I've disappointed you."

"You certainly have," Sadie snapped bitterly. "And what really angers me is that I wasn't even so anxious to get married anyway."

Chris' tone was patient. "You're just lashing out now, because you're hurt and you want to hurt me too. Believe me, Sadie, I know how you must be feeling."

"I can most certainly assure you that you do not know how I am feeling."

"Well, if you don't want to get married, and I can't get married, I don't see what we're arguing about, do you?" When Sadie didn't reply, he suggested, "What I think we both need right now is a good night's sleep. Then we can make some plans for what we're going to do about you tomorrow, when we're both feeling fresher."

He started the car and began to drive in the direction of his home. Neither of them spoke the rest of the way.

The week Sadie had been staying at the Hollington home, she noticed that Chris slept late each morning and she had accustomed herself to doing the same thing. But the next morning she was up before daybreak. She listened to the house. It was far too early for anyone to be stirring. She dressed quickly and quietly opened her bedroom door. Without a sound she made her way down the hallway and then down the stairs and through the living room to the kitchen. She peered in—no one was there. She went to the stove, and moving as quietly as she could, put on the kettle for hot water. When it was ready, she fixed herself a cup of tea, then looked about for the sugar cubes so she could drink it Russian style the way she had seen her grandparents do. She sat, sipping the tea through the sugar cube, and waiting.

A short time later she heard footsteps on the back

porch, and then Mona, the old black housekeeper, came through the door.

"What you doing up so early, honey?" she wondered aloud the moment she saw Sadie. "And look, you already done gone and fixed yourself a cup of hot tea."

Sadie ran her tongue over her lips. "Mona, I was wondering if you could help me with something. Actually, it's for me and Chris both."

Mona looked at her with mild interest. "Sure, darlin'. Anything I can. Ain't nothin' Mona can't do if she sets her mind to it."

She sat down across from her as Sadie folded and unfolded her hands on the table top. "Well, you see, I need someone who's a special kind of doctor. It wouldn't even have to be a doctor really. Maybe it could be a nurse, just someone who has medical knowledge and who knows how to help women when they've got . . . uh, certain problems, a certain physical problem she wants to get rid of."

"You speaking about female trouble?"

"Yes."

Mona stood up. "I know what you talking about now, honey. I know what you want. You're telling me you're carrying a baby, ain't you?"

Sadie nodded reluctantly.

"And you don't want to be. Now, what does Mr. Chris say about this situation, seeing as how he's your special friend and all?"

"We're not getting married, if that's what you mean."

Mona studied her for a few moments. "I don't know, honey. You sure you want to do this? There ain't no gettin' off this train once you board it. I want you to be real certain."

Sadie answered without hesitation. "I'm certain." What else could she do, she asked herself. There was no way she and Chris could be married. Obviously a Jewish wife wasn't good enough for him. And besides, she didn't want that anyway. As his wife she would be expected to live here in this town with him the rest of her life, away from *Bubbe* and *Zeyde,* and her parents and even Adam Dov and Zosa, and the city she had grown up in. She would be expected to stay home and have children, who would all grow up knowing little of her side of the family and who would invariably talk with Southern instead of New York inflections. She would have to give up everything and he would be giving up nothing. But there wasn't any use in thinking about all that anyway because they wouldn't be married. Nor did she want to keep the baby. She just wasn't ready to be a mother and she knew she'd be a bad one if she were just doing it because she had no other choice.

She never could abide feeling like a prisoner, when all she really wanted was just to be free and feel the wind in her hair as she drove down the road in her tin lizzie. And she couldn't see any point in letting him make the decision about what she was going to do, the way he had suggested last night. It was her life, not his, and she didn't think much about it being his baby, especially since he didn't seem particularly interested himself.

"I'm certain," she repeated, this time even more firmly.

Miss Mona was just as Chris had described her. If she couldn't do for you what you needed done, she knew the person who could.

Three days later Sadie, pale and tired, boarded a northbound train for Atlanta, where she transferred to the train that would take her the rest of the way to New York. Every mile farther away from Chris, the more pleased she was. She didn't want anything more to do with him or his kind. She just wanted to go back to her grandparents in New York, to something solid and lasting.

As she watched the green flatness of Florida and southern Georgia give way to rolling hills and then the smoke-begrimed brick buildings of the seaboard cities, Sadie felt strangely relieved. At first she wondered if she was still weak from the abortion, but the moment she thought that, she knew that wasn't really the cause of her uneasiness. It was funny how she had never thought before of being from someplace, of being a native of anywhere, of being a New Yorker. But as she looked out the window of the train and saw the congested tenements along the railroad tracks, the skyscrapers shooting upward in the distance, she felt oddly comforted. She was indeed coming home.

When Adam Dov returned from Europe, Elke insisted on giving a party to welcome him home. Zosa, her belly now swollen in her sixth month of pregnancy, had been looking forward to it ever since her mother had told her what she was planning. Now, as she sat in the drawing room of her parents' home, wearing her new dress of midnight blue georgette that draped softly over her rounded stomach, she felt profoundly disappointed, even though the house was full of their college friends and Adam Dov was sitting next to her and talking animatedly.

"So Zosa, you must tell us what names you and Leonard have chosen. What's your favorite boy's name and what's your favorite girl's name?" As he spoke, he turned his head often in the opposite direction to include in the conversation the young woman he had brought to the party whom he'd introduced as Nancy Allen.

Nancy had a job as a commentator with a new radio station in New York. She had been on the same boat to Europe as Adam Dov, traveling partly on assignment and partly for pleasure. She was encouraging him to come work for the same station the next year when he finished his degree, and she felt she could be of some help to him in getting hired.

Zosa couldn't help feeling crestfallen as she watched the two together. Nancy Allen was certainly not dressed in the mode of the day, but nevertheless she projected her own distinct and confident style. She was slightly on the tall side, with an angular face that had high cheekbones, a strong chin and a generous mouth. Her dishwater blonde hair was bobbed and lightly marcelled, but her Scotch tweed skirt was longer than was in vogue and her brown shoes were what definitely would be called sensible. She obviously was alert to everything going on around her and had a ready wit.

As Zosa listened to Nancy talk about her and Adam Dov's travels through France and Germany, she found her comments entertaining and perceptive, and for that reason, the more she listened to her, the more dowdy and dull she felt, until Zosa finally decided she didn't like this Nancy Allen at all.

Deliberately snubbing her brother's friend, Zosa began to allow her attention to drift around the room until it settled on Sadie. When Sadie saw Zosa watching her, she picked up her plate of food and came to sit on Zosa's side.

"Mother tells me you're going back to college after all," Zosa mentioned a little wistfully.

"Thanks to *Bubbe, Zeyde* finally relented. But the only way he would agree to another year is if I promised to pay back my tuition for all three years if I didn't do well this coming semester. I even put it in writing," she revealed, thinking of the typed document Wolf had insisted she sign as proof of her commitment. She tried to laugh and make light of the situation, but somehow she couldn't. She knew how close she had come to not being able to return to college at all, and she was grateful for Marya's intercession. Ever since she'd returned from Florida, it seemed it wasn't as easy for her to regard things as lightly as before.

Zosa too had noticed a change in Sadie. She seemed less frivolous, more inclined to engage in a discussion of a serious nature. Perhaps she really would settle down and do well in college this term, Zosa thought, and tried not to be envious.

Zosa heard a burst of laughter coming from her other side where Adam Dov and Nancy sat. Sadie looked over at them. She's lovely, she thought to say as she watched Nancy holding Adam Dov in rapt attention, but something stopped her, and instead she said, "It's good to have Adam Dov back, isn't it?" But as soon as she'd said it, she realized that didn't seem a whole lot better than what had first been on her lips.

Zosa absent-mindedly patted her swollen belly as she suddenly had an overwhelming feeling of being trapped in a marriage she didn't want, with a man she didn't want, and a baby she didn't want. From where he stood on the other side of the room talking to the men, her husband Leonard looked over at her and saw her pat her stomach. He smiled because he liked to see his wife acknowledge her pregnancy, and he looked forward to his role as father of that child. All in all he was quite pleased with his life. He had acquired a beautiful and intelligent wife; he would soon have a baby; and because of this experience, he had finally made up his mind that his specialty in medical school would be pediatrics.

Zosa felt the panic rising. She tried not to look at Nancy Allen. She finally signaled her husband to come to her side. After a whispered conference, she stood up, her increased girth making her a little unsteady, and turned to Adam Dov. "We have to go now. Will you come visit me? I'd like to hear more about your travels," she glanced quickly at Nancy who was looking up at her and Adam Dov, "when we have a chance to be alone and talk privately."

As Adam Dov also stood, he tried to read the message underlying his sister's words and glimmering in her eyes. He thought he saw there a pleading, but he couldn't be sure. Nancy got to her feet next to him and stood very close. She felt warm and that warmth made it difficult for him to concentrate on Zosa's unspoken message the way he usually could. He took Zosa's hand

and noticed it felt uncharacteristically cool and damp. "I most certainly will come. This Sunday?"

Zosa regarded him intently. "Come Monday, when Leonard will be away." She glanced quickly over her shoulder at her husband who stood waiting slightly behind her and attempted a light laugh for his sake. "That way we won't bother him with our endless chatter." She glanced back at Leonard again and was relieved to see that he was smiling pleasantly at what she said.

"You promise now?" she asked, wishing she weren't sounding so intense, wanting to reestablish the easy banter they had once shared between them.

"Nothing could keep me away from you," Adam Dov assured her. He watched his sister leave the room, puzzling over her meaningful tone of voice and look. Then he caught the gentle scent of Nancy's hair.

Zosa's eyes fluttered open to the sound of Adam Dov's voice. It took her a second to realize where she was. Then she saw the sterile whiteness of the room and remembered. "The baby?" Her voice was a whisper.

Adam Dov answered her. "Zosa, the baby didn't live."

She blinked slowly as if she didn't understand his words. Then she looked up. "It's my fault."

He gripped her shoulders tightly. "Zosa, listen to me. It's not your fault. How could it be? It's not anyone's fault. These things happen. Many women have miscarriages, especially with their first."

Her face was strangely placid. "It is my fault. It's my fault because I didn't want it. I never wanted that baby, and it knew."

"Hush, Zosa. You don't know what you're saying."

Her voice was soft and lilting. "I do. It was a part of me and it knew what I was thinking. It knew it was all a horrible mistake, this whole marriage, everything. It was because I got jealous when you—"

"Shhhhh." His expression was masked. "I don't want you to talk too much. You'll get excited. Just rest now."

She kept looking at him raptly and he saw that there were no tears on her face or in her eyes. All her anguish was constricted inside of her, trickling out little by little in her words. He stood over her. "Zosa, you're going to be all right. Leonard will be here with you in a moment, and I'm here, and you're going to be all right."

"What day is it?" she asked suddenly.

"It's Monday."

She lifted her hand to him. "Dear Adam Dov, you were so kind to keep your word. Here it is the day you promised to come see me. You said nothing could keep you away and here you are."

Adam Dov was beginning to become alarmed. Something in her voice and her mannerism troubled him. She seemed somehow too distant. He doubted she understood what had really happened.

"Of course, you had no idea we would be having tea at the hospital instead of at my home. But that's my fault too."

He shook her. "Zosa, don't you know what happened? Nothing is your fault. You slipped in the bathroom. It was an accident. The woman downstairs heard a loud noise and then crying. When she came up with the building superintendent to investigate, they found you passed out from the blow you got on your head when you fell."

Her voice was still eerily calm. "I don't remember anything like that. No, that can't be what happened."

"It is. You have a gash over an inch deep in the back of your head to prove it."

"It's my own fault."

He tried to keep his voice from rising. "Zosa, will you stop saying that? It was an accident." He cautioned himself that she was still suffering from the blow, that she wasn't in her right mind yet, and that maybe he should let her rave. Then it might make her feel better.

She reached her hand out to him again and spoke in a very low voice. "Adam Dov, there's something I've always wanted to tell you about you and me. Come, put your ear by my mouth." As he leaned over to hear her better, she suddenly stopped talking. She was looking past him to the woman who sat in the chair on the other side of the room, waiting. Zosa visibly stiffened as she lay there under him.

"Zosa," he said, "you remember Nancy, don't you? She came to the hospital with me when we got word about what had happened."

"Hello, Zosa," Nancy said softly from across the room. "I'm sorry about what happened, but we heard from the doctor you're going to be all right, and we're so thankful."

Whatever else she said Zosa didn't hear. Her eyes were on Adam Dov and he was frightened by the look he saw there. He felt like she was staring at him from down a long, black tunnel, like an inverted telescope, and as he watched she seemed to diminish before him, becoming smaller and smaller.

"Zosa!" he called, revealing the alarm he felt. "Zosa!"

She just stared at him with a fixed look that he knew was that of one betrayed and she refused to speak.

Chapter 31

Sadie sat by the radio and wondered how many hard things in a row she was supposed to endure. She had heard that bad events always arrived in threes. Was it possible they sometimes came in fours?

As she whirled the radio's tuning knob, searching for a news announcement, crackling and sputtering sounds filled the room.

"Not so fast," Kathy, Sadie's senior classmate and roommate for the last three years, said with a hint of annoyance. "You're spinning past the stations too fast to hear anything."

Sadie made an effort to slow down. The past year, she and Kathy had not gotten along as well as they had their first two years. Last spring, in their junior year, the faltering friendship had come to a head over a seemingly minor issue. Sadie declined an invitation to go with Kathy to see "The Jazz Singer," the new talking movie with Al Jolson. When Sadie had begged off, explaining she had to study, Kathy had tossed her peroxided locks in disdain. "What's happened to you, anyway? You act like you think the things we used to do—like parties and drinking and going out in your car—are all wet. What's the matter? You've become too high-hat for us?"

Sadie had tried to explain that she just didn't get the same enjoyment out of those things as she used to, and that besides she had a big test coming up in biology that she wanted to do well on.

"Sure," Kathy had snapped, "that's what you always say. You read so much you're even starting to talk like a book." Kathy put on a formal, dry accent in imitation of Sadie and intoned, "One must apply oneself rigorously to one's endeavors or one won't succeed, will one? Rather a pity. Have you noticed how people like you say one, and rather and quite all the time, as if they were college professors? Well, if that's how you want to be, you can sit alone forever. Nobody's going to look to you for fun anymore." She had slammed the door behind her, and it had taken several cold, angry months before the two women had come to an uneasy truce. Sadie was relieved when their relationship had become a little more amiable again this year.

Now she found on the radio what she had been looking for. The announcer's voice was crisp and hurried as he listed the stock prices: ". . . Allied Chemicals, down thirty-five; American Can, down sixteen; American Machine and Foundry, down twenty-five and three fourths; American Telephone and Telegraph, down twenty-eight. . . ."

"I can't believe it," Sadie whispered, as the announcer continued through the alphabet. "I just can't believe it."

"What are you getting so excited about?" Kathy grumbled. "Prices fell drastically last Thursday, too, but I heard that Thomas Lamont from J. P. Morgan's bank said it was just a little distress selling because of a technical condition of the market, and Merrill Lynch and Company was even encouraging customers to take advantage of this opportunity to buy good securities. So I wouldn't worry if I were you."

Sadie nevertheless went out to the telephone in the hallway and tried to put a call in to Wolf's and Marya's home.

The operator was brisk and efficient, but not at all reassuring. "I'm sorry, miss. All trunks are jammed. I'm unable to get a single call into New York."

"Thank you, Central. I'll try again later." When she returned to the room, Kathy was putting on her coat.

"What say we forget about all these gloomy thoughts and go find some high jinks somewhere? Maybe we'll run into a couple of lounge lizards on the loose."

"I wish I could, Kathy, but I just have to get hold of my family. I won't be good for anything, I'm afraid, until I do."

"Have it your way then," Kathy replied a little huffily as she swept out the door.

Sadie stretched out on the bed, wishing she could close her eyes and sleep, but powerless to stop the thoughts that were whirling through her brain. "Threes," she said aloud, "bad events shouldn't come in more than threes. Oh God, please let it be so."

She couldn't help but think back over the past sixteen months. First there had been the abortion, which had affected her more than she'd anticipated. Seeing Chris' real nature wasn't what was so bad; she had determined she didn't want him anyway long before she left St. Augustine. What lingered from that summer was the firsthand exposure to a point of view—to prejudice—she had only heard about before, but had never directly experienced.

And she sometimes found herself thinking about the baby, wondering if she had really done the right thing. Shortly after she returned to New York to face her family's anger and disappointment, Zosa had suffered a miscarriage from a fall in her bathroom. That was in September. Sadie marked that event as the one that had made her first begin to wonder if she had done the right thing in having the abortion. It was strange for her to think that she and Zosa had been pregnant at the same time and now neither of them had children to show for it.

What was the most painful of all was what had happened to Zosa. When Sadie had gone to see her in the hospital, Zosa had stared at her blankly, as if she didn't know who she was and had refused to talk. Adam Dov tried to explain to her later that Zosa was that way with everyone and she shouldn't take Zosa's remoteness personally. Zosa hadn't reacted to anyone or spoken in days, not since the day of the accident when he had rushed to the hospital to see her. She responded to no one—neither to him, nor her husband, Leonard, nor her parents, nor the doctors.

Days and then weeks passed and still Zosa didn't speak or even appear that she'd heard what was addressed to her. Physically, the doctors said, she was doing fine, but evidently the shock of losing the baby was more than she could accept. October came and went, and then November and December, and still Zosa was not better. In January her parents and grand-parents called everyone in the family together. Zosa herself, attended by the nurse Wolf had insisted on hiring to take care of her, was there.

After a great deal of discussion the family decided to put her in a special home where she would be able to have round-the-clock care and the attention of professionals who might be able to bring her out of herself. Again, Wolf insisted on bearing the full expense, in spite of Jacob's protestations, and Sadie could tell from the look in his eyes how difficult it was for him to accept that this had happened to one of his own. It was almost impossible for her to accept that mental illness had crept into their family, one which seemed otherwise to be so physically and mentally graced, and that Zosa might never recognize any of them again.

And now Sadie wondered if there was to be another awful event for her to endure. The bottom had obviously fallen out of the stock market, and no matter what Kathy predicted, Sadie had an intuitive feeling that things could be very bad for a long while. She had learned in her economics classes of the dangerous combination of forces her professor had predicted could destroy the market and the economy: a banking system where failure of one bank would lead to a run on the others; an international balance of trade where the U.S. had become a creditor and foreign countries were defaulting on their loans to the detriment of American investors; scores of dubiously financed investment trusts and holding companies; and an economy that was dependent on five per cent of the population, which was receiving one third of the country's personal income, to keep on spending and investing without disruption.

Now she fervently prayed that her grandfather had not gone ahead with his plans for MW Enterprises to go public. But even if he hadn't, she knew things were still going to be bad. She went back into the hall and tried again to reach New York. She had no luck.

She went back to her room just long enough to grab her coat, then hurried out into the street. She would send a telegram, she decided, telling them she would be arriving on the morning train. She had to see for herself firsthand what was happening.

Sadie was surprised by how worn Wolf looked when she walked into his office the next day. Marya was sitting in an easy chair across from him and Michael was sitting on the other side of her. Sadie caught what Marya was saying in midsentence.

". . . no reason to try to hold on to everything. The best thing would be to cut our losses, if we still can."

"I agree," Michael spoke up. "We can get along without the exports and instead concentrate on our holdings in this country."

Sadie slipped into another chair and didn't interrupt.

"But not the mills," Wolf insisted. "I've been

wanting to let those go for some time. Let's sell the mills immediately. Even if we have to take a loss, we'll probably get more for them right now than a year or two from now. Britain's economy is worse off than ours, so disbanding our export operations is the logical thing to do. Then, with the mills and the exports gone, we might be able to maintain the factory and the chain stores. We'll have to cut back on production, of course, and. . . ."

He trailed off and Marya finished the sentence for him. "That means we may have to let some workers go."

Wolf brought his fist down on the desk. "If there's any way we can keep from doing that, I make that my first objective. I'll keep this factory operating with its present employees as long as I can."

No one said anything for a few moments. Then suddenly they all noticed Sadie at the same time.

"I just had to be here," she explained in answer to their barrage of questions about why she wasn't at the college. "There's always been an MW Enterprises in my life, ever since I was born. I just couldn't sit in my room up there and wonder what was happening. I tried to call but I couldn't get through. So coming down myself seemed to be the most sensible thing to do. Besides I'm probably going to get more of a lesson in economics by being here at this time than I would sitting in the classroom listening to a lecture. It won't hurt to take a couple weeks off. This year I think my grades can take it."

But in the next couple of weeks, Sadie felt at loose ends. Wolf was making all the decisions, with assistance from Marya and an occasional opinion from Michael. It was clear that she was not needed, or particularly wanted, so she packed up and went back to Cambridge before she had planned to. As she listened to her economics professor, she heard only gloomy analyses and predictions. By mid-November, according to his reports, the New York Stock Exchange alone had paper losses of thirty billion dollars. She watched that winter as the Gross National Product started plummeting from its high of one hundred and four billion dollars in 1929 to what looked to be considerably less in 1930.

In the months that followed, the reports she received from Marya and Michael not only confirmed the gloomy observations of her professor, but made it sound as though he had been too conservative in his predictions. Although MW Enterprises had succeeded in cutting back the export operation, they had been forced to sell the textile mills at an even greater loss than they'd anticipated. Production had fallen at the factory by half and three of the six chain stores were on the verge of going under. Nobody was buying new dresses; everyone was reining in.

Still, even with production down, Wolf refused to let any of the factory workers go. Finally he was forced to cut back their hours and the decision had been an excruciating one for him to make. Sadie could tell from Marya's letters how concerned she was becoming over the state of his health. "He doesn't have as much energy as he used to, probably because he works so late into the night trying to salvage what he can of our operations."

By midterm of her final semester, MW Enterprises was in serious financial difficulty. Sadie was beginning to open the letters from Marya with dread now, fearful to learn what further cutback had been made. Only one of the chain stores was still open, the one operating in New York. The others had been forced to close their doors because the inventories wouldn't move.

In April, when she returned to New York at her spring break, she discovered two upsetting things had taken place. Wolf had been forced to make the first cuts ever in the factory's work force; it was no longer enough just to cut back his employees' hours and then ask them voluntarily to take a cut in pay: men and women had to be told they no longer had a job.

When she walked into Wolf's office at the factory, Sadie made another discovery. She saw with her own eyes that Wolf had suddenly become an old man.

He looked up when she came in. "I've always prided myself on being a businessman. A good one," he said slowly. "Day after day I tell myself there's got to be a way out of this pit our livelihood is in, that the whole country's in. As a businessman, I should be able to find a way. But each night I return home exhausted with the realization that I have no solutions. Everyone looks to me for an answer, and I have none. Nobody does."

Elke knew that Jacob was up to something in his old workroom in the back of the house, but she wasn't sure what. He had been in there a long time. She and Mrs. Chotzinoff had been listening for the door to open for a couple of hours. When Jacob finally came out, he was dressed in his heavy winter coat even though it was a relatively mild fall day, and he was carrying a black satchel. "I'm going out for a while," was all he said as he let himself out the front door.

Elke grabbed her coat and watched him from out the parlor window as he walked down the sidewalk and turned the corner. Then she too let herself out the door and followed the route she had seen him take, determined to keep an eye on him. That proved easy to do because Jacob had always been a slow walker, and now that he was in his late sixties, he was even slower. Twenty blocks later, he stopped outside a nondescript building, hesitated a moment, then went in. Elke hurried up to the door and read on the brass plate next to it, "Collectors of Rare Art."

When she read those words, she had a sinking feeling. She knew she couldn't go in after him; to do so would wound his pride forever. Instead, she retreated to a doorway half a block down and on the other side of the street where she could wait for Jacob to come out. As the minutes changed into a half hour and then an hour, Elke changed her mind about staying there any longer and began to retreat down the street in the direction of home.

When Jacob finally returned several hours later, she was waiting for him. He looked tired and pale.

"Have some hot tea, Jacob. It's all ready. I only have to pour it for you."

"Just a minute, Elkeleh. I have something to do." He went down the hall to his workroom and shut the door behind him.

Elke lingered outside the closed door. What if she were simply to open it and walk in? But she had never done that before. She had always respected his privacy in that room and had never entered it unless he invited her. She returned to the parlor to wait until he was ready. Only ten minutes passed before she heard the door opening, but it seemed like an hour. Then he was filling up the doorway with his girth. Rubbing his hands together, he attempted to speak casually. "Now, Elkeleh, I will have that cup of tea you tantalized me with."

After he had gotten settled, Elke watched him as he carefully sipped the hot tea. She ran her tongue over her lips and folded and unfolded her hands in her lap. "You went out just now to sell the *kesubahs*," she finally said.

He lifted his eyes to hers as he continued to blow lightly on the tea. "Yes."

"Jake, I don't want you to do that."

He spoke slowly, in measured words. "They are mine, Elke. Surely I can dispose of them if I wish."

"They are too precious to you. There are other things we can do. But I will not have you sell those beautiful, rare artworks. I want you to tell me how many you sold."

He chucked her under the chin. "And why do you want to know such a thing? Since when did you develop an interest in business, my pretty girl?"

"I want to know because I am going to find a way

to get them back. I simply will not have you selling them, Jake. We can get money some other way, but not that way. Now tell me. How many have you sold?"

He sat back in his chair and eyed her. This was a side to her he hadn't seen before. "How did you know I went to sell them?"

"Never mind that. How many did you sell?"

He looked into his tea. "None."

She didn't know whether to be relieved or even more alarmed. "None?"

"Nobody, it seems, was interested just now. That is because they know even worse times are ahead." He paused. "They are waiting for my price to fall."

Elke managed to sound calmer and more confident during this discussion than she actually felt. During the twenty-five years of their marriage, Jacob had never taken her into his confidences regarding their finances or his business. The world outside the house was his domain; the world inside was hers, and she had always been content with that arrangement. But she knew nothing could make Jacob part with this collection of ancient marriage contracts that he had so painstakingly and lovingly built up over the years—nothing but the direst of financial circumstances. She also knew he would never admit their plight to her. But if it had come to selling the *kesubahs*, she decided something had to be done right away.

Two days later, wearing her best dress, which she rarely wore because of its bright color, Elke stood outside the Metropolitan Bank president's office. She was not unmindful that the emerald green voile of the dress brought out the color of her eyes. In front of her was a secretary, a tall, shapely woman. On her desk stood a brass sign identifying her as Mrs. Fenster, Secretary to the President. She was firing questions at Elke with military precision, clicking her teeth at the end of each sentence.

"No, I don't have an appointment, Mrs. Fenster."

Elke replied, mildly annoyed with the secretary's rigid demeanor.

Mrs. Fenster arched an eyebrow. "Mr. Sheffield has a very tight schedule. I'm afraid that without an appointment, there's just no way I can fit you in today. He will return from lunch any minute, and then he'll have to leave immediately for a meeting across town. These are very grave times, I'm sure you must realize."

"I'll take my chances. I'll wait here for him anyway." Elke stationed herself in one of the heavily upholstered chairs outside his office. A few minutes later, her heart leapt as she saw him come in the front door. She knew he hadn't seen her sitting there, which gave her a chance to study him openly as he drew nearer. It had been over five years since that last hurried and awkward visit to his office, and she was startled to see that these five years had taken more of a toll on him than the previous twenty had. His red-brown hair was now mostly grey and his face was lined around the eyes and mouth. His step was slower and he had put on more weight. Yet to her, he was still a good looking man. She imagined he must have gone through a lot recently, what with the stock market crash last year, banks being forced out of business and now the whole economy reportedly spiraling downward.

When he was only a few feet away, she suddenly stood up and called his name. He looked at the tall, handsome woman standing in front of him and stopped abruptly as if stunned. "Elke! My God, I don't believe it." He guided her into his office. "I'm so glad you've come. Sit down, sit down."

Mrs. Fenster called out after him. "Mr. Sheffield, let me remind you of your meeting with Mr. Markingham at two in the Chrysler Tower."

"Yes," David acknowledged and closed the door. "She should have been leading the troops in the Battle of Verdun," he nodded in Mrs. Fenster's direction. "It would have changed the outcome."

Elke tried to laugh and feel more at ease. She told herself perhaps this wasn't going to be as hard as she had feared. Yet every bit of her pride and dignity was crying out the opposite. She came right to the point. "I have to tell you right away, David, that this is more than a social call."

David picked up a pen and ran it back and forth between his fingers. "Elke, I'm glad for a chance to get to see you, no matter what the reason."

She noticed he seemed nervous but continued doggedly. "Perhaps you don't know, but my husband Jacob retired a few years ago. He was a very successful diamond merchant, and provided very well for us. When he retired, he maintained a small inventory of diamonds, as an investment. He also placed a great deal of our money in the stock market, where he, like so many others, enjoyed considerable success."

David grew more somber. "Naturally. Everyone thought it was the smart place to be. Even shopgirls were managing to double or triple their take-home pay by stock investments."

"Of course, like everyone else, we lost all that a year ago. Since then, I know my husband has been selling off the diamonds one by one so that we might live. I have reason to believe that he has sold, or must be close to selling, the last one. Once the diamonds are gone, there is nothing else that . . ." she faltered for the right words, "that he can sell." It was true, she thought, for she would never let him sell the collection of ancient *kesubahs*. That was her whole reason for being here. "And so," she took a deep breath, "the reason I'm here is to . . . to apply for a loan . . . under my own name."

David blinked rapidly. "You don't want your husband to know what you are doing?"

"That's right. He is a very proud and old-fashioned gentleman. He can't know where I've gotten the money. So I have come to fill out an application for the loan in my name."

David put down the pen and tried to think of a way he could tactfully educate her about the demands of modern banking and her complete lack of status as a woman in the financial world. No bank would ever give her a loan, even assuming it was in the position to do so.

"You realize the banks are not in the solvent state that they once were," he stated gently.

"Yes. I know the banks have had a hard time and I know there's a chance I could get turned down."

David couldn't say aloud what he was thinking. Not only would she be turned down, she would be laughed out of the bank. A married woman, without a job, applying for a loan without any collateral or ostensible means of repayment, all at a time when the banks not only weren't making loans, but were counting themselves lucky to be still in existence. Even a man so naive as to request a loan at this particular time would be laughed at.

He tried to be as tactful as he could. "You are quite right, there is always the chance you could be turned down." He thought about what she had told him. He was well aware of the collapse of the gem markets during the past year and he knew that nobody buys diamonds in a depression. He could imagine how her husband had to sell the diamonds at an incredible loss. The import of rough diamonds was already down twenty-two per cent, with indications of going twice as low the coming year. He had even heard rumors that De Beers in London had enormous quantities of diamonds stored in large milk cans in its Charterhouse London offices.

He picked up the pen and began to run it idly through his thumb and index finger again. He said nothing for a few moments, contemplating his pen. He glanced up at her, sitting there with the same luminous eyes that had captivated him so many years ago, and he had to admit, still did. "I'm quite sure," he finally said, "that there should be no problem with a loan in

your case." As she started to say something, he continued, "However, I have a request to make. Since our arrangement is somewhat unorthodox, given . . . given"—
he thought to himself, given that I am advancing you
the money totally out of my own funds, rather than the
bank's—"given the tight money policies that exist, and
given that you don't want your husband to know of
this financial arrangement, I must ask you that you
tell no one of the loan and of our . . . agreement."

"That is what I would want too." Elke was visibly
relieved. "For not a soul to know, ever."

Later, as David was on his way across town in the
bank's chauffeur-driven limousine, he asked himself
why he had done what he had. If he had not given her
the loan, perhaps, just perhaps, but no, he had given
up a long time ago thinking that Elke's marriage to
someone so much older might not last. Elke was the
kind of woman who would make it work, no matter
what. And that quality in her was, unfortunately, part
of what he couldn't let go of.

Neither of them had discussed how she would pay
the money back.

"Close the factory down?" Sadie repeated, unable
to believe what she was hearing. "Shut down the whole
thing, all of MW Enterprises?" She grabbed the bro-
caded back of the chair for support. She'd come down
from Cambridge for the weekend to offer what moral
support she could to her grandparents as they struggled
to hold on to what was left of MW Enterprises, but she
was not prepared to hear anything like what Marya
was not telling her.

Marya tried to soften her announcement. "Just
temporarily." But Sadie noticed something evasive in
her voice, something that unnerved her even more.

Shifting the topic, Marya gestured toward the
bedroom. "I think you should see him, Sadie. He's
resting and doesn't know you're here." She left the
room for a few minutes and went down the long hall

toward the bedroom, her footsteps muffled by the thick carpet. While she was gone, Sadie surveyed this large room with its expanse of mirrors and luxurious furniture, trying to take comfort in the sheer beauty of this home over the river where her grandparents had decided to move a few years ago.

When Marya returned, Sadie noticed her smile was strained. "Why don't you go into the bedroom, dear? He's still a little too tired to get up yet, but he wants to see you."

Nothing could have prepared Sadie for the sight of her grandfather. When she had last seen him at spring break, he had looked old and worn. But now he looked sick. His usual strong coloring was gone and he appeared weaker than she had ever seen him. When she put her arms around him, she noticed a faint acrid smell, the odor of sickness. She fought back a strong urge to yell at him to get up, stop pretending to be so worn-out looking, to stand tall and vigorous as he always had and stop scaring her this way.

But when he spoke, she was relieved to hear his voice as full and hearty as ever. Perhaps this sickness, whatever it was, would pass quickly and he would soon be back at the helm of the company again. They talked for almost twenty minutes, with Wolf asking most of the questions and Sadie giving the answers. He wanted to know about her classes and questioned her in detail about the observations of her economics professors regarding their expectations for the nation's financial well-being.

When Sadie came back into the living room, she found Marya still sitting where she had left her at the small, ornately carved table in the corner with what was now a cold cup of tea. Sadie realized her grandmother hadn't moved for the whole time she had been in with Wolf. Marya looked up, and the moment Sadie's eyes met her grandmother's she found herself on the verge of tears. She struggled to fight them back. "What's wrong with him, *Bubbe?*"

"He's taken the downturn of the business very hard. He's not been himself since it all started. There have been hard years before, back in '93 and in '07, but it wasn't like this. He feels personally responsible for not being able to figure a way out this time."

"What does the doctor say?" She heard her voice and wished she could keep it from breaking.

Marya laughed with soft resignation. "What doctor? I can't get him near a doctor and he refuses to let one in the house. The only time your grandfather has ever let a doctor come near him was when he was unconscious and didn't know what was happening. Once was when he had pneumonia before we were married and the second time was when I called an ambulance for him." She laughed softly, remembering how it had been. "When he woke up and found himself in the hospital, he would have gotten up right then and there if he hadn't been so heavily bandaged and tied to the bed as a precaution. Now he's insisting he just needs to rest a little and then he'll be fine."

Sadie wanted desperately to take reassurance from the tone of Marya's voice. But the image of her grandfather, pale against the pillows, kept coming back to her, and along with it came the memory of Zosa the same way, and then the memory of her own face as she had seen it reflected in the mirror the day after she had followed Miss Mona to a tarpaper shack in the pine woods outside of St. Augustine where she had gotten rid of her unborn baby. She tried to shake her head free of these images, but the more she tried the more insistent they became until she felt she was starting to break. The next thing she knew, Marya was holding her against her shoulder and she was sobbing, "It isn't fair, it isn't fair."

Marya patted Sadie's head as she held her. "What isn't fair, Sadie?"

"It's too much all at once, *Bubbe*. Now *Zeyde* is sick, and the factory's closing, and before that it was

Zosa, and before that Zosa's baby, and before that ...
before that ... Florida."

Marya started to ask her what had happened in
Florida, but stopped. All along she had had a sense
that something more significant had happened that
summer than Sadie ever had revealed, something that
had marked her deeply. But she knew this wasn't the
time to probe into that wound.

Sadie lifted her head and her eyes were red and
watery. "It's all just too much sadness, *Bubbe*. I just
can't take anything else going wrong and any more of
this ... this ugliness and pain. I don't know what I'm
going to do. I feel I just can't go on."

Marya tightened her grip on Sadie's shoulders and
pushed her away from her so she could look her in the
eye. "Listen to me, Sadie. I want you to stop this talk
about not being able to take it. You most certainly can
take it. You're stronger, far stronger, than you recognize and I want you to remember this: no matter what
happens, the most horrible thing you can imagine, you
can always stand it. If your grandfather, God forbid,
were not to live, if something were to happen to me, if
you should see your mother and father killed right before your eyes, no matter how awful it would be, you
could take it."

Sadie was shocked at Marya's intensity. Marya
spoke to her with the conviction and passion that had
taken a lifetime to forge. Sadie realized Marya was
speaking to her of her own sorrows and the events that
must have occurred in the course of her own life. That
realization stunned her.

Marya was looking at her fiercely. "You have gotten through whatever it was that happened in Florida,
and you've gotten through the death of Zosa's baby and
the fact that Zosa is perhaps forever lost to us. So no
matter what happens next, you will survive it and
you'll go on. I know it, Sadie. I know it because I
know what your bones are made of, and I know the
blood flowing in your veins." Her voice rose loud and

sure. "Do you hear me? Whatever happens, you will go on, and you will be stronger than ever for it."

Sadie saw an expression in her grandmother's eyes she had never seen before. It was a combination of anger and tenderness at the same time, and as Sadie felt that look penetrating into her, she began to accept her grandmother's words and believe that she did indeed have a strength greater than she had ever thought possible. How could she not? She was from this strong woman's loins. She would endure, she resolved. Then she stopped crying.

"Now I want you to sit here a moment," Marya instructed. "There's something I want to show you." She left the living room and when she came back, she was carrying an old faded purse, the kind that had been in vogue some thirty or forty years ago.

Marya placed the purse on the table. "Open it."

Sadie opened the purse and was struck by the old, musty smell that emanated from it. She reached in and withdrew from the bag what appeared to her to be folded wads of currency. She looked at her grandmother, clearly puzzled.

"Go ahead. Take it all out."

Sadie unpeeled bill after bill and laid each one out on the table. She was astonished to see that no bill was smaller than one hundred dollars. She continued until the table was covered with what was probably over ten thousand dollars. She could only stare at her grandmother in amazement and wait for some kind of explanation.

"Some of this money I have had for more than forty years. It was a gift from your grandfather. Only he didn't present the gift to me in this form. And some of the money I have saved from a windfall." Marya chuckled softly, thinking about Wolf's jewels and her casino outing with Andrew. Sadie kept perfectly still, wanting her to go on.

"Your grandfather, as you know, is a man of the old country, and he came from a wealthy family there.

It has always been part of his dream to accomplish here what his father accomplished in St. Petersburg. He always had to prove, I suppose, that he was worthy to be his father's son, especially when he and his father couldn't agree on the course the family should take in the face of the czar's harassment of the Jews. That is when he left, you know. When I became his wife, he wanted to dress me in jewels, the way his father had adorned his mother. Only," Marya sighed, "my dream was not exactly the same as his. I did not feel like myself, draped in such glitter. I have always loved fine things, it is true, but more than fine things I wanted to make sure we had, before anything else, a firm foundation under us. You see, our people," she paused before she said the word, "the Jews, we were not allowed to own land in Russia, or, for that matter, in most parts of the world. I wanted so much for us to buy a piece of property of our own here in America, perhaps a tenement which we could acquire with another couple to get started, something we could hold on to and always have for security."

Sadie broke in. "But you could have worn those jewels with the beautiful dresses you designed."

"I didn't want to wear those jewels. To me they still are like the badges of an aristocracy, be it the Russian or the American. Although I know little of the Russian upper classes, I've learned much of the American ones, and I have not always liked what I learned. I've spent time in their company, but to tell the truth, although I still have a friend or two among them, I never could respect them the way I have supposedly more ordinary people. And so, over the years, whenever I had an opportunity for a good price, I cashed the stones in."

"And *Zeyde?* What did he say? Didn't he wonder why you didn't wear his jewels?"

Marya sighed. "I was not so wise there. I hurt him deeply, of course. I was too blind to see it at the time. Our marriage was not always as peaceful and

happy as it is now, and we both went our separate
ways most of the time. He thought I didn't wear his
jewels because I didn't love him. So as the years
passed, he gave them to me less and less often, and his
enthusiasm dampened."

Sadie was stunned. Ever since she could remember, her grandparents had been like newlyweds, affec-
tionate and content in each other's company. It was
hard for her to picture the things her grandmother was
telling her. It was hard for her to imagine that two
people as in love as they were had once gone their separate ways, as her grandmother said.

She saw that Marya was looking at her with a
fixed expression. "Sadie, I have not given up my
dream. That's why I've continued to hold on to this
money without touching it all these years."

Sadie practically sputtered. "But you could have
used it to save the business! We can still use it!"

Marya shook her head. "There is a lot of money
on this table, but not enough for that. How much and
for how long could this money really help MW Enterprises? The expenses of the business are so high that
they would eat through this money in less than a
month. And then where would we be? Exactly where
we are now, only without the money."

Sadie knew what her grandmother said was true.

Marya began to brush the bills into a pile in the
middle of the table. "Sadie, I want you to take all this
money, and I want you to use all your intelligence and
intuition and whatever you may have learned in college
in order to buy property and land for our family. There
is enough here for us to get started. You must accept
that the factory is gone for the time being. The only
chance we have now is to buy property with this
money . . . now while the prices are low and people
are selling cheap, especially if they can get cash. Then
we will hold on to the property until better days, and
then perhaps, your grandfather can reopen MW Enterprises. That is the only hope."

Sadie, her face sober, stared at Marya. "You want me to do that? Not Adam Dov or . . . or Michael?"

"You must know Adam Dov has no real interest in business. His passion is politics. And Michael is still too young. He has another year of high school and he isn't ready. He doesn't have your . . . sense of things. You are the logical one. You'll be finished with college in a few months. And besides, you have always had a special concern for the factory, which has always been the lifeblood of this family."

"And the factory, is it really to be closed?" She still couldn't believe it. .

"Yes, at least for the time being. It's losing money now at a frightening rate. Your grandfather needs to rest. He's not well enough to run it, no matter what he may tell you. I've talked him into liquidating some of our holdings and with that money we'll be able to live until times are better."

Sadie was looking at her soberly.

"There's something else, Sadie. As far as your grandfather knows, the jewelry he gave me is hidden away in a dusty box somewhere, never worn and never looked at. He knows nothing of this money. And I do not think now is the time to tell him any of this. The last thing he needs to hear is that we've begun to speculate in land while the world is collapsing around us."

Marya stood up and began to walk around the sumptuous living room. She came to a stop in front of the expansive windows that held a spectacular view of the East River. "From here you can almost see the Lower East Side. We're not that far from it." She inadvertently sighed. "I tell myself this isn't really starting over. It's not like after the fire . . . you wouldn't know about that, your mother was just a little girl then. We're not completely back where we started forty years ago. We have a richness we didn't have at that time. We have you, our children and grandchildren."

Sadie began to sort out the bills that were now

heaped into a pile on the table. She carefully arranged them so they were all smooth and facing the same way. Then she slowly counted them. "Fourteen thousand and five hundred," she announced when she was finished. She placed the pack of bills back on the table and stared at it respectfully. Even though she had worked in her grandfather's factory when she was a teenager, she had always taken money—both her grandparents' and parents'—for granted. Now, except for this small tower of green in front of her, her family's money was virtually gone. Here before her was her grandfather's dream, transmuted from jewels to greenbacks, and waiting to be transmuted again into her grandmother's dream, one of land and a secure prosperity. As she gazed at the money, she gradually began to recognize the responsibility with which her grandmother was entrusting her. She desperately hoped she was worthy of that trust.

Sadie looked up and saw her grandmother watching her. "You can do it, Sadie. I know you can."

Chapter 32

A few months later, Sadie told Marya she had found a tenement building for sale at a very low price on Second Avenue. After Sadie took her to see it, Marya said without hesitation, "Buy it." Three months later, Sadie announced she had found another. It was on Third Avenue and could be had for an even better price than the first one. Again Marya went with Sadie to look at it with the same result. "Buy it."

In the next year, Sadie found two more buildings. These Marya decided she didn't need to inspect. Sadie could handle it on her own.

"Now I think we should diversify," Sadie told Marya after her fourth purchase. They were sitting in the living room of the small house located in the Williamsburg section of Brooklyn. After they had sold the lavish home in Sutton Place, Wolf had wanted to rent, rather than buy, the modest little house in Williamsburg.

"Why buy a house that we don't want permanently?" he had asked. Marya had sensed that it was almost a superstition with him that to buy that house might mean they would seal themselves in it forever. Sadie had been able to finish her college because the tuition and room and board had all been paid for in advance before the crash, but as soon as she had graduated, Wolf had invited her to move back in with them in order to cut down the family's expenses.

He'd extended the same offer to Jacob and Elke, well aware of what had happened to the diamond market since '29, but Jacob and Elke seemed somehow to have had an unexpected reserve of cash and were able to make do on their own although in considerably reduced circumstances. They'd brought Zosa home to live with them and they still had Mrs. Chotzinoff, who by now was too old to work, and she had become like one of the family, receiving the respect and deference given to an elderly but well-loved aunt.

So the four of them—Wolf, Marya, Sadie and Michael—lived together modestly and quietly, doing their best to conserve the little money that remained from the sale, made at a painful loss, of the Sutton Place residence.

Now Marya was assessing her granddaughter's words. "Diversify?" Marya looked at her and marveled at how Sadie had grown in confidence and maturity these last two years. Her face had lost its round girlish look, and although she still had an impish sparkle in her eyes, her countenance was more thoughtful and reflective. Marya felt Sadie had borne her sorrow well, and the painful events of the last few years had seemed to strengthen rather than weaken her resolve. The almost imperceptible stress lines highlighted her face, giving her an astonishing beauty, of which she seemed quite unaware.

"Yes, diversify," Sadie repeated with a sudden shyness. "This will probably sound silly to you, but please don't laugh. I sometimes get feelings about things. They're kind of like hunches, and I just know something is going to happen."

Marya smiled in spite of herself. "That doesn't sound foolish to me at all, Sadie."

Sadie returned the smile and appeared less bashful. "It doesn't?" But then, she thought, she should have known her grandmother would understand. Over the years Marya had always understood what she was thinking or feeling better than anyone else.

Marya shook her head. "No, not at all," she repeated.

Sadie's confidence returned and she went ahead eagerly. "When I was in Florida in the summer of '28, I learned of the land opportunities there. Remember how everyone was buying lots in the early twenties? And then the bust set in a few years later when those hurricanes hit? In spite of all that, I'd like to see us buy some land there, solely as an investment because I know I never want to live there. It must sound mad, but I know those prices must be even lower now than ever. And somehow I just can't see that they're always going to stay that low. In spite of the hurricanes and the bugs and the terrible summer heat, people are going to want to go there when this country gets back on its feet. They're going to want to get out of the cold winters and as they get older, they'll want to find a pleasant place to retire. Maybe it's just a hunch, but I believe it's true. We should buy."

"Sadie, if your feelings are that strong, I think you should go ahead and follow them. And I think the best thing would be for you to go back down there and see for yourself just what the lots look like. You might even be able to persuade Michael to go with you this summer."

"Summer?" Sadie gasped. She had no desire ever to return to Florida, and the prospect of going there in the summer was unthinkable. Yet that was the only time Michael was free. She and Marya had held out a small portion of the money from the jewels so that Michael could attend City College. Sadie knew that going to Florida alone was out of the question, so summer it would have to be and with Michael.

Marya paid her gasp no heed. "He could help you drive that old car of yours, if it still runs."

* * *

Sadie was aware she was being watched. If she hadn't been trying to cope with a very messy plate of fried catfish, she wouldn't have minded so much, because it was a very handsome man who was watching her. She gnawed the breaded catfish as far as the tail, which unlike the people of this area, she refused to consider the choicest part. "Michael," she asked suddenly. "Do I have grease grinning from ear to ear?"

"Uh huh," said Michael, and snatched up the tail she had just set down. "You're a regular gusher."

"Oh. I wonder if that's why that man keeps staring at me. Look at how immaculate he looks in that white suit. He can probably tell I eat catfish like a Yankee." Since coming to the South again, she realized that she was in the eyes of the locals not a Northerner, but a Yankee, as if the war between the states were still on.

Michael concentrated on his fish without looking up. "Maybe he just likes the way you look. Some men like a woman with a shine to her," he chuckled, and without asking helped himself to one of the fillets still on her plate.

Sadie stole a few more glances at the dark man in the white suit and concluded she didn't like him. Too polished, too much like Chris.

After lunch, she and Michael decided to take a walk along the pier. They were at the waterfront in Miami Beach. She felt a lot more comfortable here than she had in St. Augustine, much to her surprise. It wasn't the weather that made the difference, she decided, because it was just as humid and hot as in St. Augustine. Here, for some reason, she felt more accepted and more at ease. Maybe not being with Chris, but with someone who truly loved her was what made the difference.

She and Michael leaned over the pier and watched the slightly choppy waters of the Atlantic below them. A slight breeze ruffled her hair. It had been a long time since Sadie had felt so happy. She thought about the lists she used to make when she was a girl, where she would line up the things she liked and didn't like about her life. If she were to make a list at this moment, the column of "likes" would be full and the column of "don't likes" almost empty. She was buoyed by her grandfather's improved health, the closeness she felt with both Michael and her grandmother, and the sense she had that she was contributing something important to the family's well-being.

Just about the only thing she didn't like and hadn't been able to accept was what had happened to MW Enterprises, and it rankled her that at least some vestige of it wasn't in operation. But, maybe, if the family was able to make some money in a few years on the property she'd been purchasing and could put a little money aside, the company could reopen on a small scale.

She turned to gaze back down the pier at the land behind them, with its flat horizon and hundreds of palm trees. As she did so, she noticed the man who had been watching her a short while ago in the restaurant. He was also out on the pier, standing not too far away and staring southward down the coast. He was of average height, with a slender but well-proportioned frame, and he had a great deal of straight black hair that was being tossed every which way by the steady breeze.

She started to turn back toward the sea when Michael caught her eye. In the last year he had finally begun to put on a little weight and it suited him well. He was no longer the broomstick he'd been since he was ten years old. He was as energetic as ever, but that energy had never been channeled into athletics or even the factory, despite his interest in the business world. At this moment he was looking at her with his darkly fringed eyes and she could tell he was getting ready to tease her about something.

"Michael," she began before he could say anything, "have I told you how much fun it is having you on this trip with me? You actually make the temperature bearable."

"That's a trait we uncles have."

They laughed and began to stroll back down the pier. The dark-haired man from the restaurant was still standing there a short way ahead. As they drew near, he looked up and smiled. "Hello," he nodded and raised his straw hat slightly. He smiled at both of them and at Sadie in particular.

To her consternation, Sadie saw Michael stop. "Hello," he returned, and put out his hand. "I'm Michael Luminov, and this is my niece, Sadie Molnar."

Sadie had no choice but to shake the man's hand also, noticing as she did so that his skin felt remarkably cool and not at all sticky from the humidity.

"I'm Benjamin Moses de la Fuente Cordoba," he introduced himself with a slight trace of an accent.

The name rolled off his lips so fluently and quickly that for a second she and Michael were too amazed to say anything in response.

"I'm sorry," Michael finally managed to reply. "I didn't get your name at all."

He laughed genially, flashing extremely white teeth. "Of course, I should have said it less rapidly. Most Americans are not used to the Mexican sounds." He gave his name again, only a tiny bit more slowly, and still neither of them could have repeated it.

Sadie's cheeks turned red at the impossible name. She heard Michael say, "One more time, please, and much slower." She wondered why he was bothering to get his name straight when they would probably never see him again.

The man was not at all embarrassed or in a hurry. "Say after me," he instructed. "Ben-hah-meen. It's like your American name Benjamin, only with a Spanish pronunciation."

"Oh! It's Benjamin," Michael said suddenly, giving the name its customary English pronunciation. "Of course. Now I recognize it."

Sadie didn't say anything and felt distinctly uncomfortable. She didn't like the way this man's black eyes kept straying over to hers.

Benjamin slung his white jacket over his shoulder. "Then that is all you need to know. The rest you can learn later, if you like, while I buy you and your niece, did you say?"—he turned toward Sadie, raising an eyebrow—"a refreshment."

Sadie was about to decline politely when Michael surprised her by accepting the offer. She hurled him a stabbing glance but had the distinct impression that, mischievous as he was, he avoided looking at her.

As they seated themselves in the small oceanfront café, Sadie was struck again by how clean and cool Benjamin looked. His white suit was perfectly pressed and he appeared to be completely unaffected by the heat. As soon as they'd finished ordering, Benjamin startled them by leaning forward intimately, his dark eyes lit with intensity. "I could not help but overhear your conversation in the restaurant earlier today as you talked about the parcels of land you are considering for purchase."

Sadie felt a moment of embarrassment. She hated to think someone had listened in on their somewhat amateur discussion of local land values. She also recalled how messy she must have looked eating the catfish. She forgot her embarrassment as she was struck by the slightly formal rhythms of his English and his precise way of speaking.

"You are from New York, I believe? And not from this region?"

When they nodded, he quickly continued, "Ah, then you must not think me forward if I say I can be of some assistance to you. You see, I am an architect, and I am here in the Miami area to survey the location of a new building that my family—we are a family of architects—has been awarded a contract to design.

From previous visits here, I have some knowledge of this area and the kind of lots that are available. And I have reason to believe that the lots you were discussing are not for you."

"Why not?" Michael protested slightly skeptical. Sadie was even more skeptical.

"I know for certain that one of the pieces that you were talking about is swampland that has been filled in. It is completely unstable and could not be built on in its present condition."

Sadie sat up straight. "What else do you know?" she asked, at the same time doubting they could trust him any more than anyone else.

In response to her question, he replied, "If you have transportation, I will take you to look at some land that I think would be a good investment for you."

Once they were in Sadie's now somewhat dilapidated tin lizzie, he insisted on spending the afternoon with them, directing them to a number of sites where he was able to point out the advantages and disadvantages of each parcel of land.

But for some reason Sadie couldn't relax. Even though he wasn't American and of course not a Southerner, his smoothness reminded her of Chris. A couple of hours later, after he had shown them a particularly attractive plot near the ocean, and clearly and logically explained its merits and demerits, she began to see that he was not strongly advocating any particular parcel, but instead trying to indicate basic things they should know.

Michael was beaming. "Being with you is like getting a fast course in real estate. We deeply appreciate how much time and trouble you're taking on our behalf."

"It is no trouble," he replied, "when the company is as charming as you and your niece. There are always many shady characters trying to sell land in this area," he warned. "We must see that you do not meet up with any of them. I don't like to see people taken unfair advantage of."

Five hours had passed quickly. To the west they could see one of Florida's spectacular sunsets. Sadie noticed this man still managed to look immaculate, impervious to the grueling climate.

Michael shook Benjamin's hand. "I don't know how we will be able to repay you for your generosity," he said as it finally came time to part.

His eyes lit up. "I know one way, if again I would not be too bold. You see, I will be in New York in a few months on business. If you and your niece would be so kind as to allow me your company for dinner one evening during that time, I would feel myself more than amply repaid."

Michael was quick to reply. "Of course. That would be no problem at all," he accepted the invitation before Sadie could start forming her own answer.

Later that evening, as Sadie and Michael were walking along the powdery white beach, their shoes in their hands, Sadie cleared her throat in an exaggerated manner. "There's something I have to ask you. Since when have you started speaking for me?"

"What are you talking about?"

"You know, Michael. Don't be coy with me."

"Oh, that? It's time you got to know some men. You know what they say about all work and no play."

Sadie reddened. Ever since Chris, she hadn't wanted anything much to do with men and she hadn't accepted a single date. Then in her last two years of college her studies had devoured all her time.

"Michael, you may be right. Maybe the time has come for me to open my eyes to the other half of the human race. But I can tell you one thing. I don't want to start with Benjamin." She paused. "He's too pretty and doesn't look like the kind that would have much to him. Anyway," she changed the topic, "I'd rather not think of men right now."

As the cool sand squished between her bare toes,

she was aware of how happy she was to be walking on a broad beach in the moonlight with almost nothing in the "debit" column of her life. Under those circumstances, who needed a man?

The house was dark and all the shades drawn. It smelled slightly musty, as if nobody had been there for quite a while. "*Bubbe? Zeyde?*" Sadie called. Michael set their valises down, as perplexed as Sadie. They looked at each other. Then Michael went into every room, looking for his mother and father.

He returned a minute later, looking no less baffled. "They're not here."

Sadie picked up the telephone and dialed her parents' house. The phone rang for a long time and finally Mrs. Chotzinoff answered in a crackling voice.

"Mrs. Chotzinoff. It's Sadie. Michael and I are at my grandparents'. We just got back and there's nobody here. Do you know where they are?" As she waited for the slow-talking housekeeper to respond, a sharp dagger of dread hung over her head.

Mrs. Chotzinoff's voice cracked more than ever. "You must come, Sadie. Come at once." Before Sadie could ask her another question, the housekeeper hung up on her.

On the drive to her parents' house, neither Sadie nor Michael spoke. Sadie was only aware that the dreadful feeling of anxiety was back. Since that summer when she'd first gotten back from Florida, through what happened with Zosa until the crash of the stock market and her grandfather's illness, a tight knot of pain had always hovered nearby and now had suddenly returned, just when she had let herself believe it might be gone for good.

As they pulled up in front, she noticed her parents' house also had the shades drawn. She and Michael ran up the steps and into the house.

Sadie saw Marya sitting alone in the parlor, staring into the fire. She burst in upon her. "*Bubbe,* what's happened? What's going on? I have a terrible feeling something awful's happened."

Marya looked up, her face expressionless. "Come here, Sadie, and sit down next to me."

As Sadie did so, Marya said, "Give me your hand." She noticed Michael still standing in the doorway. "Come in, Michael. I want to talk to you, too." When he sat down on the other side of her, Marya also took one of his hands in hers. Although she was holding on to both of them, it was Sadie she was looking at. "A week ago, your father became violently ill after supper."

Sadie's heart contracted as the arrow of dread finally hit its target. At her grandmother's words, she felt suddenly light and disconnected from the earth, as if all this were a dream and she might float up and out of it. "What happened? He's all right, isn't he?"

"The doctor said he suffered a stroke. He died a couple of hours later that night, right here at the house . . . in his bedroom."

Sadie felt a rush of fear and pain sweep over her. She tried to pull her hand away but Marya held it tightly. From somewhere far away she was aware of her grandmother's voice going on, saying something about how the doctor had said that Jacob mercifully hadn't suffered.

"We had no way of reaching you," Marya explained. "We wanted you here for the funeral."

She twisted and turned in her grandmother's grip and heard a young woman's voice, as if at a great distance, yelling hoarsely, "It isn't fair! It isn't fair!" Then she realized that the voice was her own, and the next thing she knew she was curled against Marya's shoulder the way she had done when she was a little girl, and she cried softly. She had no idea how much time she passed curled up like that, but finally she felt she could open her eyes again.

The first thing she saw was her grandmother, staring at her with that same mixture of fierceness and tenderness she had once seen in the living room of the house at Sutton Place. Marya's words came back to her unbidden. You will survive. No matter what happens, you can endure it. It is in your blood to bear this. Sadie silently repeated the words to herself and found that they helped. The pain was still there, but along with it now was an acceptance that this event was part of her life and that she must embrace it. And then she remembered her mother. "Where is Mother?" she asked suddenly, sitting up.

"Your mother is in the bedroom. She's been very distraught and has refused to leave the room where your father died. Your grandfather and I have been here with her for the last week. We want her to come live with us, but she is in no condition to face a change yet. But we can't leave her alone here. Mrs. Chotzinoff is unable to look after her." Marya sighed. "Elke needs her family around her at a time like this."

"And *Zeyde?*" Sadie asked.

Marya sighed again. "He is with Elke now. He doesn't say much, but I can tell this has shaken him deeply. You know, your father was a friend of your grandfather many years before he became a part of our family."

As Sadie listened to Marya's voice calmly answering her questions, she sensed again how strong her grandmother was and how much she must have endured in her own life. She wondered if her grandmother ever cried. She couldn't remember ever having seen her do so.

That evening, everyone sat on low stools in the parlor on this last day of shivah, the seven-day period of mourning, while Adam Dov recited the Kaddish, the mourners' prayer. As Adam Dov's low voice rose up in this prayer that testified to the everlasting peace to be found in the coming of the Messiah, Sadie looked at the members of her family gathered there. Elke was crying softly. She was dressed all in black, her blouse slightly torn; the *keriah* she had made in display of her grief. Her grandfather's shirt bore a similar tear, as did the garments of everyone else in the room except her and her grandmother. Someone had even made a rip in Zosa's skirt, and she sat among them, her eyes staring and uncomprehending, like a universal monument to death.

As she looked at each member of her family, Sadie pictured this bearlike father of whom she had always been a little afraid, as he had been with each of them. He had always impressed her more with his strictness than with anything else. Even though she had not felt particularly close to him while she was growing up, she nevertheless loved him, and as she had come to realize as she grew older, he had loved her too. They had never understood each other, yet she had his blood and was of his flesh, and to this extent she would always carry him with her. She felt as though she was just beginning to know and appreciate him. Now it was too late.

Tears sprang to her eyes again as she felt something awaken in her, a desire she had never had before. She suddenly wanted to share in these religious rituals of comfort taking place around her. She took hold of the front of her dress, and with her sharp nails, pierced a hole to let out the sadness trapped inside her.

In the weeks that followed, Sadie was filled with a restless energy. She tried to explain it to her grandmother when she and Wolf finally returned to the house in Williamsburg a month later. One day Sadie found Marya sitting alone with a book at the kitchen table and she burst out without prelude. "I don't know if it's father's death or what, but I have a terrible sense of time passing while I just sit here. I know I'm looking for investments, but that doesn't take all my time, and besides, it could be a long while before any of them start to pay off. All of a sudden I want to make things happen now. I want to take ideas that have only been just that and turn them into something real and tangible. Something that gets results sooner than the land and property will."

During this declaration, Marya closed her book, and watched Sadie pace back and forth across the kitchen as she talked. "What sort of ideas?"

Sadie stopped abruptly and turned to face her. "MW Enterprises is still on my mind. I just can't stop thinking about it. At night as I lie in bed, I get ideas of things that we could do to get it going again. Some of the ideas are crazy but at least one of them isn't."

"Sadie, I have to caution you not to get your hopes up. You know we don't have the resources to open the factory, and frankly, I don't know when we will. The economy gets worse every year. I read in the paper this morning that the Dow Jones Industrials have been steadily dropping from twenty-two per cent in 1930 to forty-one per cent in '31, and they're predicting fifty-two per cent for this year."

"It's got to bottom out somewhere, and I have a hunch that this year and maybe next year are the worst. And when it ends, I want us to be ready to jump in. Women are going to have to start buying dresses again. When they do, I want us to be in a position to take off." She sat down across from Marya. "Will you listen to my plan, just listen?"

Marya nodded. "Listen, yes. Approve of? That I wouldn't want you to count on."

"First of all, we can't afford to open the factory and run it the way we used to. I won't argue with that. But I think we can start putting out dresses bearing the MW label again without opening the factory." When she saw that Marya was looking at her with patient skepticism, she hastened to explain.

"I had this idea when I was eighteen years old, and I've always thought it could work. Please just listen to me all the way through."

"I'm listening already."

"Remember how I said it would be possible to run MW out of just a showroom? I still believe that.

We let go of the factory. It takes too much time and money, not to mention energy, to manage anyway. First, we come up with the designs."

"We?"

"Well, not *we*, actually. You. I can't even draw a stick, you know that." Before Marya could react to having been assigned a role in the new plan, Sadie rushed on. "Once we have the designs, we make up a prototype or sample. We place a custom order with the textile mills to get the prints and colors that we want in the fabrics we want. Then we turn it all over to outside sources."

"You mean go back to outside contracting? I'm afraid your grandfather would never go for that."

Sadie wasn't the least deterred. "Who says we have to tell him? We can go ahead with this on our own. What will convince him will be our success. That way, we don't have to try to persuade him of anything in advance. Anyway, so many people are out of work, they'll jump at the chance to stitch our clothes up using their own homes as workshops. We could probably even get some of the people who used to work for us. Then," she paused long enough only to take a breath of air, "once the dresses are assembled, we inspect them and sew our MW label into them, and just like that, we're back in business." The room was suddenly silent as she waited for Marya's response.

For a moment Marya just looked at her blankly. "The main thing I want to know is," she finally said, "who's this we you keep referring to? You and who else?"

"You and me, of course. Who else is there?"

Marya started to laugh, shaking her head. "I can think of lots of people who might be who else."

"But *Bubbe*, I need you to come up with the designs and to help with the sizing and selection of fabric. You're the one with the experience. I just have the idea, but you're the one who can make it all happen."

She grabbed hold of Marya's hand. 'Say you'll help me with this. Say you'll at least give it a try."

"It sounds like you're the brains and I'm the brawn," Marya sighed, but Sadie could see the twinkle in her eye as she said it. "Since you're the brains, how are you proposing we get the money to buy the fabric?"

"That's easy. We still have some of the cash left from your jewels."

"You're really sure you want to do this?"

"You told me some time ago to follow my hunches. Well, I have a hunch this can work."

In the next few months, Marya was to learn that Sadie had boundless enthusiasm and an answer for everything regarding her project. The very next day after their discussion, Sadie appeared suddenly and insisted she was taking Marya to see a movie. She stood by the door, already wearing her coat.

"We shouldn't be spending our money on movies," Marya scolded. "And besides, it doesn't seem right, so soon after your father's death."

"Nobody will know but us." Sadie reached into the hall closet for Marya's coat, her mind obviously made up. Marya resigned herself to being bundled off to see Helen Hayes in "The Sin of Madelon Claudet." When they emerged from the ornate movie palace two hours later, Sadie boomed full of enthusiasm. "Well?"

"Well?" echoed Marya, not getting the point.

"Don't you see? Remember how I used to try to make myself into Clara Bow when I was a teenager?"

Marya laughed. "Oh! So that's who you were supposed to be when you cut off your hair and then your skirts!"

"I used to go around pretending that I had 'It,' whatever 'It' was. I'm not sure I knew myself. But the point is I was crazy over the movies, and as far as I can see, everyone else still is. Movies set the trends now. Any time actresses like Bette Davis or Norma

Shearer or Helen Hayes wear something new, everyone else wants one just like it. So I think we should design to attract that audience. That's why I brought you here, so you could see what Helen Hayes was wearing and get some ideas."

Following Sadie's instructions, Marya sketched out a few possibilities for dresses similar to the ones movie stars were wearing in current popular pictures. Marya was amazed that these young women had become such celebrities. She could remember how in the earliest movies around 1921, there had been no big stars. But once Sadie pointed out to her the slavish devotion to the trends set by the films, she knew instantly her granddaughter was right. So Marya designed her first dress for their new line. It featured a longer skirt that fit at the hips, a natural waistline, generally more feminine lines, and it looked best worn with one of the new off-the-brow hats.

Sadie clapped her hands when she saw it. "That's exactly right! Every woman in New York will want one the minute she sees it."

When Marya wanted to know where their workroom, or showroom as Sadie had taken to calling it, was going to be, Sadie had an answer for that too. They could go ahead and fashion their prototypes in the most logical place of all—the factory. "Why not?" Sadie said. "It's sitting down there boarded up, having no use, and it would be the perfect place to store our bolts of yardage. In fact, I already went ahead and made arrangements without you to have the yard goods delivered there. Oh," she added before Marya could say anything, "we should use the electric cutting machines down there too. That will speed up things a lot."

In the next few weeks while they were assembling their prototypes, Marya and Sadie managed to come up with a series of excuses to explain why they weren't at home. Several times they were supposedly at the library; once they were taking a long "constitutional";

another time they were even visiting Jacob's grave. "It's not such a terrible lie," Sadie kept reassuring Marya. "Especially since it's for a good cause, the well-being of the family."

Marya had looked askance at Sadie's rationalization. "I suppose you're going to tell me Jacob would have wanted it this way?"

Sadie giggled. "How did you know? He would have, too. I just have a hunch."

Once, as they sat in the empty factory working across from each other, Marya had looked up to see Sadie surrounded by fabric parts, a piece of tailor's chalk in her mouth, her auburn curls falling forward into her face as she leaned over her work. For a moment Marya was carried back in time to the days when MW Enterprises was a one-room operation in the tiny two-room flat that was her and Wolf's first home. She would have never dreamed that over forty years later she and her granddaughter would be back to doing the same kind of labor, as if they were newly arrived immigrants. She sighed, wondering when she would ever get the feeling that they had something secure under them.

Once the prototypes were made and the pieces cut for a modest first lot of fifty garments based on two of Marya's designs, they waited eagerly to see the results. When the completed dresses finally arrived from the outside contractors, Marya had to admit she was as excited as Sadie. The two walked around the racks where the finished dresses were hanging. "They're beautiful," Marya proclaimed. She looked at Sadie who was overflowing with confidence and energy. At that particular moment, she thought she had never seen a woman look more beautiful or alive.

Sadie nodded her head in agreement. "The only thing to do now is sew in our MW label and get them out to the stores to see if they sell." Then she looked at her grandmother and was startled to find her close to tears.

* * *

Sadie was so immersed in the details of her project that she was thoroughly taken aback when she picked up the telephone one afternoon a few months later and an accented voice informed her, "This is Benjamin Cordoba. I'm in town for a while and would consider it an honor to have a chance to see you, with or without your Uncle Michael."

Flustered, she found herself speaking for Michael and agreeing they would have dinner with Benjamin the next evening at the Plaza Hotel. As soon as she hung up, she tried to get hold of Michael to make sure he could go with her, and when he begged off, she was immediately suspicious, remembering how he had been trying to set a trap for her down in Florida when they'd met Benjamin. Once again, she realized, it had worked all too well. Her first thought was to cancel. But she felt they owed Benjamin Cordoba at least some sign of gratitude for the help he'd given them in Florida, guiding them to a safe buy.

The next evening she arrived alone at the fashionable hotel across from the southern entrance to Central Park at the appointed time. Benjamin was already waiting in the lobby for her, and as she spotted him, she was struck again by his elegance. The crisp white summer suit of the tropics had given away to a one-button, single-breasted coat in the style called the English drape, with loose trousers pleated at the waist. As he strode toward her, she was impressed with how at home he seemed in this aristocratic setting. Yet it was that very elegance and poise she still mistrusted. Chris, according to the fashion of the midtwenties, also had been elegant, and she now was wary of anything that possessed too smooth and effortless a facade.

"And our uncle, where is he?" Benjamin asked as soon as they were together, guiding her in the direction of the dining room.

"He said he had some previous appointment he just couldn't get out of." Sadie tried to sound convincing, especially because she herself couldn't believe

Michael's excuse. "But he does want to have a chance to see you while you are here. How long do you think that will be?"

"That depends on many things. Possibly as long as two months. Then from here there's a good chance I'll be going to California where my family is about to buy some land."

The mention of land drew her attention like a magnet and made her momentarily forget her discomfort in his presence. She wasn't so caught up in resurrecting MW Enterprises that she had forgotten about the remaining money she'd set aside for a final land purchase. As soon as they were seated, she prompted, "Land, did you say? You are looking at some land to buy?"

"Yes. In the Ojai Valley in California. Have you heard of it?"

She shook her head. She knew almost nothing about any area outside of New York and Cambridge. She knew even less about California than she had about Florida.

"Ah, yes, I had forgotten how provincial you New Yorkers are," teased Benjamin. "You really don't make good travelers."

Sadie was tempted to retort that why should New Yorkers make good travelers; they had everything they wanted right in Manhattan. But she resisted an argument. What she really wanted was information.

"It's a beautiful and rich valley about eighty miles to the north of Los Angeles and a little to the east of a small town called Ventura. The land is ideal for ranching or for establishing citrus, avocado and nut groves."

Sadie had no idea what sort of thing an avocado was, but she listened avidly as Benjamin continued to describe the valley and its potential for agriculture. She knew the farmers in the Midwest had been hard hit by the collapse of the economy, but California hadn't been struck so badly. Such an area, she decided, could have possibilities as the place for her final investment. All along she had been reluctant to sink all the money from the jewels in just one part of the country or in just one kind of property. A piece of raw land in California that might be put to use once she got a little bit of working capital from the dress line, that sounded like a wise investment. Unlike the land in Florida, it wouldn't just be lying fallow.

"Now you must tell me a little more about yourself," Benjamin requested after he had answered all of Sadie's questions about the Ojai Valley. "I know virtually nothing about what you do with yourself all day or anything about your family."

Sadie was astonished. Talk about herself to this man? It would be easier to talk about the family. She explained to him the nature of her family's business. When he showed interest, she told him about her grandmother and grandfather and tried to capture their personalities for him. She was somewhat surprised to find herself unfolding such things to him, although she had now decided she somewhat liked his extreme courtesy and gracious manners. She also told him about the secret project with her grandmother to rebuild the family company.

He listened attentively and was obviously impressed with the enormity of her undertaking and her concern for her family. "Now you've told me some very nice things about yourself. I must tell you I find you even more remarkable than I first thought."

As she had been talking about her family and their business, she had indeed been revealing a great deal about herself. By the time he walked her to the curb later that evening and waited with her until the doorman had summoned a taxi for her, she admitted to herself that the evening with him had been quite pleasant.

"We will see each other again soon," Benjamin leaned over to kiss her hand.

Sadie suppressed a giggle at his romantic gesture.

Then he pressed into her hand a small card. "Please give this to your uncle. It has the telephone number where he can reach me. He and I have much to talk about, including our admiration for a beautiful and intelligent lady."

Sadie was distressed that the dinner for Benjamin at the house had not gone well. Michael had made the arrangements and her mother had prepared a tasty dinner of baked stuffed peppers. Everyone had been perfectly polite, but she had sensed that her grandfather in particular had not welcomed Benjamin's presence. She thought it might be because *Zeyde* was thinking Benjamin would be Catholic. But then Benjamin had startled them all during a discussion of the observation of Jacob's *yahrzeit,* the anniversary of his death.

"Yes," he said. "I'm familiar with the practice. We call the anniversary of the death the *nahalah* instead of the *yahrzeit.*"

"Is that a Spanish term?" Michael asked.

"No. It's Ladino. Now you are probably wondering what that is."

Before anyone else could reply, Wolf interrupted. It was the first time he said anything to Benjamin since they had all come to the table. "Ladino, did you say? You speak Ladino?"

"Yes. And I speak Spanish too, of course, since I'm from Mexico City."

Wolf was staring at him. "Then you are a Sephardic Jew."

"Yes," Benjamin replied.

Sadie was astonished. "You're Jewish?"

Michael remained confused. "I still don't know what Ladino is."

Wolf answered him. "It's a language spoken by the Sephardic Jews, most of whom had ancestors who lived in Spain and were forced to leave during the Inquisition. It's a dialect of Spanish with many Arabic,

Hebrew and Turkish words in it now. I imagine your family came from Spain or Portugal?"

"That's right. Spain. And one branch of the family came from Turkey." He addressed himself to Michael. "Many Jews who left Spain went to Holland, but some also went to Mexico and South America. There was another migration when the Ottoman Empire broke up. The similarity of appearance and customs and, of course, language made it easy for the Sephardic Jews to gain acceptance in the Latin countries. Ladino is a form of Spanish, and is spoken by my people the way Yiddish is spoken by yours. For example, you call a synagogue a *shul*, but we call it a *snoga*. The Passover service is a *seder* to you, but *haggadah* to us, just as a rabbi is a *ribbi*. Our family was what were called Marranos. That means swine, and was the name given to the Jews who, in order to save their lives, had to live outwardly as Catholics, while secretly still practicing their Jewish beliefs. There are many stories in my family of close calls they had while they were forced to live this double life."

Sadie expected that this revelation of Benjamin's background would soften Wolf's attitude toward him. Now he need not worry that she was keeping company with a Gentile. But to her surprise, while everyone else in the family was fascinated, Wolf became even cooler. She was at a loss to understand his attitude and resolved to find out its cause.

Later that evening after Benjamin had left, she opened the subject. "Michael and I would like to have Benjamin to our house again. But I have the feeling you wouldn't like that."

Wolf looked up from the newspaper. His granddaughter was watching him intently, and as usual, he found it flattering that it mattered to her what he thought. But he knew he wouldn't be able to give her the affirmation she probably would be seeking in this conversation. "You do what you wish, Sadie," he said noncommittally and returned to his reading.

"But you don't seem to like him," she persisted.

He put down the newspaper. "Must I like every human being on the face of the earth?" he asked a little more strongly than he had intended. He recognized an expression of old come over her face. Her eyes hardened slightly, and her jaw was set.

It occurred to her that Benjamin didn't deserve her grandfather's coolness, especially when, as far as she could tell, there was no basis for it. "Well, I for one intend to keep seeing him, I just want you to know," she announced before she left the room, aware that her voice was starting to rise the way it used to many years ago.

When she was gone, Wolf wished he knew how to tell her what he was thinking, but he found that he was actually ashamed. He didn't like to admit it even to himself, because having so many times in his life been the victim of prejudice, he hated it more than anything else. But deep down, he had to admit, he just couldn't consider the Sephardic Jews on the same level or quite as worthy as the other Jews.

He had seen the look in Sadie's eyes, the rebellious quality they used to get when she was a teenager, and he fervently hoped this friendship would be short-lived and the Sephardi would go back to Mexico where he'd come from. He didn't know what kinds of friends they were now, but it bothered him to picture Sadie and this Benjamin together.

Chapter 33

"Daniel's son Joshua is coming here from Palestine to visit us," Marya announced in a soft voice one morning in the midst of breakfast. Startled by her words, everyone stopped eating and looked at her, but it was Wolf she was watching.

She saw the blood rush to his face and his eyes met hers. She had told him long ago that Daniel and Alma had a son, but Wolf had never expressed any desire to know more. Now he would have to confront the past he had avoided for twenty years. She tried to read the look on his face, but it changed too fast as a series of emotions flashed across him.

Sadie drew her attention. "Why's he coming? For a visit?"

"And when's he coming?" Michael asked, full of excitement.

Marya tried to answer each of them while she pretended not to see the tears in Elke's eyes. "I believe it's mostly business that brings him here. Something about wanting to study soil chemistry or agricultural techniques in California. And I don't know when exactly. He just said probably sometime in the next year. At any rate, I don't expect he would be here for long because he would just be passing through on his way to the West Coast."

Michael and Elke and even Mrs. Chotzinoff were all asking questions at once. But Sadie had heard the word California and was off on a different track. California was where Benjamin was right now. She hadn't told her grandmother yet, but with the last of the jewel money, she had gone ahead and bought some land that Benjamin had told her about. She had felt shy about telling her about the land because it meant she would probably have to talk about Benjamin too, and she hadn't been able to sort out her feelings about him yet. But if this cousin of hers, Joshua, were going out West to look at farming techniques, she knew she wanted to go with him. As far as she was concerned, the sooner he got here the better. But then, she wondered, who would take care of her new dress business? She lamented the fact that lately she always seemed to have more ideas than time to do them.

After breakfast, Sadie managed to get Marya alone. "We have to go to the factory today, *Bubbe*. There's something I have to show you."

"What is it?" Marya asked.

"I can't tell you, I just have to show you."

Marya wanted to be near Wolf that day in case he wanted to ask her something more about Daniel's son or even about Daniel. Ever since the factory closed, she had tried to spend as much time with him as she could, for it was clear he was at a loss with himself. Yet she could see from the way Sadie could hardly stand still that she couldn't disappoint her by not going to the factory. Sadie obviously had something important to show her.

Wolf came into the living room as they were putting on their coats. "Where are you two off to again?"

"Oh," answered Marya vaguely, "we're just out for a bit of air."

As soon as the two of them got to the factory and entered the part of the loft they had designated their workroom, Sadie turned and made an announcement. "I've just bought a piece of land, sight unseen. And not only have I not seen it, but it's nowhere even close to here. It's in southern California, in the Upper Ojai Valley."

Marya looked puzzled. "That's not what you brought me all the way down here to tell me, is it? And where in the world is the Upper Ojai Valley? I've never heard of it."

"I'll have to show you on the map. And once we get enough money, I'm going to take us all on a trip out there to see it. It'll be your first vacation."

"That would be some trip, Sadie. And it'd take a lot of money."

"That gets me to the real reason I wanted you to come down here." She ran over to the side of the loft and wheeled over two empty clothes racks. "Look!" she pointed to them. "We've sold out! All our dresses are gone. How about that!"

When Marya couldn't say anything, Sadie cried, "What's the matter? Don't you believe we've done it? Then wait till you see how fast our second lot is going to go and this time I'm doubling the number of dresses we're going to make."

Finally Marya found her voice. "I just can't believe this, that's all." She pointed at the empty racks. "I can't believe you're actually producing these dresses and they're actually selling." She still hadn't moved from where she was standing.

"Will you stop saying you? I told you a long time ago this business involves both of us. It's we who've done it, not just me."

Sadie ran to the corner and picked up several bolts of yardage. "I want you to see the new yardage I ordered. I hope you approve. It's lightweight. Just the thing the modern woman will want her clothes made out of." After dumping the bolts on the worktable in front of Marya, she began to unwind each of them so that her grandmother could examine the goods.

Marya, moving as if in a dream, took up a handful of the cloth and rubbed it between her fingers to assess its texture and weight. "I know I keep saying this, but I just can't believe it. We're really back in business!"

"And this is only the beginning!" Sadie threw her arms around her grandmother for a fast hug before hurrying on to the next thing she wanted to do.

They got out Marya's second series of designs, again produced according to Sadie's suggestions, and Marya draped the fabrics around Sadie's body to get a rough idea of how each would look made up.

They were engrossed in these comparisons when Sadie suddenly cried, "Stop!" in a half whisper and looked frantically at Marya. They both froze in position and continued looking at each other. Both had heard a noise coming from some other part of the factory. They stayed like that a few moments, perfectly still, waiting to see if they would hear the noise again.

"It sounded like a door slamming shut," Sadie said in a low voice. Then they heard a different kind of sound, that of footsteps.

"Someone's coming!" Sadie whispered. "Who? Nobody knows we're here." For the next couple of moments a succession of images raced through her mind. Was it just some tramp who'd wandered in, looking for shelter? But Sadie thought she remembered having locked the side delivery door behind them. Yet maybe someone had forced his way in, having seen them enter a short time ago, and they were going to be robbed or gunned down in this abandoned factory, where nobody would ever think to look for them. In the next few seconds, which seemed like hours, she imagined a whole series of frightening possibilities.

The footsteps drew nearer. Finally she saw Wolf appear in the doorway. She didn't know whether to be relieved or even more upset.

He quickly looked from Marya to Sadie to the yards of fabric spread out on the table along with the sketches and then back to Marya. "What the hell's going on here?"

For a second neither of them moved. Then they both tried to talk at once, until Sadie kept quiet and Marya took over. "What's going on is MW Enterprises. We're back in business," she announced with a proud calm that Sadie found herself envying.

Wolf's eyes kept darting around the workroom and he still wasn't looking happy. "What do you mean we're back in business? I don't see anything that looks like business to me."

Sadie broke in. "Here!" She indicated the empty clothes racks. "Two lots of a hundred dresses each were hanging here a couple of weeks ago. And now they're all gone—sold! And we're getting ready to start our next lot."

Wolf still looked unbelieving. "Where are your workers, your crew? I don't see any pattern graders, any cutters, basters, stitchers, fellers, finishers, pressers. How the hell can you be back in business? Or are you going to tell me this is a factory-paid holiday?" he added sarcastically.

"What Sadie is trying to tell you, Zavel, is that she and I are doing the creative part, the designing, pattern making and sizing, choosing the fabrics. The rest we're jobbing out."

Sadie jumped in again. "That way we don't have the overhead of keeping the factory going. And we've already made a profit. It's not much, but it's a start. And I know we'll make even more with these dresses we're working on now." She paused, making an effort to speak less rapidly. "We need you, *Zeyde*. We need a manager. It's going to get too big for just the two of us to handle and there's so much about the financial end we just don't know. What I'm trying to say is . . . we need you back in your position as president of the company, now that we have a company again."

When Wolf still didn't say anything, Marya spoke

again. "Sadie's really got some excellent ideas, Zavel. I think you're going to be impressed."

"You mean to tell me this is where the two of you have been disappearing to all the time?"

"Yes," they said in unison.

"Isn't it wonderful what Sadie's done?" Marya prompted. She came up to Wolf and put her arms around him. "This whole thing was her idea. I just came along for the ride, as they say." When he still didn't say anything, she coaxed, "Don't you realize, Zavel, Sadie's put us back in business? The child certainly has your blood coursing in her veins."

Wolf finally turned to Sadie. He spoke slowly. "You know me well enough to know how hard it is for me to say this. But all these years, I didn't think you had it in you. I didn't take your interest in the business seriously, and frankly, I didn't think you could do it." He hesitated. "You've proved me wrong. I guess what I mainly want to say is I'm very proud of you, more than my words are telling you."

She ran to him and threw her arms around both him and Marya at the same time. "Then you approve? It's okay, and you'll help us?"

Wolf was tentative. "I'm not sure you need my help. Apparently you've done all right for yourselves."

"Oh, but we do. It's going to get big again—soon—and we need you. Please say you'll help us. It's your factory, after all, and any knowledge I have comes from you. But I still don't have enough."

Wolf looked beyond them at the comforting signs of work in progress on the table. "Well then, since you put it that way, I just might be able to give you a little advice every now and then."

Sadie was relieved to see he was finally smiling.

"I might even be able to show you how to handle the whole thing when I retire and move to Florida."

Sadie and Marya glanced at each other uneasily. But Sadie quickly realized there was no way Wolf could know about that venture too. It had to be just a coincidence that he had mentioned Florida. Sadie responded casually. "Florida? Why not make it southern California?"

"Why California?" Wolf asked.

Sadie again glanced quickly at Marya before she answered in as noncommittal a tone as she could. "Oh, no particular reason, other than it's warm and pretty, and there's more variety to the scenery than in Florida, and there's much more to do. That's where I'd go if I were you and wanted to take a vacation or find a place to retire."

Wolf laughed. "Whatever you say, Sadie. Whatever you say. Anyway, I've never taken a vacation, and retirement is still a long time off for me, especially now that you've got things going again."

In the next six months, Sadie managed to triple then quadruple the production of the new MW line of dresses. And just as she had anticipated, when the business started expanding, she found herself seeking advice from Wolf more and more often. She was pleased with how things were going and felt absolutely content. It was as if she had finally found something on which she could focus all her energies. Now that Wolf had given his approval to her plans and she no longer had to hide the fact that she went to the factory each day, she spent more time than ever in the workroom, often with him, sometimes with Marya, but most often alone.

One afternoon Marya appeared at the factory unexpectedly. "Since I haven't been down here in a week, I wanted to see what you were up to." She sat down on the other side of the table where Sadie had spread out the account book. "You remind me of your grandfather, sitting hunched over a book of figures like that. For so many years when we were first married, he would sit that way in the evenings, muttering numbers to himself."

Sadie closed the book. "Your being here gives me

an excuse for a break. Would you like a cup of coffee?" She went to the corner of the room where they had set up a small table with a teapot and a coffee urn.

As she busied herself with preparing the coffee, Marya watched her. As always, she marveled at the beauty of her girls. Sadie wore her thick auburn hair shoulder length now and was dressed in a Guatemalan dirndl skirt bordered in bright embroidery. There was no doubt that Sadie was a fashionable young woman sporting one of the popular styles, yet just for the moment the colorful costume reminded Marya of the bright clothes sometimes worn by the Russian peasants, and for an instant she could see Sadie in another lifetime, another world, looking startlingly like the great-grandmother she had never met. The illusion quickly passed and it was a totally modern, American Sadie who brought her the cup of steaming coffee.

As Sadie sat across from her, Marya now noticed the tiny lines around Sadie's eyes. "We're all so proud of you, Sadie. But I hope you're not pushing yourself too hard. You must allow yourself a little time off."

"What would I want any time off for? I'm doing what I like best. To me this isn't work; it's fun. It's even relaxing."

"Still, Sadie, it can't be good to do just one thing so many hours. You need to keep a balance. Go out and take a walk, see a movie—just for relaxation, not to see what the actresses are wearing, talk to people. You might even go out with a young man occasionally."

"Like who? I don't know any men anymore."

Marya tried to catch Sadie's eyes, but they were downcast and peering intently into her coffee cup. "You're almost twenty-six. I should think you might want to start a family one of these days."

"I have nothing against that. Only right now I'm just too busy. And besides, I don't know anyone."

"Isn't there any man who interests you just the slightest bit? You must meet salesmen, at least."

Sadie hesitated. "Well, yes, there is one man. But he's not a salesman." She saw Marya nodding, encouraging her to go on. "You've met him. It's Benjamin. He's the only man I've met in years that I'd like to see again, which is funny because I didn't even like him at first. Now he's living in California and he's in town so seldom that I don't get much of a chance to see him. And I know that *Zeyde* doesn't really like him, although I can't imagine why."

Marya too had noticed Wolf's aloofness to Benjamin the night he came to dinner and subsequently whenever his name came up. It was almost as if he were prejudiced against Benjamin for being darker and foreign, and perhaps even for being Sephardic. Yet she found it hard to believe that Wolf would actually dislike someone without cause. It just wasn't like him. "Don't worry about *Zeyde*. He's come to trust your judgment. I'm sure he just wants you to be happy. Now tell me what you like about this young man, Sadie."

Sadie laughed out loud. "Your question reminds me of the lists I used to make when I was a girl. When I was in high school, I had one for my ideal man. There was a 'must have' column and a 'must not have' column. In my 'must have' column were all kinds of foolish things the poor man had to be blessed with or own, like a raccoon coat, a radio with a loudspeaker, a Packard, bright blue eyes, blond hair, a flare for the Charleston and a strong sense of humor. The only thing on that list that Benjamin has is the sense of humor. And even on that point we sometimes have difficulties because of the language difference. Yet, there's just something about him. I guess what I like the most is the way he's so courteous and attentive. He always seems interested in what I'm doing or saying. But then I think that's just how he is. He's interested in what almost everyone says or does. And he has a sense of fairness. Probably the only reason we met is that he wanted to make sure I didn't buy a bad piece of property in Florida and get taken advantage of. And he's romantic. When I'm with him, he makes me feel like the most important person in the world, and I love that feeling. I don't have to be witty or follow the latest trends. He just takes me as I am. But best of all, behind those smooth manners, I really think there's something solid about him."

"Those are important qualities."

Now that Sadie had finally admitted her feelings about Benjamin, she wasn't ready to stop. "Oh, and there are other things, too. The first thing that caught my eye is how handsome he is. I just like to let my eyes linger on him, if that doesn't sound too silly."

"No, it doesn't. I still like to let my eyes linger, as you say, on your grandfather. He's still a handsome man to me."

"I like the way Benjamin always looks so . . . well, clean. Like he's at ease and he doesn't let little things bother him much or muss him up." She stopped and shrugged. "But the more I try to tell you exactly what it is, the more it gets away from me." She stopped all of a sudden, aware she'd been chattering on like an infatuated schoolgirl.

"I know. It's hard to put certain feelings into words. They never account for all the different ways you feel. So what are your reservations about him?"

Sadie looked down again. "It's not him, exactly. It's . . . it's . . . well, ever since that summer I ran off to Florida, I've just not felt like I could really trust a man again."

"It must have been very painful." Marya waited, giving Sadie a chance to talk about it if she wanted to. She knew what it was like to be afraid and remembered that it hadn't been until a long time after she met Wolf that she could start to trust again.

Sadie nodded yes. But she couldn't say any more about it. She looked out across the loft that was still largely empty. "For the time being, my job is here. I have something to accomplish right here in this loft before I can start thinking at all about Benjamin with any future in mind."

Marya thought for a moment. "When I first came to this country, I spent a lot of time reading, trying to improve my English and to learn everything I could about this new land I was living in. I remember reading a line from Mark Twain that stuck in my mind and confused me. He said that something's either easy . . . or it's impossible. In so many ways, nothing seemed easy in those days. But now that I've lived longer and acquired more experience, I come to look at those words from a different angle. So perhaps you're right. It just isn't the time yet to be with a man, or else you would find it easy to do so."

"Right now it's the work that's easy, and everything else is impossible." Then she laughed. "My father would be so proud of me. I just thought of a line from the Bible that says the same thing. 'To every thing there is a season, and a time to every purpose under heaven.' It's just not my season yet, I suppose."

Wolf thought for a few seconds that it was Daniel he saw coming through the door. The tall, broad-shouldered young man had the same curly brown hair, the same walk, and even the same set to his face as Daniel. During that second, Wolf's heart had started to beat wildly, and even when he realized that this must be Daniel's son Joshua, it took a while for him to regain his composure.

As Joshua entered the room, valise in hand, he automatically ducked his head, as if accustomed to low doorways. He was with Sadie and Michael who had gone to the boat to pick him up. As Michael relieved Joshua of the valise, which he had, until now, insisted on carrying himself, Sadie took him by the hand and led him to Marya and Wolf, who were standing together next to the sofa in the living room. "This is your *Bubbe* and *Zeyde*," Sadie said, then laughed self-consciously. "Oh, but you probably don't speak Yiddish, do you? So I should say your grandmother and grand-father."

Joshua offered Marya his hand, then impulsively threw his big arms around her, dwarfing her in his embrace. "I have wanted all my life to see you and my grandfather," he said quietly.

Marya was surprised at the roughness of his hands and at his low, almost gruff voice that carried the soft, melodic accent of Hebrew. For some reason it hadn't occurred to her that this grandchild of hers would speak English only as a second or even third language, and that he would be more at home in Hebrew. She looked up into the wide face, with its hauntingly familiar black eyes so like Daniel's and Wolf's, and its strong jaw and nose. There was no doubt that this young man she had never laid eyes on before was one of theirs. "We've wanted to see you too, Joshua. You are welcome in our house for as long as you want to stay." She stood on tiptoe and kissed him.

His eyes shining, Joshua then turned to Wolf and gave him the same warm embrace. As the two big men hugged each other, Marya saw that Wolf's face had lost some of its customary reserve. There was some of the intense feeling built up from so many years of waiting to have contact of some kind with his son.

"My God," Wolf finally pulled away, "you're every bit as big as Daniel, if not bigger. It must be something in the air over there."

Joshua smiled awkwardly, searching for something to say that his English could handle. Sadie jumped in, relieving him from having to say anything. She introduced him to Elke, who still wore black, and who had begun to cry softly to see this nephew who looked so much like the Daniel she had last seen. Finally she introduced him to Mrs. Chotzinoff, who she explained was like one of the family.

"So there you have it," Sadie said. "This is your American family. Now, you must be starved, and wait until you see what your Aunt Elke has fixed for you. She's one of the best cooks in the country."

They sat down to an early dinner of borscht, brisket and sauerkraut, with a matzo farfel ring and carrot tsimmes for side dishes. When Joshua saw the amount of food on the table he was amazed. "Such food is all very new to me. My father has told me of these wonderful foods you have here, which he misses very much. But living on the kibbutz, I have gotten used to a diet of things like *hummus,* made from chick peas, eggplant salad, and *tahina,* a dip from ground sesame which we eat with out pita bread. In the north especially near the Sea of Galilee, water is not a problem, but much of the countryside near our kibbutz is desert, and we have to eat foods that our dry land lets us grow."

"What's living on a kibbutz like?" Michael asked, noticing the well-formed muscles under Joshua's shirt. "I imagine it's a lot of hard work."

"Yes, for both the women and the men. My mother works as hard in the fields as my father does. There's hostility all around us, from the land, which is arid and must be irrigated, to of course the Arabs, who raid our settlements, destroying our crops and shooting down our people."

Michael had been on the verge of asking what they did for fun, but Joshua's mention of people being killed made him feel his question was too frivolous. He changed to a more serious topic. "I've heard you've come here to study agriculture."

"More specifically, I will be studying soil chemistry. I must go to California for that. My kibbutz is paying for me to study at the University of California at Davis, where I'll be looking for new methods and products that I can take home to my kibbutz with me."

Throughout the meal, Wolf was attentive to Joshua's every word. Marya wondered if he saw any of himself in this strapping young man who had to live by his wits and instincts, and also she wondered what the sight of him did to his feelings about Daniel, so long buried.

After dinner, Sadie suggested that she, Michael and Joshua go for a walk to let the rich food digest and so that Joshua could see what an American city looked like. As they walked past the two-story brownstones and the tidy red brick tenement buildings of three and four stories, Joshua looked about him with awe. "This is a rich country. I can't imagine what it would be like to live in a big house like this with just a few other people. We all live together on the kibbutz. All single people, from the time of their birth until they marry, which is much younger than here, I believe, sleep in the youth dormitory." He pointed to one of the many trees that grew along the Williamsburg streets. "And look, you have a tree on every block, a bit of green. What a richness that is, too. And trolley cars to take you where you want to go, or even your own car. We are a poor people, although we count ourselves fortunate."

Sadie grew reflective. "Listening to you, I realize how much we have here, and how lucky we are, even though the whole country is still deep in the Depression." She again realized how fortunate their family was to have the cash which Marya had given her, the cash that had allowed MW Enterprises to struggle to its feet again and that had allowed her to make a few investments for the future.

They came to the Williamsburg Bridge, its span arched over the East River. Sadie pointed to the skyline. "That's Manhattan."

Joshua studied the sparkling city across the river. "The most famous skyline in the world. At night I look out across the desert into black nothingness. But I like it."

For a moment they all fell silent. "What about California?" Michael finally asked. "How long will you be there?"

"The kibbutz has money enough to pay my expenses for two years. Then, if I've done well, and if they have by that time raised more money, I will study another two years and earn my degree."

"I would love to see California," Michael said wistfully. "I wish I were going with you."

Sadie had been unusually quiet all this time. Now she startled them both by speaking up suddenly. "Listen you two. There's something I want to tell you. You must promise you'll tell no one else."

The two men looked at her expectantly.

"We—our family—owns some land in California." She saw Michael was looking at her as if she were crazy. "It's land I bought with some money *Bubbe* set aside a long time ago. I haven't told you about this land, Michael, because I've been so busy at the factory with our fifth line of dresses. But it's in a place called the Upper Ojai Valley, and its supposed to be a rich area, where fruit trees grow easily."

"Like the northern part of Palestine," Joshua put in.

"The land is an investment because we know the prices will not always stay low. But it bothers me to think of that land lying unused all this time until it becomes valuable again. As you were talking just now, I had an idea. We could all three of us go to California!"

"Sadie, you're nuts," Michael pronounced immediately. "How could we afford it? And what would we do once we got there? Joshua has plans, but what about you and me?"

Sadie was undaunted by his outburst. "With what you know about growing things, Joshua, you could look at the land and see if we could be growing anything right now. Maybe we could turn that land to some profitable use."

Michael looked skeptical. "That still doesn't account for why all three of us should go."

They were startled by another outburst from Michael. "Now I've got it!" He was looking at her with a playful gleam in his eye. "I know why you want to go to California. That's where Benjamin is."

"Michael, that is not the reason. It's because we have an investment out there and I think it bears looking at. Also, with my work at the factory still small enough not to require us to work year round the way we used to, the timing is perfect. We can go now and be back by midsummer to start the next season of clothes."

Michael pulled a hank of her hair. "Sounds to me like you've got more than one kind of investment going in California."

Sadie put her hands on her hips. "Please be serious, Michael. Do you like my idea or not? Tell me."

Michael looked at Joshua. "I'm not sure our cousin necessarily wants company in California."

Joshua was looking from one to the other of them. "I'm not sure I understood such a fast conversation, but if I did, my answer is yes, I would like to have my family with me. I'm not used to living alone, you know, and it would be a great pleasure to me to have two people who are both friends and family in this new country."

The more Sadie thought about it, the more she liked the idea. In fact, why shouldn't the whole family go?

"So you would like me to draw up a will for you and your husband?" Andrew asked, as they walked up and down the rows of Easter lilies being exhibited for the last time in the Central Park Conservatory. When Marya had telephoned him, he had suggested they meet in this enormous glass building, which was three buildings actually, and despite its size, delicate and light as Oriental filigree. He wanted to visit this gigantic conservatory one more time before the city went through with its plans to destroy it, he explained, and meeting there would give them a chance for a leisurely stroll and private talk.

As they made their way along the paths, breathing in the heady perfume of the flowers, Marya responded to his question. "We have a will which was drawn up some time ago, but our financial holdings have changed considerably since then. I don't suppose you would know, but MW Enterprises had a hard time of it after the crash. We had to close our doors completely."

"I'm sorry to hear that." Andrew walked slowly, his hands folded behind his back. He was almost seventy years old now and had finally begun to show more signs of age. He walked a little more slowly, and although always a reflective person, he tended to deliberate even longer when he spoke and to choose his words even more carefully than he had previously.

"My granddaughter Sadie must be credited with resurrecting our garment business. I do wish you could meet her. She's really a marvelous young woman."

Andrew caught her eye. "Like her grandmother?"

She laughed. "How you still flatter me, Andrew." And to herself she thought what a relief it was to be talking together with ease, unlike the last time they had met seven or eight years ago. "Another reason I wanted to consult you is that the entire family is about to take its first trip together. A vacation, my granddaughter calls it. Imagine," she laughed again, "going on a vacation! Neither I nor my husband has ever been on a vacation in our lives. And although we have a lot less money now than we did, we're bending to Sadie's wishes and using some of what we do have to take a trip out West, to California. So I would feel a lot better if this matter of the will were taken care of first." Marya acknowledged it was prudent to take care of matters like that before a long trip. But she also knew that with the plans for the trip had come a desire to see Andrew again. Maybe it was a superstition, since she had not taken such a long journey since the one that had brought her to this country, and she hadn't been out of New York even once. Now she wanted to take care of loose ends, as the expression went, before she left New York, even temporarily.

"Then you must make another appointment, this time in my office. And we will arrange to review the old will and draft the new one," Andrew was saying in his businesslike tones.

They continued to walk up and down the paths of the lush indoor garden as their conversation drifted to more general topics. "I think I'd like to sit down," Andrew proposed after a while, indicating a bench just a little way ahead. They rested in the warm sun, the light streaming in through the panes of glass arching high above them.

"I've known you longer than almost anyone else in this country." Marya watched the motes of dust spinning lazily in a shaft of sunlight. "You've heard me speak of my dreams for my work, of my children, even my grandchildren, and more than anyone else, you are aware of my little victories as well as my disappointments over the years. And here we are, almost a lifetime later, together in the sun like two lizards."

Andrew looked somber. "Yes, we know a great deal about each other, Marya. I've never told you this, but after we decided not to . . . not see each other again, I couldn't get you out of my mind."

Marya's heart fluttered, and out of nervousness, she couldn't resist interrupting on a lighter note. "Is that why you consoled yourself with women young enough to be your daughter . . . or granddaughter?"

He shot her a mock withering glance, then became serious again. "I'm afraid I went a little further than that. You see, since I couldn't have you with me, I had to content myself just knowing about you." He took a deep breath. "In short, Marya, I think I understand you better now. I know more of what you've gone through. What I'm trying to say is that I know that your present marriage was not your first."

Marya spun to face him. She tried to say something, but no words came out. Nothing had prepared her to hear Andrew say this, especially not when so many years had elapsed since they'd spoken this way.

"And there is more, Marya. I know that you and your first husband had a child, who was lost to you and presumed dead. His name was David. And so I now understand why you have had this obsessive interest in David Sheffield all these years. And I see that I was quite off the mark in guessing at your real interest in the young man. It wasn't because he might be the son of a former lover at all, as I had thought."

Marya suddenly clutched at him and her voice rose. "Is David Sheffield my son? If you know all that about me, you must know that. You must have found that out! Tell me!"

Andrew responded in his same smooth, deliberate manner. "I couldn't establish that. I don't know if he is or isn't."

Marya slumped back down. She was oblivious to the sunlight and the lush scent of the greenery. She was torn with emotion. Then she looked at him, incredulous. "How long have you known about my first husband and son?"

"A long time, Marya. Many, many years. I learned about them while we were still seeing each other."

Marya was aghast. "Why did you do all this? All these years, Andrew, you've known. And you've never said anything?"

"Not to anyone."

"But why, Andrew? Why?"

"Because I've never stopped loving you. Because I hoped someday you would turn to me again, and if I myself weren't a strong enough incentive to keep you with me, perhaps the information I held would be. At least that was my reason at first. I had planned to tell you what I'd learned that night I came to your house. And then, I realized that I didn't want to hold you that way. I just wanted you to want me for myself, without any trimmings or . . . or emotional blackmail. And if you didn't, well, you just didn't." He looked out over the rows of foliage and fell silent.

"I did want you, Andrew. I loved you. I still do. But—"

"You don't have to say it," Andrew interrupted. "We said all that to each other over fifteen years ago."

It was Marya's turn to fall silent and she stared down at the worn path. Then she looked up determinedly. "I know David Sheffield is my son, Andrew. And before I leave on that trip, I plan to tell him. It may be my last chance."

Andrew grabbed her by the shoulders, suddenly impassioned. "You mustn't do that, Marya. You have no proof for what you're saying, just a desperate hope."

Marya's voice was strangely calm. "There are some things I've always just known to be true, Andrew. Call it a trait left over from the old country that somehow managed to survive being uprooted and transplanted in a new country. But I know he is my son."

"Then keep your knowing to yourself. You just can't confront a person with something like that after forty years of his life, not when you can't offer anything more substantial than a hunch to go on. You cannot do that."

"Don't you understand, Andrew? If he's my son, how can I not?" Her voice was strangely serene.

"You cannot because he is a grown man, with a life that may or may not have included you. Even if it did, it wasn't for more than a couple of years. You can't disrupt his present life that way and destroy what serenity he may have."

"I don't see how that would destroy it."

"It most certainly would. Especially when you can't offer him any real evidence beyond the coincidence that you have the same hair color." Andrew's words grew even more impassioned. "Marya, I beg you not to do this. You could be hurting both of you deeply. Leave well enough alone. *Please*."

Marya introduced herself to the secretary outside the president's office of Metropolitan Bank. "Tell him it's an old friend," she said.

Within seconds, the door burst open and a grey-haired man was standing in front of her. "I don't believe it! Marya Luminov!" He guided her into his office.

Marya recognized David's voice, so this man had to be David. She tried not to stare at him, but she was shocked by how much older he looked. Although he was fifty years old and entitled to grey hair and a few lines, she had not thought of him as growing any older than the last time she had seen him. Whenever she thought of him, he was still a young man in his midtwenties, with red-brown hair and a lithe, athletic way of moving.

"You're still lovely, Marya," he admired her as soon as they were out of earshot of the secretary. "I want you to know I've thought of you many times over the years." He hesitated. "And of Elke."

Marya wondered if she blushed. She had never been able to accept her role in breaking off their romance, and she wondered if David still bore her any ill will, for she knew he had once held her partly responsible.

She glanced around his office, trying to glean from any personal mementos there what his life now must be like. "I hear you're married and have a daughter." She felt she had to make at least a little small talk before she got to the heart of why she had come.

"Yes," he smiled. "Lisa—that's my daughter—is the joy of my life."

"Listen, David," Marya sat up on the edge of her chair, determined to get to the purpose of her visit, "there's something I'd like to tell you about."

David was at that moment leaning over, rummaging through his bottom desk drawer for something. "Just a second," he said, his voice slightly muffled. "Since we were talking about Lisa, I want to show you something."

Marya had no choice but to wait until he found what he was searching for. Finally he pulled out a small leather binder. "Look, these are pictures of Lisa when she was a baby. I want you to see what a little charmer she was. I think you'll appreciate these." He flipped open the photo album and slid it across the desk toward her. "Here—take a gander at this one. She's only six months old here."

Marya peered at the naked infant, lying on her stomach and laughing into the camera as she kicked her feet up behind her.

"Why, she looks like Sadie," Marya said before she realized it. The baby had the same round face, button nose and thick shock of hair that stood straight up like Sadie's as an infant.

David was busy turning the pages, jabbing his index finger at other pictures that were also his favorites. "Sadie?" he asked absently. "Who's Sadie?"

"My granddaughter, Elke's girl." Marya was dismayed with how the conversation was going. She hadn't come here to talk about Elke or other children. She just wanted to talk about her and him. Then she noticed him looking at her strangely. "How is Elke?" he asked.

"She's quite well now. You know her husband passed away, didn't you?"

David looked startled. "No. I didn't." He gave a hard look, but Marya could tell he wasn't really seeing her. He was lost in thought and staring through her. Then he shook himself lightly and began to turn the pages of the photo album again.

Marya viewed a pageant of an infant turning into toddler, then a little girl, and emerging into a comely young lady, all within the space of a few minutes. She saw snapshots of Lisa in the bathtub, Lisa's first birthday party, at the menagerie in Central Park, on a swing in someone's garden. There were several of her sitting atop David's shoulders and a couple where she was playing in the snow. As Marya watched the little girl grow up before her eyes, she couldn't help but notice how proud David was of her.

As he turned another page, Marya was suddenly looking at one large photo of him, Lisa and the woman who must be his wife. The woman was seated in a chair, Lisa was on her lap, and David stood alongside them. Unlike most family portraits of the time, they were both smiling and gazing up at him. Marya stared at the picture, and a strange feeling came over her. She felt almost as if she were down on her knees, peering through a keyhole into his private life, a life she had often wondered about but had never been able to see in any detail. An now here it was in front of her.

She continued to study the large picture of the three of them, then glanced up at David. She could see Gershon in him, of that she was positive. And in these pictures of Lisa she felt she could see Sadie. Andrew's words came back to her. "But you have no proof. You can't just crash in and upset a person's life like that." David was obviously a completely grown man now, with a daughter who was also grown and a wife who was growing old along with him, who shared his own understanding of who he was and how he'd come to be where he was in his life. She suddenly wondered if what she had come here for was entirely self-serving. To tell David of her beliefs, what would that accomplish for David? Would it help him to know that he had been in love with his half sister? Would he be glad to know he was suddenly Jewish, although he had been raised to other beliefs and worked and socialized in banking circles that were rigorously non-Jewish? Could he be expected to have any feelings for her as his mother, when it was not she who had cooked, cleaned and held him in her arms all those years but another woman? Would he thank her for what she yearned to tell him? These questions pounded in her head.

Finally David shut the album. "Now, what is it you were starting to say before I got obsessive about showing you these pictures. My daughter is my weakness, in case you haven't noticed."

Marya looked at his green eyes, so familiar, the eyes she saw every morning in the mirror. She didn't care what Andrew said about having positive proof, she knew.

She saw David looking at her expectantly. "Oh, nothing important. I was just going to say how glad I was that you had pictures of your family here that I could see. And I can understand how a child can become a weakness, even an obsession." She tried to keep her voice from breaking as she got up to leave. "You've led a very fortunate life, David."

He smiled broadly. "You couldn't have said anything more true, Marya. And you can't know how your dropping by so unexpectedly like this after so many years has delighted me. I think old friends should always stay in touch."

Chapter 34

To the south and west of them stretched miles and miles of green valley, filled with groves of fruit trees and an occasional ranch. Around them rose the Topa Topa Mountains, impressive outcroppings of sandstone and shale that formed a crown around the valley. As they gazed at the splendor of this panorama from the Upper Ojai Valley, Benjamin again unfolded the topographical map of the Sulphur Mountain area. Sadie, Michael and Joshua pressed in close and studied it avidly, searching for the boundaries of their land.

"There it is!" shouted Michael, glancing rapidly back and forth between the map and the view of the valley in front of him. He pointed to a location about a quarter of a mile away.

The four of them ran across the rocky fields, eager to stand on this spot of California land that was theirs. When they reached the right location, Sadie spun in a circle and again surveyed the view. "Even if we can't grow a weed on this land, it's worth having just for the magnificence of the surroundings!" she exclaimed. "I can hardly wait for *Bubbe* to see this place."

Marya and Wolf were scheduled to arrive at

Union Station in downtown Los Angeles in three days without Elke, who at the last minute had decided she didn't want to leave home. Sadie was excited about their arrival, just as she had been excited about everything she had seen or done since setting out from New York in her aged but functioning tin lizzie with Michael and Joshua a month earlier. As they had left behind the rolling hills of the East for the endless plains of the Midwest, Sadie had been astounded to see for herself this vast wheat field, extending through four states and relieved only here and there by a desolate farmhouse and windmill. The two summers she had gone to Florida, she had also been thrilled to see the landscape of the North give way to flat countryside and the lusher, wetter green of the South, but the change had not been nearly as dramatic as this.

Almost every morning as they had continued their cross-country trek, Joshua had expressed his amazement. "I knew America was big, but I never imagined it to be so immense as this and full of so much variety."

When the plains finally had lifted up into the foothills of the Rocky Mountains, they had been ready for a change in scenery. They had felt like a little speck, barely moving as they'd hurtled down the highway at close to the car's top speed. Yet no matter how fast they had driven as they'd crossed Nebraska, they'd always felt as if they'd been standing still. As they'd wound up into the Rocky Mountains, Sadie felt she had never seen any place more beautiful. "Now these are mountains. They make what people in the East call mountains look like miniatures." They had dropped down into the dry heat of Utah and Nevada, while the terrain had changed to the dramatic browns, reds and purples of the desert. When they had finally emerged through California's Cajon Pass, a wonder of towering granite boulders, they had been ready for the palm-lined streets of Riverside, a fashionable resort seventy miles east of Los Angeles. With its Spanish-style architecture in the heart of town, miles of rosebushes down Victoria Avenue and everywhere breezes scented with orange blossoms, it was a fitting introduction to what awaited them in southern California.

In spite of all the beauty she had seen coming across the country, Sadie was still impressed with the rich greens, oranges and browns of Ojai. "What do you think?" she asked Joshua. "Can you tell from just looking at this land what it might be suited for?"

Joshua knelt down and dug in the dirt, kneading the soil between his fingers. He held it up to his nose. "I want to run a chemical analysis to be sure," he said, not wanting to get anyone's hopes up prematurely. They continued to survey the acreage, noting the trees, how the rainwater must drain and the angle of the sun.

All of a sudden Joshua stopped and pointed about twenty feet ahead to a dark black spot. "Do you know what that is?" he asked excitedly.

"Looks like tar," Michael offered.

"That's right. This is a tar seep." Joshua's accent grew much thicker as he hurried to tell them his thoughts. "Do you know what this means? It means there's oil being formed somewhere in this area, maybe even under this land." He addressed himself to Benjamin. "Do you know if oil has been found anywhere in this valley?"

"I've heard that Shell-Union and a few other companies have some operations here. But I don't know where or anything more than that."

Joshua kept staring down into the pool of tar. "I say the first thing we do is find a geologist. If there's oil down there, we can forget about my doing soil samples to see what we should grow here." He looked at Benjamin again. "You know this area better than any of us. Do you think you can round up a geologist for us? The sooner the better."

The next morning the geologist Benjamin had contacted was already out walking across the Luminov acreage with Joshua and Michael, Sadie having elected to wait for them at Benjamin's home in the Hollywood Hills. The geologist was a stocky middle-aged man with balding blond hair, and as if to make up for the scant hair on his head, an extremely bushy red beard. When he walked, he rocked from side to side with his legs slightly bowed. He studied the area that Joshua and Michael indicated and pulled on the ends of his beard.

"The first thing I need to do is an outcrop study. We need to know if there's the potential for an anticline here."

"Anticline?" asked Michael.

"That's a porous rock formation, a trap to hold the oil in the ground. We know from this tar seep that oil is definitely being formed, but we also know that means there isn't much pressure in the rock where this seep is. What we're looking for now is a trap."

Joshua asked quickly, "How long will it take to do such a study?"

"Just a short time. It involves making a surface map of the geology for your acreage, and then estimating from those surface formations the chances for oil. I can probably get to the outcrop study tomorrow. But I can tell you right now that the area's geology suggests that this horizon, or formation, could be productive. This region in general is rich with Miocene Monterey shale, and we're near what's called the Sisal Fault. So there's a good chance we'll find oil. The question is where the pay zone is and whether it's on your land."

Back in Los Angeles, Benjamin was trimming the oleanders growing alongside the deck of his home overhanging the city of Los Angeles, while Sadie watched him from her vantage position on the outdoor lounge. "Has anyone ever told you you're as graceful as a cat?" she asked as he manipulated the big shears. He was stripped to the waist and the sun glistened off the smooth muscles of his chest. She thought she had never seen a man that could manage to look so handsome, no matter what the occasion, or his attire.

"Graceful?" He smiled. "Nobody, just you." He put down the shears. "But graceful is what you are, not I."

She made room for him on the end of the lounge, and as he sat down next to her, she saw his eyes move up the length of her legs. She was wearing a blue halter top and a pair of white shorts, and in the short time she'd been in California, had already managed to acquire a respectable start on a tan during the day when Benjamin was at the office. This was the first time he had seen her so scantily dressed, and it was with great difficulty that he kept his eyes on the oleanders instead of her. He was sitting very close now and she was keenly aware of the warmth of his body next to hers.

Before she realized what was about to happen, he leaned over and kissed her on the lips. Almost immediately she pulled away.

He was surprised. "I shouldn't kiss you? I have waited a long time for this moment."

"No. I mean yes. Yes, you should kiss me. It's just hard for me to . . . to relax."

He took her hand and held it in his. She noticed how cool it felt and reassuring. He was watching her carefully. "You are afraid? I frighten you perhaps?"

Sadie's heart was beating wildly. "No. It's not you."

"Ah, then someone else you are thinking of." He looked down.

She rose up on her elbow. "No, that's not it either. It's just that it's been so long since I've let anyone hold me. I guess I've forgotten how to let it happen."

"But you would like to again? To let it happen?"

She hesitated. "I guess what I want is something I know I can't have, some kind of guarantee that it will all end happily." She looked up at him. He was watching her intently. The sun glinted off his black hair and smooth skin. He was simply dazzling. She knew she wanted him. Why couldn't she just let go? In spite of her early impressions, she had no doubt now that Benjamin was not another Chris. Still she was afraid.

Benjamin leaned forward again and kissed her very lightly. "There is no hurry, Sadie. I just want to be with you, however I can."

As soon as he said that, she felt herself start to relax a little. "Perhaps," she said shyly, "I need to be taught again, very slowly."

He kissed her a second time, and this time the kiss was longer. She didn't pull away. He put his arm around her shoulders, the touch of skin on skin exciting her.

Then he eased her softly down onto the lounge and looked in her eyes. "Sadie, what makes you think I can't give you that guarantee you want? I have been in love with you since I met you. I don't ever want to leave you."

"I want to believe you."

"You must. I have never met a woman like you."

He kissed her again and this time she could feel his heart beating strongly against her breasts. The sun shone down on them, making her warm and lazy. She reached up and put her arms around him. "I'm going to try."

Gently he picked her up and carried her into the cool of the house.

"Benjamin, how long can we go on like this?"

They were lying out on the lounge again, side by side. Sadie had finally gotten dressed again.

He pulled a handkerchief from his hip pocket and mopped his brow. "You mean making love? Or do you mean with me on the West Coast and you on the East Coast, and three thousand miles in between?"

Sadie laughed, glad to be able to banter again. She hadn't felt this secure, this loved by a man ever. "That's exactly what I mean," she continued. "I don't like it. I would like to be able to see you more. In fact, I think about you all the time."

"And I of you."

"I know. That's why I think we should get married."

"Married?" he echoed, taken aback. "Are you proposing to me?"

"I most certainly am. I learned a long time ago that if you want something, you have to go after it. It was my grandmother who taught me that."

Benjamin was still staring at her incredulously. "I was wondering when the Sadie I was accustomed to was going to return. Are you really proposing to me?"

She nodded and put her arms around his neck again.

"But what about your grandfather? My feeling was that he has never really approved of me. What did your grandmother teach you to do in a case like that?"

"Follow my hunches. And my hunches tell me we should go ahead. Besides, I know my grandfather won't stand in the way."

"Just like that, you say? I am a Latin, and we are romantics. I am accustomed to wooing and poetry. Where is the moonlight, where is—"

Sadie laughed. "Won't sunlight do? After all, we met in sunlight—unbearable sunlight, as I recall. Isn't it romantic enough here amidst the severed oleanders?" She waved her hand at the branches lying on the deck and then turned onto her side facing him. "Well, isn't it customary to give a proposal an answer?"

Benjamin ran his eyes along the curve of her hip, then gathered her up in his arms. "If you want an answer, I insist on giving you one in my own way. And it will be a romantic way, I assure you."

He carried her into the house again and into his bedroom, which had a spectacular view of the city and ocean and sometimes the island of Catalina. He let her down onto the bed, then buried his face in the curve of her breasts above the halter. "Do you have any idea what my answer is yet?" he asked as he began to untie the halter's straps she had just a short while before tied up again.

"Not yet," Sadie murmured. "I think you'd better keep showing me."

Benjamin took her in his arms and followed every instinct he had to show her that his answer was yes.

Afterward, as she lay curled in his arms, completely satisfied, she thought briefly of Chris, the only other man she had ever made love with, and of how different it was with someone she really loved and who loved her. That first time with Chris, she had barely been conscious, so intoxicated with alcohol had she been and here she and Benjamin had already known each other for two years. But it made all the difference in the world to make love with a man she truly was in love with. "Perhaps," she said aloud, "I've found my season."

"What?" Benjamin asked drowsily.

"Oh, nothing. It was just a line from the Bible that means you're a sitting duck now. You couldn't get away even if you wanted to."

The three of them—Sadie, Michael and Joshua—were beside themselves with excitement as they hastened to explain the findings of the geologist's outcrop study to Marya. Wolf was out walking along the cliffs overhanging the ocean outside their Santa Monica hotel, so they felt this was the perfect time to tell Marya about what they had learned in the last few days before she and Wolf arrived.

Sadie picked up where Michael had left off. "The geologist's words were encouraging. He says there's definitely the potential for an oil trap on our land."

"So what's the next step?" Marya asked, trying to sort it all out. She could hardly believe that they might have oil-rich land. And even if they did, she wasn't sure just what that would mean for them. How much oil would have to be down there for it to be worth their while to go after it? She looked from Sadie to Michael, then to Joshua, hoping to find one of them with a more cautious and sober attitude. It just seemed to her they were getting their hopes up in a situation where the odds were against them.

Michael was eager to explain. "Our next step is to raise the money to drill. We need to hire a drilling company to set up a rig on the land so we can bore in and see what's under there."

Marya was even more skeptical. "Set up a drilling rig? That sounds expensive."

"It is," Sadie confirmed. "It will probably cost fifteen thousand dollars. We've already done some sleuthing around and found out that's about what we'd need for what's called an exploration well."

"But if we can get a loan from a bank, once we strike oil, we'll have no trouble paying it back," Michael took up the explanation. "In fact, they'd probably be forcing more money on us, encouraging us to drill more."

"I don't want to dash your hopes," Marya put in cautiously, "but what bank will lend you the money? Neither of you have any collateral of your own or, for that matter, experience."

But her words did not deter them. The next day they approached the Bank of A. Levy, the main bank in Ventura County, where the Ojai Valley was located. That afternoon, when they returned to the hotel in Santa Monica where Wolf and Marya were staying, Marya was waiting for them.

"Well?" she asked.

They'd had no luck. The bank's loan officer had courteously but firmly told them they hadn't a chance of getting a California bank to loan them the sum of money they were asking for. Not only were they young and without oil experience, as Marya herself had said, but they were from out of state. Even if they already knew for certain that oil was there and were seeking funding for a development well rather than a wildcat well, they would still be turned down. Furthermore, even if they were to strike oil, the unstable price of California crude was not encouraging. It had gone from one dollar and ten cents a barrel in 1929 to eighty-one cents in 1932, down to seventy-two cents the following year. Although it had come back up slightly to ninety-two cents recently, it had just dropped again to eighty-two cents. Nor did it matter that Sadie was even willing to put up part of MW Enterprises as collateral. The whole venture was just too risky for any bank to touch.

"Can't you do something?" Sadie asked Marya. "Isn't there someone you know who can advise us about this?"

Marya started to shake her head. "Well, yes," she lit up suddenly. "There is someone." She looked at her watch. "But we'll have to wait until tomorrow before I can talk to him. He's on the East Coast."

The next day before she and Wolf left for a tour of Paramount Studios in Hollywood, Marya telephoned the Metropolitan Bank in New York and asked for David Sheffield. She explained to him about the land and the findings of the geologist's report. When she told him they were looking for a loan to finance the drilling, David's voice grew reluctant. "I'd have to tell them the same thing the bank president in Ventura County told them, which is the same thing the chairman of the board would tell me if I tried to put this loan through, and that's even assuming we had any money to loan," David said quietly. "They're requesting too much money and they've too little experience. Frankly, Marya, I think there's a better way for them to go than taking out a loan, and that's to raise the money through private investors."

"Private investors?" Marya was dismayed. "Where could they possibly find an individual willing to invest that kind of money?"

"First of all, it's not an individual you want, it's several individuals, each putting up a third or fourth of the total. As to where to find those people, do you forget the circles we once traveled in Marya? Despite the crash, there are still a lot of very rich people around, just looking for something to do with their money. If you really want to go in this direction, I could contact several persons who might be interested in such a venture."

"And then what?"

"I have to know from the beginning what kind of percentage split your family would be willing to offer the investors. That, of course, is what will pry them off their wallets. When you know those figures, when you're quite certain you don't want to offer the project to someone with a rig for a fifty or sixty per cent interest, then notify me, and I'll get to work on it."

When Marya passed on the details of her telephone call with David Sheffield, Michael, Joshua and Sadie were elated.

When they began to talk figures, Michael took over. "Let's first see if we can get the private investors. If we've no luck in enticing some rich folks looking for some easy cash, we'll still have the possibility of interesting someone with a rig to do it on a percentage basis later. The percentages for us will be much better if we go with the investors. Rather than the fifty-fifty split, we can offer a thirty-three per cent interest for them, and a sixty-seven per cent interest for us."

Throughout her grandchildren's spirited discussion, Marya was amazed at their confidence and optimism. To them, the oil was already a sure thing. It was just down there waiting for someone to come along and coax it up. They had all the fresh hope and enthusiasm of youth and to their minds there was no way they could fail. She told herself she would be content just to have the land, whether or not they ever did anything with it. Maybe one of them could even have a home on it. She watched now as Michael in the heat of discussion jabbed the air with his finger to make a point, and suddenly she was reminded of Wolf when he was their age, full of passion and complete confidence, never doubting that MW Enterprises would make a go of it, when the rule for the small manufacturing house was to go under eventually. Yes, she realized, they are only doing what is in their blood. Yet, somewhere, she thought she felt a chill wind blowing.

Early next morning, before she and Wolf set out on another day of sightseeing, she managed to find time to slip away from Wolf again and call David to give him the figures he had requested. After that, a week went by without anyone hearing anything. During that week, Marya and Wolf spent time walking barefoot along the Santa Monica beach where they collected sand dollars and bits of unusual shells. They took the train to Tijuana one day for some sightseeing in that colorful border town. "Do you realize, that's the first time we've set foot out of the United States in almost fifty years?" Marya asked. After the day's excursion to Mexico, she sensed that Wolf was finally tiring of sightseeing. He seemed quieter, more withdrawn than he had in years. As the train from San Diego rolled past the splendid beaches of San Clemente, Marya saw that Wolf wasn't looking out the window any longer. His eyes were closed and he looked tired, yet she knew he wasn't asleep.

"Southern California is beautiful and diverting, but I think it's about time for us to go back to New York," she proposed softly.

His eyes fluttered open. "Yes. I'm ready to go home now," he agreed, then closed his eyes again.

When they returned to the hotel, Marya announced to the grandchildren that she and Wolf planned to draw their vacation to a close and return home the next day. "You must realize," she tried to joke by way of explanation, "that since we've not had a vacation before, it's work for us to rest this much. Besides, Elke will be missing us, and your grandfather wants to take care of a few details at MW Enterprises."

When Wolf was out of earshot, Michael also had an announcement. A few nights before the family had decided that Michael was to act as their spokesman for all business matters concerning the well, and Joshua for all physical aspects of the deal. Sadie had adamantly refused a role, claiming that her hands were full with MW Enterprises, and that she was thrilled the land just could be put to use.

Now Michael cleared his throat. "It is in my official capacity of business spokesman that I wish to make this announcement," he intoned with mock formality. "It so happens that luck is blowing our way. Your friend David Sheffield has already managed to round up five investors, each willing to sink up to five thousand dollars into this wildcatting venture. We've had a number of telephone conferences, and David is ready to draw up the paperwork. All that awaits are the signatures, and a bank draft will be ours."

"That's wonderful!" Marya exclaimed. "Then you'll be returning to New York, too!"

Michael looked at Sadie. "Michael and I are leaving the same day you do," she took over. "Josh will stay here and watch over the drilling."

Marya was suddenly very glad that Michael and Sadie were coming back home too and that they would all be together. It bothered her to have her family strung so far apart. She only wished that there were some way Joshua could come too. He had already fit into the family so smoothly that it seemed like he ought to be coming home as well.

Chapter 35

There was such a chill in the air that Marya looked out the window of their Brooklyn house to see if it might be snowing. Even though it was a mild winter, she just couldn't get warm. Reluctantly, she took her heavy coat from the closet and slipped it on, determined to brave the elements at least long enough to get to the post office and back. She hoped she wasn't being precipitous in mailing the letter, but it was just something she felt compelled to do. After posting it, she hurried back to the house, already savoring the cup of hot tea she was going to make to warm herself.

Elke and Mrs. Chotzinoff had started taking afternoon naps, so she moved quietly in the kitchen, trying not to awaken them. She noticed that it was almost four o'clock now, and that meant Wolf would soon be home from the showroom, as Sadie still persisted in calling the factory, and Michael would be returning from City College. Sadie had mentioned she might be dropping by for a few minutes before she went home to Benjamin at their new house in Riverdale. Marya wished Joshua could be there with them, but he was still in California, supervising the drilling, which he reported to be going well.

The derrick had been erected by the time they had all arrived back in New York, and the last few months had been given to installing the rotary table and the drill pipe, which would be suspended into the hole for what was going to be straight-hole drilling, according to Joshua's reports. Soon it would be time to connect the heavy gears that would turn the drill to the steam engine. Marya was amazed at all the new terminology she was learning. She now knew about drill collars, drill bits, mud pumps and shale shakers, and whenever she, Sadie and Michael were alone together, they bandied the terms back and forth as if they knew what they were talking about. The drilling was likely to begin any day now and even she had put aside her earlier reservations and become excited.

She heard footsteps outside on the porch, and Sadie and Wolf appeared in the kitchen a moment later. Without asking, Marya put on more water for tea. Sadie was brimming with her usual energy, but what startled Marya was the way Wolf looked. He seemed tired, as if Sadie had all the energy for the two of them, and his face was washed out.

Sadie began talking instantly. "This man you married, *Bubbe,* has to be the most stubborn man in the world. I spent all afternoon showing him—with exact numbers—how feasible it is to sell the factory and move MW to a smaller set of rooms somewhere. We certainly don't need all that space. The place is mostly empty except for the area where we do our cutting and store our fabrics. And it's costing us money. We could take the profits we'd get from the sale and next season offer an expanded line. We could even try something out of nylon, that new artificial silk." She pointed to Wolf. "But will he budge?" She threw her hands up in the air, pretending to despair.

"I don't see any reason to be in such a hurry," he countered patiently. "We're certainly not going to get any price for it that will give you the wild profits you think. We've held on to it this long. It won't hurt to keep it a while longer and see what happens."

Sadie wanted to cry out that nothing was going to happen other than losing money by not being able to invest what they got from its sale. But something in Marya's eyes told her to keep quiet.

After Wolf went in the other room, Marya took Sadie aside. "Can't you see? He just can't let go of that factory. It's been his reason for getting out of bed for the last fifty years."

"I know," Sadie said softly, sorry she had allowed herself to get so excited earlier. "It's just annoying when he's so stubborn and gets that fixed set to his jaw. Then I get carried away."

Early the next morning, Marya was awakened by Wolf tossing restlessly next to her in the bed. "Are you all right?" she asked.

"It's nothing, just a pain in my chest," Wolf replied. "It'll go away."

But even though he tried to make light of his pain, Marya was alarmed. This was not the first time lately that Wolf had awakened during the night not feeling well. She lay there until dawn unable to go back to sleep. Wolf, she knew, did not sleep either.

Nor did he sleep well the next five nights. Whenever Marya would try to question him about how he felt, he would become visibly annoyed. "It's just a little pain in my chest. I've had it before. It'll go away," he dismissed the subject, obviously not wanting to be fussed over.

One afternoon a couple weeks later, Marya was in the living room when Wolf answered the telephone. Even from where she was across the room, she could hear the shouting. "What the hell are you yelling about, Joshua?" Wolf demanded. There was a pause. "No," Wolf contradicted, "this isn't Michael. It's your grandfather. And what the hell is this about our land? We don't have any land."

"Oh my God," Marya whispered half aloud, running to take the telephone from Wolf.

She found Joshua practically screaming in her ear. "Zerzol! Zerzol!" he kept saying. He was so excited his Hebrew accent had returned full force and it took her a moment to realize what he was yelling about.

"Joshua, now tell me again what you're saying and this time slow down!"

It was only slightly slower, but at least she could make out the words this time. "Are you saying we've hit oil?" she repeated to make sure. "Our land has oil on it after all?" She saw Wolf staring at her, but it was too late to bluff her way out of this now.

"Yes!" Joshua shouted.

"Oh my God, I can't believe it!" She let herself down into a chair. "Are you sure?"

Joshua was laughing. "There's no mistaking what it looks like, especially when you've got it all over you. Yesterday the drilling contractor wanted to try this new technique of taking core samples from the pay zone. They gave us a positive indication of oil. That's when we got really excited. Today, when we reached it, I was so happy, I was rubbing my hands in it like a baby."

Marya joined his laughter. "That's wonderful! Wait till I tell the others! I wish they were here to hear this from you firsthand."

"What's next is to bring in the jack lines, the pumps. The drilling contractor says it looks like we're going to be able to pump one hundred to two hundred gallons a day out of that hole."

Marya laughed again. "You've got all the oil language, Joshua. You're talking like a real wildcatter now." She saw Wolf give a start.

"That's because I am, *Bubbe*. I mean *we* are!"

As soon as he hung up and before Wolf could stop her, Marya telephoned Sadie and then Michael. "You got to come home at once," she told each of them. "There's something I've got to tell you. It's good news," she added. "So don't worry."

As she put the phone down, she heard Wolf's growl. "What the hell is going on here, Marya? What are you up to this time without telling me?"

She turned to face him and tried to make her face serious to match his. But she was so elated with the news she'd just heard that she couldn't stop laughing as she talked. "We've struck oil on our land, our land in California!"

He wasn't sharing her laughter. "What land? How did we get any land in California? And with what?"

"Sadie bought it." She saw that he was waiting for her to go on, and she knew she was going to have to tell him everything. The time had come. "With cash that I had." She sat down on the sofa and pulled him down next to her. "Zavel, I have something to confess to you. I just hope that after all these years you won't be angry with me."

"I don't like the sound of this, Marya."

"Remember how you used to give me jewels on my birthday and other times during the year?"

"Jewels which you never wore."

"I couldn't, Zavel. I just couldn't. I know you did it because you loved me, but I never felt right about them. It seemed we needed so many other things in those days. And so . . . so I sold them, a few at a time and whenever I could get a good price. I wanted us to be secure, to always have a nest egg we could fall back upon."

She saw he was looking at her strangely, but he didn't interrupt.

"When we lost everything after the crash, I turned it over to Sadie and told her to take advantage of the low prices of land. That way when prices rose again, we'd be able to pull ourselves up, and maybe one day get enough ahead to open the factory again. And there you have it." Now that she had told him everything, she was suddenly frightened. She waited for his reaction.

He put his head in his hands. "I don't know whether to laugh or be angry. All those years, Marya. All those years that you didn't wear those stones and I didn't know why, especially after I chose each of them so carefully."

"Those jewels were beautiful, but I *couldn't* wear them. I put them to the use that seemed best to me at the time. I was wrong not to explain to you what I was doing. I know I hurt you and that's what I regret more than anything."

When he didn't say anything, she went on. "Those jewels aren't really gone, not completely lost, Zavel. They've only changed form. They've become land. Their value isn't lost to us. And now the land has oil and that means those stones have become worth more than we could have dreamed."

As soon as Michael, Sadie and Benjamin were all at the Williamsburg house, they sat down in front of Marya like little children waiting to be told a story. Wolf sat alone on the other side of the room. When she gave them the news from Joshua, they all jumped to their feet in the same second.

Marya was quiet. She thought, there was no doubt their future would finally be secure. And even if the well ran dry, they would always have the land. She glanced at Wolf and noticed he was looking at her, a stern expression still on his face. She went over to sit next to him.

Noticing her go, Sadie got up and went to sit on his other side. "Well, *Zeyde,* you haven't said a word. What do you think about all this?"

"I'm not sure just what to think."

Michael joined in. "Aren't you at least a little proud of us? We've got a new business for the family."

Wolf shrugged. "I guess what's hard for me to accept is that this wasn't all my idea. My children and grandchildren seem to be doing quite well on their secret ventures without me."

Sadie stood up, her hands on her hips. "What do

you mean without you? What makes you think any of this would have been possible if you hadn't come along first and paved the way? We're all building on what you started. If it hadn't been for you, I would never have learned a thing about the garment business, and if it weren't for you, we would have never had the capital to buy the land. Can't you see that you and *Bubbe* have been the inspiration for all of this?"

Wolf attempted a smile, and he was hoarse with emotion. "Nothing would make me happier than to believe that. It's just that things are happening a little too fast, that's all." He smiled again, this time more convincingly.

Marya didn't have to say anything. She knew that Sadie had said the one thing that could remove Wolf's reservations. It appeared that in ways Wolf never could have foreseen, he had finally realized the dream he had labored for all these years, a line of sons, and a daughter—carrying on in his name.

The next morning Marya was awakened early by the sound of a moan. She didn't know if it came from her or Wolf. She had been dreaming of a wintry Russian landscape where a lean, wild animal was running on all fours with fevered single-mindedness as it searched for food. Its eyes and nose were alert to every smell, every movement. But it found nothing. The more the creature ran, the hungrier and more desperate it became until finally it began to gnaw at its own forelegs. Suddenly a flock of white doves appeared and bore the tormented beast away into the sky.

It was almost light outside. Marya turned and looked at Wolf. What she saw frightened her. His face was contorted in an expression of pain and was covered with drops of perspiration.

She forced herself to stay calm as she got out of bed. "I don't care what you say this time, Zavel. You're going to the hospital."

Wolf started to protest, but she didn't stay to listen. She hurried into the other room and called the ambulance service, the sound of the clicking telephone dial grating harshly in the morning stillness. She took care to make all her movements steady and deliberate, with no wasted motion. But no matter how she tried, she couldn't stop the shaking in her hands.

Within half an hour the ambulance arrived and the whole house was astir. Feeling helpless, she watched as Wolf was carried out on a stretcher, doubled over in pain.

The next five days were a nightmare. As Marya and her family haunted the halls of the hospital, doctors in ghostly white smocks appeared and disappeared, sometimes stopping to mutter a few words of explanation or kindness, more often hastening by with averted glances.

As they sat lined up in chairs along the cheerless green corridor, Sadie and Elke held Marya by the hand the whole time. "The doctors are running tests," Sadie explained. "They're not sure what the problem is." Sadie had never seen Marya so subdued and pale, almost like a colorless shadow.

"I know what the problem is, I know what the problem is," Marya kept whispering softly, but when they asked her what she meant, she declined to say anything more.

Sadie's attention wandered to Adam Dov where he sat across the hall from her. She had seen little of him these last few years since he'd gone to work at the radio station. She knew he still saw Nancy Allen, but she was at a loss to understand why they had never married. She thought of how once she would have been so excited to see him five days in a row like this. But under these circumstances his presence just made her shudder.

By the end of the week they had a report. A young, grey-eyed doctor stood before them in the hallway, shifting his weight nervously from foot to foot.

"I'm sorry to tell you that Mr. Luminov has cancer of the lungs," he said in a neutral voice.

From where he stood on the edge of their group, Adam Dov asked, "What does that mean we can expect, Doctor?"

"We'll begin treatment immediately. Depending on how he responds to the treatment, he may live another five days, five weeks or even another five years."

After the doctor left, Marya sunk back down in the chair. Sadie sat down next to her and seized her by the arm. "You will endure this, *Bubbe,*" she whispered fiercely. "No matter what happens, you will pass through it and be all right." She tightened her grip until Marya was forced to look at her.

Marya sighed from somewhere deep inside her. "Yes, I will. I must believe that."

Sadie was still holding her firmly by the arm. "You do believe that already. I know."

Marya looked at her granddaughter and tried to smile. How could she explain to Sadie how much it hurt her to see Wolf suffering this way? That she couldn't imagine her life without him, that it would all be so empty and cold if she couldn't see those intense black eyes every morning when she awakened? That she had already endured more than one person should have to and now to lose Wolf, too?

A few hours later, when Marya was allowed to go in to see him, she stood by the bed. Wolf was sleeping and as she looked at his closed eyelids, she thought she caught an acrid smell in the room. In the past week he seemed to have shrunken in size, and it pained her to see him slipping away before her eyes. She yearned to see him get up out of that bed and walk out of there with those long strides of his. When he was awake, he still looked strong and spoke with confidence, so it was harder to see the signs of his illness upon him. Asleep, his vulnerability showed though, and Marya was glad the children hadn't seen him at this moment.

The next week passed and then the next. Wolf

seemed to respond to the treatment, but he clearly didn't like being in the hospital. "I want to go home," he told Marya. "I don't like this place. I want to be at home with you and my family."

Marya was torn. She wanted him home too, but she knew the doctors didn't. "They want to operate, Zavel. They think they can help you."

"I don't want them to touch me."

"But, Zavel, perhaps they can slow down the spread of the disease."

He rose up off the pillow. "What for, Marya? What kind of life would I have afterward? I'd be a feeble old man, condemned to hanging on until the next operation. Each day I'd be able to do less, until finally I might as well be dead."

She wanted to cry out, But at least we'd be together! But she couldn't. She knew he was too proud and dignified to bear the humiliation of slowly wasting away.

When Joshua returned from California, the family was gathered in the hospital hallway. The nurse came out of Wolf's room. "You can go in now," she said, inappropriately cheery. Marya led the way, with Sadie and Michael following, and Adam Dov coming after, leading Zosa by the hand. They filled the small room and pushed in close around his bed.

Wolf looked up at them and smiled weakly. "The Luminov clan assembles," he said. "Am I that sick?"

Please God, Marya thought, not even realizing it was a prayer she was uttering, let me be doing the right thing. "We've come to take you home," she informed him.

Marya had the telegram in the pocket of her skirt. Every few minutes she patted it reassuringly to make sure it was still there. It was just a matter of waiting five more days. But these five days truly could be a lifetime. Each day Wolf grew visibly weaker.

On the morning of the fifth day, Marya was in their bedroom changing the linens on Wolf's bed. "I'm going to wash your hair today," Marya announced.

"My hair? Why in the world? You just washed it three days ago."

She tried to joke. "I know, but I want to have you looking your best at all times."

"I'm not sure I know what to make of that statement."

She laughed. "There's nothing to make of it. Just let me have my way with you."

That afternoon Marya was alone in the living room when she finally heard the knock she had been waiting for. She hurried to the door before anyone else could and threw it open.

"Daniel!" she cried. She didn't even take time to look at him. She just threw her arms around him and held him as tightly as she could.

"Mama, I left as soon as I got your letter," he said, his voice breaking with emotion.

When they finally let go of each other, she was astonished to see how much older he looked. His hair was completely grey, and although he looked fit, he had put on weight. But then, why shouldn't he look older? she said to herself. He was in his midforties now. He couldn't forever stay a twenty-five-year-old.

"Come," she whispered quickly, "before anyone else sees you." She led him down the hall to their bedroom. She rapped gently, then pushed the door open. Wolf's eyes met hers for a second just as she came in, then his attention flickered past her to the tall man still standing shyly in the doorway.

His voice was hoarse. "Daniel? Oh my God. Daniel, is that you?"

"Yes, Papa," he said, still standing in the same spot. "I just had to talk to you. I've had so many conversations with you in my mind these last twenty years. I figured it was time I told you all these things myself."

"What a man you've become." Wolf continued to

stare at Daniel. "What a man you've become. Come here, son."

Marya stepped to one side, and as Daniel went past her toward the bed, she saw the tears in his eyes. She quietly closed the door behind her as she left the room. After Daniel's arrival, Wolf gathered strength. He looked better, his color improved and he was eating more. Then when everyone had begun to allow themselves to hope, he took a turn for the worse.

Marya was at his bedside constantly. One day, after he had been asleep for a long time, Wolf opened his eyes and spoke very clearly. "All I have to look forward to now is pain."

Your pain is my pain, Marya thought as she watched him close his eyes again. If only there were something she could do so he wouldn't have to suffer like this. She was still by his side when he opened his eyes the next time. "Are you sure you don't want to go to the hospital? They have medicines there that can stop the pain."

"That's all they can stop. They can't stop what's happening to me."

That night Wolf didn't sleep at all. He turned his head from side to side restlessly and when Marya went to check on him, she found his sheets drenched in sweat.

He saw her hovering over him. "I believe you love me," he said suddenly.

"With all my heart."

"Then give me something to stop this?"

She went cold all over. "Stop this? Stop the pain?"

"No," he whispered. "To stop everything." When she didn't say anything, his voice grew amazingly strong and clear. "I don't want to go on like this, withering a bit every day until there's nothing left of me. You know what to do. You used to work in the apothecary shop. You can give me something." He put out his hand and took hers in it. To Marya's surprise, it felt cold and unyielding, as if he were already dead.

"I don't want our children and grandchildren to see me turn into a stump. I want them to remember me upright, arguing with them, giving orders, maybe even laughing, but not like this."

They spent the rest of the night like that, hand in hand. "It's like we've come back to the beginning," Marya said softly at one point. "You're in bed and I'm nursing you. We could be still seventeen and eighteen years old and living on the Lower East Side, and all this in between is just something we imagined together, just a dream."

The next morning, Marya set a teacup of pale yellow liquid down next to the bed. "I won't give this to you because I just can't. But it's there if you want it."

"I remember those vile potions you used to force on me," he said, attempting to make her smile.

She caught an acrid smell, and she knew it was the smell of death. "This one is the bitterest of all," she said unsmiling, wondering why it was she couldn't cry.

Epilogue

The bells . . . the bells . . . they had finally stopped their tolling. Marya shook herself loose from her nap, opened her eyes and looked out over the East River. From the bench where she sat she could see the Williamsburg Bridge, and if she were to follow the bridge across the river, she'd be on Delancey Street, in the heart of the Lower East Side. She knew that even today, fifty years later, she could turn down those tumultuous streets and find the same signs in Yiddish and English, crowds of vendors along Hester Street, the clothing stores lining Division Street, the smell of spices and the lure of forbidden pleasures on Allen Street. Maybe there no longer were horses bedecked in little straw hats, or colorful wash snapping in the breeze in the Italian area south of Washington Square, or men struggling with large wooden barrels of herring on their backs. There weren't as many Jews there now either, but it was undeniably a Jewish homeland, and the first place in her life she had ever felt like she was truly safe from the tyranny of the czar and his Cossacks, free to strive for a better life as a Jew and as a woman.

As she looked across the water at the uneven

roofs of the East Side, a picture of Wolf, vibrantly handsome and permanently young, came to her as he had looked when he ran his fingers through her short red curls and pulled her to him on their wedding night. She pictured him as he was two years later, his arms laden with bolts of fabric as he took the steps of their first tenement flat two at a time, eager to hold her and explain his newest idea for the fledgling MW Enterprises. And then she saw him a few years after that, balancing their infants on his knees, Daniel on the right, Elke on the left, and then many, many years later with Michael in his arms and streaks of grey in his hair. Those were the images she loved the most and would always hold of him. She thought again of the pale and already skeletal man in the bed—her husband, who no longer existed except in her memories.

Without warning, the words from the prophet Isaiah came to her: "Upon a high and lofty mountain thou hast lain thy bed."

Wolf was gone. The bells had tolled for him—for both of them. She felt the tears in her eyes.

It had been a very long time since she had allowed a line from the Torah to enter her heart. Now she spoke out loud: "The voice of my beloved, behold, he cometh leaping upon the mountains, skipping over the hills."

Then slowly and deliberately, as she allowed herself to weep for her husband, she began to rend the edge of the blouse she was wearing.

She heard footsteps behind her. "Here you are," Sadie was saying, her voice subdued. As she came around to the front of the bench, Marya looked up and smiled tranquilly. The sun had finally come out, and as it glinted off of Sadie's red hair, Marya gazed at this new president of MW Enterprises—vigorous, talented and beautiful—and she felt a strange calm.

Sadie sat down next to her. "I've been looking everywhere for you. The last thing I knew you just stepped out this morning to take a walk." She hesitated, seeing tears in her grandmother's eyes for the first time in her life, and knowing that Marya already knew what she was going to say. "I came for you because I wanted to tell you that *Zeyde* died peacefully in his sleep a short time ago."

"Yes," said Marya, "I know. I saw it all here," she pointed to her kerchiefed head, "in my mind."

The sky was lit up even brighter now, and as the sunlight fell across Sadie, Marya reached out to touch her auburn hair that had grown long and luxurious again. As she did so, she admired the swell of Sadie's belly and the new life growing there. Wolf's strength would live on and prevail.

LOOK FOR . . .

THE IRISH

A powerful American saga of the young and old, uprooted from Ireland and borne to a new continent on the strength of a promise and a dream . . .

For Nora and Sean O'Sullivan, the voyage to America was a long and terrible journey into the unknown. But they had the courage and the skills to begin again, even in the face of incredible hardship. From the poverty-ridden streets of New York to the New England mills and sweatshops, seeking to find a place they could call their own, they would bring to America their own special gifts, their loves and their memories of a life left behind forever.

ANOTHER POWERFUL DRAMA IN THE STORY OF A NATION'S NEW BEGINNING

COMING SOON
WHEREVER DELL BOOKS ARE SOLD